*Managing New Product
and Process
Development*

KIM B. CLARK
STEVEN C. WHEELWRIGHT

Managing New Product and Process Development

Text and Cases

FP

THE FREE PRESS
New York London Toronto Sydney Tokyo Singapore

The Free Press
A Division of Simon & Schuster Inc.
1230 Avenue of the Americas
New York, N.Y. 10020

Printed in the United States of America

printing number

   3 4 5 6 7 8 9 10

Library of Congress Cataloging-in-Publication Data

Clark, Kim B.
    Managing new product and process development : text and cases /
Kim B. Clark, Steven C. Wheelwright.
       p.   cm.
    Includes bibliographical references.
    ISBN 0-02-905517-2
    1. New products—Management.   2. Product management—Case studies.
3. Production planning—Case studies.   I. Wheelwright, Steven C.,
II. Title.
HF5415.153.C58   1993
658.5'75—dc20

                            92–29067
                              CIP

To
Our Parents
Merlin and Helen Mar Clark, and
Max and Deborah Ann Coulam Wheelwright,
who provided the foundation upon which any
of our successes and good works have been built

Contents

Preface

*I*n the vast majority of manufacturing firms—whether in Japan, Europe, or the United States—senior managers identify product and process development as an area of great opportunity, and an area where the firm needs much stronger capabilities. Yet if one asks those same managers how effectively their organizations carry out development activities and how close they come to achieving their desired targets, one hears a litany of past frustrations and little hope that current projects will achieve dramatically improved results. Similarly, if one were to poll faculty and deans of leading business schools, they would be nearly unanimous in targeting product and process development as a critical area of opportunity they hope their institutions will address in the 1990s. Follow-up questions regarding the current number of faculty doing outstanding research and course development, courses offered, and books and papers in the area, however, would reveal far less activity than one might expect. How is it that such an important topic could garner this level of recognition, yet command so few resources and so limited a knowledge base? Our work with manufacturing firms throughout the world as well as leading business schools in Europe, the United States, and Japan suggests that three factors have contributed to this situation.

First has been the view, prevalent in the early 1960s and, for business schools, widespread still, that good managers can manage anything. As initially espoused by conglomerates, this view held that the vast majority of managerial skills required for outstanding performance was generic, and effective managers needed only a cursory, high-level understanding of the related technologies. As subsequent competitive results confirmed, such a premise was never well-founded. Consequently, by the 1990s, practitioners agreed that most competitive settings required a much better balance between industry knowledge and focus, and general managerial talent and leadership.

Related to this premise has been the second view, especially prevalent in selected high-tech firms, that technology and management could be effectively separated in terms of career paths and organizational focus—technologists need not know a lot about management, and managers need not know a lot about technology. Issues could be decomposed into their managerial and technical components and the appropriate skills brought to bear. This separation was reinforced in universities: business schools included departments covering all the major functions except engineering, which was housed in a separate school that focused on the discipline's theoretical and analytical foundations and its application in practice.

A third factor has been the belief that functional excellence is the primary source of competitive advantage. This belief posits that low-cost manufacturing, technology patents, and domination of marketing channels are the foundations of distinctive advantage. While functional advantages are important, a handful of firms—Motorola, Honda, and Chaparral, for example—have based outstanding performance on cross-functional capabilities: they have learned to integrate system solutions that combine low cost, high quality, and excellent time to market. The implication is that functional excellence may no longer provide sufficient advantage in the coming decades.

The result of these three factors has been a tendency to see development as a technical engineering activity that is either ignored in business schools or examined from a narrow functional perspective—whether marketing or R&D. Missing is an integrated framework that treats development as a business process linking technical, commercial, and managerial issues. The primary purpose of this book is to develop such a framework, drawing on almost a decade of our own research, course development, and consulting activities. We have used as our primary unit of analysis—as is common in companies—the development project. This is the vehicle by which the relevant skills, abilities, processes, and procedures are focused to transform a product and/or process concept into a commercialized, effectively delivered process, product, and service.

While the development project is the reference point for this book, we also address those activities that must set the stage if each project is to accomplish its objectives and achieve its full potential. Similarly, we include conclusions and insights regarding the capture and application of learning from individual projects to further strengthen and build an organization's development capabilities. Thus, the book is organized into three parts—sets of chapters and cases dealing with pre-project activities and concerns, with issues in managing projects, and with post-project learning and ongoing improvements.

The ideas presented in this book have been tested in research and classroom interactions with hundreds of executives and put into practice in many companies. In all of these interactions, we have tried to find the general principles that guide executive action and ground them in an understanding of the details of practice: the actual day-to-day work of development. Like the components of a great product, a crucial part of the magic in a great development process is in the details of strategy, planning, designing, engineering, testing, and implementing. But a great process is not complete unless the details coalesce into an effective whole. How managers and their organizations facilitate the coming together of these details to create an effective pattern of development is the primary theme of *Managing New Product and Process Development: Text and Cases*.

Many people have contributed significantly to the writing of the text and cases in this book. Literally thousands of managers, engineers, designers, and functional specialists in many different companies throughout the world have shared their experience, insights, and perspective. Without their cooperation we could not have conducted the research, written the cases, nor learned first-hand what it meant to develop new products and processes and apply new technology. Although we can not recognize them here by name, we continue to thank them personally and would like to acknowledge their support.

We have also been blessed with great colleagues and a stimulating, supporting environment at Harvard Business School. We are especially grateful to Dean John McArthur for his encouragement and for the faith he had in us when it was not clear that any of this would actually work and prove valuable to practitioners. Jay Lorsch headed up the Division of Research and was always there when we needed support. Bob Hayes chaired our area and took a lot of flak while keeping our administrative burdens relatively light (we have been in his debt for many years; he is finally starting to collect!). Earl Sasser co-authored the first paper on maps and Taka Fujimoto (now on the faculty at Tokyo University) was involved in much of the initial work on product development in the auto industry. They were among the first of our colleagues to recognize the crucial role of product and process development. Kent Bowen, Jai Jaikumar, Dorothy Leonard-Barton, Marco Iansiti, Dave Upton, Gary

Pisano, and Brent Barnett have worked with us on related research. We have benefited from their field work and ideas. Our doctoral students past and present, especially Taka Fujimoto, Rebecca Henderson, Marcie Tyre, Michael Watkins, Clayton Christensen, Dave Ellison, and Jonathan West, have been a crucial source of research assistance and stimulating ideas. We especially want to thank Michael Watkins for his help with the text of Chapter 9 and Dave Ellison for his many contributions to the text of Chapter 10.

Several of our colleagues have willingly agreed to share their cases and teaching notes for this book. We are especially grateful to Geoff Gill, who worked as a research associate and case writer on many of these cases. Contributing authors that we particularly want to recognize include Dr. Margaret Graham [Ampex Corporation: Product Matrix Engineering], Professor Marco Iansiti [Intel Systems Group and Honda Today], Dr. Brent Barnett [Ceramics Process Systems (B)], former students Bill Kennedy and Steve Zuckerman [Applied Materials], Professor Nan Langowitz and Dr. Brian Westcott [Plus Development Corporation (A)], Professor David Garvin [Lehrer McGovern Bovis Incorporated (Abridged)], Professor Clayton Christensen [Quantum Corporation—Product and Business Teams], Dr. Karen Freeze and the Design Management Institute [Braun AG: The KF 40 Coffee Machine (Abridged)], Professor Bruce Chew [Design for Manufacturability at Midwest Industries], Dr. Margaret Graham and Professors Dick Rosenbloom and Marcie Tyre [Bendix Automation Group (B)], former student Sandeep Duggal [Associated Instruments Corporation—Analytic Instruments Division], and Professor Gary Pisano and DBA student Jonathan West [Eli Lilly and Company: Manufacturing Process Technology Strategy (1991)].

We are pleased that product and process development is a rapidly growing area for research and teaching. Many colleagues have contributed ideas, offered encouragement, used our case material, and otherwise helped us in our work while establishing their own complementary research agendas. We are especially indebted to members of the Manufacturing Vision Group, a research consortium of five companies and engineering and business schools in four universities that for the past five years has focused on product and process development. The results of that effort should appear in early 1993 as *Vision and Capability: High Performance Product Development in the 1990s* (New York: Oxford University Press). We have been part of the group since its inception and have benefited greatly from our involvement. We would like to thank Kent Bowen, Tom Eagar, Jim Solberg, Carolyn Woo, Phil Barkan, Chuck Holloway, Richard Billington, Bill Hanson, Gordon Forward, Hal Edmondson, Sara Beckman, Max Jurosek, Jack Rittler, John Owen, Robin Farran, and Doug Braithwaite, as well as others who helped on some of the project's subprojects.

Throughout the writing of this book and the preparation of its manuscript, important supporting roles have been filled by a number of people. Bill Handy, Director of Development at the *Wichita Eagle*, and a former executive student of ours, was kind enough to apply his critical reading, editing, and creative skills to the final manuscript. He supplied us with many improvements and suggestions. We appreciate the time and energy he spent making a significant contribution to this effort. Bob Wallace, our editor at The Free Press, was an enthusiastic supporter from the beginning and kept after us to make it happen. Elisabeth Peter kept the office humming along and helped us with some of the drafts and revisions. Jean Smith managed the manuscript, made numerous and extensive case revisions, designed and executed the graphics, and kept us all organized and focused on meeting deadlines—we could not have done it without her help. Barbara Feinberg provided invaluable editing assistance on many of the cases.

Finally and most importantly, we would like to thank our families for their enduring love and support. From our earliest years, our parents sought to instill a love of learning and discovery mingled with a heavy dose of practical reality. To the degree that we have been successful in balancing the many demands on our time and achieving some measure of success in tackling these important topics, we owe it to them for their diligence and commitment in teaching us the fundamentals that pointed us in the right direction. For our immediate families, we also offer our heartfelt thanks for their love and support. For the Clark children (Bryce, Erin, Jonathan, Andrew, Michael, Jennifer, and Julia) and the Wheelwright children (Marianne, Melinda, Kristen, Matthew, and Spencer), we appreciate their letting us pursue such a work and willingly accepting the royalties from it into their trusts. Finally, our thanks and appreciation to Sue and Margaret, who lovingly support our efforts at such projects, but help us keep things in perspective and successfully integrate our professional and family lives.

Boston, MA
March 1992

Competing Through Development Capability

Overview

This chapter introduces product development as a central focus of competition in the 1990s. While firms have developed new products since the Industrial Revolution, in industry after industry, the importance of doing product development well has increased dramatically in recent years. This chapter identifies the forces driving the importance of product development—changes in competition, customer demands, and technology. An important theme in the chapter is that these forces have created a competitive imperative for speed, efficiency, and high quality in the development process.

In reading the chapter it is important to establish a basic idea of what product development involves—both what makes it difficult to achieve, and the competitive power it creates when done well. To provide perspective on what we mean by product development, the chapter briefly summarizes the major sequence of activities involved in taking an idea from initial concept through prototype building and testing, and into commercial production. A key theme is that product development is a process involving all the major functions in a business. With the development process as background, we then use the example of the Northern Electronics Company and its problems with the A14 stereo project to illustrate the difficulties in development.

The problems on the A14 project—missed schedules, cost overruns, and a poorly designed product—reflect a mismatch between the way the project is organized and managed and the requirements of the development process created by the product's complexity and the rigorous and uncertain competitive environment in which Northern Electronics competed. Exhibit 1–5 summarizes the characteristics of problematic projects as well as their consequences. The exhibit also identifies key themes that characterize outstanding projects—clarity of focus, integration across functions, a strong focus on time to market, doing things right the first time, and effective substantive leadership—thus summarizing many of the important themes developed in the book.

Our intent in this first chapter is not only to highlight the challenge and characterize what an outstanding project might look like, but also to illustrate the competitive power created in the organizations that do development extraordinarily well. To underscore that power we close the chapter with a review of the competitive interaction between Northern and Southern Electronics in the compact stereo market. Historically these two companies mirrored one another in terms of their market approach. But in the 1980s, Southern built a new strategy around superior capability and product development. In effect, Southern embarked on a strategy to become a fast-cycle competitor. In reading through this history, it is useful to note the way in which Southern linked its product development capability with its strategies in marketing and manufacturing. In fact, the way Southern exploited its advantage in speed and efficiency over its slower Northern rival was precisely by integrating its development capabilities with its actions in marketing and manufacturing. The history also sheds light on the A14 stereo project referred to above. Here, we see what happens when a senior management team attempts to achieve substantial improvements in performance without making basic changes in processes or in capabilities. The chapter closes with a summary of the advantages that effective product development capability conferred upon Southern.

*I*n a competitive environment that is global, intense, and dynamic, the development of new products and processes increasingly is a focal point of competition. Firms that get to market faster and more efficiently with products that are well matched to the needs and expectations of target customers create significant competitive leverage. Firms that are slow to market with products that match neither customer expectations nor the products of their rivals are destined to see their market position erode and financial performance falter. In a turbulent environment, doing product and process development well has become a requirement for being a player in the competitive game; doing development extraordinarily well has become a competitive advantage.

The New Industrial Competition: Driving Forces and Development Realities

The importance of product and process development is not limited to industries or businesses built around new scientific findings, with sig-

3

nificant levels of R&D spending, or where new products have traditionally accounted for a major fraction of annual sales. The forces driving
development are far more general. Three are particularly critical:

- *Intense international competition.* In business after business, the number
  of competitors capable of competing at a world-class level has grown
  at the same time that those competitors have become more aggressive.
  As world trade has expanded and international markets have become
  more accessible, the list of one's toughest competitors now includes
  firms that may have grown up in very different environments in North
  America, Europe, and Asia. The effect has been to make competition
  more intense, demanding, and rigorous, creating a less forgiving environment.
- *Fragmented, demanding markets.* Customers have grown more sophisticated and demanding. Previously unheard of levels of performance
  and reliability are today the expected standard. Increasing sophistication means that customers are more sensitive to nuances and differences in a product, and are attracted to products that provide solutions
  to their particular problems and needs. Yet they expect these solutions
  in easy-to-use forms.
- *Diverse and rapidly changing technologies.* The growing breadth and
  depth of technological and scientific knowledge has created new options for meeting the needs of an increasingly diverse and demanding
  market. The development of novel technologies and a new understanding of existing technologies increases the variety of possible solutions available to engineers and marketers in their search for new
  products. Furthermore, the new solutions are not only diverse, but
  also potentially transforming. New technologies in areas such as materials, electronics, and biology have the capacity to change fundamentally the character of a business and the nature of competition.

These forces are at work across a wide range of industries. They are
central to competition in young, technically dynamic industries, but also
affect mature industries where life cycles historically were relatively
long, technologies mature, and demands stable. In the world auto industry, for example, the growing intensity of international competition,
exploding product variety, and diversity in technology have created a
turbulent environment.[1] The number of world-scale competitors has
grown from less than five in the early 1960s to more than twenty today.
But perhaps more importantly, those twenty competitors come from
very different environments and possess a level of capability far exceeding the standard prevailing twenty-five years ago. Much the same is true
of customers. Levels of product quality once considered extraordinary

are now a minimum requirement for doing business. As customers have grown more sophisticated and demanding, the variety of products has increased dramatically. In the mid 1960s, for example, the largest selling automobile in the United States was the Chevrolet Impala. The platform on which it was based sold approximately 1.5 million units per year. In 1991, the largest selling automobile in the United States was the Honda Accord, which sold about 400,000 units. Thus, in a market that is today larger than it was in 1965, the volume per model has dropped by a factor of four. Currently over 600 different automobile models are offered for sale on the U.S. market.

Similarly, technological change has had dramatic consequences. In 1970, one basic engine-drive train technology (a V8 engine, longitudinally mounted, water cooled, carbureted, hooked up to a three-speed automatic transmission with rear wheel drive) accounted for close to 80 percent of all automobile production in the United States.[2] Indeed, there were only five engine-drive train technologies in production. By the early 1980s that number had grown to thirty-three. The growing importance of electronics, new materials, and new design concepts in engines, transmissions, suspensions, and body technologies has accelerated the pace and diversity of technological change in the 1980s. Simply keeping up with those technologies is a challenge, but an often straightforward one in comparison with having to integrate them in development efforts.

Similar forces have been at work in other traditional, mature industries. In textiles and apparel, for example, firms such as Benetton and The Limited have used information technology to create a production and distribution network which links retail outlets directly to distribution centers and back into factories and suppliers in the chain of production from fiber to finished product. The thrust of these networks is the ability to respond quickly to changing customer demands at relatively low cost.[3] Fueled in part by availability and in part by growing demands for differentiated products, product variety has expanded significantly. In plant after plant, one finds vast increases in the number of styles produced and a sharp decline in the length of production runs. These are not changes of 10 or 20 percent; in the 1980s, it was common for apparel plants to experience a four- to fivefold increase in the number of styles produced. These increases in garment variety have pushed back into the textile plants as well. For example, the average lot size for dying at Greenwood Mills, a U.S. textile firm, declined in the 1980s from 120,000 to 11,000 yards.

Changes in markets and technologies for automobile and textile firms have accentuated the importance of speed and variety in product development. But changes in competition, customer demand, and technology have also had dramatic effects on newer, less mature industries in which product innovation has always been an important part of competition. In industries such as computer disk drives and medical equipment, already short life cycles have shrunk further and product variety has increased. In addition, competition has placed increased pressure on product reliability and product cost. In disk drives, for example, the market for Winchester-technology hard disks has expanded from a base in high-end systems for mainframe computers to include a spectrum of applications ranging from notebook personal computers to large-scale supercomputers.[4] Even within an application segment, the number of sizes, capacities, access times, and features has increased sharply. In addition to this *explosion of variety*, firms in the hard disk drive industry have had to meet demands for *dramatic increases in reliability* (tenfold in five years) and *decreases in cost* (5 percent to 8 percent quarterly). These have been met in part by incremental improvements in established technologies and in part through the introduction of new design concepts, production technologies, materials, and software.

Much the same has been true in the market for new medical devices. Innovation has always been important in the creation of new medical devices, but by the 1980s success required the ability to follow an innovative product with sustained improvements in performance, application to new segments, improved reliability, and lower cost. In the case of devices for angioplasty (a procedure using a balloon on a small wire to expand clogged arteries), the initial innovation was followed by a variety of developments that offered the physician greater control of a smaller device, making access easier and creating additional applications. In concert with process changes that substantially improved or reduced variability of performance characteristics, changes in the product have opened up new applications and treatment of a more diverse set of clinical problems and patients, worldwide.

The Competitive Imperatives

Rigorous international competition, the explosion of market segments and niches, and accelerating technological change have created a set of competitive imperatives for the development of new products and processes in industries as diverse as medical instruments and automobiles, textiles, and high-end disk drives. Exhibit 1–1 identifies three of these imperatives—speed, efficiency, and quality—and suggests some of their implications. To succeed, firms must be responsive to changing customer demands and the moves of their competitors. This means that they must be fast.[5] The ability to identify opportunities, mount the requisite development effort, and bring to market new products and

EXHIBIT 1–1

The Development Imperatives

Required Capability	Driving Force	Implications
1. Fast and Responsive	Intense competition; changing customer expectations; accelerating technological change	Shorter development cycles; better targeted products
2. High Development Productivity	Exploding product variety; sophisticated, discerning customers; technical diversity	Leverage from critical resources; increased number of successful development projects per engineer
3. Products with Distinction and Integrity	Demanding customers; crowded markets; intense competition	Creativity combined with total product quality; customers integrated with truly cross-functional development process

processes quickly is critical to effective competition. But firms also must bring new products and processes to market efficiently. Because the number of new products and new process technologies has increased while model lives and life cycles have shrunk, firms must mount more development projects than has traditionally been the case utilizing substantially fewer resources per project. In the U.S. automobile market, for example, the growth of models and market segments over the last twenty-five years has meant that an auto firm must mount close to four times as many development projects simply to maintain its market share position. But smaller volumes per model and shorter design lives mean resource requirements must drop dramatically. Effective competition requires highly efficient engineering, design, and development activities.

Being fast and efficient is essential but not enough. The products and processes that a firm introduces must also meet demands in the market for value, reliability, and distinctive performance. Demanding customers and capable competitors mean that the ante keeps going up—requirements of performance, reliability, ease of use, and total value increase with each product introduction. When competition is intense firms must attract and satisfy customers in a very crowded market. More and more this means offering a product that is distinctive; that not only satisfies, but also surprises and delights a customer. Moreover, attention to the total product experience and thus to total product quality is critical.

The Opportunity and the Challenge

Firms that step up to the challenge and meet these competitive imperatives enjoy a significant advantage in the market place. The development of outstanding products not only opens new markets and attracts new customers, but also leverages existing assets and builds new capability in the organization. Getting a succession of distinctive new disk drives or a string of new medical devices to market quickly and consistently requires the solution of technical problems that builds know-how. Moreover, it stimulates the creation of greater capability in problem solving, prototype construction, and testing that can be applied in future projects. All of these skills and capabilities enhance a firm's ability to compete. But there is more. Successful new products also unleash a virtuous cycle in reputation and enthusiasm within and outside the organization. Inside, successful new products energize the organization; confidence, pride, and morale grow. The best employees remain challenged and enthused. Outside, outstanding new products create broad interest in the firm and its products, enhance the firm's ability to recruit new employees, and facilitate the building of relationships with other organizations. The organization's momentum builds and reinforces itself.

While the potential opportunities to be realized in developing new products and processes are exciting, making them happen is a demanding challenge. New product or process development entails a complex set of activities that cuts across most functions in a business, as suggested by Exhibit 1–2, which lays out the phases of activity in a typical development project—a new product. In the first two phases—concept development and product planning—information about market opportunities, competitive moves, technical possibilities, and production requirements must be combined to lay down the architecture of the new product. This includes its conceptual design, target market, desired level of performance, investment requirements, and financial impact. Before a new product development program is approved, firms also attempt to prove out the concept through small–scale testing, the construction of models, and, often, discussions with potential customers.

Once approved, a new product project moves into detailed engineering. The primary activity in this phase of development is the design and construction of working prototypes and the development of tools and equipment to be used in commerical production. At the heart of detailed product and process engineering is the "design-build-test" cycle. Both products and processes are laid out in concept, captured in a working model (which may exist on a computer or in physical form), and then subjected to tests that simulate product use. If the model fails to deliver the desired performance characteristics, engineers search for design

EXHIBIT 1–2
Typical Phases of Product Development*

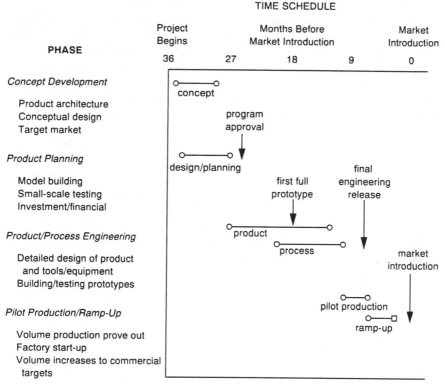

TIME SCHEDULE

PHASE	Project Begins	Months Before Market Introduction			Market Introduction
	36	27	18	9	0

Concept Development

  Product architecture
  Conceptual design
  Target market

Product Planning

  Model building
  Small-scale testing
  Investment/financial

Product/Process Engineering

  Detailed design of product
    and tools/equipment
  Building/testing prototypes

Pilot Production/Ramp-Up

  Volume production prove out
  Factory start-up
  Volume increases to commercial
    targets

* This development process assumes a thirty-six-month cycle time and four primary phases. Vertical arrows indicate major events; horizontal lines indicate the duration of the activities.

changes that will close the gap and the design-build-test cycle is repeated. The conclusion of the detailed engineering phase of development is marked by an engineering "release" or "sign off" that signifies that the final design meets requirements.

At this time the firm typically moves development into a pilot manufacturing phase, during which the individual components, built and tested on production equipment, are assembled and tested as a system in the factory. During pilot production many units of the product are produced and the ability of the new or modified manufacturing process to execute at a commerical level is tested. At this stage all commercial tooling and equipment should be in place and all parts suppliers should be geared up and ready for volume production. This is the point in development at which the total system—design, detailed engineering, tools and equipment, parts, assembly sequences, production supervisors, operators, and technicians—comes together.

The final phase of development is ramp-up. The process has been refined and debugged, but has yet to operate at a sustained level of high-yield, volume production. In ramp-up the firm starts commerical production at a relatively low level of volume; as the organization develops confidence in its (and its suppliers') abilities to execute production consistently and marketing's abilities to sell the product, the volume increases. At the conclusion of the ramp-up phase, the production system has achieved its target levels of volume, cost, and quality. In this phase, the firm produces units for commercial sale and, hopefully, brings the volume of production up to its targeted level.

An obstacle to achieving rapid, efficient, high-quality development is the complexity and uncertainty that confronts engineers, marketers, and manufacturers. At a fundamental level the development process creates the future, and that future is often several years away. Consider, for example, the case of a new automobile. The very best companies in the world in 1990 could develop a new car in three to three and a half years. At the outset of a new car development program, therefore, designers, engineers, and marketers must conceive of a product that will attract customers three years into the future. But that product must also survive in the marketplace for at least another four to five years beyond that. Thus the challenge is to design and develop a product whose basic architecture will continue to be effective in the marketplace seven to eight years after it has been conceived.

The problems that uncertainty creates—e.g., different views on the appropriate course of action, new circumstances that change the validity of basic assumptions, and unforeseen problems—are compounded by the complexity of the product and the production process. A product such as a small copier, for example, may have hundreds of parts that must work together with a high degree of precision. Other products, such as the handle of Gillette's Sensor razor, appear to be fairly simple devices but, because of very demanding performance requirements, are complex in design and come out of a manufacturing process involving sophisticated equipment and a large number of operations. Moreover, products may be evaluated across a number of criteria by potential customers. Thus the market itself may be relatively complex with a variety of customers who value different product attributes in different ways. This means that the firm typically draws on a number of people with a variety of specialized skills to achieve desired, yet hard to specify, levels of cost and functionality. To work effectively, these skills and perspectives must be integrated to form an effective whole. It is not enough to have a great idea, superior conceptual design, an excellent prototype facility, or capable tooling engineers; the whole product—its design system, production process, and interaction with customers—must be created, integrated, and made operational in the development process.

But an individual development project is not an island unto itself. It interacts with other development projects and must fit with the operating organization to be effective. Projects may share critical components and use the same support groups (e.g., model shops, testing labs). Additionally, products may require compatability in design and function: models of computers use the same operating system, and different industrial control products conform to the same standards for safety. These interactions create another level of complexity in design and development. Critical links also exist with the operating organization. A new design requires the development of new tools and equipment and uses the skills and capability of operators and technicians in the manufacturing plant. Further, it must be sold by the sales group and serviced by the field organization. Of course, new products often require new skills and capabilities, but, whether relying on new or old, the success of the new product depends in part on how well it fits with the operating units and their chosen capabilities. Thus, effective development means designing and developing many elements that fit and work well as a total system.

Assessing the Promise and Reality: The A14 Stereo Project

The uncertainty and complexity that characterizes the development of new products and processes means that managing any development effort is difficult; managing major development activities effectively is very difficult. Thus, while the promise of a new development project is often bright and exciting, the reality is often quite different. The following story, based on a composite of several situations we have encountered, illustrates typical problems in product development.

In September 1989, Marta Sorensen, product manager for mid-range stereo systems at Northern Electronics Company, a large consumer electronics firm, laid out a plan for a new compact stereo system utilizing advanced technology and providing superior sound quality. Sorenson's marketing group at Northern felt that the company needed to respond quickly to the expected introduction of a new compact system by one of its toughest competitors. The plan Sorenson presented at the beginning of the concept investigation stage called for a development cycle time of one year, with volume production commencing in September 1990. (See Exhibit 1–3 for the initial schedule and subsequent changes.) This would give the factory time to fill distribution and retail channels for the all-important Christmas season in late 1990.

As the exhibit suggests, the schedule began to slip almost immediately. Because of problems in freeing up resources and scheduling meetings, and disagreements about desired product features, the concept investigation stage was not completed until November 1989, six weeks later than originally planned. At that point, no change was made to the schedule for commerical introduction or start of pilot production, but two months were added to the prototype build and test schedule. This additional time was needed as a result of the selection of a new speaker technology that the engineering group had lobbied for during the concept development stage. It was assumed that the time originally allowed for pilot production could somehow be overlapped and/or compressed.

By February 1990 new design problems had emerged. The compact size of the product created unexpected difficulties in fitting the components into a small space while maintaining sound quality. Furthermore, delays with a chip supplier and the speaker technology supplier set back the project schedule several weeks. A revised schedule, established in February 1990, called for completion of the design in April and completion of the prototype-build-test cycle by June. However, no changes were made to the schedule for pilot production or ramp-up. This meant a significant compression of the time between completion of prototype testing to commerical production; process engineering and manufacturing groups were asked to begin preparing the process for production even though the design was still incomplete.

Design engineers worked hard to solve problems with product size, and cost and completed the design in May 1990. By that time, however, new problems had emerged with the prototypes and with the production process. Part of the delay in prototyping reflected late deliveries of parts from suppliers, overambitious testing schedules, and problems in scheduling meetings for milestone reviews. But part of the delay also reflected technical problems with the introduction of surface mount technology in the printed circuit boards for the product. Moreover, process engineering had experienced difficulties with production tooling. There had been a significant number of engineering changes to accommodate changes in exterior appearance as well as performance problems with the product. As a result, the completion of prototype testing was rescheduled for August and pilot production and ramp-up were scheduled to occur in rapid fire succession thereafter.

Even the new schedule proved optimistic. As the fall months wore

ExHIBIT 1–3

Schedule Slippage in the A14 Stereo Project at Northern Electronics*

Anticipated and Actual Phase Completion Dates

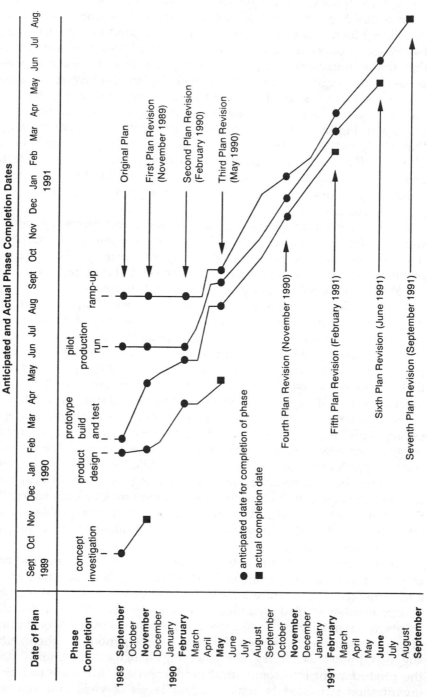

*Each row indicates the phases completed (■) and planned completion dates (●) for remaining phases as of a given date.

13

on and the project continued to slip, Sorenson and her marketing team realized that they would not meet the critical Christmas season deadline. Much of the latest delay had been caused by interaction between the product design and new automated assembly equipment that the manufacturing organization had installed. In order to meet product cost targets, manufacturing had chosen to move to an automated assembly system that would significantly reduce variable cost on the product. However, while design engineering was aware of the manufacturing plan, there were many subtle details of product design that conflicted with the capabilities of the automated equipment. These conflicts only surfaced late in 1990 as attempts were made to run full prototype units on the automated equipment. These problems required additional product redesign and slowed the completion of prototype testing.

Engineers eventually corrected the problems and prototype testing was completed in February 1991. While compression of the schedule had made product and process engineering operate in parallel, the completion of prototype testing did not mark the end of design changes nor the alleviation of production problems in pilot production.

Although Sorenson and the marketing group were happy to see the product make it through prototype testing, the fact that it was almost a year late had serious consequences for its potential attractiveness in the market. Sound quality and features were adequate and the cost and pricing were in line with expectations, but some of the product's aesthetics were out of synch with recent market developments. Thus, during the spring and summer of 1991 marketing pushed through a redesign of the product's exterior package to make it more attractive and contemporary. This caused some delays as engineering put through a crash program for new tooling and testing, but the redesigned exterior was put into production during the early fall. While the design of the new exterior was being developed, the manufacturing organization struggled to debug the new equipment and achieve consistent levels of quality. By September the plant had solved most of its major process problems and attention was shifted to increasing volume and filling channels for the 1991 Christmas season.

Market acceptance of the new product was satisfactory, but did not meet the projections originally laid out in 1989. Further, the engineering and manufacturing organizations soon found themselves confronted by a large number of field-identified quality problems. Exhibit 1–4 documents the engineering change history of the product from the beginning of pilot production to its post-Christmas sales period. As the exhibit suggests, there was a flurry of engineering change activity shortly after the product went into commerical production and the manufacturing organization struggled to achieve target levels of yield and volume.

Exhibit 1–4

Engineering Changes in the A14 Stereo Project, May
1991–July 1992*

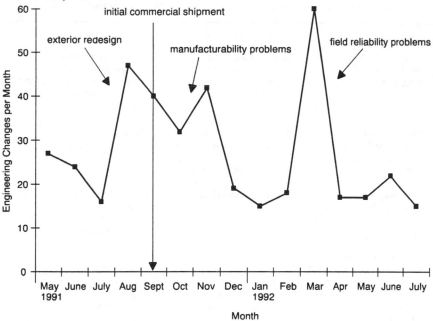

* Arrows indicate major events against which the monthly rate of engineering
changes can be referenced. The peak in November 1991 resulted from feedback from
early adopters; in March 1992 from feedback from Christmas season customers.

Many of these engineering changes were intended to improve manufacturability. The significant peak in March 1992 reflected consumer experience with the product following the Christmas season. In February
and March of 1992 design engineering launched a crash program to
solve several field problems with product reliability.

The Characteristics of Effective Development

The experience of Northern Electronics with the A14 stereo system is not
a pathological example. It reflects experience that is all too common in the
world of product and process development. The failure of the A14 project
to meet its original potential and expectations was not due to a lack of

15

Exhibit 1–5

Central Themes in Ineffective and Effective Development Projects

PROBLEMATIC PROJECTS		OUTSTANDING PROJECTS
Characteristics	*Consequences*	*Selected Themes*
• Multiple, ambiguous objectives; different functional agendas	• Long planning stage; project becomes vehicle for achieving consensus; late conflicts	• Clear objectives and shared understanding of project's intent throughout organization; early conflict resolution at low levels
• Focus on current customers and confusion about future target customers	• Moving targets; surprises and disappointments in market tests; late redesigns; mismatch between design and market	• Actively anticipating future customers' needs; providing continuity in offerings
• Narrow engineering focus on intrinsic elegance of solutions; little concern with time	• Slipping schedules; schedule compression in final phases	• Maintaining strong focus on time-to-market while solving problems creatively; system view of project concept
• Reliance on engineering changes and manufacturing ramp-up to catch and solve problems; "we'll put a change order on it when we get to manufacturing"	• Poor, unrepresentative prototypes; many late changes; poor manufacturability; scramble in ramp-up; lower than planned yields	• Testing and validating product and process designs before hard tooling or commercial production; "design it right the first time"
• Narrow specialists in functional "chimneys"	• Engineering "ping-pong"; miscommunication and misdirected effort; use of time to substitute for integration	• Broad expertise in critical functions, team responsibility, and integrated problem solving across functions
• Unclear direction; no one in charge; accountability limited	• Lack of a coherent, shared vision of project concept; buck passing; many false starts and dead ends	• Strong leadership and widespread accountability

creative people, management desire, technical skills, or market under-standing. The company had excellent marketing information, good re-lationships with its dealers and customers, recognized competence in engineering and design, and was known for its technical expertise. The A14's problems were rooted far more in the inability of the organization to bring together its insight and understanding and the expertise of its people in a coherent and effective way. In short, the A14 had problems because Northern lacked critical capabilities for integration.

Column 1 of Exhibit 1–5 summarizes typical characteristics of problematic projects like the A14, and column 2 identifies some of their implications. Problems on the A14 were rooted in the nature of the development process and its organization and the absence of a coherent and shared cross-functional plan for competing in the compact stereo market. Different functional groups (e.g., marketing and engineering) had different agendas and there was no organizational process to resolve issues before they surfaced throughout the phases of the A14 development effort. This led to delays and miscommunications throughout.

The development process itself contributed to delay and poor design. The many late engineering changes reflected in part a poorly organized and executed prototyping process. Some prototype parts came from suppliers unfamiliar with the commerical production environment at Northern and were late and poorly built. Delays getting into manufacturing were caused by a narrow focus on product performance in design choices (no design for manufacturability) and barriers to communications between engineering and manufacturing. Management treated the development of new products as the responsibility of the engineering group. Manufacturing was not of primary concern, at least not until problems with the new automated process began to surface. Without strong leadership, problems in the project went undiscovered, surfaced late, and were difficult to resolve.

In contrast to the A14 experience, column 3 in Exhibit 1–5 lays out selected themes in an outstanding development project. Objectives and accountability are clear and widely shared and stem from a concept development and product planning process that brings marketing, engineering, and manufacturing together. Moreover, early-stage development builds on clear strategies in the organization for the product line and major functions. In effect, the outstanding organization starts development projects with concept development on a firm foundation.

Once the concept has been developed and plans for the product have been laid out, execution in outstanding programs has a distinctive character. Guided by strong leadership, engineers with broad skills work in a coherent team with skilled people from marketing and manufacturing. "Integrated" describes day-to-day problem solving across departments and functional groups right down at the working level. Strong, collaborative relationships across departments are rooted in intensive communication, a shared responsibility for product performance, and an appreciation of the value to be added by each group. In this context an excellent engineering design is one that not only achieves outstanding performance but also is manufacturable and comes to market rapidly.

Indeed, time-to-market is such a critical dimension of performance in the outstanding project that all of the processes, systems, and activities in development are geared to fast action. This is particularly true for the critical design-build-test cycles that are at the heart of problem solving in development. Thus, the outstanding project has a prototyping process that creates representative components, subassemblies, and complete units of high quality. These prototypes in turn come out of a design process in which careful and simultaneous attention to the details and behavior of the product as a system catches numerous problems and identifies important opportunities early in the process. In this setup, engineers concentrate on eliminating redesigns caused by mistakes, poor communication, and lack of process understanding, and maximizing product performance and distinctiveness for its target market. "Design it right the first time" is critical because it creates products of high quality and saves valuable time.

Outstanding projects of this kind are not possible without leadership. In contrast to problematic projects where direction is lacking and responsibility diffuse, the excellent project has a project leader who gives conceptual direction and stimulates and nurtures working-level integration. Moreover, that leadership extends to linkages with critical suppliers, customers, and the market. The outstanding project leader fosters internal integration and integrates customer needs into the details of design. Effective product development is not the result of a single individual, but strong leadership makes a difference.

The Fast-Cycle Competitor

The themes that characterize outstanding development projects—clarity of objectives, focus on time to market, integration inside and out, high-quality prototypes, and strong leadership, to name a few—reflect capabilities that lead to rapid, efficient development of attractive products and manufacturing processes. The power of such capabilities lies in the competitive leverage they provide. A firm that develops high-quality products rapidly has several competitive options it may pursue. It may start a new product development project at the same time as the competitors, but introduce the product to the market much sooner. Alternatively, it may delay the beginning of a new development project in order to acquire better information about market developments, customer requirements, or critical technologies, introducing its product at the same time as its competitors but bringing to market a product much better suited to the needs of its customers. Furthermore, if it also has achieved speed and quality in an efficient way, it may use its resources to develop additional focused products that more closely meet the demands of specific customer niches and segments. Whatever the mix of customer targeting, speed to market, and product breadth the firm chooses to pursue, its advantages in fundamental capabilities give it a competitive edge.

For a firm like Northern—with slipping development schedules, late design changes, and problems with field failures—competing against a firm capable of rapid but effective product development can be a bewildering, discouraging, and ultimately unprofitable experience. Exhibit 1–6A illustrates just such an episode in Northern's history. Consider first Panel A, which graphs the price, cost, and product generation experience of Northern and its principal competitor, Southern Electronics Company, from 1978 until 1985.

Until 1985, both Northern and Southern followed standard industry cycles in new product development, pricing, and manufacturing costs. With a product development cycle of eighteen to twenty months, both firms introduced new generations of product every two years. Between major generational changes in products there were frequent model upgrades and price declines as the cost of key components and manufacturing fell with increasing volume. Thus, until the mid 1980s, both Southern and Northern had prices and costs that tracked each other closely, and both mirrored industry averages.

Improvement Efforts at Southern Electronics

In the early 1980s, changes in Southern laid the foundation for a significant change in the nature of competition in the industry. Stimulated by the efforts of Greg Jones, the new vice president of engineering, Southern embarked on a concerted effort to reduce its product development lead time. Without compromising quality, Jones and the entire organization began to develop the characteristics sketched out in column 3 of Exhibit 1–5. Stronger leadership, more effective cross-functional integration, greater attention to issues of manufacturability and design, more effective prototyping, and a revamped development process gradually led to a reduction in development lead time from eighteen to twelve months. By 1986 Southern could develop a comparable compact stereo system about six months faster than Northern.

As Panel B of Exhibit 1–6B suggests, Southern began to use its new development capability in early 1986. At that point it broke with industry tradition and introduced its next generation of stereo product about six months sooner than expected. With a more advanced system and superior performance, Southern was able to achieve a premium price in the marketplace. Although Northern followed six months later on a standard cycle, its next generation stereo was unable to command its

Exhibit 1–6A

Panel A: Standard Competitive Patterns for the Compact Stereo Market*

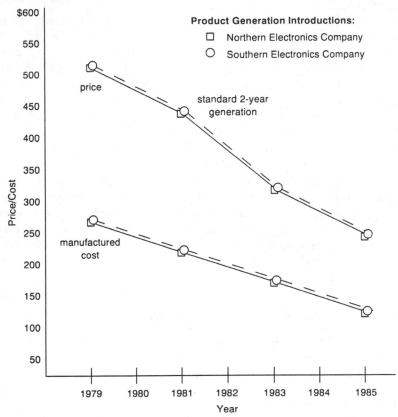

* Prior to 1986, both competitors introduced their new stereo products on the same two-year cycle, adopted similar pricing strategies, and experienced comparable manufacturing costs.

---

traditional market share. As a result, Northern's volume increased more slowly than expected and its cost position began to erode slightly relative to Southern.

Southern Electronics introduced its next generation product eighteen months later in the fall of 1987. Once again the product achieved a premium price in the market. However, Southern did not fully exploit its premium pricing opportunity. Instead, it lowered prices somewhat to increase further its market share. At that point, not only was Northern

EXHIBIT 1–6B

Panel B: Competition on Rapid Development Capabilities in the Compact Stereo Market*

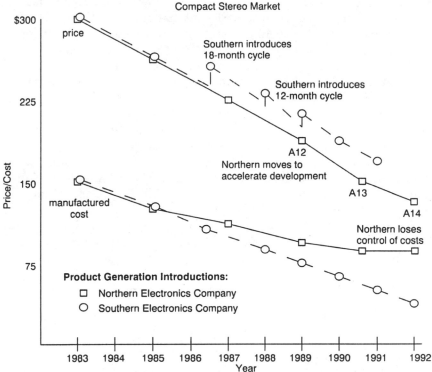

* Beginning in 1986, Southern moved first to an eighteen-month product introduction cycle and then to a twelve-month cycle; Northern moved to an eighteen-month cycle only in 1990. The consequences were continuing price premiums and cost advantages for Southern.

behind in product features and technology, but Southern's aggressive pricing posture put even more pressure on Northern's sales volume and margins. Although Northern fought back with price discounts, increased advertising, and promotions to dealers, it was unable to stem the erosion of its historical market position. The result was an even greater disparity in the cost positions of Northern and Southern Electronics.

Northern's Competitive Reaction

In late 1988, Northern introduced its next generation stereo system, the A12. Developed under the motto "beat Southern," Northern's executives felt that the A12 would be the product to regain their former competitive position in the market. Much to their surprise, however, the rollout of the A12 in early 1989 was met by Southern's introduction of its next generation stereo system: Southern had moved to a twelve-month product introduction cycle in late 1988. At that point Northern was a full generation of technology behind Southern in its market offerings. Northern's management determined that the only course of action open was to accelerate development of the next generation system, the A13. They thus embarked on a crash development effort to bring the A13 to market in early 1990. At the same time Sorenson and her colleagues began development on the A14, which they targeted for the Christmas 1990 selling season. The A14 was to get them back into the competitive ball game on solid footing—a "close the gap" strategy.

While Northern's strategic intent was to catch up to Southern with accelerated product development, the reality was much different. Northern brought the A13 to market in early 1990, but the development process was so hectic and the ramp-up in manufacturing so strained that the company effectively lost control of its costs. The product came to market but was much more expensive and less effective than the company had planned. Because of its many problems, scarce development resources that were to have been moved to the A14 in early 1990 were focused instead on correcting problems and cleaning up the A13's design. To make matters worse, Southern continued to follow its twelve-month introduction cycle and actually beat Northern to the market with its next generation product. The result for Northern was a further erosion in margins and market position.

Without making fundamental changes in its development process, which management considered neither necessary nor within the charter of Sorenson and those working on the A14, Northern's attempt to push ahead with the A14 for the 1990 Christmas season was a dismal failure. The A14 product had so many problems in the field and was so expensive to manufacture that the product line became a serious financial drain on the company.

The Sources of Advantage

The key to Southern's success in the compact stereo market was its consistent ability to bring excellent products to market before its competitors. This ability was rooted in fundamental changes that Jones and others had made in its development process. These included obtaining broad-based organizational and individual buy-in to key project goals, at the onset, and empowering and encouraging development teams to modify the development process while developing the needed products. In addition it harnessed that capability to a marketing and pricing strategy that was well targeted at Northern's weaknesses. In effect, Southern changed the nature of competition in the industry; Northern was forced to play a game for which it was ill suited—a game Northern never fully comprehended until it was years behind in capability.

Southern Electronics' ability to bring a competitive product to market more rapidly than its chief rivals created significant competitive opportunities. How Southern chose to exploit those opportunities depended on the nature of its competition and its own strategy. But the ability to move quickly in product development created at least three potential sources of advantage:

- *Quality of design.* Because Southern had a twelve-month development cycle, it could begin the development of a new product closer to the market introduction date than its competitors. Whereas Northern had to begin eighteen to twenty months before market introduction, Southern's designers and marketers could gather and refine an additional six months of information before setting out to design a new product. In a turbulent environment, designers face a high degree of uncertainty in the early stages of development about which set of product characteristics will be most attractive to target customers. Additional time to secure feedback on the most recently introduced generation and to learn about market developments and emerging customer preferences may mean the difference between winning and mediocre products. Although the product may use the same basic technologies, additional market information may yield a much better configuration. The product's features and aesthetics may be fresher, more up-to-date, and more closely matched to customer expectations. Thus, Southern could exploit its lead time advantage by waiting to launch its development effort until more and better market information became available. Even though its product would arrive on the market at the same time as its competitors, its product would offer the customer a superior experience.
- *Product performance.* A much faster development cycle gave Southern Electronics the opportunity to launch a new product program well in advance of its competitors. It could use that lead to introduce the next generation of product technology. In this case, the advantage of speed lay not in superior market or customer intelligence, but rather in the ability to exploit technological developments and bring them to market faster than its competitors. The gap in performance this created is depicted in Exhibit 1–7 for a single product generation. As illustrated in the exhibit, a six-month jump on competitors in a market accustomed to eighteen- to twenty-four-month design lives can translate into as much as three times the profit over the market life of the

EXHIBIT 1–7

The Impact of Market Introduction Timing on Lifetime Profits of a Major New Product*

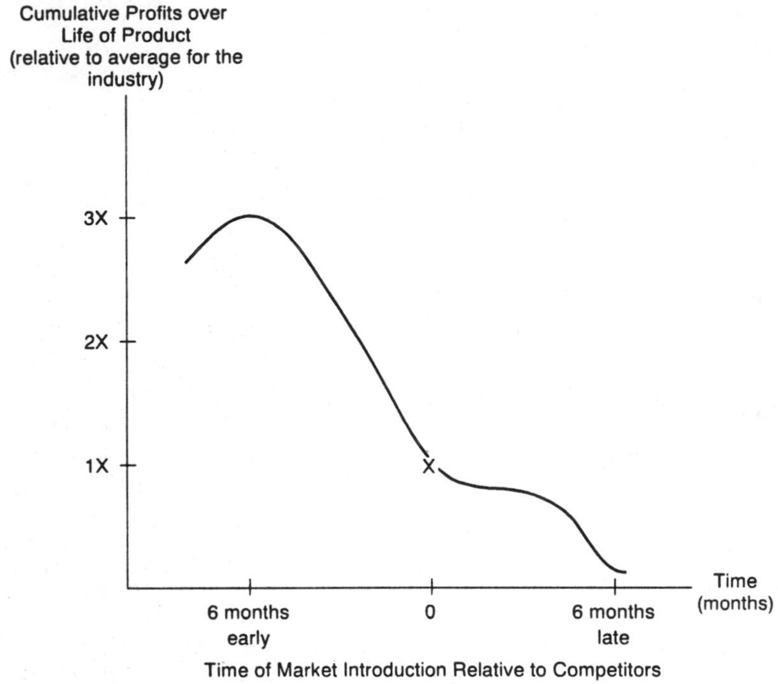

Time of Market Introduction Relative to Competitors

* Introducing at the same time as competitors (0 on the horizontal axis) leads to average profits over the life of the product (1x on the vertical axis). Introducing a new product six months ahead of competitors can triple (3x) total profits over the life of the product; introducing six months behind competitors may mean simply breaking even. Note that getting too far ahead of the market (greater than six months) can be less than optimal.

---

design. Conversely, being late to market with a new product can lead to break-even results and zero profit. This provided Southern with the leverage to control not only their own profits and returns, but also those of their chief competitor, Northern. Putting a sequence of such developments together further widens the competitive gap, as depicted in Exhibit 1–8. The slow-cycle competitor brings new technology to market every two years. The fast-cycle competitor, in contrast, achieves the same performance improvement every twelve months. While the initial advantage of the fast-cycle competitor is relatively small, the ability to move quickly to market eventually creates a significant performance gap. To the extent that customers can discern the difference in performance and to the extent that the gap offers them valuable improvements, a faster time to market creates a superior product.

Exhibit 1–8

Fast-Cycle Development and the Technological Gap*

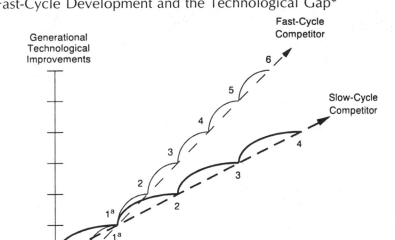

ᵃIndicates product generation.

* This example assumes both competitors incorporate similar amounts of technological change in each generation of product, but the slow competitor lets twice as much time elapse between product generation introductions as the fast competitor. This is what was happening between Northern and Southern Electronics in the compact stereo market (see Exhibit 1–6B, Panel B).

- *Market share and cost.* A better product design and superior product performance gave Southern the opportunity to achieve premium prices in the market. However, a firm may also choose to price its product to create superior value for its customers, thereby translating advantage in design and performance into increases in market share. Where lower costs are driven by growth and increases in volume, increases in market share may translate into improved cost position for the fast-cycle operator. Thus, even if two competitors operate on the same learning curve, the fast-cycle competitor will achieve a cost advantage. However, it may also be the case that the capabilities which underlie fast development cycles create a steeper learning curve. Speed in development is rooted in the ability to solve problems quickly and to integrate insight and understanding from engineering with critical pieces of knowledge in manufacturing. This set of capabilities likewise is critical in achieving cost reductions in established products. Thus, when costs are sensitive to volume and fast-cycle capability enhances a firm's overall learning capacity, the fast-cycle competitor enjoys double leverage in improving its manufacturing costs.

25

How a fast-cycle competitor chooses to exploit the potential advantages in design, product performance, and manufacturing cost will depend on the competitive environment and the firm's strategy. In the case of Southern Electronics, all three dimensions of advantage were important. Initially, Southern used its six-month advantage in lead time to obtain better market information and still introduced its 1986 compact stereo about six months before its competition. In the second generation, however, Southern accelerated its model introduction and began to exploit its development capacity to achieve superior product performance. By 1990, Southern was a generation ahead of its competitors in product technology. It used its superior design and performance to achieve some price premium in the market, but it did not raise prices as much as its performance advantage warranted. The result was a superior value for customers, increases in market share, and steeper slopes on its manufacturing learning curve. Thus, Southern used its advantage in performance and cost both to expand its market share and increase its margins.

But perhaps the most powerful effect of Southern's fast-cycle capability was its ability to change the nature of competition. By improving its development productivity and shortening the time between product generations, Southern forced Northern to play a competitive game that Northern was not prepared to play. Northern would have faced competitive difficulties no matter how it responded to the Southern challenge, but it compounded its problems by failing to change fundamentally its approach to product development. By attempting accelerated development in the context of its traditional systems, Northern created internal confusion, strained its resources, and actually reduced the effectiveness of its development organization. In addition, previously enthusiastic, capable, and hard-working product managers such as Sorenson became frustrated and disappointed. Thus, at the start of the 1990s, Northern Electronics faced the challenge of undertaking a major overhaul of its development process while its margins were eroding, market position was slipping, and morale among some of its best development people was declining. Southern's fast-cycle capability had clearly put Northern and its other major competitors at a significant competitive disadvantage while generating additional enthusiasm and competence among people such as Jones and individual project contributors. Southern was continuing to build momentum as Northern and other competitors continued to lose it.

Achieving competitive advantage through effective development capability is not just a theory. Effective fast-cycle competitors have emerged in a wide range of industries. Firms such as Honda in automobiles, Applied Materials in semiconductor production equipment, ACS in angioplasty, Sony in audio products, Matsushita in VCRs, The

Limited in apparel, Philips in computer monitors, Hill-Rom in hospital beds, and Quantum in disk drives have made the ability to bring outstanding products to market rapidly a central feature of their competitive strategy. Once achieved, and subsequently maintained as the organization grows, an advantage built around fast-cycle capability seems to be strong and enduring. In the first place, the advantage is based on capabilities—human and organizational skills, processes and systems, and know-how—that are difficult to copy. Moreover, effective, rapid development creates superior products and offers customers superior value. It therefore helps to create a market franchise and brand equity. A real product advantage rooted in difficult-to-copy capabilities and a translation of that product advantage into a fundamental market franchise that reinforces its own momentum is a powerful combination. Although product development is difficult, doing it well confers significant advantage. Furthermore, the more challenging the development requirements, the more dramatic the potential impact.

The Plan for the Book

In this book we lay out concepts for the effective organization and management of product and process development. Each chapter frames a particular problem or issue in development, provides a set of ideas for effective management, and illustrates those ideas and their application with several examples. The cases accompanying each chapter in the College version provide an opportunity to apply and develop the concepts and ideas in a practical context.

The first part of the book focuses on the front end of the development process. In Chapters 2 through 5 we discuss the concept of development strategy, the use of maps and mapping to chart an organization's path through the development terrain, the creation of an aggregate project plan to guide a portfolio of development efforts, and the challenge of creating an overall development process that effectively initiates and selects projects and focuses the organization's resources to bring the most attractive projects to market rapidly and efficiently. The thrust of these chapters is laying the foundation for effective development efforts. While the actual development project is a natural locus of attention and effort in organizations, individually effective development projects depend on a strong foundation in strategy, a shared understanding across functional organizations, and an overall process that effectively allocates and concentrates time, energy, attention, and resources on the most attractive opportunities.

Chapters 6 through 10 focus on the management of individual development projects. We first work through an overall framework for evaluating development efforts, including identification of the important phases of development, the measurement of performance, and the critical areas of leverage and choice for managing projects. We then examine the problems of cross-functional integration. A central theme in this part of the book is the power of integrated problem solving. Chapter 8 deals with the problem of organizing development projects. Our emphasis is on the organizational structure, the processes the organization uses to carry out development, and the impact of development leadership. We lay out four contrasting approaches to development project organization and focus particular attention on what we call heavyweight project teams.

The challenge of integration applies not only to large functional organizations like marketing, manufacturing, and engineering, but also at the working level within those organizations and across departments and work groups with different disciplines, tasks, and experiences. Chapter 9 focuses on recent developments in systematic methods and tools for product (and process) development. Concepts such as quality function deployment, design for manufacturability, computer-aided design, and computer-aided engineering represent new design and development methodologies. Much of the thrust of these methodologies is the creation of more effective integration in the development process. In Chapter 10 we examine prototyping, testing, and convergence to a final design. Much of development is a sequence of design-build-test cycles in which prototyping and testing play a central role. Effective management of prototyping is therefore a critical element of effective development capability.

In the final chapters of the book, we shift our attention from the planning and execution of specific projects to the problem of managing the improvement of the development organization and its processes. In Chapter 11 we examine the problem of learning from individual development experiences. This involves not only capturing the insight and understanding that come from current experience, but also capturing that experience in the form of changes in the development process. In addition, learning from experience involves building resources and capabilities to conduct development efforts more effectively in the future. Thus the major focus of Chapter 11 is on mastery of the building blocks for superior development capability and the associated investment in people, skills, tools, and systems.

The book concludes with a chapter on making it happen. We examine alternative improvement paths and focus on the peculiar nature of the development process and consequent issues that managers must examine in pursuing an overall improvement plan. A central theme in this final chapter—and, indeed, throughout the entire book—is the importance of learning by achieving consistency and balance across a wide range of development activities. There are no "three easy steps" to effective development performance. The capabilities that allow an organization to move quickly and efficiently to the market are rooted in people and their skills, organizational structure and procedures, strategies and tactics, tools and methodologies, and managerial processes. This is what makes it so difficult for organizations to improve—and why they acquire such a strong competitive advantage when they do.

Study Questions

1. Product development has been a part of competition at least since the Industrial Revolution. Apparently, doing things faster, more efficiently, and with higher quality has always been an advantage. In what sense, therefore, has product development become more important in competition in recent years? Do you agree that increased speed, efficiency, and quality have become competitive imperatives? Are they imperative under all circumstances?
2. Consider Exhibit 1–2. What is the rationale for dividing the development process into phases? What distinguishes the first two phases from the last phases of Exhibit 1–2?
3. In the A14 stereo project, what explains the differences between the original plan of September 1989 and the third plan revision of May 1990?
4. Consider Exhibit 1–5. Pick one of the characteristics of problematic projects and compare it with its counterpart theme in the outstanding projects. What might explain the problematic characteristic? Where does it come from? What makes moving from problematic to outstanding difficult?
5. What are the key elements in Southern's "fast-cycle" strategy? What explains Northern's response to Southern's strategy? Was Northern's response predictable? Inevitable?
6. The fast-cycle strategy conferred significant advantage upon Southern. Will a fast-cycle strategy work this way under all circumstances? Why or why not?

Ampex Corporation: Product Matrix Engineering

TO: T. Burroughs
FROM: M. Hirschfeld
DATE: March 30, 1979
SUBJECT: Product Matrix Engineering—
          Future Plans

I meant what I said yesterday, Ted. You and your PME Group deserve much of the credit for the success of our VPR$_2$ program start-up. We were so involved with other matters in our discussion that I neglected to ask for your views about the future of PME. Now that you're moving into the Data Systems Division, I would appreciate your recommendations. Do you think PME should become a permanent organization, or should it be disbanded as such ad hoc organizations have been in the past? If PME does become a permanent organization, we will have to define its place in the organization and its charter very carefully.

The note from Morris Hirschfeld raised several issues that Ted Burroughs had thought about often. He was confident that the PME experiment had been a success, and he had a definite opinion about what should be done.

AVSD=Audio Visual Systems Division; ECN=engineering change notice; MRP=materials requirement planning; NAB=National Association of Broadcasters; PME=product matrix engineering; SMPTE=Society of Motion Picture and Television Engineers; VTR=video tape recorder.

This case was prepared by Assistant Professor Margaret B. W. Graham; names of individuals and certain data have been disguised.

The Company

The Ampex Corporation manufactured magnetic tape and magnetic tape equipment, serving a worldwide market with sales of nearly $400 million in 1979 (see Exhibit 1 for financial data). Headquartered in Redwood City, California, it had manufacturing operations in several western and southern states and in a number of countries including Mexico, Brazil, Taiwan, and Japan.

Ampex placed special emphasis on its position as a technological leader in its industry, employing some of the most highly respected design engineers in its Redwood City Engineering Center, a university-like research center that was located with Ampex headquarters near Stanford University. More than half the products sold in 1979 had not existed only five years previously.

At the heart of Ampex's business was the Audio Video Systems Division (AVSD), which supplied high-performance audio and video recording and editing equipment to professional broadcasters. AVSD accounted for 35% of Ampex's sales and more than half of the company's earnings. Ampex had attained its leadership position in broadcast equipment by introducing the first professional transverse scan magnetic video recorder, the Quadruplex VR 1000, to the industry in 1956. During the next two decades, Ampex dominated the quadruplex video recording market claiming a 65% share compared to RCA's 35%. (By 1976 it was estimated that 10,000 quadruplex VTRs had been sold worldwide.) Ampex had extended its line of professional video products to include other proprietary equipment such as the slow-motion disc recorder famed for its instant replay when used to broadcast sports events such as "Wide World of Sports."

The division continued to reaffirm its commitment to scientific excellence through new product introductions every few years. Its latest technological first was an experimental digital video recorder which it demonstrated to the March 1979 convention of the Society of Motion Picture and Television Engineers (SMPTE). That product would not be commercially feasible until the mid-1980s, but Ampex saw it as the kind of product that would keep the company at the forefront of its industry.

Two Video Tape Recorder Technologies

Ampex AVSD's principal product was traditionally the Quadruplex Video Tape Recorder (VTR) for professional broadcasting. The *quad* ma-

EXHIBIT 1

Four-Year Summary of Operations
($ in thousands except per share data)

	1978	1977	1976	1975
Net sales and other income[a]	$322,050	$287,429	$257,935	$244,903
Costs and operating expenses[a]	291,811	262,264	239,153	226,075
Interest expense	6,747	7,736	9,350	13,829
Earnings from continuing operations before nonrecurring income and taxes	23,492	17,429	9,432	4,999
Gains on sales of facilities	—	—	2,473	1,031
Income from nonrecurring royalties, licenses and agreements	—	—	—	13,000
Earnings from continuing operations before taxes on income	23,492	17,429	11,905	19,030
Taxes on income	10,250	8,640	5,520	9,200
Earnings from continuing operations	13,242	8,789	6,385	9,830
Earnings (loss) from discontinued operations, net of taxes	—	—	292	(3,848)
Earnings before extraordinary items	13,242	8,789	6,677	5,982
Extraordinary items: Utilization of tax carry-forwards	6,500	5,435	2,480	4,300
Settlement of class action suits, net of taxes	—	—	(1,125)	—
Net earnings	19,742	14,224	8,032	10,282
Research, development and engineering:				
Research and development	18,123	16,522	15,991	b
Engineering	5,096	5,027	3,758	b
Total company sponsored	23,219	21,549	19,749	20,097
On contract for others	3,077	3,934	6,630	3,411
Total	$26,296	$25,483	$25,379	$23,508
Working capital provided from continuing operations	$21,964	$17,427	$16,863	$22,289
Working capital	134,372	121,338	112,537	126,130
Total debt	92,222	96,284	110,010	143,480
Shareowners' equity	104,386	84,525	70,166	62,134
Current ratios	3.2-1	2.1-1	2.9-1	3.2-1
Debt-equity ratio	0.9-1	1.1-1	1.6-1	2.3-1
Return on equity	19%	17%	11%	17%

[a] Excluding discontinued operations.

[b] Research and development expense as defined in FASB Statement No. 2 cannot be determined.

chine was a large (6 feet high by 3 feet wide) piece of equipment containing expensive parts and delicate circuitry and selling for over $100,000. It recorded its video information in a crosswise (or *transverse scan*) pattern on two-inch magnetic tape (Figure A). The quad recorder was suitable primarily for studio use because of its size and complexity of operation. It was generally sold with accessories such as the slow-motion disc recorder ($100,000) or a computerized editor ($50,000) to form a complete magnetic tape editing system for broadcast production purposes.

FIGURE A   Transverse Scan

Ampex also manufactured and sold a second form of magnetic video tape recorder, the helical scan VTR. Helical recorders were smaller, lighter, and cheaper (base price $5,000–$25,000) than quad. They offered features such as still frame and slow motion that quad recorders did not have, and because they recorded their information on one-inch magnetic tape (see Figure B) at slower recording speed, their tape consumption was roughly one-third of the quad's (helical: 10 square inches per second; quad: 30 square inches per second).

FIGURE B   Helical Scan

During the 1960s helical scan performance had been unacceptable for broadcast use. Its recording format was less forgiving to operate than that of its quad counterpart, requiring constant adjustment to reduce tape tracking errors that caused picture defects. Consequently the helical video recorder had been sold as a low-priced, high-volume product for the institutional market with margins about one-half those of quad equipment. (Helical video recorders contained fewer expensive parts and simpler electronic circuitry.) Ampex had shared the industrial recorder market with numerous Japanese recorder manufacturers including Toshiba, Matsushita, and Sony. Each manufacturer had a different tape format, but since interchangeability of tapes between machines was not crucial in the institutional market, no standard tape format was adopted.

In the early 1970s an auxiliary device called the digital time-based corrector appeared, compensating for the helical recorder's previous quality problems. With their special features, light weight, simplicity and low cost of operation, the improved helicals were ideal for television news gathering from remote locations. Major broadcasters such as Westinghouse and CBS began to demand improved-for-broadcast helical machines.

Some industry observers speculated that potential sales for helical recorders for professional uses could be 20,000 systems. Other experts had been saying for some time that at a price lower than $50,000 the distinction between industrial and professional recorders would disappear and that the total primary market for helical might reach 100,000 systems worldwide.

In 1974 Sony introduced a new model helical recorder that quickly dominated the institutional and industrial market. Ampex withdrew from that market and focused its attention on the professional recorder, launching a program to do a new helical design for broadcast use. John Roberts, product manager for the Ampex video recorder line, recalled:

> It was difficult to persuade first-line engineers who had devoted their entire careers to transverse-scan recording to switch to designing helical machines. They hated to see quad sacrificed on the altar. To them, helical was inferior and would always remain so.

In 1975 the Ampex design team produced a helical video recorder designated the VPR$_1$. The VPR$_1$ offered "outstanding recording and playback with capability of 1/5 speed slow motion and still-frame pictures of broadcastable quality" made possible with the addition of an automatic scanning module (the Ampex AST). To avoid introducing a new tape format to a market already crowded with helical tape formats, the designers of the VPR$_1$ retained the Ampex A format, which they had used in their latest institutional and industrial models. As Doug Grantham, systems manager, explained, "In quad the format never changed. The first quad tape made can be played on the newest machine. We wanted to push for that kind of stability in helical technology too."

Standardization

At the National Association of Broadcasters (NAB) convention in March 1976 the Ampex VPR_1 announcement was closely followed by Sony's revelation that it intended to penetrate the professional video recorder market for the first time with a helical machine called the BVH 1000. Sony's demonstration model equalled Ampex's in major features and price. Sony elected to introduce a different tape format from those it used in earlier helical recorders, one that was similar to Ampex A but not compatible. A third company, Germany's Bosch-Fernseh, announced its intention to market another incompatible version of the helical recorder, which it advertised as rugged, reliable, and less expensive than either of its competitors.

The reception of new recorders by potential customers was enthusiastic, but actual orders were limited because of the standards issue. Major customers wanted the ability to interchange tapes among machines without regard for make of equipment. The Fernseh product was too different for compatibility to be considered, but Sony and Ampex were enough alike to warrant standards negotiations. At the behest of the major customers, CBS and ABC, a standards working group comprising representatives from Sony, Ampex, and several other SMPTE members negotiated a compromise format in 10 months. By January 1978 the new C Format, essentially Sony's format modified for use with Ampex's automatic scanning module, was formally accepted by the SMPTE. Both companies had made concessions that would cost them some months' design rework. The helical machines that the companies had already sold could, under the terms of the agreement, be upgraded with kits to use the C Format.

VPR_2 Design Program

Under pressure to produce their design speedily, the Ampex design team turned to its task of designing a second-generation helical video recorder. The Ampex team adopted three original design goals: 1) to adapt their product for use with the C Format; 2) to keep as many parts and processes compatible with the VPR_1 as possible; 3) to correct known problems with the VPR_1 design. Grantham discussed the effort:

Exhibit 2
VPR$_2$ Configurations and Price List, January 1, 1979

Like the VPR-1, the VPR-2 is available in various configurations to suit any need.

Basic Machine

In its basic configuration, the VPR-2 can be rackmounted, or installed in the convenient "tabletop" housing.

Mini-Console

When used with the Ampex TBC-2 Digital Time Base Corrector, the VPR-2 and the TBC can both be installed in the optional mini-console.

Studio Console

This optional console provides space for the VPR-2, a TBC-2, and other options and accessories.

Studio Console with Monitoring

When fully equipped with optional monitor bridge, the VPR-2 system includes a color picture monitor, a waveform monitor, and vector display.

When mounted in one of the console configurations, the VPR-2 can always be removed and used in its basic record-playback configuration.

We soon realized it was easier to design a new machine than to fix all the problems with the old one. After two weeks we assigned three engineers to do the upgrading kit for the VPR$_1$ while the rest of us concentrated on producing a good C Format machine. When we were finished, the VPR$_2$, with an entirely new scanner assembly that was three times more accurate, was a substantially better machine than the VPR$_1$.

Of course the manufacturing people were unhappy about the new design. We had passed the design deadline, and the manufacturing people claimed the machine was impossible to manufacture. But we were far more concerned about the manufacturing aspects of the design than usual. We've not only given the factory the product design, we've shown them how to make it. One of our best engineers spent time designing tooling for the scanner. In fact, the tooling is the chief proprietary aspect of the product [see Exhibit 2 for VPR$_2$ product information].

Manufacturing

In the early days of the company, audio-video manufacturing had been located in the Redwood City headquarters complex. By the late 1960s taxes and union wage rates had risen sharply in northern California, and

EXHIBIT 2 (cont.)

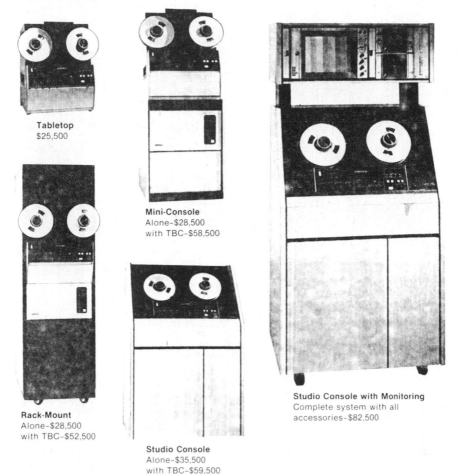

Tabletop
$25,500

Mini-Console
Alone-$28,500
with TBC-$58,500

Rack-Mount
Alone-$28,500
with TBC-$52,500

Studio Console
Alone-$35,500
with TBC-$59,500

Studio Console with Monitoring
Complete system with all
accessories-$82,500

Ampex had moved a large part of its manufacturing 1,000 miles away to nonunion plants in Colorado Springs, where Ampex built a large (250,000-square-foot) two-story plant that housed both its fabrication facilities and its audio-video assembly and test operations (see Exhibit 3 for AVSD organization).[1] Colorado had begun its operations by assembling mature high-volume audio products. By 1978 the plant housed

---

[1] By 1978 assembly workers in Colorado were making $8 per hour, including benefits, while California assembly workers of comparable skill level were receiving $10 per hour, including benefits.

EXHIBIT 3
AVSD Organization Chart, January 1978

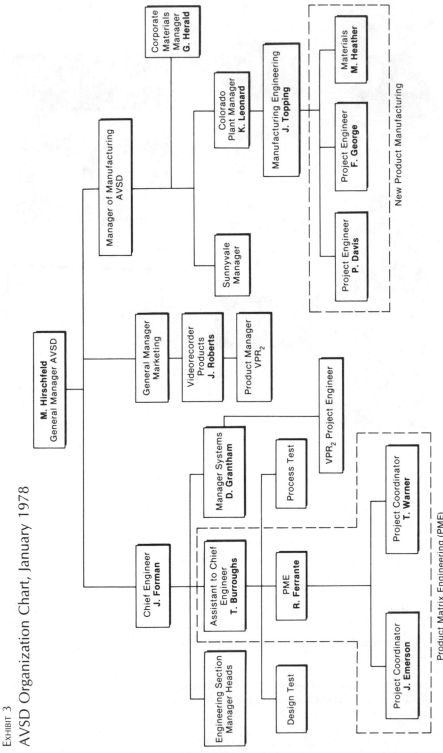

80–90% by unit volume of AVSD's manufacturing capacity and employed 1,800 people.

Ampex AVSD also employed 300 people in Sunnyvale, California, about 20 miles from Redwood City. Sunnyvale handled special projects and small-volume products that did not seem suited for Colorado's large-scale approach. Most of Sunnyvale's engineering staff had transferred from Redwood City.

Some members of the corporate engineering staff said the Colorado plant ought never to have been built; most expressed a low regard for its performance. They said the factory had a history of being unresponsive to their needs, and they complained that it paid less attention to quality and on-time delivery than to keeping down manufacturing costs. Terry Warner, a member of the engineering support staff, described the Colorado plant's approach to manufacturing.

> The philosophy at Colorado has always been to deskill the operator; make the machines do all the thinking. When it comes to assembling new products, that's a problem because the assemblers lack the skills and the necessary judgment to assemble tight tolerance subassemblies, for instance. It's no wonder manufacturing engineering insists that tooling be *foolproof*.

Ken Leonard, plant manager at Colorado Springs, responded to the criticisms from Corporate Engineering:

> Manufacturing has to worry about reliable details and unrealistic schedules. We are responsible for keeping materials costs down and getting volume production up on time. We are always squeezed between an optimistic product delivery date set by marketing and a pessimistic part delivery date set by a supplier with a long lead time. Designers are impractical, undisciplined people who can never make up their minds. Their prototypes are put together by engineers with sandpaper fingers who know exactly what effect they are trying to achieve. These designs defy assembly by a bench worker working for $5 an hour from a vague set of blueprints and a list of approximate specifications.

A major burden on AVSD manufacturing at Ampex were the engineering change notices. (ECNs were official notifications from the design team to the factory engineering staff and purchasing people that a part substitution had been made.) The Colorado plant typically had 31,000 separate parts on hand of which about half were purchased. Typically 15% of this number changed over in one year. To cope with the task of inventory control the factory installed a computerized materials requirements planning (MRP) system in the early 1970s, but recording and updating the data base placed such demands on the materials people that the system had not been reliable.

In 1977 Gary Herold, who joined Ampex from the computer industry, was appointed corporate director of materials and given the task of gaining control of the materials situation in Colorado. Herold said:

> When I arrived in October 1977, we had a horrendous inventory problem. We had 300 people in materials handling, and they were costing us 20% of direct materials. We were coping with 80 ECNs per week of which 60 were marked mandatory. It took a week to put a change through.
>
> I came in and set up a new system. First we separated new product parts from the rest and controlled them off line. We made a rule that we would only enter a part in the data base when the part had already been tested out and the design released, and we wouldn't accept an ECN until there was a high degree of certainty it would be used. We are down to 20 ECNs a week. I think we've influenced the engineers to become much more accurate.

Product Transfer

New product transfer from design to manufacturing had long been a problem area for Ampex. When audio-video manufacturing had been located in Redwood City, the transfer had been accomplished by putting design engineers in the plant to do the early training of assemblers when necessary.

Later, when manufacturing had moved away from headquarters, several different approaches to transferring the product had been tried. First, a limited production line had been set up in Redwood City, where the design was debugged and then transferred to the Colorado plant. When that had resulted in friction between engineering and manufacturing, Sunnyvale had been used as a start-up facility from which the product was transferred to Colorado Springs only when the design was considered firm. Redwood City's engineers could easily visit Sunnyvale.

The VPR_1 project had gone through start-up in Sunnyvale. The experience had been costly in both time and money. Sunnyvale procedures and processes were typically quite different from those employed in Colorado, and the difference was accentuated because the VPR_1 was a higher-volume product (at 75 units a month) than either plant was accustomed to turning out in video products.

The two-phase transfer had resulted in two complete workups for the product. Not only had VPR_1 been totally redocumented for Colorado but certain tools and test equipment had been purchased twice. Colorado blamed the loss of learning on the early units for keeping the factory from bringing down costs and achieving target production volume on schedule. The transfer of information between the two plants' materials control systems had also caused substantial losses on materials. It was rumored that the project had dropped $37,000 in two weeks because of typographical errors alone. Overall, inaccurate part numbers and unrecorded or belatedly recorded changes pushed the materials wastage figure to $150,000 over budget by $100,000. Eighteen months had elapsed before saleable units were being produced in Colorado Springs, and customers had waited for their VPR_1 units as much as a year after ordering them.

Gary Herold commented on the types of problems that had occurred in the VPR_1 program:

> Engineering worried only about its design. They let manufacturing worry about how to make it work: if manufacturing couldn't make the design work then manufacturing was incompetent. Here at Ampex, engineers have always missed design schedules, and they've always been allowed to run over because to enforce a design date would be to stifle creativity. Meanwhile, the factory has always been held to its original product introduction date. This has left the factory with the largest amount of work to do in the shortest amount of time.

As a result of the experience on the VPR_1, it was decided to put the VPR_2 directly into Colorado Springs from Redwood City. The new Colorado Springs plant manager, Ken Leonard, set up a New Product Manufacturing Team especially to handle the interface with Redwood City engineering. The new product group contained two project engineers and one purchasing manager: the first time these functions had answered to a common boss in Colorado (see Exhibit 3). Previously, new products had been handled by the regular staff.

Everyone knew that the VPR_2 was going to be a very important product for Ampex and much different from the VPR_1. Original marketing projections had been 600 units the first year, but by January 1978 1,200 units were on backorder and revised forecasts kept appearing from marketing as further orders came in from new types of customers. To meet new projections Colorado would have to produce 260 VPR_2 units per month. At the new rate the VPR_2 would constitute 70% of the Colorado plant's total unit volume when it was being produced at full volume.

Ampex manufacturing personnel saw the VPR_2 as a formidable manufacturing task in other ways as well. Attention to quality would be paramount, since Sony was known for its high-quality manufacturing. Cost control would be even more significant than it had customarily been because helical recorders were lower-margin products than quads had been. Scrap was budgeted not to exceed $500,000.

The schedule established in July 1977 allowed four months to complete initial design and nine more months before the first 20 sale units were to be delivered early in September. Full-volume production was to be reached in January 1979, by which time it was hoped that labor content might be approaching the steady state goal of 21 hours per scanner. Prompt delivery would be crucial for broadcasting customers, especially those who had ordered hundreds of units for use in the winter and summer Olympics of 1980. According to marketing, inability to promise early delivery might be the determining factor in European sales, where Bosch would be a strong competitor.

Product Matrix Engineering

By October 1977 the VPR_2 design team was still not willing to give out much information about its design. Advance indications of product specifications alarmed the manufacturing staff. The tolerances of the new scanner mechanism were said to be 10 times more exact than those of the VPR_1. Eighty to 95% of the VPR_2 parts were to be new. Essentially only the motor and the transport mechanism remained compatible. In all likelihood these differences would mean major changes in the way the product had to be manufactured. Higher skilled assemblers, an environment controlled for temperature and humidity, and a complex testing procedure might all be necessary.

The Colorado plant's New Product Manufacturing Team members were anxious to gain information to give to their prospective vendors, especially since components were likely to be higher precision than usual. However, the designers would commit to very little, and they resisted taking time to put their specifications on paper until they were ready to call the design firm. Lacking definite information, the manufacturing people could do little in advance without risking substantial materials wastage.

In October a decision was made to establish a liaison effort between new product engineering and manufacturing on the VPR_2 project. The frequent arguments between engineering and manufacturing were becoming heated. Although it was doubtful that the design team would meet its scheduled deadlines, Richard Rothmann, Ampex's executive vice president, had warned the Colorado plant that no slippage would be tolerated in the September 1978 product shipment date.

Ted Burroughs, a former Ampex employee who had left to manage a smaller company several years before, was hired to coordinate the liaison function as an engineering support group. Named assistant to the chief engineer AVSD, Burroughs decided to adopt a matrix form of project management, which he called product matrix engineering.

Burroughs explained the philosophy of his group as follows:

> PME was envisioned as a natural buffer between Manufacturing and Engineering. Previous attempts to establish a high-level liaison had been unsuccessful. When I was hired there was more discussion as to whether the head of PME should be at general management level; but the key idea was to start at the grass roots level this time, to resolve conflicts before they reached higher levels. It was important that neither side felt that the PME head was in the opposing camp. We represented the factory to Engineering and Engineering to the factory.

Burroughs's criterion in selecting people to be on the PME team was what he called the "green beret principle," requiring each to have experience in more than one function. Bob Ferrante, for example, Burroughs's next-in-command, had been with Ampex for 17 years. He had worked first on the limited production line in Redwood City and later at Sunnyvale, always with skilled people on small-volume or custom products. Later, as a junior engineer, he had become involved in interfacing with the Sunnyvale factory on several projects.

At first the role of PME was loosely defined. In general the group concerned itself with aspects of the product start-up that mattered most to the factory: documentation, cost structure, and materials control. Its responsibilities evolved partly in response to the VPR$_2$ design. As the design became more complicated and the start-up and production tasks it required began to exceed the previous experience of the manufacturing group, PME assumed more responsibilities.

PME devoted several months to improving the amount and quality of information that passed between engineering and manufacturing, especially discovering the advance information the factory needed about critical parts before the design was released. (Critical parts were those that had long lead times or were exceptionally difficult to procure either because there was a limited number of qualified suppliers or because a part was unusually exacting in its specifications.) PME members also notified the New Product Manufacturing Team when meetings were held on program decisions that would affect them. Gradually they gained the confidence of the Colorado New Product Team, but Engineering also had to be convinced. Terry Warner recalled that it was six months before the design team also trusted him.

To assure continuity and accuracy of information, the PME team developed new procedures and documentation devices for Ampex. A drawings tree (the Xmas tree) identified by number the drawings that were needed for each subassembly. A material status chart was a bill of materials color-coded to indicate PME's confidence level concerning the likelihood of a part being used in the final design. Such documents formed the basis for frequent project reviews and served as control feedback documents. Warner explained:

> As soon as we could get any information at all about a part of the VPR$_2$ design, we would publish an initial compilation which would stimulate responses from the design engineers. Then we would update and republish our charts and documents immediately and repeat the same procedure. Each new piece of information was factored into the schedule to come up with some idea of a critical path. And each time we were reasonably confident about a new part number, we would pass it along to Colorado.

Procedures were also established for document control of engineering changes. Every ECN had to go through the same people both in Redwood City and in Colorado in the same order. Setting up documents and procedures alone took several months of full-time work.

By March 1978 most members of the PME had been accepted as individuals, and the group began taking on tasks that were more than simply interface responsibilities. Burroughs insisted that the group farm out everything it possibly could to the factory, but a number of tasks had arisen, such as precision part purchasing or fixture testing, that the factory did not have the resources or the time to handle. Since an expanded role for PME would require top management approval, Burroughs proposed a more formalized PME structure that would also act as project interface for other new products to be transferred between Redwood City and satellite factories. The VPR$_2$ program would continue to receive highest priority until it was completed.

Burroughs requested and received a budget of $500,000 for equipment and permission to hire assemblers. This allowed him to set up a small scanner assembly laboratory and to take on a supplementary role in purchasing and prototype building.

The new PME organization consisted of 17 people (see Exhibit 4). Initially it was agreed that PME should order parts for, build, and assist in testing 14 engineering models of the VPR$_2$ system.

As soon as the initial design was completed, the first prototypes were built. The PME assembly group proved to have real advantages as prototype builders and fixture testers. They could give engineers instant feedback on the product design and fixtures, from people who were more representative of bench work labor available in Colorado than the engineers would be. The nine PME assemblers were medium-skilled

Exhibit 4

PME Organization Chart, March 23, 1978

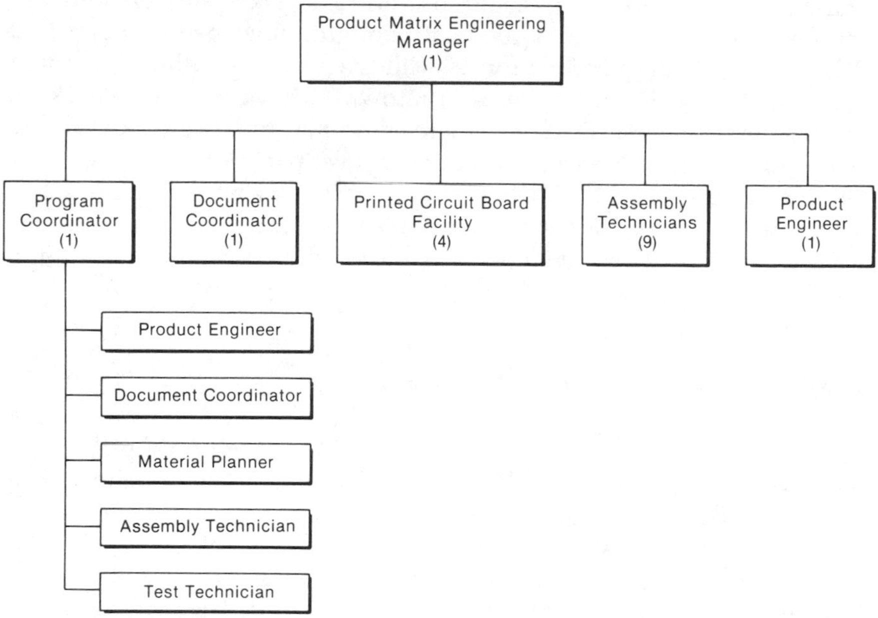

```
                    ┌─────────────────────────┐
                    │ Product Matrix Engineering│
                    │         Manager          │
                    │           (1)            │
                    └─────────────────────────┘
```

| Program Coordinator (1) | Document Coordinator (1) | Printed Circuit Board Facility (4) | Assembly Technicians (9) | Product Engineer (1) |

Under Program Coordinator:
- Product Engineer
- Document Coordinator
- Material Planner
- Assembly Technician
- Test Technician

NOTE: Personnel in parentheses totals 17.

technicians paid $8.50 per hour. They could read blueprints, and they each learned to do a variety of jobs. All of them learned to put together major parts of an entire scanner.

As time became short, Burroughs proposed to do 100 scanner modules in Redwood City, while Colorado geared up for the system assembly first. PME would calibrate scanner assembly fixtures, assemble and test the engineering models, and then assemble and test the first saleable units. Then personnel from the Redwood City scanner laboratory would transfer to Colorado Springs to help assemble the first scanners there. Meanwhile, PME would assemble and ship the 20 saleable units to be delivered in September.

Disagreement arose over the number of scanner units that Redwood City should build. The engineers were pleased with the PME assembly's early performance and argued that at least 200 saleable scanner modules should be produced by PME. Colorado argued that it needed to have control over those important parts of the VPR$_2$ systems. Prime costs, both materials and labor, would be twice as high in Redwood

City. Labor rates in general were higher in Redwood City than in Colorado, and parts were much more expensive. While Colorado purchased in larger lots and could promise longstanding relationships with reliable suppliers, Redwood City bought only small numbers and was known among vendors for its willingness to pay a high premium for immediate delivery. It was also known to have no entry check on parts so that material delivered there often had to be reworked in the model shop. The adapter casting, one critical part of the scanner, cost $90 when purchased by PME in a lot of 150, $25 when purchased in an 800-unit lot by Colorado from the same vendor. In the end, the number of 70 saleable scanners was accepted as a compromise figure for PME to assemble.

Outcome

The VPR$_2$ program met each of its stated goals. Twenty completed systems were shipped on schedule in September 1978. The Colorado plant was turning out completed systems at the rate of 100 per month by January 1, 1979, though it had yet to assemble saleable scanners. Seventy scanners had not been enough to debug the new tooling, and Burroughs had transferred them later than planned. The material scrappage cost charged on the VPR$_2$ product start-up was $10,000, a fraction of the amount budgeted.

Manufacturing engineers at the Colorado plant noted, however, that there had been additional costs associated with PME's handling of the VPR$_2$ start-up that had not been captured by conventional measures. Since printed circuit board purchasing had been handled by the PME Group, for instance, rework in the model shop of perhaps $50,000 had been absorbed into engineering overhead rather than charged to manufacturing (see Exhibit 5 for unit cost information about the first 150 scanners assembled). The 11 complete systems assembled at Redwood City had prime costs 50% higher than expected steady state system costs were likely to be, while the first 10 assembled in Colorado were only 25% higher than steady state.

Customarily the Manufacturing Engineering Group in Colorado handled tooling for new product assemblies in their own plant. It had been a blow to their morale to be passed over on VPR$_2$. Redwood City's decision to design the fixture for the VPR$_2$ scanner was interpreted as a sign of low esteem for their capabilities at headquarters. They complained that the fixtures designed in Redwood City were $100,000 more expensive than they might have been, and that the tooling required too much judgment from assemblers. Peter Davis, an engineer at the Colorado plant, explained the consequences:

Exhibit 5
VPR$_2$ Scanner Cost History, First 150 Units

	Scanner Prime Cost Index		
Number of Units	*Labor*	*Material*	*Total*
1 NAB prototype	3	3	6
10 demonstration models	.7	2.9	3.6
120 PME limited production	.48	1.32	1.8
20 Colorado early models	.36	.94	1.3
Expected steady state	.33	.67	1[a]

[a] Base = prime cost (labor and materials) for scanner in steady state. Scanner represents one-eighth of total system prime cost. Labor accounted for 33% of scanner prime costs as compared to 60% of system prime costs. Total factory cost includes additional 300% factory overhead.

So far, we've been trying to put together the scanner here at the plant using selected employees with their old job grades and giving them merit pay for scanner work. But we may have to hire a more skilled grade of employee to get the consistent quality output we have to have. An extra $1 per hour will increase the prime cost significantly, but getting good output the first time will put less strain on our testing capacity and improve our volume performance considerably.

Because of the evident success of the VPR$_2$ program, many key PME members were promoted out of the group. Burroughs was named operations manager in the Data Systems Division. Ferrante was given the title of engineering section manager when he succeeded Burroughs as PME head. Jerome Topping, head of Manufacturing Engineering in Colorado, praised the PME Group but expressed concern about the effect the promotions might have:

PME worked well as our eyes in Redwood City. But I am worried about what's happening now. The key to this type of group is continuity. It took us a long time to learn to trust the PME people as individuals to represent our interests fairly when we weren't there. Of course, the matrix structure and the new control procedures were partially responsible for PME's success, but I'd have to say that it was probably 70% people and 30% procedures. PME needs very strong interface types with a high level of authority, people who can insist on getting a part order released, for instance, where it's appropriate.

Even though no new products as critical as VPR$_2$ were expected during the next year, there was clearly more than enough work to keep a

PME group occupied. Already under Ferrante, PME was being deluged with requests to take on new types of work that the group had not originally been set up to do. Because of the small assembly group's skill and flexibility, several product managers wanted PME to build their saleables for custom products. PME had also earned a reputation as a good training center for lead assemblers through its training of the scanner assembly team from Colorado. Ampex's plant in Juarez, Mexico, wanted to send a group of leadmen to be trained by PME to assemble a new solid-state computerized editing system. Taking on either the training work or the assembly of saleables would soon require a larger PME staff, but Ferrante thought he could easily find 20 more people (mostly college students) to work as PME assemblers during the summer. The old PME quarters, located between Design Engineering and the model shop, would be too cramped to accommodate any extra people, but Ferrante knew of some unused storeroom space on a floor two stories below, where PME could set up expanded quarters.

PME was having some problems with other new product transfers it was coordinating. The VPR_{20}, portable version of the VPR_2, was supposed to be transferred to Sunnyvale, but had slipped far behind schedule at the prototypes stage. The design engineer in charge of the VPR_{20} had taken the project out of PME to build the demonstrator models in Engineering on a six-week crash effort before the NAB convention in March 1979. PME members blamed the delay on a single-source part that had not been delivered on schedule, while the designer blamed PME for paying so much attention to building saleable VPR_2 scanners that they missed their deadlines on his lower-priority project.

PME Future

Inside Ampex, ideas differed as to the role PME should play in the aftermath of VPR_2. Certain design engineers argued that their new products should now go directly to Colorado. They cited recent quick response time from the plant as evidence that Colorado's New Product Manufacturing Team was becoming effective. Warner wondered whether institutionalizing PME would make it a less effective form of organization to use in a crisis—"a peacetime army."

Doug Grantham, as new engineering manager, wanted to keep PME as a short-run production facility under the control of Engineering. It could continue to produce prototypes and demonstration models, and it could do saleables when its services weren't otherwise required. "Of course what I'm really saying is I trust Bob Ferrante, not PME. PME without Bob Ferrante, I'm less sure of. Who knows whether the person who succeeds him will be as capable?" Herold commented:

> Ampex can do better than PME. What really needs to happen is for the factory to be involved directly in the design process. Now that the New Product Manufacturing Team has some experience, they should be able to manage the transition alone. We might consider a small liaison group at Redwood City, but they should be factory generated and under factory control.
>
> Of course, it suits Engineering to keep manufacturing capabilities limited. Your average high-technology company represses innovation in the factory because it inhibits innovation in design. But we're no longer in a controlled marketplace willing to wait for its products.

Past and present members of PME also disagree as to if and how their group should continue. Ferrante wanted an ongoing organization with a flexible role, "You can't have fixed and hard rules about what should be done for every project ahead of time. On some we just check the documents; on some we can proof the design; for some we handle purchasing, and for some we might go so far as to build saleable units."

Burroughs' Response

Burroughs began writing his answer to Hirschfeld:

TO: M. Hirschfeld
FROM: T. Burroughs
DATE: March 31, 1979
SUBJECT: PME Future

As I see it, Morris, you have three options. You can keep PME as it is, a grass roots organization reporting to Engineering; you can put an end to it and leave its most important functions to be picked up by the New Product Manufacturing Team, or you can give PME the status I think Ampex's business now demands and appoint the head of PME as a general manager reporting directly to you.

Such a person could be involved in the earliest project planning session and could take part in new process decisions that would affect many new products. The decision whether to adopt automatic component insertion equipment for electronics subassembly is an example.

This person would have the power to keep good integrators in the group and develop them, not have them promoted away when they showed capability. Finally this manager could insist that it be standard procedure for all new products to go through PME before entering the factory.

Braun AG:
The KF 40 Coffee Machine
(Abridged)

"If we're going to do it, we've got to quit stalling," exclaimed Albrecht Jestädt, head of development for a new coffeemaker at Braun AG. "I've said all I can about polypropylene, and I'm convinced we can go with it," he added, taking another sip of his beer.

At the end of the day in January 1983, Jestädt and his colleagues were discussing Braun's newest design: an elegant, cylindrical coffeemaker, called the "KF 40," destined for the mid- and upper end of the mass market. To meet management's cost targets, however, they would have to use polypropylene, a much less expensive plastic than Braun's traditional material, and whether so doing would jeopardize Braun's reputation for quality was a matter of intense debate throughout the company. Unlike the very expensive polycarbonate, Braun's traditional material, polypropylene could not be molded into large, complicated parts (like the KF 40's "tank") without suffering so-called "'sink" marks on surfaces that were supposed to be flawlessly even. So the designers had devised a solution that involved a major departure from the smooth, winter-white surfaces characteristic of all Braun household products. (See Exhibit 1 for a prototype.)

"The decision is obvious," claimed Gilbert Greaves, business director for household products. "We need this product *now*, and we have to stop being quite so picky."

"I think we should be picky," said Hartwig Kahlcke, the industrial designer on the project. "But we feel that the rippled design for

Exhibit 1

Prototype for Braun's KF 40

the tank actually enhances the surface appearance, without compromise."

"Maybe," said Hartmut Stroth, recently appointed director of corporate communications. "But it's no trivial matter. It's true that if we lose a year, we might not get in the market at all. Yet *nothing* is worth losing our reputation for superior quality. Not even the mass market." Stroth, who had served for over a decade in various communications positions at Braun, was very sensitive to the importance of Braun's "visual equity" and the need for maintaining it: "Not only do we have to think hard about how this corrugated surface design would fit into the Braun 'look,' but also about what that look represents. The idea of using design to mask sink marks bothers me in principle, and it may not work in practice, especially if the stuff doesn't hold up. I'm anything but risk-averse in this business, but I need to be convinced."

"Then let's go ahead with the trial tooling," Kahlcke responded. "The chairman has already okayed it; maybe that will convince you." Not waiting for Stroth's response, Kahlke inquired about the chairman's views to date. "I know he liked the design, and I know he wants the product. What does he think about the material at this point?"

"You tell me," answered Lorne Waxlax, chairman of the board and Braun's CEO. He would have to make the ultimate decision and had just dropped in, as was his custom, to get the latest thinking on the KF 40.

Company Background: Braun by Design

Braun AG began as a family-owned radio and small appliance business founded in 1921 by Max Braun. In the 1940s, Braun developed a novelty, the electric razor, which he introduced in 1950. After Braun's death in 1951, his sons, Artur and Erwin, took over, and three years later they asked their friend, Fritz Eichler, an artist then working in the theater, to help them find a new approach to their struggling business. In 1955, looking for an architect to help build a new office building, the company hired Dieter Rams, just two years out of architecture school.

Rams became Eichler's protégé, and together they built a small, intense design department at the company's headquarters in Kronberg, Germany. Convinced they could change the taste of their fellow citizens, Eichler, Rams, and colleagues set out to design and build a new kind of product. (See Exhibit 2 for Rams' ten commandments of good design.)

Eichler and Rams believed that their design philosophy should permeate the company, providing a recognizable identity not only in its products, but in every aspect of its relations with customers. (See Exhibit 3, "The Principles of Braun's Corporate Identity.") In Rams' view, achieving that identity required top management support of good design, and team work—constant interaction among disciplines. But designers also needed certain responsibilities and authority; otherwise, they would arrive, at most, at "superficial product cosmetics."

According to Rams, designers needed four things. First, they had to be responsible for configuring all elements of the product that would influence its final appearance. Second, designers needed the authority to determine the dimensions of a product—e.g., the positioning and ergonomic design of its operating functions; third, they must be the ones to decide on surface structures, colors, product labeling and imprinting; fourth, they needed to cooperate with the engineers on construction problems—e.g., manufacturability—whenever the form of a product directly depended on the construction.

53

EXHIBIT 2

10 Principles of Good Design

1. Good design is innovative.
2. Good design enhances the usefulness of a product.
3. Good design is aesthetic.
4. Good design displays the logical structure of a product; its form follows its function.
5. Good design is unobtrusive.
6. Good design is honest.
7. Good design is enduring.
8. Good design is consistent right down to details.
9. Good design is ecologically conscious.
10. Good design is minimal design.

"Braun has an uncompromising commitment towards the pursuit of excellence in performance-oriented design. Every product designed and manufactured by Braun must adhere to these commandments of good design. So, too, should every consumer demand such quality in the selection of a product—be it furniture, clothing, an automobile or a home appliance."

—Dieter Rams
Braun's Chief Designer

EXHIBIT 3

The Principles of Braun's Corporate Identity

"Braun regards the consumer as a *partner* in its business, not as an *object* of its strategy that is open to manipulation.

"Braun believes that consumer desires relate to genuine needs, and employs its expertise, inventiveness, know-how, etc. to satisfy these needs.

"Braun seeks to satisfy these needs in an optimal way, perhaps even better than the consumer expects.

"However, Braun refuses to persuade people to buy its products on the basis of a presentation which meets—or pretends to meet—entirely different needs (which are not amenable to rational consideration) for prestige, ego-support, ostentatious consumption, cosmetic effectiveness, etc.

"Braun refuses to exploit human weaknesses to improve its results, and rejects any means of 'hidden persuasion.'

"Braun also rejects all methods involving purely superficial attraction: in place of this, it has demonstrated that firm concentration on product design which is as good and functional as possible—including external aspects—is also experienced as aesthetically satisfying."

Although Rams was not without critics, his work was an effective counterweight to the popular assumption that designers merely dreamed up the external form of a product. Moreover, he adamantly stood by his own definition of "functional": that the purpose of good design is to fulfill the *primary function* of a product, including its need to be appealing to the user so it would be a welcome object in his or her environment.

By the mid-1970s Braun had built a thriving business, primarily in small home appliances (e.g., shavers, coffeemakers, and mixers), with additional sales in consumer electronics (e.g., cameras and hi-fi equipment). Further, the Braun design group was succeeding in its mission. One of their first products, a heavy-duty kitchen mixer (1957), was still in production and selling well. Most famous was their shaver, familiar to men all over the world. Many Braun products had won design awards; 36 of them, including Braun's first coffeemaker, had found a permanent place in New York's Museum of Modern Art.

The company's mission was carried out not only in its products, but in its people. The company's principles had permeated its corporate consciousness and were second nature even at lower levels in the organization. Almost any employee could tell a visitor that Braun's values were embodied in its products, which had to have three characteristics: (a) first-class design; (b) superior quality; and (c) functions or features ahead of the competition. "We'll never bring out just a me-too product" echoed in every department.

The Gillette Connection

In 1967, the Braun brothers sold the company to an American consumer products giant, Gillette, well known for its mass-produced, mass-marketed products like razors, blades, and toiletries that had been marketed in Europe since the turn of the twentieth century. For the first several years, Gillette left Braun's product strategy intact while infusing some of its management expertise into the organization. In fact, very few people knew that this German company *par excellence* had an American owner. But Braun soon began to expand its operations in other countries and extend its target markets beyond the opinion leaders it had originally cultivated.

For example, in 1971, Lorne Waxlax, a Gillette manager since 1958, took charge of Braun's Spanish plant. He largely refocused the operation, emphasizing product development, sophisticated manufacturing, market research, and television advertising. The plant manufactured Braun's first successful mass-produced kitchen appliance, the hand blender, and served as the training ground for Braun's mass-produced appliance motors. By the early 1980s, Braun's sales exceeded $400 million (see Exhibit 4).

Braun's Organization and Operations

Braun AG in 1983 was organized into three main functions: business management, technical operations, and group sales. (See organization chart in Exhibit 5.) Business management, a coordinating group established in 1976, was essentially strategic marketing. Until Gillette came along, Braun had assumed that if one made a good product, it would sell. And it generally did. But in 1975, marketing became more important, as the domestic and international marketing people came together under a single group. A director for each product group reported to the head of business management, as did the director of communications, which included packaging.

Braun invested heavily in technology, and all key technically related disciplines were based at company headquarters under Dr. Thomas H. Thomsen, recently appointed director of technical operations. Previously, he had been head of engineering for Gillette in both London and Boston. Technical operations comprised four functional groups: R&D, Manufacturing, Quality Assurance, and Industrial Design.

The research and development department employed 220 people and included scientists and engineers working on advanced technology, as well as those involved in product development. R&D was headed by Dr. Peter Hexner, an American ex-army colonel who had directed Gillette's advanced technology department for 10 years. He commented on the challenge of balancing technology with the demands of design: "We have the classic conflicts. Design wants an elegant shaver a centimeter thick, and I have to knock reality into their heads: 'You can't fit a motor into a case a centimeter thick.' "

Process development and manufacturing engineering were part of the manufacturing organization, which managed Braun's component and assembly plants. Over three-quarters of Braun's manufacturing activity took place in its two large state-of-the-art plants in Walldürn and Marktheidenfeld (smaller operations were located in Spain, Ireland, Mexico, Argentina, and Brazil). Because of German labor's high cost, the manufacturing organization was continually pressured to produce efficiently, particularly in a plant like Marktheidenfeld that produced a wide variety of low volume products including kitchen appliances.

EXHIBIT 4
Braun Group Financial Information (millions of dollars)

	1980	*1981*	*1982*
Net sales	$496.1	$451.4	$403.4
Profit from operations	23.6	22.8	33.3
Identifiable assets	384.3	325.2	301.5
Capital expenditures	21.5	23.6	20.4
Depreciation	17.3	18.9	16.6

EXHIBIT 5
Corporate Structure

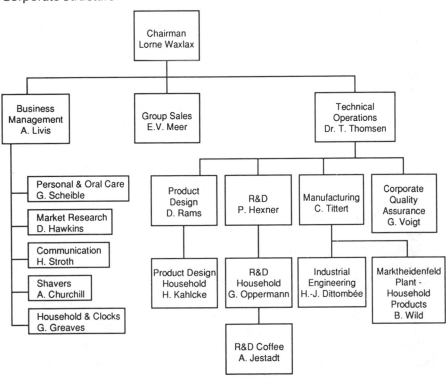

(For example, the plant produced around 700 units of the KF-35 coffeemaker per day.) While efforts to improve operations included automation, especially assembly, more challenging was designing a product so it required minimal assembly. "Anyone can make a cheap product with many parts and hire cheap labor offshore to screw them on. But not everyone can reduce as many parts as possible to one," said Bernard Wild, plant director at Marktheidenfeld. "We can prove that advanced industrial nations don't have to forfeit manufacturing just because their labor costs are high. Our resources are in our brains and imaginations-our know-how."

Quality assurance was responsible for analysis of competitive offerings and rigorous testing during the product development process. Because Braun insisted that all its products be better than those of all the competition, the quality group relentlessly pursued the smallest detail with very high standards. As Werner Utsch, a quality engineer, commented, "We take them apart down to the last screw."

The fourth group in technical operations, industrial design, had an impact on the company far beyond its 16-member size. Indeed, Dieter Rams, head of the department, felt that small size was an important ingredient in its success. The department employed seven designers, most of whom had won the Braun Prize, a design award the firm had offered to design students since 1968. By 1983 Rams' international stature often resulted in his being equated with Braun design almost exclusively. Yet he found this star status awkward: "I constantly have to stress that I don't do everything; I'm simply the motor that drives the department. I try to give other people the credit they deserve."

Until recently, Rams had reported only to the chairman. But because of time limitations, Waxlax assigned industrial design to technical operations, where most problems could be solved. The direct line to the chairman remained, but was used only for the most important issues and impasses. Rams noted, "I've had a good understanding with every chairman I've worked with. But often designers aren't so lucky. We often educate business management people to the point where they begin to understand design and are supportive to us, but then they leave."

Product Development: The Triangle of Power—Design, Technology, Marketing

Product development had been relatively informal until 1980, when three people, representing R&D, business management, and manufacturing engineering, came together to develop procedures to make the process more operational and efficient. The result was a product development manual, introduced in 1981, that covered the responsibilities of key persons in a team (called a MTS team, for marketing-technology-strategy), definitions of elements in project development (e.g., different kinds of models), product specification guide, stages ("categories") and signoff points in the process. (See Exhibit 6 for the project manual's table of contents.)

The "product program manager" (PPM) was responsible for maintaining these procedures; he or she chaired team meetings and represented the team vis-à-vis management, reporting directly to the head of technical operations or business management. The team itself had no formal leader. Various people took over as the stage in the product development process dictated, and stronger personalities could be influential; Jestädt, for example, first as product program manager, then as R&D manager for coffee, had quickly emerged as the de facto leader

Exhibit 6

Contents of Product Development Handbook

	Chapter
Project Procedures for New Products	1
Introduction	1.1
Goals	1.2
Assumptions	1.3
Tasks, Competence, Responsibilities	2
Project team	2.1
Project manager	2.2
Project team representatives	2.3
Project Development Procedure	3
Assumptions/principles	3.1
Implementation	3.2
Definition of terms	3.3
Exceptions	3.4
Project Profile	4
Explanations	4.1
Forms for project profile	4.2
Project Reporting	5
Project book	5.1
Reporting to the chairman	5.2
Summary	6
Product development flow chart	6.1

of the coffee machine project. (See Exhibit 7 for the PPM's and team's formal responsibilities.) In addition to the core team, people from other groups and disciplines—sometimes as many as 40—became involved as the project proceeded.

The team's monthly reports to the chairman had a standard format, divided into four sections: Description, Status, Further Steps, and Problems (or Risks). Although these monthly reviews were considered effective in motivating people to move toward the project goal, Waxlax did not like to use them as a threat: "The trick is to know whether the deadline is truly viable or not. It's easy for marketing to insist on a deadline—they don't have to do the work. I believe the engineers know better than I how fast the team can go, and for that reason I don't want to force it unduly."

Waxlax saw the meetings as an efficient way to keep up to date on all that was going on and to keep on top of problems and conflicts as they arose. He didn't believe in minimizing conflict, but saw it as positive for the company: "It's often the guy who is against something who forces it to become better." He also viewed the monthly meetings as "a chance for me to encourage people," he added.

The point at which a project became formal and began to adhere to the *Projektablauf* [Project Procedures] varied. If, for example, a project had proceeded informally rather far in its development before entering the formal product development process, it might simply be formalized and have product specifications delineated. In its early stages, a project like the KF 40 might have provided monthly reports to the chairman for some time before becoming a formal project. (See Exhibit 8 for the Braun product development process line.)

The industrial design department played a central role in development, particularly at the front end of the process. Because most key disciplines at Braun were located in the same building, much communication about development took place informally, and no one really kept track of where ideas came from and when they first got together with a colleague from another department. That design, because of its reputation, often received disproportionate credit for a product occasionally irked some engineers and scientists, whose contributions were less visible. Well aware of this problem, the company's chairman accepted the responsibility of keeping the rivalry healthy.

Industrial design's relationship to other departments varied. Within the "triangle of power" (design-technology-marketing), design felt most akin to technology. The designers kept up with new developments in such fields as materials science, for example. "We under-

EXHIBIT 7

Formal Responsibilities of the Project Manager and Project Team Members*

The Project Team

Tasks

- Collective development of the project goals and procedures (the Project Profile) on the basis of the product concept determined by the MTS team as well as the product profile.
- The assignment of functional-specific tasks to the relevant team member.
- The independent solving of problems in order to reach the goals articulated by the project profile.
- The development of alternatives when deviations from the project profile are necessary and the formulation of written proposals for changes for approval of the MTS team.

Authority

- Shortening of the planned course of product development when possible through changes in the project profile.

Responsibility

- The responsibility of the project team consists of the responsibility of the individual team members and the project manager.

The Project Manager

Tasks

- Overall coordination of the project from planning to production startup and control over fulfillment of project goals.
- Requisition of representatives from functional departments and the establishment of a project team.
- Calling and running of project meetings; preparation of meeting reports.
- Maintenance of the Project Book.
- Written records of project assignments.
- Planning and implementation of phase reviews at the end of each development category and whenever needed.
- Reports to product line manager.

Authority

- The right to direct information from team members and their superiors in the respective departments.
- The right to make necessary changes in the project profile and to submit written proposals for changes for approval by the MTS team.

Responsibility

- For coordination of
  - individual assignments in all functions.
  - project procedures.
  - information flow (including among team members).
  - supervisions of costs, deadlines, and performance in accordance with the project profile.

EXHIBIT 7 (cont.)

- For the content of the project profile and project reports.
- For assuring that any changes in the product objectives set by the MTS Team are made only in exceptional circumstances and only with the approval of the MTS team.

The Team Members

Tasks

- Handling of tasks in his functional area.
- Assure readiness, in cooperation with the product line supervisor, for his department's contribution to the project.
- Timely reports to the project manager about the completion of his department's tasks or deviation therefrom, in accordance with the project profile.
- Communicate information from his product line superior and other colleagues in his department.
- Nominate further representatives from his department (in agreement with the product line supervisor).

Authority

- Each team member can request that the project manager call a team meeting.
- Each team member has operating room, within the project profile, for solving problems.

Responsibility

- The team members of individual departments bear responsibility for the technical performance of their part of the work.
- The team members are responsible for ensuring the flow of information from their departments that pertains to the project.

* From *Handbuch Projektablauf von neuen Produkten*, section 2.

---

stand technology, so when we have an idea, it is not unrealistic technically. We don't come up with totally impossible ideas," explained Rams. Likewise, with manufacturing, the group knew what it meant to design a product for manufacturability; if they were having difficulties, all they had to do was to go down the hall and across the parking lot to the engineering building. Such interaction among all disciplines was daily fare at Braun.

Marketing was something else, however. Business management often had conflicts with design because, said the marketers, the latter insisted on certain principles that were not always viable in the marketplace. "The problem with designers," Greaves, director of household products, sighed, "is that they think they design for eternity. Rams will hand me a 1965 design and expect me to go for it today." Sometimes the conflicts were trivial. For example, "one time we argued with Kahlcke (an industrial designer) over the baseplate of the

EXHIBIT 8

Product Development Procedures Outline and Definitions

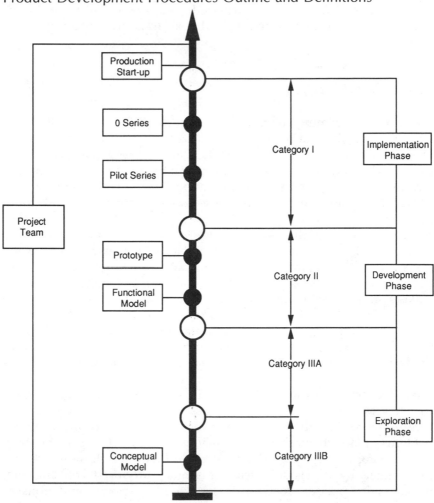

mixer. Because of his obsession with details, he wanted it changed. I told him that was ridiculous, since no one would ever see it," recounted Greaves. "The cord storage was not in the base, so there was no reason whatsoever to turn the mixer over. But Kahlcke got his way!"

People in industrial design had a different perspective. Noted Rams: "I don't mind if technology has greater influence than design; we understand each other and can work things out. But when mar-

keting gets power, it can be bad." For example, sometimes marketing got its way with regard to color. "Why should we pay attention to color fads? Just because red cars are popular one year,
why should we have a red hair dryer? It is not integral to the
design."

A New Strategy

Lorne Waxlax became chairman of Braun in 1980. After his five-year
stint in Spain, he had managed Braun's non-Central European export
business for three years, and then headed business management for
two. Waxlax had long wanted to encourage Braun to get rid of cameras
and hi-fi and to focus more effectively on its core technologies in the
personal care and appliance businesses. As chairman, Waxlax could
proceed with this strategy.

While narrowing the product line, Waxlax also saw opportunity
in six segments of the consumer appliance business: coffeemakers,
irons, toasters, hairdryers, shavers, and food preparation products. They were big, and they were constant; the market for coffeemakers in Europe alone was over 9 million units per year. Even
a small percentage share would make a good business, but Waxlax
was "always going for a big share." Both business management
and Braun's designers eagerly embraced this new strategy. Rams
made very clear his philosophy: good design should be for everyone.

By 1983 Braun was well established in several product families. Electric shavers were their biggest and most widely marketed product line,
accounting for half the company's revenues. In many countries Braun
held first place in market share; wherever they were present, they
were among the top three. The household division, whose image was
represented by its classic kitchen machine, produced coffeemakers,
mixers, juice presses, food processors, food choppers, and irons as
well. In the personal care area, hairdryers and curling irons were the
most successful, having achieved market leadership in Europe.
Braun's exports were continuing to grow: in 1982 exports accounted
for 75% of its turnover.

Waxlax and his top managers wished to focus on Braun's core products and expertise, its reputation for excellence in design, and the opportunities within grasp at the upper end of the mass market. Balancing
these three dimensions of the company—technology, design, and business management—while maintaining the integrity of its corporate mission was management's key challenge.

Coffeemakers: The KF 40 Project

One August day in 1981, when half of Germany was on holiday and the other half getting ready to leave, Waxlax wrote a memo to Gilbert Greaves, asking him to check into the possibilities for Braun in coffeemakers, a key element in the new strategy. Braun had entered the coffeemaker business in 1972 with the KF 20, a novel cylindrical design that won many design awards and was enthroned in the Museum of Modern Art in New York. (See Exhibit 9.) Available in strong red and yellow, it had entered the consciousness of upper-income coffee drinkers in both Europe and the U.S. It was, however, a very expensive machine, and expensive to produce, retailing at about DM 120.

A few years later, the company introduced the KF 35, a sleeker version of the then popular "L-shape" epitomized by Mr. Coffee. It cost about 40% less than the KF 20 to produce, retailing at about DM 90. The

Exhibit 9

The KF 20

design department was not fully satisfied with it: "I always thought it looked like a chemical lab sitting on the table," declared Rams, disdainfully. (See Exhibit 10.) The unit enjoyed only average sales, about 150,000 units annually.

Braun's major competitors in the middle-to-high-end coffee machine segment were two German companies, Krups and Rowenta. Braun's market research defined this segment in terms of price points: DM 70 retail or above. In Germany and France, two of the biggest markets for coffeemakers, half the units were sold in that range. The market researchers were confident that a new Braun coffeemaker family offered across the entire spectrum from DM 72 to DM 136, would be competitive in Europe, where the greater part of the market (about 70% of 9 million units annually) was for replacements. An open question was how soon Krups and Rowenta would copy Braun's design, as was their custom.

The U.S. market was considerably less certain yet crucial if Braun was to attain a volume permitting a tolerable return on investment. "You don't go for the small appliance business because of the margins, You have to have high volumes," remarked Waxlax. Americans

Exhibit 10
The KF 35

had been introduced to filter coffee systems through Mr. Coffee, a low-end product. Would they be willing to pay for Braun quality? With the currency exchange rate at DM 2.40 to $1.00, it was reasonable to expect imports to the U.S. to grow. The market for filter coffee machines was already running at about 11 million units, and penetration was still low. Braun's distribution system in the U.S. was practically nonexistent, however, and Waxlax wondered if it could be sufficiently developed in time.

Upon receiving Waxlax's coffee machine memo in August 1981, Greaves set to work with his people and in two months came up with a rough description of a product Braun could sell:

> It should have a shortened filter, slimmer jug [than the competition]; it should come in different colors, the water tank should be opaque, the tubes should be completely covered up, the filter should be tight and compact, the thermal jug should be more elegant, lighter, handier, taller, slimmer, and presentable on the coffee table.

That idea, which marketing articulated in October, 1981, evolved into a "product profile" that Greaves circulated to key people on December 2, 1981. In this memo Greaves discussed, as Waxlax had asked, the issue of the cost/volume relationship, and presented the direct costs and price points in connection with assumed volumes. He also analyzed the market segments and defined those segments where Braun could realistically compete. He determined that (a) a range of models—at least two—would be necessary; (b) this range was defined so that it could be constructed on a "building block system" to "minimize tooling investments"; and (c) the range would enable Braun to compete in medium to high price segments, at retail prices about DM 70. This would mean that Braun had to compete with key players—Krupers, Rowenta, Siemens, and AEG—on feature, not price. To be profitable, it would have to cost fully one-third less in direct costs than the KF 35, or 60% less than the KF 20. (See Exhibit 11 for summary of Greaves' memo.)

When the document was sent to R&D for feasibility analyses, R&D's first reaction to the target costs was "Nonsense! You can't make a coffeemaker for DM 23 in this company!" Nor did engineering take the idea well: "To be honest," confessed Hans-Jürgen Dittombée, manager of industrial engineering, "we thought the cost targets were impossible. We are responsible for technical planning and didn't see how we could get there."

Working with Greaves on the project was a young, energetic product program manager, Albrecht Jestädt, a mechanical engineer with expe-

67

Exhibit 11

Excerpts from Memorandum "Product Profile—Coffee Machine Range" from Gilbert Greaves to G. Voigt

---

December 2, 1981

Background:

A key element in determining the viability of a filter-coffee machine entry is the investment/volume required. The problem is that volume depends on the range offered. [But a wide range] necessitates different tools for housings, water tanks, etc., thus increasing the investment cost for entry.

A further element determining the range is price segmentation. In Germany 52% of the unit volume is sold under DM 59; [this would require] a direct cost we cannot realistically expect from Braun.

Conclusions:

1. A range of models will be needed.
2. A range has been defined which can be constructed on a "building block" system to minimize tooling investments.
3. This range will enable Braun to compete in medium to high price segment only . . . retail sales prices above 70 DM. We will have to compete on feature, not on price.

This document, [based on a market survey], will serve as an input to R&D to evaluate costs, feasibility, and timing based on the [following] volume estimates.

Range:

The Braun range will be differentiated from competition by the following characteristics:

1. The premium model in the range will have a thermal flask. Into this thermal flask the coffee can be filtered direct. Coffee can be held off the hot plate in the flask at 80° Celsius for 45 minutes. This prevents evaporation and aroma loss.
2. All models in the Braun range will be compatible with a special "Coffee ground dispenser." This stores 500g of ground coffee in an airtight hopper and has a metering system allowing the coffee ground to be dispensed by cups into the coffee machine filter.
3. All models in the Braun range will have a laterally pivoting filter allowing the filter to be swung out of the machine and underneath the hopper so that the consumer does not need to handle the coffee ground at any time. The filter can be lifted out to dispense with the paper filter and coffee ground.

---

rience in production and engineering. Upon hearing R&D's and Engineering's reactions, Jestädt refused to take "no" for an answer, and set about looking for alternatives. If Braun can't manufacture it, at least we can sell on OEM product that we design, he reasoned. Over the next year, he explored options in and outside of Germany and managed to find a manufacturer in Switzerland who could meet the cost requirements.

Exhibit 11 (cont.)

The range will consist of the following models:

	1	2	3	4	5	6	7
Standard Features							
Cup à 125 cc	8	8	8	12	12	12	12
Anti Drip	x	x	x	x	x	x	x
Pivoting Filter	x	x	x	x	x	x	x
Translucent Tank	x	x	x	x	x	x	x
Pilot Switch	x	x	x	x	x	x	x
Warming Plate	x	x	x	x	x	x	x
Cord Compartment	x	x	x	x	x	x	x
Optional Features							
Glass Jug	x	x	x	x	x	x	
Thermal Jug							x
Coffee Dispenser			x			x	x
Calcification Indicator			x			x	x
Detachable Tank		x	x		x	x	x
Fixed Tank	x			x			
Target Direct Cost	22	23	29	24	25	31	36
Target Price Point DM	74	78	99	82	85	105	122
Target Price point £	18.5	19.5	24.75	20.5	21.25	26.25	30.5

Annual Volume Assumptions (000)								Total
Year 1	150	50	60	50	50	40	100	500
Year 2	225	75	90	75	75	60	150	750
Year 3	300	100	120	100	100	80	200	1000

The KF 40: Problem Solving in Development

In the meanwhile Jestädt and the designer for household products, Hartwig Kahlcke, teamed up and began to develop the product. Kahlcke, a quiet contrast to the ebullient Jestädt, had come to the design department 10 years earlier, and worked on the KF 35. Kahlcke had also dealt extensively with the Spanish group because they did so many household products. "We share a vision," Jestädt declared, "and we're both willing to do what we have to to realize it." That vision had as its starting point the KF 20 and its still novel cylindrical design. How could they use the cylinder within the cost parameters? They had to use less material and only one heating element to start with. "Our first design was really terrific—the water tank completely surrounded the filter. But then we realized that we had to think modularly, so manufacturing costs would be minimized, and so we had to drop it," Jestädt recalled.

Jestädt and Kahlcke knew that the cylindrical form not only was appealing, but it used less material than the "chemical lab," the KF 35. Going back and forth they came up with five or six blue foam models before settling on what they believed was the optimal configuration: a cylinder within a cylinder, operating on the same principle as the KF 35 but much more compact. The main novelty: It would be operated from the front, and thus it would take less space and look even slimmer on the kitchen counter. (See Exhibit 12 for initial concept.)

At the same time, other disciplines continued working on the project. R&D, after exclaiming "impossible" at the very idea, took up the challenge and looked at how to get the cost out of the heating element and many other dimensions of the machine. The cost target presupposed a single heating element for both heating the water and keeping the coffee hot, rather than the two needed for the KF 20. Within those parameters, they finally decided that they could go for aluminum rather than copper in the heating element, which would be cheaper, but it would mean different dimensions for the various parts because of differences in conductivity. Keeping the coffee temperature at 82°C was considered an

EXHIBIT 12

Initial Concept for the Cylindrical KF 40

absolute must by the designers and marketing alike, even though they knew it was essentially an insoluble problem because of the length of time that coffee might be held.

R&D also responded to new design concepts. Kahlcke and Rams, for example, wanted to glue the handle on the pot, and asked Engineering to explore adhesives. The design reasons were both aesthetic and functional: The conventional means of attaching the handle to the coffee jug was the metal band, which both interrupted the line of the jug and collected dirt. In the course of working on the adhesives, it had become clear that manufacturing engineering would have to design an automated gluing process, in order to keep the costs down. The good news by spring 1983 was that the design and manufacturing process was expected to cost less than the conventional metal-band method. R&D still had not found the ideal adhesive, however, one that would hold for years under heat, impact, and moisture.

R&D had other challenges. The marketing people had found that an anti-drip device would be very attractive for customers, but Braun wanted to go at least one step beyond the competition. The idea was to prevent drips either from the filter (when one pulls out the coffee-pot) or from the water tube (when one swings the filter out). It was supposed to be a relatively easy assignment but, as Gunter Oppermann, head of R&D for household products, pointed out, "Simple is most difficult," and that was what the project was about. The drip-stop was a case in point. "It has to be dual-action (stopping the flow when either the pot *or* the filter was pulled out), and we have to go around some outside patents. We thought about toilet flushers as a model and started from there. We didn't want the device to stick, and yet it must be sturdy."

Quality assurance was working on several aspects of the new machine, including its end product. "We found that we didn't really know anything about coffee," quality engineer Werner Utsch confessed, "so we had to analyze and test some more, and that has led us to work with the coffee producers." The tests revealed valuable information: "We have found that our competition doesn't know much about coffee either." The next step would be blind taste tests, for which they needed a functional model.

The market researchers continued gathering data as well. In October 1982 they tested the thermal jug concept and determined that it would be an essential selling feature. The next month they tested filter systems; the swivel filter won hands down. At this time, contrary to results a year earlier, the market wanted a detachable, transparent water tank. It was "significantly preferred over a nontransparent one" and "should be included . . . if the price is not prohibitive to the customer." (See Exhibit

71

13 for market test results.) Jestädt and Kahlcke had, however, already developed a modular design that could not accommodate a transparent tank.

Operating from the principle that "no parts = no assembly costs," Jestädt and Kahlcke were striving to collapse the number of parts into as few as possible. This was where Rams' motto, "To design means to think [Designarbeit ist Denkarbeit]," converged with Bernard Wild's view of Braun's know-how. Working with machine tool experts, headed by Friedhelm Bau, Jestädt and Kahlcke had designed a configuration that incorporated many large and small parts that in the past would have been screwed together. The water tank was now part of the appliance housing, and the whole large piece, known simply as the "tank," was now central to their product concept, for it accounted for a good chunk of the savings in assembly costs. (See Exhibit 14.) It was, however, the largest, most complicated part ever attempted in polypropylene injection molding at Braun, and as such would be risky. (Exhibit 15 explains injection molding.)

Manufacturing and toolmaking engineers were involved from the beginning of the project. Bernard Wild had prepared an analysis of plant

EXHIBIT 13

Report on Coffee Maker Tests*

Title	Date of Report Month	Year	Comments
Coffee machine group discussions	10	1981	Desired improvements of the Braun coffee machine with thermal jug: Shortened filter, slimmer jug, should come in different colors, the water tank should be opaque, the tubes should be completely covered up, the filter should be tight and compact, the thermal jug should be more elegant, lighter, handier, taller, slimmer, and presentable on the coffee table.
Thermos jug concept	10	1982	The concept of a thermos jug with aroma test protective lid is preferred by the majority of respondents over a conventional glass jug with removable hot plate. There's a theoretical potential for a detachable heating or heat protection device.
Coffee filter system	11	1982	The best filter system for our new coffee acceptance test machine would be a swivel filter and the best water tank would be a transparent one.
Coffee machine features	12	1982	BMR would recommend the following concept test features to be considered for the new coffee machine range: built-in decalcifier, jug with heat and aroma preservation, swivel filter system, transparent detachable water tank, capacity 10-12 cups.

* Source: Company documents.

Exhibit 14

Prototype of the KF 40: The "Tank" Configuration

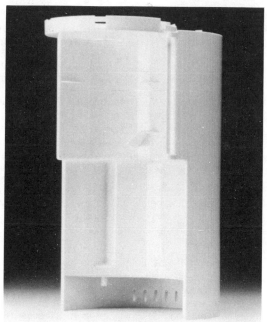

requirements in order to achieve the projected volumes for the new coffeemaker. As soon as polypropylene was proposed, Bau's toolmaking department started working with plastic suppliers and toolmakers in Berlin, who had experience with designing large tools for polypropylene. Bau was convinced that the large tank could be molded on the three 330-ton molding machines (presses) available at Marktheidenfelt. One machine could make 1,500 moldings (tank units) per day. With estimated volumes at 500,000 the first year, ramping up to 2,000,000 units the fourth year, the plant needed to be prepared to manufacture 10,000 units per day, given the 220 days per year that the plant operated. They were assuming a one-minute cycle time for the "tank" part, but could not be certain of it. They could start with three molds (or "tools"), one each for the 10- and 12-cup units and one for the thermal carafe, but they preferred to have the flexibility offered by five molds—two each for the 10- and 12-cup units.

If the product took off as expected, they would need four more molding machines and at least as many molds. Each machine cost about DM 500,000. The estimated cost for each tank mold was DM 250,000 and the lead time for tooling was around nine months for the

Exhibit 15

Note on Injection Molding

Injection-molding technology permits the high-speed molding of thin, often complex parts out of metal or plastic. It involves (a) melting the material to a liquid state; (b) injecting the liquid under pressure into a metal mold; (c) waiting a number of seconds until the liquid cools and solidifies; (d) opening the mold; (e) withdrawing the part; (f) closing the mold again. To be precise and consistent, the process needs computer controls and robotized handling.

The easiest form to mold in this way is the cone, because it comes out from the mold easily. As soon as there are straight sides and protruding features, the design problem is vastly more complicated. Industrial designers, engineers, and tool designers work together to develop a design that can be produced effectively. For example, the mold needs to open at some point, and a flash line, preferably a very thin one, will show. The designers need to determine where the line's effects are minimal, and design the mold accordingly.

In the case of plastic injection molding, the material is not held in liquid form. Rather, it is fed to the machine in small beads, like small white beans, which are melted instantly under pressure at the nozzle. This way the temperature can be controlled and there is less waste.

An important point in the design of a mold is the cooling rates of the plastic. This rate is determined by the properties of the plastic itself and by the shape of the part—its thickness at any given point and the distance of that from the nozzle through which the liquid is injected. Because the part cannot be removed until all of it has solidified, these problems must be taken into consideration when designing the part. Moreover, the injection temperature of the plastic and the temperature of the cooling water have to be kept constant via computer controls.

A mold may be very complicated, with more than one axis. Then the order in which the parts of the mold are opened and removed has to be carefully thought through. The "tank" part of the Braun coffee machine incorporated parts that would conventionally have been cast in at least five separate components and then screwed or snapped together. To save labor costs, the company invested in knowledge and tooling up front. This enabled them to keep production in high-wage Germany.

Some plastics are easier to cast than others. Those with low density, like polypropylene, are less stable, and this needs to be compensated for in the design of large parts. A large wall, for example, needs to be thicker or have a supporting shape built into the design. Because of the design implications of the variations in plastics, the same mold cannot be used for multiple kinds of plastic.

The quality of the molded part is determined not only by the design of the mold, but also by the interior surface finish of the mold. The quality of the metal, usually a special alloy steel, and the finishing technology used (e.g., erosion, grinding, polishing) determine how well a mold can meet its tolerances and how long it will last.

large molds. Because the molds were not interchangeable for various types of plastics, the choice of plastic was crucial to engineering's planning.

Polypropylene: A Question of Braun-ness

Braun had pioneered in the use of plastics as early as the 1950s, when it rejected fake wood and overstuffed designs for its products. Its designers, engineers, and toolmakers were experienced in making both clear and opaque parts from several different kinds of plastic. For the outer housing of its appliances, the company had traditionally used polycarbonate, a dense, stable material that could be fashioned into precision parts with smooth surfaces. Polycarbonate was, however, too expensive for the new coffee machine's requirements.

For that reason, Jestädt had begun working with ABS, which sold for about half of polycarbonate's going rate (see Exhibit 16). Even that, as it turned out, would probably be too expensive. The alternative, polypropylene, was the material of choice for low-end producers, but had never before been considered by Braun, except for interior parts that could benefit from its lower density and other features. The amount of polypropylene needed for each KF 40 unit was estimated at 700–950 grams. The problem with polypropylene for use in injection molding was its instability during the cooling process. Having a lower specific weight than the denser plastics, it tended to shrink unevenly and fall off, or "sink," at edges and meeting points. The resultant "sink marks" marred the surface and looked "cheap." Nor did polypropylene become as rigid as the more expensive materials, thus posing additional design challenges. Large parts were therefore especially vulnerable to a flimsy feel and had to be designed with the need to control that problem. It might mean

EXHIBIT 16

Properties of Plastics

	Polycarbonate	ABS	Polypropylene
Cost DM/kg (1983)	8.5 DM	3.95 DM	2.8 DM
Specific weight	1.2	1.05	0.9
Melting temperature	220°C	200°C	165°–170°C
Softening temperature	160°C	140°C	120°C
Color-fastness	yes	no	yes
Shrinkage	0.5–0.7%	0.3–0.9%	0.3–2.5%
			(1–2.5% unfilled)

thicker walls or a shape in the mold that would buttress the form from within.

When polypropylene was first suggested, many colleagues familiar with its problems immediately objected: It will not be a *Braun* product if we use this cheap stuff, they warned. Despite such adamant objections, Jestädt and Kahlcke began working with chemical suppliers and toolmakers to explore ways of improving the quality of polypropylene parts. In fall 1982 they achieved a breakthrough: Why not let necessity be the mother of design in this case? If we can't get a perfectly smooth surface, let's minimize the effect of the sink marks by treating the surface in some way. This inspiration led to the idea for a corrugated surface that would both mask flaws and actually enhance the design as well.

NO! said the purists, for whom Braun design was synonymous with absolutely smooth, winter-white surfaces. "It's a compromise," said Utsch, "and I don't like compromises." Utsch, head of quality assurance for the project, kept pointing to polypropylene's tendency to scratch: "It's just too soft. Even a fingernail can scratch it. And if you wipe it off with the same sponge you wiped the counter off with, you can scratch it with food particles or coffee grounds." Even Rams was skeptical at first, but eventually came to support the solution. "It is the obvious way to go, given the project requirements."

Polypropylene did have some advantages other than its price, Oppermann pointed out: "It doesn't absorb water, so it won't stain easily. And, as far as we can tell, it won't get brittle as fast as polycarbonate, so it won't chip easily."

Jestädt, ever confident, explored further. Wiling to take risks, R&D director Hexner supported R&D's involvement in trying to make polypropylene work. Like everyone else, he knew that if it didn't work, it would be extremely costly. "They are talking about a *huge* and very complicated tool for the tank. If it doesn't work, we'll have to throw it away and be another year behind." But Hexner didn't see any choice: "We've been given the job of making this thing at a ridiculous cost. My people say that it's possible only with polypropylene, and I agree." To Hexner the "purists" were entirely unrealistic. "If a Braun product *has* to have a smooth surface, then you have two choices: Go with flaws, or forget it. And that is ridiculous!"

Hexner's boss, Dr. Thomsen, did not think it ridiculous to consider further choices. Nor did Waxlax. "We could make a business with, say, ABS. But it would be a different business," Thomsen contended. Waxlax was worried about the U.S. market implications: "We'd either have to drop the U.S. market, and that means low volumes, or restrict it to the higher-priced department store segment."

Jestädt and Kahlcke, meanwhile, were not insensitive to the design concerns. The ridges of the corrugated surface would have to be absolutely smooth, with no peaks or valleys, so that they would not catch any dirt. That job was turned over to the toolmakers. By the end of 1982 Bau's department was confident that the job could be done using the 330-ton molding machines at Marktheidenfeld. An outside consultant had suggested that the molding machines should be larger (500-ton) for a part the size of the tank, but that would mean an additional investment of DM 2 million for two new machines and upgrades of the old machines. Because the larger machines were much slower than the smaller ones, it would take five of them to produce the same number of units per day as the three 330-ton machines could produce.

In December, 1982, Jestädt had presented his plan for a Swiss company to manufacture the new design. At the same meeting, someone brought in a cheap DM 29 coffeemaker from a supermarket and challenged those present, "If these guys can sell a coffeemaker for DM 29, you can surely make one for DM 23." As the discussion proceeded, the group realized that the new design was so special that it would be dangerous to let it out to a subcontractor; they would have to keep it inside in order to assure a competitive lead.

At that point it was proposed to take three months and build a trial tool to test the material; Waxlax approved DM 140,000 for the test and the tool, if the team chose to take that step. The proposal was, according to a project report for December 12, simply to "clarify if polypropylene is suitable for the appliance housing material." That was the point, according to Dittombée of industrial engineering. "I am confident that we can master polypropylene *technically*," he said, "but the discussion is about whether *Braun* can—or should—use it." For the purists, such a trial was far better than ordering the production dies and finding out polypropylene wouldn't work in this design and product.

A Material Decision

Over the next four months the coffeemaker project became more intense. At the report to management at the end of January 1983, drawings for the functional model were presented, and a schedule established (see Exhibit 17). The new 10-cup coffeemaker now had a name: the KF 40. A second model, the KF 45, would have a 3–4 cup switch, costing one DM more. According to this schedule, the functional model would be ready by the end of March, with final tool drawings complete on May 16. The formal go/no-go decision would be

EXHIBIT 17
Project Report, Coffee Maker KF 40, Version 1

January 26, 1983

Product Description:
KF 40: 10-cup version with swinging filter, anti-drip, and cord storage
        DC target: FY 1982/83: 23.50 DM
KF 45: same as the KF 40, but with switch for brewing 3-4 cups
        DC target: FY 1982/83: 24.30 DM

Status:
Blueprints for the construction of a functional model have been prepared, and it is currently being built.

Further steps:

- Prepare drawings for parts and tools   by 28 January 1983
- Requisition parts and tools; produce the A.R.   by 18 March 1983
- Have the A.R. approved   by 29 April 1983
- Finish the functional model   by 25 March 1983
- Test the functional model by QC   by 16 March 1983
- Build the design model   by 30 March 1983
- Complete drawings for tool models   by 16 May 1983
- Go or no-go decision   by 17 May 1983
  If go, then Category 1 release
- Planned startup of production   April 1984

Risks:
The above schedule does not include the production of prototypes. Only if the tests of the functional model reveal no major problems will it be possible to meet the planned deadlines.

Project: Coffee Makers KF 40 and KF 45   Signed: A Jestädt, Project Mgr.
Project Number: 542   Date: 26 January 1983   Version: 1

---

made on May 17, followed by a "category I" signoff, which released the drawings so that tools could be ordered. Production ramp-up was estimated to begin in April of 1984, to reach 3,000 units per day within three months.

All this assumed that the KF 40 could be made with polypropylene and that all the other problems, such as the drip-stop, could be solved in time. By producing this schedule, business management had already cast its vote of confidence. Waxlax knew that Greaves tended to be conservative in his forecasts, and therefore one didn't have to worry about unrealistic figures in his analyses. Neither engineering nor design wanted to be pushed, however, and that Waxlax respected. The decision was a strategic one: a big risk—but one with a big payoff if they succeeded. The risk was not so much financial, though a million DM in molds and two years in development costs would not be insignificant. Should they go ahead without trial tooling, take three months for the trial test, rethink their positioning with a more expensive plastic, or walk away from the project? What risks were they willing to take and how far should they go before modifying the business strategy? Waxlax intended to take his time in listening to all points of view.

The Concept of a Development Strategy

Overview

In Chapters 2 through 4 we explore what we call the "front end" of development. We begin in Chapter 2 by focusing on the concept of development strategy. While much of the activity in product development occurs in projects, there are many things companies do before projects get started that lay an important foundation for effective development. In this chapter, we focus on the front end of the development process with a discussion of several problems that typically arise in development projects. We trace many of these problems to two fundamental gaps in companies' development activity. The first gap is the mismatch between senior management attention, which normally occurs at the end of the development project, and senior management influence, which is much higher and more effective at the early stage of a project and even before a project is launched. Where this mismatch occurs senior management gets involved in projects at the wrong time, and usually in the wrong way. The second gap is the mismatch between the business planning and strategy process inside the company, and the set of projects that the company has underway. There is too often little connection between these two areas of business activity. The result is that the projects often fail to reflect the direction and intent of the business. The implication of this gap is that issues of marketing and technology strategy, for example, tend to arise after the projects have been started, and generally make the project itself a much more complex managerial problem than it should be.

Setting the stage for the remainder of the book, this chapter identifies development strategy as a way to create an effective framework within which these gaps can be closed. It provides a means for senior management to interact and shape the development process in a timely and effective way. In addition, it provides an explicit link between the business planning and strategy process and the shaping and selection of specific projects.

The concept of a development strategy adds two primary mechanisms for linking the business planning process to projects. The first is development goals and objectives: the firm translates its business strategy into specific requirements for the development organization. These requirements focus on both the performance of development, in terms of lead times, productivity, and number of new products created, as well as development capability. The second mechanism is the aggregate project plan, in which the firm determines the specific mix to types of projects that fit within the business strategy, gauges its capacity to undertake those projects, and defines the appropriate set of projects given its opportunities and constraints.

Our focus on the front end of the development process in this chapter identifies three themes that have a substantial influence on development performance: (1) what goes on before the project is initiated is crucial to the project's success; (2) an effective front-end process provides a framework for timely senior management involvement, and explicitly links business planning processes to project identification and selection; and (3) development projects not only create new products but build new capabilities. Thus, development strategy comprehends not only the activities the firm must undertake to create an attractive set of new products and processes in the next generation, but also identifies the critical capabilities that need development and cultivation in order to lay the foundation for effective development in the future.

CHAPTER *2*

Perhaps no activity in business is more heralded for its promise and approached with more justified optimism than new-product and new-process development. The anticipated benefits almost defy description. This is true whether the business is engaged in an old-line manufacturing-intensive activity such as steel or machine tools, the manufacture of consumer goods such as appliances or personal care products, the production of industrial products such as material transfer systems or heavy equipment, or the creation of technology-intensive products such as pharmaceuticals or electronics.

The potential benefits of effective development efforts are of three types—market position, resource utilization, and organizational renewal and enhancement. In terms of *market position*, ideally a new product can set industry standards—standards that become a barrier to competitors—or open up whole new markets, such as the Sony Walkman or Polaroid camera. Superior products and processes are a means to get a jump on the competitors, build on existing advantages by creating stronger competitive barriers, establish a leadership image that translates into market dominant designs, extend existing product offerings, and increase market share.

Anticipated benefits in *resource utilization* include capitalizing on prior

R&D investments (applying lab discoveries), improving the return on existing assets (such as the sales force, factories, and field service network), applying new technologies for both products and manufacturing processes, and eliminating or overcoming past weaknesses that prevented other products or processes from reaching their full potential. The potential leverage on a variety of resources can be substantial.

Perhaps the most exciting type of development benefit is the prospect of *renewal and transformation of the organization*. The excitement, image, and growth associated with product and process development efforts capture the commitment, innovation, and creativity of the entire organization. This success, in turn, enhances the firm's ability to recruit the best people, improve their integration, and accelerate the pace of change. Furthermore, development projects themselves often are the vehicle by which new approaches and new thinking are adopted and take on institutional reality.

Finally, it is anticipated that all of these benefits will drop to the bottom line, providing rich financial rewards such as improved return on investment, higher margins, expanded sales volume, increased value added, lower costs, and improved productivity. Little wonder that development prospects build excitement and anticipation throughout an organization and its people.

Unfortunately, in most firms the promise is seldom fully realized. Even in many very successful companies, new product development is tinged with significant disappointment and disillusionment, often falling short of both its full potential in general and its specific opportunities on individual projects. In fact, many individuals directly involved in creating new products and processes suffer burnout or a longing to return to the status quo (business as usual), and may even depart from the company.

Problems in New Product and New Process Development

To understand what causes the great disparity between promise and reality, and, more important, to take corrective action, it is useful to explore some ways in which development problems manifest themselves. From experience in a variety of firms and industries, a handful of obvious pitfalls emerge.

The Moving Target. Too often the basic product or process concept misses a shifting technology or market, resulting in a mismatch. This can be caused by locking into a technology before it is sufficiently stable, targeting a market that changes unexpectedly, or making assumptions about the distribution channel that don't hold. In each of these cases, the project gets in trouble because of inadequate consistency of focus throughout its duration and an eventual misalignment with reality. Once the target starts to shift, the problem compounds itself: the project lengthens, and longer projects invariably drift as the target continues to shift. Dramatic examples of such mismatches include the Ford Edsel in the mid 1950s, Texas Instruments' home computer in the late 1970s, and Kodak's disk camera in the 1980s. Even very successful products like the Apple Macintosh can experience a rocky beginning and have to iterate through revisions into an appropriate focus and positioning because of moving targets.

Mismatches Between Functions. While the moving target problem usually reflects a mismatch between an organization and its external environment, mismatches also often occur within an organization. What one part of the organization expects or imagines another part can deliver may prove to be unrealistic or even impossible. For instance, engineering may design a product that its factories cannot produce, at least not consistently, at low cost and with high quality. Similarly, engineering may design features into the product that marketing's established distribution channels and selling approach cannot utilize fully or existing customers do not need. Or manufacturing may assume a certain mix of new products in planning its requirements, while marketing makes different assumptions, confident that manufacturing can alter its mix dramatically on short notice when, in fact, it cannot. Such mismatches may result from a lack of communication among the functions or from a sequential, over-the-wall approach to project management; in either case, development suffers. One of the most startling mismatches we've encountered was at an aerospace firm where manufacturing built an assembly plant using one set of new product specs only to find that it was too small to accommodate the wing span of the aircraft it ultimately had to produce.

Lack of Product Distinctiveness. Often new product development terminates in disappointment because the new product is not as unique or defensible as the organization anticipated. If the organization gets locked into a concept too quickly, it may not bring differing perspectives to the analysis. The market may dry up, or the critical technologies may be sufficiently widespread that imitators appear overnight. Plus Development introduced Hardcard®, a hard disc that fits into a PC expansion slot, after a year and a half of development work. The company thought it had a unique product with at least a nine-month lead on competitors. But by the fifth day of the industry show where Hardcard® was introduced, a competitor was showing a prototype of a competing version. And within three months of Plus's market introduction, the competitor was shipping its new product.[1]

Unexpected Technical Problems. Delays and cost overruns often can be traced to overestimates of the company's technical capabilities or simply to its lack of depth and resources. Projects can suffer delays and stall in midcourse if essential inventions are not completed and drawn into the designers' repertoire before the development project starts. An industrial controls company encountered both problems: it changed a part from metal to plastic only to discover that its manufacturing processes could not hold the required tolerances and that its supplier could not provide raw material of consistent quality.

Problem-Solving Delays. Every new product development activity involves uncertainty, with regard both to specific problems and conflicts that will inevitably arise, and the resources required to resolve them. Too often organizations allocate all of their development resources to known project requirements, leaving little or no cushion for the unexpected. Subsequently, when the inevitable, unanticipated problem occurs and the project experiences delay, managers rob Peter to pay Paul. This siphoning of resources cascades into delays on other projects. Once delays occur, costs increase, pressures mount to cut corners, and further problems erupt. The cycle is familiar. A major project gets into trouble, and managers pull key people off of other projects only to discover that the reassigned people take weeks to get up to speed—thus, the project is almost as late as it would have been without them. In addition, several other projects suffer delays and escalating costs.

Unresolved Policy Issues. A number of very specific choices and decisions must be made during any product or process development project. If major policies have not been articulated clearly and shared, these choices often force a decision on the policy issue for the entire organization. While such forcing is not inherently bad, it inevitably involves more senior levels of management in resolving specific issues. Resolving policy issues during the "heat of the battle" and at senior (more politically oriented) levels of the organization inevitably engenders delay and further complications. One industrial products firm that lacked a clear policy on make-versus-by and vertical integration changed the manufacturing location for a new product four times—from a headquarters plant to offshore Mexico, to offshore Japan, to a local subcontractor—before actual start-up. Each change entailed months of delay and costly design modifications. In effect, the project became the forum for making major strategic decisions.

The reality is that much can and does go wrong during development projects in most firms. When it does, most often it is not because the project team was not smart or was unwilling to work. Nor is it because they do not want to do a good job or that senior management lacked good intentions. The problem is a much more fundamental one—managers fail to plan sufficiently in advance to provide the requisite skills and resources, to define the project and its purposes appropriately, and to integrate the development project with other basic strategies. Rather, managers often seek to respond to problems as their importance becomes apparent; at that point they are unavoidable.

A visit we made to an automotive plant revealed the shortcomings of a focus on "after-the-fact" problem solving rather than problem prevention through effective pre-project planning. In touring the assembly line, we were surprised to find a workstation where the worker's tools consisted of a rubber mallet and a two-by-four. The tour guide explained that the worker was aligning the doors so that each automobile would pass the subsequent leak test. Further questioning revealed that the designers had gone to a new aerodynamic design that eliminated rain gutters and had the doors joining the roof at a point over the driver's (or passenger's) shoulder. This required much tighter tolerances than on previous models—tolerances that this plant could not meet routinely. While several long-term options were available, the short-term fix was a rubber mallet and a two-by-four.

Additional investigation found that the pattern of management's involvement in the development of this particular car and its production start-up followed the pattern shown in Exhibit 2–1. In the early part of the development effort, when management had the ability to make a substantial impact on the eventual outcome, they had been only minimally involved. It was not until pilot production started and the factory discovered it could not make a watertight passenger compartment that management got heavily involved. While the engineers thought the rubber mallet and two-by-four had solved the problem, when the factory began shipping the car in volume, dealers experienced heavy warranty claims for leaks. The problem was that as customers leaned (or hung) on the car door, it again became misaligned. This caused a second flurry of management attention. Subsequently, dealers were trained in the use of rubber mallets and two-by-fours.

This example provides a vivid illustration of why worrying about a development project only when problems become apparent (late in the development cycle) leaves the organization behind the power curve and in a reactive mode. Under such circumstances tremendous amounts of management, technical, and functional expertise do get applied, but largely to avoid competitive disaster rather than to provide competitive advantage. Managers need a much more comprehensive approach—creation and pursuit of an overarching development strategy—in order to apply development resources, including senior management's time, in a manner that is preemptive, proactive, and of maximum value.

EXHIBIT 2–1

Timing and Impact of Management Attention and Influence*

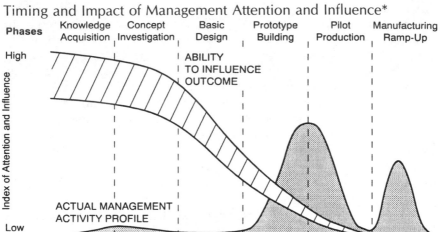

* Management's ability to influence a development project's outcome is high early in development (diagonally shaded area). Yet typically, management's actual activity profile (darkly shaded area) is very limited early on and only becomes significant late in the project, when the effort is in trouble.

SOURCE: R. H. Hayes, S. C. Wheelwright, and K. B. Clark, *Dynamic Manufacturing* (New York: The Free Press, 1988), p. 279. See also F. Gluck and R. Foster. "Managing Technological Change: A Box of Cigars for Brad." *Harvard Business Review* (1975, September–October), p. 141.

A Framework for Development Strategy

In reality, too many firms use an approach to product and process development (depicted in Exhibit 2–2) in which the critical elements of strategy—a plan for technology and a plan for product-market position—are only connected (and then loosely) in individual projects. The major shortcomings of such an approach are (a) a failure to bound and focus the individual project sufficiently to guarantee its rapid, productive execution; (b) a failure to provide sufficient up-front planning to effectively link individual development projects to these two key strategies; and (c) an unreasonable burden on the individual project, so that it must address policy issues, functional mismatches, and other fundamental organizational needs, as well as meet the challenges inherent in any development project. As a result, individual projects fall short of their potential to implement the technology and product market strategies and to capture market position, improve resource utilization, and facilitate organizational renewal.

EXHIBIT 2–2

Conventional Approach to Development Projects*

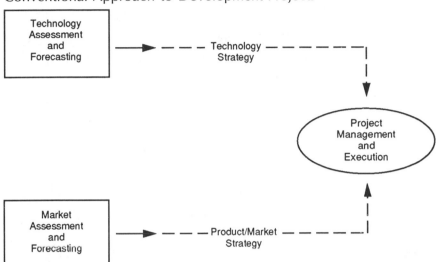

* Traditionally, most firms make only a loose assessment and forecast of technology and market evolution. Futhermore, even the technology and product/market strategies are not explicitly integrated with individual product development projects.

Our research on and experience with firms that have superior development capabilities suggests that a much more comprehensive framework for development strategy, as shown in Exhibit 2–3, provides a far more secure foundation for individual projects. This framework addresses the four main purposes of a development strategy.

• Creating, defining, and selecting a set of development projects that will provide superior products and processes.
• Integrating and coordinating functional tasks, technical tasks, and organizational units involved in development activities over time.
• Managing development efforts so they converge to achieve business purposes as effectively and efficiently as possible.
• Creating and improving the capabilities needed to make development a competitive advantage over the long term.

This expanded framework accomplishes these purposes by adding two pre-project focal points—development goals and an aggregate project plan—where technology strategy and product/market strategy can be discussed and integrated. These explicit pre-project activities

Exhibit 2–3

Development Strategy Framework*

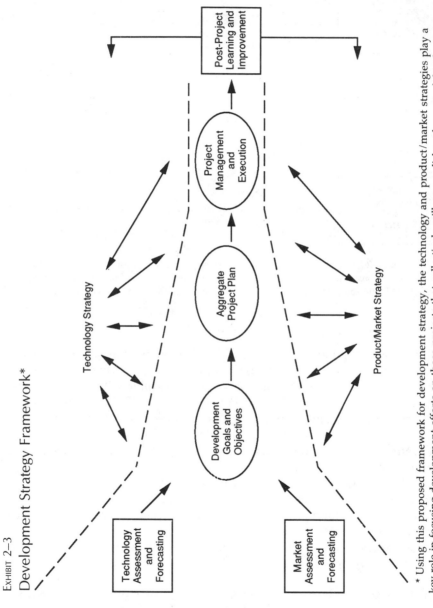

* Using this proposed framework for development strategy, the technology and product/market strategies play a key role in focusing development efforts on those projects that collectively will accomplish a clear set of development goals and objectives. In addition, individual projects are undertaken as part of a stream of projects that not only accomplish strategic goals and objectives, but lead to systematic learning and improvement.

provide a way for managers to address policy issues and cross-project concerns, and to set bounds on individual projects. By limiting the scope of individual projects, senior executives make projects more manageable and facilitate refinement and improvement of project management procedures. The framework thus recognizes the need for ongoing learning and provides mechanisms for capturing and applying learning beyond the local efforts of individual team members. The framework provides much more robust phases for pre-project planning and post-project learning that complement and support work on specific projects.

In the remainder of this chapter, we discuss and illustrate each of the elements of the development strategy framework. We place particular emphasis on pre-project steps and their linkages to technology and product/market strategies. Chapters 3, 4, and 5 then deal with concepts, tools, and procedures that have proved extremely effective in operationalizing and implementing these pre-project elements. We will touch only briefly on the project and post-project phases of the framework, since they are the primary focus of Chapters 6 through 10, and Chapters 11 and 12, respectively. We conclude this chapter with an example of development strategy in action.

Technology Planning and Strategy

The objective of technology strategy is to guide the firm in acquiring, developing, and applying technology for competitive advantage.[2] Linking this element of development strategy to the success of a specific development project requires a clear understanding of what technology is, the characteristics of a strong technology strategy, the key issues such a strategy must address, and a plan for achieving it through a set of projects and complementary actions that build the organization's technical skills.

A strategy for technology must confront, in the first instance, what the focus of technical development will be. The question is what technologies are critical to the firm's competitive advantage. In this context, technology must include the "know-how" the firm needs to create, produce, and market its products and deliver them to customers. While some of this knowledge may be based on years of practical experience, some may be rooted in science and scientific research. Such knowledge is "know-why"—a deep understanding of why the products or processes work as they do. While technical knowledge and understanding may therefore have different sources and take different forms, what matters for competition is the firm's technical capability—its ability to use its "know-why" and its "know-how" to achieve very specific results in its products and processes.

As the first step in creating a technology strategy, *focus* defines those capabilities where the firm seeks to achieve a distinctive advantage relative to competitors. For most firms, there are a large number of important areas of technological "know-how" but only a handful where the firm will seek to create truly superior capability. In the steel industry, for example, a firm might seek to build an advantage in the quality and speed of its continuous casting operations. This is a technology based on the sciences of metallurgy, thermodynamics, mechanics, and electronic control; it requires know-how in machine design, computer modeling, materials development, metallurgy, and electrical engineering. There are many other areas of know-how required to be an outstanding competitor in the steel business, but a technology strategy focuses attention on those few areas of distinct advantage. The strategy additionally defines those areas where the firm will seek mastery, if not superiority, and may also define areas where it will rely on generally available, standard technologies.

Establishing focus defines targets for investment in technical capability, but leaves open the question of *source*. This is the second critical aspect of technology strategy. Technological capability may be developed internally through investment in people, equipment, facilities, and methodologies, or through advanced development projects. But technology may also be acquired from outside the firm through sponsored research in universities, joint ventures, licensing, and outright purchase. Inside and outside sources are not mutually exclusive. Indeed, the specific mix of internal and external sources is a crucial dimension of the strategy. Although one source may be dominant, the other usually plays an important role. For example, our steel firm that seeks an edge in continuous casting might engage in significant internal development— building experimental machines, developing prototype control systems —but also may enter into a partnership with equipment suppliers in the development of advanced controls and fund university research on heat transfer modeling. Even where the primary source is external (e.g., licensing coating technologies for special applications), the steel firm needs some internal capability to evaluate the external work and to integrate it into the internal operations. Thus, the key questions the technology strategy must answer about sources are: (1) what roles will external and internal sources play, and (2) how will they be integrated?

Having determined the focus of technical development and the source of capability, the firm must establish the *timing and frequency of implementation*. Part of the timing issue involves developing technical capability, and part involves introducing technology into the market. Our steel firm, for example, may decide to pioneer a new technique for metal forming by conducting advanced development projects, but may choose to delay market introduction until others have paved the way. Though the firm will be a relatively early player in the game, others are the commerical pioneers. Without the advanced development work, the firm's only choice would be to be a follower (possibly a slow follower).

The frequency of implementation and the associated risks will depend in part of the nature of the technology and the markets involved (disk drive technology changes more frequently than automotive engine technology, for example), but in part on strategic choice. At the extremes, a firm may adopt what has been called the "rapid inch-up" strategy—frequent, small changes in technology that cumulatively lead to continuous performance improvement. In the case of the steel company, this would involve introducing many new technologies into the continuous casting process as they are developed. The polar opposite is what might be called the "great leap forward" strategy. In this approach, a firm chooses to make infrequent but large-scale changes in technology that substantially advance the state of the art. In the steel case, this would involve collecting all the individual pieces of new technology and creating a totally new system that is implemented in one large project.

Critical Issues in Technology Strategy

Integrating technology strategy with specific product or process development projects requires managers to articulate the strategy in terms of a plan for development and implementation of capability. Advanced development projects and external acquisitions need to be phased to connect in time with the planned development of products and processes. In developing these plans and linking them to specific development projects, there are two critical issues: separation of technology invention from technology application and integration of product and manufacturing process technology paths.

The *first* issue—separating invention from application—is one of the few development guidelines upon which everyone (practitioners and academics) seems to agree. When invention (for which the timing, prerequisites, resources, and specific outcomes are largely unpredictable) is included in a development project, it invariably causes delay, backtracking, and disappointment. However, when done in advance so that its results are available for application, development of new technology may contribute significantly to project success. The implication is that required inventions should be proven (i.e., feasibility demonstrated) beforehand, off the critical path of commerical development.

The challenge lies in foreseeing when the guideline is likely to be violated and taking the pre-project actions needed to prevent it. A comprehensive process for creating a development strategy can do much to address this issue by forcing clarification of the technology strategy, articulating the relationship of its goals and objectives to those of the

EXHIBIT 2–4

Development Strategy at Hewlett Packard Emphasizing the Separation of Technology Invention and Its Application in Development Projects*

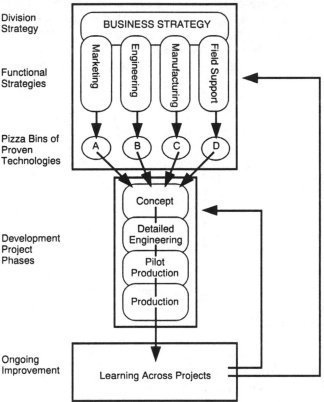

* Hewlett Packard conceives of the business and functional strategies as key drivers in assessing which technological opportunities hold the greatest promise for a business. Advanced development projects around those technologies then prove technical feasibility *prior* to their application in specific development projects. (Note that HP uses a standard four-phase process in development, followed by efforts to consolidate learning across the set of projects.)

development strategy, and defining a set of advanced technology projects (as part of the aggregate project plan) that ensure required inventions precede their application in development.

To highlight the importance of separating the invention of technology from its application, one of Hewlett Packard's major businesses created what they refer to as the "pizza bin" approach. As shown in Exhibit 2–4,

EXHIBIT 2–5

Aligning Product and Process Technology Efforts at IBM*

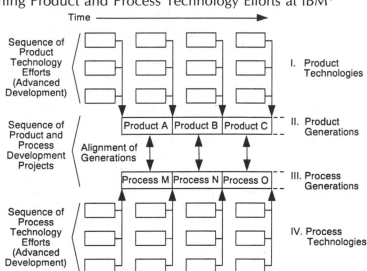

Time ──────────────────────────▶

Sequence of Product Technology Efforts (Advanced Development)

I. Product Technologies

Sequence of Product and Process Development Projects

Alignment of Generations

| Product A | Product B | Product C |

II. Product Generations

| Process M | Process N | Process O |

III. Process Generations

Sequence of Process Technology Efforts (Advanced Development)

IV. Process Technologies

* IBM seeks to identify critical product (I, II, and III) and process (IV, V, and VI) technologies, and then uses a string of advanced development efforts to push each along as fast as possible. Only proven technologies are then applied in each generation of development effort. However, generations or "windows" of product and process development are matched to create superior products and processes.

their framework for development strategy requires explicit identification of the technologies required in each of the primary business functions *before* proceeding with a development project. It also recognizes the desirability of having several technology options "on the shelf" so that development projects can apply those that are most appropriate.

The *second* critical technology issue—integration of the paths of product and manufacturing process technology evolution—also can be largely preempted through use of the comprehensive development strategy framework. While this issue is not as universal as the separation of invention and application, it is frequently a major pitfall. Basically, the issue arises because most firms develop a rather narrow technology strategy—one that addresses only product technology. In the framework of Exhibit 2–3, technology strategy is defined broadly (as Hewlett Packard did in Exhibit 2–4) and covers manufacturing process and service delivery technologies, as well as product technology.

All too often "development projects" means "product development projects," the assumption being that process technology can be acquired easily if and when the need for it becomes obvious. Unfortunately, such a view results frequently in the full benefits of the product technology never being realized—the manufacturing process simply cannot deliver the quality, cost, or timeliness the product requires. In addition, the potential for competitive advantage from superior process technology, either by doing things others cannot do (at least, not easily) or by protecting proprietary product technology, is never realized.

A comprehensive development strategy can do much to address this issue by providing a long-term focus on product and process technology evolution and an intermediate-term focus on development projects that apply those technologies in an integrated and complementary way. Many of IBM's businesses, for example, have detailed this aspect of development strategy as shown in Exhibit 2–5. There are four subparts in IBM's approach: pursuing long-term inventions in product and process as part of the technology strategy, engaging in medium-term advanced development projects to refine and prepare technology for commerical application (filling the pizza bins), executing numerous near-term product and process development projects to apply technical advances, and matching product and process "windows" (generations) in order to maximize the competitive benefits of product and process improvements.

Product/Market Planning and Strategy

A product/market strategy for a business addresses four important questions:[3]

- What products will be offered (i.e., the breadth and depth of the product line)?
- Who will be the target customers (i.e., the boundaries of the market segments to be served)?
- How will the products reach those customers (i.e., the distribution channels to be used)?
- Why will customers prefer our products to those of competitors (i.e., the distinctive attributes and value to be provided)?

From the perspective of product and process development, the critical issues in the product/market strategy are the number of platform (or core) products, the number of enhanced (or derivative) products, and the frequency of new product introductions. Development projects are, after all, the primary vehicle by which such changes in the product line are accomplished.

There are a variety of patterns of platform and derivative projects. Some firms choose to have relatively few core product offerings that change only infrequently, but offer a variety of product variations based on the core product. Steinway, with its handful of upright and grand piano models, introduced only one major new model between 1970 and 1990. It customizes each piano, however, making it a work of art. Thus Steinway offers no two identical pianos, yet produces only a handful of core models. Other firms choose to have a few core products that change much more frequently, in addition to offering numerous variations. Sony's Walkman (a portable, personal audio system with earphones) illustrates this strategy. By 1990, Sony offered over 180 models of Walkman, with almost half of them introduced in the preceding twelve months. That wide variety, however, was derived through incremental changes to one of three platform products. Each of those platform products in turn was redesigned to provide a "next generation" core product every eighteen to twenty-four months.[4]

In other industries the frequency in performance improvement increments of platform products is set largely by an industry standards group, with firms free to offer as much variety around those platforms as they think appropriate. The alternating current (AC) electric motor industry in the United States, with its seven-year cycle of rerating standards set by the National Electrical Manufacturers Association (NEMA), is an excellent example of this. Reliance Electric chooses to offer extensive variety around current standards, while Emerson Electric's variety is more limited. In relatively young industries, such as medical instruments, every development effort appears to be a platform effort (to broaden the firm's market coverage), with incremental changes targeted primarily at correcting deficiencies in the platform products (as originally introduced).[5]

Critical Issues in Product/Market Strategy

Linking product/market strategy to specific development projects raises two critical issues: (1) the number, timing, and rate of change of platform products, and (2) the number, timing, frequency, and relationship to the product/market strategy of derivative products.

The way a firm deals with the first issue defines the generations of platform products. There are five specific factors involved in the choices the firm makes about platform generations:

1. *Technology evolution.* The rate of technology change impacts how much new knowledge is available, and when it can go into a next-generation platform product.
2. *Competition.* The rate and time at which competitors introduce new generations of platform products affects how long an existing generation can remain in the marketplace and still be viable.

3. *Return on investment*. The investment required to develop the next-generation product (and its associated process), in concert with the contribution margins generated by the new product, determines the cumulative sales volume required for that product to provide a sufficient return before the next-generation product is introduced.
4. *Customer support*. Providing a continuous flow of products that meets the needs of targeted markets and channels for product "freshness," customization, and performance affects the timing and structure of the generational products offered.
5. *Available resources*. Generally, next-generation platform development efforts require significant resources over an extended period. Available resources—constrained by existing people, productivity, and the R&D expenditures the business can support—usually can execute only a handful of generational projects every couple of years.

What the firm does with platform generations will affect its approach to derivative products. Derivative products range from defeatured, cost-reduced versions of platform products to enhanced and even hybrid versions. While the marketplace often makes only minor distinctions among platform and derivative products in the line, for development planning (and manufacturing) the distinctions are significant because of the differences in resources required to develop and support them. The development strategy, in conjunction with the product/market strategy, needs to bring these differences into sharp focus and address these concerns:

- The timing of derivative products and developments and market introductions *relative* to the timing and life cycle of platform generation developments from which they derive.
- The fraction of sales expected to come from derivative versus platform products.
- The nature of the markets and channels served by the derivative products (e.g., niche or custom segments) in contrast to those served by platform products (e.g., the volume segment or the early adopters).
- The leverage on development resource investments as well as operating investments (e.g., sales force, factories, field service) to be provided by derivative products.
- The role of derivative products in extending the life cycle of platform products and "holding" market position (preempting competitors) until a next generation can be completed and introduced.

These choices and the factors related to them need to be addressed at both the strategic and tactical levels. At the strategic level, choices must be made such that the product/market strategy and the longer-term development and business goals are compatible and do-able. At the tactical level, decision rules and disciplines must be adopted that enable the aggregate project plan and individual projects to implement successfully the product/market and development strategies.

The leverage provided by effective integration of the product/market strategy and the development strategy can be significant. Consider the experiences of two companies, a scientific instruments firm and an electric hospital bed firm. Historically, the scientific instruments firm had developed and introduced a highly featured, generational platform product every four or five years, followed by a cost-reduced derivative product and some minor "fixes" a year or two later. As part of a comprehensive development strategy, they decided to develop and introduce the derivative, low-cost model concurrent with the high-end platform model and to target the derivative product at the high-volume market segment. Through the use of software options, a common manufacturing process, and extensive testing to design in reliability, they were able to introduce two winning products off a single platform, and achieve very aggressive business and development goals while implementing a new product/market strategy.

A leading hospital bed company consolidated a formerly "all things to all people" product line around three platform products while maintaining breadth of line through modularized options. This increased significantly their return on development and manufacturing investments, enabling them to expand into other related product fields. Through additional investments in technology and market research, they began shortening the time between platform generations. This in turn increased the value of their products to customers, making it attractive to hospitals to replace beds more rapidly. The result was increased volumes, market share, and profit margins.

Development Goals and Objectives

A strategy for technology and for products/markets gives the development effort guidance and direction. But to ensure consistency and coherence across these strategies and to link them explicitly to business as well as development objectives, a firm must define its basic development goals and objectives. At the aggregate level, the goals and objectives need to be made explicit and then juxtapositioned to examine their compatibility and complementarity. The purpose of this process is to provide integration both in the aggregate and at the level of the individual project. Typically, these goals range from market share (by customer segment and channel) to revenues and profits, and from dates for platform generation introductions and technology achievements to new

Exhibit 2–6

Motorola Life Cycle Planning—Relating Business Goals to New Product Development and Market Introductions*

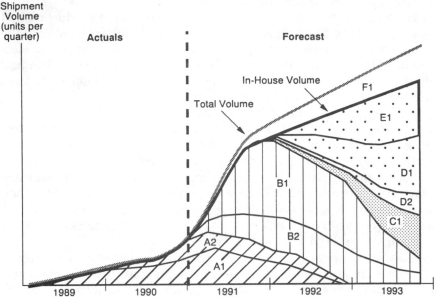

* Starting with development plans for product families (A through F), business unit revenue planning and budgets can be linked to individual development projects (A1, A2, B1, etc.), their market introduction dates, and their product life cycles.

source: Adapted from C. H. Willyard and C. W. McClees, "Motorola's Technology Road-map Process," *Research Management*, vol. 30, No. 3 (September–October 1987), pp. 13–19.

product/new process performance objectives. When effectively tied together, these goals provide an organization with confidence that their strategies will generate the business performance desired. They also can serve as a guide for investment decisions and a benchmark for monitoring ongoing progress.

For such goals to be credible, they must be linked directly to the set of development projects the firm intends to undertake. That is, the sum of the parts (the projects) must provide the aggregate performance desired. One way of determining whether this will indeed be the case is to model financially the development projects and their expected results. Exhibit 2–6 illustrates the use of one such model applied at a Motorola business unit. In 1990, this business offered a single platform (A) in two primary forms (A1 and A2). The plan is to introduce a second platform (B) in 1991, again in two forms (B1 and B2), that will replace the current

Exhibit 2–7

Establishing Generational Development Goals that Tie Product
Families to Business Strategy Goals at Northern Electronics*

	1990	1992	Mid 1993
Family generation	I	II	III
Number of components	3100	1250	1150
• PC Boards	27	11	8
• ICs	90	32	27
• Semiconductors	400	140	170
Defective units (final assembly)	28%	14%	5%
Service call rate	32%	11%	6%
Services costs/set sold (indexed)	100	50	20
Volume (indexed)	100	125	320
Factory cost (indexed)	100	70	40
• Work content	100	60	34
• Material	100	65	42
• Overhead	100	80	40

* In the late 1980s, Northern Electronics prepared plans for three generations (I, II, and III) of a consumer product, to be introduced in 1990, 1992, and mid-1993, respectively. They then set performance goals for both product and process development that would first close the competitive gap, then achieve parity, and finally provide a competitive advantage by the third generation.

---

platform (A) by the end of 1992. They also expect to add another primary platform offering (F1) in 1991, but that will be produced by a supplier. Finally, by early 1992, they plan to introduce three more platforms (C, D, and E). Similar graphs could be developed to show factory utilization, development resource commitments, revenues, profits, or any other measure of interest.

In addition to meeting aggregate business goals, the collective set of projects also must meet technical performance goals. Consider, for example, the competitive interaction between Northern and Southern Electronics discussed in Chapter 1. When Northern found itself slipping behind, they could have looked carefully across the product generations and established goals to regain competitive position. Exhibit 2–7 presents an example of what these goals might have looked like. Such goals would have helped significantly in linking individual projects to the longer-term strategic problems at Northern.

At the operating level, there is also a need for goals that can guide the individual project, yet connect its contribution to longer-term objectives. Typically, firms that measure development focus their attention on either resource productivity (especially of engineering) or design quality

EXHIBIT 2–8

Performance Measures for Development Projects

Performance Dimension	Measures	Impact on Competitiveness
Time-to-Market	• Frequency of new product introductions • Time from initial concept to market introduction • Number started and number completed Actual versus plan • Percent of sales coming from new products	• Responsiveness to customers/ competitors • Quality of design – close to market • Frequency of projects – model life
Productivity	• Engineering hours per project • Cost of materials and tooling per project Actual versus plan	• Number of projects – freshness and breadth of line • Frequency of projects – economics of development
Quality	• Conformance – reliability in use • Design – performance and customer satisfaction • Yield – factory and field	• Reputation – customer loyalty • Relative attractiveness to customers – market share • Profitability – cost of ongoing service

(delivery of new features). Only recently have time-to-market and production quality (manufacturability) gained widespread attention as important measures for individual projects. In most competitive environments, however, managers need multiple measures on all four performance dimensions. Moreover, the primary emphasis must be on improving all of the dimensions simultaneously. As part of the development strategy, it is important to define what measures are to be used and why, and to apply them consistently in evaluating development performance. Exhibit 2–8 presents examples of performance measures and their connection to competition.

Taken together, time, quality, and productivity define the performance of development, and, in combination with other activities—sales, manufacturing, advertising, and customer service—determine the market impact of the project and its profitability. In order to integrate the dimensions of development performance so that general management, the functional areas, and the development team can better monitor, evaluate, and learn from individual projects, Hewlett Packard has defined what they call "the return map." As shown in Exhibit 2–9, this concept presents graphically the relationship of several key measures important to development projects. For example, it captures both money and time, as well as market acceptance. This single diagram conveys the time-to-market for a project, its break-even time (when cumulative product contribution has repaid the development and start-up investments), and the return factor (the ratio of contribution to original investment over a given sales period). Hewlett Packard found that since it shows

Exhibit 2–9

Hewlett Packard's Development Project Return Map*

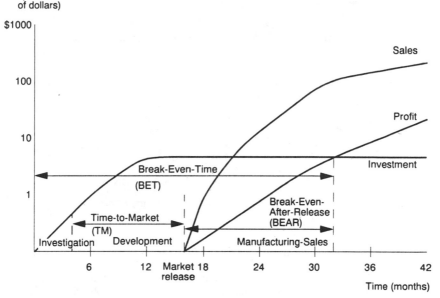

* As a way to make comparisons among projects, Hewlett Packard has developed and refined the set of measures shown here. These are now used as management tools by both the team and senior management on all product development projects.

SOURCE: C. H. House, and R. L. Price, "The Return Map: Tracking Product Teams," *Harvard Business Review* (1991, January–February), pp. 92–101.

investment, cost, revenue, and profit over time, a variety of groups charged with making decisions that impact the development strategy can use the map as a common reference point.

The Aggregate Project Plan

The process of working out development goals and objectives integrates technology and commerical plans from the standpoint of purpose and intent. The aggregate project plan brings a second stage of integration down to the level of specific projects and resources. The purpose of creating such a plan is to ensure that the collective set of projects will accomplish the development goals and objectives *and* build the organi-

Exhibit 2–10

Four Types of Product / Process Development Projects*

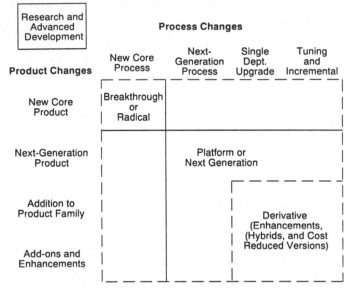

* The amount of product and process change determines the type and magnitude of the development effort required. Research and advanced development involves proving the feasibility of new technology. The other three types of projects involve the application of proven technologies to create commercial products and manufacturing processes that will achieve business objectives.

---

zational capabilities needed for ongoing development success. While an aggregate project plan is absent in the vast majority of firms we have studied, the concept is relatively simple and straightforward. (Chapter 4 deals with the practical challenges that must be addressed to operationalize the concept fully.)

The first step in developing an aggregate project plan is to ensure that development resources are applied to the appropriate types and mix of projects. For most firms, development projects—both product and process—fall into one of the four types shown in Exhibit 2–10. Briefly, these are defined as follows:

- *Research or advanced development projects.* These aim at inventing new science or capturing new know-how so that required knowledge will be available for application in specific development projects. Often they are conducted by a research or advanced development group that is separate from the main development organization.

- *Breakthrough development projects.* These involve creating the first generation of an entirely new product and process. They are "breakthrough" in the sense that their core concepts and technologies break new ground for the organization. If successful, they are likely to constitute a whole new product/process family for the organization.
- *Platform or generational development projects.* These are the platform or core development projects mentioned earlier in this chapter. Typically they have a design life of several years and establish the basic architecture for a set of follow-on derivative projects.
- *Derivative development projects.* These tend to be substantially narrower in scope and resource requirements than platform projects. They refine and improve selected performance dimensions to better meet the needs of specific market segments. Often they are referred to as "incremental."

While these four project types may vary in the degree of product and process change they incorporate, a fifth type can be distinguished by who does the work. In *alliance or partnered projects*, the firm "buys" a newly designed product and/or process from another firm. The possibility of subcontracting a development project to a partner needs to be included in the aggregate project plan because it can leverage in-house effort, yet requires some resources for coordination and integration.

By indicating the number and mix of these types of projects the aggregate project plan helps an organization allocate its efforts in proportion to the need for and benefits from projects of each type. In addition, it makes explicit the connection between research projects and development projects. Finally, the mix by type translates the product/market and technology strategies into more specific bounds for development efforts and gives the organization the ability to deliver on intermediate-term operating objectives and goals.

The second step is to develop a capacity plan. In virtually all organizations, the demands or opportunities for development projects far exceed the capacity of available resources to work on them. Furthermore, when organizations overextend their resources, productivity declines, the number of projects "in process" increases, projects take longer to complete, and the rate of project completions declines.

As part of the aggregate project plan, the expected resource requirements for representative projects of each of the five types need to be estimated. These estimates, multiplied by the number of projects of each type, can be compared with the available resources to estimate the capacity utilization levels. Initially when this is done, it is not unusual for project commitments to exceed available development capacity by 50 to 100 percent or more. Over time, as demand and capacity are brought into better balance—usually by reducing significantly the number of projects underway at any given point in time—more refined estimates of project requirements can be developed and used to schedule at a detailed level.

The final step in the aggregate plan is to examine the effect of the proposed projects on fundamental skills and capabilities required for future development projects. This includes planning net additions to development resources, but more importantly, providing a set of projects wherein individual contributors, project leaders, and teams can sharpen their skills over time. This aspect of the plan comprehends the fact that development projects build skills and capability, in addition to creating new products and processes.

Project Management

The aggregate project plan and the goals and objectives set the stage for execution of individual projects, a subject we examine in detail in Chapters 6 through 10. But the firm's approach to project management is also part of its development strategy. Since a primary objective of development strategy is to better focus, bound, and set the stage for individual projects, individual projects must build on prior planning by starting with their own planning phase. In essence, each project needs to create its own project strategy and plan that fits with the development strategy. Thus, at the front end of an individual project, the firm needs a process to connect the project in its details to the broader strategy and direction of the business. An important part of that connection is the establishment of clear, measurable goals that can guide development and ensure the project's contribution to overall development objectives.

With the project firmly linked to the business's overall strategy and objectives, project leaders have a much clearer sense of mission and purpose. That clarity in turn simplifies the project and brings focus to the actual work of development. Getting that work done is a matter of detailed design, engineering problem solving, building and testing of prototypes, marketing planning, process planning and development, and manufacturing ramp-up. But the way the firm approaches that detailed work—how it is broadly structured and organized—is part of its development strategy. There may be several different "models" or "approaches" that the firm may develop to apply to different kinds of projects. Crafting a complete development strategy, therefore, involves deciding what those approaches need to be and how they ought to be developed and used in different circumstances. As Exhibit 2–11 makes clear, the key components of individual project management must be not only integrated among themselves, but also linked effectively with the aggregate project plan and the other elements of the development strategy.

EXHIBIT 2–11

Integrating and Linking Project Management Elements to
Development Strategy

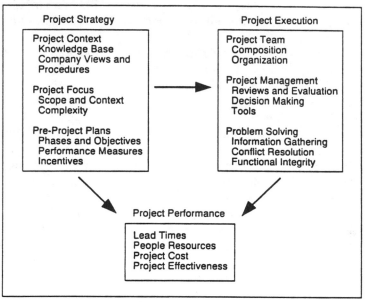

Development Strategy Context

Post-Project Learning

The final element of a development strategy, the focus of Chapters 11
and 12, is post-project learning. Its goal is to ensure that the lessons
available from each project are identified, shared, and applied throughout the organization. In doing so, it closes the loop on continuous improvement by strengthening the foundation for the next iteration of the
development strategy.

Learning from individual development projects has proven to be an
elusive goal for too many organizations. This is due in part to the prevalent view of how such learning occurs. Many firms think of improvement in development as fixing problems. Unfortunately, the "ideas" for
improvement are often little more than short-term reactions to problems
the firm has experienced. Taken together, they may add new procedures, steps, tests, and organizations that only increase the bureaucracy
of the process. The accumulation of fixes then sets the stage for a major
overhaul of the development process in which the firm strips away all
the added steps and procedures. Overall performance, therefore, goes

up and down, but on average changes very little. In contrast, the most successful organizations at learning *and* improving are those that follow a path of continuous improvement in the fundamental capabilities that drive development performance. Each project results in an incremental, but cumulatively significant, improvement in the capabilities of the organization.

Another reason many firms find improvement and learning elusive is that they fail to plan for learning across a sequence of projects. Their goal on each project is to get the product or process into the marketplace (or factory) as rapidly as possible, without significant regard for the means by which they accomplish it. They fail to capture and embed learning in people's behavior, complementary tools, supporting systems, and the organization's structure during each project. Furthermore, even across generations of product and process or even in derivative projects, they fail to plan systematically for the performance and capability improvements they desire.

To make continuous improvement a reality, the post-project phase of the development strategy needs to address the how, who, what, and where of such learning. A particularly effective part of *how* is the project audit, described in detail Chapter 11. Such audits seek to identify the lessons learned and determine how best to apply them. The *who* consists of the entire organization. However, focused steering committees, continual management attention, and a cadre of trained project managers help ensure that the lessons identified in the audits get applied fully. The *what* involves investing—in training, new tools, and new skills. This investment is both in people and procedures, ranging from support groups to the development engineers, and from project planning systems to computer-aided design tools. The *where* is largely in the development projects themselves, targeting some to demonstrate new tools, others to train new people, but all to improve incrementally the organization's collective capabilities.

Honda: An Example of Development Strategy in Action

Honda's competitive performance in the world auto industry over the last decade illustrates the power of a coherent development strategy. Beginning in the 1970s with the Civic, Honda has successfully expanded its product line and established a reputation for innovative products that offer outstanding performance and reliability. Honda's development process has been crucial in establishing that reputation. Continued growth and market success will depend on ongoing improvements in development skills and capabilities.

The challenge that Honda faces in the 1990s is to meet distinctive demands in different regions and market segments, and yet offer a consistent image and product character across models. As Honda moves from its position as a niche player to a full line producer, it must nurture and sustain its reputation for innovative, exciting products while meeting increasingly rigorous competition on cost and quality. Moreover, the global nature of Honda's business and the regional nature of markets means that Honda's product development process must address the need to be both local and global at the same time.

To address the challenges of the 1990s Honda has organized regionally with capability for marketing, manufacturing, design, and engineering established in each of the major regions of the world—Asia (Japan), North America, and Europe. Compared to the challenge of the 1980s, Honda's product line is more complex, its technical requirements more demanding, and its target markets more diverse. Nobuhiko Kawamoto, Honda's CEO, has made it clear that more and more effective up-front planning is crucial to Honda's continued success.

Honda's development strategy has several distinctive elements. Advanced technology has always been a centerpiece of Honda's approach to competition. But at Honda, advanced technology has a particular character. Consider engines, for example. Honda's roots are in motorcycles where highly efficient yet powerful small engines are critical to success. This philosophy has carried over into automobiles. Honda has used Formula 1 racing activities to test and refine engine concepts that deliver very high performance with a minimum of weight and space. Moreover, Honda's engines deliver high performance without add-on devices like turbochargers. In engines, as in other technologies such as four-wheel steering, the hallmarks of Honda's approach are innovation and simplicity.

Looking forward, Honda (and the rest of the world auto industry) faces major technical challenges from the environment (i.e., emissions and recyclability), energy use, safety, and ergonomics. It is likely that meeting these challenges will require the integration of science into the R&D program at Honda. Individual projects will need more focused, deeper technical knowledge and advanced components and systems that have been developed and tested prior to the project's launch. The need for depth and advanced development places an even greater premium on close links between planning for technology and advanced development, and planning for the product line. In our terms, the aggregate project plan, including advanced development as well as commercial products and processes, will be crucial.

Honda's experience with the Today, a micro-mini car sold in Japan, illustrates the power of a close link between advanced development and the product plan.[6] Changes in government regulations in 1988 created new standards for engine and body size for micro-mini cars in Japan. Honda had done advanced work on engine designs for micro-minis that fed directly into the Today redesign. The total development process for the Today took twelve months (compared to a normal development cycle of twenty-four to thirty-six months for such projects), a speed that would not have been possible without the advanced engine development work.

Not all of Honda's development efforts have been unmitigated successes, but the company seems to learn rapidly from each of them. Indeed, the capability for learning seems to be a significant part of Honda's overall success in development. Consider, for example, the project to develop the 1990 Accord, a mid-size family sedan. Honda chose to develop models for the U.S. and Japanese markets from essentially the same platform (body structure, interior, chassis) with different engines, but the two markets proved to be quite different. While a conservative design worked well in the United States, Japanese customers in that segment seemed to be much more interested in innovative concepts and advanced technology. Honda's senior managers have learned that the next generation Accord not only must be more exciting and innovative, but that the two markets probably need different concepts and possibly different platforms. The 1994 Accord project, therefore, is likely to be really two or three projects with distinctive concepts, conducted in a way to achieve coordinated development that leverages common skills and technologies.

One part of the changing development strategy to meet the challenge of multiple platforms yet common identity and character is Honda's approach to project leadership and project teams. For incremental projects, they have defined a type of "small project leader" who, having worked on a preceding development effort for that car model, is given management responsibility for a derivative product or enhancement. A more expanded type of leader is the "regular project leader," who heads a platform effort such as the one resulting in the 1990 Honda Accord. Above this regular project leader is a "large project leader," having responsibility for a group of projects such as the three Accord platforms that will be introduced in 1993–1994. Finally, at the corporate level, there is an executive, or "large, large project leader," who oversees all projects in a broad part of the product line (e.g., one each for small, medium, and large cars).

A final aspect of Honda's project management has been the creation of and continued improvement in the tools and techniques used for carrying out projects. An integral part of this effort has been improving the transfer and introduction of newly designed products into Honda's worldwide manufacturing network. In the future, Honda anticipates that R&D will increasingly focus its attention on platform and technical projects while manufacturing and sales and marketing organizations will handle more of the incremental, derivative, and enhancement projects. One of the reasons for giving the operating organization more development responsibility is to create the same opportunities for renewal and innovation as the R&D organization has. This also would provide a means for implementing a fundamental tenet at Honda: "every organizational unit must break old habits, even good ones."

Honda has used development strategy to build distinctive capabilities and to address the issues raised at the outset of this chapter: avoiding the moving target syndrome, aligning the efforts of individual functions, creating distinctive products while avoiding unexpected technical problems, shaping policies in advance of individual projects, and avoiding unanticipated delays. The success of Honda's efforts is evident in individual projects such as the "Today" as well as in rapid development time for platform projects (three to three-and-a-half years—among the fastest in the worldwide auto industry) and in the completion of factory and supply chain changeovers for new car models in a single weekend, thereby avoiding costly plant shutdowns. Honda has occasionally stumbled in the past, and it faces significant challenges in the future. However, its experience illustrates the power of a development strategy and suggests that continual success will be found by paying close attention to pre-project planning, linking technical strategy to the aggregate project plan, and creating an approach to leadership and organization that matches the need for distinctive, innovative products that create an attractive, coherent image in the marketplace.

Study Questions

1. Pick two of the problems identified at the beginning of the chapter. Compare these problems in terms of their root causes. How are these problems related? What are their underlying sources?
2. Consider Exhibit 2–1. What explains the curves depicted in the exhibit? Why is management's ability to influence a project high at the outset of the project and low later on? Why might management's activity profile be low at the early stage of a project, but high later on?
3. A firm's technology and product/market strategies apparently play a key role in focusing development efforts on projects that will accomplish a clear set of development goals and objectives. In what way does technology strategy or product/market strategy focus development efforts? What are the key choices in technology and product/market strategy that provide such focus? Evaluate the following comment:

"As far as development goals and objectives are concerned, the only goal that matters is profitability. Therefore when we set out to establish our development goals and objectives we should define them in terms of the investments we make in new products relative to the profits they generate."

4. What is the relationship between Exhibit 2–1 and the aggregate project plan?

5. What are the key elements of Honda's development strategy? What is your evaluation of those elements in light of the framework developed in this chapter?

Resotech, Inc.

In closing, I want to remind each of you what this company is all about. When we founded Resotech in 1982, we envisioned a firm at the cutting edge of MRI technology. We were committed to developing MRI equipment with performance and capabilities which set industry standards. I think we're there. We know we can never be the biggest; what we strive for is undisputed leadership in ultra-performance systems.

With those words, Ray Kumasaka, the diminutive but charismatic co-founder and CEO of Resotech, Inc., closed his message to employees at the annual company picnic on July 1, 1986. Resotech, maker of magnetic resonance imaging (MRI) scanners used in diagnostic medicine, was celebrating a milestone in the company's short history. Two weeks previously, they had shipped their fifteenth RS-1000, a highly advanced, $2 million MRI system purchased by prestigious teaching hospitals. Resotech had built an extraordinary machine, and the medical imaging trade journals were labeling them something of a "giant killer." The development process had not always been smooth sailing: the firm's first fully operational prototype was installed in October, 1985, nine months behind schedule. Yet Resotech's scientists had pulled together into a tight-knit group and morale was high.

While Kumasaka was confident, he faced several pressing issues. Foremost in his mind was the Coastal Hospital Consortium contract. Soon after the release of the RS-1000, Coastal Hospital Consortium, an elite group including many of the Western States' wealthiest medium-sized for-profit hospitals, had approached Resotech about building mobile MRI machines capable of servicing several hospitals. Kumasaka was intrigued and somewhat surprised by CHC's overtures:

This case was prepared from general industry information by Research Assistant Brandt Goldstein under the direction of Professor Kim Clark; some names and data have been disguised.

This contract would mean greater revenues than we'd expected at this point. Mobile scanning has a significant share of the market, and we may have at least one and perhaps several other customers besides CHC if we go mobile. But there is a lot of disagreement in the company about this contract. We have some exciting things in development and we've always thought of Resotech as a "big machine" operation. On the other hand, a mobile machine could be a perfect expansion opportunity. Whatever we decide, we've got to do it fast. CHC's board wants an answer quickly and I'm sure they'll go to Picker International if we decline.

Industry Background

Magnetic Resonance Imaging, or MRI, was a relatively new technology in medical diagnostic imaging. Researchers first produced in-vivo images with MRI in 1973; by 1980, production prototypes were capable of imaging an entire human body. Industry analysts estimated that 650 machines would be in use in the U.S. by the end of 1986. In that year alone, vendors were predicted to ship more than 300 units to hospitals, outpatient clinics, and mobile vans.

The Technology

MRI produced an image by exposing the body to a strong magnetic field. Atoms in the body with a "north-south" axis responded by lining up parallel to the field's north-south axis. A clinician would then tilt one type of atom off the north-south axis using a specific radio frequency (different radio frequencies were used for different atoms). When the radio wave was stopped, the atoms began realigning along the north-south axis, and the realignment motion produced an electric current in a detector outside the body. Uniformly varying the magnet's field strength allowed a computer to calculate an image reflecting the location and concentration of the specific type of atom targeted, as well as the effect of adjacent atoms and molecules on that atom.

When MRI became clinically useful in the early 1980s, it captured the interest of the medical profession for a number of reasons. Since bone did not interfere with MRI signals,[1] physicians could obtain clear views of areas such as the brain stem and spinal cord. A promising future application of MRI involved the spectroscopic analysis[2] of atoms such as

---

[1] MRI was usually used to image hydrogen atoms, and bone contains very little hydrogen.

[2] Spectroscopic MR techniques provided biochemical information about the body, rather than imaging it. Spectroscopy analyzes substances based on their electromagnetic energy absorption characteristics.

sodium and phosphorous, which would allow physicians to assess stroke damage and many other biological malfunctions. Several technical improvements would be necessary to achieve clinically useful MR spectroscopy. Because MRI employed radio waves and magnetic fields rather than ionizing radiation, it eliminated the risk of X-irradiation caused by conventional x-ray technology and CT scanners (more politically than scientifically significant).

MRI units were large. A permanent installation could be eight feet tall and equally thick, incorporating a doughnut-shaped magnet weighing from 10 to 100 tons with a magnetic field 20,000 times that of the earth's. A system was composed of three main components: field magnets; radio transmitter/receiver and antenna; and computers controlling data acquisition, storage, processing and display.

The most powerful MR machines used superconducting magnets. These magnets operated at a few degrees above absolute zero, where their niobium-titanium wire coils lost all electrical resistance. The electrical current providing the magnetic field could circulate for years without significant decay. Superconducting magnets of 1.5 Tesla[3] were commonplace; GE and others had created prototypes, but no commercial products, with field strengths of up to 4 Tesla (spectroscopic MR depended on very large magnets).

Superconducting magnets were extremely expensive, accounting for one third of a system's cost. The liquid helium used to cool the magnets was both costly and difficult to handle. The magnets required extensive shielding, since they could damage electronic equipment up to sixty feet away. Despite these drawbacks, most first used superconducting magnets because of their superior field strength.

Radio equipment consisted of a tunable radio frequency generator which broadcasted a signal through a coil antenna surrounding the patient and located inside the field magnets. Shielding was necessary from outside radio transmissions. Computer hardware and software handled three different tasks: controlling the test scan, including the variation in strength of the magnetic field and the generation and reception of radio frequency signals; data acquisition and storage; and image processing enhancement and display.

Mobile MRI Equipment

Although the first MRI systems were all permanent installations, some companies began developing a version of the product that could be moved from hospital to hospital. Hospitals could then share an expen-

---

[3] Magnetic fields are measured in gauss or in Tesla; 1 Tesla equals 10,000 gauss. The earth's magnetic field is about 0.5 gauss.

sive MR system, but mobilizing MRI technology posed a number of formidable problems. The greatest difficulties involved the magnet. The equipment rode in a semi-trailer (usually called a "van" by the industry), putting a premium on weight reduction and space; magnets therefore had to be smaller and lighter, but maintain enough field strength for quality images. A mobile superconducting magnet had to be ramped up every time it was moved. This required computer-directed ("intelligent") power supplies that minimized ramp-up time and cost. Because the environment constantly changed, stringent shielding measures had to be taken to protect the magnet's extraordinarily fine adjustments. Many of the sensitive components (e.g., disk drives and computers) had to be mechanically stabilized to prevent damage during transport.

The Market

Technological advance had fueled dynamic growth in the diagnostic imaging market and industry analysts expected imaging firms to prosper into the 1990s. In 1983, while there were perhaps 50 MRI units in clinical use, the technology was not commercially available. In 1984, the FDA first approved MR equipment for commercial sale. Technicare and Diasonics received approval in April, Picker International in May, and Forar in October. By August, 1984, 145 MRI scanners were in use throughout America, and the number was expected to reach 650 by the end of 1986. Estimates varied somewhat on the exact figures, but all observers agreed that MR would grow more rapidly than any other diagnostic imaging modality. Market Intelligence Research Company of Palo Alto, California, predicted in 1986 that sales of MRI equipment would increase from $554 million in 1985 (15.8% of the medical imaging industry) to about $1 billion in 1991 (20% of the industry), while overall sales of medical imaging equipment would expand to $5 billion in 1991.

Industry observers put mobile products at 20%–25% of the whole MR market; this percentage was not expected to change in the next several years. There were approximately 70 mobile systems operating by January 1, 1986, concentrated mostly in California and Florida followed by Texas and Ohio. These figures represented a dramatic increase from early 1985, when the mobile market was nonexistent. Previously, the term "mobile" had meant machines standing full-time in the parking lots of large hospitals providing interim service until fixed units could be installed. In 1986, however, "mobile" began to mean "units in motion": smaller hospitals (250–300 beds) started sharing MR equipment, scheduling anywhere from a day to a week with a van following a scheduled route (which might cover hundreds of miles).

New hospital reimbursement regulations that became effective in October, 1983, somewhat inhibited the medical imaging industry's expansion. Previously, the Medicare system had simply reimbursed hospitals for their costs. Under the new Diagnosis Relation Groups (DRG), Medicare paid hospitals, clinics, and doctor's offices a fixed fee for each of 476 diagnoses, regardless of the length or intensity of service given a patient. This legislation spurred efforts by hospitals to cut costs, somewhat reducing medical imaging equipment expenditures. MRI equipment was among the industry's most expensive, ranging from approximately $1.0 million for some small magnet systems to approximately $2.2 million for GE's flagship Signa system. Analysts believed that in the future, an MR system's price would increasingly affect buyer behavior.

Price was considerably less important for the large teaching and research hospitals than for smaller and for-profit hospitals. Consequently, most large hospitals had permanent MRI installations, usually with the best, most recent technology. Other hospitals relied on either freestanding MRI clinics or mobile MRI machines. Clinics were often operated by entrepreneurs seeking to capitalize on high patient throughput. Mobile equipment circulated among several hospitals, usually on a weekly basis.

Competitors

In the early days of the industry, few machines were actually sold; rather, firms competed for collaborative research contracts and clinical placement sites at major teaching hospitals around the country by installing scanners without charge. By 1986, GE led the market with a share of 31% (see Exhibit 1). Several other companies had a significant

EXHIBIT 1

Estimated MR Unit Shipments for 1986

Firm	Number	Market Share
General Electric	98	30.6%
Diasonics	56	17.5
Siemens	35	10.9
Picker International	30	9.4
Philips	28	8.8
Fonar	27	8.4
Resotech	23	7.2
Technicare	15	4.7
Others	8	2.5
Totals	**237**	**100.0%**

SOURCE: Casewriter estimates based on industry sources.

117

share of the MRI market in 1986, with Diasonics, Siemens, Picker, Philips, and Fonar all expected to ship more than 25 units by the end of the year.

The market experienced consolidation in 1986. Picker International and Philips announced plans to merge and General Electric acquired Technicare, a subsidiary of Johnson and Johnson. Technicare, which sold CT scanners, ultrasound devices, and other medical imaging products in addition to MRI equipment, had recorded a loss of $40 million on revenues on $270 million in 1985, and a total loss of $260 million since Johnson and Johnson had bought the company in 1979. Technicare was estimated to have had the most mobile units in operation through April, 1986, followed by Picker (shipment figures were unavailable for either firm). Analysts cited a number of reasons for Technicare's failure, including competitive, low-cost CT scanning equipment from Japan. GE stated that while it would support Technicare products already in the field, it would produce no new Technicare equipment.

Technicare's departure appeared to create a significant opportunity in the mobile field. Only Picker was clearly established, but Diasonics quickly challenged Picker by introducing a mobile machine with an Applied Superconetics superconducting magnet. Diasonics hoped to ship as many as 30 mobile units in 1986. Producers sold approximately 75% of their mobile units to mobile MRI service companies such as Mobile Technology of Los Angeles, Motion Scan, Inc. of San Diego, and Scientific Imaging of Farmington, Connecticut. The balance of sales went to hospital chains such as Humana Corp. and Voluntary Hospitals of America, and to local hospital consortiums.

Company Background

Ray Kumasaka and Glenn Lee founded Resotech in August, 1982 (see Exhibit 2). Since 1977, Kumasaka, a radiology fellow at Stanford Medical School, and Lee, a physicist from Cal Tech, had collaborated on several diagnostic imaging research projects. By mid-1982, the two were convinced that they could design and build MRI equipment "at least as good and probably much better" than the prototype projects they had seen from Diasonics and Technicare, the first two firms to get FDA licensing for scanners. In August of 1982, Lee had developed the basic architecture for a machine and Kumasaka had sketched out a rough business plan. After two months of interviews, meetings and negotiations, Kumasaka and Lee obtained funding from two venture capital firms, and Image Science, Inc. (later renamed Resotech) was launched.

Backed by venture capital, Kumasaka and Lee initially hired eight other people, including Sarah Pines, a software engineer from Hewlett-

EXHIBIT 2
Selected Biographies (1986)

Ray Kumasaka

Resotech's culture derived from the personalities of Ray Kumasaka and Glenn Lee. The son of Japanese immigrants, Kumasaka, 53, was patient, slow-spoken and deliberate, the glue of the organization. He was born and raised in San Francisco before attending Harvard College, where he had a reputation for being extraordinarily calm during exam period. Kumasaka traced his grace under pressure to a three-year stint at Camp Manzanar, where the entire Kumasaka family was interned during World War II. "I was very young at the time, but I learned how to be patient and calm under intense pressure and uncertainty. My parents didn't try to hide what was going on." On the strength of excellent grades and outstanding recommendations, which repeatedly praised his perseverance in laboratory work, Kumasaka was accepted to the University of Michigan medical school in 1954, where he ultimately chose to specialize in radiology.

Kumasaka returned to the Bay Area in 1959, where his parents still lived, because his mother had been diagnosed with terminal lung cancer. He was a radiology intern at Berkeley until 1963, when he moved to Stanford to assume a radiology fellowship. He met Glenn Lee in 1972 at a medical imaging convention. Lee had come to hear another physicist discuss the potential medical applications of MRI. While the talk attracted only a few listeners, Kumasaka and Lee had both been fascinated, and stayed after to discuss the topic.

While he rarely showed it, Kumasaka had an entrepreneurial streak in him:

> Where it came from, I'm not sure, but since I can remember, part of me liked the idea of my own business. Until Resotech, I avoided taking risks because I saw my parents work very hard for very little. Being a doctor was stable and secure. But the chance to work with Glenn, creating a new medicine and running my own show, was too good to pass up.

Glenn Lee

If Kumasaka was the glue of Resotech, Lee was the driving, innovative force. Constantly in motion, forever chewing gum as if he always needed something to do, Lee had inordinate amounts of energy and drive. He was, in his own words, "an obsessive-compulsive," hardly able to tear himself away from his work. When he was not working, he ran, biked, and climbed. He once finished second in the "Vertical Mile," a timed race up the stairs of the World Trade Center. "I always have to tell people it's not a joke," he explained in a serious tone.

Lee, 42, the son of a mathematics professor and a violinist, was raised in Connecticut and New York. After winning what one of his old teachers described as "every national high school science award that ever existed, and some that didn't," Lee went to study engineering at Cooper Union in New York City. As an undergraduate, he became more and more interested in research physics, ultimately deciding to leave engineering. "It wasn't that I didn't like EE. I loved it. But physics I could do all night, every night, without ever getting bored or tired. It was like a new kind of food." At Cooper, Lee also discovered that his work was marketable. He made money by turning student stereo equipment into "thundering towers of sound. I'd modify their amplifiers, warning them that it would ruin their speakers. No one cared, everyone just wanted noise. It made me pretty wealthy for a student."

After completing a doctorate in physics at Princeton, and a post-doctoral fellowship at SUNY Stony Brook (where he collaborated in producing the first two-dimensional MRI image in 1971), Lee took a position at Cal Tech. His work in magnetic fields culminated in 1982 with the founding of Resotech: "I decided to quit telling other people how to build these things and do it myself."

Kener Jain

Thirty-six-year-old Kener Jain completed his Ph.D. in electrical engineering at Cal Tech in less than three years. He was, in the words of his undergraduate thesis advisor at MIT, "so naturally gifted it's frightening. It seemed to me that he solved problems in sort of a continuous flow process." Lee remarked, "The word genius is used too much these days, but I thoroughly believe that Kener is the real thing."

Jain's office was a shambles, "a paper blizzard," according to a colleague. Kumasaka said,"It's often a mystery how he gets things done, and how he keeps track of everything. Sometimes he doesn't. Other times, he'll solve something before the problem is out of your mouth. He's the nicest guy in the world, but you have to make sure you've got his attention. It seems that the gears inside are constantly grinding."

Jain came to Resotech in late 1984 from the systems architecture group at MIT. He had known Lee at Cal Tech. "I liked Glenn a lot. I contributed, if only a small bit, to a couple of his research projects at Cal Tech. They needed someone to help with the math. When I found out about Resotech, I gave Glenn a call because I was looking for a change. He's a great scientist, a good person to work with."

Clayton Jackson

Jackson, 34 years old and VP of Marketing, was born and raised in Atlanta. He received a bachelor's degree in marketing at Georgia State University before joining Market Design, Inc., a San Francisco consulting firm which specialized in market research for hi-tech firms. Jackson attended business school at UCSF, graduating in 1980. He then returned to Market Design as a full associate. One former colleague at Market Design described him as "hardworking and bright. He's often got great insights. Also, he really works to understand the technology he's dealing with." Jackson joined Resotech full time in 1986 after having served as a marketing consultant to the firm for two years.

Allison Selvala

Allison Selvala, VP of Finance, held a BA and an MBA from the University of Arizona. Forty-two years old, she had worked in San Francisco as an investment banker for ten years before starting a venture capital firm in 1976. Selvala had invested in Resotech in 1982 and became good friends with Kumasaka. She sold out to her partner in 1984 for $6 million. By 1986, Selvala discovered that she was "tired of retirement. I wanted the challenge of building a high-tech firm." Ray offered Selvala the position the day after she called him. Kumasaka explained: "From the moment she invested in Resotech, Allison gave us better financial advice than anyone."

David Malm

David Malm, 32 years old and VP of Operations, graduated with a degree in mechanical engineering from Berkeley in 1976 and worked in operations at Hewlett-Packard for three years. He attended UCLA Business School, specializing in operations management. "I came to Resotech because I'd always wanted to work in a small-firm environment," he explained. "Kumasaka and Jackson are great people to work with, and Lee is an amazing character." Lee called Malm "enthusiastic and very willing to learn."

Packard and Garth Van Hull, an electrical engineer from Texas Instruments, as well as other technical support staff. Lee planned to focus on the magnet work, and to create at least a partially operational unit, he needed the software expertise involved in imaging processing and the engineering expertise necessary to integrate the machine's various components. He handled the radio work haphazardly, sometimes getting help from old colleagues at Cal Tech; occasionally collaborating with a Ph.D. candidate from Berkeley.

Funding problems slowed development. The prototype project burned money at an alarming rate, and within a year Resotech's venture capital proved insufficient. The niobium-titanium wire in a superconducting magnet cost over one dollar per foot and Lee needed still more than the 160,000 feet already purchased. The insulating mechanisms for the magnet, called dewars, were taking far longer to build than expected, and leak problems cost Resotech over $1,500 each week in evaporated liquid helium. The coil which would produce the necessary radio waves had caused more unexpected difficulties.

In August, 1983, Kumasaka decided that they had to have stronger financial backing; he felt Resotech needed a partner with deep pockets if it was ever going to compete with the companies already far along on their own MRI projects. In October, Kumasaka approached a number of medical products firms that might support Resotech's project.

After several weeks of negotiations, Bauer-Behm, the German pharmaceutical company, bought out the venture capitalists and put in additional equity funding, acquiring a 45% stake in the company. Bauer-Behm, with sales of $16 billion in 1985, saw the partnership as a positive diversification move. Analysts predicted high growth in the MRI market, and Resotech's emphasis on innovative technology and high performance fit Bauer-Behm's corporate strategy. Bauer-Behm put three people on Resotech's board and also offered the technical assistance of its instrument group, which, although unfamiliar with MRI, had significant expertise in computer systems and sensors.

By judiciously using stock options and exploiting their connections at a number of universities, Kumasaka and Lee were able to assemble a small team of first-rate scientists (see Exhibit 3). All were highly competent; a few stood out. In addition to Sarah Pines, the programmer from HP, they brought in a graphics expert from Brown University, Michael Lippman. Lippman had a wealth of experience in imaging processing and had worked on the 1984 project which had achieved pseudocoloring of magnetic resonance images using NASA programs designed for aerial photography enhancement. Princeton physicist Stephen Anderson specialized in magnetic field research and had helped design a number of superconducting magnets. Kumasaka saw electrical engineer Kener Jain as a particularly significant coup. Jain had spent

Exhibit 3
Selected Research and Development Personnel

Name	Age	Experience/Background
Glenn Lee	42	Ph.D. Physics, Princeton Professor of Physics, Cal Tech
Ray Kumasaka	53	M.D. (Radiology), University of Michigan Radiology Fellow, Stanford Medical School
Kener Jain	36	Ph.D. Electrical Engineer, Cal Tech 8 yrs, MIT Systems Architecture Group
Sarah Pines	32	M. S. Comp. Science, Carnegie-Mellon 6 yrs. Software Development, HP
Michael Lippman	30	Ph.D. Comp. Science, MIT 5 years. Graphics Research, Brown
Stephen Anderson	36	Ph.D. Physics, UC-Berkeley Associate Professor of Physics, Princeton
Sabra Cyzais	31	M.S. Material Engineer, University of North Carolina 5 yrs. Design Group TFI Magnetics
David Lurie	37	B.S. Electrical Engineer, Purdue 8 yrs. Design Engineer, Xerox
Steven Kliman	37	Ph.D. Electrical Engineer, University of Texas, 7 yrs. MIT Systems Architecture Group
Eric Shaw	32	M.S. Physics, University of Chicago, 4 yrs. Prod. Feasibility Group, Comsat
Pam Wasserman	35	M.S. Material Engineer, Cal Tech, 7 yrs. GE Materials Group
Garth Van Hull	34	Ph.D. Chemistry, University of Texas, 6 yrs. R&D, Medchem Electronic
Rob Bingham	30	M.S. Operations Research, University of Wisconsin, 4 yrs. Research Associate at Cray Research
Sarah Eaton	37	M.D. (Radiology), Northwestern, 6 yrs. Radiology Research, UCSF
Jorgen Hammerstrom	33	M.S. Electrical Engineer, University of Stockholm, 4 yrs. Engineer Staff, Baylor College of Medicine

eight years guiding a systems architecture group at MIT and his colleagues considered him a genuine genius.

Company Operations

From the beginning, Lee and Kumasaka had worked closely together on every aspect of the business. However, each had particular interests and assignments. Kumasaka's main concern had been selling the RS-1000 to the large research and teaching hospitals where he had long-standing relationships. Until 1986, Resotech's sales force consisted of Ray Kumasaka and whoever happened to be traveling with him on a particular day (he often took one of the scientists with him on hospital visits). In addition to sales, Kumasaka assumed principal responsibility for building the management team.

Glenn Lee concentrated on managing R&D. Lee's approach to management was described by one of his colleagues as "managing by hanging around." Knowledgeable about every aspect of the project and unbelievably energetic, Lee seemed to be everywhere. He described his organization:

> We organized teams around each of the main components of the system—the magnet, the radio equipment, and data processing (see Exhibit 4). After the first few months, each team worked pretty independently, although we had lots of meetings. The team leaders were the key to the whole project. They really set the focus in their own groups.

Michael Lippman, co-leader of the data-processing team, talked about how R&D worked:

> The boxes that you see are just lines on paper. When somebody has a problem around here, they go to whoever can help them. The whole group is small, and usually we all know what's going on. Glenn's no bureaucrat. He's made Resotech a pretty fluid place.

Lee made it a practice to hold design reviews every Thursday at lunch. Different parts of the machine were featured each week, and the lunchtime sessions involved everyone. Eric Shaw, a member of the magnetics team described the atmosphere:

> I don't know if you've ever sat in a high-powered seminar at a place like Cal Tech, but that's what this has been like. We've had raging battles over tech-

EXHIBIT 4

Organization of Resotech R&D Group

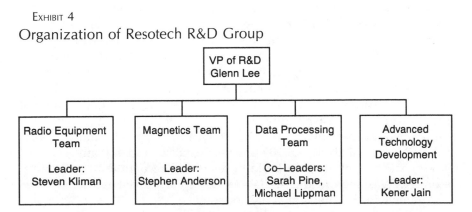

nical design issues. When Jain and Lippman go at it, it's incredible. Those lunch meetings are largely why the RS-1000's such a good machine.

Although David Malm was responsible for operations, Kumasaka and Lee subcontracted out nearly all parts manufacturing; Resotech's machinists made several of the small items themselves. High level assembly was done in a facility next to the research lab. The first few RS-1000s were completed largely under Lee's direction. All testing was done on site in Santa Clara. The first objects to be scanned in the experimental prototype were inanimate; testing later progressed to laboratory animals, and finally, to human beings. In the beginning, worried about legal complications, Lee himself played the guinea pig. While several members of the team had experienced headaches and dizziness around the magnet, Lee was extremely eager to test his first prototype, and in December, 1984, he had Kumasaka scan his chest. Lee experienced no side effects, and he and Kumasaka took turns in the machine during 1985. Several terminal cancer patients in the Bay Area offered themselves as subjects during that time. After the testing became routine, it was led by Resotech employees Sarah Eaton, a radiologist, and Rob Bingham, an operations research specialist, using Resotech personnel and occasionally nearby hospital patients.

Resotech created a five-person service and support group for the RS-1000, led by Jorgen Hammerstrom. Service contracts in the MR industry were extremely lucrative, often running 10% of the system cost each year. Resotech's contract, which was 9% of the scanner price, covered preventive maintenance and an insurance policy for malfunctioning.

The RS-1000

Resotech completed final testing of the first fully operational RS-1000 in October, 1985, two years after the Bauer-Behm deal (and more than nine months late). Their first placement was with the radiology department at Stanford Medical School. While an experimental prototype had been completed in late 1984, numerous setbacks, particularly with magnet insulation, kept Resotech out of the marketplace until 1986. With Kumasaka and Lee on hand, the first scanner was installed at Stanford by the Resotech service group in cooperation with hospital support staff. Resotech also won research contracts with the radiology department at the University of Washington in Seattle (October) and the radiology department at the University of Texas Health Science Center in'Dallas (November). All three RS-1000s were installed and initially serviced gratis, as Resotech tried to build support and recognition for the new scanner. Washington and UCLA agreed to work out reimbursement programs with Resotech at a later date.

The RS-1000 was a highly advanced machine by any standard, offering significant improvement in image quality, speed of data collection, and image examination. Anderson's group had created an impressive 1.5 Tesla superconducting magnet, as powerful as any in the business, which provided the highest quality images available on a commercial basis. He had overcome some of the massive shielding difficulties with a novel approach, counter-winding the magnet with superconducting wire that had an opposing orientation. This measure had effectively eliminated much of the troublesome fringe field. To speed data collection, the RS-1000 offered a new option called HFI, or Half-Fourier Imaging. This technique utilized half a data set to reconstruct an image, thereby reducing scanning time by nearly 50%. The Stanford researchers working with the first RS-1000 believed HFI would be particularly useful for rapid screening studies of the brain. HFI promised improvement in patient throughput and greater patient comfort, although it suffered a reduction in signal to noise (S/N) ratio.[4] Several machines offered still faster data collection, but with considerably reduced image quality. A final feature of the RS-1000 which had really impressed the industry was the machine's off-line examination system. This system allowed the radiologist access to forty-eight images simultaneously, including hard copies of the images; the previous on-line image maximum had been four.

Response from the teaching hospital community had been phenomenal, both because of Kumasaka's rapport with a few very influential buyers and high praise through word of mouth. By June 20, Resotech had shipped 15 RS-1000s to leading research hospitals, and Kumasaka anticipated sales of perhaps 8 more units by year's end. He noted, "After years of waiting the revenues suddenly came pouring in. We were all extremely excited" (see Exhibit 5). Lead stories in several industry trade journals spread Resotech's name to small- and medium-sized hospitals. While most of these hospitals were not expected to purchase Resotech equipment, the name "Resotech" had earned a "Rolls-Royce" image among hospital administrators.

Plans for upgrading the RS-1000 headed the company agenda during 1986. Lee, however, had already begun work with several others on the next generation MR machine, the RS-2000. Production of the new model was slated for October, 1989. Morale was exceptionally high both because of rapid progress on the 2000 and the commercial success of the 1000. For the RS-2000, Resotech was focusing on research magnets with field strengths exceeding 3 Tesla, capable of spectroscopic analysis of

---

[4] This ratio compares the amount of useful information in an image (the signal) to the amount of interference or disruption in that image (noise).

125

Exhibit 5
Summary of Financial Statements

Consolidated Statements of Income
(in thousands of dollars)

	1986[a]	1985	1984
Net Sales	29,430	—	—
Cost of Goods Sold	19,198	—	—
Operating Expenses:			
Research and development costs	3,212	2,102	2,915
Selling, general and administrative expenses	3,503	2,380	801
Operating Profit	3,517	(5,482)	(3,716)
Other Income (expense):			
Dividends and interest income	88	160	120
Interest expense	(212)	(275)	(260)
Income Before Provision for Income Taxes	3,393	(5,597)	(3,856)
Provision for Income Taxes	1,212	—	—
Income Before Extraordinary Credit	2,181	(5,597)	(3,856)
Extraordinary credit:			
Reduction of income taxes resulting from tax benefit of net operating loss carrying forward	1,212	—	—
Net Income	**3,393**	**(5,597)**	**(3,856)**

[a] For the nine months ending June 1986.

Assets
(in thousands of dollars)

	June 30, 1986	Sept. 30, 1985
Current Assets:		
Cash	1,642	(471)
Accounts receivable	6,279	—
Notes receivable	256	21
Inventories	2,217	1,105
Prepaid expenses	363	505
Total current assets	10,757	1,160
Property and Equipment:		
Research, development and demonstration equipment	3,014	2,032
Offsite research scanner	1,301	—
Machinery and equipment	947	742
Furniture and fixtures	502	311
Accumulated depreciation and amortization	(1,901)	(887)
Other Assets:		
Cost of acquiring technology and license	2,295	1,977
Patents and other assets	1,217	802
Total	18,132	6,137

Liabilities and Stockholders' Equity		
Current Liabilities:		
Notes payable	1,000	922
Current portion of long-term debt and capital lease obligations	587	453
Accounts payable	6,048	848
Accrued liabilities	1,325	746
Customer advances	2,511	—
Total Current Liabilities	11,571	2,969
Other Liabilities:		
Long-term debt and capital lease obligations	2,251	1,512
Stockholders' Equity	3,310	1,656
Total Liabilities and Stockholders' Equity	18,132	6,137

sodium and phosphorous. The entire R&D group expected the 2000 to be at least as revolutionary as its predecessor.

The CHC Contract Offer

On July 29, 1986, CHC made a formal offer to Resotech, requesting the development and production of twenty-five mobile MRI units to be purchased by CHC over two years, beginning in October 1988 (see Exhibit 6). Dean Williams, a radiologist and highly influential member of Coastal Hospital Consortium's board, had known Ray Kumasaka for more than ten years. Williams had called the RS-1000 the "sharpest machine I'd ever seen. Unfortunately, most CHC members could not use something so huge and expensive. But if Ray ever decided to go a little toward the lower end, I told him we'd be interested." In December, 1985, and again in February of 1986, Kumasaka and Williams had discussed a slightly less advanced product from Resotech, perhaps a mobile machine, but Kumasaka had made it clear that his firm was focused on the high end.

Williams had kept his discussions with Kumasaka private until late April. At that time, CHC was preparing a contract offer to Technicare, the leader in mobile equipment sales. The contract, however, collapsed when Johnson and Johnson sold Technicare to GE. Williams then told the CHC Purchasing Committee about his discussions with Kumasaka, adding that a firm order might convince Resotech to build a mobile machine. Along with three other administrators who knew either Kumasaka or Lee and were extremely impressed with what they had read about the firm, Williams persuaded the committee to explore a Resotech contract before going to Picker or Diasonics.

127

EXHIBIT 6
CHC Contract Offer Cover Letter

Coastal Hospital Consortium
Purchasing Division
380 Montgomery St.
San Francisco, CA 94104

Dr. Ray Kumasaka
Resotech, Inc.
12 Research Park Circle
Santa Clara, CA 05051

Dear Dr. Kumasaka,

Enclosed are the specific details of the contract offer initially negotiated in our phone conversation of August 19.

To briefly summarize, we expect shipment of thirteen (13) mobile units (vans to be supplied by Calumet Coach) during the 1988 fiscal year, five (5) in October, four (4) in November and four (4) in December. We expect shipment of twelve (12) mobile units during the 1989 fiscal year, beginning with two (2) in January. Shipping dates for the final ten (10) units shall be determined at a later date. See Appendix A (pp. 3–25) for complete details.

We have set our final offer at $1.5 million per unit for the 1988 fiscal year. As agreed in our phone conversations of August 18, 19, and 20, the price for the 1989 units shall be determined at a later date, with the prices not to exceed $1.6 million per unit. Also as agreed, the service contract shall be 8.5% of the cost of each machine, per year.

The payment schedule agreed upon requires payment in full for each unit, within sixty (60) days of receiving it in working condition. An initial payment of $1 million will be made upon satisfactory examination of the experimental prototype scheduled for fall, 1987. An additional $2 million payment will be made upon satisfactory examination of a commercial prototype scheduled for May/June, 1988. See Appendix B for pricing, payment and financing details. Appendix C discusses the service contract.

Expected equipment performance capabilities and standards are discussed in Appendix D. We draw specific attention to pages 29–57, which describe the expected capacity for upgrading; pages 92–113, which describe imaging quality specifications; and pages 129–146, which describe shielding requirements.

Additional legal information is contained in Appendix D.

We look forward to a successful association with Resotech.

Sincerely,

Emily Ceisler
VP Purchasing

The decision to approach Resotech was based on the reputation of the RS-1000 and the demand for MRI technology. Many of the consortium's members were lobbying for new MRI equipment. The hospitals in CHC were generally known for their emphasis on the best in medical technology—"The finest medical care available, without a 'large hospital' environment" typified their marketing message—but few of the members had the capital necessary to install a cutting-edge machine. Mobile scanners, which most CHC hospitals were using,[5] allowed members to share costs—a must, given the current DRG regulations. The problem was that mobile MRI equipment had not equaled the performance of the big, permanent machines, particularly in overall image quality. Williams believed Resotech could close the performance gap. Not all the hospitals would need everything Resotech had to offer, but the board believed there were two key advantages in going with Resotech: better medical care and significant marketing leverage.

To persuade Resotech to take the contract, Williams suggested to Kumasaka that R&D funding might be possible, perhaps up to $250,000. Williams observed:

> We believed that an order for 25 units would attract them. I believe that mobile equipment is a positive direction for Resotech. More and more of the small- and medium-sized hospitals will be using MRI technology in the future, and many will rely on mobile equipment.

On August 5, one month after the company picnic, Kumasaka, Lee, Jain (who headed Advanced Technology Development), Jackson (VP of Marketing), Selvala (VP of Finance), and Malm (VP of Operations) met to discuss the CHC contract. Gunther Stein, an executive from Bauer-Behm's North American headquarters in New York City, attended the meeting.

The Meeting

Kumasaka opened the meeting with a review of the situation:

This is how I see it. We're running out of time on CHC's contract and we have to decide if we should go mobile. The contract looks attractive, but I don't know whether we can keep on track for the 2000 in '89 if we take it. I don't want to slow down on the 2000's spectroscopy work. We plan to announce the 2000 next June, and if everything's on time, production will start in October, 1989. We can't lose momentum on this project.

JACKSON: I don't think we have a tough decision here. This is exactly what I discussed in my memo to Ray last week: we need to be more knowledgeable about the market and sensitive to what our customers

---

[5] At the time, CHC owned seven units and leased three mobile units from Technicare.

want [See Exhibit 7]. Our success depends upon pursuing marketable technologies. I'm worried that we are committing resources to a product which may have a very narrow customer base because it's so advanced. Here we have a customer who will buy 25 units of a product we have the capacity to develop today. It's exactly what we should be doing—attuning our R&D agenda to the customer.

JAIN: Clayton, the reason Resotech is so successful is because we didn't follow the crowd. I know we've got to be sensitive to the market, but look at the RS-1000. That machine pulled in top research hospitals because of its superior technology.

MALM: That's true, but I think Clayton has a point. Look at the Computer Enhanced HFI project, for example. Maybe it won't turn out to be as big a deal to the hospital as it is to us. Lippman's pretty high on this idea of intelligent image enhancement, but the guy's not a radiologist, and frankly, I'm not sure we're as close to practice as we need to be.

JAIN: I disagree. Mike knows what's going on out there, but his idea is to take some leadership. Besides, being sensitive to the market is not

EXHIBIT 7

Jackson's Memo to Kumasaka

MEMORANDUM

TO: Ray Kumasaka

FROM: Clayton Jackson

DATE: July 22, 1986

RE: New Marketing Group

Ray:

I think last month's meetings on our long-term agenda revealed some problems in the RS-2000 design focus. In my opinion, your R&D group is too occupied with the technology for its own sake, and not concerned enough about the 2000's marketability. Should we really be channeling so much research capital into a product with no well-defined customer base?

To shift the focus back to the customer, I recommend that we form a special marketing group to assess customer needs and wants. We can thereby reshape the 2000 and the upgraded 1000 into higher-demand products. I envision a team composed of application and bio-medical engineers who understand academic medicine, combined with leading-edge doctors, people who use MRI regularly. (Perhaps we should retain some practicing radiologists as consultants.) Our new group would be able to identify customer interests and related product opportunities and then filter that information down to R&D, giving Glenn and his people a clearer product development focus.

I will get back to you on this in depth.

the issue here. The issue is do we divert attention from our primary focus?

JACKSON: Developing a mobile version of the RS-1000 is fully consistent with exploiting our technology. It's not a diversion. It's what we need to do to build the company.

KUMASAKA: Before we get too wrapped up in the issue of the 2000, let me repeat myself: We are going to do the 2000, period. If we decide to do the mobile system, we'll have to hire almost an entirely new team to do it. But nothing gets in the way of the 2000.

SELVALA: Ray, is this mobile product consistent with our strategy? It seems to me it is. I know it wasn't planned, but CHC is a leading edge customer, and our product will be the leader in that niche.

KUMASAKA: Well, I'm not sure. Part of the problem is that we've never thought about something like this. It came out of the blue. On the surface, it looks pretty good, but I'm worried about diversion even if we have new people. On the other hand . . .

STEIN: Ray, could I break in here? I think we're having another very nice conceptual discussion, but I suggest that we—how do you say?—come back to earth. This contract has something we need: revenue and profits. Your expenses on the 2000 are looking very high, and this kind of contract is what will fund the advanced system. I think we go here with first things first.

MALM: We're talking like a mobile unit is a piece of cake, but I'm not so sure it's all that simple. Glenn, what's involved in this thing?

LEE: Well, there's not a whole lot that's new except for the magnet. But getting a really good mobile product out is definitely not a piece of cake. There's some very tough engineering involved. I can tell you one thing, though, and that's that I'm going to have a difficult time getting everyone geared up to do a mobile 1000.

JACKSON: But if we do it we're talking about new people anyway, aren't we? Or did I miss something?

LEE: We'll need to hire a lot of new people. I've done a rough study, and I think I'm gong to need at least 20 people and about 20–25 months to really do the mobile job right. We're going to need engineers to work on rigidizing and size and weight reduction. We'll also need people to do insulation modifications and I'm sure there will be problems with the magnet. I've worked up a memo on some of the other costs involved [see Exhibit 8].

SELVALA: We haven't completed all the work on analyzing the contract yet. But so far it looks like a pretty profitable project. If we decide to do it, the real problem I see will be meeting the delivery schedule.

LEE: Getting the people on board will be the biggest problem. If we

EXHIBIT 8

Lee's Mobile MR Development Cost Memo to Selvala

MEMORANDUM

TO: Allison Selvala
FROM: Glenn Lee
DATE: July 29, 1986
RE: Mobile Development Cost Estimates

Allison,

The estimates here are very rough. I just sat down and sketched out the bare minimum, so you may want to think $2–300,000 higher. Give me a ring after you've looked it over. CHC says first exp. proto by Oct. '87—gives us 13 mos. if we start in Sept. Commercial proto due around May '88; only eight months to work out everything. Then first shipment August. Means less than 2 years. Magnet is the time problem.

Hardware Development Costs—One-Time Purchase

Magnet Wire (mostly niobium-titanium)	$250–300,000

Data Processing Equipment
  Includes: boards, CRT's, drives, modified graphic
            systems
	$125–150,000

Radio Equipment Includes: coils, new generator, other	$250,000

Miscellaneous
  Includes: shielding equipment, rigidizing hardware
            and materials, other
	$200,000

Contingencies	$100,000
Total	$825–900,000

Recurring Costs

Motion Simulators (2) for Equipment Test (probably for 6 months)	$19,500/month
Liquid Helium (about 40 weeks)	$1,500/week (avg.)
Other (for all 20–25 months)	$1,000/week (avg.)
Total	$520–540,000

get going, we probably can pull a team together by the first of the year.

MALM: I think we may be able to get a leg up on the lead-time problem. If we buy the magnet, we could get this done much quicker. I got word this morning from an old friend in New York who told me that IGC [Intermagnetics General Corporation] has a swollen inventory because Technicare's not buying their magnets anymore. IGC's talking with Diasonics and they're already working with Picker, but we may be able to get somewhere with them.[6] Steve [Anderson] and his group may want to make a mobile magnet themselves, but in the interim we can buy the magnet in order to meet deliveries.

JAIN: I'm sure we can do this if we want to, but I think it's a mistake. It just doesn't look right.

KUMASAKA: Well, we need the financials and a time schedule before we can make a decision. Can we meet tomorrow morning?

[6] Information was sketchy, but it appeared that an IGC magnet might cost $400–$450,000.

Dayton Electric Corporation[1]

In late January 1991, Rick Rawlins, manager of the Motor Division of Dayton Electric Corporation, had to decide where to add the capacity needed to produce the next generation of redesigned medium-sized DC motors. In less than two weeks he was to meet with Dayton's board of directors to review his recommendations and get the board's approval for the required capital investment. For several months, Rawlins' staff had investigated a variety of alternatives so that a decision could be made with sufficient time to support the planned early 1993 market introduction of the redesigned line. It had gathered and analyzed data and presented its conclusions to the division's management team. All had recently agreed that there were two good options to choose from. One was to expand the existing motor plant in Indianapolis, Indiana. The other was to build an entirely new plant at a previously approved site in Florence, Kentucky.

Unfortunately, a conversation a day earlier with Rawlins' director of engineering, Bill Vogel, had revealed an additional complication in the current capacity deliberations. In a nutshell, Vogel proposed that the soon-to-be completed redesign of the medium DC motor (known as the Mark II)—the one for which a capacity decision was needed—be put on hold and a three-month crash redesign program be undertaken. The goal of this crash program would be to see if a significantly higher performance design alternative could be identified.

If successful, the resulting design would most likely require another $1 million in development costs to avoid delaying the planned 1993 market introduction. It also would require approximately $2 million of

[1] Data have been disguised to protect the competitive and proprietary interests of Dayton Electric Corporation.

unanticipated additional investment if Florence was selected as a manufacturing site, but little or no unanticipated incremental investment if Indianapolis was selected. Finally, it would send ripples through other development efforts that were following the division's traditional approach to new product creation.

Rawlins was inclined to take Vogel's objections to the Mark II redesign seriously. Not only was Vogel a first-rate engineer with intimate knowledge of this class of product, he had worked on the development of the division's current medium DC motor (the rectified power motor, or RPM), which had been wildly successful following its market introduction in 1985.

Rawlins knew Dayton's board would expect a firm capital investment figure as part of his proposal and would ask about the status of the development project for which the new capacity was intended. Thus he needed to resolve the design issue as far as possible, as well as the capacity options, before the board meeting.

Company Background

Founded in 1920 and quickly becoming a major industrial manufacturer in the Dayton, Ohio, area, Dayton Electric originally manufactured and sold electric motors and controls; it was split into two major groups, and made a handful of diversified acquisitions during the 1970s. By 1991, the company continued to be organized largely along functional lines in its traditional business (see Exhibit 1).

Brett Sorenson, CEO of Dayton, emphasized effective operations management and the accomplishment of corporate plans and objectives; his management philosophy stressed strong internal management based on systematic planning. As a guide, Sorenson had provided a set of ground rules, including 18% aftertax return on capital employed and 20% aftertax return on stockholders' equity. Each segment of the business was expected to equal or better these goals.

The thrust of the overall corporate strategy was to concentrate on segments of chosen markets and to serve them extremely well. This was described as serving "selected customers and selected markets" on the basis of product features and product performance. Strong corporate performance suggested that this approach was indeed working (see Exhibit 2).

In the mid 1980s, the Motor Division faced some major challenges. Brian Canann, executive vice president, recalled:

> Sorenson made it very clear that in order for the corporation to make a major commitment to the business, substantial improvement was needed in our

Exhibit 1

Corporate and Motor Division Organization Chart, 1991

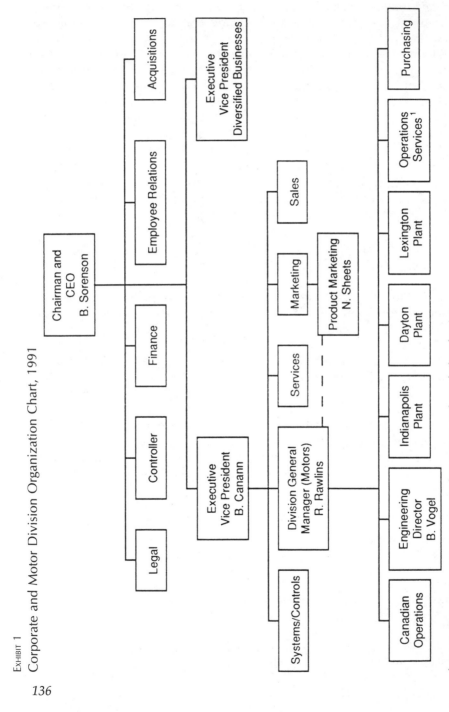

[1] Handles industrial engineering, new product start-up, and new facility planning.

EXHIBIT 2

Four-Year Corporate Financial Summary for Dayton Electric
Corporation

	1990[1]	1989	1988	1987
Net Sales (millions)	$643.1	$580.0	$484.4	$399.3
Net Earnings (millions)	$ 35.0	$ 28.9	$ 23.2	$ 15.4
Net Earnings/Net Sales	5.4%	5.0%	4.8%	3.9%
Return on Equity	19.4%	18.1%	15.9%	11.2%
Net Earnings/Share	$ 2.48	$ 2.10	$ 1.68	$ 1.11
Dividends/Share	$ .875	$ .80	$ .725	$ .70

[1] Approximately 20% of corporate sales and 50% of net earnings came through the
Motor Division in 1990.

operations and performance. This was highlighted in 1987 when our pretax
margin dropped to an all-time low of 10% on sales, while sales continued to
increase. At that point, we knew that immediate action and clearly positive
results from that action were necessary to gain credibility. That credibility
was required before additional funds would be made available for future
growth and development of the business.

Rawlins, with engineering and manufacturing experience, was chosen
to direct the operating and engineering efforts of Dayton's motor business in early 1987. He had already established himself in the company by
directing and coordinating the important and successful 1985 program to
redesign the medium-sized DC motor line, an effort that saw the company's first use of a tiger team. Although an exception to the company's
traditional approach of many subfunctions each doing their well-defined
set of tasks, the approach resulted in the RPM DC design, which gave
Dayton technical leadership in the medium DC motor business.

During 1987, under Rawlins' direction, the Motor Division drew up a
plan to cut spending, attack its marketing problems, and redesign its
products to reduce manufacturing costs. By 1991 pretax profits were
almost double those in 1987, sales were growing 25% per year, and
return on investment (ROI) was continuing to increase. With that
record, Rawlins now expected the corporation to make major long-term
commitments to the motor business.

The Dayton Motor Division and Product Lines

The Motor Division's two major product lines were AC and DC motors.
Dayton based its motor business reputation primarily on high quality

and reliability and its skill in filling customers' motor needs. Each motor line included many possible sublines consisting of several combinations of frame size, performance capabilities, and enclosures.

Both AC and DC motors provided basic converting functions for industrial applications—converting electrical energy to mechanical power (torque). AC motors, the most economical means of obtaining such power conversion, were used throughout industry to operate fans, pumps, conveyors, and other equipment that was run continuously. The drawback of AC motors was that they were fixed-speed devices. DC motors were used when variable speeds were required, for example, in running take-up reels on paper machines, in steel mills, and in other start/stop applications. DC motors could provide an extremely wide range of shaft speed and yet be powered by the rectified AC power delivered by electric utilities.

AC and DC motors were described in terms of horsepower and frame size. The frame sizes were specified by industry standards to ensure that motors from different manufacturers could be used interchangeably on a wide range of equipment. Because the frame sizes were based on physical dimensions (base size and height), similar frame sizes in AC and DC represented equivalent-sized motors.

As a result of their greater complexity, DC motors were usually sold for three to five times the price of their equivalent frame-sized AC counterparts. This price difference accounted for much of the difference in product volume. Industrywide sales of AC motors exceeded sales of DC motors by a factor of 10 or more.

Nathan Sheets, product marketing manager for the motor business, summarized several other characteristics of the AC and DC markets:

> In the AC business, the market tends to be very competitive. Products are almost commodity items, and product redesign has to meet strict National Electronics Manufacturers Association (NEMA) standards. NEMA members agree upon such standards approximately every seven years, which helps industrial users plan and design their own upgrade and replacement systems. For AC motors, these standards specify the horsepower (rating) that can be associated with each frame size. As a practical matter, the industry leader in AC motors (General Electric) pretty much sets the standards that are adopted by NEMA. With our current 10% share of the AC markets we serve, we're probably fourth or fifth (after GE, Emerson Electric, Exxon, and possibly Westinghouse) among the competitors in overall importance.
>
> In spite of the fact that NEMA establishes standards for all AC motors, individual manufacturers can use different materials in constructing their motors and vary the design of the enclosure and basic components. Given Dayton's strategy in the marketplace, we tend to offer specialized enclosures, such as are needed for underwater use or in mines where explosion hazards

exist. We also offer special product features, such as greater breakaway torque or positive braking capability, that are not available on standard AC motors supplied by other manufacturers.

While many of the same production processes and similar equipment are used in manufacturing DC and AC motors, the markets and competitive environments are substantially different. DC motors tend to be less standardized—only physical dimensions are specified by NEMA—than their AC counterparts. Because of the smaller volumes and much greater product variety of DC motors, the margins tend to be higher than for the AC product line. Also, Dayton is number one in share in DC motors, followed by Exxon, GE, and several European firms.

DC motors are generally used in combination with a power source and a control mechanism to provide a drive system for an industrial application. In recent years, these DC drive systems have begun to encounter competition from AC systems that are equipped with variable frequency speed control. However, these AC modifications so far have made such systems substantially more costly than their DC drive counterparts. Though we expect that in the future such AC systems will make considerable inroads into the DC market, our current position as the market share leader in DC should be defensible.

Our DC motors are sold primarily to original equipment manufacturers (OEMs) who incorporate them into their systems. This is common in major process industries such as paper, metals, textiles, and plastics. They are also used heavily in specialized industries that have DC power available, such as mining. Our AC motors are sold to both OEMs and final users. Those sales are handled both directly and through distributors. Typical industries that use Dayton AC motors include shipboard marine, food processing, machine tools, electric utilities, and those mining applications where AC is the only available power source.

Motor Division Operations (1991)

Electric motors rarely used state-of-the-art technology; developments were usually incremental, and often involved adapting materials and processes previously created in other industries. Systematic analyses done by Rawlins, Vogel, and others in the early 1980s had identified a number of long-term trends in motor development. One of the most significant among those related horsepower rating (for a given frame size) to time (see Figure 1), showing clearly that ratings for a given size increased roughly 40%–45% each decade. This and other trends appeared to be continuing, making it somewhat easier to set targets for the primary redesign programs Dayton undertook every seven years. Bringing out redesigns with performance superior to that predicted by the trend line, as Dayton had done with the 1985 RPM medium DC, provided a significant opportunity to gain market share.

FIGURE 1

AC Motor Ratings History and Projections 405 Frame

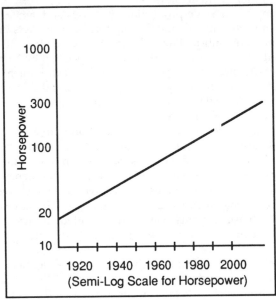

Product Development and Manufacturing

As part of its business strategy, the Motor Division stressed continued technological improvements, which included incremental improvements as well as more radical innovations such as the 1985 RPM motor design. Many product feature enhancements came from new applications of existing motors based on customer feedback. In the seven-year cycle of motor redesign, Engineering initially worked with Marketing to determine the desired improvements; then came the product engineering phase to accomplish them. Manufacturing became involved early in product redesign to be certain that a workable and economic production process was available before product design choices were finalized. Finally, once the product was introduced, Engineering continued to work with customers to improve existing products and to adapt and customize designs to meet specific needs.

Since becoming division manager, Rawlins had pushed his intention to make the division's AC products' manufacturing requirements as compatible as possible with those of their DC counterparts, and vice-versa. He hoped to minimize the diversity of materials required, to

140

increase the volumes produced of common components, and to increase manufacturing equipment utilization. He also hoped that it might become increasingly attractive to consider combining AC and DC motor manufacturing operations for a given size range within a single plant. The production equipment used in making motors could economically produce only a subset of the full range of frame sizes—for example, 5000 to 9000, 180 to 360, or 280 to 440. As the sizes produced moved away from the point where the manufacturing equipment performed best, utilization became less efficient. Product engineers strove to achieve compatibility, although they were not always successful.

Both AC and DC motors were manufactured in two stages. The first stage, component manufacturing, was a mechanical process and involved considerable machining work. This was generally done in batches on components that were then placed in inventory until needed for specific orders. The manufacturing done in the mechanical stage included shaft production, frame and bracket machining, and lamination punching. The second stage was electrical and involved winding, connecting the windings, making the rotor for AC products, and completing the armature for DC products. In the final steps of the electrical stage, the electrical components and remaining mechanical parts were assembled into the final unit and tested.

Because the AC motors were more likely to be standard, off-the-shelf items, the division usually planned AC production on a make-to-inventory (i.e., make-to-forecast) basis. DC motors were generally planned on a make-to-order basis for the electrical stage of production and on a make-to-inventory basis for the mechanical stage. However, given that some AC motors were made to order and some DC were largely standard items, no absolute rule separated AC from DC in terms of production scheduling.

The manufacturing processes uses in each of the division's three motor plants were somewhat similar except for differences in equipment size and in the degree of automation, the material handling, and the control of the process, although there was no absolute criterion as to what process was likely to be found in which plant. Each plant had different capabilities and capacities (see Exhibit 3), and consequently, different costs (see Exhibit 4). However, with regard to cost structure, Rawlins made it clear that "Lexington, Kentucky, is the only plant meeting my objective of 35% contribution. Possibly we should consider it the ideal plant in terms of focus and size."

Exhibit 3

Manufacturing Facilities, 1991

	Dayton, Ohio	Indianapolis, Indiana	Lexington, Kentucky
Products	Special, medium and large AC and DC; Prototypes; Special vertical integration into component parts	Special, custom and standard medium AC and DC	General purpose medium AC
Capacity (units/week)	AC–180 and DC–40	AC–1750 and DC–250	AC–750 and DC–0
Capacity[1] (annual net sales billed)	$22,000,000 (35% DC, 65% AC)	$46,000,000 (25% DC, 75% AC)	$35,000,000 (100% AC)
Number of Hourly Production Employees (at capacity)	175	220	155
Production Process	Modified job shop	Modified assembly line	Modified assembly line
Frame Size	400, 500, 580, 680, 800 AC 5000, 6800, 8000, 9000 DC	180, 210, 250 AC 180, 210, 250, 280, 320, 360 DC	280, 320, 360, 400, 440, 447/449 AC
Horsepower Range	200–3000 AC 100–3000 DC	1–15 AC 1–75 DC	15–150 AC
Specials for Selected Industries	Frame sizes as above plus larger	Frame sizes as above plus larger	None
Other	Oldest plant, built in early 1920s; Has made virtually all products in the line at some time.	Plant built in the late 1920s, located 115 miles from Dayton; Has been producing RPM medium DC line since mid-1980s.	Plant built in 1985–1986, incorporating newer production processes and focusing on a narrower range of product; Located 97 miles from Dayton.

[1] Assumes two shift, five day per week operations.

Eₓₕᵢᵦᵢₜ 4

Comparison of Plant Costs (1990)

	Dayton	Indianapolis	Lexington
Labor Rates			
Hourly	$12.50	$11.60	$ 8.25
Fringe	3.60	3.10	2.10
Total	$16.10	$14.70	$10.35
Major Costs[1]			
Total Factory Cost	100%	100%	100%
Materials	36%	38%	41%
Direct Labor	18%	14%	9%
Factory Overhead	23%	19%	15%
Contribution	23%	29%	35%

[1] Differences in cost structure and contribution were a result of a number of factors: direct labor cost, overhead, support, age of plant, volume and scale, and products manufactured.

The Design of the RPM Medium DC Motor Line (1983–1985)

The division's current version of a medium DC motor, the RPM, had been a special situation for Dayton. Designed as a three-year effort lasting from 1983 to 1985, its first objective was developing a DC motor that would operate satisfactorily on rectified power. With the spread of solid state technology in the early 1980s, solid state rectifiers replaced rotating generators as the source of direct current. It was soon discovered, however, that rectified direct current was not smooth, as generated current had been, which caused a number of performance problems. Competitors were forced to sell external choke systems to mitigate the effects of the rectified power; chokes, however, were costly, cumbersome, difficult to install, and slowed the response time of the drive system.

Dayton's original design team worked for a year without cracking the rectified power problem before Rawlins was asked to work on the project. He organized a companywide task force or tiger team composed of some of the best engineering talents Dayton had. Vogel headed one of the four concept groups on that task force.

The RPM design program was unusually successful. As Vogel recalled, "We killed all the sacred cows in DC motor design and came up with a totally new concept in DC motors." The result was the first major new DC motor design in decades. It operated well on rectified or generated power, exceeded previous DC motors of its size in electrical performance (energy efficiency) by as much as 35%, weighed 35% less, used 35% less space, and had improved insulation and cooling systems that prolonged the motor's operating life.

The RPM also had a completely different shape from its predecessors and was constructed differently. Previous motors were round—the conventional "rolled ring" design—while the RPM was square, allowing more efficient use of the cubicle space. Where the rolled ring motors had solid steel frames, the RPM had the first laminated frame: it was the laminations that suppressed the eddy currents produced by the rectified power. (See Exhibit 5 for RPM product information and Exhibit 6 for product information on the E-line, the comparable medium AC line at Dayton.)

Dayton's major competitors responded with redesigns of their competing medium DC products to deal with the problem of rectified power. They all kept the old rolled ring and solid frame concept. Although those designs came close to staying on the long-term performance trend line, they did not match the Dayton RPM in several key dimensions of performance.

The Medium DC Redesign Effort (1989–1991)

In mid-1989, in concert with the next generation of NEMA standards for medium DC motors, the division appointed a team of development engineers to start work on the follow-on to the RPM medium DC design (see Exhibit 7 for a map of various product generations). That team consisted of engineers from various subgroups within the division's engineering function. They were given the following objectives (with a deadline of January 1991 for being close to achieving them):

(a) design the division's next generation of medium DC motor to achieve the usual improvements in cost and performance consistent with the long-term trend lines for that class of product;
(b) reduce noise levels significantly from those associated with the RPM design and correct other problems identified by customers over the past several years; and
(c) make the medium DC line (sizes 180, 210, 250, and 280) compatible with the medium AC line of the same dimensions. (Because standards for the F-line of AC motors were not expected to be promulgated until the mid-1990s, the team chose to concentrate on standardizing its design on the already familiar product line, the medium AC E-line.)

EXHIBIT 5

Product Literature (late 1980s) for Dayton's Original RPM Medium DC Motor

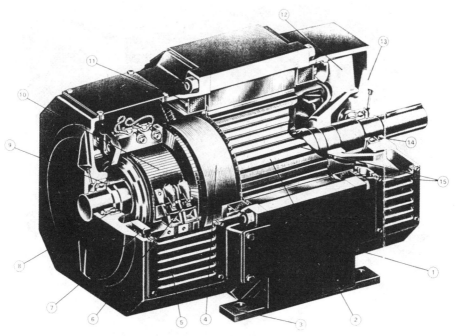

1. **Laminated frame** minimizes eddy currents for improving commutation of rectified power and gives rigid support and alignment of internal components.
2. **Armature core** has low inertia for a high torque-to-inertia ratio and fast dynamic response.
3. **Bar style feet** maintain maximum rigidity and strength. Bolt holes are readily accessible for easy mounting.
4. **Banding on coil heads** is non-conducting and strong, adding to the reliability of the insulation system.
5. **Access openings** are extra large for easy brush inspection and convenient replacement.
6. **Brush holders** with reaction type design maintain constant tension without adjustments throughout the brush life.
7. **Brush rigging assembly** has precision modeled rocker for precise spacing and rigidity.
8. **Anti-friction (ball) bearings** are deep grooved, and double shielded to seal out contaminants.
9. **Grease seal** keeps lubricant in the bearings and out of the motor for long, trouble-free motor life.
10. **Commutator** incorporates design changes that give high stability and excellent heat dissipation for cool operation.
11. **Armored field coil** has steel bobbin and a new high-thermal capability insulation system for long life.
12. **Fan** is made of lightweight cast aluminum for efficient cooling and low inertia.
13. **Machined end brackets** have a large contact area that forms an effective, leak-free seal against the frame.
14. **Metermatic lubrication** adapts the RPM DC motor to your present maintenance schedule without danger of overgreasing or undergreasing.

Exhibit 6

Product Literature (late 1980s) for Dayton's Medium AC Motor (E-line design)

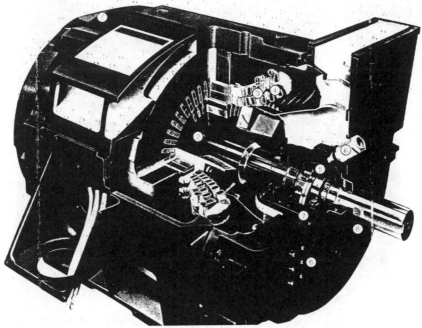

1. Rigid cast-iron frame holds alignment true over years of operation.
2. Lightweight die-cast aluminum rotor improves starting and heat dissipation for longer life.
3. Matched stator and rotor reduce current densities for greater electrical efficiency.
4. Two performance-proved insulation systems assure electrical integrity for both corrosive and non-corrosive atmospheres.
5. Anti-friction or split-sleeve bearings allow you to choose the right bearing system for your application.
6. Sight gauge and bull's-eye on sleeve bearings afford fast visual verification of proper lubrication for longer life.
7. Bearing locking device eliminates bearing rotation to assure proper bearing performance.
8. Oversized shaft assures a large safety margin in transmitting torque.

After 18 months of effort, the team was well along in creating a redesigned medium DC line—referred to as the Mark II—that was married wherever possible to the AC E-line. Although the Mark II redesign was cheaper both in material and labor costs than the RPM (see Exhibit 8), as of late January 1991 it had not quite reached its performance goals. However, it seemed reasonable to hope that further optimization over the next few months would enable it to do so before commitments were made to equipment and material suppliers and it was put into produc-

Exhibit 7

Generations of AC and DC Motors (dates approximate market introduction)

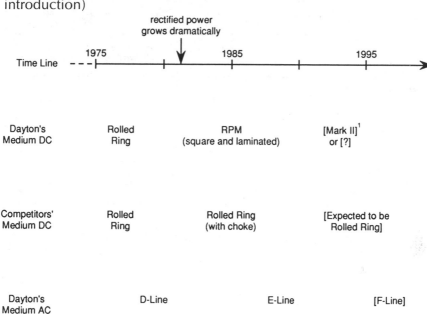

		rectified power grows dramatically	
	1975	1985	1995
Time Line			

Dayton's Medium DC	Rolled Ring	RPM (square and laminated)	[Mark II][1] or [?]

Competitors' Medium DC	Rolled Ring	Rolled Ring (with choke)	[Expected to be Rolled Ring]

Dayton's Medium AC	D-Line	E-Line	[F-Line]

[1] The Mark II design was a hybrid, returning to the standard rolled ring form but with a laminated frame. It was developed to be manufacturing compatible with the AC E-line. Vogel has proposed as an alternative[?], a crash program to develop a second generation RPM design (square and laminated). It would be compatible (in concept) with the AC F-line, scheduled for redesign and introduction in the mid- to late 1990s.

tion. The primary obstacle to reaching the performance objectives was the severe space limitation of the new design which made it necessary to cram in the coils in such a way that cooling system features were limited, causing difficulty in getting the desired rating from the coils.

The design team had abandoned the unique RPM square frame concept to make the Mark II DC motor compatible with the AC E-line in frame, selected structural parts, and certain manufacturing processes. In its place was introduced a "hybrid," a combination of rolled ring shape and laminated steel frame construction (see Exhibit 9 for a diagram comparing basic DC motor design concepts).

Motor Division Capacity Plans

Meanwhile, as part of its long-range planning during fall 1990, the Motor Division had looked at its capacity requirements through 1997 in

EXHIBIT 8

Comparison by Product Design of Direct Manufacturing Costs

	1990 Cost Estimates			1995 Cost Estimates
	Dayton's AC E-Line[1]	Dayton's DC Original RPM[2]	Competitors' DC Rolled Ring[3]	Dayton's DC Mark II Design[4]
Materials ($/unit)	$104	$344	$325	$296
Direct Labor (hours/unit)	2.0	13.3	15.0	8.6
Direct Labor ($/unit)	$29	$196	$180	$105

[1] Dayton's AC E-line introduced in the late 1980s.

[2] Dayton's DC original RPM introduced in the mid–1980s.

[3] Based on competitor analysis and reverse engineering of selected medium DC products.

[4] Dayton's DC proposed Mark II design scheduled for introduction in the early 1990s. Dayton engineers expected to improve these projected Mark II costs by at least 10% prior to introduction.

---

order to relate those to its existing facilities. As shown in Exhibit 10, it was clear to all that additional capacity would be needed soon, even if the three existing plants could be utilized 100%. The redesigned medium DC line, scheduled for market introduction in early 1993, was viewed as a logical catalyst for planning the first step in such an expansion. Based on considerable work, two options had gained widespread support—expansion at Indianapolis or development of a new facility in Florence. All work had been done assuming that the product would be the "Mark II" redesigned medium DC line.

In line with Dayton's corporate requirements, Rawlins had his staff compare these two options in terms of their cash flows (see Exhibit 11). While the Florence option required $3 million more in capital because it was a new site, it also would generate over $2 million more in annual operating contribution once established because of its newer equipment, improved processes and flows, and lower labor costs. In comparing the qualitative difference between these two options, a number of key points had been highlighted. Rawlins felt that both short- and long-term considerations were important:

148

EXHIBIT 9
Comparative Medium DC Motor Configurations

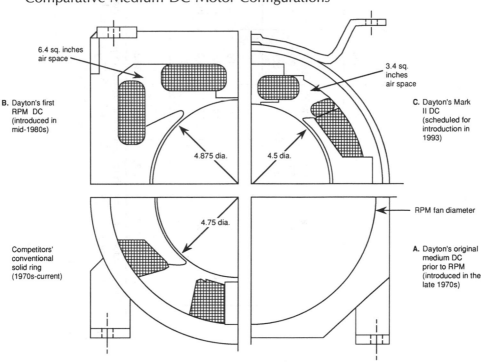

6.4 sq. inches
air space

B. Dayton's first
RPM DC
(introduced in
mid-1980s)

3.4 sq.
inches
air space

C. Dayton's Mark
II DC
(scheduled for
introduction in
1993)

4.875 dia.

4.5 dia.

4.75 dia.

Competitors'
conventional
solid ring
(1970s-current)

RPM fan diameter

A. Dayton's original
medium DC
prior to RPM
(introduced in the
late 1970s)

In the short term, we could manufacture the redesigned line in Indianapolis, because that is where the previous line is manufactured and where most of the relevant production experience resides. However, in the longer term, we might want to place the medium DC line into a new plant, as was done in the second half of the 1980s with the somewhat higher volume and larger size AC line now produced in Lexington. Florence is not too far from Lexington [about 50 miles] and thus offers some economies in corporate visits to the plants and would ease certain support problems.

Both the Indianapolis plant manager and the division controller had made numerous arguments supporting an expansion in Indianapolis. Chief among those were the opportunity to improve significantly that plant's cost structure, to utilize more fully existing equipment and capital investment, and to avoid having a major investment dependent on a limited, cyclical part of the division's product offerings. In sharp contrast, Vogel and some of his engineers were strong supporters of the

EXHIBIT 10

Existing Manufacturing Capacity and Projected Demand[1]
(in millions of constant dollars sales)

	Frame Sizes	1991 Existing Capacity	1991	1992	1993	1994	1995	1996	1997[2]
Dayton Product Lines		$22 million							
Special Medium AC	(400		$ 3.5	$ 4.1	$ 4.8	$ 5.8	$ 6.7	$ 7.7	$ 8.6
Large AC	(500–800)		8.3	8.5	8.8	9.1	9.5	9.9	10.4
Large DC	(5,000–9,000+)		4.1	4.3	4.6	4.9	5.3	5.7	6.0
Indianapolis Product Lines		$46 million							
Existing Medium DC	(180–360)		9.2	8.5	6.8	4.1	4.0	4.0	4.0
Existing Medium AC	(180–250)		32.0	34.8	37.0	40.0	42.5	42.0	41.8
Redesigned Medium DC[3]	(180–280)		—	1.5	10.4	14.1	17.9	18.8	19.8
Redesigned Medium AC	(180–280)		—	—	—	—	3.2	6.3	7.1
Lexington Product Lines		$35 million							
Medium AC	(280–449)		24.3	25.7	27.2	28.8	30.5	32.3	34.1

[1] Forecasts for 1991–1997 assumed some increases in market share for the division as well as growth in total demand. The improved market share assumptions were felt to be consistent with the projected competitive environment and the division's market performance over the past few years.

[2] The division's long-term forecasts were for about 8% real growth (constant 1991 $).

[3] This was the line for which Rawlins faced design and production location decisions in early 1991.

EXHIBIT 11

Florence versus Indianapolis Expansion:[1] Incremental After Tax Cash Flow Analysis (in 1991 $000s)

	1993	1994	1995	1996	1997	1998[2]
A. Cash Flow *with* Florence						
1. Florence Plant:						
Funds from Operations	$ 450	$ 2,200	$ 3,600	$3,800	$4,100	$4,500
Capital Expenditures	(9,000)[3]	(2,700)	(50)	—	(90)	(90)
Working Capital Changes	(900)	(750)	(1,200)	(30)	(450)	(450)
Net Florence Cash Flow	(9,450)[3]	(1,250)	2,350	3,770	3,560	3,960
2. Indianapolis Plant:						
Funds from Operations	4,300	4,450	4,600	4,750	4,750	4,700
Capital Expenditures	(1,200)	—	—	—	—	—
Working Capital Changes	(1,550)	(310)	(400)	(400)	(400)	(400)
Net Indianapolis Cash Flow	1,550	4,140	4,200	4,350	4,350	4,300
3. Total Cash Flow (*with* Florence)	$ (7,900)[3]	$ 2,890	$ 6,550	$8,120	$7,910	$8,260
B. Cash Flow *Without* Florence						
1. Indianapolis Plant:						
Funds from Operations	$ 4,400	$ 5,400	$ 6,100	$6,200	$6,300	$6,400
Capital Expenditures	(7,400)	(900)	—	—	(90)	(90)
Working Capital Changes	(1,900)	(700)	(1,400)	(700)	(700)	(700)
2. Total Cash Flow (*without* Florence)	$(4,900)	$ 3,800	$ 4,700	$5,500	$5,510	$5,610
C. Difference in Cash Flow						
(With Florence minus without Florence)	$(3,000)[3]	$ (910)	$ 1,850	$2,620	$2,400	$2,650

[1] Added capacity under either option would be about 1,800 units/week (220-DC plus 1,580-AC), representing capacity for annual net sales billed of about $30 million.

[2] Beyond 1988, cash flows were assumed to continue at the 1998 level.

[3] The initial capital expenditure on Florence would increase by approximately $2 million—resulting in these 1993 outflows increasing by $2 million—if the three month redesign being proposed by Vogel was successful and adopted as the medium DC design.

Florence option, in part because of what they considered its longer-term possibilities. Vogel elaborated:

A new plant that initially could build only medium DC motors, but eventually could add AC motors of similar frame sizes (180, 210, 250, and 280) might be very attractive. Such a plant would provide economies for both AC and

DC product lines that have many production steps and processes in common. Also, it would encourage cost reduction on the DC line since AC is more cost-oriented, given its competitive environment. Additional production advantages would include the possibility of longer runs and lower inventories due to commonality of materials and some parts.

The possibility that Florence, if built, might eventually be given similarly-sized medium AC motors as well, was particularly unsettling to Sheets and some of the marketing people. They noted:

> The less competitive attitude of those traditionally involved with the DC motors might adversely affect AC production in that plant. The AC line might well become less competitive, rather than the DC line becoming more competitive. Additionally, the marketplace for AC and DC motors will not necessarily follow the same track in the future as they have in the past. This could mean that eventually the product lines would need to be split apart, resulting in a costly relocation for one or the other product line. This issue probably tips the balance in favor of Indianapolis.

A third opinion, raised in early discussions and supported by the Lexington plant manager, was to put the redesigned medium DC motors into Lexington for the first few years (e.g., until 1994) and then move them to a new facility. The Lexington plant manager had argued that major facility investment for medium DC would thus be postponed for a few years (increasing the division's ROI), Lexington's capacity would be better utilized in the near term, and a new facility for medium AC and DC, when built, would have greater initial volume (and thus better ROI). Furthermore, it might be easier at that point to tailor the facility to medium AC and DC motors since the next generation of medium AC would be well along in its redesign. Vogel had not been enthused by this option, in part because it would broaden the range of frame sizes in Lexington and in part because it might result in Lexington becoming larger than the $30–$35 million sales revenue he considered optimal.

Vogel's Design Concerns

As Rawlins' staff was finalizing its analyses on the capacity issue, Vogel was harboring growing concern over the medium DC redesign (the Mark II). He had voiced this to Rawlins in late January:

> Ordinarily, I would have spoken up long before this, but for a while I thought it was my close involvement with the original RPM design that made the new Mark II design strike me as unacceptable. I expected to have trouble read-

justing to any redesign, and I wanted to give it time. But I've lived with the new proposal for several weeks now and I still don't believe it's the right way to go. It would take me a lot more study to prove it, but I have a strong hunch that the Mark II is just too much of a compromise. It may be acceptable, but I still believe that square laminated frame you and I developed is superior.

As Rawlins probed Vogel's position, Vogel summarized his perspective around two points:

First, the proposed redesign (the Mark II) has not produced the performance we should be able to expect from a major redesign. It's true the design team is likely to achieve better ratings before production starts, but with those coils all jammed in that way, it's clear it will take brute force. There is no space to have a better ventilation system, and where's the room for future improvement? Contrast that with the ample space in our square design. *Second*, standardizing on the E-line of AC when we know that the F-line ratings will be along in no more than four or five years bothers me. When that rerate comes, if we put medium AC in the same plant as medium DC, it will mean changing the tooling for both AC and DC rather than just one of them.

Rawlins discussed these points with Vogel at considerable length, eventually shifting the discussion to what Vogel would propose at this late date. Vogel commented:

Postpone the final design decision for three months and set up a crash redesign tiger team. Assemble a top-flight, dedicated group of the most creative people in the company and tell them to start with a clean slate to design the ideal next generation medium DC motor. Give them the goal of doubling the horsepower per frame size. Tell them to study the AC motor concepts too and see if they can agree on the most likely concepts to govern the F-line when it comes. If they are able to determine with a fair degree of certainty where they think AC should go, then they can work to standardize the DC design on the future F-line concepts rather than on existing E-line concepts. While they won't be able to complete the design in three months, they should be able to get an initial prototype that we can compare with the Mark II option.

Rawlins' Decision

While there was no guarantee that a three-month tiger team would come up with a significantly better design, Vogel's goals—if achieved—would have a major impact on Dayton's market position in medium DC (and possibly medium AC) over the next several years. Of course, it might also require additional unplanned development resources at an incremental cost of about $1 million. Furthermore, additional production investment (if a new site were constructed) of about $2 million would be required to procure custom equipment to handle the square shape. (Such equipment, with excess capacity, was largely in place at Indianapolis; thus, an RPM type redesign would not significantly increase the investment required for that option.)

Rawlins was uncertain about backing Vogel's proposal. Whether or not he did so, he did need to give Dayton's board his recommendations on capital spending, and that meant deciding where the next generation of medium DC product should be produced. Finally he was sure the board would want a preview of the division's longer-term capacity and investment plans as well. He mused:

This medium DC motor question is really a major motivation for reexamining our facilities. We need to be sure that they will be most appropriate not only for existing products and their volumes, but for longer-term requirements as well.

Maps and Mapping: Functional Strategies in Pre-Project Planning

Overview

One of the most important elements in laying the foundation for effective development projects is achieving alignment and integration of functional strategies. In this chapter we develop a framework and set of techniques for identifying and integrating the strategies in the functions and linking them to the overall direction of the business. We call the framework maps, and the procedure for applying it, mapping. The analogy between laying plans for a journey and charting a course for a business's product development program is deliberate. Developing a set of maps that define the competitive terrain in each of the functions of the business can be a powerful process within the organization. Done well, maps and mapping identify critical issues, build a common framework and language for communication and decision, and help to create a shared understanding among senior and functional managers about the directions of the business.

The definition of a map at the heart of this chapter is specific: a map is a graphic display of the driving forces of competition in a particular function over time relative to competitors. In reading the chapter, it is important to see how individual elements in this definition are developed in each specific map we present and the role that each dimension plays in creating a complete, useful perspective on the competitive challenges and opportunities the firm faces. In order to illustrate the technique of developing maps and to see how maps might be used to capture knowledge in a compelling way, we work through a relatively complete set of maps on a single business in the 1980s: Coolidge Vacuum Cleaner Company. (Coolidge is a disguised name, but the maps are based on real data.) The Coolidge case provides examples of specific maps in marketing, manufacturing, and engineering. In addition, we develop what are called integrated maps that bring together issues in more than one function. A key theme in this section of the chapter is the way in which the visual, graphic display of critical data highlights key issues confronting Coolidge.

In the last section of the chapter, we shift our focus from a discussion of maps to a discussion of the mapping process. The basic idea here is that what matters in laying the foundation for product development is the creation of a shared understanding and a common direction among the functions and the senior management of the company. While individual maps play an important part in creating that understanding, it is the process of developing the maps that is crucial. In our discussion of that process, a central theme is mapping as a line (as opposed to staff) responsibility. The process is led by the general manager of the business, and by the heads of the major functions within it. The definition of driving forces, the search for data to depict them over time, the development of the maps themselves, and the review and discussion of the maps and their implications are all done by managers responsible for the business. Framed in these terms, the maps and the mapping process become the starting point for developing and implementing operational plans, communicating a sense of direction within the organization, and providing a context within which plans for specific development projects may be undertaken.

The chapter closes with an application of maps and the mapping process to the history of Apple Computer in the 1980s. The discussion of Apple's experience illustrates the power of maps and the mapping process in identifying crucial gaps or mismatches between various functions in the business. By looking at a set of maps in marketing, manufacturing, and engineering we illustrate the strategic direction mapping may provide if done at the right time, with the right people involved. Although maps and mapping are not a panacea, the experience at Apple suggests they can be an important and even critical element of laying the foundation for effective product development.

CHAPTER *3*

*E*ffective managers lay the foundation for a successful development project long before the project begins. When the project starts, the project leader and members of the project team need a clear sense of strategic direction in the business and in its critical functions. A typical business plan—focused on financial and marketing information, prepared by a staff group—is not enough. Nor is it sufficient to take a business plan and add sections on functional plans. What is needed is an understanding of where the business is going, what the functions are going to do to get it there, and how this project fits into that picture. Thus, behind the foundation of a successful development project must be a process that identifies and integrates the strategies and the functions, and links them to the overall direction of the business. To see the importance of a process and a plan that links functional strategies to the details of specific projects, consider the case of a company we will call WHZ Medical Electronics.[1]

The Missing Cable

Peter Culver, project manager for a new portable monitoring unit, couldn't believe what he was reading. With only six months to go before market introduction of a new instrument, the head of electrical design for the project, Werina Milbury, had just discovered that a cable she designed into the product would not be available for commerical production. The cable was produced in one of the company's component plants in upstate New York. The plant manufactured a wide range of electrical components for several of the company's divisions. Werina learned that the plant was scheduled to be shut down and that products in the plant had been farmed out principally to suppliers; the cable she had designed into the new instrument, however, was part of a long list of components scheduled to be discontinued. Werina estimated that redesign to use available cables would require a few additional weeks of design and testing. The net effect was a two-month slip in the introduction schedule.

With the project already running behind schedule, an additional two months of delays was a major problem. To shorten that lead time, Pete put together a crash program that brought the product with its new cable to market with a delay of only one month. The crash effort was such a traumatic experience that Pete and his team spent several days trying to get at the root causes of the missing cable. What they found was sobering.

The decision to close the components plant in upstate New York and transfer many of the products to outside suppliers was made about a year before design of the new instrument started. That decision was part of a long-term strategy in the components group to sharply reduce their in-house manufacturing capacity. Thus, information on the components group's strategy and its implications for electrical components was well-known long before the new portable instrument project was launched.

Pete and his team were also perplexed to find that representatives from the manufacturing division (of which the components group was a part) had participated in the concept development stage of the instrument project as well as subsequent design reviews. Furthermore, the project team had purchased small quantities of the cable from the electrical components plant and had clearly indicated on invoices that the orders were for prototype units of a new instrument. The fact that the cable would no longer be available only came to light when the project team began to arrange for volume purchases of the cable for commerical production.

Pete's conclusion was that information about the cable was readily available in the organization long before design of the new instrument was initiated. In spite of a detailed business planning process, manufacturing feasibility studies, and design reviews to which all functions were invited—and, indeed, in which all functions had participated—that information had never been brought to bear in designing the product.

The experience of WHZ Medical Electronics is not uncommon. Our research and case writing over the last several years have brought us in contact with numerous firms that experienced similar problems. We have seen product designers develop a conservative, classically styled product for a marketing division whose advertising campaign focused on a sporty, youthful image. We have seen a manufacturing organization launch an aggressive low-cost, highly automated production process at the same time that a product development team was creating a complex new family of products requiring significant customization. And we have seen a product development team launch the design of a more sophisticated, highly featured version of an established general-purpose product while customers were demanding less complex and more tailored, customized versions. As in the case of WHZ Medical Electronics, these problems in development reflect a mismatch between the strategies of different functions. But they also reflect a failure to acquire and use readily available information. In effect, WHZ (like many other firms) failed to bring together the right people with the right information in the right forum *before* the project was launched. As a result, the team set off with a poor sense of direction and an incomplete picture of the context and setting into which their results were to be integrated.

The analogy between launching a project and setting out on a journey seems appropriate. Indeed, laying the foundation for effective product and process development is much like making preparations for an expedition into unknown territory. A central part of that preparation is developing plans for the journey, which includes acquiring all of the information available about the terrain ahead as well as likely contingencies that one may encounter. Experience has taught the thoughtful traveler than an essential part of preparation for an extended journey is the acquisition of good maps of the areas in which the journey will occur. In a similar way, we have found the mapping of the competitive terrain in each of a business's functions to be a powerful link between business and functional strategies and the details of specific development projects. Functional maps provide both the process and substance for functional integration, establish a context for a stream of development projects over time, and offer guidance and direction for an individual development project.

Maps and mapping are the focus of this chapter. We first lay out what we mean by a map and provide several examples taken from the wide variety of maps we have found useful in development. We then examine the process of mapping and develop guidelines for effective implementation. The chapter concludes with an application of maps to the story of Apple Computer's development of the Macintosh personal computer.

The Concept of Functional Maps

In every business, and every function in the business, there are driving forces that define the critical dimensions of competition.[2] In the marketing of household appliances, for example, an important driving force may be the changing nature of distribution channels as discount retailers and emerging superstores become the outlet of choice for more and more customers. In the same business, the introduction of electronic controls, plastic materials, and small but powerful electric motors may create product opportunities that open up new segments in the marketplace. At the same time, expansion of variety may be accompanied by a drive for lower cost in a highly competitive market. These forces place significant pressure on the appliance manufacturing process, where traditional approaches to cost reduction (e.g., standardization and automation) may be in conflict with the need for flexibility and expansion of variety.

Mapping has a clear objective: capture the driving forces for the business and the functions, and portray their implications for competition graphically. Defined in these terms, a functional map has the following distinguishing characteristics: it is a visual, graphic display of the driving forces in the market, and the firm's position along critical dimensions of competition over time and relative to its competitors. Each of these elements is critical. The very purpose of a map is to give managers a way to see the evolution of critical dimensions in the market, the technology and the manufacturing processes. Although good maps are based on data and analysis, we have found that pulling together that analysis in a visual format greatly enhances communication and the development of insight.

The requirement that a map show driving forces and critical dimensions of competition *over time* is central to achieving its fundamental purpose: helping managers to see where they are, where they have been, and where they may be going. Laying out developments in marketing, engineering, or manufacturing over time helps to uncover underlying trends and provides a useful context in which to evaluate alternative courses of action. In effect, putting driving forces and critical dimensions of competition in their historical context is an important element of providing strategic direction for product and process development.

With a visual, graphic display of critical dimensions of competition over time, functions in a business have a set of maps that facilitate communication, focus attention on salient issues, and provide historical context. What is missing, however, is a benchmark—a standard of comparison that creates perspective. Thus, the last requirement for an effective map is comparison with competitors. Finding out "where we are" and "where we are going" cannot be done only with internal data. The relevant standards are not past budgets or plans, but what the toughest competitors have accomplished. Furthermore, seeing what competitors have done may yield important insights into differences in competitive performance. We may discover, for example, that while our company has followed a broad line strategy, our strongest competitors have focused their marketing and development resources in a few key product areas where they dominate the business.

Such insight is invaluable in crafting a business strategy and provides an important context for decisions in new product and process development. Maps help to ensure that all functions share a collective vision of where they are going and of how individual projects contribute to their common purpose. Moreover, mapping facilitates effective mobilization of all the organization's resources, capabilities, and skills. Maps provide a tool for guiding the development of functional excellence, and they facilitate the strategic integration of that excellence around a common purpose. Additionally, maps help an organization to target its investments. By displaying underlying forces at work in the marketplace, maps help to clarify choices firms face regarding which markets to serve with which products, which manufacturing facilities to employ, what process technologies to use, and what directions to take in the development of product designs.

The specific maps that a business team chooses to develop will vary depending on the circumstances of the business, but we have found a small number of maps to be particularly useful across a wide range of businesses. These maps are listed in Exhibit 3–1, along with an indication of the specific measures used in the maps and likely sources of information. Their relation to each other, to key strategies, and to operating plans are depicted in Exhibit 3–2. To illustrate what maps such as these look like and to suggest a way in which maps may be used to identify important strategic issues in a business's various functions, we present here a set of maps developed for a company—we will call it the Coolidge Corporation—engaged in the design, development, production, and marketing of vacuum cleaners.[3] We present a small number of maps developed for the three principal functions of the business: marketing, engineering, and manufacturing. In each case, we have tried to

Exhibit 3—1
Examples of Functional Maps

Functional Area/Map Type	Concepts and Specific Measures Used	Sources of Data
Marketing		
Product profile	Product attributes; position relative to competitors	Customer interviews; market research; product testing
Channels of distribution	Sales by channel; market share by channel	Sales organization; trade publications; surveys
Product generation	Timing of new products; life cycle of models; relationship of products to one another	Sales documents
Engineering		
Critical skills	Skill composition of engineering work force	Internal personal research; interviews or comments of engineering managers
Performance tradeoffs	Range of performance combinations possible among dimensions that may conflict (e.g., weight and efficiency)	Test data; product performance specifications
Component technology	Performance of critical components using different technologies	Test data; product ratings
Manufacturing		
Process technology	Degree of automation; fraction of output in different types of processes	Production research; project data
Vertical integration	Role of suppliers; internal operations by component	Purchasing research; internal operating plans
Cost structure	Cost by volume levels; cost by factor of production	Cost accounting research

capture dimensions of competition that are central to the effectiveness of the function and to the business's competitive position. In addition to these functional maps, we also present a set of integrative maps that depict driving forces that cut across functional areas.

Marketing Maps

The mix of product attributes offered to potential customers is critical for the marketing organization. Exhibit 3–3 lays out a map of the customer and product profile for Coolidge's vacuum cleaners between 1980 and 1990. For each of the critical attributes of the product, we have identified a spectrum of performance and positioned Coolidge's offering in the middle price segment in 1980 and 1990. This provides us some perspective on the improvement in Coolidge's product performance over that period of time. In addition, we have indicated the performance position

Exhibit 3–2

Relating Functional Strategies and Maps to Other Strategies and Plans*

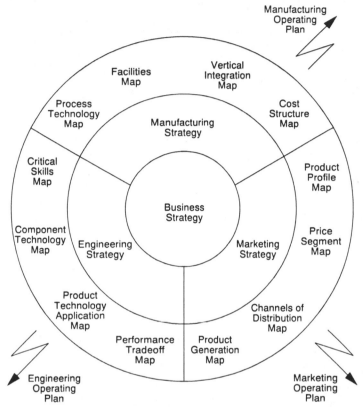

* The individual functional maps—twelve of which are shown in the outer circle—link the departmental plans to the functional and business strategies. Thus they provide an essential bridge between day-to-day activities and long-term directions.

of Coolidge's toughest competitor in 1990—the Fillmore Corporation. The diagram makes clear that Coolidge's product moved from being relatively heavy, loud, large, and somewhat difficult to operate to being relatively compact, lightweight, and easy to use. The Coolidge product offers advantages in cleaning performance and dust bag hygiene relative to its competitor, but is moderately behind in most other product attributes.

In addition to product position along the performance spectrum, we have indicated the relative importance that customers place on attributes. In the right-hand column of the diagram we have indicated a

Exhibit 3-3

Customer / Product Profile (Middle Price Segment)*

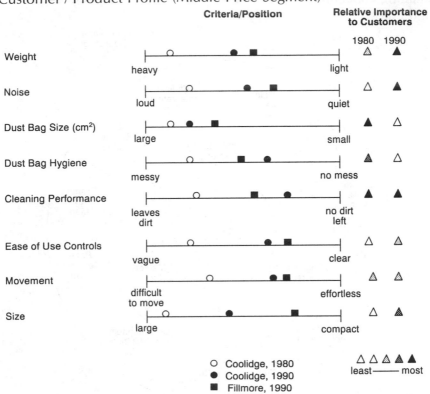

O Coolidge, 1980
● Coolidge, 1990
■ Fillmore, 1990

△ △ ⍍ ▲ ▲
least ——— most

* The right-hand columns illustrate the relative importance of each performance criterion to customers in 1980 and 1990, respectively. The horizontal continuums indicate the progress made by Coolidge between 1980 and 1990, and the position of their primary competitor, Fillmore, in 1990.

clear shift in focus of customer choice from 1980 to 1990. While customers have tended to focus on cleaning performance and dust bag size in 1980, by 1990, the principal issues were weight, noise, and cleaning performance. Overall, the map suggests that Coolidge may have some problems in the middle price segment. Except for cleaning performance, where it has a clear edge, it is at a disadvantage to its primary competitor in weight, noise, size, and ease of use, all areas of increasing customer focus.

Exhibit 3–4 maps changes in distribution channels in the vacuum cleaner business from 1975 to 1990. Vacuum cleaners are sold through multiple channels, and changes in the relative importance and mix of

Exhibit 3–4
Channels of Distribution.*

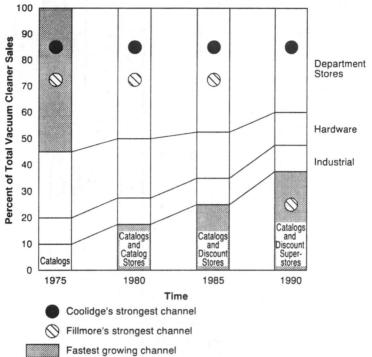

* Between 1975 and 1990, two trends in the channels of distribution occurred: the importance of department and hardware stores declined (from 80 percent to about 55 percent), and the importance of catalog and discount stores increased (from ten percent to about thirty-five percent). In the second half of the 1980s, Fillmore responded effectively to these trends; Coolidge did not.

channels may have an important influence on Coolidge's market share. The diagram shows a dramatic change in the channel mix over this period. Catalogues and especially discount superstores have become a critical factor in the business, while the share of sales going through department stores—a traditional area of strength for Coolidge—declined sharply. Looking back over the decade of the 1980s, it is clear that Fillmore moved aggressively into discount operations, while Coolidge continued to focus on its traditional channel. By 1990, Fillmore had developed its strongest position in the fastest growing channel in the market.

The final marketing map that we present for Coolidge is the product generation map. The product generation map in Exhibit 3–5 lays out the

EXHIBIT 3–5
Product Generation Maps*

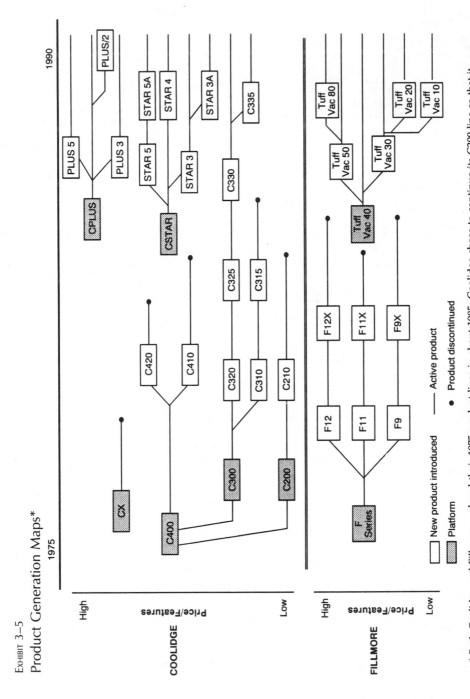

* Both Coolidge and Fillmore replaced their 1975 product lines in about 1985. Coolidge chose to continue its C300 line so that it would have three families of product in the market. In contrast, Fillmore chose in 1985 to offer a single family of products off the Tuff Vac 40 platform.

evolution of the Coolidge product line from 1975 until 1990. The diagram documents not only the major generations of product, but also how product line extensions and enhanced and lower-priced versions emerged from a core product offering. Products are arrayed in the map so that their position in the price/features spectrum is apparent; thus, high-end, high-price, high-feature products are near the top of the diagram while low-end, low-price, low-feature versions are near the bottom. The maps suggest that Coolidge systematically shifted its product line from relatively low-price cleaners to medium-price products and is moving increasingly toward more high-end offerings. In addition, the number of product families and total products offered in the market have both expanded rapidly.

The companion product generation map for Fillmore indicates a somewhat different product development strategy. Fillmore competes in the same market segments as Coolidge, but does so with a much narrower product line. Although it too expanded that line over time, its development has been much more focused. Moreover, it is evident that Fillmore leveraged a single product platform to reach diverse market segments. In contrast, Coolidge tended to launch independent development programs for specific market segments.

Engineering Maps

An important driver for the engineering function is the shifting mix of critical skills required in the design, development, and engineering of products and processes. Exhibit 3–6 depicts that shifting mix for Coolidge. This kind of map is particularly useful when product technologies, for example, are undergoing significant change. From a situation in the mid 1970s in which the engineering organization was composed of individuals with backgrounds in mechanical engineering, electromechanical design, and plastics, Coolidge has seen an increasing role for engineers trained in electronics, ergonomics, acoustics, and software. This shifting mix of skills reflects the growing sophistication of product design and the growing importance of new dimensions of the product, including noise and ease of use (electronic controls and ergonomics).

Exhibit 3–7 depicts a second important driving force in the engineering function: the shift from metal to plastic materials in the product's design, and the increasing significance of expanding the capacity for cleaning relative to the unit's weight. The diagram illustrates that Coolidge was able to expand the volume of its vacuum cleaner between 1975 and 1980 while reducing weight through substitution of plastic for metal. Between 1980 and 1990 weight declined further with only a small reduction in volume through design changes and continued use of plas-

Exhibit 3–6

Critical Skills in Engineering*

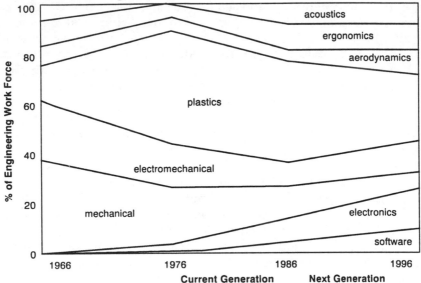

* Over time, the mix of engineering skills at Coolidge changed significantly. The proportion of mechanical engineers declined from its peak in the 1960s as plastics specialists increased and, later, electronics engineers were added. Most recently, software engineers were added, replacing some of the plastics specialists.

tic. The data suggest, however, that while Coolidge made significant progress in its volume-to-weight ratio, its competitors moved more aggressively both on design and on the use of plastic parts and by 1990 achieved an advantage over Coolidge. Fillmore, for example, offered a product with slightly less volume but considerably less weight than Coolidge. A second competitor, Harding, specialized in much smaller units.

Design changes also had an important influence on the design of motors over this period. Exhibit 3–8 documents the trajectory of motor development, again in the middle price segment for Coolidge and Fillmore. Both companies increased their cleaning performance during this time period, but adopted very different approaches to achieve it. While Coolidge (as we saw earlier) achieved significant improvement in cleaning through a larger, more powerful motor, Fillmore opted for somewhat less but equivalent cleaning performance with a substantially smaller, but much more efficient, motor. Thus, while Coolidge motors in 1990 were the same design as the 1980 model (only larger), Fillmore had

Exhibit 3–7
Engineering Design—Capacity and Weight*
(Middle Price Segment)

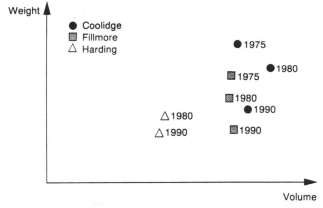

* Over time, both Coolidge and Fillmore reduced the weight of their units but did not alter their capacity (volume). Over the past decade, a third competitor—Harding —established itself with a lighter weight, smaller capacity product.

adopted a radically new motor design that offered much greater efficiency in a more compact package. The redesign of the Fillmore motor was an important element in reducing the overall size of the vacuum cleaner.

Manufacturing Maps

While the manufacturing function often finds itself involved at the tail end of product development, reacting to product designs and marketing initiatives, there are important strategic developments in manufacturing that can have decisive influence on the success of new products. It is important, therefore, that driving forces in manufacturing be evident and taken into account in the early stages of new product development. Exhibit 3–9, for example, documents trends in manufacturing processes for final assembly at Coolidge. The basic process for final assembly at the Homewood plant (the original Coolidge production facility) was a manual operation conducted with a combination of a line flow of raw materials and a stall build setup in which workers assembled significant portions of the product from parts that had previously been kitted together. In 1980, Coolidge had built a new plant (Plant A) that employed asynchronous conveyer lines in subassembly operations with a predominantly manual operation. Finishing was completed in the traditional

Exhibit 3–8

Motor Size and Cleaning Performance*

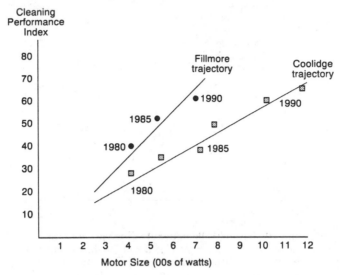

* While both Fillmore and Coolidge have improved the cleaning performance of their products significantly, Fillmore has done so with a much smaller, more efficient motor than Coolidge.

---

stall build mode. Plant B, built in 1987, added increased automation and material handing with some robotics (particularly in subassembly operations, e.g., motor and compressor assembly and the body of the unit). Plant B employed a limited number of traditional stalls for small-volume products but largely employed a manual, asynchronous assembly line process.

In contrast, Fillmore moved aggressively during the 1980s to automate the assembly process. Its main assembly plant in the mid 1970s was much like the Coolidge facility, but Fillmore engineers adopted a flow line concept in the early 1980s. Fillmore built a second line in its main assembly plant in the mid 1980s that employed robotics along with an assembly line concept. By the late 1980s, assembly at Fillmore was significantly automated with the use of robotics and material handing equipment. The main line likewise migrated from a manual to mixed mode in which people and robots shared assembly in what Fillmore called its flexible assembly system. In this system, Fillmore could assemble several of its models on the same line with minimal changeover time. The automated line was dedicated to the production of two high volume models.

Exhibit 3–9

Final Assembly Process Generations*

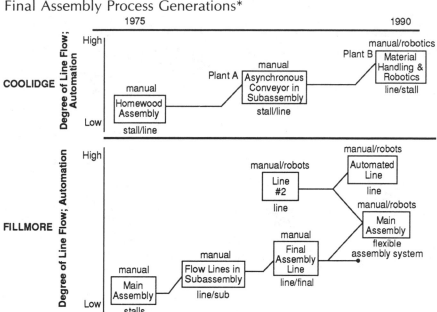

* Fillmore has been more aggressive than Coolidge in upgrading its manufacturing processes. Fillmore started in the late 1970s to redo layouts to provide line flows, then to adopt automation, and most recently, to adopt a flexible assembly system. Although Coolidge has built new facilities, they have stayed with some stall-built operations.

During the 1980s Coolidge made important changes in its level of vertical integration and in the role suppliers played in its production process. Exhibit 3–10 maps out the structure of vertical integration at Coolidge in 1980 and 1990. Whereas in 1980 Coolidge primarily focused on in-house assembly and purchased motors, electronics, plastic parts, and accessories, by 1990 Coolidge had backward integrated into motors and complex plastic parts. The drive for increased vertical integration was dictated largely by increasing pressure on margins and the vice president of manufacturing's decision to try to lower costs by bringing critical activities in-house.

Fillmore adopted a quite different strategy. The map makes clear that Fillmore was in much the same position as Coolidge in 1980, but during the 1980s chose to vertically integrate not only motors but also electronics. Fillmore additionally cultivated a network of suppliers that could provide simple and complex plastic parts and accessories and began to rely on suppliers for subassembly and assembly operations of finished

171

E×нıвıт 3–10

Patterns of Vertical Integration*

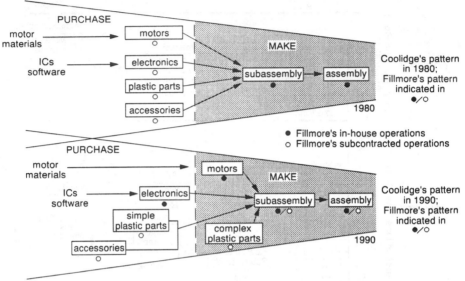

* In 1980, Fillmore and Coolidge had similar levels of vertical integration. By 1990, both firms had brought motor manufacturing in-house. Fillmore also brought electronics in-house but started outsourcing some of its sub- and final assembly requirements. Coolidge, in contrast, chose to either make or buy 100 percent of each production step.

products. Fillmore's strategy was to concentrate on control over motors and electronics while retaining flexibility to move production inside or outside in final assembly.

The final manufacturing map—Exhibit 3–11—lays out the relationship between manufacturing cost per unit and the volume of production per plant. In 1990, Coolidge operated three plants: Homewood, Plant A, and Plant B. The figure shows that Plant B, the high-volume plant, actually had a manufacturing cost per unit slightly above or equivalent to costs at Homewood. The lowest-cost facility was Plant A, the medium-volume plant. The diagram suggests that Coolidge may have suffered diseconomies of scale in Plant B. Fillmore operated a single facility in 1990 which it had broken down into two distinct plants. The main plant operated at a volume level similar to Homewood but had lower costs. Fillmore's automated line—its most efficient facility—was much higher volume but did not suffer the diseconomies of scale apparent in Plant B at Coolidge, and operated with substantially lower costs. There is also evidence in this diagram that Fillmore's costs on its automated line

Exhibit 3–11
Cost and Volume*

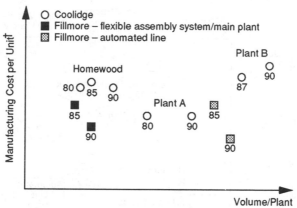

* Fillmore continued to push products toward either a low- or high-volume line and to improve its cost position at both volume levels. Coolidge neither forced products toward preferred volume levels nor pushed to reduce costs for a given volume level.

† Cost has been adjusted for product complexity and inflation.

---

declined substantially since its introduction in 1985. In contrast, costs either rose or stayed roughly the same at Plants A and B and at Homewood.

Integrative Maps

The functional maps suggest important issues confronting Coolidge as it looks to competition in the 1990s. Many of the issues, however, cut across functional areas. In order to illustrate the interaction across areas we have prepared a set of *integrative maps*. An integrative map attempts to identify important dimensions in multiple functions that interact with each other and that together provide important context for strategic decision making. Exhibit 3–12, for example, presents the product/ process matrix—a map of the relationship between the manufacturing processes at Coolidge and the evolving structure of the product line.[4]

The map suggests that Coolidge may confront a mismatch between its evolving product structure and the characteristics of the manufacturing process. The diagram shows that evolution out of its home base in Homewood has created three production facilities. Homewood concentrates on low-volume products, while Plant A uses a somewhat automated, less manual operation to produce the mid-range of the product line. Plant B produces high-volume, lower-cost, more standardized

173

Exhibit 3–12

Product / Process Matrix Assembly Plants*

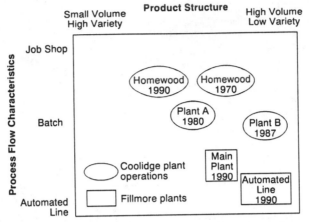

* Coolidge's choice of less automated, more batch type processes, even in their high-volume Plant B, stands in sharp contrast to Fillmore's choice of process flow characteristics.

products but does so with a production process that is still predominantly a manual assembly operation. There is some line flow at Plant B, but it is largely a batch process with heavy manual operations. The contrast with Fillmore, also laid out in the map, is quite sharp. In the standardized high-volume lines, Coolidge competes against a facility that is much more automated that the process in Plant B. Moreover, it is evident that Fillmore has focused its product line at the same time it has focused its manufacturing facilities. The result is a quite powerful advantage in terms of cost and ability to meet the requirements of specific market segments. It appears that Coolidge is at a distinct disadvantage.

The second integrative map examines interaction between manufacturing and engineering. The map in Exhibit 3–13 lays out the relationship between manufacturing cost and product complexity measured in terms of the number of parts and features in the product. A number of important developments emerge from this map. First, there is clearly a positive association between the complexity of the product and its manufacturing cost. Second, Coolidge systematically increased its product complexity and therefore experienced increasing cost in its product line. Fillmore, on the other hand, while also increasing the complexity of its products, did not experience the same degree of cost increase. This is likely a reflection of the manufacturing strategy at Fillmore in which the products are produced in a much more focused manufacturing facility

174

EXHIBIT 3–13

Manufacturing Performance and Product Complexity*
(Mid-range Family)

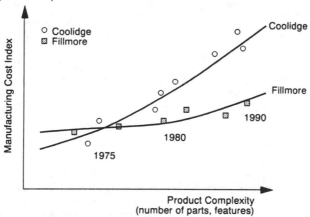

* While both Coolidge and Fillmore have seen the complexity of their products increase dramatically with time, Fillmore has controlled the increase's impact on production costs much more effectively than has Coolidge.

---

where there is greater process control and where additional complexity can be managed more effectively. The implication of this map is that Coolidge must cope with the market-driven increases in complexity much more efficiently if it is to overcome the apparent disadvantage against Fillmore.

The third integrative map—Exhibit 3–14—looks at the connections between marketing and engineering. It lays out the relationship between price and performance over time from 1975 to 1990, and makes clear that the price performance curve improved substantially. Customers could buy products in 1990 with much higher levels of performance than, but at the same price as, products they bought in 1975. In addition, it is clear that marketing and engineering combined to introduce much higher-priced products with a greater level of performance than were available on the market in 1975. In this sense it is clear that the market's range has increased. The map also underscores the advantage that Fillmore achieved over this period of time. Though in 1975 Coolidge and Fillmore had an equivalent price performance curve, by 1990 Fillmore had a significant advantage. It could offer products of equivalent performance at much lower prices than Coolidge, or products at the same price as Coolidge but with much higher levels of performance. The sources of Fillmore's advantage are evident in the functional maps out-

175

Exhibit 3–14
Price / Performance Map*

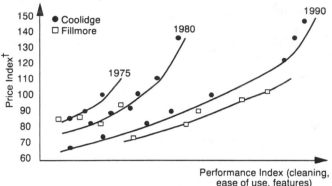

* By 1990, both firms had dramatically increased their top end product performance and the breadth of their performance offerings. However, for all but the lowest performing Coolidge product, Fillmore offered comparable performance at a lower price than Coolidge.

† $100 = average price.

---

lined earlier. Changes in product design, marketing channels, and manufacturing processes gave Fillmore a cost advantage and a performance advantage from the customer's perspective.

The Mapping Process

Maps like those developed for Coolidge underscore the critical driving forces in the business and help to clarify the important strategic decisions and directions confronting an organization. But the true power of maps is not so much in the graphs or the documents themselves, but in the process used to create them. What is important in laying the foundation for effective development projects is the creation of shared understanding among senior executives, among heads of the major functions of the business, and among engineers, marketers, and manufacturing people who make the product happen. While important insight and pieces of knowledge are incorporated into the maps, shared understanding grows out of the process that underlies them. If the maps are not actively used to structure and inform decisions and actions, they have little value. But when developed and used in an effective process, maps may play an important role in creating shared understanding.

An effective mapping process has two parts. In the first, managers define the critical driving forces in the business and the functions, and

EXHIBIT 3–15

An Effective Mapping Process*

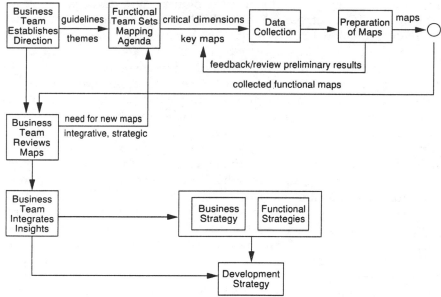

* The process for creating a set of functional maps incorporates two critical concepts. First, the business team plays a central role in establishing the context and direction for mapping and in reviewing and integrating the results. Second, the functions—those who know the specialized areas best—create the maps and work to resolve differences, gain consistency, and build consensus on future choices and detailed plans.

then acquire the data necessary to map those forces over time, against principal competitors. In the second, managers from different functions in the business develop insights from the maps and share those insights with their colleagues on the business team. In that context maps provide a new language. By visually presenting the important dimensions of competition and the business's relative position, maps give managers versed in different disciplines and endowed with different experiences the ability to communicate their ideas more effectively. Where it works well, the mapping process thus creates both a language of communication and channels within which important insights and understanding may be communicated.

Although there are many different variations of the mapping process, the central features of an effective process are laid out in Exhibit 3–15. Mapping is an iterative process carried out by managers in marketing, engineering, and manufacturing working separately, as well as jointly as a business team under the direction of the general manager. After meeting together as a business to plan out the mapping agenda, identify important guidelines (e.g., the number of maps to be developed, timing of map development, etc.), and establish overall business themes, the individual functional teams decide which maps to develop and how to get the work done. Working together as a team and involving knowledgeable individuals within the function, the functional teams identify the driving forces affecting their function and sketch out a set of maps to capture those forces. This involves deciding what dimensions to map, in what combinations, and laying out guidelines for the number of maps and methods of data acquisition. With the mapping agenda laid out, the functional teams proceed to collect data and prepare maps. Once the maps have been developed, the final step within the functional team is to meet, review the maps, discuss their implications, and develop guidelines for functional strategies.

Once the functional teams have developed a set of maps, members from each function meet as a business team to share their respective maps, identify important insights and issues, and develop guidelines for future directions and strategic choices. The business team may then identify further issues that need to be mapped, particularly those that involve cross-functional integration. In addition, the functional teams may meet again to develop strategic maps—maps that look forward and lay out the strategic direction of the business in terms of the critical driving forces captured in functional maps.

Armed with integrative and strategic maps, the business team meets again to integrate the insights, strategic directions, and plans into overall functional strategies and a business strategy. The point is not only to refine and develop the maps themselves, but also to establish guidelines for future development projects. In that sense, functional heads, project managers, and senior executives can use the maps as starting points for developing and implementing operational plans, communicating a sense of direction within their organizations, and providing a context within which plans for specific product and process development projects may be undertaken.

Getting the Most Out of Mapping

If we look at the role maps are expected to play, it is evident that the mapping process must have a certain character. We expect maps to be linked directly to development efforts. In order to be effective they must be translated into operational plans within each function and used to develop criteria for allocating resources to specific projects. One of the things that the mapping process should do is help answer questions about priorities, goals, and research allocation for the set of development projects facing the business over the planning horizon. Maps and mapping, therefore, are not simply an exercise or a tool to be used for staff analysis. Where effective, they are an integral part of the general management of the business. To make that happen, the mapping process needs to develop objectivity and to use both internal and external data sources. Managers need to evaluate performance relative to their principal competitors, not just their own internal objectives. Key people involved in the functions and the business team must be involved and committed to the maps that emerge out of the process. Mapping will not work as a staff activity, or when it is delegated to lower-level subordinates possessing little insight into the problems confronting senior managers. Additionally, if maps go into such detail that senior managers see them as tactical rather than strategic, they will lose their power and fail to play their role. Maps need to be developed in the context of face-to-face meetings involving all the major functions of the business working together as peers on the business team. In this way key issues may be raised and resolved rather than set aside or buried in a blizzard of data and detail. Finally, it is important that maps be communicated throughout the organization in order to serve as a framework and guide for development activities.

While mapping is not a panacea, it is a process that can assist in laying a foundation for effective product development. Much remains to be learned about how to use maps and make mapping effective, but our research and case writing to date suggest a number of pitfalls to avoid:

- Delegating maps and mapping to junior staffers
- Viewing mapping as "filling out forms"
- Using only internal information
- Sticking to conventional wisdom
- Ignoring historical trends
- Using only historical trends
- Getting bogged down in details
- Treating maps as an end unto themselves
- Not sharing information early
- Allowing one function to dominate
- Failing to use maps to guide and direct decision making

Apple Computer: The Need and Opportunity for Maps

Creating coherent functional strategies is essential to the success of new products and processes. Getting straight the driving forces in the business and function, the position of competitors, and the choices confronting the business is essential to picking the right projects, establishing support capabilities, and achieving effective projects. Maps can play a critical role in clarifying choices and facilitating communication. The saga of Apple Computer illustrates the potential power of maps and the mapping process. We first examine developments at Apple in the early 1980s and then review that history through a set of maps.[5]

Creating the Macintosh at Apple

In the early 1980s, Apple was riding the crest of its success with the Apple II personal computer. The product line was manufactured in both Singapore and a recently constructed facility in Dallas, Texas, while many peripheral components, such as disk drives and keyboards, were manufactured by Apple in southern California. Product development, marketing, and corporate headquarters were located near San Francisco.

In 1982, Apple's CEO, Steve Jobs, initiated the development of a new product family, the Lisa-Macintosh personal computers. The Lisa-Macintosh development effort was established as a small, dedicated team reporting directly to Jobs. Its challenge was to make major leaps in both product (hardware and software) and manufacturing process development. An extremely ambitious project, development of the Lisa-Macintosh was assigned to very capable people and had Job's personal backing and day-to-day involvement.

The Lisa, priced at $8,000 to $10,000 per unit, was initially regarded as the core of the product family. It would be the family flagship, demonstrating the power of its new technology and serving as the base from which to launch a derivative, but much higher unit-volume product: the Macintosh. Thus, the Lisa was to be developed first and was expected to provide a significant share of the family's combined profits, although not the bulk of its sales volume. The Macintosh was eventually to have its own production facility, but the low-volume Lisa was to be produced in the Dallas factory (which would also continue to make the Apple II).

In retrospect, this strategy for the Lisa-Macintosh was more wishful thinking than a well-thought-out plan. Although based on highly innovative design concepts, Lisa's sales never reached expectations, and the design of the Macintosh required a number of iterations before it could meet the needs of its evolving market. Such critical issues as customer segments, distribution channels, product support, and follow-on products had not been carefully examined. In addition, little thought was given (even in the later stages of product development) to how new and existing manufacturing facilities would be coordinated.

The absence of strategic planning within the various functional groups created two problems: additional time was spent and resources were wasted on more than one dead end. Introduction of the Macintosh was originally scheduled for March of 1983, but was rescheduled for May, then July, and then late fall (before Christmas, it was hoped). Volume shipment did not actually begin until early 1984. Even with the delay, manufacturing suffered from serious problems.

The original goal was to have a highly automated factory for the Macintosh up and running at the time of its market introduction. Although there was extensive automation of material handling and testing, within eight months of the facility's opening, $7 million worth of automation equipment (one-third of the total spent on the factory) was removed because it had not proven effective.

The delay of the Macintosh's market introduction by several quarters drove Apple's earnings down dramatically and caused the stock market's valuation of the company to fall to less than half its early 1983 value. In the restructuring that followed, Apple closed the Dallas plant, laid off several hundred people (over 20 percent of the entire work force), and took a substantial writeoff. By late 1985, Apple had gone through great agony and emerged a vastly different company. Much of this had its roots in the shortcomings of the Lisa-Macintosh development effort. Although errors were certainly made during the actual execution of the project, the seeds of most of Apple's major difficulties were sown beforehand.

Using Maps: The Apple Case Revisited

Our discussion of Apple's development of the Lisa and Macintosh illustrates the problems that can occur when product and process development projects are launched without clear strategic direction. We have suggested that mapping can provide such direction. But would the existence of such maps have made any difference to Apple? Did information exist from which it could have gained valuable insight through a mapping process? We believe it did. In fact, the Apple case provides a good example of the power of functional mapping. Each of Apple's three main functions—marketing, design engineering, and manufacturing—confronted issues in the development of the Lisa-Macintosh product line that maps could have helped clarify.

Marketing. The Lisa and Macintosh were viewed primarily as engineering projects, and thus marketing issues—though they had a profound influence on both product design and ultimate sales—received secondary attention. Marketing thought of the Lisa as a high-end office product; the Macintosh was slated to serve the lower end of that market, with some application to education and home use—the phrase "appliance for the knowledge worker" summarized its basic concept. Yet information

EXHIBIT 3–16

Personal Computer Market Segments and Product Development Factors, 1982*

Buyer/ Development Factors	Market Segments						Development Emphasis	
	Home	Education (K-12)	University	Home Office	Small Business (and professional)	Corporate Office	Lisa	Macintosh
Performance	◎	◎	●	◎	◎	◎	●	◎
Price	●	●	◉	●	●	◎	○	●
Features	◎	◎	◉	◎	◎	◎	◉	◎
Reliability	◉	◎	◎	◎	◎	◎	○	◎
User friendly	◉	◉	◉	◉	◎	○	●	●
Connectivity	○	○	○	○	○	●	○	○
Field support	○	○	○	○	○	●	○	○
Application software	◎	◎	◉	◉	◉	●	◎	◎

● Highly significant factor   ◎ Of some importance
◉ Important factor   ○ Little role in decision; secondary factor

* In 1982, Apple identified six primary market segments, with the Lisa targeted at the corporate office and the Macintosh targeted at business and education. This chart suggests that the Lisa was a poor match with its primary target, the Macintosh, however, was a reasonably good fit with education but was not well positioned in the business market.

---

available in 1982 indicated that this concept ignored several important issues.

Exhibit 3–16 describes the major personal computer market segments in 1982, along with the emphasis placed on different criteria by each segment. A comparison of the importance placed on different criteria in Apple's development program (the right side of Exhibit 3–16) and the needs of different market segments suggests that the Lisa was a machine without a market. Additionally, though Apple intended the Macintosh for large corporations, it appeared better suited to the needs of small businesses and universities. The map thus highlights a mismatch between development objectives and market requirements that should have been apparent in 1982.

Design Engineering. The Lisa was to be both a high-end machine for offices and a technology platform for subsequent products like the Macintosh. But apparently little thought was given to the way that the Lisa itself would evolve. Nor does it appear that the Lisa-Macintosh devel-

EXHIBIT 3–17
Product Generations at Apple*

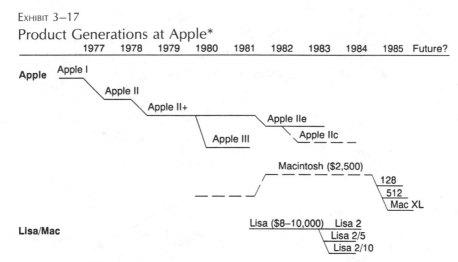

| | 1977 | 1978 | 1979 | 1980 | 1981 | 1982 | 1983 | 1984 | 1985 | Future? |

Apple — Apple I
Apple II
Apple II+
Apple IIe
Apple III
Apple IIc

Macintosh ($2,500)
128
512
Mac XL

Lisa/Mac — Lisa ($8–10,000)   Lisa 2
Lisa 2/5
Lisa 2/10

* For its first several years of existence, Apple had only one product family and simply brought out a sequence of product generations, each replacing its predecessor. While the Lisa and Macintosh were conceived as a related but entirely separate family from the Apple line, over time the Macintosh was expanded to include multiple concurrent offerings. Due to poor market fit, Lisa was dropped after only a few years.

opment team understood the implications of evolving component technology. Exhibit 3–17 is a product generation map that shows the evolution of the Apple and Lisa-Macintosh product families through 1985.

The Lisa was based on the Motorola 68000 microprocessor and employed new concepts in software (windows, icons) and user–machine interaction (the mouse). Higher-performance models were unveiled after initial introduction, but they simply incorporated additional memory. The original design of the Lisa, despite its innovativeness, did not lend itself to future evolution and development. Not only was it very expensive to manufacture, but its use of many unusual parts and design concepts made it difficult to modify. The Macintosh also was based on the 68000 microprocessor, however, and the price of memory was dropping rapidly. As a result, the Macintosh soon was able to provide most of the capabilities of the original Lisa at a fraction of the price. A product generation plan, together with a forecast of the likely evolution of component technology, would have suggested in 1982 that the Lisa was likely to be a dead end product.

Manufacturing. Apple's production experience as of 1981 had been limited largely to labor-intensive assembly in a batch processing environ-

EXHIBIT 3–18

Product / Process Matrix Assembly Plants*

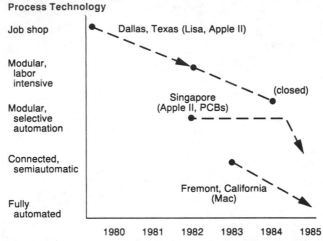

* As Apple's oldest, least automated plant, Dallas found it increasingly difficult to compete against the higher volume Singapore plant and the focused, automated Fremont plant. Eventually, with the discontinuance of the Lisa line and the relentless drive for higher volume products, Apple's senior management chose to close Dallas rather than make the imvestment required to automate it.

ment. Although the Singapore facility had some experience with automation, it was a relatively recent addition to the manufacturing organization. The Lisa required only manual assembly and fit well with Apple's capabilities, but the Macintosh was a different story. It was decided that it should be the vehicle for developing Apple's capabilities in both line-flow (as opposed to batch) processes and automated manufacturing.

Exhibit 3–18 depicts the evolution of Apple's manufacturing, from simple manual to fully integrated, automated processing. The figure highlights the major leap that the new plant—designed to use automated materials handling, automated component insertion, and (eventually) robotic assembly—represented in manufacturing technology and systems. The plan was to make the transition from unskilled workers with solder guns to automated lines in a single step. However, the various parts of the organization apparently did not have a shared understanding of what this implied, the kind of organizational capabilities that would have to be developed, or the alternatives. Thus, even where subparts of a plan existed, they were often incomplete and contradictory.

The concerns raised in this brief discussion of the Lisa-Macintosh development process do not reflect simply good hindsight; this information was widely available at the time and no tricks were involved in processing it. Had a set of functional maps been developed before the project began, these issues would have surfaced at Apple before it made commitments to specific target markets, product designs, and manufacturing equipment. Some decisions might have been altered as a result, but even had they remained the same, Apple would have been in a better position to manage their risks and develop the necessary supporting capabilities.

Fortunately, the lessons of this experience did not go unheeded at Apple. By 1986 it focused significant attention on its pre-project development procedures as well as on its project management capabilities. Each of its manufacturing facilities defined its process improvement path over time. The product development and advanced technology groups established clear targets for forthcoming product generations and the technologies they would enjoy. Moreover, marketing realigned its coverage of distribution channels and customer segments to better capitalize on the anticipated wave of new products. As a result, the introduction of several new products took place, well configured for their target markets and largely on schedule.

Study Questions

1. What explains the episode of the missing cable at WHZ Medical Electronics? Given the efforts of engineering and the involvement of manufacturing in the project, how could the cable problem occur?
2. What is the definition of a map used in this chapter? Consider each element of the definition. What purposes are served by each of the elements? Why, for example, does the definition require that a map depict data over time?
3. Consider Exhibit 3–3. What is your evaluation of Coolidge's position as depicted in this map? What might explain Coolidge's position relative to Fillmore in the product profile?
4. What is the relationship, if any, between Exhibit 3–5 (the product generation map) and Exhibit 3–11 (the relationship between cost and volume in manufacturing)? What explains the pattern observed here?
5. Given your understanding of the situation at Coolidge, what additional maps would you like to see? For each of the functions (marketing, manufacturing, engineering) identify a map and the associated issue it would be designed to address.
6. What should be the role of senior management in the mapping process? What issues must functional managers confront in carrying out the process depicted in Exhibit 3–15?

Sun Microsystems, Inc. (A)

In August 1985, Scott McNealy, CEO of Sun Microsystems,[1] strolled into the Asimov conference room to greet the key players on the development team for Sun's Carrera workstation. The team had been given full resources to develop the Sun 3 workstation family, of which Carrera was the first product. It was now time to decide finally whether to announce Carrera on September 10. Although the hardware, marketing, and finance managers were generally enthusiastic, their counterparts from software, manufacturing, and customer support had some serious doubts.

Background

Sun Microsystems was incorporated in February 1982 by Andreas (Andy) Bechtolsheim, Scott McNealy, and Vinod Khosla. Bechtolsheim, the company's technical hardware guru, had been an engineering doctoral student at Stanford developing the hardware that became the Sun, and which he had tried, unsuccessfully, to get vendors to produce.[1] The hardware included a CPU (central processing unit) printed circuit board, a video board, and a power supply. Khosla had heard about Bechtolsheim through the Silicon Valley venture-capital network and proposed they start up a company, with McNealy, his Stanford Business School classmate, handling the operations side of the new venture. When McNealy had graduated from Stanford, companies wanted to hire him only for strategic planning; he had to fight his way into the factory—to be what he called "a real manager." McNealy was therefore delighted to run operations for the new company.

---

[1] "Sun" standing for Stanford University Network

This case was prepared by Dr. Nan J. Langowitz under the supervision of Professor Steven C. Wheelwright.

Workstation Development

A workstation unit (or system) was a high-performance desktop technical computer that for an engineer, for example, combined the functions of a calculator, a personal computer, and technical data manuals; it could also be used for applications such as computer-aided design or engineering. (One application Sun first provided was computer-aided software development.) Workstations could be interconnected to form a network of anywhere from two to several hundred systems through which they could communicate, share a mass storage unit, or access a common peripheral, such as a laser printer.

A basic workstation system had five key elements: (1) a CPU, or logic component, (2) memory, either RAM (random access memory) or disk-based, (3) a high-resolution monitor, (4) the operating system, and (5) network capability. The CPU, memory and monitor were physical elements of the machine (hardware); the operating system and network capability were embodied in a computer program (software). The specification of the system, particularly in terms of the functioning of these five elements, was given in what was called the system's "architecture." The architecture gave a blueprint of the basic parameters of the workstation's performance: speed, timing, memory capacity, and interaction among the five elements. Both hardware and software designs were based upon the specifications of the architecture. Other peripherals to the workstation included central file servers (for networked machines) and mass memory storage devices.

A product family had a common architecture. Within the family might be several models or versions that exploited a different aspect of the base architecture; each version was considered a separate product. Different products within a family were often categorized as high-, mid-, or low-end products. A high-end product, priced above $50,000, was used for graphics-intensive work such as simulation or modeling. Mid-end products were most commonly used for computer-aided electronic or software design and were priced in the $25,000 to $50,000 range. Low-end products were priced below $25,000 and were used for technical publishing and less complex computer-aided design.[2] A product's positioning from low- to high-end depended upon the amount and expandability of main memory, the computing speed, and the graphics capability of the workstation.

Several developments in the early 1980s set the stage for Sun's entry into the computer market. First, technological advances had been made in areas such as computer networking and high-speed computer mem-

---

[2] These range definitions appeared in "Workstation Vendors Clash for Dominance in Unsettled Market," *Computerworld*, February 17, 1986.

ory systems. Second, low-cost computer components became available, such as microprocessors, memory, and disk drives. It became relatively inexpensive to build a workstation with the power of a minicomputer. Third, early workstations had been built using proprietary designs. Although these workstations had high performance, their unique and closely guarded designs often limited future adaptability, application, and compatibility.

The first Sun 1 machines were shipped in May 1982 and by August the company was profitable. At the same time, Bill Joy, the developer of the Berkeley 4.2bsd version of the UNIX (a trademark of AT&T) operating system the Sun 1 ran on, was asked to join the firm. As Joy recalled: "They thought I had offers from lots of companies. The truth was, no one ever asked me before." In November 1983 the Sun 2 product line was introduced, and Sun opened its first European sales/support office shortly thereafter. In October 1984, Eastman Kodak invested $20 million in Sun, which quickly became a leading supplier of workstations for the technical computing market; company revenues jumped from $39 million in fiscal 1984 to $110 million in fiscal 1985. By taking advantage of a window of opportunity, Sun became a major player in the workstation segment of the computer market—a segment it was instrumental in establishing. (See Exhibit 1 for a breakdown of market share in the workstation market.)

Sun's Design Philosophy

Sun's product-design philosophy centered on "open systems" architecture and "single board" design.

According to the company's profile, "Sun's products are designed around industry standards for hardware, software, and data communications." These standard technologies included the UNIX operating system (AT&T), VME systems bus (Motorola), Ethernet local area network (Xerox), and 6800 series microprocessor integrated circuits (Motorola). Noted Bill Joy, "There's truth and right and IBM in this industry; if you have two on your side you're okay." The use of standard components in the open system architecture was a means of keeping truth and right on Sun's side. Moreover, Sun constantly scanned future technological trends to make sure it picked the right standards. The director of product marketing, John Hime, called Sun people "nerd managers" because they were always reading and keeping up with technical developments: "It's not optional not to keep up; the worst thing is to be in a meeting where you don't know what's going on and can't contribute."

Open system architecture provided several advantages to the customer: compatibility among Sun's products, enhanced ability to interface with other vendors' products, adaptability to future hardware

EXHIBIT 1

Worldwide Workstation Market

Market Share in the Workstation Segment

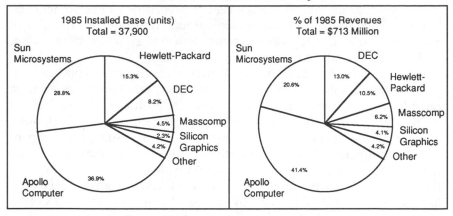

Projected Sales in the Workstation Segment

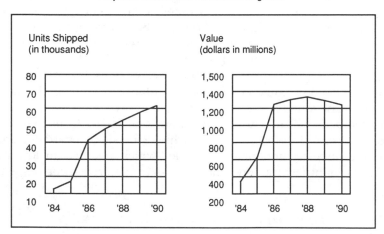

SOURCE: International Data Corp.

developments, portability of applications programs, and availability of many third-party software packages.

There were advantages for Sun as well. First, using standard components limited the technical options and allowed the machine's design to be well-specified, which, in turn, made possible easier and more extensive testing. Second, with existing standards, third-party vendors could develop products, particularly software, that complemented Sun products and enhanced their marketability. Third, the open system approach enabled Sun to bring new products to market more quickly. Other start-up companies tried to do everything in-house, and larger companies often had internal processes that slowed down development. Finally, Sun could concentrate on its unique contributions: the central processing unit, the operating system software, graphics, networking, and general-purpose tools for technical professionals.

Software was a key focus at Sun. Whereas other small computer companies often bought the operating system and other software from an outside vendor, Sun had software expertise in-house. These "kernel designers"—programmers who understood the guts of the UNIX operating system—beginning with Bill Joy, were an unusual group of people. According to Howard Lee, director of engineering, there were "very few UNIX hackers in the universe," and Sun had a large number of them. These "experts" were able to advise the hardware engineers on how to design a better machine by taking advantage of the UNIX operating system's capabilities. In turn, the software engineers could then implement UNIX to best take advantage of the hardware design.

Focusing on its unique contributions carried over into Sun's manufacturing strategy. Sun relied on a number of vendors for standard parts as well as subassembly of its machines. Only testing, final assembly, and configuration were done in-house. (The typical production process is shown in Exhibit 2.) By 1985, approximately 9,000 Sun 2 family machines had been built using this process.

The second aspect of Sun product design was the "single board" design. A single printed circuit board contained the logic, display, and memory functions for the workstation. Even within a product generation, competitors often used more than one board to encompass the basic functions of a workstation. To achieve the single board design, Sun used the fewest components possible, which resulted in lower cost, increased manufacturability, and savings in materials procurement.

The Competitive Environment

In addition to workstations, the general computer market comprised mainframes, minicomputers, and personal or microcomputers. In 1985, minicomputer prices ranged from $30,000 to $100,000, workstations from $15,000 to $60,000, and personal computers from $1,500 to $20,000. Sun believed that workstations, because of their increasing price/performance, to some extent fed off both the minicomputer and personal computer market segments. (See Exhibit 3 for computer market growth.)

In the early 1980s, typical workstation customers were universities

Exhibit 2
The Production Process at Sun, 1985

The process begins with a bill of materials for a customer's order that authorizes materials to be pulled from inventory. Except for sample testing on bare printed circuit boards and RAM, no incoming testing is done on the components. Instead, sample testing, including OEM peripherals such as disk drives, is performed by an outside test house before components arrive at Sun.

"Kits" of components are then assembled for specific boards and sent to outside subcontractor for "'stuffing," i.e., inserting the components. (Some manual vendors are used for regular production, others for quick turnaround.) However, some manual insertion is done in-house, for example when a chip needs programming (such as a PAL—programmable logic array) or is expensive (such as a microprocessor).

Completed boards undergo two in-house tests. First, a "bed of nails" automatic tester checks for subcontractor errors, faulty chips, and mechanical problems. (This is the board-level test.) Second, a system test checks the functionality of the board as part of the system.

The boards are then "burned-in." They are placed in ovens for 48 hours at 55 degrees Celsius, while run through a series of software diagnostics that test for temperature sensitivity and weed out component and design problems.

Meanwhile, after being assembled and tested for focus, linearity, and other functions, the monitor is packaged in its plastic shell.

Three types of production stations, corresponding to the three workstation options (rack mount, desktop, and pedestal models), then perform final mechanical assembly; this is followed by a mechanical inspection by quality assurance.

Next, the appropriate logic and memory boards are inserted according to customer order. Because every system is different, there are an enormous number of configurations; 150–200 switches must be flipped to the correct positions. Afterwards, more system testing is done, and functional quality assurance follows.

System "burn-in" then takes 48–55 hours, while the systems are tested by a series of diagnostics and tasks.

Systems are then boxed and sent to a consolidation area in another building, where all parts of an order (i.e., the system, keyboard, file servers) are put together to complete that order. The product is then shipped.

SOURCE: Casewriter notes from plant tour.

---

and sophisticated end users who followed technological developments and often discovered Sun's products through the technical grapevine. By 1984–1985, the customer base broadened to include *Fortune* 1,000 companies who were either end users or original equipment manufacturers (OEMs). The trend from early adopters to more traditional customers was expected to continue.

Sun's main competitors were Apollo Computer and Digital Equipment Corporation (DEC). In 1981 Apollo was the first company to introduce a technical workstation; Sun introduced the Sun 1 in February 1982. (Exhibit 4 depicts how Sun and Apollo envisioned workstation environments.) From 1982 to 1984 other start-up companies, e.g. Data General, tried unsuccessfully to enter the workstation segment. And

Exhibit 3

Computer Market Growth, 1984–1986 (millions of dollars)

Segment	1984	1985	1986 (projected)
Personal/Micro	3,554	3,868	4,621
Workstation	789	1,057	1,483
Minicomputer	5,870	6,395	7.099
Supermini	6,545	7,060	7,836
Mainframe	8,290	8,870	9,897
Supercomputers	520	840	1,020
Total Systems	25,568	28,090	31,956

SOURCE: *Electronics*, January 6, 1986, page 43.

DEC briefly offered proprietary CPU workstations: its 1984 offering, the Vaxstation I, did not do well. In May 1985 DEC introduced the Vaxstation II, also with a proprietary CPU, and in July 1985 Apollo introduced a 68020-based product. By summer 1985, however, it was too early to tell how the DEC and Apollo products would fare. Further, IBM was expected to enter the workstation segment, probably in the fall of 1985. (Exhibit 5 compares workstation product features from Apollo, DEC, and Sun.)

Sun's Customers

Along with end users, Sun had two types of OEM customers. The first group purchased complete workstations and incorporated them, labeled with the OEM logo, into the OEM's product. For example, a company in the printing industry might offer a computer-aided publishing (CAP) workstation product by developing CAP software and printing protocols for use in a Sun workstation bearing the OEM's nameplate. In this way, an OEM could offer a workstation-based product without actually developing the workstation. A second type of OEM customer purchased Sun's logic board—the guts of the workstation—and incorporated the board into workstation hardware and an operating system of the OEM's own design. Companies producing workstations for special applications, such as air traffic control, might use Sun's logic board but custom-design the remaining hardware and operating system to suit the specific application. Product development time varied for either kind of OEM. Some had speedy design-to-market cycles and wanted to see new Sun products as early as possible. Sun might consult these customers during the final product development stages and show them new product prototypes prior to announcement.

EXHIBIT 4

Comparison of Sun and Apollo Workstation Environments

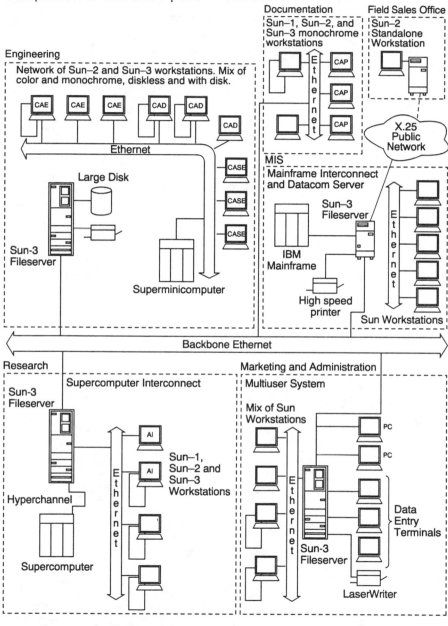

SOURCE: Company documents.

EXHIBIT 4

Comparison of Sun and Apollo Workstation Environments (*continued*)

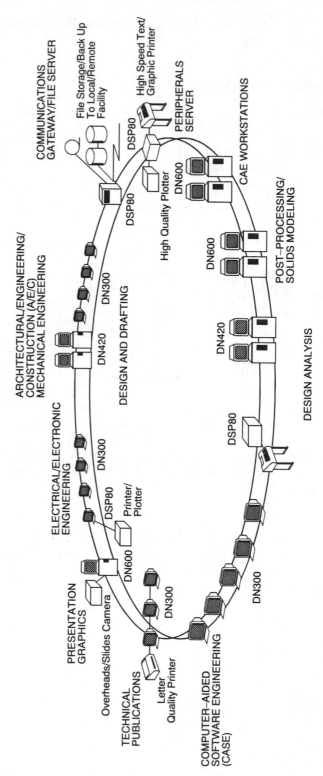

SOURCE: Company marketing materials.

EXHIBIT 5

Comparison of Leading Workstation Product Features

Vendor/ Product	CPU Micro-processor	Clock Rate	Perform-ance (MIPS)[a]	Main Memory Range (Bytes)	Hard Disk Storage		Operation System	Networking	Support	Graphics			System Price Range
					Minimum Configuration (Bytes)	Maximum Configuration (Bytes)				Resolution (pixels)	Dedicated Graphics Chip or Board	Dedicated Floating-Point Processor	
Apollo DN570, DN580	68020	16MHz	1.3	2.3–16M	69M	308M	Aegis (proprietary) AT&T UNIX System V Univ. of Calif. Berkeley 4.2	Proprietary, Ethnet, TCP/IP X.25, IBM's System Network Architecture	Siggraph Core Digital Research, Inc. Graphics Kernel Systems 4014	1,024 by 1,280	Yes	Yes	$29,900–70,000
Digital Equipment Corp. Vaxstation II	Proprietary	NA	NA	2M–9M	33M	213M	UNIX (proprietary version), VMS	Ethernet, TCP/IP, Decnet	GKS	1,024 by 864	Yes	Yes	$26,500–48,000
IBM[b]	Proprietary	NA	1.6–2.1	1M–3M	40M	40M	UNIX (proprietary version)	Proprietary	Proprietary	1,024 by 768	No	Optional	$11,700–19,500
Sun Microsystems 3–160C	68020	16.67MHz	2	4M–16M	71M	1.3G	Berkeley 4.2	Ethnet, TCP/IP, X.25, IBM's SNA	GKS, Siggraph Core, CGI	1,152 by 900	Optional	Yes	$34,900–50,000

[a] The companies included in this chart responded to a telephone survey by *Computerworld*. Further product information is available from the vendors.

[b] Information based on industry expectation of IBM entry.

SOURCE: *Computerworld*, March 10, 1966, pp. 45–54

The life of a workstation design was short because the base technology of the workstation, the microprocessor, was continually improving in speed and performance. Sun products were based on Motorola's 68000 family of microprocessors. The Sun 1 had been a 68000 design, the Sun 2 used the 68010, and the Sun 3 would be based on the 68020. (See Exhibit 6 for a technical comparison of the Sun family product lines.)

Sun's open system architecture was directly affected by changes in standard industry technology—microprocessors, floating point chips which allowed for high-speed mathematical computation, and networking protocols. Sun was particularly subject to Motorola's developments in the 68000 family line, and that company tended to announce and promote new products in advance of their availability. Customers often used a standard set of metrics, or "fundamentals," to compare workstation products, such as CPU performance, floating point performance, main memory size, mass storage (memory) size, networking capabilities, software windowing capability, and monitor attributes (color versus monochrome, size of screen, and resolution). So when customers heard that a new microprocessor or floating point chip was coming out, they expected Sun to incorporate the new technology in their machines. In this way, Motorola and other vendors essentially dictated not only Sun's product design but the life of that design and the timing of the next product introduction.

Overall, Sun was constantly working against time. The average period for an end user to order a new Sun product was 18 months. OEM purchasing behavior worked differently: they generally considered new products during their first year. If an OEM chose a Sun product to use

Exhibit 6

Technical Comparison of Sun 1, 2, and 3 Product Families

	Sun 1	*Sun 2*	*Sun 3*
CPU	68000	68010	68020
CPU clock	9.83 MHz	9.83 MHz	16.7 MHz
FPC	NA	NA	MC68881
FPA	NA	NA	yes
MMU	Sun 1	Sun 2	Sun 3
Virtual Memory	NA	16 K-Bytes	256 K-Bytes
Page Size	2 KB	2 KB	8 KB
Physical Memory	2MB	1–8MBytes	2–16 MBytes
Memory Bus	16-bit	16-bit	32-bit
VMEbus	16-bit	16-bit	32-bit
Memory Bandwidth	4.9 MBytes/sec	4.9 MBytes/sec	14.8 MBytes/sec
CPU-VME Bandwidth	3.3 MBytes/sec	3.3 MBytes/sec	9.5 MBytes/sec
MIPS	0.5	0.7	2.0

in its own product line, Sun might receive orders for it for as long as three years. Taking production time into account, this meant that the product might be actively shipped for five years at best. (Exhibit 7 shows a product time line.) Thus, the name of the game was time-to-market.

Sun's Workstation Products

Sun tried to be proactive in its new product introductions and to improve performance over existing entries. Noted Andy Bechtolsheim, "You have to obsolete your own product. Any time you try to protect your past you're in trouble, because the future is cheaper." Revenues from a new generation product typically replaced the existing revenue stream in three to six months, given its compatibility, better cost performance, and competitive features. Therefore, new product offerings were a high risk.

Sun's approach to architectural choices reflected its competitive strategy. By focusing on the "fundamentals" of the workstation, Sun tried to have faster CPU and floating point performance, more main memory, and better graphics and monitors. (The open systems architecture was another distinctive feature of its products.) With Sun 1 and 2 the firm had outperformed its competitors along these metrics and did so approximately 20% cheaper than Apollo. Much of Sun's price advantage stemmed from its use of a single board design with standard components. Except for Apollo's July 1985 product offering (which used the Motorola 68020 microprocessor), Apollo, as well as DEC, used propri-

EXHIBIT 7

Time Line of Workstation Product Life

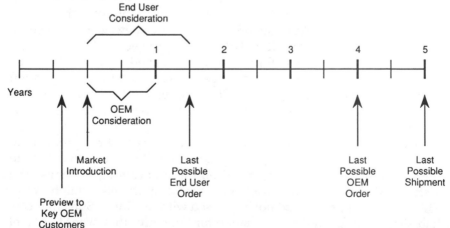

197

etary CPUs and networks in their workstations. Both companies also relied primarily on outside vendors for their software. While Apollo's products performed better than DEC's, Sun believed that neither company came close to the technical performance of its products.

Sun's average selling price for a single workstation unit, $15,000 in 1985, was expected to drop to $10,000 within two years, whereas Apollo's price was approximately $20,000. Price was a function of selling effort and support, as well as cost, and revenues increased as a customer built a unit into a network that might include other workstations, a file server, or a laser printer. Sun's goal was to add value without raising prices.

Sun believed that it would be hard for competitors such as DEC (and IBM, when it jumped in) to adapt their corporate revenue structures from a model based upon lower volume, higher-priced equipment to one based upon higher volume, lower-priced equipment. Sun conceived of its cost in terms of MIPS (millions of instructions per second), expecting to be at 1 MIP = $1,000 within a few years. It believed IBM and DEC would not be able to compete with them on this parameter and still maintain their revenue; the only thing protecting IBM was its installed base. Nonetheless, Sun agreed that brand name was important in the industry. Though Sun now had such a name, it still considered IBM and DEC among their biggest threats. In 1985 Sun had almost 600 customers and approximately 20% of workstation segment revenues. John Hime summed up Sun's market goals: "10% share is sustainability, 20% is a nice share of the pie."

The Sun 3 Development

The Sun 2, based upon the Motorola 68010 microprocessor, was introduced in fall 1983, but by June 1984, given Motorola's recent announcement of the 68020 microprocessor, Sun knew it would need a 68020-based workstation. It initiated three projects: (1) a high-end workstation, code named Sirius, newly designed and based on the 68020 microprocessor; (2) a mid-range product, code named Carrera, which would be a redesign of the Sun 2/50, using the 68020 instead of the 68010, and (3) a low-end product, called M25, which would use the old 68010 technology.

In October 1984, Sun executives previewed these three products to their largest OEM customer, Computervision, to induce that firm to design its own new products based on these upcoming offerings. The visit would also enable Sun to add features Computervision might want. This preview approach had not been used with the Sun 2: Sun engineers had simply designed the workstation for "the guys they went to school with," Howard Lee remarked. By 1984, however, a changing market increased the importance of customer input into new products.

During the Computervision visit, Sun managers realized that their three new products did not make sense as a family; they did not have the same architecture and were not software-compatible. Over the next six weeks, Sun redesigned and consolidated the three products to form the Sun 3 line. The goals for the revision were: (1) the products had to be high-, mid-, and low-end; (2) their operating differences should be transparent to the user; (3) their hardware should be transparent to the software; and (4) they should be compatible with the later model Sun 2 (Exhibit 8 compares the Sun 2 and Sun 3 product families.)

EXHIBIT 8

Relationship Between Sun 2 and Sun 3 Product Families

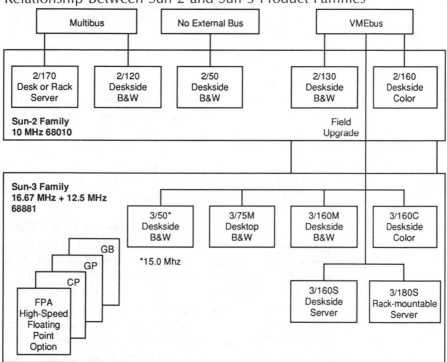

Key:

FPA = Floating Point Accelerator
CP = Floating Point Co-processor
GP = Graphics Processor
GB = Graphics Buffer

SOURCE: Company marketing materials.

The revised architecture was finalized in November 1984 during a series of meetings involving all key development people: representatives from hardware engineering, software, customer support engineering, advanced manufacturing technology, product engineering, product marketing, and manufacturing. In consolidating three different product designs, all the features of each product could not be maintained. Compromises had to be made, and not without difficulty, for each engineer had a vested interest in certain features and ideas. To facilitate these compromises, the group set up a special voting system. The two technological gurus, Bechtolsheim and Joy, shared one vote, and hardware and software each had one vote. Bernie LaCroute, then vice president of engineering, said that if they could not agree, he would simply flip a coin to decide, rather than vote. In the end, the group agreed on an architecture document outlining the hardware and software specifications for the three Sun 3 products, and this document, closely guarded by a separate manager who became "the keeper of the book," held everyone on the development team together. (See Exhibit 9 for a description of Sun 3 family features.)

The Carrera Product

A sense of urgency surrounded the Carrera development project. As the mid-end product, it was scheduled to be the first of the Sun 3 family to be introduced. The team had eight months to develop Carrera (by summer 1985). Given the tight schedule, it could be tempting to skip steps—simulating the design or not fully evaluating a new component—in order to get the project done quickly. Yet everyone at Sun knew that a skipped step had the potential of cost later on, and that the cost magnified as development progressed.

Among several technical issues considered in Carrera's final design, the first was how the machine's CPU would access memory. The choice was between a "cache-based" design and a "wait state" design. In a cache-based machine, the microprocessor accessed a special cache of high-speed RAM in order to retrieve data. This design gambled that when the microprocessor looked for appropriate data in the cache it would have a continually high hit rate, or success. In a wait state machine, the microprocessor accessed regular RAM and experienced a slight pause, or wait, while it retrieved the data, and with this approach a high hit rate was more easily guaranteed.

Sun rejected the cache design because the special memory was expensive, the cache could not be fit onto a single board design, and, as Lee noted, "cache is still an art." In fact, it was hard to predict exactly how well any given design would perform. Theoretically, a very well-designed and well-executed cache machine had a 10% performance edge

EXHIBIT 9
Carrera Product Line

Sun–3 Features

Sun–3 Model	75M	160	160C	160S	180S
Function	Desktop workstation	Expandable deskside workstation	Deskside color workstation	Deskside fileserver	Rack-mountable fileserver
MC68020 clock cycle	16.67 MHz	16.67 MHz	16.67 MHz	16.67 MHz	16.67 MHz
MC68881 floating-point coprocessor	12.5 MHz	12.5 MHz	12.5 MHz	12.5 MHz	12.5 MHz
Main Memory	2–8 MB	2–16 MB	2–16 MB	2–16 MB	2–16 MB
Display					
Type	19″ mono	19″ mono	19″ color	N/A	N/A
Resolution	1152 × 900	1152 × 900	1152 × 900	N/A	N/A
Refresh	66 Hz	66 Hz	66 Hz	N/A	N/A
Card Cage					
Bus	N/A	VME	VME	VME	VME
Slots	N/A	12	12	12	12
Serial Ports	2	2–16	2–16	2–16	2–16
Floating Point Accelerator	N/A	yes	yes	yes	yes
Graphics Processor/Buffer	N/A	N/A	yes	N/A	N/A
4-Channel Synchronous Controller	N/A	yes	yes	yes	yes
Disk Drives	71 MB	71, 130, or 380 MB	71, 130, or 380 MB	71, 130, or 380 MB	130 or 380 MB
Tape Backup	¼″ tape	¼″ or ½″ tape	¼″ or ½″ tape	¼″ or ½″ tape	¼″ or ½″ tape

Sun–3 Industry Standards

Microprocessor	MC68020
Buses	32-bit VMEbus, Multibus (IEEE 796 Adapter)
Floating Point	IEEE Standard 754, Version 10.0
Local Area Network	Ethernet
Disk Interface	SCSI 5-¼″ Winchester drives; SMD 8″ and 10-½″ drives
Operating System	UNIX
Network Protocols	TCP/IP, ISO OSI Model; Sun Network File System (NFS)
Data Communications	SNA, S.25, Bisync
Languages	ANSI F77, Pascal, C, Common Lisp, Prolog, Ada
Graphics	ACM Core, GKS2, CGI, PHIGS, Sun Pixrect, PostScript™

SOURCE: Company marketing materials.

over a wait state machine, but Sun believed that such a differential would not exist in practice because their competitors had not yet come up with a high-performance cache.

A second issue was how much virtual memory the Carrera machine architecture would support. Virtual memory was not hardware, like a RAM chip or a disk drive, but a software application that allowed the CPU to address memory stored on a disk so quickly that it appeared to be accessing RAM. The Sun 2 could address 16Mbytes of virtual memory, and Computervision had requested that Carrera address 64Mbytes. The design team eventually chose to have Carrera address 256Mbytes of virtual memory because Apollo had a product with that amount.

The third set of choices—for the entire Sun 3 family—involved software. One question for designers was how the microprocessor would coordinate or handle on-board (on the logic board) devices such as memory or the Ethernet networking chip. The design could either use an "interrupt-and-poll" system or an "auto-vector." In the interrupt-and-poll method, the devices would ask the microprocessor for service and then wait for a response: that is, "poll" microprocessor availability. In the auto-vector method, a device would ask the microprocessor for service and get an immediate response. The hardware engineers were in favor of the interrupt-and-poll method, but the software engineers preferred the auto-vector method. The compromise was to use one method in the low-end machine and the other in the mid- and high-end machines.

A final technical issue concerned Sun's confidence in the chips used in the Carrera design. Although the 68020 would likely become an industry standard, based on the history of its earlier family members, it was nonetheless a new chip. And there was always risk associated with a new chip. Sun generally designed at the top of the chip's learning curve, when the chip was still relatively expensive, and bet that the curve, and therefore the cost, would move down. Because Sun thought about the prices of components as if they were a commodity, it tried to guess the future in terms of the number of suppliers, customers, exchange rates, and production yields. The risk seemed acceptable, however, since at low volumes the company could probably debug any problems on early parts by having excellent technicians on hand.

On Carrera, Sun faced this risk with the 16 MHz speed of the 68020 and the PALs (programmable logic arrays); both chips contributed to the high-performance speed of the machine. In spring 1985, Motorola was having trouble producing full-speed 16.67 MHz parts and could only offer 12.5 MHz reliably. But according to Howard Lee, who was both director of engineering and Carrera project manager, the 12.5 MHz part "wasn't interesting." Lee told Motorola that Sun would only ship 16.67 MHz parts and asked for parts partially tested to run at 16.67 speed;

these were called 12AF parts. Sun built machines using 12AF parts on the Carrera pilot production line during July, testing them internally for 16.67 MHz reliability. It seemed important to risk the 12AF parts because the pilot machines were those sent to early OEM customers for testing and adjustment to their hardware. However, it was not clear when Motorola would be able to guarantee the 68020 at 16.67 MHz. Thus, the microprocessor speed issue seemed likely to remain a problem if Sun announced Carrera in September.

The Carrera Team

With each product that Sun designed, the development process improved. Sun 1, of course, had gained little benefit from manufacturing input, as Andy Bechtolsheim was still at the Stanford engineering lab when he designed it. The Sun 2 was Sun's first real product, but problems in the field had led key engineers from both design and manufacturing to stay up three nights running to upgrade its design. The Sun 2 episode was typical for a start-up company; in the early stages, a company never had enough resources or team experience to get a "clean" product. Nonetheless, the Sun 2 was a success. Now, Sun 3 was the first product family to be developed with full forethought, careful management, and discipline. (See Exhibit 10 for a summary of Carrera's eight-month development.)

Sun's best hardware designers were assigned to Carrera, and although the three key designers had different work styles, they worked with Lee to coordinate the project and keep it on schedule. Because of the sum-

EXHIBIT 10

Milestones in Carrera's Eight-Month Development

December 1984. The first Motorola 68020 part arrives just prior to Christmas, is plugged into a 68010 socket, and runs on the logic board. Sun tells Motorola they "had a machine running," which gives Motorola incentive to provide more parts to them.

February 1985. Prototype design review with Computervision.

April 1985. The first "stuffed" board comes back from the subcontractor and the UNIX operating system can run on it. Being able to run UNIX for more than one minute was considered a success. Manufacturing technicians are brought into the engineering lab to help debut the board.

July 1985. To get additional customer feedback, an early Carrera machine is privately shown to key customers in a hotel suite during the Siggraph industry trade show. (These customers are asked to sign nondisclosure agreements prior to examining it.) No orders are taken for the machine and it is not considered a public market announcement.

---

mer deadline, there were many contingency plans. Extra money was spent to maintain team morale and project momentum. For example, Fourth of July weekend 1985 was a four-day holiday at Sun, but the Carrera team worked nonstop. On the factory floor, people were offered two days off for every day they worked during the holiday.

Lee used what he called "best-guess scheduling" to manage the project, setting target dates for key milestones. The team did not hit a single target. Each target date had an associated "wave-off date," however, and Lee used these to coordinate lead times when targets were missed. A blank check from management to "do what you have to do" was particularly helpful in getting the project accomplished quickly. It also helped that Sun hired very experienced people: the norm was eight or ten years' previous experience at a single company such as Hewlett-Packard, General Motors, or Data General. Although this policy produced expertise among key team members and managers, the "melting pot" phenomenon was sometimes a problem, for there was no critical mass of "Sun" people.

Lee tried to anticipate manufacturing needs for Carrera. Manufacturing technicians began working in the engineering prototype lab in April. An informal new product introduction group was formed—something new for Sun—including hardware engineers, test engineers, manufacturing technicians, and manufacturing managers. The group worked together to design the Sun 3 production process, which superficially resembled the Sun 2's. But while in "gross stages [there was] no change, finer modules changed a lot," according to Curt Wozniak, director of manufacturing. On the Sun 3 there was more production process feedback on quality, reliability, and testing. Another new approach in the design-manufacturing interface was for engineering to buy forward in materials from prototype to pilot. A special engineering inventory account was set up that did not require assigned part numbers, even though the parts were not yet approved for purchase. Engineering therefore had responsibility for them, and bore the expense if they did not get used. Manufacturing was wiling to accept these parts as long as the cost was not their responsibility. This reduced the lead time between prototype and pilot manufacture because parts were already on hand.

The August 1985 Meeting

Now assembled in the Asimov conference room the Carrera team represented marketing, customer support, hardware, software, manufacturing, and product engineering. Howard Lee opened the discussion: "Look folks, it may still be summer but September 10th is coming up fast, we've got to make a final launch decision today."

Everyone in the room realized that the computer industry was in a slump, and that Sun 2—approaching the end of the 68010 life cycle—had been experiencing a falling backlog. (See Exhibit 11.) Digital Equipment had recently released its Vaxstation 2, and Apollo had announced its

EXHIBIT 11

Sun 2 Backlog and Bookings as of July 1985

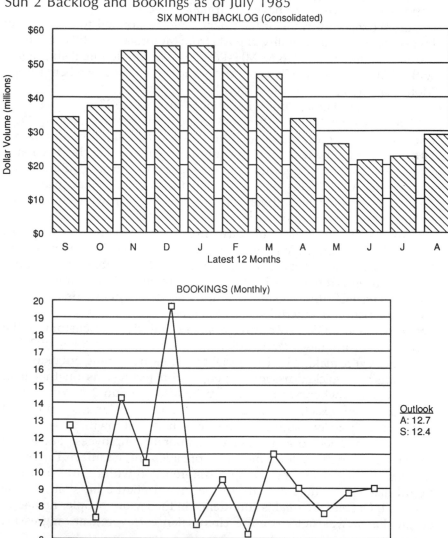

SOURCE: Company planning documents.

68020 product at the Siggraph trade show in July. IBM was rumored to be ready to announce a workstation product, its first entry in this segment, during early fall.

John Hime, director of product marketing, responded. "We're under a lot of external pressure out here. You all know what our competitors are up to, but let me remind you that our customers are anxious for this product. The OEMs who have been testing the pilot Carreras are hot to move. I'd like to go for September so we can keep our customers happy—but we've *got* to have a shippable product."

Curt Wozniak, director of manufacturing, responded to Hime. "My biggest concern is availability of parts from Motorola. We still don't have a steady supply of fast [16.67 MHs] 68020s. We can do initial shipments with 12AFs, as we have in pilot, and swap out later but we better hope Motorola gets its act together soon."

"Okay," said Hime, "but what about Carrera itself?"

"I think Carrera's in pretty good shape," answered Wozniak. "You know how it is in this industry, John. It's got to be slightly underdone. How could it not be with an eight-month development cycle? The hardware took nearly half that time to develop, and software couldn't even begin until April." This was a familiar Catch–22. The hardware was needed to develop the software but, in turn, the hardware couldn't be debugged without the software.

Paula Sager, coordinator of software release, then spoke. "The software's coming along. We're putting more people on it. The pilot version has nearly full functionality; it's just not yet fully testable. Our customers have been through this before. Just tell them we'll upgrade in a few moths. The FCS [first customer ship—the date when a final version would be ready] is scheduled for December."

Lee rejoined: "Okay, we can go ahead and give the customers the product with upgrades later. But what if Carrera really takes off? The machines we're making in the special pilot area are coming out okay, but there are hand-picked assembly people and technicians on that line. What happens when we put Carrera in with the Sun 2s? Will it fly?" Wozniak knew exactly what Lee was getting at. Manufacturing had been through a slow summer. They had had no growth, little investment, and had let go a number of temporary employees. Further, a search was underway for a new vice president of manufacturing since the current one would be taking a different job within Sun, and that might make the whole manufacturing organization a bit shaky in the early fall. Despite Wozniak's confidence in the factory people, he had to admit that it was not clear the circumstances favored an aggressive ramp-up.

Bob Caporaso from customer support had other qualms about a September release. While Sun was trying hard to build up its support organization, it didn't yet have strong leadership, as it had just recently begun a search for a vice president to head the function. "Don't forget that Carrera really has to be ready when we ship; there are high warranty costs otherwise and we'll need a big field service effort. It's true we've run that risk before, and so has Apollo, but the game may change if IBM jumps in the ball park," he asserted. IBM was renowned for its service organization.

"You're right Bob," said Bernie LaCroute, executive vice president. "But even IBM shouldn't make us think twice. What should make us think twice is our own credibility in the market. Sun is a visible company now. The Sun 2 put us on the map and we've got a good reputation in the business. We've got to think about that, especially with our initial public offering coming up."

Carol Bartz, vice president of marketing, pushed back her chair and started pacing. "All right, so where are we on this? You know, from marketing's standpoint this announcement is going to take a lot of doing. Sun's a big deal now. We need at least three weeks lead time for an effective product announcement. There are hotel ballrooms to book, media to contact, materials to develop, sales force training to do, and direct mail pieces to send out. September 10 looks awfully close to accomplish a well-coordinated introduction. If we decide to go, though, we'll get it done."

"Let's face it folks, we've got to get Carrera out there," said Mo Virani, from finance. "The Sun 2 backlog is consistently dropping and it's our main revenue stream." (See Exhibit 12.) With the industry segment's short life cycles, Virani estimated that for every month Sun delayed a product it lost 10% of sales volume, because the product had less time to actively sell.

Bill Joy added, "I agree with Mo about launching, but for other reasons. It's important to maintain our reputation for technology leadership." Sun aimed to be first with added functionality and speed in its machines. The Sun 2 had been twice as fast as the Sun 1, but the Carrera would be nearly three times as fast as Sun 2. Joy continued: "Carrera is an exciting product and so far no show-stopper bugs are showing up in pilot manufacture. Even if IBM does come out in the fall, you *know* we've got a better product than they do: they're never state-of-the-art. If we could outperform IBM on design, it would be tremendous plus—in both the financial and workstation markets."

The pros and cons were on the table, and Scott McNealy understood that the project team was waiting to hear his opinion. As the CEO he believed it wasn't his decision to make, he could only apply pressure. If he applied pressure to announce, he knew expediency would increase

Exhibit 12

Sun Financials by Quarter, Fiscal Year 1985 ($ millions)

	Q1	Q1	Q3	Q4	FY85
Bookings	$34.4	$42.6	$26.8	$19.5	$123.3
Revenues	19.7	24.3	33.9	37.3	115.2
Gross Margin	47%	45%	45%	48%	46%
RD&E	2.4	3.5	3.9	5.3	15.2
SG&A	3.7	5.0	6.3	8.9	23.9
Total Exp	6.1	8.6	10.3	14.2	39.1
Operating Inc.	3.1	2.5	5.1	3.8	14.5
%	15.5%	10.2%	15.1%	10.2%	12.6%
Net Income	1.8	1.4	3.0	2.4	8.5
%	8.9%	5.8%	8.8%	6.4%	7.4%
Cash used (Generated) From Operations	$ 4.4	$ 2.6	$ 5.0	$(6.2)	$ 5.9

SOURCE: Company financial documents.

the chances of other problems later in the fall as ramp up occurred. That would make manufacturing more difficult and customer support more critical. McNealy also knew that in this market you could never really have a perfect product and still be a technological leader. Given the stakes for Sun, which way should he lean?

TRUS JOIST Corporation

In early March 1975 Peter Johnson, president of TRUS JOIST,[1] was attempting to formulate his manufacturing plans for the remainder of 1975 and early 1976. With a mid–1975 turnaround anticipated in the lagging construction products industry, Johnson was concerned about strains that might be placed on the company's manufacturing operations in the coming months. TRUS JOIST, a young growth-oriented company that had expanded both its sales and product lines rapidly for several years (*see* financial statements, Exhibits 1, 2, and 3), had recently developed and announced a new product line that, based on preliminary analysis, appeared destined to be much more successful than originally expected. As a result of this and the projected increased demand for the company's other lines as construction picked up, Johnson decided that it was now necessary to carefully review and analyze all factors critical to planning both the company's over-all manufacturing strategy and its specific capacity requirements. From this analysis he expected to develop his final program for managing TRUS JOIST's manufacturing operations.

The planning dilemma Johnson faced originated from the company's response to the economic downturn in 1974. That year, TRUS JOIST's dollar sales had leveled off and its unit volume had declined slightly due to the precipitous decline in residential and commercial construction. In order to utilize idle capacity at its capital-intensive, raw material manufacturing plant located in Eugene, Oregon, the company had added a new product to its line of floor and roof joists.[2] (See Exhibits 4, 5, and 6, respectively, for illustrations of TRUS JOIST products, applications and

---

[1] Registered trademark.

[2] A joist is a support beam used in both floor and roof systems to support the decking material (usually plywood) over which the finished floor or roof is laid.

Copyright © 1975 by the President and Fellows of Harvard College. Harvard Business School Case 675–207.

Exhibit 1

Consolidated Balance Sheets TRUS-JOIST Corporation

	December 28, 1974	December 29, 1973	December 30, 1972
Assets			
Current assets			
Cash and short-term investments	$ 2,039,522	$ 809,168	$ 776,133
Receivables, less revenues of $320,000, $100,000 and $54,400	2,565,685	3,707,497	2,506,498
Inventories at lower of FIFO or market	2,968,868	3,249,475	2,473,440
Prepaid expenses	28,074	24,663	174,695
Total current assets	$ 7,693,149	$ 7,790,803	$ 5,930,766
Property, plant, and equipment Land	$ 579,062	$ 473,524	$ 267,559
Buildings and leasehold improvements	5,841,133	4,185,251	3,521,031
Machinery and equipment	5,676,987	4,020,252	2,888,046
Autos and trucks	144,960	151,509	134,910
Office equipment	931,900	800,956	266,038
Total	$13,174,042	$ 9,631,492	$ 7,077,584
Less accumulated depreciation	3,554,711	2,501,817	1,661,062
Total	$ 9,619,331	$ 7,129,675	$ 5,416,522
Other assets	349,218	244,545	287,743
Total assets	$17,661,698	$15,165,023	$11,635,031
Liabilities and stockholders' equity			
Current liabilities			
Notes payable	$ —	$ 275,000	$ —
Current portion of long-term debt	314,575	231,107	135,102
Accounts payable	1,265,386	1,893,561	1,505,825
Accrued liabilities	1,155,435	1,313,881	747,358
Income taxes payable	189,822	777,983	526,268
Total current liabilities	$ 2,925,218	$ 4,491,533	$ 2,914,553
Long-term debt, net of current portion shown above	$ 7,060,583	$ 4,282,444	$ 4,319,550
Common stock, par value $1.00, authorized 10,000,000 shares, outstanding 1,740,313 and 1,691,785	$ 1,740,313	$ 1,691,785	$ 317,512
Paid-in capital	88,815	9,029	975,862
Retained earnings	5,846,769	4,690,232	3,132,303
Total	$ 7,675,897	$ 6,391,046	$ 4,400,927
Less treasury stock at cost 1,320 shares	—	—	24,750
Total liabilities and equities	$17,661,698	$15,165,023	$11,635,031

EXHIBIT 2

Consolidated Statements of Income TRUS JOIST Corporation

	December 28, 1974	December 29, 1973	December 30, 1972
Sales	$41,640,576	$40,928,782	$26,988,696
Cost of sales	$28,677,880	$28,075,659	$18,292,315
Selling expenses	5,661,018	5,452,779	3,677,531
Administrative expenses	4,544,101	3,784,116	2,856,611
Interest	578,040	438,920	187,122
Total costs and expense	$39,451,039	$37,751,474	$25,013,579
Income before provision for income taxes	$ 2,189,537	$ 3,177,308	$ 1,975,117
Provision for income taxes			
Federal	$ 1,039,000	$ 1,476,000	$ 907,000
State	93,000	127,000	112,000
Investment tax credit	(99,000)	(115,000)	(80,000)
	$ 1,033,000	$ 1,488,000	$ 939,000
Net income	$ 1,156,537	$ 1,689,308	$ 1,036,117
Earnings per share	$.65	$.96	$.61

production operations.) Called the 50/60 line, the new joists utilized TRUS JOIST's raw material, MICRO=LAM,[3] produced by a revolutionary new type of wood-lamination process developed by the company's research and development group. Preliminary analysis indicated that the 50/60 line might be so successful that major changes in the company's manufacturing facilities could be required in a fairly short span of time in order to supply sufficient MICRO=LAM.

Johnson believed that the company had two alternatives with regard to the new product line, each of which had strategic implications affecting the company's long-term goals of maintaining a flexible operating stance in its cyclical industry and exploiting products and processes whose capital requirements were low enough to allow continued company expansion with only internally generated funds.

The first alternative continued the strategy that the company had followed prior to the construction downturn of 1974 and before the development of the 50/60 line. This option involved proceeding in a very controlled way and intentionally limiting the appeal of the 50/60 series rather than letting it take over a larger and larger percentage of the company's product line. Johnson felt this could be done either by raising

[3] Registered trademark.

EXHIBIT 3
Six-Year Sales and Profit Summary

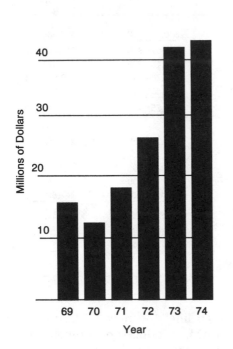

Net Dollar Sales

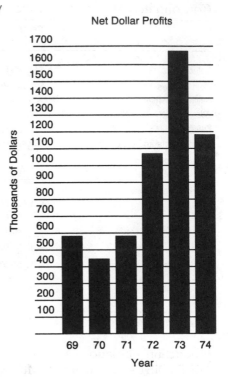

Net Dollar Profits

prices on the 50/60 series as it began to catch on, thereby restricting it to filling a gap in the existing product lines, or by carefully allocating MICRO=LAM capacity among competing TRUS JOIST products. In this way, the company could gradually adapt existing assembly facilities as demand materialized and could delay any expansion of its capital-intensive raw material manufacturing operations at Eugene, Oregon until 1977.

The second alternative entailed full use of the attractive characteristics of the 50/60 product line and adjustment of other aspects of the company's activities to fit that opportunity. This would involve increasing the market share of the 50/60 products as quickly as possible. Johnson believed this strategy would require several actions, namely: (1) ordering long lead time equipment for a second MICRO=LAM manufacturing plant; (2) obtaining a material supply contract for veneer with one or more major forest products firms; (3) searching out sources of long-term debt financing, and (4) undertaking a major marketing effort in the eastern United States. This strategy had particular appeal because it

EXHIBIT 4

TRUS JOIST Corporation Products

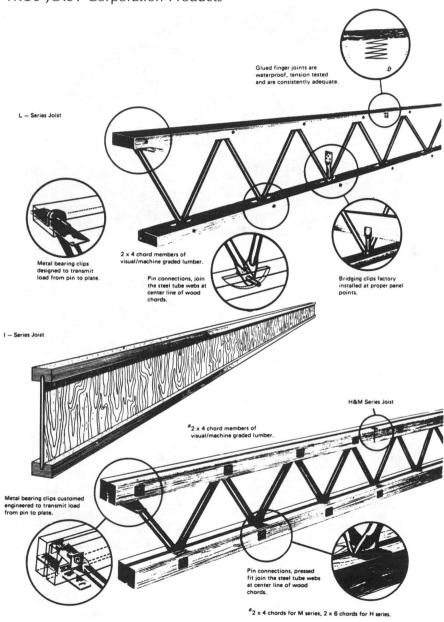

Glued finger joints are waterproof, tension tested and are consistently adequate.

L — Series Joist

Metal bearing clips designed to transmit load from pin to plate.

2 x 4 chord members of visual/machine graded lumber.

Pin connections, join the steel tube webs at center line of wood chords.

Bridging clips factory installed at proper panel points.

I — Series Joist

H&M Series Joist

Metal bearing clips customed engineered to transmit load from pin to plate.

ᵃ2 x 4 chord members of visual/machine graded lumber.

Pin connections, pressed fit join the steel tube webs at center line of wood chords.

ᵃ2 x 4 chords for M series, 2 x 6 chords for H series.

213

ExHIBIT 5

TRUS JOIST Corporation Product Applications

EXHIBIT 5
TRUS JOIST Corporation Product Applications (continued)

Exhibit 6

TRUS JOIST Corporation Production Operations

Portion of the interior of a TRUS JOIST plant where L Series are manufactured.

A close-up of a new joist. The TJ/50 and TJ/60 are the first of a family of five wood and steel open web joists to incorporate MICRO=LAM lumber.

MICRO=LAM billets as they exit from machine at Eugene, Oregon plant are 80 ft. long, 2 ft. wide and 1½ in. thick.

would help ensure full utilization in the future of the Eugene MICRO=LAM facility and would help the company achieve its earnings per share objective of 30 percent annual growth.

Corporate History

The TRUS JOIST Corporation of Boise, Idaho was founded in 1960 by Harold Thomas and Art Troutner. Thomas was a lumber distributor and salesman; Troutner was an architect and builder who had invented a new type of roof and floor joist. Troutner's open web joist had used top and bottom chords of 2 × 4 lumber connected to tubular steel webs with steel pins. (See Exhibit 4.)

From the outset, the strategy of the founders was to design and develop lightweight roof and floor structural systems that represented new technologies, used proprietary production processes, and could command sufficient margins to justify sales by a company-owned sales force. Given the cyclical nature of the industry, the company also sought manufacturing procedures and product designs that minimized fixed costs. By the early 1970s, it had become clear that the company had a viable strategy and the resources necessary to follow it successfully. In 1973 sales had reached $41 million with after-tax profits of 4 percent of sales.

Despite the success of TRUS JOIST's strategy, the company was still subjected to the same cyclical swings and seasonal variations that were so much a part of the construction industry. For example, the sales during a typical calendar year were distributed so that 18 percent occurred in the first quarter, 25 percent in the second, 35 percent in the third, and 22 percent in the fourth quarter. Since all TRUS JOIST products were made to order, this meant that the company's level of operations in the third quarter was roughly twice that of the first quarter, even without any sales growth.

Management's objective was to have a major public offering of the company's stock at some point within the next few years so that current investors could diversify their investment holdings if they so desired, and so that the company could grow even more rapidly through the use of equity funds. A strong equity market was viewed as important in the long run, because the company envisioned that once its sales exceeded $100 million, its investment requirements would increase substantially.

In 1975 the founders were still actively involved in the business although additional management skills had been added to cope with the requirements of a growing company. Thomas was chief executive officer of the company and chairman of the board while Troutner was vice president of research and development. Peter Johnson, a Dartmouth College MBA who had been with the company since 1969, was president and chief operating officer. Reporting to Johnson were two operating managers—one with responsibility for TRUS JOIST's four geographical regions in the United States and Canada (covering both sales and production), and the other with responsibility for MICRO=LAM operations.

Product Line

The company's original product had been the L series joist and in 1974 it still accounted for over 40 percent of dollar sales volume. This joist

(Exhibit 4) consisted of top and bottom chords of 2 × 4 lumber connected by tubular steel webs attached to each chord with steel pins. L series joists were particularly well suited for lightweight roofing systems that covered open spans of 20 to 40 feet. While improvements had been made in the production process used on this product, the design was essentially the same as it had been in 1960.

Shortly after the introduction of the original L series, the M and H series had been offered. These products utilized double top and bottom chords of 2 × 4 and 2 × 6 lumber respectively (Exhibit 4) and were designed to perform the same function as the L joists, but for spans of 30 to 70 feet. In contrast to the L series, the M and H series required substantially more material and labor to produce.

Throughout the 1960s, the L, M, and H series had represented the bulk of TRUS JOIST's product line. In 1970 the company had added the I series joist. This product line (Exhibit 4) consisted of 2 × 3 top and bottom chords connected by a vertical plywood web. The line had been an immediate success and had found wide acceptance as a structural floor system in apartments, town houses, and condominiums. Thus it had complemented the company's line by providing a product whose normal use was as an integral part of the floor system (as opposed to the L's, M's, and H's which were most commonly used in roofs) and which was particularly attractive in multifamily residential construction (as opposed to commercial and warehouse construction).

MICRO = LAM

Of even greater significance in the development of the company's product lines was the introduction of MICRO=LAM lumber in 1971 following five years of research effort costing over $1.5 million. MICRO=LAM consisted of 12 or 16 sheets of veneer fed into one end of a specially designed press that produced an 80-foot long billet, 24 inches wide and 1½ inches thick.[4] The cross section of such billets looked much like an exceptionally thick piece of plywood (Exhibit 6). The MICRO=LAM billets could be ripped to any size to produce a piece of high-grade structural lumber that was markedly superior to natural lumber in its strength, predictability, and uniformity.

The company believed the product would be particularly significant to TRUS JOIST as a raw material for joist products and to other major forest product firms because it allowed a substantially larger percentage of the tree to be used and because it randomized defects in the veneers. This

---

[4] A billet foot is one foot of MICRO=LAM 24 inches wide and one and one-half inches thick. An 80-foot MICRO=LAM billet contains 80 billet feet.

latter property made it possible to use a smaller piece of lumber to perform a certain job than was the case for sawn lumber.

TRUS JOIST management felt that eventually MICRO=LAM could become a substantial business, much as plywood had. However, they had not yet determined how that could best be exploited—through TRUS JOIST products, through licensing agreements with major forest product firms, or through some other arrangements.

As soon as the MICRO=LAM plant in Eugene, Oregon, was completed, the I series joist underwent modification to replace the top and bottom chords of sawn lumber with comparable pieces of 2 × 3 MICRO=LAM lumber. This modification greatly improved the performance characteristics of the I series joist and reduced the amount of scarce high-grade sawn lumber required by the company.

MICRO=LAM production was highly capital-intensive compared to the company's other production operations. Management estimated that in 1975 the cost of a second MICRO=LAM plant with maximum annual output of 6 million billet feet would run $3.5 million to develop and would have annual fixed costs (including $350,000 of depreciation) of almost $900,000. In order to cover the annual fixed costs on a breakeven basis, the plant would need to be operated at roughly 50 percent of capacity. If operation of such a plant could be maintained at 100 percent of capacity, over the course of a year it would generate approximately $1 million in contribution in addition to covering these fixed costs. This contribution was based on an established transfer price between the Eugene plant and the company's plants utilizing MICRO=LAM for other products.

Development of the 50/60 Product Line

During late 1974, as the slumping construction industry had its impact on demand for TRUS JOIST products, the company focused its research efforts on speeding the development of new products to add to its product line. For several months, the research and development group had worked on a product that would complement the existing line by bridging a gap that currently existed between the L line and M's and H's. It was apparent from market reports that, although the company's existing products would technically meet the requirements in middle-range spans of 38 to 50 feet, they were not cost-competitive in that range. To fill that gap, R&D had worked on a new line of joists.

With the sudden downturn in the construction industry, management had focused renewed effort on the development of a product line that would fill the gap in the existing product line, would increase manufacturing productivity over existing levels for M's and H's, and would utilize much of the company's idle MICRO=LAM capacity. (This capacity had been idled when demand for the I joist—used in multifamily residential floor systems—had evaporated in the fall of 1974.) In addition, TRUS JOIST management hoped that any new product could be sold as a second-generation product that could eventually replace existing lines and thereby gain wider acceptance in the marketplace.

By late November the research staff had completed development of a product line, the 50/60 series. This product could be produced on M and H production lines with a relatively modest investment in new equipment. (It could not be produced on L lines.) The product line itself looked much like the existing M's and H's but rather than using sawn 2 × 4's and 2 × 6's as support chords, it utilized MICRO=LAM chords ripped from the 2 × 80-foot billets produced in Eugene.

By early January 1975 the company had developed the equipment necessary to convert the existing M and H production line at the Boise, Idaho, plant for production of the 50/60 series. As prototype production began, the company found that the 50/60 product not only accomplished the objectives of utilizing MICRO=LAM and filling a gap in the existing product line, but also the 50/60 series could be priced competitively and offer better margins than existing products. The company also found that conversion of an M and H line could in fact be done very quickly with an investment of only $100,000, as compared to a cost of $175,000 for adding a new 50/60 line to an existing plant.

Moreover, it was found that a single production line could turn out twice as much 50/60 product as M and H product. This doubling of productivity was due to the uniformity and longer length of the MICRO=LAM chord as compared with sawn lumber. In the 50/60 product it was no longer necessary to spot knots and other defects in the chord before proceeding with drilling and pinning, and it was no longer necessary to splice chords together in order to obtain the desired over-all length of up to 70 feet. One possible disadvantage of the use of MICRO=LAM in this product was that increased inventories would be required since the raw material used to manufacture the chord material of MICRO=LAM would need to be produced about six to nine weeks prior to 50/60 fabrication rather than being purchased just two or three weeks in advance of joist production.

Before sending product literature to individual salesmen, an analysis was done to compare the 50/60 series with the company's other products for a typical roof system. This comparison, shown in Exhibit 7, indicated that the series not only filled a gap in the existing line but also was cost-competitive with much of the market for the L, M, and H series. Exhibit 8 explains the basis for this comparison. While it was indeed rewarding to have a product with such strong promise for success, the

Exhibit 7

Cost Analysis of TRUS JOIST Products for a Typical Roof System (Pacific Northwest Region)

	Lowest Cost of Using 50/60 Product[a]			Lowest Cost of Using TRUS JOIST's Other Products[a]	
Joist Product	Total Cost per Square Foot[b]	Span	Joist Product	Total Cost per Square Foot[b]
	not appropriate	22	L[c]	$ .85
	not appropriate	24	L[c]	.85
	not appropriate	26	L[c]	.85
	not appropriate	28	L[c]	.85
50[c]	$ .89	30	L	.99
50[c]	.89	32	L	1.00
50[c]	.90	34	L	1.00
50[c]	.91	36	L	1.01
50[c]	.92	38	L	1.02
50[c]	.93	40	L	1.21
50[c]	.94	42	L	1.22
60[c]	1.00	44	L	1.23
60[c]	1.01	46	L	1.25
60[c]	1.01	48	L	1.25
50[c]	1.14	50	M	1.31
50[c]	1.15	52	M	1.31
60[c]	1.23	54	M	1.32
60[c]	1.25	56	H	1.58
60[c]	1.28	58	H	1.57
60[c]	1.30	60	H	1.56
60	1.55	62	H	1.55
60	1.57	64	H[c]	1.55
60	1.61	66	H[c]	1.56
60	1.65	68	H[c]	1.58
60	1.89	70	H[c]	1.59

[a] Joist configuration may vary in terms of on-center spacing and depth. This simply indicates the cost per square foot for the least expensive configuration.

[b] Includes costs of joists, decking material, installation, and access during construction. Differences in square foot costs for L, M, and H products and 50/60 product are due mainly to differences in joist cost.

[c] Indicates TRUS JOIST product with lowest cost per square foot covered.

Exhibit 8

TRUS JOIST's Basis for Comparing Costs

As a basis for comparing the cost of installing a TRUS JOIST roof support system in a standard application, an analysis of competitors' costs was recently made in the Seattle area. The pricing information for this comparison was based on local sources which were thought to be very reliable. The parameters used in developing the information were as follows:

Grid System	(40' × 40')
Roof load	25 psf live load 15 psf dead load
System components	primary carrying member (TJ 50) roof decking material labor to install joists and decking only
Exclusions	columns and footings all ledges insulation built-up roofing secondary framing

Given the above information, five alternative systems were analyzed for their material costs and installation labor. These analyses gave the following square foot costs:

TRUS JOIST = *$1.02 per square foot*
Tim Joist[a] = $.99 per square foot
Berkeley Panelized = $1.20 per square foot
Metal Gusset Plate[a] = $.98 per square foot
Steel Girder and Bar Joist[b] = $1.31 per square foot

Management considered this comparison to be somewhat more favorable to TRUS JOIST than anticipated. However, it was felt that it could be explained because it was in the northwest where TRUS JOIST was generally well accepted, and it was prepared at a time when the company was seeking to substantially increase the sales of its products.

[a] Typical competitor systems encountered when selling TRUS JOIST systems in western US.

[b] Typical competitor system encountered when selling TRUS JOIST systems in eastern US where steel costs tend to be comparatively lower and wood systems more expensive.

---

new product also had manufacturing planning implications for TRUS JOIST management.

Research and Development

Since the company's founding, major emphasis had been placed on research and development. In 1975 the corporate research and development group, headed by Troutner, included a staff of 20 professionals.

The work of this group was spread about equally between the development of new products and the development of new processes. TRUS JOIST had found it most economical to design and build all of their own production equipment. This strategy had further enhanced the proprietary nature of its product since it allowed the company to patent the production equipment as well as to patent the production processes and the products themselves.

One of the guidelines that had been used by the research and development group in its product design was that of product and component rationalization. In 1975 the company's full line of products required only a couple of dozen components. This allowed tremendous flexibility in the manufacturing operation and minimized the need for maintaining large inventories of a wide range of materials.

The research and development group had, for several years, been turning out new products and new process ideas and improvements at an even faster rate than they could be utilized by the company. Some of the new products they had considered recently involved the application of MICRO=LAM as a raw material. These included decking (for semitrailer trucks), scaffolding, recreational stadium seating, and a hollow, square telephone pole. Unfortunately, while many of these were large markets (almost of a commodity nature), they tended to require substantial capital for entry, and TRUS JOIST management was hesitant to make commitments to pursue such opportunities at the present time.

Marketing Efforts

For the past several years, the company's selling efforts had focused on increasing market penetration of both residential and commercial construction. This had involved selling through a direct sales force to architects, engineers, and contractors. Due to the proprietary nature of the company's production processes and the patents that it had obtained on all of its products (with the exception of MICRO=LAM,[5] TRUS JOIST had been able to compete effectively with sawn lumber and structural steel. The company had considered its product lines the Cadillac of the industry and had sought to maintain their proprietary nature and high margins through additional research and development.

---

[5] Although the MICRO=LAM product was not patentable, the process of manufacturing it using a unique traveling press was protected by TRUS JOIST patents. Johnson knew of one major forest products firm that had invested substantial resources in an unsuccessful effort to develop an alternative process for manufacturing a product equivalent to MICRO=LAM. He believed that if the product did turn out to have substantial market potential, major firms would increase their efforts to develop an alternative process.

The company's selling strategy for its product line had involved tailoring every order to the particular requirements of the job rather than selling from a finished goods inventory. Following receipt of a customer order, the plant designed the product so that it would best meet that customer's needs at minimum cost to TRUS JOIST. This strategy had helped the company to further differentiate its products from the commodity nature of most roof and floor structural systems and to promote the proprietary nature of its products.

TRUS JOIST's use of a direct sales force and a selling strategy that compared the total cost of floor (or roof) systems incorporating the company's joists were only two aspects of its marketing approach that had been unique to the industry. In addition, TRUS JOIST stressed service (three-week delivery was guaranteed on every job), quality, and creative solutions to customer problems that provided the best value per dollar of cost. Customers included architects, engineers, and contractors with the relative importance of each depending on the type of project and the industry's characteristics in particular geographical regions.

The typical sequence of steps in obtaining an order for one of the company's products started with the salesman's call on an architect or engineer who was designing a construction project. Through the use of price estimates showing the cost per square foot of area covered for various TRUS JOIST configurations, the salesman would present the architect or engineer with a product that would best suit his needs. The aim was to have that product specified on the construction plan. When the contractor received the plan from the engineer or architect, he would note TRUS JOIST product specification and would subsequently place an order for the specific joists required. (Normally, the salesman also called on the contractor to ensure that the contractor understood the advantages of the TRUS JOIST system.)

When the contractor placed an order, he stated the area to be spanned, the quantity, depth and length of joist, the performance characteristics desired, and the product line desired. The TRUS JOIST manufacturing plant receiving the order then prepared a set of working drawings incorporating the design and performance specifications for that particular order and had them checked by the customer and the architect. Once the contractor approved those working drawings, TRUS JOIST used a proprietary computer program to determine the optimal design that would meet the requirements shown on the drawings and yet minimize manufacturing material and labor costs.

Market Share and Competitive Pricing

One of the performance measures Peter Johnson used in evaluating the company's marketing efforts was that of market share by geographical area and type of construction. These figures were obtained by comparing company sales with the appropriate McGraw-Hill construction activity data. In early 1975 TRUS JOIST estimated its national market share to be 3 percent of those construction projects where its product was suitable. However, this varied widely by geographical area and was probably closer to a 20 percent market share in the northwest and northern California and considerably less than 3 percent in the eastern part of the United States.

Management felt that the disparity of the market share figures between east and west was largely due to the fact that the company had started in the west and had concentrated the majority of its early efforts there. Western contractors were also more accustomed to using wood-based floor and roof structural systems than were eastern contractors who worked mostly with steel and concrete. Because of this, sales in the east required a greater "missionary effort" than did sales in the west.

In recent years TRUS JOIST had undertaken to substantially strengthen its east coast market share. This involved training new sales people, teaching them to sell the joists in competition with structural steel (as opposed to sawn lumber), and developing regional delivery facilities that could provide three-week delivery.

As a general proposition, management estimated that a TRUS JOIST roof or floor support system in place would, on average, be 10 to 50 percent more costly than a comparable steel or plated rafter-all wood system, at least in most markets and most applications. The company considered its heaviest competition in the east to be steel joist systems and in the west to be plated rafter and other competitive wood systems. From time to time the marketing group prepared comparative cost analyses for various market segments and various types of buildings, as already shown in Exhibits 7 and 8.

Both marketing and top management at TRUS JOIST stressed that generalizations regarding the cost of various joist systems tended to break down in particular building applications. It was management's best estimate that perhaps 25 percent of the structures that the company sold were, in fact, applications where the TRUS JOIST system represented the lowest in-place cost; in the bulk of the remaining applications where the company was successful, the cost disadvantage of the TRUS JOIST system was no more than 15 percent. In almost every area of the country at any particular time, there were some building applications where TRUS JOIST would "fit" particularly well and where, in fact, it was the least-cost solution. Finding those situations and others where the company's cost disadvantage was not too severe and, then, convincing the customer of the advantages of the TRUS JOIST system were the primary functions of the direct sales force.

225

Manufacturing

While TRUS JOIST viewed itself as an innovative, new wood technology-oriented marketing organization, it also developed and carefully executed a manufacturing strategy that complimented its marketing efforts. This strategy historically involved minimizing fixed costs and plant and equipment investments while maximizing production efficiency, flexibility, and reliable service.

Manufacturing the company's joist products involved three steps. The first two, done in parallel, were tube fabrication and chord fabrication. These fabricated parts were assembled into finished parts. Because of the design differences in the M and H and the L series, a separate production line was required for L's while both M's and H's were produced on the same production line. For the I series floor joist, basic units 80-feet long were manufactured at the MICRO=LAM plant and I series production plants simply performed a cut-up operation.

With the exception of the MICRO=LAM operation and I joist fabrication at Eugene, Oregon, each of the company's plants consisted of a combination of production lines that could produce L's, M's, and H's, or cut-up I's. In early 1975 the company had fourteen such plants, as shown in Exhibit 9. Although they were not all in operation in March of 1975, they included five I cut-up lines, twelve L lines, and five M/H lines.

The Boise plant, typical of the company's larger plants, was equipped with one M and H line and two L lines. A full shift on each of these three lines required approximately fifteen direct labor people per line. The company tried to locate its plants in small productive communities and had never attempted to run more than two shifts a day, five days per week, although it did schedule occasional overtime on weekends. The rate at which a given production crew could operate depended both on the experience of the crew and on the specific product. Typical production rates for an experienced crew and MICRO=LAM utilization rates are given in Exhibit 10.

Production did not require a high level of operator skill. It did, however, take two to three months for a new crew to achieve an average level of efficiency. Because of the substantial seasonal fluctuations in demand for TRUS JOIST products, the company had often found that in the third quarter productivity dropped substantially. This decrease occurred because of the number of new workers that had to be hired and given on-the-job training.

Over the years, TRUS JOIST had placed particular emphasis on improving productivity and reducing labor input per unit of product. It was management's feeling that the company had been able to do this consistently and that if appropriate data were available, it would be possible to show a marked learning curve effect in the production op-

EXHIBIT 9

Production Capabilities and Typical Production Rates

Plant	Production Facilities
Boise A	Equipment shop (produced all equipment needed for TRUS JOIST manufacturing)
Boise B	1 M/H line and 2 L lines (the M/H line converted to also handle 50/60 in February 1975)
Chino A	1 M/H line and 1 I cutup line
Chino B	1 L line
Portland	1 M/H line and 1 L line
Iowa	1 M/H line and 2 L lines
Canada	1 M/H line and 2 L lines
Santa Rosa[a]	1 L line
Phoenix[a]	1 L line
Virginia[a]	1 L line
Eugene A	MICRO=LAM facility and 1 I manufacturing line
Eugene B	1 I cutup line
Colorado	1 I cutup line and 1 L line
Texas[a]	1 I cutup line
Summary:	5 I cutup lines (4 operating in 1975) 12 L lines (9 operating in 1975) 5 M/H lines (1 equipped to also handle 50/60)

[a] Closed in early 1975.

eration. This pattern would probably also be true in the purchasing area where for several years the company had centralized purchasing the basic material components and simply had individual plants issue ship orders to meet their particular needs. This procedure had enabled the company to purchase its materials at the lowest prices possible, to ensure its sources of supply, and to minimize its materials inventory.

Historically, TRUS JOIST had followed a capacity strategy that provided 20 percent more production line capability than was expected to be required in the peak season (third quarter). Because of the minimal investment in plant and equipment, and the marketing strategy to provide three-week delivery, top management had felt it was well worth any extra costs involved to maintain this excess physical plant capacity. (It had typically been insufficient skilled labor that led to overtime during the third quarter rather than the lack of physical plant and equipment.)

By late fall of 1974 it had become apparent to management that the industry slowdown had reached critical proportions and that if the company were to maintain profitability, immediate action was required. All nonessential programs were postponed, operations were reduced to a skeletal level, management salaries were reduced 10 to 25 percent, and

EXHIBIT 10
Typical Production and Utilization Rates

Maximum Production Rates in Regional Plants (single shift)

Product	Feet per 40-Hour Week
1 L line	25,000
1 M/H line	10,000 (M) or 7,500 (H)
1 I line	250,000
1 50/60 line	20,000 (50) or 20,000 (60)

Existing Eugene Facility Production Rate (three full shifts per week for entire year)

I manufacturing 25 million feet per year

MICRO=LAM 7.2 million billet feet per year

MICRO=LAM Utilization Rates
One billet foot MICRO=LAM produces

5 feet I joist
or 3 feet 50 joist
or 2.5 feet 60 joist

---

a review of all employees and managers was expedited. Included in these moves was the closing of four production plants (in Santa Rosa, Phoenix, Virginia, and Texas) which management anticipated would be in mothballs for at least one year and would be considered for reactivation when justified by demand.[6] A key management objective in these actions was to maximize liquidity so that the company could capitalize on the construction upturn anticipated in late 1975 and early 1976.

Future Considerations

One of the issues in Peter Johnson's mind upon reviewing the cost analyses shown in Exhibits 7 and 8 and the cost-competitiveness of the new 50/60 series was that while no problem existed in the short term of supplying MICRO=LAM for the product line, there might well be a problem of doing so in the longer term. He reasoned that as the 50/60

---

[6] On average, each plant closing had resulted in one-time costs of $12,000 to $15,000 and was expected to require annual outlays of $35,000 on each closed plant.

series, with its requirements for MICRO=LAM, began to replace the existing L, M, and H series, and as the construction industry began to recover, the company's need for capital would increase. While Johnson knew that this would not happen overnight, he wanted to be sure that he had thoroughly investigated the available alternatives before it became necessary to deal with either a capacity shortage or a capital shortage at TRUS JOIST. Some of the major factors he thought he should consider in doing his analysis planning included the following:

1. *Veneer supply.* At the present time, TRUS JOIST purchases all its veneer required for MICRO=LAM production on the open market in the Pacific northwest. However, management agreed that if purchases in that market were increased substantially to supply a second MICRO=LAM plant, the price would become prohibitive (because the company would be competing against itself for the supply of veneer in that market). The alternatives for obtaining additional veneer were either to build its own veneer plant at a cost of approximately $6 million, or to negotiate a long-term supply contract with one of the major forest products firms that had its own veneer operation. In either case, the company thought it would probably be most attractive to make these arrangements in the northwestern United States, since the company's experience had been with veneer of the type produced from forests in that region.

2. *A second MICRO=LAM plant.* It was management's feeling that it would take between 6 and 12 months to construct a new MICRO=LAM plant, and it would cost about $3.5 million. It would be possible to shorten that time if some of the longer lead-time equipment components were ordered immediately and then stocked for when the plant would actually be built.

3. *Eastern markets.* One of the real attractions of the new product line was that, because of its lower cost, it could be a substantial help to the company in penetrating eastern United States markets. The firm's sales force was most enthusiastic about the 50/60 line and the help it was expected to give them in reaching sales and profit goals.

4. *Production line requirements.* The fact that the product could only be produced on converted M and H lines meant that replacing a major portion of the L, M, and H products with equivalent MICRO=LAM products would render most of the existing production lines obsolete. It was felt that because of the higher production rate for 50/60 products, substantially fewer production lines would be required to meet existing levels of demand, and that this space could be used to house additional capacity to meet the requirements of future growth.

229

Exhibit 11

Product Economics and Sales Mix (Late 1974)

Joist product cost structure (in percent)

Net selling price (excludes freight)		100
Cost of goods sold	43[a]	
Direct labor	8	
Plant administration	4	
Fixed and variable overhead	12	67
Gross margin		33
Division overhead		2
Sales cost		15
Corporation general and administrative		8
Pretax profits		8

Typical product prices and product mix

Product	Selling Price per Linear Foot	1974 Sales	Percent	1975 Sales (in percent)[b]
L Series	$1.50	$19,360,000	(46)	(51)
I Series	$ .78	13,860,000	(33)	(27)
M Series	$3.00	3,650,000	(9)	(9)
H Series	$4.50	1,980,000	(5)	(6)
50 Series	$1.90[c]	—		
60 Series	$2.05[c]	—		
Accessories and other		3,150,000	(7)	(7)
Total sales		$42,000,000	(100)	(100)

[a] Where materials included MICRO=LAM, it was assigned a cost equal to the company established transfer price.

[b] Estimates made prior to decision to introduce 50/60 Series.

[c] Prices announced in February of 1975. These prices gave about a 40 percent gross margin for 50/60 joists as compared to the 33 percent gross margin on other products. (The 40 percent gross margin did *not* include the contribution of the MICRO=LAM plant.)

NOTE: Since a linear foot of 50/60 is a stronger joist than a linear foot of L but not as strong as a linear foot of M or H, a given roofing system would require different configurations and amounts of joist depending on whether L, M, H, 50 or 60 products were used. Exhibits 7 and 8 illustrate the company's approach to comparing such alternatives based on cost per square foot covered.

5. *Rate of market turnaround.* An important consideration in Johnson's planning was that the actions be timed so they would best fit with the anticipated turnaround of the residential and commercial construction markets. Obviously, Johnson wanted to utilize existing MICRO=LAM

capacity as fully as possible in order to cover the high fixed costs associated with that operation. He reasoned that with recent federal legislation, it was conceivable that residential construction might come back more quickly than it had in the past and thus shorten the time span TRUS JOIST would have to gear itself to adjust to increased demand. This was a particularly important consideration given the company's historical emphasis on guaranteeing three-week delivery through the maintenance of excess production capacity.

Since I joist sales had gone from $4 to $8 to $16 million in 1971, 1972, and 1973, respectively, Johnson knew that once the market demand for this product returned to normal, sales would exceed even 1973 levels. His best estimate, prior to the introduction of the 50/60 line, was that by early 1976 the company would be selling at a seasonally adjusted annual rate 50 percent higher than 1974 with over one-third of that likely to be in I series products. At the prices announced for the 50/60 line (Exhibit 11), Johnson felt that 50/60 might add as much as $10 million of new business to 1976 sales in addition to the 50 percent increase.

6. *Financing.* Johnson had made recent contacts with financial institutions. They suggested it might be at least two years before a company like TRUS JOIST could obtain attractive prices for its stock in a new equity issue. The company had obtained a $2 million line of credit in early 1975 from United California Bank to help meet its possible short-term needs.

The Aggregate Project Plan

Overview

This chapter continues our focus on the front end of the development process. It introduces the concept of an aggregate project plan and lays out the steps firms need to follow in developing one. As noted in Chapter 2, many firms establish little connection between their business planning processes and the processes they use to identify and select individual product development projects. The aggregate project plan is designed to fill that gap. In order to motivate the need for an aggregate project plan and to illustrate how such a plan may be developed, the chapter carries through an analysis of development projects and their resource requirements at PreQuip, Inc., a manufacturer of precision equipment.

The experience at PreQuip highlights two critical themes that the aggregate project plan is designed to address. The first is the problem of balancing opportunities for conducting projects with resources and capacity. As in many firms, PreQuip simply has too many projects relative to its capacity. The second theme is the problem of achieving the right mix of projects, so that the resources are allocated in ways that enhance the business's strategic direction. In a company such as PreQuip, not only are there too many projects, but many of the resources

233

in the organization are devoted to solving short-term problems rather than building the foundation for long-term market success. The aggregate project plan addresses those issues explicitly by examining the question of the appropriate mix of projects given the business strategy, by identifying available capacity, and by laying out a sequence of projects that reflects that constraint.

An important starting point for an aggregate project plan, therefore, is to identify the types of projects the firm needs to undertake. We propose five types of projects, but concentrate attention on what we call platform projects. The notion of a platform is crucial to understanding the development of the aggregate project plan. Such a project represents a new "system" solution for customers, and provides a base for a family of products to be developed in subsequent projects. In addition to platform projects, we also highlight the importance of breakthrough projects in creating new technical or market categories as well as incremental or derivative projects that build off of previous platforms. These project types are relatively general as presented here. The central idea in this part of the chapter is that firms need to tailor the definition of each project type to the specific circumstances they confront so that those types can become the basis for analysis and planning.

In addition to identifying the types of projects in the business, an aggregate project plan specifies the mix of projects pursued at any point in time, as well as the sequence of projects to be conducted over time. Thus, the firm needs to pay attention to how platforms, breakthroughs, and derivative projects will be sequenced over the planning horizon. Examples of the issues in the sequencing of platforms and derivative projects are drawn from the experience of Kodak's reusable 35 mm camera and Hill-Rom's advanced electric hospital bed.

The chapter concludes with a look at how PreQuip implemented the concept of an aggregate project plan. We outline the steps that PreQuip went through to establish an aggregate project plan. An important element in this discussion is the notion of engineering or development capacity. The procedure we outline identifies the existing mix of projects and the utilization of the existing development resources. This provides the firm with a perspective on its current situation. In the case of PreQuip, there were two to three times as many projects as there were resources to complete them on schedule. The second phase of the aggregate project planning process, therefore, is to identify the future desired mix of projects, available capacity to complete them, and to define the mix of projects to be undertaken over the planning horizon. An important theme of this discussion is the need of senior management to redefine and reshape individual projects to reflect the strategic direction of the business and to only launch projects that the company has the resources to complete. A second theme is that projects build capabilities. An effective aggregate project plan not only defines a sequence of new products, but also the building of new capabilities.

*I*n a vast majority of organizations, the management of development efforts focuses primarily on managing individual projects. Yet in reality, all but start-up firms almost always engage in multiple concurrent projects. Thus, they engage in a set of development efforts (both product and process) that changes as products get to the market and as new projects come up for approval. For management, this involves deciding on the set of projects to be added to the "active list," how those projects are to be scoped and defined (and their objectives), when those projects are to be started and completed, what resources will be allocated to them in what time periods, and how they will accomplish, collectively, the firm's strategy. As discussed in Chapter 2, management and direction of these activities constitutes the aggregate project plan—an important building block in the development strategy.

All firms have a set of projects that are on an "active" list—projects that have been started and not yet killed or completed. Relatively few firms arrive at such a list through a systematic process of review and decision about what the *set* ought to be. The aggregate project plan has several functions and offers firms that develop and use it several advantages. As a starting point, the plan specifies the types and mix of projects that the firm plans to undertake over the planning horizon. Laying the plan out explicitly makes it possible to balance the demands of individual projects for critical development resources with existing capacity. In technology-intensive environments, for example, it is crucial to make sure that the demands for scarce engineering talent balance appropriately with the number of engineers available.

Those demands need to be balanced over time. The aggregate project plan lays out the sequence of projects the firm plans to undertake, as well as which will be actively supported at any one time.[1] The planned project sequence establishes a framework for future decisions about adding new projects, and thus the demands on the organization resources. But it also makes explicit the kinds of capabilities the firm will be building over time. Development projects serve as a primary vehicle for building people and organizational skills. The aggregate project plan helps senior executives ensure that, collectively, individual and group project assignments make sense over time, enhancing and expanding the organization's critical capabilities.

In this chapter we examine the issues managers must confront in developing an aggregate project plan, and suggest a process for dealing with those issues in a systematic way. The first section of the chapter compares the promise of the aggregate project plan with the often problematic reality we have found in many of the firms we have studied. Simply put, most firms have too many projects. As a result, resources are overcommitted and the organization scrambles to satisfy competing development demands. Solving that problem must begin with defining the types of projects the firm is to undertake and choosing the appropriate mix of projects over time. This is the issue we examine in the second section of the chapter. We use a number of examples to explore in detail the major types of projects, paying particular attention to what next-generation or major platform projects the firm might undertake. In the third section we look at the mix and sequencing of projects over time. Two critical issues addressed in this section are the relationship of advanced development projects to platforms, and the strategy for products derived from the platform. In the last section of the chapter we lay out a process for developing an effective aggregate project plan and illustrate the implementation of the approach in an organization that had never planned its aggregate project "plan." As that company's experience suggests, the promise of the procedure we outline in the last section is to replace a weak, undermanaged aggregate project planning approach with one that is robust and effectively managed.

Aggregate Project Plans: Promise and Reality

An aggregate project plan lays out the specific development projects a firm will undertake over the relevant planning horizon. The plan establishes the types of projects the firm will complete and the relative resources the firm plans to commit to them. Thus, the plan not only lays out the sequence of projects, but also identifies the desired dates of market introduction and the associated resources required to bring each project to the market. The plan therefore establishes absolute resource requirements and explicitly allocates them to different types of projects over time.

By making explicit the set of projects a firm plans to undertake and by laying out their sequence over time, the aggregate project plan creates a framework in which the firm may address such questions as the balance between available capacity and expected requirements, and the fit between the business strategy and the specific projects a firm plans to undertake. The projects that make up the aggregate plan include new products as well as new processes and advanced development efforts. As a framework, the aggregate project plan thus helps to focus both resources and attention on the balance of effective capacity and development requirements, and on the effectiveness of the proposed set of projects in implementing the business strategy.

Part of the power of an aggregate project plan lies in the focus and direction it gives to individual development projects. Indeed, a list of the benefits and the promise of the aggregate project plan—e.g., adequate resources for project completion, a clear mission and purpose for individual projects—may sound like "nirvana" to experienced project leaders who have tried to carry out projects without an aggregate project plan. To understand this apparent inconsistency, consider the experience of a precision equipment company that we will call PreQuip, Inc.

The Overcommitment of Development Capacity

In mid 1989, the management of PreQuip became concerned about the performance of their product development process. Worried by what seemed to be a rash of late projects and a development budget that was increasing while the number of projects completed seemed to be declining, senior executives undertook a review of their active project list. Much to their surprise, they discovered that PreQuip had thirty active development projects—far more than they anticipated, and, they suspected, far more than the organization could support. For each project they obtained estimates of the remaining labor months of effort required

239

EXHIBIT 4–1

Engineering Requirements for Active Projects Compared to Available Engineering Resources at PreQuip, June 1989– December 1991*

Active Projects (formal development projects by number)	Engineering Months Required for Completion	Months to Completion (desired)	Implied Engineering Resource Allocation (engineering months)		
			1989	1990	1991
1	54	8	40	14	0
2	123	24	38	62	23
3	86	12	50	36	0
4	286	20	92	172	22
5	24	4	24	0	0
.					
.					
.					
26	352	36	48	150	120
27	75	9	62	13	0
28	215	30	40	80	95
29	153	18	60	93	0
30	29	3	29	0	0
All Other Engineering Activity (customer support, troubleshooting)	—	—	430	430	430
Total Engineering Requirements	—	—	2783	2956	2178
Available Engineering Months	—	—	960	960	960
Rate of Utilization (percent)	—	—	289.9	307.9	226.9

* This list of commitments at PreQuip indicates that for the thirty active development projects to meet their target completion dates *and* other ongoing, "sustaining" engineering activities to be carried out, almost three times as many engineering resources are needed than are currently available.

for completion and identified the expected and desired project completion dates. They compared these requirements to available development capacity, including particularly the critical resources—such as design engineering—available to support development projects.

The data developed by PreQuip's senior management are presented in Exhibit 4–1. By its own estimate, PreQuip had committed to and launched two to three times as much development activity as it was capable of completing over the 1989–1991 time period. In such an environment, it is inevitable that projects will be much later than top management expects, and much later than participants have planned in their product proposals. Furthermore, if any one project runs into unexpected trouble, there is no slack available, and it will be necessary to take resources from other projects. This causes subsequent trouble on other projects and the effects cascade. As costs of development increase and deadlines pass, there is pressure to cut corners and the firm may suffer quality problems.

This tendency to substantially overcommit development resources has been characterized by John Bennion and his colleagues at Bain and Company as the "canary cage approach" to aggregate project planning. If one thinks of a firm's existing development resources as dimensioning a canary cage, and the individual development projects as canaries, there is an optimal number and mix of sizes of canaries that can thrive in the given cage. However, what most firms do is to continually add canaries to the cage without considering how many are already in it. As each new canary enters, it becomes more crowded and the fight for survival between canaries becomes more consuming. Eventually, weaker canaries find themselves pushed to the bottom of the cage, dumped on by their fellow canaries, and they become sick, and die. Even the remaining canaries find it difficult to grow and develop in a normal way because of overcrowding in the cage.

Overcommitment of available development resources also tends to mean that a handful of key individuals show up repeatedly and concurrently on different projects. Such individuals may be key functional engineers, development specialists important to each of several projects, and even support personnel (such as an analytical test person) needed on a variety of concurrent projects. When aggregate capacity is overcommitted by 100 percent or more, these individual contributors find themselves spread across several projects at a time. The justification offered for such concurrent assignments is that, because such individuals are a scarce resource, it is important that they not have any idle time. The logic is that it is better for a project to wait for such a key resource than to have the resource waiting for the next project. While that sounds appealing, it seldom works that way in practice.

The problem is that as the number of projects increases above one, productivity rises and then falls. Extensive proprietary studies by a major computer firm and our own observations of several medical electronics firms indicate a pattern like that shown in Exhibit 4–2. When an engineer focused on a single project is given a second one, utilization often rises slightly because the engineer no longer has to wait for the activities of others involved in that single project. Instead, the engineer can move back and forth between the two projects. However, if a third, fourth, or even fifth project is added, the percentage of time spent on value-adding tasks drops rapidly, as an increasing fraction of valuable time is spent on non-value-added tasks—coordinating, remembering, or tracking down information, for example.[2] In addition, the engineer becomes the bottleneck on all of the projects to which he or she is assigned.

Exhibit 4–2
Productivity of Development Engineering Time*

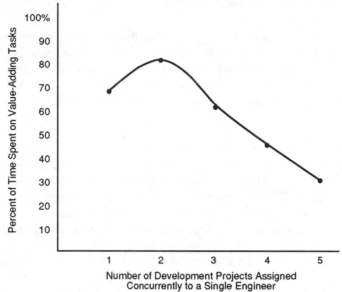

* In the studies underlying this graph, the activities engaged in by development engineers were grouped into two categories—those that added value to a development project, and those that did not. This graph shows the percent of an engineer's activities in value-adding tasks.

A Reactive Mix of Development Projects

For the senior managers at PreQuip, the news that their development organization was two to three times overcommitted was bad enough. They also discovered, however, that their development resources were not focused on the critical issues for the business. After reviewing how engineers were actually spending their time, senior management discovered that the bulk of their critical resources were not focused on the major projects required to implement their business strategy. Rather, the development organization was focused on reacting to near-term pressures. This is a common problem. Short-term pressures occur daily and come from existing customers, products, competitors, and distribution channels—often with information about existing products' problems and shortcomings. This gives rise to projects that extend existing product market offerings or solve very specific customer problems. Their focus is to "sustain" the business and keep the organization's product market position viable with existing customer segments, distribution channels, and product categories.

In the PreQuip case there was no formal system to track types of projects, but a rough estimate by the vice president of engineering suggested that 60 to 70 percent of the company's development resources were devoted to "sustaining" projects or activities (much of the work was never formalized into projects). When those activities were compared to the strategic potential of developing new technology (e.g., advanced control systems) and the need to break into new markets (e.g., a smaller, lighter machine for the Asian market), and taking into account the age of the company's bread and butter product line, it was clear to PreQuip's senior management that the corporation's critical development skills and capabilities were woefully misallocated. By piling on project after project, failing to identify critical projects, and succumbing to short-term pressures, they had systematically underinvested in the most important projects for the company.

The problems at PreQuip are not unique. Most organizations fail to realize the strategic potential in new technology or markets and next-generation projects because there are too many projects, and because they pay too little attention to the strategic mission of the development effort and too much attention to short-term pressures. But it is also true that planning, shaping, and initiating longer-term, more strategic projects requires a very different kind of managerial activity. Managing next-generation (or advanced development) projects, or breaking into new markets, is much more comprehensive, ambiguous, and uncertain than reacting to short-term problems. An essential element in dealing effectively with these challenges is a well crafted aggregate project plan. The first step in developing such a plan is to define clearly the types and mix of projects the firm needs. It is to that task that we now turn.

Types of Development Projects

While a number of different dimensions could be used to classify development projects into different categories or types, perhaps the most useful relies simply on the degree of change represented by the project. As illustrated in Exhibit 4–3, the degree of product change and the degree of manufacturing process change can be combined to define several types of development projects. Distinguishing types of projects is important not only because it clarifies management's thinking about planning, staffing, and guiding of individual projects, but also because it aids in developing an aggregate project plan since each of the project types requires a different level of resource commitment. These same types also can be used in creating product and process maps, as discussed in Chapter 3.

Exhibit 4-3

Defining Primary "Types" of Development Projects*

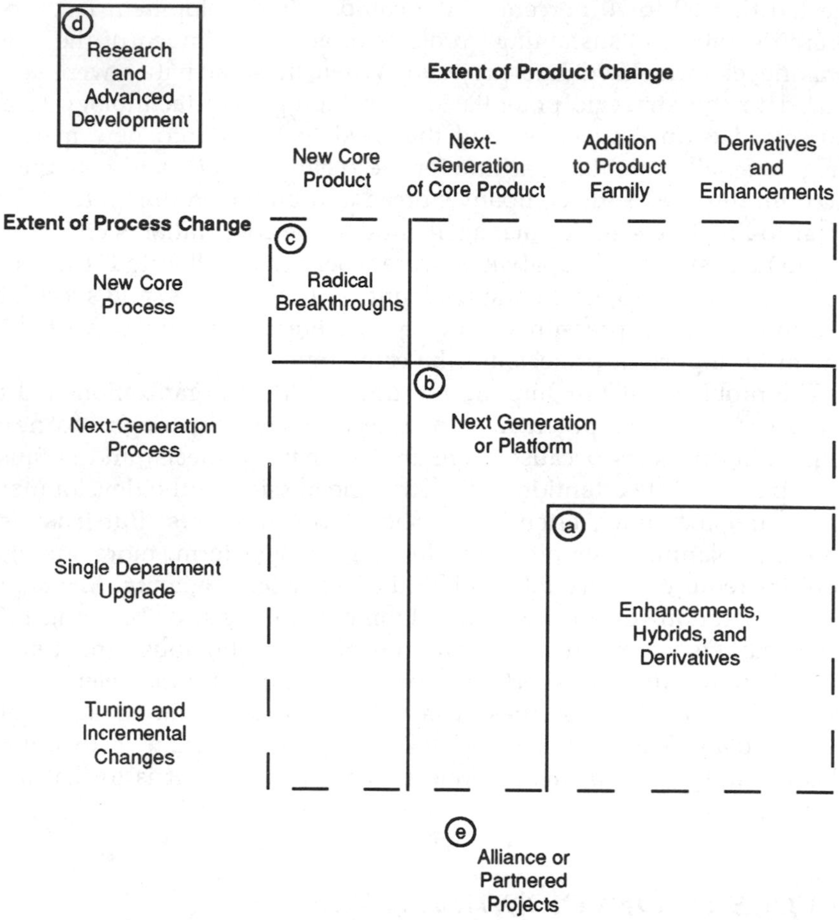

* The four primary types of projects, a through d, differ in the degree of change they require in product and process technology. The fifth type—alliance or partnered—involves joint work with another organization. While any of the four types could be partnered, it occurs most often with those involving substantial change, not with incremental or enhancement projects.

R&D/Advanced Development Projects

The boundaries of the diagram in Exhibit 4–3 define the range of commerical development projects carried out inside the firm. Two types of projects lie outside those boundaries: research and advanced development projects, and alliance or partnered projects. While projects within the primary diagram in Exhibit 4–3 focus on the introduction of viable, profitable products and processes, the focus of research and advanced development projects is the creation of knowledge—know-how and know-why—as a precursor to commerical development. Explored in more detail in Chapter 5, separating technological explorations and investigations from the application of known technologies in specific marketable products is a broadly accepted principle of technology management. Typically firms conduct advanced development in a separate group, staffed with a different set of people and equipment, than commerical development. However, over time people may move from advanced development projects to commerical development. Thus for aggregate planning purposes it is useful to include advanced development in the overall plan.

Alliance or Partnered Projects

Alliance or partnered projects also need to be considered in preparing the aggregate project plan. This type of project represents a different mode for conducting the project rather than involving a different extent of product or process change. In fact, any project could be done in a partnered mode. That is, an organization could form an alliance or create a partnership with another organization to conduct research or advanced development, to pursue a new product concept, or to develop a simple line extension. Instead of using the organization's resources alone, the partner firm often provides unique and/or significant resources (and sometimes all of the resources) and may manage the execution of the project. In recent years, firms increasingly have used partnered projects to fill in when their own resources were not delivering the development results required or when strategic opportunities were initially identified by other (often smaller) firms and acquiring a new product or process appeared less expensive or faster than duplicating the work in-house. Including partnered projects in the aggregate project plan is important because they invariably require some of a firm's own development resources, even if the partner firm does the bulk of the work. Even when the project is executed by the partner's organization, transferring the results of that project into the acquiring firm's product line, sales force, and often factories requires some of the same resources that otherwise would be available for in-house development efforts.

Incremental or Derivative Projects

In the lower right-hand corner of Exhibit 4–3 are projects that create products and processes that are derivatives, hybrids, or enhancements—what we have called sustaining projects. These range from cost-reduced versions of an existing product to add-ons or enhancements to an existing production process. As suggested by the positioning of that class of development effort, such projects include incremental product changes with little or no process change, incremental manufacturing process changes with little or no product change, and products involving incremental changes on both dimensions. Such projects usually require substantially fewer resources than projects that break new ground, because they leverage existing products or processes by extending their applicability.

Breakthrough or Radical Projects

At the other end of the spectrum are projects that involve significant change in the product and process. These "breakthrough" projects, when fully successful, establish a new core product and a new core process. They may create a whole new product category for the business or spearhead the entry of the firm into a new business. Much of the focus in such projects is on the product, because it often represents a new application or function and depends for its success on attracting and satisfying new customers. But breakthrough projects also involve significant process development; indeed, the process is likely to be critical to the success of the product. Senior management may give teams assigned to breakthrough projects some latitude in choosing the manufacturing process rather than constrain the team to use the existing plant or existing equipment and operating techniques.

Platform or Next-Generation Projects

In the middle of the spectrum between derivatives and breakthroughs lie what we call next-generation or platform projects. These projects, representing new "system" solutions for customers, involve significant change on either the manufacturing process dimension, the product dimension, or perhaps both. They provide a base for a product and process family that can be leveraged over several years, and they require significantly more resources than derivative or incremental developments. When carefully planned and executed, platform projects provide a significant base of volume and a fundamental improvement in cost, quality, and performance over the preceding generation. Thus they often are referred to as "next generation" efforts.

Platform projects deserve special emphasis in developing the aggregate project plan. Not only do they offer great competitive leverage and untapped potential in established markets, but senior managers—like those at PreQuip—often find that their organizations systematically underinvest in creating them. Understanding why, recognizing the consequences for performance, and developing guidelines for integrating platforms into the aggregate project plan thus present a significant opportunity.

Next-generation platform projects do more than create a single product and its manufacturing process. To function as a platform, a next-generation project must establish a product and a process with three essential characteristics:

1. *Core performance capabilities that match primary needs.* The solution the project develops needs to be a targeted, system solution to the needs of the core group of customers.
2. *Support of an entire product/process generation.* Platform projects create products and processes that subsequent development efforts can expand and enhance through the addition or removal of incremental features, thus creating a product and process family. While the platform must address the needs of the core customer group, it must also be adaptable and expandable.
3. *A link to previous and subsequent generations.* Platforms provide a migration path for customers, facilitating movement from one generation to the next. This ensures stability for customers as well as distribution channels, and enables the firm to leverage more fully its position and resources. Platforms do not disrupt the customer's world.

In effect, a platform project creates products (and processes) that embed an architecture for the system solution to be provided to customers. In fact, it is the architecture of the system that enables other features to be added or existing features to be removed in tailoring derivative products to special market niches. Making explicit the platform architecture helps designers, marketers, manufacturers, and general managers identify the role the platform should play in the aggregate project plan. For example, a critical choice in the aggregate project plan is whether the initial platform offering should be a fully featured version that later can be stripped down and focused as derivative products are created, or whether it ought to be a stripped-down version to which features can be added to create subsequent enhanced products. Both strategies have been pursued in similar markets. Polaroid's instant photography strategy has long been to start with a highly featured platform project, introduce it at a premium price, and then gradually remove features and create more cost-competitive versions as subsequent derivative offerings. In contrast, Kodak's single-use camera strategy in the late 1980s was to introduce a stripped down, bare bones platform—the FunSaver—to which other options and features (a panoramic lens, waterproof container, and flash) could be added to form enhanced products that were higher priced and higher performance than the original platform offering.

Using Project Types: The Benefits

The categories defined in Exhibit 4–3 are general; more specific and tailored categories may be useful in specific businesses. Explicit recognition that projects differ in ways that matter to the individual firm, and are not precise universal categories, is important. Each type of project has a different role and provides a different competitive contribution. Each requires different levels and mixes of resources, and typically generates very different results. Furthermore, because of the differences in the scope of projects and the issues associated with each of the types, requirements for success also differ.

Take, for example, the differences between platforms and derivatives. The most important of these is the front-end planning activity. While derivative projects often can represent specific, targeted responses to the requirements of small groups of customers, platform projects represent the bundling and packaging of a set of improvements into a new system solution for a much broader range of core customer needs. A successful platform project must embody sufficient improvement across a range of performance dimensions that customers will see it as a significantly better solution than either the prior platform or its targeted derivatives. Second, the new platform must combine a range of improvements in a way that no single customer may yet have thought of. Thus much more creativity, insight, and initiative are required at the front end of a platform project than a derivative project.

In addition to the challenges of front-end planning, two other differences distinguish the development of platform versus derivative projects. One is that getting convergence to a final set of specs is significantly more challenging on a platform than a derivative effort: there are many more specs that need to be defined and far fewer that are already constrained. In a derivative project, most of the issues already have been closed or severely bounded by the earlier platform effort.

The other difference characteristically highlighted is that platform projects require much more cross-functional problem solving and integration because so many issues must be defined. On a platform project, setting the specs in detail at the front end is often impractical. Instead, the project must converge over a series of months as cross-functional problem solving and conflict resolution take place. On a derivative project, setting the specs at the outset is commonplace. The focus of the project is delivering those specs by having individual functional contributors address the issues that they influence.

Getting capacity requirements clearly identified and linking projects to business strategy are first-order effects of using project categories as a framework for planning. But there are critical second-order effects that bring the organization significant advantage, particularly in making clear the interactions across projects. For example, these categories provide a useful way to link product and process development activities and plan for them jointly. Making the categories explicit highlights the similarities in needs, scope, and approaches for process and product development projects. Our experience is that most organizations spend far more time worrying about the degree of product change than about the degree of process change. In a large number of industries, achieving a better balance in the concerns and attention given to both dimensions can provide substantial competitive leverage.

There are other subtle, but substantial, effects of thinking about future projects in these terms. Project categories, for example, provide a framework for thinking not only about products and processes, but also about building development capability. Combined with a long-term planning horizon, laying out the future portfolio of projects facilitates the training and development of individuals involved in development. The primary goal of development projects is a defined product and/or process, but projects also create capabilities—particularly in human resources. A natural training path for engineers as well as marketing and manufacturing people is to begin their involvement in development by working on derivative projects, then to move to next-generation platform projects, and perhaps, for a much smaller number, to become centrally involved in breakthrough projects as experience and skills accumulate. Furthermore, key resources can be moved between research and commerical development types of activities to facilitate technology transfer and to ensure that advanced development is focused on those aspects of technology that will have the highest payoff in the market place. All of this grows out of establishing project categories as the first step in the aggregate project plan.

Choosing the Mix and Sequence of Projects

Establishing the appropriate types of projects for a particular business is the starting point for the aggregate project plan. But to put the categories to work and link them to business strategy, the firm must choose the appropriate mix of projects over the planning horizon. The mix is indicated by the percentage of a firm's development resources that are allocated to the various types of projects. Most established firms spend the majority of their development resources on incremental or derivative (sustaining) projects, whereas start-up firms spend the bulk of their development activity on radical or breakthrough projects. Additionally, some start-up firms dominated by scientists and engineers often find it difficult to make the transition from primarily research and advanced development efforts to commerical development projects. For all these types of firms, however, the issue of mix in the aggregate project portfolio needs to be readdressed periodically.

There are a number of factors that determine the most appropriate allocation of a firm's development activities across the primary types of projects. Some forces come from the firm's environment. Particularly important are industry maturity and the rate of technological innovation in the industry. As an industry matures, the opportunities for advanced development and breakthrough projects decline relative to opportunities (and customer demands) for derivative and platform projects. In fact, it is the evolution of the existing customer base, distribution channel, and competition that leads many mature firms to spend the bulk of their efforts on enhancement and derivative projects. But mix also depends on the firm's capabilities and its strategy. Given its engineering skills and manufacturing processes, for example, the returns available from enhancements and derivative projects may be quite attractive. If its strategy is to use that capability and its distribution strength to exploit market segments and niches pioneered by others, the aggregate project plan will have a higher mix of derivative projects than if the firm relied heavily on breakthrough projects. In the final analysis, the mix of project types is a strategic choice senior management makes in light of the firm's opportunities, capabilities, and strategies. The following examples illustrate how these factors combine in different firms and industries.

Changing Technology and a Focus on Platforms. In the early stages of an industry's development, firms typically compete and gain market position through products with dramatically superior performance on one or two dimensions of interest to the customer. As an industry matures and the opportunity to hit distinctive home runs on one or two technical dimensions decreases (often because technology becomes mature and shared more broadly), competitive success increasingly depends on giving customers an integrated, high-quality, system solution rather than a solution that is outstanding on only one or two dimensions of performance. In this context, platform projects become critical. Competitive success for a next-generation platform project tends to be determined by the system's collective capabilities and the excellence of the total solution on a number of different dimensions, not simply being superior on one or two dimensions.

One of the considerations in deciding when it is appropriate to go to a next-generation platform project is when there have been sufficient advances made in technology, features, and knowledge of customer needs on a range of dimensions so that they can be bundled together into a significantly better next-generation platform project. The difference between two platform generations in a given product family is not a home run on one or two dimensions, but rather greater or lesser degrees of incremental improvement on several dimensions simultaneously, integrated into a significantly better system solution. This gives the new-generation system an overall performance that is significantly superior to that achieved by the prior generation.

In the hospital bed industry, firms involved in designing, manufacturing, selling, and servicing electric hospital beds historically have faced a mature market under substantial pressure to contain capital expenditures and operating costs. In addition, technologies long had been considered mature and the payoff from new innovations largely incremental. In such a setting, it is not surprising that product generations (new platforms) have lasted from eight to twelve years. Derivatives and enhancements, however, have followed two quite different patterns. In the 1970s, as a number of hospitals in the United States were renovated and new hospitals were built, the prospect of an order for several hundred beds led firms to respond by customizing designs (doing derivative development) on almost every bed proposal. The result was extensive product line proliferation with most of the development resources being spent on derivative, incremental efforts.[3]

In the 1980s, with increased pressure for cost containment and much less new construction and renovation, Hill-Rom, the leading electric bed manufacturer, dramatically changed its resource allocation. Hill-Rom focused on developing three platform products—which shared many common parts and production processes—and providing add-on options to those basic platform designs. As a result, the mix of development projects at Hill-Rom shifted dramatically between the 1970s and 1980s from largely reactive, sustaining projects to proactive, next-generation platform efforts. In the early 1990s, with a variety of new technologies available and hospitals demanding beds that dramatically improved patient recovery and nurse productivity, Hill-Rom anticipated that generation life cycles would shorten and even more of its resources would be focused on platform projects.

Managing the Platform to Achieve Hyper-Variety. As markets mature and customers become more knowledgeable and sophisticated, the attractiveness of a standard product declines; customers seek tailored solutions. This tendency may be exacerbated if the product has a high fashion content and is sold through multiple distribution channels. In such environments, effectively managing product variety is crucial to competitive success. The market for portable cassette tape players and radios—"Walkmans"—pioneered by Sony illustrates the nature of these development challenges.

In the late 1980s Sony continued to dominate this market with over 200 models of Walkman available in 1990 alone. Yet these models were built off of three platforms, each of which had gone through periodic generational redesigns. The great bulk of Sony's development efforts were directed at a wide array of derivatives, enhancements, hybrids, and line extensions that offered something tailored to every niche, distribution channel, and competitor's product.[4]

These satisfied the full range of distribution requirements and end customer desires. Sony credited its continued dominance of the industry on this broad range of models and offerings. By basing 200-plus models on only three platform products/manufacturing processes, however, they were able to leverage their manufacturing investments dramatically and support continued improvements in cost and price in concert with continued improvements in performance. Clearly their project portfolio planning was an integral and essential part of their development and business strategies.

Choosing the mix of projects establishes how the firm will allocate resources at any point in time. But the aggregate project plan sets out how the portfolio of projects will evolve over time. Thus, choosing the sequence of projects is a critical element of the planning process. All of the project types are part of the sequence strategy, but of central interest are major platform projects for a given product family and the timing of derivative projects that will enhance and leverage that platform. When a new platform product is introduced, it usually replaces an older platform and its derivative offerings. If the new platform represents a significant improvement in system performance, several customers previously served by niche derivatives on the old platform will return to the core customer group because they will find the new system's capabilities superior to the derivative niche solution off the old platform. Thus a solid next-generation product will consolidate demand and build core volume soon after its introduction, providing leverage and scale for the primary operating assets of the firm. One reason for not usually introducing derivative products simultaneously with the next-generation platform is to take advantage of that consolidation and the competitive strength of the new platform. In addition, this allows development resources to be better leveraged: rather than working on the platform and derivatives concurrently, work can be done sequentially, without incurring any penalty in the marketplace. Experience in the world auto industry illustrates the issues involved in sequencing major platform projects.

In an extensive study of the world auto industry in the late 1980s, Clark and Fujimoto found that, on average, European platform generation designs changed every twelve years, U.S. generations changed every eight years, and Japanese generations changed every four years.[5] In exploring the sources of those differences, they discovered that European firms typically looked for larger performance improvement steps in the system solution provided by next-generation products, which took longer and were more costly to develop. When combined with lower volumes per model, this required higher prices (consistent with the higher performance characteristics) and longer design lives to earn a good return on development investments. Firms in the United States, which historically had not sought as much "perfection" in their next-generation platforms and had higher volumes per model, had found that a pattern of eight-year platform design lives was attractive. Finally, Japanese firms, faced with a more turbulent domestic market and with significant (i.e., two to one) advantages in development productivity, capitalized on performance improvements with shorter time spans between platform generations. They used development approaches that required fewer resources yet captured the latest improvements possible, enabling them to shorten the design life of platform generations to four years.

While all of the auto firms engaged in derivative enhancements in the interim years, those with longer design life patterns found it increasingly difficult to compete with the short, efficient, and system solution-oriented efforts of the Japanese firms. This competitive interaction scenario was analogous to that of the consumer electronics industry described in Chapter 1.

The timing of major platform efforts establishes the window of opportunity for derivatives and enhancements, but firms confront a number of strategic choices within the window. While many strategies for sequencing derivative projects are possible, the two depicted in Exhibit 4–4 illustrate the range of choices. Panel A of the exhibit presents the "steady stream" strategy. This scenario is often followed by business units offering a single product family derived from a single platform. Typically all of the unit's development resources will be focused on the platform during its development. Following its introduction, the team will go to work on a set of derivative projects, but their introduction will be spaced in a fairly steady stream until the development resources again focus on creation of the next generation platform and its introduction.

A very different pattern is the "secondary wave" of derivative projects, illustrated in Panel B. Business units with multiple product

EXHIBIT 4–4
Timing Platform and Derivative Project Sequences*

Market Introduction Year

		1	2	3	4	5	6	7	8

A. Steady Stream Strategy

Current
Platform: | Intro (year 1)

Derivative   1   Intro (year 3)
Projects: 2   Intro (year 4)
      3   Intro (year 5)
      4   Intro (year 6)

Follow-On
Platform: | Intro (year 7)

B. Secondary Wave Strategy

Current
Platform: | Intro (year 1)

      1   Intro (year 5)
Derivative   2   Intro (year 5)
Projects: 3   Intro (year 6)
      4   Intro (year 6)

Follow-On
Platform: | Intro (year 7)

* The steady stream strategy focuses first on a new platform, follows it with a steady stream of derivative projects, and eventually moves to the next generation platform. The secondary wave strategy does no enhancements immediately after the platform introduction, but instead uses derivatives later to extend the platform life and hold market share until the new platform is introduced.

lines, each having their own base platform, often pursue this strategy. The scenario works as follows: a critical mass of development resources is focused on a next-generation platform; once introduced, the key people go off to work on a platform for another product family. The recently introduced platform is left in the market for a couple of years with little or no derivative effort. As it begins to age and is challenged by competitors' newer platforms, development resources are refocused on derivatives in order to strengthen and extend the viability of the product line's existing platform in the marketplace. The wave of derivative projects provides training and feedback to those working in development and serves to prepare them for conducting the next-generation platform project. They receive market feedback on the prior platform, information on competitors' platform offerings (many of which may have been introduced recently), and information on market needs, some of which are to be addressed by the derivatives under development. Key people then bring that information together to shape the front-end definition of the next-generation platform project. Hill-Rom's electric bed approach, described earlier, is representative of this strategy.

An important variant of the "secondary wave" involves shortening the time between market introduction of major generations or platform offerings in a product family. Rather than sending the development team off to work on another product family immediately following the introduction of a new platform, they go to work immediately on a set of derivative models. This of course requires more real-time assessment of market response to the platform they have just introduced and much shorter feedback loops regarding competitors' products. Once the flurry of derivative products have been developed and introduced, the team then goes to work on the next-generation platform project for that same product family.

An excellent illustration of this secondary wave strategy is the single-use camera operations at Kodak, referred to earlier.[6] Prior to 1987, Kodak conducted a series of advanced development projects to explore alternatives for a single-use (disposable) 35 mm camera—a roll of film packaged in an inexpensive camera; once used, the film is processed and the camera discarded or recycled. A commercial version of a camera that used 110-size film was developed in the mid 1980s but without substantial market success. During 1987, a focused group of Kodak development people went to work on a first-generation platform project, largely in response to Fuji Film's demonstration of a 35 mm single-use camera. The Kodak project resulted in market introduction and volume production of the Fling 35 mm camera in January 1988 (later renamed the FunSaver). As that platform project was being completed, the front-end development resources were reassigned to two derivative projects: the Stretch (a panoramic, double-wide image version) and the Weekender (a waterproof version). By the end of 1988, both derivative projects were introduced and shipping in volume. As true derivative projects, the Stretch and Weekender took significantly less development time and fewer resources than the platform project, and required much less new tooling since they leveraged the existing automation and manufacturing process.

Thus within a year, Kodak had introduced a platform single-use camera and two derivative products. At that time it contemplated using those same resources on a third derivative product, a single-use camera with a built-in, single-use flash. However, after a couple of months of exploration, it was decided that rather than doing the flash version as a derivative project, competitively, it would be better to do it as the next-generation platform product for Kodak's 35 mm single-use family of cameras. Two things led to this conclusion. First, because of the electronic controls and connectors necessary for the flash version, substantially more development was required than for either the Stretch or Weekender derivative products. If Kodak had attempted to do the flash version as a derivative, it would have been somewhere halfway between a derivative and a platform product. The other consideration was that while the first generation was designed as disposable (and even referred to as such in some of the early advertising literature), market response suggested that Kodak would be better off positioning its cameras as single-use and recyclable. This would require a number of changes so that once the film processor removed the film, the remaining camera, lenses, and other parts of the single-use system could be recycled and reused.

The combination of both factors led Kodak to conclude that the flash version should be the first offering of the next-generation product. The product would incorporate a number of improvements to provide a better system solution, be recyclable (satisfying market desires and lowering costs), and, because the flash version would be the first to be introduced on that new platform, it would represent substantial performance improvement. In late 1990, Kodak introduced the FunSaver flash 35 mm camera and announced that, within a year, its three existing single-use offerings (FunSaver, Stretch, and Weekender) also would be recyclable. These three products were to be derivatives developed off the second generation platform—the FunSaver flash unit.

Developing an Aggregate Project Plan

Our discussion of different project types, the choice of an appropriate project mix, and the sequencing of platforms and derivatives underscores the power and importance of the aggregate project plan. Senior management at PreQuip grasped the importance of the concept as they learned about it and began to implement it. A procedure we have defined (and the one PreQuip's management followed) consists of eight sequential steps. Like any aggregate planning activity, the process does need to be repeated on a periodic basis, such as every six or twelve months.

PreQuip's management went through the first four steps of this procedure to identify the desired mix, estimate available capacity requirements, and take stock of the situation.

Step 1: Define the types or classes of development projects that are to be covered by the aggregate project plan. Most firms find it useful to start with the five categories or types outlined in Exhibit 4–3, and then refine them by specifying the characteristics to be used in deciding when individual projects encountered are of each type. This results in a set of criteria that can be used to classify any project as one of the five types.

Step 2: Define for a representative project of each type the critical resources and cycle time required for its complete development. Most often firms decide that the critical resource is the human resource, and seek to determine the full-time equivalent (FTE) development engineers, product marketing people, and manufacturing people required to go from project conception through market introduction. The cycle time is the calender time required for these activities. Firms also find it useful to specify the expected dollar cost of a representative project of each type, since that helps the organization shape its expectations and further distinguish the types of projects.

Step 3: Identify the existing resources available for development efforts (particularly the critical human resources for which the full-time equivalents were defined in Step 2) and currently active projects, with their requirements for completion. This results in explicitly identifying the available capacity and existing set of projects that will make demands on that capacity.

Step 4: Compute the capacity utilization implied by the results of Step 3. This can be done using a chart like Exhibit 4–1 that shows for appropriate time periods the amount of resources required for each of the currently "active" projects. The result is the capacity utilization of development resources over each of the next several time periods if projects are to be completed on schedule.

At the conclusion of Step 4, PreQuip's senior managers developed the summary data presented in Exhibit 4–1. The numbers were surprising. They found that total requirements over the next two quarters to complete the active projects were almost three times the available capacity. But the project mix itself was also out of balance. By breaking projects into categories based on the degree of change, they found that over 60 percent of their resources were devoted to derivative projects.

The next step for PreQuip (and for our planning procedure) was to forge a much closer link between its project mix and its strategy. Steps 5 through 7 create an aggregate project plan with this characteristic.

Step 5: Establish the desired future mix of projects by type. This entails balancing strategic choices against practical realities, in determining what percent of the critical resources should be committed to each of the five

Exhibit 4–5

Presenting the Aggregate Project Plan at PreQuip, 1990–1991*

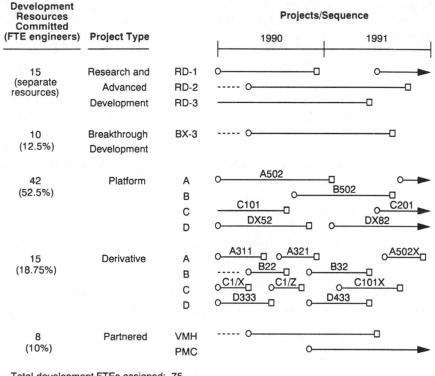

Development Resources Committed (FTE engineers)	Project Type		Projects/Sequence	
			1990	1991

Total development FTEs assigned: 75
Total development FTEs available: 80

O Project start   ------- Pre-project planning and analysis
□ Project completion   ——— Actual project

 * In 1990–1991, PreQuip developed an aggregate project plan that matched its strategic requirements. It included advanced development (fifteen dedicated engineers working on up to three projects), breakthrough (ten engineers on one project), platform (forty-two engineers on up to four projects), derivative (fifteen engineers on up to four projects), and partnered (eight engineers on up to two projects).

types of projects. (See the left-hand column of Exhibit 4–5.) In established firms, it is common for management to conclude that half or more of the development effort should be focused on next-generation platform projects, with 10 to 20 percent focused on derivative developments and 10 to 20 percent focused on each of the other three types—research and advanced development, breakthrough development, and partnered development. It is important that the mix specified be achievable in the time horizon for which the aggregate project plan is being created and that it be appropriate given the firm's strategy, innovation opportunities, and existing product-market requirements.

Step 6: Estimate the number of projects of each type that can be undertaken concurrently with existing resources. For instance, if the critical resource is development engineers and a firm has 100 full-time equivalents in development engineering, it can use the desired mix of projects (identified in Step 5), combined with the number of full-time equivalents required for a representative project (from step 2), to determine how many projects can be undertaken concurrently. For example, if the firm wants 50 percent of its effort spent on platform projects, and it has 100 development engineers, then on average, 50 development engineers will be committed to platform projects. If representative platform projects take eight quarters to perform, and, on average, require 15–20 full-time equivalents per quarter, then the firm can undertake three platform projects concurrently given its existing resources, its estimated requirements for a typical platform project, and its desired mix of efforts.

Step 7: Decide which projects to undertake. This includes reassessing the existing projects to make sure that they should be continued, as well as determining how many new projects of each type should be started and in what time periods. This is more than just "picking projects" from the existing list. The firm may need to repackage and reformulate projects in order to define the set that offers the greatest opportunity given the firm's strategy and resources. In the example just cited, if four platform projects are already underway and it is going to be another nine months before the first two are completed, the firm should not add another platform project for nine months. If it adds one sooner, it will be pursuing the canary cage approach described earlier. A firm that is unhappy with its mix of existing projects and its overcommitment of development resources may decide to drop projects currently on the active list, add new resources, or subcontract some of its yet-to-be-started projects in order to transition faster to its desired mix and level of capacity utilization.

In PreQuip's case, senior management believed that platform projects were critical to its competitive success and required much more attention and focus. After reshaping and redefining its platform projects, PreQuip developed the aggregate project plan presented in Exhibit 4–5, which lays out a sequence of platform projects for the four product families in PreQuip's line. The painful part of the planning process is evident in the resources devoted to derivative projects. The plan calls for a substantial reduction in resources devoted to "sustaining" projects, and this required PreQuip to kill or postpone several projects. Senior management believed, however (and their belief was confirmed in subsequent events), that a more focused effort would improve development productivity. This would permit the organization to get more actual work done over the three-year planning horizon, even though there would be fewer projects in process at any one time.

Taking into account the platform and derivative resources and the engineers allocated to breakthrough projects and partnerships, the plan called for commitments of only 75 of the 80 full-time equivalent engineers in the development organization. PreQuip, thus, provided for a small "capacity cushion" in the plan. Where aggregate planning is a well-known and practiced discipline (e.g., operations management), firms have discovered that the higher the level of uncertainty about individual project requirements, the greater the need there is for a capacity cushion (slack in capacity commitments) so that those uncertainties can be accommodated without delaying all future projects. The analog in product and process development is recognizing the need to leave some percentage of the total aggregate development capacity (in PreQuip's case, 5 FTEs) uncommitted to specific projects so that as uncertainties occur throughout the year those resources can be used to cope with them.

The plan laid out in Exhibit 4–5 addresses the sequence of products and associated processes PreQuip will bring to the market over the three-year planning horizon. But if it stops there, it is incomplete. The plan must also address how these projects and other related activities will improve the performance of development. Thus, the final step of the aggregate planning process:

Step 8: Determine and integrate into the project plan changes required to improve development performance (speed, productivity, and quality) over time. Projects not only create new products, but also have the potential to build new development capability. A project may be the vehicle for introducing a new computer-aided design (CAD) system or a new approach to project organization. In addition, new systems and procedures—such as a new engineering change process—need to be planned and coordinated with ongoing development projects. Thus, the aggregate project plan needs to identify where the firm intends to make significant changes and how the changes will be connected to product and process development. In PreQuip's case, for example, the major changes were a restructuring of the engineering organization (e.g., far fewer projects per engineer) and the introduction of a new CAD system. Management planned to phase in the restructuring during the first year of the plan, while the RD-3 advanced development effort would be the pilot project for the CAD system.

As senior management at PreQuip discovered, developing an aggregate project plan involves a relatively simple and straightforward procedure. But actually carrying it out—moving from the largely ad hoc "active" project list to a robust, effective set of projects that matches and reinforces the business strategy—involves hard choices and discipline. In PreQuip's case (and in the case of every other company we have studied), the difficulty and significance of those choices have made strong leadership from senior management imperative. Without that leadership, organizations that have habitually overcommitted themselves will have great difficulty killing and postponing projects, or resisting the short-term pressures that drive the organization to spend the bulk of its resources "fighting fires."

Getting to an aggregate project plan is not easy, but working through the procedure is a crucial part of creating a development strategy. Indeed, it is crucial to understand that the specific plan itself is not as important as the planning process. The plan will change as events unfold and managers make adjustments. But choosing the mix, defining the sequence, and creating the projects to support raise crucial questions about how product and process development ought to be linked to the firm's competitive opportunities and challenges. Laying the results out in a specific plan over time gives clarity and direction to the overall development effort and helps to lay the foundation for outstanding performance in specific projects.

Study Questions

1. Consider Exhibit 4–1. What explains the relationship between engineering requirements and available engineering capacity at PreQuip? What are the implications of the patterns you observe in the exhibit?
2. What is a platform project? How does it differ from a breakthrough project? What specific criteria would you recommend that firms establish to define platform projects?
3. What considerations are important in determining the appropriate mix of development projects?
4. Consider Exhibit 4–4. What is the difference between a steady stream and a secondary wave strategy? Under what conditions will the one be more appropriate than the other?
5. What problems might a firm like PreQuip confront in defining its development capacity? How would you propose to address those problems?
6. Suppose you were in charge of the aggregate planning process for a manufacturer of computer printers. You discover that the firm has fifteen projects underway, but only has the resources to complete six to eight of them. How would you recommend the firm proceed to reduce the number of projects? What issues must the firm confront?

Ceramics Process Systems (B)

In early July of 1989, Bob Block, manager of sales at Ceramics Process Systems (CPS) Corporation, walked into the office of Cathryn Sundback, manager for molded products process engineering, with proposals for three new products—a sensor package, a turbocharger rotor, and an integrated circuit substrate. "Here's what the customers are looking for," Block remarked. "Can you take a look at the list of their requirements? I'd sure like to get a bid from you by the end of the week so we can move on it. We have to keep the pipeline moving."

Sundback looked at the sheet on her desk. Block was right about keeping the pipeline moving, but the real problem was to get things into *and out* of the pipeline. The projects looked possible, but the current backlog was a problem. She would have to talk things over with her people and get everyone on board. The engineers always had something to say and getting their consensus was important. As she read through the project descriptions, Sundback reflected on where CPS had been.

> Two years ago we failed with a project very similar to this sensor project. But we have learned a lot since then, and I think this one is doable now. The customer wants a delivery promise but you never know for sure on projects like this. One little unexpected tooling change could set us back weeks. Customers are willing to work with us, but given the uncertainties of their own development, they want us to get it done as quickly as possible. And we have a lot on our plate right now.

Of course, there was more to the decision than delivery time. Over the last few months, Peter Loconto, president and chief executive officer of

This case was prepared by Research Fellow Brent Barnett under the supervision of Professor Kim B. Clark.

CPS, had been pretty blunt about the need to find projects with real commercial potential. Sundback knew that the proposals on her desk might be just what CPS should be doing. But with several of her current projects late there was a lot of pressure not only to get product out the door, but to learn how to make the development process run better.

The Company

CPS, the brainchild of a group of MIT scientists, was founded in 1984. From the outset, CPS was a technology-focused company, having been formed with the explicit mission to commercialize a new approach to making ceramics, applying new scientific knowledge to the age-old art of ceramics processing. As the director of R&D, Bruce Novich, explained, "We go on the principle that if you don't understand ceramic processing you can't control it. People in ceramics have never understood what was really going on. We want to change that."

CPS produced a wide range of ceramic products used in industries from advanced engines to biomedical devices to steelmaking. The firm focused primarily on the microelectronics market, however, where it aspired to be a U.S. technology leader in the market for packaging and interconnecting high performance, high-density integrated circuits. Its technological advantage was based on a number of proprietary processes which enabled it to manufacture products exhibiting more uniformly superior strength, surface smoothness, and wear resistance than typically available from existing products and more traditional suppliers. (See Exhibit 1 for typical products.)

While much of CPS's initial funding had come from venture capital, the firm had also pursued joint development agreements with a number of large corporations, including Alcoa, Hoechst-Celanese, Vesuvius (a leading producer of refractory products), and General Motors. For CPS, such agreements provided funding for the development of their technology and comprised a large portion of the total revenue. For the partner firms, such joint agreements allowed them access to new developments in ceramic processing which might be crucial, as in the case of GM, were ceramics to find application in automotive engines.

In its first few years, CPS had grown rapidly. By the time it went public in July 1987 the company employed over 150 people. The past year, however, had brought many changes. A major product line had been discontinued resulting in a work-force reduction of 50 manufacturing employees. Operations had been consolidated from two facilities in Cambridge and Watertown to a modern 36,000 square foot facility in Milford, Massachusetts, thirty-five miles west of Cambridge. Loconto, previously head of CPS's superconductor subsidiary, had been installed as president

263

Picture and Description of Typical Products Custom Molded Ceramic Components

 Capability

Ceramics Process Systems proprietary QUICK-SET™ Molding Process produces cost-effective net-shape ceramic components with:

> *Complex geometries*
>
> *Tight dimensional tolerances*
>
> *High-density microstructures*
>
> *Uniform material properties.*

The QUICKSET™ Molding Process produces components made of virtually any ceramic material system. In addition to the material systems listed, Ceramics Process Systems will engineer a custom material to meet your specific requirements.

Left to right: Silicon Aluminum Oxynitride rotor; Aluminum Nitride cavity substrate; Silicon Nitride tappet; Aluminum Oxide nozzle; and Zirconia toughened Alumina die.

 Applications

Custom molded ceramic components produced with the QUICKSET™ Molding Process have a wide variety of uses.   Illustrative examples include:

> *Integrated circuit package components with superior thermal conductivity.*
>
> *Rotors and other components for gas turbine engines with superior high temperature properties.*
>
> *Nozzles and dies with excellent wear and abrasion resistance.*
>
> *Bulk superconductors in complex shapes for research applications.*
>
> *Tappets for automotive engines with superior strength-to-weight ratio.*

and chief executive officer. Revenues continued to grow, reaching $1.8 million in the second quarter of 1989, which represented a 100% increase over the second quarter of 1988. However, CPS's venture capitalists had become alarmed at the rate at which the firm was using up its capital and piling up operating losses (see Exhibit 2). The past year had been spent instituting stricter cost controls to bring costs in line with revenues, an effort that had gone a long way in reestablishing confidence among investors.

EXHIBIT 2

Financial Statement

	Quarters Ended		Six-Months Ended	
	1 July 1989	*30 June 1988*	*1 July 1989*	*30 June 1988*
Statement of Operations				
Revenues				
Collaborative Development				
Agreements	$1,616,156	$ 780,000	$ 3,006,025	$ 1,530,000
Product Sales	179,007	206,566	468,848	363,373
Total Revenue	1,795,164	986,566	3,474,873	1,893,373
Expenses				
Research and Development	909,587	1,257,510	1,524,620	2,601,914
Manufacturing Costs	429,286	1,389,257	952,468	2,486,401
General and Administrative	607,362	1,080,262	1,309,431	1,793,555
Total Operating Expenses	1,946,235	3,727,029	3,786,519	6,881,870
Operating Loss	(151,071)	(2,740,463)	(311,646)	(4,988,497)
Interest Income	109,733	156,135	221,782	373,419
Interest Expense	(34,313)	(42,226)	(61,698)	(66,903)
Net Other Income	75,420	113,909	160,084	306,516
Net Loss	($ 75,651)	($2,626,554)	($ 151,562)	($4,681,981)
Net Loss Per Share	($0.02)	($0.55)	($0.03)	($0.99)
Weighted Average Number of				
Shares Outstanding	4,919,250	4,752,097	4,910,758	4,734,503

Condensed Balance Sheet	1 July 1989	31 December 1988
Cash and Short-Term Investments	$3,611,930	$ 5,600,783
Other Current Assets	531,571	713,153
Property and Equipment, net	1,181,954	1,520,551
Other Assets, net	889,840	393,618
Total Assets	$6,185,295	$ 8,228,105
Deferred Revenue	$ 545,736	$ 1,561,872
Current Portion of Long-Term Debt	544,329	602,687
Other Current Liabilities	1,148,703	1,828,642
Long-Term Debt	355,210	515,118
Stockholders' Equity	3,591,317	3,719,786
Total Liabilities and		
Stockholders' Equity	$6,185,295	$ 8,228,105

This Statement is Unaudited

Advanced Ceramics Markets

During the late 1970s and throughout the 1980s, advanced ceramics had found applications in a variety of global markets. These markets generally were grouped into two broad categories: structural and electronic. Structural applications of advanced ceramics included potentially large volume uses as a substitute for metal in gas turbine and diesel engine components. Less eye-catching, but potentially more important, were electronic packaging applications for integrated circuits. Currently a billion dollar business, electronic packaging was expected to grow to $5 billion by 1995. This market was segmented into two parts—basic packaging and high performance. In the low end, basic portion were simple Cerdips (ceramic, dual in-line packages) and pin grid arrays (PGA), often selling for a few cents per package. In contrast, for high performance ASIC (application specific integrated circuit) chips, in some cases costing $800 a unit, manufacturers were looking for greater reliability and performance in the ceramic substrate. The market for high lead count, high interconnect packages was expected to grow from $40 million to $500 million by 1995. Thus, while past growth in the high-end had been slow, it appeared to be gaining momentum.

Overall, the market for electronic ceramic packages was dominated by Kyocera, a Japanese firm. Kyocera had taken the ceramics world by storm in the late 1970s by moving quickly into the burgeoning semiconductor industry to gain a commanding market share in microelectronic packaging, displacing much more established ceramic firms along the way. In the ensuing ten years Kyocera had continued to grow rapidly, in step with the rapid growth of the semiconductor industry. Although market share had shrunk somewhat due to inroads by other Japanese ceramic manufacturers, Kyocera still enjoyed an enviable reputation for technical prowess as well as manufacturing efficiency. The word in the industry was that Kyocera had 1,500 people in its development labs, a tremendous resource which could be directed at a wide variety of problems. As one CPS employee described it, "For Kyocera, it isn't a question of whether they can do it, it's whether they want to do it. If they want to do it, they will."

The challenge to CPS was to find applications where they could apply their proprietary technology in growing markets. With this strategy, CPS avoided "me-too" products where they would be a second source on an established product. Instead they hoped to get in early on the development of next generation products. To make this strategy work, interaction with customers was crucial. This meant that CPS had to become part of the customer's development process, where their materials and processing expertise could be used to solve difficult problems.

In its short lifetime, CPS had, however, developed a reputation for solving hard problems for customers. CPS's unique expertise allowed them to land prestigious contracts such as a recent Defense Advanced Research Projects Agency (DARPA) contract for development of super-conducting wire for electric motors and a joint development contract on gas turbine rotors with another firm. And a number of new contracts came from customers who had approached one of the larger, more experienced firms like Kyocera only to discover that those firms were unable to or unwilling to solve their problems.

In microelectronic circuit technology, the ceramic packaging had for many years been considered routine. Now, with the increased use of VLSI chips, the packaging had become the limiting factor in the performance of the circuit. In response, computer and electronic firms were scrambling to find new packaging solutions. For some firms this meant going to outside suppliers for the first time. Although reluctant to work in joint development projects, electronic firms often were desperate enough to at least try such arrangements.

The same was true in structural applications. Here the customers were often traditional manufacturers with expertise in forming and finishing metal parts. In the rapid push toward new materials, these companies were looking for solutions that offered higher heat resistance and lighter weight for applications like internal engine components and turbocharger rotors. Structural products also had a variety of uses in medicine and high temperature industrial processes. In all of these environments, joint development contracts were a good solution both for CPS and potential customers.

CPS Technology—The Manufacturing Process

Production of a typical ceramic part began with the combination of a clay or mineral powder in a ceramic slurry, a solution of water or organic chemical. This slurry could then be poured or injected into a mold to form ceramic parts, extruded into pipes or spread as a sheet to form ceramic tapes before being placed in an oven for firing. Research efforts at CPS had focused on two different forming methods or "processes" for making high-performance ceramics, tape casting and injection molding. Both of these processes were known to be difficult, "the toughest processes known to man," according to one researcher. But in each case unique powder preparation and control of microstructure gave CPS a unique processing advantage.

In the first process, tape casting, ceramic slurry was spread out in a thin film, dried and cut into shapes, and then stacked and joined with

267

adhesives to form laminated substrates for electronic applications. In this arena, CPS's proprietary slurry preparation steps imparted exceptional smoothness to the substrate, thus allowing reliable deposition of fine-lined metallic patterns.

The second process, injection molding, was an established technology for molding ceramics, having been adopted many years before from the plastics industry. But in the view of CPS engineers, traditional ceramic manufacturers had never recognized how different molding ceramics was from molding plastics. As expressed by one CPS engineer, "Ceramics firms have used the exact same molding equipment that people use in plastics. But ceramics are very different. In fact, the only thing they have in common is that you can get them to flow into a mold but how you do that is quite different."

In the CPS proprietary QUICKSET™ molding process, ceramic slurry was prepared using a specific mixture of components, and then the slurry was injected into the mold using a modified syringe. The filled molds were then allowed to set. For a typical mold, 30 parts could be molded in an eight-hour day. Once the slurry had set, the parts were removed from the mold and put into a drier. Normally drying took one day's time, but for larger parts it could take several days.

After drying, the parts were fired and then ground to their final shape. CPS currently used outside vendors for the grinding but it was anticipated that the grinding step would eventually be eliminated entirely. This was, in fact, one of the crucial advantages of the CPS technology. CPS engineers felt that the CPS process allowed unusual control of shrinkage, leading to more predictability in the size of the final part and hence less need for grinding. Elimination of the grinding step could give CPS a real cost advantage in the marketplace.

The QUICKSET™ process was itself still in development, having never been applied on a large-scale manufacturing line. The current implementation used hand-operated injection devices and inexpensive prototype molds; more automated facilities would be required for larger volume production. Recognizing this, CPS had developed a pilot low-pressure injection molding operation in a joint agreement with another firm. This operation was being used to test out the process on a larger scale. Don Page, vice president of manufacturing, explained the underlying philosophy of the test line. "What we want to do is get the basic capability in-house so that when we are ready to go into volume production we have all the expertise and understanding in place. We are still a ways from that point but we don't think it is too early to start thinking about the issues of scaling up the process."

This experimental line was capable of producing parts on a three minute cycle time. That cycle time would allow production rates up to 200 parts per day for a single machine. Page continued, "We anticipate having 10 of these machines in a row all working continuously. That is one of the real advantages of the molding technology—flexibility. The ability to do many kinds of parts and give quick response time will allow us to achieve a manufacturing advantage. You can start with a technical advantage like we have, but eventually someone will copy you. We need to have that first-mover advantage, but also have an established sustainable advantage in manufacturing."

At this point, neither of the CPS processes was free from difficulty. Although a fundamental belief of the founding scientists had been that process control would improve yields and provide increased reliability, the current state of the art was still far from those visionary anticipations. Both the tape casting and molding processes suffered from high failure rates and low overall yields. Yet little by little, progress was being made, and R&D engineers confidently predicted that overall yields would easily top 90% in eventual volume manufacturing, a yield unheard of in high performance ceramic applications.

Organization

In June of 1989, CPS employed 75 people. Of those, roughly fifteen were administrative, another five were in marketing and sales, and ten were manufacturing employees. In R&D, ten engineers were devoted solely to CPS Superconductor while the remainder belonged to the main R&D organization. The organizational structure of R&D had evolved gradually over time. Initially all R&D personnel had worked on one or two major projects. But as the customer base had grown, engineers gradually acquired expertise in particular products, materials, and process steps. R&D was eventually organized into formal groups: materials development, headed by Ran-Rong Lee; process development for molded products, headed by Sundback; process development for laminated products, headed by Ellen Tormey; and design engineering, headed by Kevin Fennessy. The manager of each of those areas reported to Novich, the director of R&D (see Exhibit 3 for an organization chart).

While the formal organization was important for directing project assignments and allocating funds and equipment resources, the group was small enough that there was a lot of interaction between materials development engineers and process engineers. Sundback explained how this often worked. "Officially the material engineers report to Lee. But in practice, I work directly with them on a regular basis. Since I have been here longer than just about anyone else, my influence can sometimes extend beyond my group."

The materials development group was composed of both B.S. and Ph.D. level ceramics engineers who had acquired extensive knowledge

Exhibit 3
Organization Chart

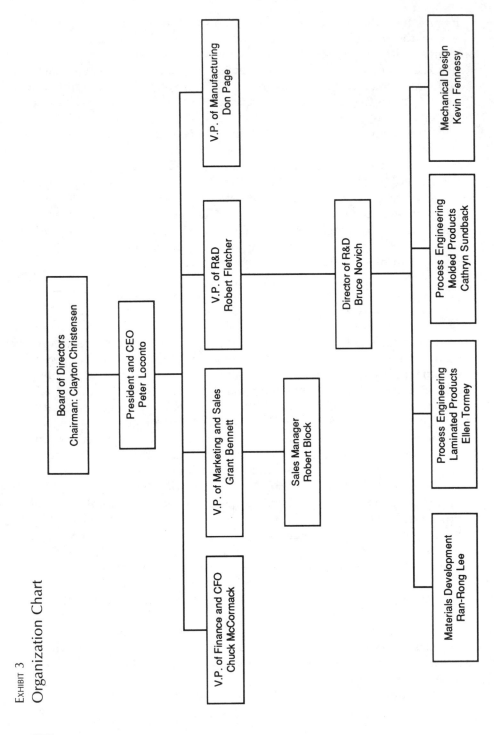

of the basic properties of materials and how different ceramic materials could be mixed and fired to achieve certain properties. The two process development groups, on the other hand, included a few ceramics engineers but were composed primarily of people with experience in chemical engineering. These engineers specialized in the principles of flowing and processing solutions and powders. They could take a particular material composition and design a dispersion with good flow properties by adjusting the powder size distribution and mix of additives.

The R&D group was, however, far from homogeneous. Novich, for example, had a Ph.D. in chemical engineering, having studied soil mechanics for his Masters' work. CPS was proud of the diversity of its engineering talent. In the view of management, the diversity among the R&D engineers was a necessity in solving the hard problems inherent in a new field. They pointed to the QUICKSET™ process as a prime example of the importance of this interdisciplinary approach, it being a direct application of technology from an entirely different industry.

Equipment used by the molding group was housed in the prototype molding shop. On a normal day this room, about 20' × 40' in size, was a flurry of activity, with individual engineers preparing slurries, pouring molds, and drying parts. In an adjoining room, the furnaces for firing were also busy with activity. Many of the molded products required a special high vacuum furnace. Recent customer orders had increased demand on this furnace so much that it was used to capacity, even after following strict scheduling guidelines.

Product Development

Ideas for new development projects originated with the marketing department. In laminated products, many projects came from contacts that CPS marketing representatives initiated with users of microelectronic packages. On occasion, a Kyocera customer looking for a second source would approach CPS about trying to qualify. But for molded products, new contacts were mostly the result of word of mouth, which brought to CPS customers looking for solutions to difficult problems. Generally such customers knew very little about CPS but were anxious to solve a particularly hard problem and had heard of CPS's reputation.

Initial customer requests were followed up with visits by Block. With his background in technical ceramics, Block was able to understand and characterize the needs of individual customers. Often the challenge was helping customers to understand their own needs. In the increasingly competitive world, many customers found themselves in a new technological arena where they were unable to specify their technical requirements. They just needed something that would work.

Quoting

Until recently, all potential molded products were channeled through Novich. With the growth in the number of products, however, it had become standard procedure for Block to approach Sundback directly. Sundback would then prepare a proposal or quote after consulting with Novich and other engineers in the product group. The quote would then be passed through Block to the customer, who would either accept or reject it. While the quoting process in laminated products led to only one in ten quotes being accepted, in molded products there had never been a quote that was not accepted.

In the past year CPS had learned a lot about making quotes for molded products. Originally quotes were based on estimates of production costs for single parts. Soon, however, they recognized that the real development costs were much higher. As one engineer explained, "While a per-piece pricing approach might work in a high volume environment, for just a few pieces, the non-recurring engineering (NRE) expenses were killing us. We would quote a certain cost and then when we ordered the tooling it would cost more than the value of the entire order."

CPS had since hired a design engineer who prepared estimates of tooling costs for each potential product. The result was that the quoted cost now more accurately reflected the true costs of development. Block commented, "Of course we had to get customers to pay for the tooling. But that was really a matter of convincing them of the fact that small volume development is a different game. You have to remember that they have never done this before either."

To estimate lead times, Sundback calculated the time required for the entire development from rough estimates of the time required for the major engineering stages (see Exhibit 4 for a description of the engineering sequence). In general, the core activity of development was experimentation with the process of making parts. This process of experimentation introduced a large degree of uncertainty into the development. While CPS engineers were confident that they could find a way to solve almost any problem, it was mostly a matter of how many different experiments they would have to try to find a way that worked. One scientist compared the development process to Edison's discovery of the light bulb, explaining, "You just have to keep thinking of things that might work and keep trying them. Sometimes you get it on the first try and sometimes it takes you a thousand tries."

In general, however, Sundback had found that engineers needed an average of three or four experimentation loops at each development stage, that is, they had to try three or four ways of solving the problem before they narrowed in on a viable solution. Knowing approximate times for each loop thus allowed her to get an estimate of the total time

EXHIBIT 4

Flow of New Projects

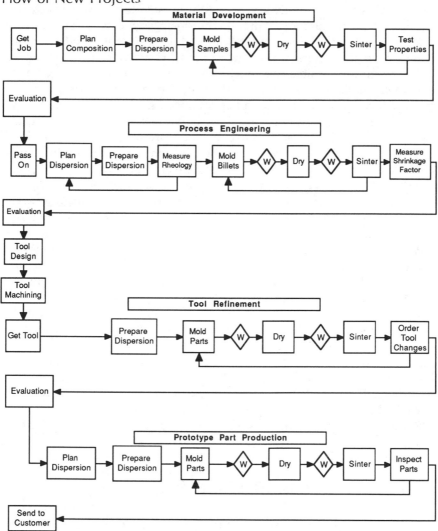

required to finish the project. For projects that posed particular difficulties at certain stages, she generally used the "factor of two" rule, multiplying the average time for those stages by two when estimating development times. For simple modifications, on the other hand, the experimentation time could often be cut in half since it took only one or two experimental loops to fine tune a particular step in the process.

There were, of course, many nuances of each new project that might prove exceptionally difficult. These had to be anticipated but could never be completely accounted for in advance. This was always a concern in quoting delivery times. Experience with the technology was invaluable in making the tough judgments. As Sundback suggested, "I look at our past experience in doing similar things. But I also look at what unique things have to be done. Is it a new material? How tricky is the molding? What might be possible roadblocks? And then I allow some extra time for problems. You have to allow time for the inevitable crisis. On one project, for example, our supplier stopped making the powder. We went to powder from a new supplier but then we found that the process wouldn't work. So we had to backtrack and reformulate the process."

With the inherent uncertainty in the experimentation time, there was considerable subjectivity in the quoted delivery date. With new technology it was hard to say exactly how long it would take. "Sure, being late is a danger," argued Novich, "but we're coming down a learning curve. You're going to be late some of the time. With new technology, you run the risk of delivering late 50% of the time. Which is better: to quote short lead times and be late some of the time, or to quote long lead times and not get the contract? For me, I would rather take the risk of not delivering. If we were too conservative, we wouldn't get any contracts and we'd never come down the learning curve."

It was not uncommon, however, for engineers to feel that lead times were too short given the newness of the technology. As one engineer described it, "Bruce and Cathryn see the potential. We see the reality." But this attitude didn't bother Novich. "I know they feel that way. I have very open relationships with these people. But first of all, if you're afraid to fail, you better not be working here. Second, our engineers can usually do a lot more than they think. And while you don't want everyone to be risk-takers, Cathryn and I tend to balance each other out on that."

Product/Process Engineering

Once a quote was accepted, development proceeded through five engineering phases. This development sequence had evolved over time and was still being adjusted and reevaluated.

Materials Development (Phase 1)

For the typical CPS customer, the desired combination of mechanical, thermal, and electrical properties could not be obtained with any known material. But CPS advertised the ability to develop entirely new materials. The initial development work thus focused on developing a material which could meet the customer's property requirements. Developing the right material meant finding a mixture of chemical compounds which would give the desired properties. Based on scientific theory of the properties of ceramic materials, CPS engineers designed a material composition which they hoped would provide the required level of performance. The responsible engineer then molded five or ten simple test billets, fired them for long cycles to ensure 100% dense material, and tested them for the required property. Seldom did the theory enable engineers to hit the target the first time, but with a couple of tries, they generally got close enough to satisfy the customer.

Process Development (Phase 2)

Once a material had been developed to match the customer's requirements, the project moved on to the process development stage. The central focus in this phase was to first find a formulation or dispersion which minimized shrinkage and then measure the characteristic shrinkage or shrinkage factor of the dispersion. The central challenge in the manufacture of ceramics had always been the control of shrinkage during firing. Large variations in shrinkage were for the most part considered an unchangeable fact of the business. But these variations made manufacture of high tolerance parts virtually impossible. The CPS QUICKSET™ process, however, improved the reproducibility of shrinkage. This reproducibility was key in the CPS strategy since high reproducibility allowed consistency in the tolerance of finished parts and would thus eliminate the need for grinding.

To determine a satisfactory process, engineers prepared different dispersions and used "ideal" molds to make simple billets which would allow precise measurement of the shrinkage. The goal of such experiments was to get a high solids loading which would reduce minimize shrinkage of the part. But if the solids loading were too high, the slurry would become too thick to fill the mold well. As one engineer described it, "It is like walking along the edge of a cliff. If you get too close, one gust of wind could push you over the edge. We don't want that but we still end up pushing the limits." In practice, the engineers tended to first push the limits. Once the slurry became too thick to mold well, they pulled back to a compromise solids content for use in the actual process.

Tool Design (Phase 3)

The third phase in development was the design of a tool. Over the past year, CPS had recognized that tool design was vital not only in reducing lead time but also in controlling development cost. They found, for example, that a minor change in the design of a particular tool could often save hundreds of dollars in machining cost. Thus while the actual machining of the tool was done by an outside vendor, CPS had hired a design engineer who did all tool design and worked with outside vendors to insure that molds were made to required specifications. This arrangement had the added benefit of providing a closer relationship with vendors and thus providing a way to get quicker turnaround on rush orders.

In design of the mold, allowance had to be made for anticipated shrinkage of the part. If, for example, the shrinkage factor were 10%, the tool needed be 10% larger than the part itself. Because of this requirement, engineers had typically not worried about tooling until the process development was completed and the shrinkage factor had been defined. At some point, however, this was changed. Sundback explained, "Eventually we recognized that tooling could actually be designed and ordered before exact specification of the shrinkage factor. So now we send out the plans and the vendor does some of the work. Then, last of all, we specify the shrinkage factor. Since tool machining can take four weeks, most of which is deadtime for us, giving the vendor early information cuts our actual deadtime to less than two weeks so we save two weeks in development."

Tool Refinement (Phase 4)

When the tool was received from the vendor, it was tested and refined in use. The crucial test was how consistently parts could be extracted from the mold without breaking. Repeated molding of parts highlighted removal problems. Engineers then identified the necessary changes in the mold and the mold was returned to the vendor for re-machining and grinding. Fixing the tool was, however, not the only option open to engineers. As Sundback explained, "There are always lots of ways to fix problems. In the past, we tried getting around mold release problems by changing the process formulation. We would change the composition and try again. But with time we found that messing with the process just opens a can of worms. You can spend forever trying to find the right conditions. Now I hammer on people to just take the easy route and send the tool back for modification."

Prototype Part Production (Phase 5)

Once the engineers had a tool that worked to their satisfaction, they continued to produce parts but with a new focus on optimizing the material properties. By changing the firing schedule, for example, they could often improve the density of the material and hence the strength of the parts. During this phase, the engineers made parts in batches of

20 or 30 at a time and sent them to a vendor for polishing, a step which took two more weeks. Finally they inspected the finished parts and sent them to the customer. Yields were still not always high. Many of the parts broke coming out of the molds or in the firing step. Others broke during firing or polishing. But by molding enough parts they were generally able to fill the customer's order.

Customer Interaction

Rather than contract for the entire development at once, CPS processed all development contracts as a series of sequential orders. Orders thus fell into three broad groups: (1) initial orders specifying the material properties and shape required, (2) orders requiring changes in material or tooling, and (3) orders of parts using already developed material and tooling.

The first type of order, an initial development contract with a customer, was usually an order for a limited number (10 or 20) of test bars or parts made of the new material. Initiating such new orders required extensive interaction between CPS engineers and the customer to define the exact specifications for the customer's requirements. Rather than make parts with a variety of properties and allow customers to choose between them, CPS found it important, even at this point, to have exact specs that could serve as targets for the engineers to work toward. CPS had on occasion tried to develop materials for vague specs and had found that firms often walked away from the development still trying to define their needs. For Sundback, these specs provided more than anything a way to force the customers to define their needs before CPS invested engineering time in the development.

Customer testing of the first order of parts often suggested necessary design changes in material and tooling. In addition, since the customer was pursuing its own development cycle, new needs often arose, also requiring changes in the material or tooling of the part. Such changes were handled as change orders, orders requesting a standard lot of previously produced parts but including the necessary modifications. These modifications could be very simple or quite extensive. Marketing could approve simple changes but for extensive changes, Novich or Sundback had to approve the changes before the order could be accepted.

The third type of order was the repeat order where a customer simply needed extra shipments of parts for internal testing. Generally, in this case, the customer placed an order for a specific number of parts to be delivered on a regular schedule. Often it was a simple matter of a phone call to request an additional batch of 100 parts or order a batch of 100 to be delivered at the first of every month for the next six months. While the primary source of orders in molded products had always been entirely new materials and associated tooling for customers, with time the bulk of the orders had come to be dominated by these repeat orders of previously developed parts.

A typical customer relationship evolved from a type 1 order to type 2 and then to type 3 (see Exhibit 5). With this pattern of sequential ordering there was never a formal contract to pursue the development into volume manufacturing. But although not formalized, acceptance of each order implied a mutual willingness to pursue the development into volume manufacturing.

EXHIBIT 5

Order Types for Molded Products

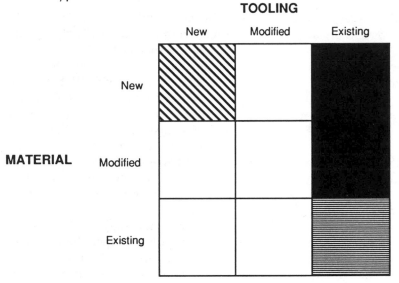

TOOLING

Standard Type 1 order: a new project requiring a new material and new tooling.

Range of possibilities for a Type 2 order: customers may request modifications in material and/or tooling.

Type 3 orders fall in this region: these call for the production of previously developed parts and require no changes in material or tooling.

Generally excluded space since orders with new material or modifications in the material inevitably require new or modified tooling.

The Atlas Electronics Project

A recent success story in molded products had been the Atlas Electronics project. It seemed to embody what CPS was good at and what they hoped to do for their customers. In 1988 the Atlas Electronics Corporation approached CPS with an interesting challenge. In the development of an advanced sensor chip they had recognized the need for a specialized substrate material which would exactly match the chip in thermal expansion. Atlas had been through the entire telephone directory of ceramics manufacturers before coming to CPS. None had been willing to take on what seemed like an extremely risky development project.

This was a project with great volume potential—easily 100 parts per day or more. And while there was some skepticism and discussion among CPS management because of the apparent difficulty of the project, when the pros and cons were discussed the pros finally won out. "After all, if we don't take on hard jobs we'll never know how good we really are," suggested one R&D manager. "It was simply a matter of needing the work," said another. They agreed on an initial fee of $30,000, plus fixed costs.

The original material development took two months. From the outset, what seemed like simple problems turned out to be much more difficult than expected. The part was to be made from a new combination of materials, whose properties were not well-known—at least relative to traditional ceramic powders like alumina. In this case, the lack of good characterization proved to be a nightmare when it came to carrying out controlled experiments. "Not every powder is like alumina," noted one engineer. "Just because you can buy it doesn't mean it is uniform or well-characterized."

Nonetheless, Atlas was pleased with the results. But as was fairly common in such development projects, testing showed that they needed something better. When they tested the product they realized that it did not have the required strength for the application. While the material met Atlas specifications, the specifications did not reflect the actual requirements of the application. "They really hadn't done their homework," explained Block, "so when they came to us the second time, they were desperate. They had their backs to the wall and were begging for help." Quick calculations indicated that any improvements in the current material could never give the desired increase in properties that Atlas needed. The project would require going to an entirely new material. Never prone to turn down a good challenge, CPS agreed to develop the new material.

But first there was the issue of cost. With the increasing financial pressures, marketing was told to "cover our costs." Block described the situation:

> I have a reputation for being the price-gouger. And in this case I lived up to my name. I had a key discussion with R&D about pricing and decided on $100 per part. So that's what we went with. It wasn't exactly right, but it was in the ballpark. If we do a hundred parts at a hundred dollars a piece that's $10,000. After all, it could take up to a full month of someone's time to do all those parts so we better get that much. Most likely we'll lose a little. Of course, when the Atlas guy heard the $100 figure, he hit the ceiling. But after he had a chance to see our facility and see how we worked, he fell in line. That has been a key to making this project work. They have learned to understand us as much as we have learned to understand them.

Work on the new material was initiated, and in spite of the newness, within a few weeks the material was ready for customer testing. It took a few iterations back and forth, but the target for thermal expansion was met. Atlas was elated and the project then moved into process development. Within two months, the dispersion system had been developed and within two more months parts were being shipped. Again Atlas was very happy with the results.

Widely credited for the success of the project was the close interaction between engineers of the two firms. As described by one CPS employee, "The marketing guys were smart enough to get out of the picture. They just left the R&D folks alone to work on the problems." Block clarified the working relationship of the two firms:

> At CPS we sometimes do things differently. When it comes to solving technical problems, for example, we believe that real problem-solving only goes on at the level of engineer to engineer and scientist to scientist. These people understand each other. You get them together and after a couple of hours they're slapping each other on the back and joking like old friends. They relate to each other. They talk the same language. They share common frustrations with management. But that doesn't mean you can leave them to do their own thing. Engineers love to change things. So if you leave it up to them, the job may never get done. I have learned to stay in close touch to insure that any changes in the order are made clear. If it isn't in the specs, it isn't in the project. And I hold them to it. What's more, in most firms we work with, the engineers don't make the final decisions, so it's my job to make sure that the people with the decision power get the full picture. I have to see to it that their engineers communicate with their purchasing people and that they and I take care of the contractual details.

Presently CPS was shipping Atlas 100 parts a month while continuing to optimize the process and material properties. Even now, though, some difficult problem had arisen in Atlas's development project, not with the CPS material itself but rather with joining of different parts. "We would love to help," suggested Block, "but we have insisted that they pay for it. We have given them some suggestions, but it's basically up to them. But while we can't tell them what to do, we have to find a way of getting our customers to uncover problems early in the design cycle. Even though it's their problem there's a lot in it for us too."

The Next Move

As chief executive officer, Loconto had brought to CPS not so much a new vision, as a vision articulated in a new way. He had continually stressed the importance of a "product engine" that would take the company from its current status as a development-stage company where revenue came primarily from development contracts to a manufacturing company where the bulk of revenue was generated by commercial products. As he often pointed out, "You have to have a product that gets you into the market. It has to be centered around one customer, but applicable in some form to other customers. We need to solve customer problems and then let those customers lead us into larger commercial markets."

And while the partnership relationship with Atlas was seen as a key element of success in the project, CPS well knew that it was not always easy to find a customer who was truly committed to joint development and the extensive cooperation that joint development required. In fact it was always a concern that a cooperative spirit be developed so that the customer didn't feel they were wasting time.

But always at the forefront was the issue of delivery. Recently it seemed that more and more orders came from marketing with ASAP (As Soon As Possible) listed as the customer request date. Although marketing avoided making those kinds of commitments, the fact that the customer needed it immediately added to the sense of pressure to get the product out faster.

Loconto was adamant that delivery had to improve. Recently he had begun the practice at the monthly company meeting of listing delinquent projects on the board and evaluating each one. This made some engineers uncomfortable—"How can they expect me to meet a schedule date when they won't buy me the equipment I need to get the job done?"—but most agreed with the thrust. As Page explained, "On this point Peter and I see eye-to-eye. If we want to be a real ceramics manufacturing company, we have to realize that there is more to being a good company than just having good technology. You have to have an attitude of quality that extends throughout the company. That means answering the phone not on the third ring but on the first ring. And it means delivering on time not 90% of the time or even 99% of the time. It means 100% of the time."

The New Orders

As Sundback put down the order sheets she had received from Block, Peter Valentine, CPS's controller, walked into her office at his usual ninety-miles-per-hour pace. "I've pulled together the information on past orders and the current backlog in molded products that we talked about. I've also got some rough calculations on engineering hours and lead time that Diana and Mark put together. It's the best we can do right now. I've got to run. Call me if you need anything else."

Sundback took a quick glance at Valentine's memo (see Exhibits 6A–F) and then hurried off to a meeting with her engineers. The Valentine memo was the first installment in an effort to get better data about delivery. With the recent emphasis on delivery performance, projects that were particularly late had been singled out for special attention. By working long hours and taking action to expedite work on these projects (e.g., moving them ahead in the queue at the furnace), they were able to get some things shipped. Sundback hoped that the data would help her identify where to make additional improvements

And then there were the new proposals (see Exhibit 7). She needed to get back to Block soon with a quote on cost and delivery, if she decided to accept them. The new proposals were interesting but it couldn't be business as usual. She felt that she needed to get more control over the projects in her group. As she walked, she commented:

> Look at this advanced alumina substrate project. We probably will have to come up with a new composition. But we've done some amazing things with the Atlas material and there's no reason we can't do it again. Our expertise is in developing new things and pushing the limits of knowledge. Isn't that the future? Besides, if we want to avoid the giants like Kyocera, we've got to come up with new, innovative materials. It doesn't look like a high volume application, but it is the kind of stuff we're good at. I'm sure if we were starting with a clean slate, it would be a clear choice. But we've got all this stuff going on. Our delinquency rate hasn't changed despite all the talking we've done, and now we're looking at even more projects. And for all I know, Bob Block is going to walk into my office next week with even more good stuff. I've got to get this sorted out.

Peter Valentine Memo

MEMORANDUM

To: Cathryn Sundback

From: Peter Valentine

Re: Report on Delivery and Engineering Workload in Molded Products

Date: 1 July 1989

As we discussed, I have pulled together information on development orders shipped, and the status of orders in the backlog. In addition, I have included data on average engineering hours and wait times by stage of development for molded products. I have used these to calculate the demands on engineering in backlog. Included are the following:

1. Shipping report for 1989 to date.

2. Report on projects in the backlog, including information on the type of project and delivery information.

3. Data on engineering hours and wait time by stage of development for molded products (these are averages Diana got from talking to the engineers).

4. Calculation of engineering workload in the backlog.

The last report requires some explanation. I used the data on average engineering hours to calculate the engineering workload left to be completed for each project in the backlog. To get even these rough calculations I used the following assumptions: a) I applied the average hours to each project; and b) the total engineering hours for a project are spread linearly over time until its ship date. All projects ship on time. In order to see the impact of yields (the yield estimates I got out of engineering are pretty rough), I did the calculation assuming 100 percent yields and using the average yields I got from the engineers.

I did a rough cut at comparing the workload with available engineering hours. What we need are *effective* engineering hours, since engineers spend a lot of time in meetings, thinking, eating lunch, etc. I think a reasonable number is 30 hours per week per engineer. Since you have five engineers, that gives you 150 effective engineering hours per week.

Exhibit 6B

Molded Products Shipping Report 1989 Year-to-Date

Customer	Material Type	Part Description	Parts	$/Part	Total Value	Order Date	Request Date	Promised Date	Ship Date
1 Ntl. Refractories	Sialon	Test Bars	6	$ 158	$ 948	9/1/88	12/1/88	1/1/89	1/1/89
2 Atlas	X	Tubes	100	$ 26	$ 2,607	1/9/89	1/9/89	2/28/89	1/30/89
3 Brown Inc.	SiC	Base & Top	15	$ 658	$ 9,871	10/12/88	2/3/89	2/3/89	2/9/89
4 Norekami	A1203	Test Bars	4	$ 198	$ 790	1/18/89	1/18/89	2/7/89	3/1/89
5 Atlas	X	0.3" Tubes	200	$ 100	$20,000	1/9/89	1/9/89	2/28/89	3/3/89
6 Atlas	X	Wafers	78	$ 51	$ 4,005	3/28/89	4/12/89	4/12/89	3/31/89
7 American	Sialon	Unfired Billet	2	$3,950	$ 7,900	3/31/89	4/20/89	4/20/89	4/20/89
8 Atlas	X	Tubes	20	$ 100	$ 2,000	3/31/89	4/14/89	4/14/89	5/5/89
9 IC Products	SiC	Substrate	10	$ 103	$ 1,027	2/1/89	2/1/89	4/4/89	6/1/89
10 Atlas	X	Tubes	55	$ 100	$ 5,500	3/31/89	4/29/89	4/29/89	6/16/89
11 Atlas	X	Wafers	114	$ 51	$ 5,854	3/31/89	5/5/89	5/12/89	6/30/89
12 Atlas	X	Tubes	40	$ 100	$ 4,000	3/31/89	5/22/89	5/22/89	6/30/89

NOTE: The composition of Material X, developed by CPS, is proprietary.

EXHIBIT 6C

Backlog Project Status for Molded Products, 1 July 1989

Customer	Material type	Description	Material	Tooling	Parts	$/Part	Total Value	Order Date	Req Date	Prom Date	Prom Time (Wks)	Weeks to Ship 7/1/89
1 Conklin	ZrO2	Ceramic Block	New	New	200	$ 55	$11,060	7/88	10/88	10/31/88	15	-35
2 Brown Inc.	Si3N4	Baseplate	New	New	15	$ 658	$ 9,871	10/88	2/89	2/17/89	18	-19
3 Atlas	X	0.8" Block	Existing	New	120	$ 75	$ 9,006	1/89	1/89	2/28/89	7	-18
4 Conklin	A12O3	Substrate as-fired	Existing	Existing	20	$ 142	$ 2,844	11/88	3/89	3/10/89	16	-16
5 Conklin	A12O3	Substrate polished	Existing	Existing	20	$ 142	$ 2,844	11/88	3/89	3/10/89	16	-16
6 Dynamite	ZTA	Piston Pins	New	New	1	$5,925	$ 5,925	1/89	1/89	5/10/89	16	-7
7 Micro	A12O3	2" Substrate w/lines	Existing	Existing	10	$ 119	$ 1,185	6/89	7/89	7/10/89	4	1
8 Columbus	A12O3	Bracket	Existing	New	50	$ 790	$39,500	3/89	7/89	7/25/89	19	3
9 Atlas	X	Tubes w/Holes	Existing	Existing	100	$ 100	$10,000	6/89	6/89	8/4/89	5	5
10 Goddard	SiC	Test Samples	Existing	Existing	120	$ 66	$ 7,963	4/89	4/89	8/23/89	19	8
11 Atlas	X	Tubes w/Holes	Existing	Existing	100	$ 100	$10,000	6/89	9/89	9/8/89	10	10
12 Atlas	X	0.2" Substrate	Existing	Existing	5	$ 490	$ 2,449	4/89	4/89	9/22/89	21	12
13 Atlas	X	0.1" Substrate	Existing	Existing	10	$ 389	$ 3,895	4/89	4/89	9/22/89	21	12
14 Goddard	SiC	Test Samples	Existing	Existing	30	$ 66	$ 1,991	4/89	10/89	10/1/89	24	13
15 Atlas	X	Tubes w/Holes	Existing	Changes	100	$ 100	$10,000	6/89	10/89	10/6/89	14	14
16 Atlas	X	Substrates	Existing	New	45	$ 43	$ 1,955	4/89	4/89	10/20/89	27	16
17 Micro	A12O3	2" Substrate	Existing	Existing	10	$ 137	$ 1,367	4/89	10/89	10/27/89	28	17
18 Atlas	X	Tubes w/Holes	Existing	Existing	100	$ 100	$10,000	6/89	11/89	11/3/89	18	18
19 Micro	A12O3	2" Substrate	Existing	Existing	10	$ 137	$ 1,367	4/89	11/89	11/18/89	31	20
20 Goddard	SiC	Test Samples	Existing	Changes	30	$ 66	$ 1,991	4/89	12/89	12/1/89	33	22
21 Micro	A12O3	2" Substrate	Existing	Changes	10	$ 137	$ 1,367	4/89	12/89	12/9/89	34	23
22 Atlas	X	Substrates	Existing	Existing	45	$ 43	$ 1,955	4/89	4/89	12/22/89	34	25
23 Micro	A12O3	2" Substrate	Existing	Existing	70	$ 137	$ 9,567	4/89	1/90	1/1/90	37	26

NOTE: The composition of Material X, developed by CPS, is proprietary.

EXHIBIT 6D
Molded Products Development Hours[1,2]

STAGE	Initial Parts	Yield Factor	Good Parts	EngTime /Piece (Hrs)	EngTime /Lot (Hrs)	Passes through Step	Total Eng Time (Hrs)	Wait Time /Pass (Days)	Total (Days)	
MATERIAL DEVELOPMENT										
Plan					1	1	1			
Make Dispersion					4	1	4			
Mold Samples	25	0.8	20	0.25	6.25	3	18.75			
Wait						3		3	9	
Dry					2	3	6	1	3	
Wait						3		3		
Sinter	20	0.5	10		2	3	6	1	3	
Measure Property					2	3	6	14	42	Outside Vendor
TOTALS							41.75	22	57	
PROCESS DEVELOPMENT										
Plan					1	1	1			
Make Dispersion					4	3	12			
Measure Rheology					4	3	12			
Mold Billets	25	0.8	20	0.25	6.25	4	25			
Wait						4		3	12	
Dry					2	4	8	1	4	
Wait						4		3	12	
Sinter	20	0.5	10		2	4	8	1	4	
Measure Shrinkage					2	1	2			
TOTALS							68	8	32	
TOOL DEVELOPMENT										
Design					8	1	8			Design Group
Machining						1		14	14	Outside Vendor
TOTALS							8	14	14	
TOLL REFINEMENT										
Plan					1	1	1			
Make Dispersion					4	1	4			
Mold Billets	25	0.8	20	0.25	6.25	4	25			
Wait						4		3	12	
Dry					2	4	8	1	4	
Wait						4		3	12	
Sinter	20	0.5	10		2	4	8	1	4	
Send out for tool changes					2	1	2	4	4	Outside Vendor
TOTALS							48	12	36	
PROTOTYPE PARTS										
Plan					1	1	1			
Make Dispersion					4	1	4			
Mold Billets	125	0.8	100	0.25	31.25	1	31.25			
Wait						1	0	3	3	
Dry					2	1	2	1	1	
Wait						1	0	3	3	
Sinter	100	0.5	50		2	1	2	1	1	
Send out for Polishing					1	1	1	14	14	Not always
Send to Customer					2	1	2			required
TOTALS							43.25	22	22	
GRAND TOTALS							209	78	161	

1. Actual yields improve over time, particularly in the prototype part production.
2. Typical yields for molding step are around 80%. Yields at the sintering step are roughly 50%.

Engineering Workload Projections—100% Yield

Customer	Order	Stage	Remain Time (wks)	Remain Hours Req	Needed Hrs/Wk	July	August	Sept	Oct	Nov	Dec
Conklin	50205	1	22	149	7	29	31	29	30	29	1
Brown Inc.	50286	3	10	66	7	28	30	7	0	0	0
Atlas	50304	5	3	25	8	25	0	0	0	0	0
Conklin	50295	5	3	25	8	25	0	0	0	0	0
Conklin	50296	5	3	25	8	25	0	0	0	0	0
Dynamite	50310	1	22	149	7	29	31	29	30	29	1
Micro	50372	5	1.3	25	19	25	0	0	0	0	0
Columbus	50316	5	3	25	7	25	0	0	0	0	0
Atlas	50338	4	5	58	12	51	7	0	0	0	0
Goddard	50321	2	8	119	16	67	51	0	0	0	0
Atlas	50338	4	10	58	6	25	27	6	0	0	0
Atlas	50354	2	12	119	10	43	46	30	0	0	0
Atlas	50355	2	12	119	10	43	46	30	0	0	0
Goddard	50321	2	13	119	9	39	41	39	0	0	0
Atlas	50338	1	14	149	11	46	49	46	8	0	0
Atlas	50311	2	16	119	7	32	34	32	20	0	0
Micro	50348	5	17	25	1	6	7	6	5	0	0
Atlas	50338	1	18	149	8	36	38	36	37	2	0
Micro	50348	5	20	25	1	5	6	5	5	3	0
Goddard	50321	2	22	119	5	23	25	23	24	23	0
Micro	50348	5	23	25	1	5	5	5	5	5	1
Atlas	50311	2	25	119	5	20	22	20	21	20	14
Micro	50348	5	26	25	1	4	4	4	4	4	4
TOTALS			307	1827	175						
				Monthly Totals		653	499	348	190	116	21.6
				per Week		152	109	81	43	27	5

EXHIBIT 6F

Engineering Workload Projections—Yielded

Customer	Order	Stage	Remain Time (Wks)	Remain Hours Req	Needed Hrs/Wk	Engineering Hours required by Month					
						July	August	Sept	Oct	Nov	Dec
Conklin	50205	1	22	209	10	41	43	41	42	41	1
Brown Inc.	50286	3	10	99	10	43	45	11	0	0	0
Atlas	50304	5	3	43	14	43	0	0	0	0	0
Conklin	50295	5	3	43	14	43	0	0	0	0	0
Conklin	50296	5	3	43	14	43	0	0	0	0	0
Dynamite	50310	1	22	209	10	41	43	41	42	41	1
Micro	50372	5	1.3	43	34	43	0	0	0	0	0
Columbus	50316	5	3	43	13	43	0	0	0	0	0
Atlas	50338	4	5	91	19	81	11	0	0	0	0
Goddard	50321	2	8	167	22	95	73	0	0	0	0
Atlas	50338	4	10	91	9	40	42	9	0	0	0
Atlas	50354	2	12	167	14	60	64	42	0	0	0
Atlas	50355	2	12	167	14	60	64	42	0	0	0
Goddard	50321	2	13	167	13	55	58	55	0	0	0
Atlas	50338	1	14	209	15	65	69	65	11	0	0
Atlas	50311	2	16	167	11	45	48	45	29	0	0
Micro	50348	5	17	43	3	11	12	11	10	0	0
Atlas	50338	1	18	209	12	50	54	50	52	3	0
Micro	50348	5	20	43	2	9	10	9	10	5	0
Goddard	50321	2	22	167	8	33	35	33	34	33	0
Micro	50348	5	23	43	2	8	9	8	8	8	2
Atlas	50311	2	25	167	7	29	31	29	30	29	20
Micro	50348	5	26	43	2	7	8	7	7	7	7
TOTALS			307	2678	269						
			Monthly Totals			988	719	498	274	167	32.3
			per Week			230	157	116	62	39	7

EXHIBIT 7

Specifications for Potential Products

CUSTOMER	Atlas	Deutsche Motorwerk	CompuChip
PROJECT NAME	Sensor	Turbocharger Rotor	IC Substrate
MATERIAL Alumina Aluminum Nitride Material X New	*	Silicon Nitride	*(Advanced)
PROCESS ENVELOPE FLAT SHAPES Size Up to 5″ Thickness Up to 0.3″ OTHER SHAPES Up to 4″ outer diameter Up to 2″ cross section	OK OK	? OK	OK More like 0.4″
TOLERANCE <0.5%	OK	?	<0.2%
TOOLING REQUIRED	New	New	Modified
NUMBER OF PIECES	100	30	10
NOTES	New modification but shouldn't be too hard. We may need to bring down current $100 price.	Really challenging shape but *big* volume potential.	Could be a good chance to develop an improved alumina.

Structuring the Development Funnel

Overview

This chapter is a bridge between our discussion of the front end of development and the management of specific projects in Chapters 6 through 10. Here we develop a framework for thinking about how firms generate alternative ideas for development projects, screen and review those ideas as development proceeds, and achieve convergence around a specific concept and design that the firm will take into the market. The basis for that framework is the concept of the development funnel—a graphic structure that depicts the firm's approach to identification, screening, and convergence in the development process. A central idea in the chapter is that the development funnel creates the "architecture" for the basic activities that occur as a part of a development project.

After a brief introduction to the basic concept of the funnel, the chapter motivates our focus on the funnel by introducing two examples of a funnel in practice in a medical electronics firm drawn by two teams of executives. These funnels are full of starts and stops, convolutions, and anything but a smooth, crisp, clear, effective process. The examples illustrate a common problem and underscore the potential within most companies for improvement through careful attention to the overall structure of the development funnel.

In reading the chapter, it is important to understand that creating an effective funnel involves choices in three dimensions: (1) the process for creating projects; (2) the process for achieving convergence in any single project to a focused concept and detailed design; and (3) the process for achieving final commitment to the market. The central theme in this discussion is that these dimensions are not independent, so that we need to understand the pattern of choices in all three dimensions taken together. We identify two patterns that we call Model I and Model II that seem to be particularly prevalent. Model I is an "R&D push" funnel in which the primary engine of the process is the R&D organization and technological change. Model II may be described as "'all the eggs in one basket," and is often used by small, start-up firms. Here the firm screens a wide variety of alternatives, but quickly coalesces around a single concept, and pushes that concept through to completion. We contrast those two models (both of which have problems) with a third model that combines a dramatic expansion of the mouth of the funnel with a subsequently focused sequence of phases and screens to achieve convergence.

An important theme in this discussion is the connection between the screens applied to potential concepts and ideas, and the overall strategy of the business. Where the criteria applied at the screens derive directly from the strategic direction of the business, the funnel provides a framework for linking the business strategy to choices about individual projects.

The chapter concludes with a discussion of a diagnostic process which may be useful in identifying critical issues in the firm's development funnel and outlining steps to improvement. The central theme in this latter discussion in the chapter is the use of the funnel to do more than simply select and focus projects. The idea here is that the processes that lie behind the funnel provide senior management with a framework in which they can train, develop, and create people capable of generating options and making decisions about development projects. Furthermore, done well, the funnel not only may be used to identify good ideas and develop them into effective products, but may also focus the organization on building future capabilities. The funnel, thus, is not only the framework or architecture for convergence on a specific project, but also for building development capability.

CHAPTER 5

The aim of any product or process development project is to take an idea from concept to reality by converging to a specific product that can meet a market need in an economical, manufacturable form. As suggested in the development strategy framework outlined in Chapter 2, the overall development process starts with a broad range of inputs and gradually refines and selects from among them, creating a handful of formal development projects that can be pushed to rapid completion and introduction. This notion of a converging funnel is illustrated in Exhibit 5–1. In its simplest form, the development funnel provides a graphic structure for thinking about the generation and screening of alternative development options, and combining a subset of these into a product concept.[1] A variety of different product and process ideas enter the funnel for investigation, but only a fraction become part of a full-fledged development project. Those that do are examined carefully before entering the narrow neck of the funnel, where significant resources are expended in transforming them into a commercial product and/or process.

The nature of the funnel is defined by the way the organization identifies, screens, reviews, and converges on the content of a development project as it moves from idea to reality.[2] The funnel establishes the

Exhibit 5–1

The Development Funnel*

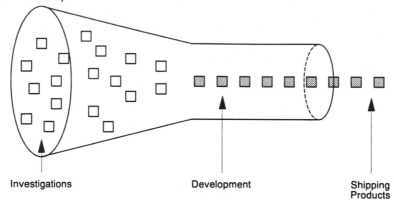

Investigations   Development   Shipping Products

* The funnel illustrates the process firms ideally go through to identify many ideas, select the few most promising for development, and focus resources to get them into the market. The small blank squares indicate ideas for investigation; darkened squares indicate ideas that are developed and applied.

overall framework for development: the generation and review of alternatives, the sequence of critical decisions, and the nature of decision making (including who is involved and the criteria used). It defines the forum for integration across and the structure within which senior managers influence the development process. In effect, the development funnel creates the architecture for the set of development activities that must occur as part of a successful development project.

In this chapter we first lay out the issues firms confront in structuring the funnel, present examples of funnels in action, and then use those examples to illustrate the power of the concept in diagnosing critical problems in the overall framework for development. In the subsequent section we turn to the question of designing the funnel for a specific business. We compare and contrast two traditional models of the development funnel, and then offer a third alternative that our work suggests is more powerful and effective. The chapter concludes with a discussion of critical challenges in using the funnel to manage development.

Basic Concepts and Their Application

Managing the development funnel involves three very different tasks or challenges. The first is to widen its mouth. To be effective, the organization must expand its knowledge base and access to information in order to increase the number of new product and new process ideas. A variety of ways of doing this—ranging from mining research labs and university relationships for more technical ideas to soliciting creative inputs from manufacturing, marketing, customers, and suppliers—will be explored later in this chapter.

The second challenge is to narrow the funnel's neck. After generating a variety of alternative concepts and ideas, management must screen them and focus resources on the most attractive opportunities. The hard part is to narrow the neck of the funnel while ensuring that a constant stream of good projects flows down it. The narrowing process must be based on a set of screening criteria that fit the company's technological opportunities while making effective use of its development resources in meeting strategic and financial needs.

Striking an effective balance between creatively widening the funnel's mouth and tough-mindedly narrowing its neck is not easy. The companies that do it best tend to combine various idea-generating mechanisms with a sequential review process. Later in this chapter we will outline alternative approaches, including front-end funding mechanisms for ensuring that ideas are ready to be screened (i.e., they receive an objective and appropriate hearing) while a systematic but fair process of screening is rigorously applied. Like capital budgeting, this task can be viewed as a resource allocation problem with all of the traditional issues of determining what data are relevant, how they should be weighted, and what they tell us about their eventual success. The goal is not just to apply limited resources to selected projects with the highest expected payoff, but to create a portfolio of projects that will meet the business objectives of the firm while enhancing the firm's strategic ability to carry out future projects.

Even with access to a number of good ideas and a process to focus on only a few, the funnel is not complete. The third challenge is to ensure that the selected projects deliver on the objectives anticipated when the project was approved. Ensuring that the project delivers as anticipated is the topic of Chapters 6 through 10. Especially relevant to this third task is Chapter 6, which considers how and when product or process specifications should be developed, when they should be modified, and how the process can be managed to convergence as opposed to being managed to a moving target.

Funnels in Practice

While the concept of the development funnel is straightforward, and the model depicted in Exhibit 5–1 apparently smooth and simple, the reality of funnels is often quite different. Even in situations where managers

EXHIBIT 5–2A

Actual Development Funnel—Medical Electronics Firm*

A. Team 1

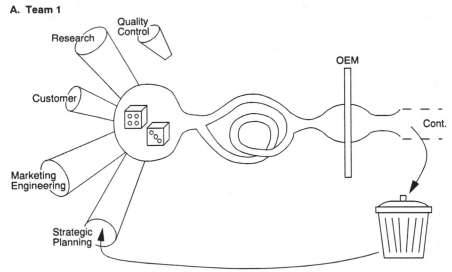

* This funnel, drawn by a group of executives, illustrates the often confused reality of actual development funnels. In this diagram, there are many funnels; choice is a random throw of the dice, and the course of development is convoluted.

have created a screening and review process, the actual funnel is not anything like the theory. To motivate a closer look at the funnel and to shed some light on the practical problems firms face in creating one, we have found it useful to have managers draw the funnel that actually exists in practice in their organization. Exhibits 5–2A and 5–2B present two examples from a medical electronics firm drawn by two teams of executives.

A few characteristics stand out in the first drawing. There is not just one funnel, but several, each with its own ideas and inputs into the development process. Some of these small funnels are important and well connected, while others (like QC) seem to be off in a world of their own. These ideas make up a large set of possibilities (notice how the funnel gets very wide at the beginning), but there is no clearly defined process for choosing among them. Indeed, Team 1 said, in effect, "We don't really know how projects get selected. It looks like we line them up and roll the dice." Those selected follow convoluted paths in development, with multiple loops and a lot of recycling until a few things find their way out into the market. Original equipment manufacturer (OEM) or subcontracted projects come in late, with little advanced warning or

Exhibit 5—2B

Actual Development Funnel—Medical Electronics Firm*

B. Team 2

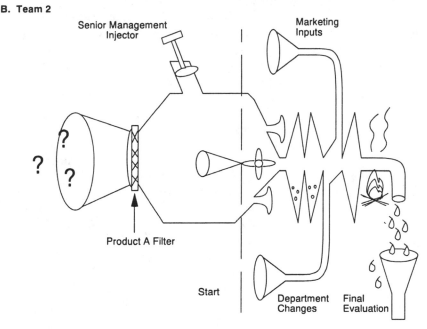

Senior Management Injector

Marketing Inputs

? ? ?

Product A Filter

Start

Department Changes

Final Evaluation

* This funnel, drawn by a group of executives, illustrates the problems firms experience with real development funnels. In this drawing, the source of ideas is uncertain, products for development get jammed up and seem to recirculate, there is a lot of heat at the end, and a few products "drip out" into the market.

analysis. Since products are often incomplete at introduction there is an ongoing development activity that lingers on. Finally, projects that fail get discarded only to be recycled through strategic planning as "new ideas."

The second funnel has similar themes. Where projects come from is uncertain, but it is clear that if the project is not a part of the Product A family (the original product line in the company) it will have a hard time getting funded. Once a project gets into the funnel, it joins many other projects that are part of the "active" list but seem to recirculate (notice the small fan in the middle of the diagram) with little progress. The team also noted that some projects enter the funnel through a special "senior management injector." These are pet projects of senior executives that seem to arrive in the development process with a big "whoosh!" behind them. Once out of the recirculation chamber, a project encounters numerous blind alleys and dead ends and also receives marketing input and departmental changes very late in its development. Finally, when something gets far enough along, senior management applies a lot of heat at the end (note the fire) and a few things drip out.

These drawings captured a sobering reality: the processes the firm used to identify, screen, select, and focus resources were fuzzy, disjointed, haphazard, and ineffective. Our experience suggests that the medical electronics company is not alone. Indeed, we have found very few companies where drawing the funnel reveals a smooth, crisp, clear, effective process. Most companies, therefore, confront a major opportunity for improving the overall development process, because getting the overall architecture of development right has great power. In the first place, getting rid of the starts and stops, the dead ends, and the convolutions eliminates a major source of confusion for the people working on the project. Additionally, an effective funnel creates a framework in which people can focus and integrate their energies and capabilities.

Creating an effective funnel, however, takes more than identifying problems and weaknesses. In addition, managers need a frame of reference to guide their choices so that the funnel they create matches the needs and opportunities they face. The first step in building that frame is to identify the critical dimensions of the funnel and how they work together to create an overall framework.

Creating the Development Funnel: Alternative Models

Exhibit 5–3 lays out three sets of dimensions that define the choices firms make about the development funnel:

- Its process for creating development projects—encouraging certain sources of new ideas and selecting which of those to support in development projects
- Its means of achieving convergence to a focused product concept and detailed design—through a set of decision-making, review, and control procedures during project execution
- Its final commitment to the market through final testing, screening, and market introduction plans

Although the large number of dimensions of choice means that in theory we could see a wide variety of funnels, in practice, many of these dimensions are closely connected. The result is that while some of the details differ, there are a few broad patterns to the choices firms make. We have presented two patterns—called Model I and Model II—in col-

Exhibit 5–3

Two Common Models of Development Funnels and Their Dimensions of Choice

Dimensions of Choice that Determine Funnel Characteristics	Model I (R&D Push/ Survival of the Fittest)	Model II (Single Project/ Big Bet)
Creating Development Projects		
Sources of Ideas		
Entry points	Primarily single function – R&D	Multiple functions
Direction	Bottom up/grass roots	Top down/senior management
Breadth	Wide within R&D/narrow for entire organization	Broad overall
Selection Process		
Purpose	Review/ready for next step	Go/no-go
Criteria	Internal/technical	External customer requirements/finance
Structure	Formal authorization	Informal/gut feel
People	Peer review	Senior management decision
Convergence to Concept/Detailed Design		
Process/Screens		
Timing	Technical milestones	Frequent/calendar
Purpose	Identify promising concepts	Go for one/adjustments
Criteria	Technical interest/performance	Customer requirements/finance
Formality	Signatures required	Informal
People	Peers/senior management approval	Senior management
Decision making	Consensus	Top management decision
Pattern of Convergence		
Number of options	Multiple/competing options	Single option
Width/length of neck of funnel	Wide/long	Narrow/short
Commitment to Market		
Criteria for introduction	Meets tests for performance	Meets financial targets
Decision making	Peers/top management	Top management

umns two and three of Exhibit 5–3. These models define approaches to the funnel that are quite common, but sufficiently different to make clear the nature of the choices firms face.

Model I

The first model is common in larger, technology-intensive firms.[3] Firms adhering to this model rely primarily on their R&D group to generate ideas for technologies and for new products and processes. They anticipate and encourage engineers and scientists to generate and explore many more ideas than will be applied in products or processes. The charge is to be creative and innovative, providing an abundance of opportunities for the larger organization to choose from.

With so many ideas, Model I then uses a series of screens—often involving peer reviews—to generate a winnowed down and manageable set of products and processes for market introduction. Early screens tend to be primarily technical in nature, focusing on technical feasibility and proof of concept. Later screens then shift to emphasize manufacturing feasibility and fundamental economics. Finally, as commercial introduction draws near, screens include added consideration of specific customer preferences, distribution channel concerns, and financial return expectations.

As a development project passes through a Model I funnel, it competes with other projects for resources. When successful, it often picks up ideas from competing projects that have lost momentum or been screened out. Many times, however, even a project that passes through the funnel successfully and is introduced to the marketplace finds itself competing with other products offered by the firm. Thus, to be successful over the long term, the resulting product must continue to compete successfully for sales, service, and customer attention, not just against products from competitors, but against products from within the firm.

The essence of the Model I funnel is a technology-driven survival of the fittest. Exhibit 5–4 graphs its characteristic funnel. The basic logic behind Model I is that of a hundred good ideas, only relatively few ever become successful products. This is due first to the fact that carrying an idea all the way from research through to market introduction is an extremely expensive proposition, and also to the notion that research can generate many more ideas than could ever be supported by the firm and absorbed by the marketplace. At each screen or hurdle, the active ideas are reviewed systematically, based on current knowledge and understanding. Only the best of those are approved for the next phase, where additional resources will be invested to prepare them for the next screen or hurdle, and to move them closer to the final form needed for eventual market introduction. But the screens are not tight enough to

Exhibit 5–4

Two Dominant Models of the Development Funnel*

A. Model I: R&D Driven, Survival of the Fittest

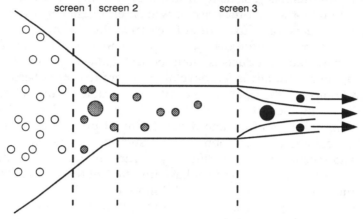

B. Model II: A Few Big Bets

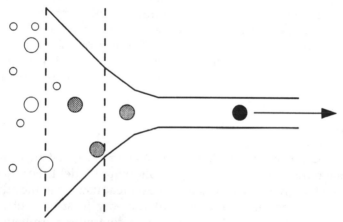

* This exhibit identifies two models of the funnel. Model I is a grass roots, bubble up model in which development is driven by R&D. Model II is a top down model common in small, entrepreneurial start-ups, in which the firm bets on a single project. The circles represent new products; shading indicates the extent of development, and size the scale of the project.

narrow the funnel substantially until market introduction is imminent.

Model I has strengths in certain kinds of markets, but a number of factors raise questions about the appropriateness of this model in a variety of industries. For many firms, a broad-ranging, exploratory research group—the vast majority of whose efforts never result in marketable products—is a luxury that few can afford. Doing such research is expensive and the forecast of which research activities would ever lead to marketable products is often too unreliable to justify such risks. Second, successful advanced development groups often become committed to turning their pet projects into marketable products, making it difficult or impractical to "kill" them. Thus, with a Model I funnel, increasing numbers of advanced development projects may find their way into commercial development. But such firms often lack the discipline and mechanisms to significantly reduce the numbers of development projects in process, and yet have insufficient resources to carry out all of them in a timely and successful manner.

A third factor that calls Model I into question is the complexity of development. As projects become increasingly complex, difficult, and expensive, it is impractical to screen out "competing projects" at the eleventh hour. While some firms respond by introducing more products to the marketplace—letting the market decide which version it prefers—this is often unsatisfactory as well.[4] Many markets simply do not grow fast enough to provide adequate rates of return by following this procedure, and too many products in the marketplace can confuse the distribution channel and final customers, and add complexity and cost in manufacturing.

Model II

Model I is a large firm model. Small firms, even those that are technically driven, have never had the luxury of following Model I. For them, the ideal model has always involved taking an idea (usually in the advanced development stage) and backing it all the way to successful product introduction. In fact, in industries such as computer peripherals, successful start-ups get that way by taking a single idea, turning it into a home run, and eventually building a product line around it. Many more start-ups have tried to imitate this approach, but failed for a myriad of reasons and disappeared in the process. When a smaller firm establishes itself using this "all-the-eggs-in-one-basket" model, they subsequently encounter a variety of challenges as they seek to repeat that success by applying the same approach on subsequent generations of products. Even mature firms, which dominate slowly evolving product market areas, often adopt this model but take more time than their smaller counterparts to execute it.

Firms that rely on the Model II development funnel generally consider a fairly wide range of ideas from a variety of sources at the outset. However, they very quickly collapse, screen, and combine them into a single project aimed at meeting a set of market needs. Most often, top management makes the call as to project boundaries, objectives, and commitment at the outset. While often influenced heavily by the backgrounds and experiences of senior management, the primary criteria for project selection, even at the outset, are market potential and financial expectations.

Throughout the execution portion of the Model II funnel, senior management requests regular reviews and updates, seeking to avoid late surprises and disappointments. With so much riding on an individual project, midcourse corrections and adjustments are common and considered appropriate. Only when serious problems arise would such a project have its market introduction postponed at the eleventh hour. Much more common is introduction as soon as feasible—even if not quite finished—with subsequent revisions and upgrades being made in the field. This flow through the funnel is illustrated in Exhibit 5–4B and can be described as a few big bets, or "all-the-eggs-in-one-basket."

While smaller firms following Model II typically have only one or two projects in process (i.e., in the narrow neck of the funnel) at any point in time, larger firms may have several projects in process under this model. However, for larger firms this most often still reflects only one or two projects per funnel for a given business unit or division. Thus in reality, even such large firms are pinning most of their new product hopes on a few bets for any given market, with many of those new products simply aimed at enhancements they hope will support and sustain an existing market position.

The success of small firms using Model II grows out of the clarity and focus that comes by necessity from betting the company on a single project. But as firms grow, using Model II may bring with it a number of problems. Model II is particularly problematic if used in large firms with multiple market segments and product families. The reality of Model II in large firms is numerous midcourse corrections, modest or even marginal market success upon introduction, and a reputation among their customers as "conservative and no longer innovative."

Exhibit 5–5 illustrates the experience of a Model II firm involved in industrial control devices in the development of a major next-generation electromechanical product. The intention of senior management in this division was to carefully serve a customer need, to apply existing technical knowledge, to identify the right product concept and features for the development effort, and then to drive that effort from advanced development through to commercial introduction in a focused project that would result in a robust, superior design, selling in volume in the

EXHIBIT 5–5

Analysis of a Specific Project's Development Funnel: Electromechanical Industrial Control Device*

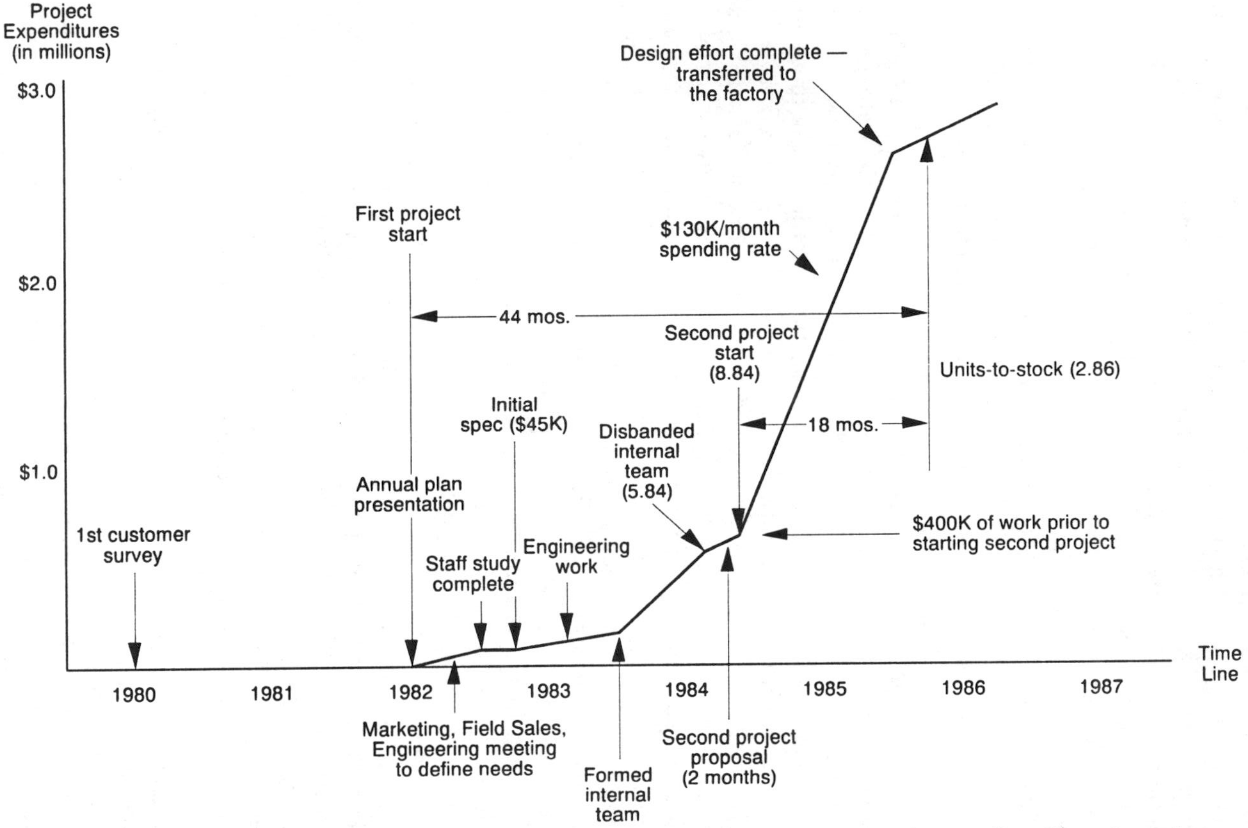

* Starting with the original customer survey and going to production units in inventory, this time line shows the major events that preceded as well as those that were part of the formal development project. It also shows the cumulative investment spent on the entire set of activities. While the "official project" was eighteen months, it was preceded by years of investigation at an identified cost of $400,000.

marketplace. As illustrated in Exhibit 5–5, initial customer surveys were done in 1980. By 1982, management felt the technical options and market requirements were known sufficiently to propose a major development effort as part of their annual plan. Over the next eighteen months, engineering spent close to $100,000 refining the product concept and ensuring that appropriate specs could be set and met. In early 1984 an internal development team was established, and over the next twelve months, worked vigorously—spending another $300,000—to bring the effort toward a marketable product. By mid 1984, however, management determined that while a new product was still needed for that major product family, it was not going to come out of the current development effort. The project was abandoned and the engineers went back to the drawing boards.

In late 1984, a revised proposal was made which included the use of corporate technical resources as well as resources from the division. A charter, including detailed specifications, a time line, and a $2.2 million budget, was established and approved by management at that point. The new team was indeed successful, and the product was launched on time and met the specifications. Unfortunately, however, the market had changed. Although the product was successful, a number of subsequent engineering changes were needed to refine and better target it. The firm concluded, however, that the second project had indeed been a successful execution of their "ideal Model II" funnel and that the problem with the first effort was a lack of focus, inadequate technical expertise, and a myriad of distractions that the second team avoided.

This experience underscores the problems in making Model II work in a changing, complex environment. First is that a high level of technical knowledge and completed scientific invention must be accessible to the development team if the project is to have a high probability of success and on-time completion. Similarly, the funnel structure requires that the firm have deep knowledge about the market, the competitors, and specific customer needs in advance. Second, disbanding established projects may sometimes be necessary, but it is particularly difficult, traumatic, and expensive. Third, by focusing narrowly at the outset, the funnel structure may reinforce a deliberate pace in exploring options and defining potential projects. But where time is of the essence, a leisurely pace is ineffective. The two years required in Exhibit 5–5 between the first customer survey and the initial project proposal, followed by another full year before the development team was staffed, is not viable in today's typical environment. Likewise, making extensive engineering change orders after introduction is disruptive in the marketplace and expensive and confusing to the firm. Thus both Models I and II of the funnel leave major gaps in what is "ideal" with respect to the development funnel. This becomes even more apparent once an orga-

Exhibit 5–6
Model III Development Funnel: Innovative and Focused*

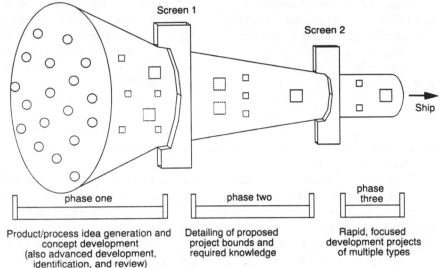

phase one	phase two	phase three
Product/process idea generation and concept development (also advanced development, identification, and review)	Detailing of proposed project bounds and required knowledge	Rapid, focused development projects of multiple types

* In Model III of the development funnel, the front end (phase one) is expanded to encourage more and better idea generation. Following an initial screening, the best of those ideas are then detailed and analyzed (phase two), ready for a go/no-go decision. At Screen 2, the approved projects are staffed and moved toward rapid introduction through a focused effort (phase three).

nization begins to sharpen its pre-project planning skills using some of the tools and concepts outlined in Chapters 2 and 3.

Model III

A much more appropriate ideal for a development funnel—Model III—combines and integrates the best features of Models I and II. In fact, it operationalizes an approach that is very close to the simple concept shape illustrated in Exhibit 5–1. We call this model "innovative and focused," and illustrate its primary characteristics in Exhibit 5–6.

The initial part of the Model III development funnel represents the concept development and idea generation for potential product/process efforts. The intent in this stage is to dramatically expand the mouth of the funnel, even beyond that envisioned in Model I. This can be done in a number of ways, gathering ideas from a variety of sources rather than just R&D.[5] One means for enlarging the mouth of the funnel is to institute procedures and incentives that encourage innovation and input from all parts of the organization as well as from customers, competitors, and suppliers. Each subfunction and group in the company needs to view itself as having significant responsibility for generating new ideas and concepts, and identifying ways in which they might be incorporated into products, services, and manufacturing processes. Providing special funding and released time for individuals to pursue and refine ideas is one type of incentive that may be needed to encourage such behavior. Recognizing individual and group contributions through competitions and awards may also be appropriate. Another way in which the need for new ideas can be addressed is through the functional maps described in Chapter 3. As each group creates those maps and plans for the activities they represent, the opportunity and need for additional development projects can be identified and responsibility for their exploration assigned.

As shown in Exhibit 5–6, a narrowing of the funnel occurs at Screen 1, which comes at the end of the product/process concept development stage. However, it is *not* a go/no-go evaluation point. Rather, it is a review by a mid-level group of managers (peers) drawn from the individual functional units to determine what additional information is needed before a go/no-go decision (Screen 2) can be made. If the organization uses a team structure to organize development, Screen 1 could be conducted by the cross-functional team. Screen 1 can be thought of as a "completeness" or "readiness" review rather than as a decision review. The intent is to periodically (at least quarterly, or perhaps monthly) review the status of those ideas in the concept development stage of the funnel. While not all ideas need to be reviewed every time, it is important that a time line be associated with individual ideas critical to carrying out the aggregate project plan. As part of this initial screen, ideas should be checked for their fit with technology and product market strategies, their potential role in executing the aggregate plan, and their appropriateness as an application of the firm's development resources. In addition, key areas of knowledge critical to the success of potential projects need to be identified and the way in which they will be accessed needs to be established.

When an idea is reviewed at the first screen, one of two outcomes is possible. If the idea is found to be complete, it can be moved into the mid-phase where project bounds are detailed and required knowledge is specified. If the idea is still incomplete and not ready to move on, then the specific tasks needed to complete it so it meets the requirements of Screen 1 can be agreed upon, assignments made for completing them, and the time at which it will next be reviewed (hopefully with all the steps completed) at a Screen 1 meeting established. In this way the product/process concept development stage can be completed effectively and efficiently, and the standards for moving to the next stage applied consistently.

An important aspect of the concept development phase that deserves highlighting is the role of advanced development. Typically, advanced development projects seek to push a technical idea or concept to the point where it is ready for inclusion in a commercial product or process development effort. The output of such advanced development projects—"proof of technical feasibility"—usually becomes a key kernel of knowledge or core concept for a specific product or process development project or provides a foundation for multiple projects. Thus advanced development projects occurring in the funnel prior to Screen 1 ensure that invention is clearly separated from commercialization.

Initiation of advanced development projects can result from different triggers: (a) a *function* may decide that an advanced development effort around a specific topic is important to their ongoing development efforts and success; (b) those involved at *Screen 1*, reviewing the development of a specific concept or idea, may recommend an advanced development effort as a way to answer specific questions (both technical and market-based) that need to precede a go/no-go decision; and (c) *senior executives* dealing with technology and/or product market strategy may identify the need for specific advanced development efforts in anticipation of subsequent development projects.

In order to coordinate resource requirements for such advanced development efforts and to ensure that the sequence of steps followed is appropriate to achieve the results desired, many organizations put the relevant resources and their management into the individual functions (engineering, marketing, and manufacturing). The logic is that most advanced development efforts are fairly narrowly focused (or can be subdivided and focused) and thus do not require cross-functional teams. The drawback in doing this is that since each of the functions has a number of operating responsibilities, they may put such advanced development projects on the "back burner," resulting in low priority. We have seen some firms counter this by separating out the key resources (primarily engineering) that will focus on advanced development, and having them handle only such requirements. Often firms transfer a few people from an advanced development effort to the follow-on commercial product or process development effort to facilitate effective "technology transfer" and ensure that those in the advanced development group do not get too far removed from the marketplace. Whatever the particular form of advanced development organization, the firm may need to create a screen prior to Screen 1 to identify promising advanced development ideas. This advanced development screen links choices about individual technologies to the aggregate project plan.

Besides reviewing ideas for completeness, Screen 1 carries out a second, important function. It begins to identify competing concepts, ideas that might be integrated into platform development projects, and those that might be most effectively embedded in enhancement or derivative projects. This sets the stage for the activity that is to take place between Screens 1 and 2—defining and creating the appropriate sequence and set of platform and derivative development projects. Thus, rather than making go/no-go decisions about potential projects as they naturally arise as individual ideas, the development group reshapes and recasts them to provide an appropriate set of platform and derivative projects to support and strengthen the product family and its coverage of the targeted markets. This also operationalizes the stated business and functional strategies. This mid-funnel phase links the development projects under consideration directly to the stated strategies and objectives of the business.

At Screen 2, senior management reviews product and process development options and selects those that will become development projects. Thus Screen 2 is a go/no-go decision point, and any project passing it will be funded and staffed with every expectation that it will be carried through to market introduction. That is, while subsequent project reviews and updates will be held with management once the project is underway in the narrow neck of the funnel, at Screen 2, management commits itself to fund the entire development effort or stops the potential project from going into formal development.

While the second phase of detailing the project bounds and required knowledge usually takes only one to two months, it has a very specific purpose: to take the data and information developed during Phase 1 (concept development) and put it in a form that will enable senior management to evaluate proposed projects against competing and complementary projects under consideration, the functional strategy maps, the aggregate project plan, and the available development resources. If approved, this statement of a project's bounds and the knowledge required for its completion become the starting point for Phase 3 project execution by the development team.

As Exhibit 5–6 indicates, under the Model III development funnel, for any product family, multiple projects typically would be in the execution phase simultaneously. However, those would generally consist of one, or at most two, platform projects and a handful of smaller derivative and enhancement projects. As a set, these projects would match the development resources available and appropriate for this product family and its associated markets, and have a high probability of delivering on the strategies and objectives specified for that business. Thus the real power of the Model III development funnel is derived from three sources: avoiding the problems inherent in Models I and II, folding a creative set of innovative ideas into a logical set of development projects, and ensuring those projects tie directly to the business strategies.

Diagnosing and Correcting Critical Issues in the Development Funnel

Shaping and managing the development funnel gives managers a tool to address a number of important issues that set the stage for success on individual development projects. The first phase in shaping the funnel involves diagnosing the characteristics, form, and underlying logic of the existing funnel.

We have found a straightforward four-step process extremely effective in guiding this analysis. The process is an audit of the organization's existing funnel that characterizes the pattern of choices the firm has made. The audit sets the stage for a diagnosis of the strengths and weaknesses as well as opportunities for improvement.

The *first step* in applying the funnel concept as a diagnostic tool is to lay out the basic dimensions of choice and the role the funnel plays in development with a diverse group of middle managers and functional contributors in the firm. These people should have direct knowledge of the firm's development practice. The *second step* is to divide the managers into a half dozen randomly composed teams who are asked to do three things:

- Identify the salient characteristics of their organization's actual development procedure
- Draw the organization's development funnel
- Present the drawing (through an overhead transparency) with the other five groups

In the teams, participants are encouraged to consider such characteristics as the sources of ideas for the firm's development projects, the way in which narrowing occurs, the possibility of inputs that arrive later on, and the likelihood of extra iterations during development. Participants should understand that their charge is to be creative and make it fun, but to capture graphically the essential characteristics of their organization's development funnel. The funnels presented in Exhibits 5–2A and 5–2B at the beginning of the chapter came out of precisely this process. The teams were made up of about seven people drawn from a variety of different parts of the medical electronics company.

After approximately 45 minutes of work, the *third step* is for the entire group to reconvene and for each team to present its "picture" and explain its essential elements. The funnels drawn by Teams 1 and 2 (see Exhibits 5–2A and B) are typical of the creativity that often comes out of this process. (One team we worked with drew a large pinball machine, labeling the blocking "bumpers" as different executives or departments;

the projects—as pinballs—get bounced around between bumpers, often repeatedly.)

The *fourth step* in using the funnel concept as a diagnostic tool is to have a discussion of the common themes that appear across characterizations of the development funnels made by the different teams. In the case of the medical electronics firm, the ideas from Teams 1 and 2 were reinforced in the five other teams that made presentations. Indeed, the breadth and depth of insight this simple exercise developed was remarkable. The drawings and the discussions revealed seven critical themes:

1. Ideas for new product and new process developments came from many sources, but tended not to be managed or guided.
2. The "start point" for development projects was ill defined; the tendency was to approve anything that looked reasonably good, put it on the "official list," and then see what happened.
3. During the development process, there were a number of bulges and subsequent constrictions—the funnel did not converge consistently or according to any set pattern. Some of the causes of these bulges included late redefinitions of products (the moving target), fuzzy definitions at the start point, mixing research (invention) with development (application), changing midstream the key participants assigned to individual projects, and making some decisions early that did not seem to stick later on.
4. A number of inputs that could occur early in the development process actually occurred quite late, requiring additional recycling and extra iterations.
5. Toward the end of a project, management added considerable heat to push for market introduction—often creating difficulties for other projects in process, and in many cases resulting in the introduction of products before they were fully ready.
6. A lot more went into the development funnel as "approved projects" than ever came out. Many projects simply seemed to die over time as a result of inattention and lack of progress. Of the products that did get out, it was much more likely that they would be part of Product Family A than B, even though the firm's stated strategy was to build rapidly its revenues and profits from Family B.
7. Subcontracted or "OEM" projects (referred to in Chapter 2 as "alliance projects") tended to come in very late in the process—thereby requiring considerable iterating to fit with other ongoing efforts in the firm, or getting introduced without such iterating and never quite fitting into the product line.

These themes had been discussed individually at one time or another in the medical electronics firm, but the funnel provided a framework in which their implications became clear. Moreover, the diagnosis identified opportunities for substantial improvement.

The four-step diagnostic exercise can, in a relatively short time, result in a fairly accurate description of a firm's development funnel and suggest where efforts for improvement might be focused. While some changes may be made fairly quickly and still have significant impact, others may require additional resources, involve basic changes in behavior, and take much longer. This suggests the need for a more systematic funnel improvement plan to be followed over a longer time horizon. Often such a plan can be built around three critical issues common across all development funnels—the roles of management, competition among projects, and the mix of projects pursued.

Managerial Roles. The first issue is the advisory and decision-making roles of senior and middle management. Having observed a variety of splits in these responsibilities, we think the only viable long-term solution is for middle management to do more of the day-to-day planning and decision making. Senior management does not have the time, patience, or inclination to run individual projects or to micromanage the development process. This they must delegate. However, senior management should set the agenda, determine the organization's focus, and provide many of the incentives and supports that enable middle management to do what is needed. People at the midlevels of the organization must create the rich set of options, ensure that they have been sufficiently explored, elaborated, and prepared for decision making, and be directly involved in executing the resulting development projects. Senior management trains, develops, and creates systems that encourage and make them capable of doing that. In organizations that have moved considerable distance in this direction, often the approval of all but the platform projects is delegated to those down in the organization.

The opportunity and need exists for senior management to use the development funnel as a vehicle in building the organization, the people, and their collective capabilities, not just to select development projects for top management approval and funding. The challenge is for top management to spend sufficient time initially, to start the organization down a path of improvement, and yet to be able to withdraw as appropriate and transfer greater responsibility for these activities and their continued improvement to those down in the organization. The placement of screens in the funnel is one way to formalize middle and senior management's key responsibilities.

Competing Projects. A second critical issue is when, where, and how competing concepts and projects should (or should not) be encouraged or even allowed. One of the places where we think such competition is good is in the initial phase of concept development, often through advanced development projects. There is frequently insufficient information early on to know which ideas will eventually gain market acceptance and dominance, and which will prove too limited or narrow for extensive application. Thus, many of the concepts under investigation in the front end of the funnel represent competing approaches for addressing similar issues or competing projects for meeting market requirements. (These need not be just competing technical solutions, but also might be competing marketing, field service, or distribution solutions as well.) Such competition should be allowed to continue until the second screen, the go/no-go decision point. Beyond that point head-to-head competition generally is inappropriate.

Once a development project is underway, it makes most sense to put all the resources on the best possible platform project and an associated set of derivative projects rather than divide them between an ad hoc set of projects. Only where extreme time pressures exist have we seen it make sense to have competing development projects in the execution phase. Where viable options do exist, an organization is best served by exploring them thoroughly prior to the development project phase, or tailoring alternative development projects toward markets that will sufficiently support those multiple efforts. That is, rather than have them be direct competitors for the same customers, it may make sense to target them at different subsegments and then, based on market results, decide which options and approach to push hardest in subsequent generations.

Project Mix. A third issue is providing a mix of development projects that builds both market position and desired development capabilities in areas where they have not existed previously. For example, this is particularly important in hardware companies which find their challenges shifting more toward software and manufacturing processes. If the vast majority of ideas and options that are in the funnel at a given point in time continue to be primarily hardware, the firm will increasingly find itself at a disadvantage as competitors increase their proportion of software and manufacturing process technology development projects. The need to increase the proportion of these types of projects is accentuated because collective knowledge about managing software and manufacturing process developments is much less than collective knowledge regarding hardware efforts. Similarly, if distribution channels are changing, a firm wants to be certain that its mix of development projects matches future distribution opportunities and needs, not just past channels. Managers can address the issue of project mix through the criteria they use to screen projects, and the process they use to make decisions.

For the thoughtful organization, diagnosing the reality of its existing development funnel, outlining the idealized model that best fits its environment, and implementing changes that will move it toward that improved funnel is an opportunity as well as a challenge. By creating and adopting procedures that build its capabilities through selection of a mix of ideas and practices that improve all three phases of the funnel, a firm is much more likely to have the capabilities and knowledge required for effective development projects than if it works only on improving individual projects and their outcomes.

Study Questions

1. Consider Exhibits 5–2A and 5–2B. What explains the patterns observed in these funnels? Why don't the funnels drawn here look like the funnels in Exhibit 5–1?
2. Compare Models I and II depicted in Exhibits 5–3 and 5–4. What is your evaluation of these models? What are likely to be their strengths and weaknesses?
3. What are the primary differences between Models III and I? What problems is Model III likely to encounter?
4. What is the relationship between the funnel depicted in Exhibit 5–6 for Model III, and the aggregate project plan discussed in Chapter 4?
5. What are the fundamental challenges management faces in expanding the mouth of the funnel? In narrowing the funnel once projects are underway? How can each set of challenges be addressed?
6. What is the appropriate role for senior management in the development funnel? How might your answer to this question be affected by different competitive environments?

Honda Today

On the afternoon of December 10, 1988, Masami Kamimura, the Large Project Leader (LPL) of Honda Motor Co.'s Today team, was concluding a presentation to the company's senior management. One month earlier the Japanese Diet had approved a sweeping tax reform package to take effect in April 1989; one direct consequence would be to reduce some of the advantages "micromini" vehicles (those with an engine displacement of 550 cc or less) such as the Honda Today had enjoyed. Doomsayers were predicting an overall market decline for microminis of anywhere from 10 to 20%.

When rumors of the proposed tax changes had started circulating at the beginning of 1988, the Japan Automobile Manufacturers Association (JAMA) formed a micromini task force both to lobby for an exemption from the tax, and to come up with recommendations for new micromini specifications in the hope of making these cars more appealing to buyers in the wake of the new tax laws.

Over the months, the specification issue was hotly contested; there were disagreements on engine volume (displacement), and body length and width. For its part, the government (i.e., the Ministry of Transportation [MOT]) indicated that it would consider the matter of changing the specifications only when JAMA reached consensus on its recommended set of specifications.

As a micromini manufacturer, with a 13% market share in 1988, Honda had participated in the JAMA discussions, though it had not taken an explicit position in the debate. But it was keenly aware of the dilemma it faced, as Kamimura reminded the small audience of senior managers:

This case was prepared by Professor Marco Iansiti and Barbara Feinberg with the assistance of Professor Takahiro Fujimoto; some data have been disguised to protect company confidentiality.

315

We have word that the JAMA committee is very close to reaching a decision on specifications—it might even come tonight. I believe that they will suggest a significant increase in the limits for both the engine size and the length of the car. As we have discussed over the past few months, we must be prepared to act. It's clear that there will be some increase in engine displacement, but as you know, how big an increase is something that has divided the JAMA group. Moreover, we don't know for sure that the MOT will agree with the recommendation—or when it will come up with final specifications. But the stakes are very high here, for everyone in this market.

After a day of long meetings discussing the most likely JAMA recommendations, the possible MOT response, the possible impact on the demand for micromini cars, and Honda's options for redesigning the Today engine, Kamimura was tired. In his experience at Honda, where he had started 25 years earlier as a vehicle body engineer, he had rarely encountered a situation like the current one. The change in regulation was likely to trigger a head to head product development race between all micromini manufacturers. Kamimura began summarizing for the senior managers at Honda:

We want to introduce our new Today as close as possible to the date that the MOT puts the new specifications into effect, because we know our competitors will do the same. Currently, our best guess is that once the MOT announces the specifications, they will pick a date about 12 months out when the specifications will take effect. Since 12 months is an extremely short period for developing a new car, anything we can do now to focus our efforts and get started will be beneficial, assuming MOT follows JAMA's recommendations.

Kamimura had spent much time thinking about the costs and benefits of several options open to Honda in responding to the impending regulatory changes. His eyes lit up as he pointed to the various engine design possibilities displayed in charts arranged on the wall, and continued:

We basically have four options for increasing the size (and thus horsepower) of the Today engine. Three involve adapting the existing 550 cc[1] engine design, by (a) increasing the stroke length, (b) expanding the bore,[2] or (c) changing both the stroke and bore. Fourth, we could redesign the en-

---

[1] "cc" is an abbreviation for cubic centimeter. 16.4 cc is equal to one cubic inch; 1,000 cc corresponds to one liter. The number of cubic centimeters in an engine indicates its volume. Usually, the larger the volume, the greater the horsepower rating, and the lower the fuel economy. Honda's existing 550 cc engine had a horsepower rating of 31 HP. Typical engine volumes for compact cars in the United States usually ranged between 1,800 and 3,000 cc.

[2] See Exhibit 4 for a description of "stroke" and "bore."

gine entirely, expanding the width of the engine block. In choosing one of these options, we must remember that the project will have to proceed quickly, given the urgency of the situation.

After a brief but vigorous discussion, the meeting came to a close, with Honda president Tadashi Kume and Managing Director Nobuhiko Kawamoto[3] both thanking Kamimura for his efforts. Kume added, "We have always had confidence in your decisions, and know that in this situation you will once again make a good choice."

As Kamimura left Honda's headquarters in Tokyo to take the bullet train to the company's main R&D center in Tochigi (100 kilometers northwest of Tokyo), he mulled over the meeting and hoped that the president's confidence wasn't misplaced.

Honda Motor Company, Ltd.

Since its founding in 1948 by Mr. Soichiro Honda, Honda Motor Co., Ltd., had grown from a small manufacturer of engine-powered bicycles to become one of the world's largest engine manufacturers and the largest motorcycle producer; Honda ranked tenth worldwide in automobile production as well (see Exhibit 1). Honda's engineering excellence had won the company, and people within it, countless awards, a large proportion of which were first-place racing prizes for both motorcycles and cars. Mr. Honda was frequently recalled as pointing out: "In a race competing for a split second, one tire length on the finish line will decide whether you are a winner or a loser. If you understand that, you cannot disregard even the smallest improvement."

Tenacious striving for improvement infused the company. Early on, R&D had been spun off as a separate entity, the idea being to provide top-grade engineers—what the company sought—"an environment without constraints in order to maximize their creative energies."[4] Overall, Honda—the man and the company—welcomed the toughest design and manufacturing problems and challenged themselves to solve them innovatively and quickly. They also believed that the primary method of communicating Honda's philosophy was through their products. Honda engineers were particularly proud of their accomplishments in engine development, as well as in elegance and efficiency of interior and exterior design.

Organizationally, the company's renowned egalitarianism transcended similar uniforms, open-office arrangements, and other

[3] Mr. Kawamoto was also president of Honda R&D Co., Ltd.

[4]*Honda Corporate Outline*, April 1989, p. 20.

Exhibit 1

(a) Unit Production of Cars and Trucks in 1988

Rank	Company	Production (millions of units)
1	General Motors	5.1
2	Toyota	4.0
3	Ford	3.3
4	Nissan	2.2
5	FIAT	2.0
6	Peugeot	2.0
7	Volkswagen	1.9
8	Chrysler	1.7
9	Renault	1.7
10	Honda	1.3

(b) 1987 Honda Sales by Car Model in the Japanese Market

Model	Engine(s)	Sales (units)
Legend	2700 cc	12,800
Accord	1800 cc, 2000 cc	70,854
Vigor	1800 cc, 2000 cc	9,856
Prelude	2000 cc	52,978
Integra	1500 cc, 1600 cc	43,128
Civic	1300 cc, 1500 cc, 1600 cc	106,428
CR-X	1500 cc, 1600 cc	9,383
City	1300 cc	34,101
Today	550 cc	100,660

nonstatus-oriented signposts; people were actively encouraged to think, to participate, to experiment—and to increase their performance daily. These specific forums and policies reflected a philosophy called the "Honda Way."

By 1988, the company employed 58,000 people worldwide (including 6,700 in R&D), and was located in nearly 40 countries. Worldwide, Honda espoused the following "management principles":

- Proceed always with ambition and youthfulness.
- Respect sound theory, develop fresh ideas, and make the most effective use of time.
- Enjoy your work and always brighten your working atmosphere.
- Strive constantly for a harmonious flow of work.
- Be ever mindful of the value of research and endeavor.

Automobile Development

Developing an automobile entailed several complicated sets of tasks. Generally, for most automakers these were divided into four basic groups—concept development, engine development, vehicle design and development, and process engineering. Beginning with *concept development*, planning discussions considered several alternative approaches for designing the car and possible target market segments for the car. In addition, the appropriateness of different styling themes was explored as were performance goals and the specifications for technical components. The output of this first stage was typically summarized in a document stating the vehicle concept and/or specifications. These served as a guide throughout all subsequent steps in the development project.

Engine development began with several advanced engineering projects that explored novel engine designs and assessed their possibilities. The emphasis was on building prototype engines for testing in order to obtain performance data. Based on the data and concepts generated in these projects, specifications were set for developing the actual engine (in concert with concept development), and the engine was then designed. The emphasis during engine design was on optimizing and refining the detailed design. Engine development also involved designing the engine's production process, including the design of required dies and castings, and of techniques for machining and assembling the different engine parts. (Honda produced its engines in factories that only made engines, and then transported them to the final assembly factories.)

Vehicle design and development included the following tasks: "styling," i.e., designing the car's interior and exterior; "packaging," i.e., specifying the layout of the car's many components; and "body and chassis" and "component" engineering, i.e., detailing the engineering of the car's body, parts, and components.

Finally, *process engineering* entailed designing, refining, and testing the car's production process (for all elements except the engine). This included the design of the dies for stamping the body panels and creation of the assembly process.

In most automobile companies, engine, vehicle development, and process engineering were performed by separate organizations. Most often, a single basic engine design was employed (with minor refinements) in several car models. New engines were also introduced much less frequently than new car models.

In general, the development of a brand-new automobile (referred to as a "major" program) took from three to six years, whereas minor additions and modifications could require as little as one year. The most capital-intensive part of the process occurred during the process engineering stage when tooling and equipment at the production plants had to be modified to accommodate model changes. It was not unusual for a major new car development program to entail more than a thousand person-years of engineering effort and significant capital investment in tooling, equipment, and facilities (amounts exceeding $500 million were occasionally possible, if both engine and vehicle had been completely redesigned). Investment and staffing requirements for minor changes were considerably smaller.

Honda's Development Process

In most automobile companies, individual development engineers identified closely with their functional subspecialty (e.g., body engineering, engine engineering, and process engineering). It was in these specialized subfunctions that they were physically located, had a defined career path, were given performance reviews, and got specific project assignments. An engineer typically worked on several development projects a year, each aimed at designing different cars. These projects were coordinated and supervised by a project manager and staff, who coordinated and tracked resources and tasks to ensure the project's completion.

By contrast, at Honda development teams were independent and focused organizational units; that is, a team of engineers was dedicated to the development of a new car model. Although the engineers were affiliated with their different functions and each nurtured distinctive skills (e.g., engine design), their primary allegiance was to the development project, with which they often remained associated through several generations of new car development programs.

In addition, while other industry competitors believed that the simultaneous design of a new engine and a new car was too risky, and thus tended to introduce new cars with old engines or vice versa, Honda engineers felt each new car deserved a new engine. Only by refining, reoptimizing, or totally redesigning the engine could the engineers achieve a coherent match between the body, chassis, and engine. Additionally, Honda engineers believed that only through such coherence could they realize the vehicle's true character. Thus, automobile development at Honda generally involved the concurrent engineering of engine and vehicle.

Large project leaders (LPLs) played a critical role in Honda's "major" development programs. In fact, their tasks began months before the development project officially started. They talked with experienced body engineers and engine experts to learn the latest technical ideas. They reviewed, and might oversee, advanced engineering projects to obtain data on future technical options. They discussed recent market trends with product planners. They might even solicit opinions from car dealers and actual (or potential) customers by visiting popular hangouts to converse with car buffs about the latest trends and fads in the marketplace. Although Honda did not believe strongly in organized market research, it insisted that its engineers, especially LPLs, understand emerging trends and thereby combine technical excellence with a passion for satisfying customer preferences.

After assembling this information LPLs focused on a particular concept for the new automobile, which included a description of the "character" of the design as well as precise engineering objectives. They then selected the cross-functional development team that would develop the car. From this point on, the LPL took responsibility for ensuring that the product concept was successfully implemented in the millions of details constituting all aspects of the car's design. From the material for the steering wheel to the sound of the engine, the goal was an overall coherence, balance, and elegance that created a consistent "experience" for the customer. For Honda, coherence or "integrity" in all components, subsystems, and the total automobile was viewed as the key to success.

The Micromini Car Market in Japan

In Japan, where both space and fuel were precious, the car market (the world's second largest) was dominated by "small" size automobiles (officially designated by engine sizes ranging from 550 cc to 2000 cc); in 1988 they represented 91.4% of the total units sold. The remaining 8.6% was composed of "standard" size (4.5%) and "micromini" (or "midget") cars (4.1%). Indeed, 1988 was a banner year for car sales in the country; not only did the market experience double digit unit growth—13.5% for the first time in a decade—but "upscale," "luxury," and import models represented 49% of the standard size category, which for the first time surpassed micromini sales. Micromini sales too, however, saw growth, of 21.1%, overcoming a four-year decline.[5]

---

[5] Figures from "1989: The Motor Industry in Japan," JAMA, p. 9.

The Ministry of Transportation set specifications that defined each of these car categories. Since 1976 the maximum specifications for microminis had been: 550 cc engine displacement, 3200 mm overall body length, and 1400 mm width. Before then, engine displacement had been 360 cc, but in 1975 micromini manufacturers unitedly and successfully argued for the increased size to enhance the vehicles' competitiveness.

Microminis were exempt from some parking restrictions and benefitted from current tax laws. In the tax reform package passed in November 1988, for example, the new sales tax on microminis was 3%, while sales of other cars were taxed at 6%. To qualify as microminis, yet achieve maximum power and roominess, these vehicles were consistently designed and manufactured to the upper limits of the MOT specifications. (As some analysts had observed, with an engine as small as a micromini's, even an increase of five horsepower could make a noticeable difference in climbing hills and passing on the highway.) Models tended to undergo a major redesign about once each six years.

About 80% of micromini owners had two or more cars per household, while the remaining 20% owned a micromini as their "first" car. The cars were particularly popular among women. Most second car purchases occurred in rural areas, where a parking space for a second car would be available, and where subways and trains were not well developed as methods of substitute transportation.

Experts felt that two considerations particularly influenced purchasing decisions in the micromini market. First, the cars had to be practical. Second, cost was considered crucial, since many of the automobiles were purchased as second cars to provide basic transportation. Other considerations—vehicle safety, technical performance, and styling—were considered of secondary importance. Technical performance was considered important in only one small subsegment of the market, that of the very young car enthusiast. Advanced technical features such as turbochargers, four-wheel drive, and anti-lock braking systems (ABS) were becoming increasingly common options for buyers in this subsegment.

Competitors in the Micromini Market

Six major domestic competitors battled strenuously for micromini business (pictures of each competitor's main micromini offering are displayed in Exhibit 2):

> *Suzuki.* The market leader with 28% share in 1988, Suzuki's micromini car, the Alto, used a tall body and upright seat configuration. Its latest model change had been released in 1988, and it exported microminis with an 800 cc engine. Suzuki was co-developing a Korean "people's car" (with Mitsubishi and Daewoo) that also would utilize an 800 cc engine.

EXHIBIT 2
1988 Micromini Models[1]

Suzuki: The birth of everybody's car

Daihatsu: A four seater sports car whose main attraction is driving feel compactly condensed

[1] Quotes are from leading Japanese car magazines.

Daihatsu. With 27% share, the company's Mira and Leeza micromini cars also had a tall body and upright seats; its latest model change had been in November 1985. The company exported microminis with an 850 cc engine. Toyota owned 14.1% of Daihatsu, and though not a Toyota subsidiary, since 1968 Daihatsu had been regarded as part of the Toyota "group."

Both Suzuki and Daihatsu, as corporations, focused on micromini car production and accordingly, compared with other auto manufacturers, had fewer small and standard size vehicles.

EXHIBIT 2 *(continued)*

Mitsubishi: The car realizes roominess of interior and cargo space that overwhelms even that of a one liter car

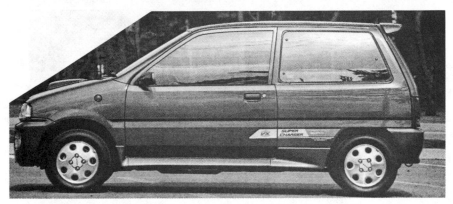

Fuji (Subaru): Solid rationalism with a high degree of perfection

---

Mitsubishi. With a 16% share, the company's Minica had a tall body and upright seats; its latest model change had been released in late 1988 and its exported microminis had an 800 cc engine.

Fuji (Subaru). With a 15% share, the company's micromini car, the Rex, also had a tall body and upright seats. Fuji's latest model change had occurred in November 1986 and its export models had a 700 cc engine. Nissan owned 4.5% of Fuji, and Fuji was regarded as part of the Nissan "group."

Honda. With a 13% share, Honda's micromini car, the Today, was configured with a low body and low seats. The product had been introduced in 1985,

EXHIBIT 2 (*continued*)

Honda: Elegant sedan with greatly improved feeling of quality

Mazda: Cute and nostalgic design

---

although it had been updated in early 1988. Honda did not export micromini vehicles.

Mazda. With a 2% share, Mazda used a Suzuki chassis under an OEM production agreement. The Carol, its micromini car, emphasized cute, nostalgic styling, and its next model change had been announced for release in 1989. Mazda did not export micromini vehicles. Ford Motor Company owned 27% of Mazda.

All of the Japanese producers of micromini cars had adopted transverse-mounted front-wheel drive configurations to maximize interior space. The engines were all in-line, usually with three cylinders, though two and four cylinder arrangements were technically feasible. (The Fuji model had a four cylinder engine.)

Typical contribution margins in this segment of the market were low, usually less than 5% of the factory selling price; the factory selling price would usually be about 80% of the retail price.

The Honda Today

Honda had been a very active participant in the early days of the micromini market. Its successful N360 model, introduced in 1966, had been the first micromini with a tall body design. In October 1974, however, the model had been discontinued to allow Honda to concentrate its resources and efforts on larger cars where contribution margins and volumes were much more attractive.

Honda reentered the micromini segment with its introduction of the Today in September 1985. In introducing it, Honda was responding to its car dealers' requests to have a micromini for their showrooms. Many of Honda's dealers had been with the company since the early days, when its business had been based on motorcycles and bicycles, which many of them continued to sell.

The 1985 Honda Today was envisioned as an entry level car, particularly for young female users who would then upgrade to Honda's main models (such as the City or Civic). In advertising, Honda consistently emphasized the Today's elegance and sophistication: the car was often described as "simple beauty" in newspaper ads and TV commercials. The Today also projected a more serious and urban image than that of its competitors. One industry expert characterized the difference between the Today and the competitors as follows:

> Rather than being a car that a father would buy for his daughter, the image is that of a daughter buying the car for herself.

According to an informal user survey conducted by Honda in 1988, out of 810 Today purchasers, 66.5% were female, whereas for the entire micromini market, 58.8% were female.

The concept and design of the Today was unusual for a micromini. In contrast with competitor models, it had a relatively low and streamlined body configuration. While not as tall as other microminis, the Today did not sacrifice roominess. Honda engineers had managed to design the car layout so efficiently that its interior offered almost as much space as competitors' models. This had been described in the automotive press as a major breakthrough.

A less attractive feature of the 1985 Today was its engine. Adapted from an existing truck engine design, it had only two cylinders. Engines offered by most of Honda's competitors had three cylinders and exhibited better performance.

The initial Today had been successful in the market. Following its September introduction, Honda had sold 36,538 units in 1985, 93,147 units in 1986, and about 100,600 units in 1987. By early December, it appeared that 1988 Today sales would be about 10% higher than the previous year, even though total industry sales for microminis were expected to be flat for the year. The retail selling price of the Today was about ¥ 640,000[6] depending on the option configuration.

Reconfiguring the Today's Engine

In January 1988, Honda introduced a new version of the Today which exhibited updated exterior styling and a new engine. The main challenge for the Today team in this development project had been a complete redesign of the engine into a three-cylinder configuration, a significant effort (and expense) that had taken about three and a half years. The effort had been significant enough for this project to be considered a major development program by the company. (A timeline of important events in the history of the Today is shown in Exhibit 3.)

The production process for the new engine had been largely redesigned and equipped, involving a large capital investment (in excess of ¥ 5 billion). All three engine production steps—casting the engine block, machining the block to tight specifications, and assembly/test of a completed engine—were altered substantially for the new 550 cc engine. Implementing each change involved considerable time and effort by both design and process engineers. New castings were required, since the engine block had been redesigned to new length, width, and height specifications. The transfer line where machining was done had been reconfigured and rearranged to accommodate the pitch and bore of the cylinders which had been changed. (See Exhibit 4 for a sketch of the engine block.) Finally, the assembly process had been reconfigured to account for the substantial changes in engine design.

Full production of the engine had begun in January 1988 and the new Today model was introduced in February. The Today team took pride in its effort: the new body design retained Honda's low body and low seat configuration while maintaining maximum internal space. The new engine was elegantly designed, integrated well with the car's design, and had a good balance of stroke and bore dimensions which ensured good

---

[6] In 1988, ¥ 140 was approximately equal to U.S. $1.00.

327

EXHIBIT 3

Timeline of Important Events in Honda Today History

	1985/9	1988/1	1988/2	1988/3	1988/4
Events regarding tax reform		Discussion on new consumption tax begins at the Diet		First draft of the tax reform package	Hearings on new consumption tax by liberal democratic party (LDP) tax committee Interim report on tax reform by LDP tax committee
Events regarding micromini standard		JAMA'S Micromini Task Force initiates study of the impact of the new consumption tax		Head of Micromini Task Force proposes that JAMA urge the government to take action to alleviate the impact of the consumption tax on the demand of micromini vechiles	
Today (engine)		New 550cc 3–cylinder engine starts production	engine expansion experimental project ▼ Project start		▼ Experimental prototype engines completed; testing begins
Today (vehicle)	Honda Today introduced	Today introduced into production after a major redesign	Market introduction of the new Today		

performance and fuel economy (see Exhibit 6; the ratio of stroke to bore in this design was 0.95). All other competitor models offered a turbocharger configuration as a popular option to boost performance; the Today team, however, believed that their engine was quite adequate without one.

The team's enthusiasm was short-lived. One week after the introduction of the new Today, rumors of the government's planned tax change circulated; two weeks later, the JAMA task force was formed to study

1988/5	1988/6	1988/7	1988/11	1988/12
LDP's outline of tax reform determined			Tax Reform Bill passes the Lower House	
			Suzuki and Mitsubishi issue a private proposal to the Chariman of JAMA suggesting an increase in engine size to 800cc Head of JAMA directs the JAMA committees to study the case based on the above proposal	JAMA issues its official request for the change in micromini standards in relation to the new consumption tax
Experimental engines assembled into prototype vehicles and further tested		Final report		

the impact the tax change would have on the micromini market and to consider the changes in micromini specifications that it would recommend to the MOT.

Experimenting with Engine Expansion

As LPL of the Today team, Masami Kamimura was especially distressed by this turn of events. Not only had his group just redesigned the Today

Sketch of Engine Block

Engine block seen from above

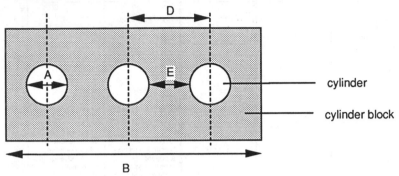

Engine block seen from side

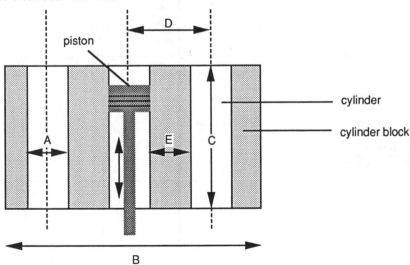

Definitions:
A = cylinder bore (diameter of cylinder)
B = engine block width
C = cylinder stroke (height of cylinder)
D = cylinder pitch
E = horizontal clearance between cylinders
Engine volume (displacement) is the sum of the volumes of all cylinders

EXHIBIT 5
Estimated Timeline for Minor Development Project[1]

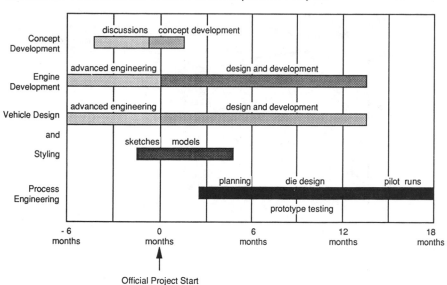

Official Project Start

[1] Estimated for a project involving a small length increase and an engine expansion (with small increases in both bore and stroke), using usual Honda staffing procedures and sequence of tasks. Timing may be changed considerably depending on staffing, project organization, number of engineering changes, and other decisions.

engine for current specifications—and at great expense—his colleagues that headed other car lines were beginning to request some of his best engineers to participate on their engine projects. Kamimura knew he had to create substantial challenges to retain his engineers' attention and to justify not letting many of them go to other projects that promised greater returns to the corporation.

As he saw it, the first task was to experiment with the existing 550 cc engine design and evaluate different options for its expansion; he understood that whatever JAMA decided, engine displacement would increase, not decrease. He further suspected that there might be a push for an increase to as much as 800 cc since several competitors produced microminis for export with engines of that size, but there was little chance it would go beyond that.

Over the past several months, he had challenged his team to increase engine volume while simultaneously keeping as much of the new 550 cc product and process design intact as possible. He also had emphasized the need for speed: he had wanted prototypes of new engine options (up to 800 cc in size) completed in slightly more than one month—a very

EXHIBIT 6

Engine Performance Data

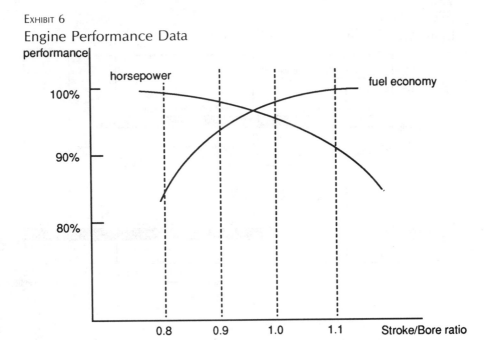

Note: These data were developed in part during the experiments on engine expansion carried out in 1988. A value of 100% corresponded to the maximum horsepower or fuel economy rating achievable with the given engine size.

ambitious goal. The point was not to develop an actual detailed design that would be manufacturable in high volumes; that would entail considerable commitment and expense—and time. Rather, the team would emphasize experimentation and data-gathering to prepare for a potential future project. How could the current design be expanded, he demanded? How could this be done cheaply while optimizing performance? What different options would be available? Under Kamimura's leadership, a variety of possibilities had been explored during 1988, and many of them eliminated on the basis of cost performance or time to convert to volume production. By early December, he and his team had narrowed the options to four (see Exhibits 7 and 8).

Decision Time

It was around 8 P.M. when Masami Kamimura returned to his desk at the R&D center. On his trip back he had collected some of the key

Exhibit 7

Engine Expansion Guidelines[1]

Design Guidelines in Expanding Engine:

The engine volume is the sum of the volumes of the engine cylinders. Expanding the volume thus involves enlarging the cylinders by increasing the bore, the stroke, or both. Another alternative involves increasing the number of cylinders.

Options:

a. Cylinder bore expansion. Expanding the cylinder bore is the easiest and cheapest option. It would only involve relatively minor tooling changes in the machining process, but no changes in the engine castings. The approximate retooling cost for this change would be about ¥ 500 million.
b. Cylinder stroke expansion. Expanding the cylinder stroke involves changing the height of the cylinder block. This would be accomplished by redesigning part of the engine block casting, as well as a few other engine parts, with an approximate investment of ¥ 1.5 billion in new tooling.
c. Expanding both bore and stroke. This option would involve the costs of both previous options plus the added design challenge and risk of changing two major design parameters in a single effort.
d. Major redesign, involving an increase of the engine block width. This option is quite expensive, since it would involve a completely new casting design for the engine block as well as a change in the cylinder pitch (total investment in tooling greater than ¥ 5 billion).

Major Constraints:

1. Horizontal clearance between cylinders. This is the thickness of the metal wall separating each cylinder from the others. Honda engineers believe that a safe lower limit for this parameter would be about 9 mm for an aluminum engine block (such as the Today's). They believed that a clearance figure less than 9 mm was feasible (down to about 6 mm), but would endanger the long term reliability of the engine.
2. Cylinder pitch change. The cylinder pitch is the distance between the centers of each cylinder (see Exhibit 4). Changing this parameter is expensive (approximately ¥ 5 billion). A change would involve a significant redesign of the engine machining process.

[1] These guidelines were developed in part during the experiments on engine expansion carried out in 1988.

---

thoughts that had been expressed thus far regarding each of the four engine options his team considered viable. First of all, he was very keen on minimizing changes to the engine production process and tooling. The expense incurred on the new 550 cc engine had been substantial and he felt it would be difficult to justify spending that much again. While he would have enjoyed the technical challenge of a substantial redesign of the engine (involving changing both the stroke and bore), he was conscious of the expense and risk. Changing the engine bore would clearly be the safest and cheapest option. However, he had been quite happy with the proportions of the 550 cc engine, and expanding the

333

EXHIBIT 8

Comparison of Micromini Engine Designs and Expansion Options

	Honda	Suzuki	Daihatsu	Mitsubishi	Fuji	Mazda
Current design details:						
engine size (cc)	548	548	548	549	548	548
number of cylinders	3	3	3	3	4	3
bore (mm)	62.5	65	62	62.3	56	65
stroke (mm)	59.5	55	60.5	60	55.6	55
cylinder pitch (mm)	80	72	75	73	62.5	72
horizontal clearance (mm)	17.5	7	13	10.7	6.5	7
stroke/bore ratio	0.95	0.85	0.98	0.96	0.99	0.85

*Implication of different design options if chosen engine volume is 650 cc:**

	Honda	Suzuki	Daihatsu	Mitsubishi	Fuji	Mazda
Engine expansion parameters:						
volume for expansion (cc)	650	650	650	650	650	650
cylinders in expansion	3	3	3	3	4	3
Option a: Increasing bore only						
bore size (mm)	68.1	70.8	67.5	67.8	61.0	70.8
bore increase (mm)	5.6	5.8	5.5	5.5	5.0	5.8
horizontal clearance (mm)	11.9	1.2	7.5	5.2	1.5	1.2
stroke/bore ratio	0.87	0.78	0.90	0.88	0.91	0.78
Option b: Increasing stroke only						
stroke size (mm)	70.6	65.3	71.8	71.1	66.0	65.3
stroke increase (mm)	11.1	10.3	11.3	11.1	10.4	10.3
stroke/bore ratio	1.13	1.00	1.16	1.14	1.18	1.00
Option c: Increasing both bore and stroke based on a stroke/bore ratio of 0.95						
bore size (mm)	66.2	66.2	66.2	66.2	60.2	66.2
bore increase (mm)	3.7	1.2	4.2	3.9	4.2	1.2
horizontal clearance (mm)	13.8	5.8	8.8	6.8	2.3	5.8
stroke size (mm)	62.9	62.9	62.9	62.9	57.1	62.9
stroke increase (mm)	3.4	7.9	2.4	2.9	1.5	7.9
stroke/bore ratio	0.95	0.95	0.95	0.95	0.95	0.95

Option d: Major redesign

* Includes estimates of possible actions by competitors, based on their existing engine designs.

---

bore would significantly change the ratio of stroke to bore length, affecting the driving performance and fuel economy of the car.

During the train ride from Tokyo to Tochigi he had also reviewed once more the timing and sequence of development tasks that experience with previous projects at Honda told him would be needed (see Exhibit 5). He had prepared the chart assuming that the development project would be focused on a small body length increase as well as an intermediate increase in engine volume (e.g., going to 650 cc). While a considerable amount of planning and advanced engineering had already been done compared to a normal Honda project, the time line would still have to be compressed considerably to get it all done by the date when the new standards would take effect.

When Kamimura walked into his office, he was still tired and a little frustrated but also hopeful that the months of indecision on the specification matter would soon come to an end. And indeed they had: there on his desk was the JAMA recommendation—an increase in displacement in the range of 650–690 cc, and an increase in overall car length of 50–100 mm.

"Well," he thought wryly, "I know more than I did this morning! But what precisely will the MOT choose? And when will they make that choice?" A few days earlier *Nikkan Jidosha Shinbun* had noted that the Ministry of Finance had been "urging" MOT to decide quickly, and that hearings would be held this month. Maybe so. There were also rumors that the new specifications would go into effect in January 1990. Kamimura knew that it would be critical to have the new engine in production as close to that date as possible. Companies achieving a timely response to the specification change would enjoy a very substantial advantage in the marketplace and would be granted considerable prestige for the feat.

Kamimura picked up the note concerning the JAMA recommendation, gathered his summary data on the four options (Exhibits 6, 7 and 8), and headed over to the conference room, where five of his leading engineers were waiting to discuss which engine option they should choose and how they would proceed with its development.

General Motors: Packard Electric Division

David Schramm, the Chief Engineer for Cable and Component Design, glanced at the RIM grommet in his hand and considered the risks and benefits. Packard Electric, a division of the General Motors Corporation, had developed the RIM (reaction injection molded) grommet as a new technology for passing the wires from the engine compartment through the fire wall to the passenger compartment of passenger automobiles.

The Product, Process, and Reliability (PPR) committee, which had the final responsibility for the new product development process, had asked Schramm for his analysis and recommendations on two issues. The first was a short term one—whether Packard Electric should commit to the RIM grommet for the 1992 model year. It was already March 1, 1990 and, because of the lead time on the equipment and tooling, the decision had to be made within the week. While many of the product development people were very excited by the RIM grommet's possibilities, many of the manufacturing people were dead set against it.

The second issue that Schramm faced was to investigate whether the new four phase product development process recently instituted at Packard would improve the product development effort. In particular, the PPR had requested that Schramm report on whether following the four phase process would have prevented the problems currently faced by the RIM project.

This case was prepared by Research Associate Geoffrey K. Gill under the supervision of Professor Steven C. Wheelwright.

Packard Electric Background

The Packard brothers founded the Packard Company in the late nineteenth century to produce carbon filament lamps and transformers. In 1899, the company moved into the fledgling automobile industry and began to produce automobiles. Eventually, the automobile business was sold, but Packard continued to be a supplier of ignition systems. General Motors bought the Packard Company in 1932, and it became the Packard Electric division of GM.

The management of the Packard Electric division had remained fairly autonomous through the years. In the first 90 years of its existence, Packard had only seven general managers. Although the majority of its sales were to GM divisions, it did receive significant business from other automobile companies.

During the 1980s, GM experienced significant competition—particularly from Japanese imports. GM's share of the U.S. market had dropped from 45% in 1980 to about 34% in 1989. Despite its parent company's problems, Packard Electric's revenues and profitability had grown steadily in the 1980s at a rate of 8–9% per year. This growth was attributed to two factors: increasing sales to other automobile manufacturers, and the growing electronic content of automobiles. By 1989, Packard Electric had over $2 billion in sales, of which 25% was to non-GM customers.

Packard's Products

Packard Electric executives referred to Packard's business as "power and signal distribution." Packard sold all the electrical cabling and connectors required to interconnect the electrical devices in a vehicle (see Exhibit 1). The business was divided into two areas—components and assemblies. The components side involved the individual pieces that made up an automobile's electrical system. Components included cables, connectors, and conduits (sheaths for holding several cables together, neatly). Packard Electric had two sets of customers for its components. One set of customers consisted of companies and GM divisions (such as Delco-Electronics and Harrison Radiators) which integrated Packard components into subsystems and then sold them to assembly customers. The other set of components customers were dealers in spare parts.

The assembly products were complete harnesses or sub-systems that could be installed directly into an automobile. Typically, Packard would sell the complete wiring system for an automobile (called a harness) which would then be installed by the automobile manufacturer on its final assembly line. Harnesses varied widely in complexity de-

EXHIBIT 1
Automobile Power and Signal Distribution System

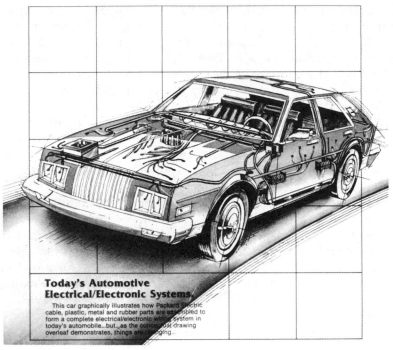

Today's Automotive Electrical/Electronic Systems.

This car graphically illustrates how Packard Electric cable, plastic, metal and rubber parts are assembled to form a complete electrical/electronic wiring system in today's automobile...but..,as the conceptual drawing overleaf demonstrates, things are changing...

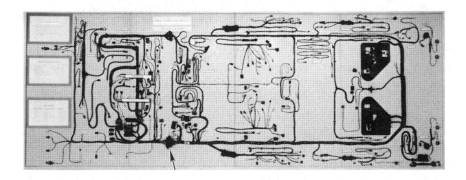

pending on the requirements of the automobile. A very complex harness for a car might have several thousand components and nearly a mile of wiring.

The design of harnesses was complicated by the fact that the engineers had to make sure that the harness be installed in the assembly line as a single unit. Furthermore, because the harnesses were manufactured at Packard plants, then shipped to the automobile assembly plant, the harnesses had to be folded for shipping. Making a harness foldable was often a difficult task because harnesses typically contained bundles of up to 150 wires. These bundles were very stiff and so the engineers had to determine a routing path that not only fit the car's design but also could be folded neatly for shipment.

The harness installation process was complicated because the cabling spanned the entire length and breadth of the car and connections had to be made at every step of the automobile's assembly process. This installation process consumed from 60 to 90 minutes of the 20 to 30 hours required to complete the final assembly of a typical automobile. As one Packard engineer noted:

> The wiring people get to know everyone in an automotive company, from design through manufacturing. They get involved at every step of the process and must work out thousands of little details. Also the easiest thing you can change in a car is the wiring, so if there are any production problems, the wiring is the first thing to be changed. What's more, customers don't notice wiring unless there is a problem, and then it's a disaster. Most companies hate wiring because of all the details and the fact that you never get any positive feedback, but at Packard this is what we do and we love it.

Because of the relative ease with which an automotive designer could change a harness, engineering change orders (ECOs) were a major effort at Packard. A harness for even a mature car had an average of two major ECOs each as well as dozens of minor ones each year. These ECOs ate up a tremendous amount of engineering time; Packard estimated that approximately 50% of the time of its 500 engineers was spent on ECOs. The part proliferation caused by these constant changes was dramatic (see Exhibit 2). Because Packard had to be able to fabricate spare parts for any component it had produced, drawings and tooling on over 45,000 parts needed to be maintained. While Schramm had never been able to get any good data on the cost of maintaining these parts, he felt sure that it was significant.

Reducing the cost of the ECOs and part number maintenance were major goals at Packard. In recent years, Packard had become better at forcing change to occur earlier in the initial design process and reducing the subsequent changes per part. The total number of ECOs had remained fairly constant, however, because the complexity of the harnesses (as measured by total length of cable and the number of connectors) was increasing by 6–8% per year with the increasing electrical content of automobiles.

Exhibit 2
Statistics on Part Proliferation and Resources Devoted to ECOs

	Applications Engineering	Components Engineering
Statistics on Parts		
Number of Active Parts	2,800	45,000
Number of Parts Added Annually	1,200	2,400
Number of Parts Deleted Annually	1,100	300
Lifespan of a Typical Part	1 year	10 years
Statistics on Engineering Effort		
Percent of Resources Developing New Parts	40%	65%
Percent of Resources on ECOs	60%	35%

Organization

Worldwide activities of Packard Electric were run by four committees which reported to the general manager, Rudy Schlais (see Exhibit 3). The *European Planning Council* had full profit and loss responsibilities for the European operations. Most of the European operations had been acquired several years earlier when Packard had purchased the Kabelwerke Reinshagen, G.m.b.H. Reinshagen supplied the electric system to many of the major German automobile manufacturers including Bayerische Motorwerk (BMW) and Audi. International operations outside of Europe and North America were controlled by the *Packard International Planning Council*.

The *North American Planning Council* had responsibility for planning and strategy for the bulk of the company's operations which were in North America, but it did not have operational or profit and loss responsibilities. Operational control of the North American business was exercised by the *Executive Committee* which consisted of the heads of each function. All of the functional divisions reported to the Executive Committee.

New Product Development Organization

Three functional groups were involved in new product development: *engineering, manufacturing engineering,* and *reliability* (see Exhibit 4). Engineering did the product design and engineering; manufacturing engineering was responsible for developing the processes for manufacturing the components, cables, and harnesses. Reliability had been given the mission of overseeing Packard's commitment to quality and excellence in all phases of its business. *Cooperative Involvement Engineering* (CIE) reported to the director of reliability and was designed to provide a direct avenue for customer feedback into manufacturing operations, engineering, and Packard upper management. Their role was that of a customer advocate and they were allowed to examine any Packard decision involving a customer.

The manufacturing engineering group was divided into several subgroups. Of these, the manufacturing engineering and industrial engineering departments were particularly important during the product development process. A sub-department under the manufacturing engineering department, manufacturing development, made a first pass at developing a manufacturing process. After manufacturing development had achieved a repeatable process, the remaining manufacturing engineering departments took over and refined and documented the process. Finally, the industrial engineering department had responsibility for training the operators, fitting the process into the plant as a whole, and coordinating the ramp-up of the process. Beneath these major departments, resources were divided along functional lines at one or two sublevels.

Four departments comprised the product engineering function. *Cable and component design* (CCD), as its name suggested, was responsible for the design of components (like connectors and pass-throughs) and cables. The design of cabling included determining the wire gage required for the application, the number of wire strands to be wound together to make up the cable, and the type of insulation to be used. *Application engineering* did the design of the harnesses as a whole—determining the number and length of cables, and the type of connectors and other components. Often application engineering would need a component that did not exist, which would have to be designed by CCD. The long term product development effort was done by the *advanced engineering* group. Finally, *product assurance* was responsible for making sure that all product designs met Packard's quality standards.

Each of these major departments were broken down into one or two levels of sub-functions. In addition to these subdivisions, both CCD and application engineering had a resident engineer program. Resident engineers were Packard engineers who were assigned to a customer and who resided at the customer's plant or design center. Resident engineers from CCD interfaced primarily with the design group at component division customers, while resident application engineers worked with the design group at car division customers. The purpose of resident engineers was to help integrate Packard's designs with customer needs. By taking responsibility for more and more of the electrical system design task, they relieved the customer of the cost of doing the design and enabled Packard to become more fully integrated into the design process.

Exhibit 3

Overview of Packard Electric Organization

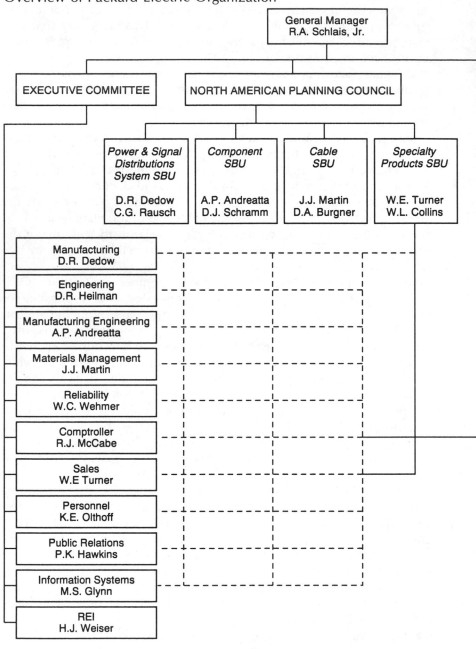

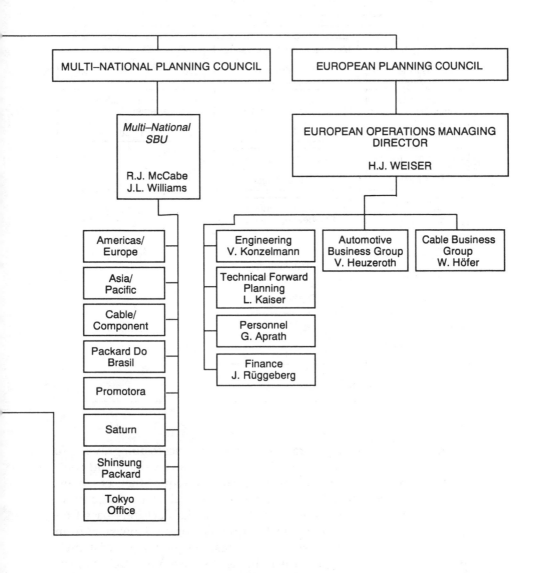

Exhibit 4

Partial Packard Electric Product Development Organization

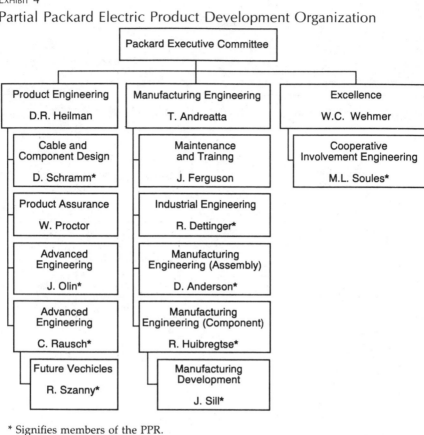

* Signifies members of the PPR.

The resident engineers program had been very successful, growing to almost 100 engineers at customer design centers and vehicle and component divisions. Many customers were eager to reduce their engineering overhead. They had been somewhat skeptical at the beginning, believing that the resident engineers would make decisions based on what was good for Packard rather than the customer. However, from the outset, Packard had stressed to the resident engineers that their responsibility was to do what was right for the customer. Packard benefitted from that program because resident engineers were expected to make sure that Packard knew exactly what the customer needed so that Packard could provide the best solution.

The resident engineering program reinforced a trend in which the customers were transferring more and more of the design task to Packard. Carl Rausch, the head of applications engineering, described the trend:

> One way to think about it is to divide the types of customer design specifi-
> cations you might get into three levels. Level 1 is a broad functional specifi-
> cation where the customer tells you what he or she wants to do but you
> design the whole power and signal distribution system. Level 2 is a system
> specification, where the customer has done a system-wide design but left the
> choice of components to you. Level 3 is a component level design where all
> that is left to do is manufacture the components to spec and assemble them
> into the product. We used to get mainly level 3 designs from our customers,
> but we have pushed towards level 1 specs. Level 1 gives us more freedom
> and leverage—we can integrate our operations much better and develop
> standard ways to attack problems. This enables us to increase quality and
> reduce overall system costs.

To integrate the efforts of all these functional departments, the Product Process Reliability (PPR) committee had been formed. This committee consisted of the managers of Cable and Component Design, Application Engineering, Advanced Engineering, Cooperative Involvement Engineering, Manufacturing Development, Manufacturing Engineering, and Industrial Engineering. Its purpose was to provide an overall strategy and process for the development effort, guide major technology decisions, and help coordinate activities between functional groups.

The RIM Grommet

Much of the cabling in an automobile's harness needed to pass through the "front of dash" area between the engine compartment and the passenger compartment. A grommet or housing was used to pass the cables through the fire wall. It had three purposes: (1) to hold the cables in place so that they did not slip and possibly disconnect or wear off their insulation; (2) to dampen engine noise and keep the passenger compartment quiet; and (3) to prevent any water in the engine compartment from entering the passenger compartment.

Packard's primary grommet, the injectable hardshell grommet or IHG (see Exhibit 5), had been developed in the late 1970s. The IHG grommet was essentially a hard plastic shell with a comb into which the cables were placed. The comb served to separate the cables and glue was injected into the comb area to seal it, preventing water from seeping through the grommet. Because the glue was quite viscous, however, it did not seal perfectly around all the wires. The resultant seal, although highly splash resistant, was not completely waterproof. It failed the

EXHIBIT 5

Contrasting the Options: IHG and RIM Grommet

IHG

RIM Grommet

most strenuous leak test—the static water test—which tested the seal with five inches of water for five minutes. (This test was commonly called the "five and five" test.)

Water in the passenger compartment had been a frequent assembly plant customer complaint in the 1980s, and Packard engineers had searched to find a solution to the problem. In July 1986, Bob McFall, a process engineer at Packard came up with the idea of using reaction injection molding (RIM) technology to form a grommet around the cables.

RIM was a type of injection molding technology that had been around for several years in large-sized applications like automobile door panels and fenders. The principle behind RIM was similar to that of epoxy—when two liquid materials were mixed, they set in less than a minute to form a rubbery solid (see Exhibit 6). Before the mixture set, it had a very low viscosity (about the same as that of water), which allowed it to seep between the cables to form an excellent seal.

Development of the RIM Grommet

From July 1986 through the end of 1987, McFall worked on a RIM grommet as a side interest (about 10% of his time), experimenting with several different materials in the Packard laboratory. By early 1988, he had developed several different configurations. During this period, McFall's principal activity had been helping design components for the electrical systems for a high-end automobile customer. Knowing that this customer was very concerned about any water leaking into the passenger compartment, McFall brought along one of his mock-ups of a RIM grommet on one of his frequent visits to the customer's plant.

The customer got very excited about the RIM grommet, and asked if it would be available for a high-end 1992 model. While McFall did not have the authority to agree to this time table, he felt that it was not unreasonable. Encouraged by the customer's reaction, McFall began to get other groups at Packard involved in the effort. During the next year, CCD expanded its level of effort and manufacturing engineering began to get involved with a low level of effort. The resident engineer at the customer's site monitored the RIM's progress but he decided not to get personally involved with the project until it was definitely "determined that it was a go."

During the next several months, McFall and others worked on several aspects of the RIM project. They worked on material development to find the RIM material that could best withstand the constant cycling between hot and cold without warping. Eventually, they determined that the RIM would need to be reinforced with an internal steel plate. They also began to look at tool configurations. Progress was quite slow,

EXHIBIT 6

Schematic of RIM Machine and Related Process Flow Layout

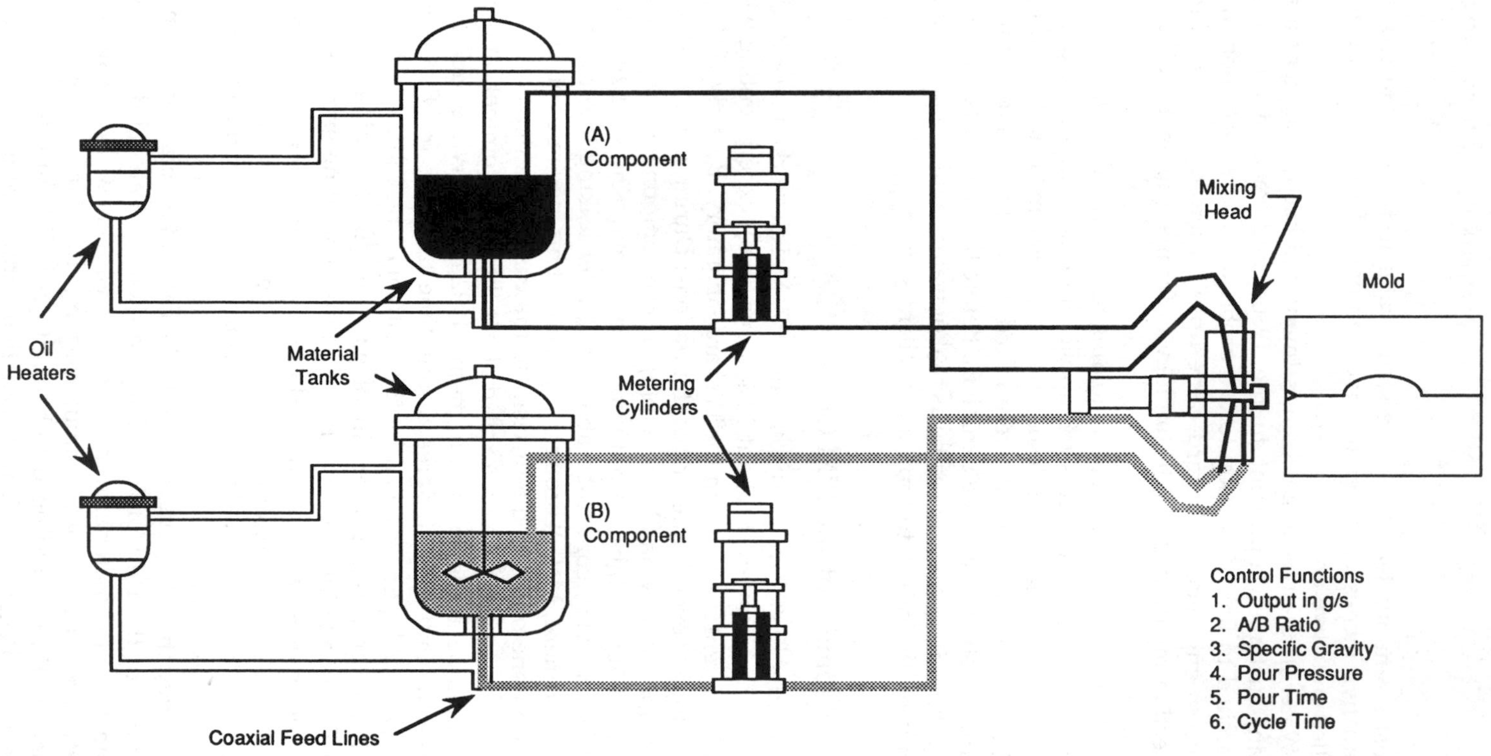

however, because all the engineers were involved in other projects which took up most of their time.

In January 1989, the customer requested a status report on the RIM project. They were not pleased with what they heard. The project had not progressed very far and it was not clear that it would be ready in time for the 1992 model year. Major RIM equipment producers had not yet provided a piece of equipment small enough to be practically used in this application. All known alternatives were expensive, labor intensive and cumbersome. The customer made it very clear that they wanted the RIM grommet and were planning to use it in 1992. With this increased customer pressure, Packard's level of effort on the RIM project was stepped up considerably.

For a while, it looked like the project would stall for lack of a molding machine that was an appropriate size for the grommet application. Most RIM machines were very large and expensive because they were designed to make large, relatively high value components. It was impossible to justify spending $300,000 for a large machine for experimentation. The project was about to be canceled, when the chief engineer from applications engineering ran across a small RIM machine at a trade show.

This RIM machine had been developed by an eight-person company. Its cost was only $80,000, and it was about the right size for Packard's application. In June 1989, the machine was ordered and it arrived in October. Unfortunately, Packard was unable to start testing the machine immediately because it discovered that, due to the toxicity of the RIM materials, EPA permits were required to run the machine. The permits arrived and testing began on the machine in January 1990. During this time, product and process development continued using RIM equipment outside of Packard Electric.

Current Status of the RIM Project

By the end of February 1990, several RIM grommets had been attached successfully to harnesses of the type required by the high-end customer. While the RIM grommet's leak performance was decidedly superior to the IHG, it was still not sufficient to pass the five and five test. Packard engineers, however, were confident they could improve this performance and pass the test. The customer was also still very much in favor of using the RIM grommet—assuming that it could be produced reliably—despite the fact that the RIM unit cost was significantly more than the IHG (initially $7.00 compared to $4.50). Exhibit 7 contains details of the differential costs.

There were a number of outstanding problems still to be solved with the RIM grommet process. Probably, the most critical set involved ma-

Exhibit 7

Operating Cost Differences Between RIM and IHG (Estimated January 1990)

	RIM Grommet vs. IHG	
Recurring Additional RIM Cost per Vehicle	*1992*	*1994*
Labor	($.80)	($.80)
Material	$.65	$.65
Burden*	$2.75	$.95
Total Additional RIM Cost/Vehicle	$2.60	$.80
*Additional RIM Cost Annually at Steady State:***	$175,000/yr	$175,000/yr
Additional Investment Required for RIM:	$350,000	$450,000

* Burden was calculated from a standard overhead rate. The overhead rate was based on non-direct charges such as salaries for management, engineering, and other non-direct labor, plant maintenance costs, taxes, and plant depreciation.

** Equaled the cost per vehicle multiplied by the number of vehicles produced in a year.

Assumptions:
1. 1992: 68,000 vehicles per year serviced by two final assembly lines, producing wiring for 300 vehicles per day.
2. 1994: 220,000 vehicles per year serviced by four final assembly conveyors producing wiring for 940 vehicles per day.
3. A full RIM or IHG setup required for each pair of conveyors.
4. One back-up system for each plant.
5. No tooling changes required.

terials handling. Keeping the two RIM materials separate was absolutely essential. For example, if the drum for "material A" was hooked up to the hose for "material B," the whole machine could be frozen permanently. This was not an idle worry; there had been incidents at other companies where a tanker truck had been filled from the wrong tank and the truck, hose, and tank had all been frozen into a solid block.

An additional problem was that "material A" froze at 64 degrees Fahrenheit, and once frozen, it was ruined. It was therefore very important to keep the material from freezing. Finally, both materials were very toxic and would require special monitoring. Because of these properties, Packard had to develop and adhere to a series of strict material handling procedures.

A second set of problems revolved around the risks if there were a failure in the production system. A failure in harness production could completely shut down the customer's assembly line—which was generally considered the worst thing that could possibly happen. Because all of Packard's customers required Just-In-Time performance, and were moving toward shorter and shorter lead times, the margin for error was decreasing rapidly. It was exceedingly important that the machine be able to run 16 hours a day without fail. Packard's limited experience with the system made it difficult to guarantee such fail-safe operations, especially considering that Packard eventually would need to install a RIM machine in its Mexican operations. Furthermore, because of the RIM machine vendor's small size, Packard was not likely to get much support from them.

The third set of problems involved repairing existing harnesses. The actual act of attaching the RIM grommet entailed some risk to the harness because the mold had to clamp down tightly on the harness to prevent the material from leaking out. If a cable were severed at this point or if the grommet were incompletely filled, the harness would have to be repaired because the harness was quite valuable (approximately $180), and could not just be discarded.

In addition to developing a repair process suitable for Packard plants, there also was a need to establish a harness repair method in the auto assembly plants, and at retail dealers. Because the RIM grommet sealed tightly around the wires, once it had set there was no way to remove a defective cable. The solution would probably entail feeding an additional cable through a hole drilled in the grommet, but many details still needed to be worked out.

Schramm estimated that four engineers would need to work for approximately three months to address these issues that were specific to the RIM grommet.

Views on the RIM Grommet

Schramm knew that the RIM grommet had become a very emotional issue for several people. The product development engineers (the engineering organization) were generally very positive about it. They felt that in addition to superior leak performance, the RIM grommet offered many other advantages, such as greatly reducing the complexity of the initial feed-through design. Because a comb was required to separate the wires in the IHG, it had upwards of 150 dimensions that had to be specified, compared to only about 30 for the RIM grommet.

The RIM grommet also reduced the variety of feed-through options required to support a broad range of automobile models. Although there was some flexibility in the number of wires that could be fit into an IHG comb, it had to be redesigned every three or four years due to changes in the number of cables in the harness. These redesigns were as costly as the initial design and typically required approximately 600 hours of engineering (at about $50 per hour) and about $13,000 in retooling costs.

In contrast, the RIM grommet had only 30 dimensions to be specified, and for this reason, the initial design of a RIM grommet took only about 100 engineering hours (and about $7000 in tooling costs). The RIM grommet was much more flexible because the number of wires that could pass through was limited only by the available area. With the current design, Packard could double the number of wires without redesigning the grommet. Furthermore, this greater flexibility meant that it might be possible to use the same grommet for different model cars—something that was unheard of with the IHG. While there would probably never be a single grommet for all models, sharing the same RIM grommet across three or four models was a distinct possibility.

An additional advantage lay in the fact that the RIM grommet saved space in the pass-through area. To achieve an acceptable seal, the IHG had to be lengthened every time the number of wires was increased. Currently, the IHG was 80 millimeters (approximately 3 inches) longer than the RIM grommet. In addition to taking up scarce space and making the harness 80 mm longer, the IHG became more susceptible to cracking (and leaking) at this length. With the trend towards increasing the number of wires in the harness, this problem was likely to get worse.

A final argument given by engineers favoring the RIM grommet was that it was a new technology. As Packard got more experience with the technology, it could expect that its costs would drop significantly. Not only would this affect the RIM grommet, but that learning would be transferable to other RIM applications. Almost everyone agreed that Packard would have future applications for which the RIM technology was suitable (although many felt it was unlikely that those applications would include the RIM grommet).

The manufacturing engineers generally felt very differently about RIM. Although they did not have statistical data to prove it, they felt that only about 15 percent of the leaks in the passenger compartment came along the wires (see Exhibit 8). The RIM grommet might help those leaks but the other 85 percent would not be affected at all. Because the RIM process would not greatly improve the leak problem, the manufacturing engineers questioned the added cost. Kitsa Aivazis, a manufacturing engineer, believed that the customer misunderstood the sources of leaks:

> The leaking along the wires is actually a small problem in comparison with some of the other leaks. The problem is that the [customer's] engineers in the auto plant do the "Dixie Cup" test. This consists of filling a Dixie cup with water and pouring it down along the wires. This test is actually equivalent to a static water test but the thing is, you don't submerge your car in water. The

EXHIBIT 8

Sources of Water Leakage into Passenger Compartment
SYSTEM LEAK SOURCES

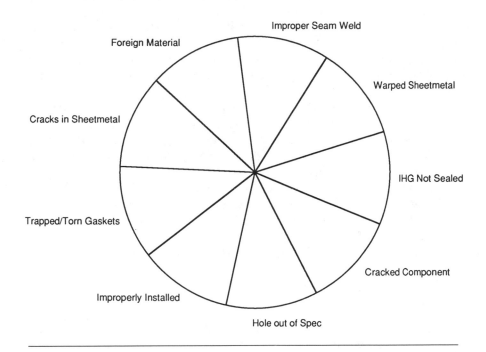

Improper Seam Weld

Foreign Material

Warped Sheetmetal

Cracks in Sheetmetal

IHG Not Sealed

Trapped/Torn Gaskets

Cracked Component

Improperly Installed

Hole out of Spec

---

grommet really only needs to pass a splash test—which the IHG can do. I think that the customers [the assembly plant] would understand this if it were explained properly, but they've formed an opinion of the IHG capabilities that is difficult to change.

A component design engineer did not dispute Aivazis' view of what caused the leaks, but felt that Packard should go with the RIM grommet anyway:

The issue is that when the customer is having leak problems, they search until they find a leak. Even if it isn't the right leak, they then tell whoever is responsible to go fix it. Well, if the grommet doesn't pass the Dixie cup test, they're going to want us to fix it and they won't be happy if we try to explain that it is really O.K. With the RIM grommet, we will pass their test, and they will have to look elsewhere for leak sources.

353

The manufacturing engineers were also worried about the process implications of the RIM grommet. Developing and implementing the strict materials handling procedures required was going to take a lot of effort and dramatically increase process complexity. Furthermore, even the act of putting the harness on the RIM machine entailed some risk because every time the harness was moved there was danger of damaging it.

The machine itself caused additional concerns. The support issue was important, and, given the size of the vendor, it was likely that Packard would be pretty much on its own. Although both the IHG and RIM machines had approximately the same throughput (both could service approximately 70,000 harnesses per year) the RIM machine was much larger—requiring approximately 250 square feet compared with 100 for the IHG. At a rate of $25 per square foot, this differential translated to $3,750 per year per machine. Because the volume estimates for the 1992 application were 50,000 to 70,000 cars per year, a single machine of either type would suffice.

Not only did it take more floor space, but the RIM was much more difficult to move. Portability was quite important because the machine was likely to be moved between plants often. The RIM machine could be moved from the Warren, Ohio plant where process development was being done to Packard's Mississippi plant where the initial manufacturing was to be done. From there, it could eventually be moved to the final harness assembly location. Roy Szanny, an applications engineering manager, pointed out an apparent conflict with Packard's strategy:

> The RIM grommet is a good product, but I'm not sure how well it fits with Packard's manufacturing strategy. Packard's strategy has been to have high-tech manufacturing of components in the U.S. and then ship the components to Mexico where the assembly is done in a low-tech fashion. The RIM machine is a relatively high-tech machine, which may be used in Mexico. The language problem and the distance would greatly exacerbate the control problems that are so important for the RIM technology.

Aivazis spoke for many of the process people when she said:

> GM management has been stressing the need to reduce costs. We've had travel reductions, hiring freezes, and even occasional layoffs. Now they are talking about spending almost twice as much for a component that complicates the process, increases risk, and may not improve performance. I don't deny that RIM is an important technology for some components, but this is the wrong application for it. Going with the RIM grommet would send a very bad message.
>
> I want to make it clear that I believe we can get the RIM grommet up and running if we want to, but it would require a lot of work, pain, and suffering. I don't think we want to do that because I just don't think that this application makes sense.

Schramm summed up the feelings of many of his subordinates, the product engineers:

> Look, if nothing else, the customer wants RIM and is willing to pay for it. They feel that it is very important to maintain their technological leadership and that RIM will help. The funny thing is that I was over at our Reinshagen subsidiary recently and I saw them experimenting with a RIM grommet for a very high-end German automaker. They didn't ask what it cost, they just said, "if it improves performance, do it."
>
> Furthermore, there are some cost savings, that no one takes into account because they are difficult to calculate. For example, with the IHG, every worker along our wiring assembly line has to insert his or her lead into the IHG's comb. With RIM that task is eliminated. Now I don't know how to calculate that improvement since it is a small amount of labor distributed among a number of workers, but there are some savings there.

The Product Program Management Process (PPMP)

The challenges and issues faced by the RIM project were not unusual at Packard, and Packard management had set out in late 1988 to develop a new method of managing product development. It turned out that other divisions of GM were studying the same problem, and Packard took much of that work and extended it to develop Packard's version of the PPMP. Although the PPMP had been developed too late to be used on the RIM project, Schramm felt that using it on RIM might have prevented some of the problems he currently faced. The PPR had, in fact, asked Schramm to look into that very issue and report whether the PPMP might have improved the RIM grommet's development process.

The PPMP had been created to provide a systematic development process featuring: customer focus, a documented framework, and a disciplined transition from development to implementation. In addition, because it was an extension of a process that GM corporate had developed, it would provide a common language with other GM divisions.

Under the new approach, the product development process had six phases (see Exhibit 9). Of the six phases, four were standard across GM. They were:

Phase 0: Concept development.
Phase 1: Prototype validation.
Phase 2: Preparation for production.
Phase 3: Production and continuous improvement.

EXHIBIT 9

Overview of PPMP as Proposed for Packard Electric
Product Program Management Process
"GM 4-Phase"

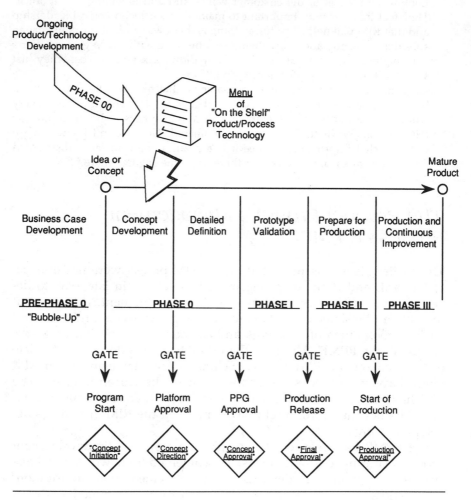

The remaining two phases were unique to Packard Electric. Pre-Phase 0, or "bubble up," was the phase in which customer input was evaluated and developed into a concept. Sales, application engineering, and the program manager analyzed the concept to determine the size of the potential market, how the concept fit Packard's overall business strategy, and the resource requirements that would be needed in Phase 0. If the analysis were favorable, the project moved into Phase 0.

The second Packard-specific phase, Phase 00, involved general purpose technology development which was done by the advanced engineering department. Once it had developed the technology to the extent that it could be readily adapted to a specific application with little or no risk of failure, it was put "on-the-shelf." In Phase 0, projects could use any new technology that was on-the-shelf, but were prohibited from using other new technology. Had the development of the RIM grommet followed the PPMP, the initial development work would have been done by advanced engineering and manufacturing development as a Phase 00 task.

At Packard, Phase 0 was to be divided into two parts: concept development and detailed definition. In concept development, the business outlook for a concept was reviewed and refined and a system level design was done. A plan for how to generate component designs and potential suppliers for required materials was developed. A component level design was generated and prototype components were fabricated in the second half of Phase 0—detailed definition. During this phase, all the technologies that were to be used were selected from the on-the-shelf menu.

The first complete prototypes were fabricated in Phase 1. Phase 1 was the first phase in which any capital purchases were permitted and any sizable expenses were incurred. By the end of Phase 1, a completed design was released. Phase 2 was the pre-production qualification and pilot production phase. All parts supplied by outside vendors were certified, production processes and trouble shooting procedures were developed, and parts were ordered for the initial production runs.

The final phase was the production and maintenance phase. Any unanticipated problems in the factory or the field were corrected, and yearly model upgrades were performed.

Each phase had a clearly delineated set of tasks and each task had a task leader, a customer and a set of deliverables. The functional departments of the task leader and customer were clearly set out. A flow chart describing the order in which tasks were to be accomplished and which tasks led into other tasks was laid out for each phase. (See Appendix A for an example of a set of such tasks.)

Schramm's Options

The RIM grommet decision was a good example of the type of situation that Packard wanted to avoid. A major decision had to be made in a hurry and there was a deep division in the views of the concerned parties. No matter what decision was made, it was very likely that one group or another was going to be faced with a challenge, either to tell the customer "no," or to develop and implement a process in a compressed timeframe.

Schramm felt that there were essentially three options that he could recommend. The first was to go exclusively with RIM for this customer's 1992 models. This was the riskiest option because if RIM failed in a major way and impacted the customer's production line, very significant repercussions would be felt by all who bore any responsibility. One way to minimize that risk was to recommend the purchase of two RIM machines, one of which would be redundant and used as backup and insurance. Schramm did not like this fallback one bit. In addition to the added expense, it seemed to be a brute force method of accomplishing the goal and removed some of the pressure from operations to perfect their processes.

A second option available was the so-called parallel development. In this case, an IHG would be prepared in parallel with a RIM grommet for this customer's 1992 requirements. The drawbacks to this plan were many and obvious. Because Packard had been planning to use the RIM grommet, an IHG grommet would need to be designed. Furthermore, it would become a logistical nightmare when the car went into production. Two sets of raw material would have to be ordered and kept track of, and both the auto plant and Packard's plant would have two different harnesses to deal with on the assembly line (the IHG harness being 80 mm longer). Furthermore, when the cars were sold, the consumers (and auto mechanics) would have two different levels of performance (although both provided a basic level of sealing).

The final option was the simplest and least risky. Schramm could recommend that Packard go with the IHG for all 1992 models. Schramm did not like giving up on the new technology, since he felt that there were many potential benefits to it. He feared that if RIM were not pursued actively at this point, it would lose momentum and not get applied in 1993 or beyond.

There was also the question of the PPMP and whether the new process would prevent situations like the RIM grommet from reoccurring. Schramm was not sure, however, that this was the only question that the PPMP should address. It was not enough to resolve all conflicts early; Packard also needed to maintain and encourage innovation. The automobile business was becoming more competitive and increasingly that competition was technology based. To become more responsive to its environment, one of Packard's main goals was to be more customer driven. The CIE and resident engineer programs were two steps that Packard had taken in this direction. However, having several groups in contact with the customer made it much more difficult to control the development process.

Schramm sighed. He had to present his recommendations to the PPR at the end of the week—both on the RIM grommet and on the PPMP plan.

Packard Electric Product Program Deliverables and Tasks for Pre-Phase 0

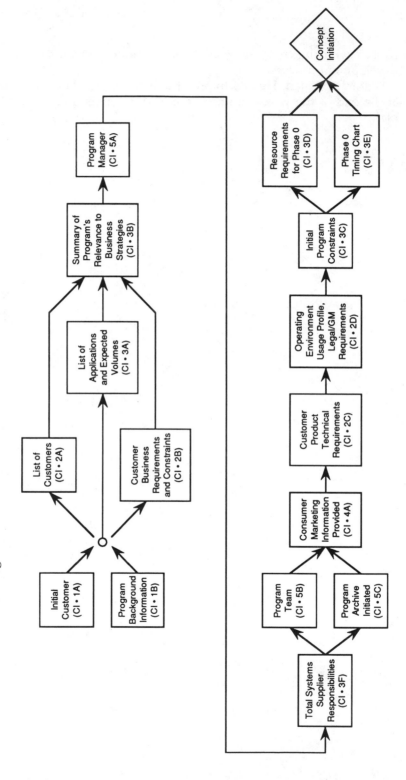

Appendix A *(continued)*

"Program Bubble Up" to "Concept Initiation"
(Sample of Representative Tasks)

Deliverable Code	Task Description	Leader	Customer
CI • 1A	Identify the customer who first initiated your participation in the program	Sales	Program File
CI • 1B	Collect the background information necessary to describe the program including the customer's primary reason for initiating the program	Sales	Program File
CI • 2A	Develop a list of all customers who come in contact with the product	Applied Engineering	Program File
CI • 2B	Identify the customer's business requirements and constraints for the program; this includes timing, piece cost, investment, volumes, and targets	Sales	Program File
CI • 2C	Work with the identified customers to develop their technical requirements	Applied Engineering	Vehicle Platform
CI • 2D	Estimate operating environment and usage profile based on the preliminary customer requirements and determine the ramifications thereof	Applied Engineering	Program Development Team
CI • 3A	Obtain a list of applications and expected volumes from identified customers.	Sales	Program File

Packard Electric Product Program Deliverables and Tasks for Pre-Phase 0

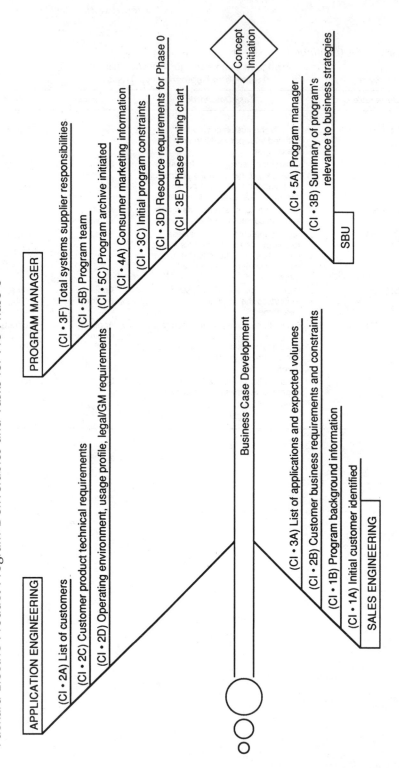

A Framework for Development

Overview

This chapter develops the framework for thinking about the overall development process—how tasks and activities in development should be sequenced, how work should be organized, how the effort should be led and managed, what milestones should be established, how senior management should interact with the project, and the way problems should be solved. This is the first chapter to deal directly with the management of specific product development projects. In subsequent chapters, we will look at the details of development. Here we look at the set of choices the firm must make about the framework within which those detailed activities will be carried out.

A centerpiece of this chapter is the case of the MEI 2010. This case describes the development of a new infant heart monitoring machine. We use this example to identify the basic elements of the development framework, illustrate the way those elements interact, and highlight the critical choices firms face in creating an effective development system. We do this by working through a history of the MEI 2010 project, organized around the phases of development in use. We then examine the 2010 experience in terms of the basic elements of the development framework proposed in this chapter. A central theme in this discussion is the importance of creating a development framework that brings a broad system perspective to the process and facilitates cross-functional integration.

In the concluding section of the chapter, we examine four models of coherent development processes. Each is quite different in its orientation, but each has its own strengths in specific applications. An important theme in our discussion of these four models is the need to match the process and its characteristics to the specific technical and competitive environment the firm faces. In addition, our discussion here underscores the importance of the total pattern of process choices the firm makes. Although the situations confronting Kodak, General Electric, Motorola, and Lockheed have been quite different, each has evolved a coherent development framework. The patterns are quite different, but each of them has met with success in its own target market.

The experience of each of these companies suggests that there is no one best development process for all circumstances and conditions. However, a close look at these patterns suggests that they share fundamental principles that drive successful development. These principles include a strong customer focus, a discipline that creates order and clarity, coherence down to the level of detail in the basic approach, a close fit with the mission of the organization, and a sharing of the total pattern throughout all elements of the organization.

CHAPTER 6

New products and processes come to the market through a process that first transforms ideas and concepts into working prototypes through detailed design and engineering, then tests and refines them, and finally prepares the product design and factories for commercial operation. The development funnel of Chapter 5 defines the way in which an organization proposes and selects concepts, and how these concepts converge to a specific product definition and design. At the other end of the spectrum of activity, day-to-day problem solving at the working level drives choices about the details of the design. Somewhere between the broad architecture of the funnel, and the details of specific tasks and problems, however, lies a whole set of choices the firm must make about the overall development process—how tasks and activities should be sequenced, how work should be organized, how the effort should be led and managed, what milestones should be established, how senior management will interact with the project, and the way problems should be framed and solved. In short, the development process as we define it in this chapter lays out the pattern or framework for development.

In trying to understand the nature and role of the development process, we have found the factory to be a useful analogy.[1] The funnel is like the layout of the factory and the basic structure of the flows of material and information within it. Like a layout diagram, the funnel does not define the detail. Instead, it establishes a higher level description of the physical structure and defines where and under what conditions material will come in and go out, what information will be collected centrally versus locally, and where and how people will be involved. It defines the architecture. The development process is more detailed and specific. From the factory perspective it is like the design of the production system, including the definition of the sequence of steps in the process and their location, the detailed information required to execute and control the process, the structure of the organization, and the definition of specific tasks the people will carry out. Within that framework, day-to-day work is done, problems are solved, products are produced, and projects are executed.

Like an outstanding factory, an outstanding development organization requires a coherent architecture and process that is well understood, highly capable, and in control. Too often our studies have uncovered businesses that regularly do development without an effective process. In some companies the process is so poorly understood that almost everything is implicit and subject to change within a project; there is, in effect, no process. In other companies there are so many detailed procedures and rules (many of which were devised to fix a long-forgotten problem) that no one understands or can keep track of them all. The process that exists on paper is so bureaucratic that those who follow it proceed slowly, if at all. Others regularly ignore the system, leading to confusion, rework, and delay.

Much like the infrastructure of a factory or a manufacturing organization, the detailed framework of development can have a powerful impact on performance. Creating that kind of capability, however, is not merely a functional detail. It requires senior management's focused effort and attention. The purpose of this chapter is to provide senior managers with a framework for thinking about and meeting that challenge. In the next section we outline critical dimensions of the development process and suggest the range of choices firms face. We then work through a detailed example that illustrates problems that arise when the process is not capable and in control. In the following section we examine four different "models" of the development process in practice at four companies. These models help to define the choices senior managers confront and the way in which those choices create development capability and influence performance on individual projects. The chapter concludes with brief observations on the basic principles that seem to govern effective development processes.

EXHIBIT 6–1

Basic Elements of a Project Management Framework*

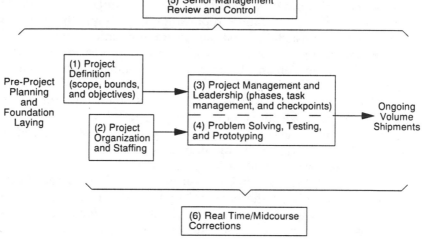

* Either implicitly or explicitly, every organization must make choices regarding these six elements in carrying out product development activities. Generally, elements (1) through (5) are considered part of the project management procedures of the organization, while element (6) is addressed on an as-needed basis.

Basic Elements of the Framework

The development process is a complex set of activities that extends over a considerable time period. As a starting point for understanding that complexity and identifying the critical choices for senior management, the six-element framework presented in Exhibit 6–1 is quite useful. Although the six elements interact to create a detailed pattern of development, they involve somewhat different issues and, at least initially, need to be understood on their own terms. Thus, before we explore how they interact, we consider the dimensions individually.

1. *Project definition.* This first element determines how the firm sets the scope of the development project, establishes the bounds for what is and is not included in it, and defines the business purposes and objectives of the project. Activities such as initial concept development, defining and scoping the project effort, obtaining both internal and external preliminary inputs, and selling the project to senior management and the entire organization are part of this element. The best indication of its completion is generally the official authorization

of the project and its associated goals, objectives, and resource commitments.

2. *Project organization and staffing.* This element defines who will work on the project and how they will organize to accomplish the work. Issues such as physical location, reporting relationships, the nature of individual responsibilities, specialized training and hiring, and the relationship to and use of support groups are items to be resolved as part of this basic element. Chapter 8, on organizing project teams, addresses this element in depth.

3. *Project management and leadership.* This dimension includes the nature and role of project leaders and the way in which project tasks are sequenced and managed. Choosing the type of individual given responsibility for program coordination and leadership, defining continuity in that assignment, and establishing expectations for how project roles and responsibilities will be executed are crucial to the mode of leadership on the project. The second part of this element includes the way in which tasks are divided and grouped into phases, how the work in each of those phases is monitored and managed, and the checkpoints or milestones used to signal completion of each phase.

4. *Problem solving, testing, and prototyping.* As indicated in Exhibit 6–1, this element is closely intertwined with the preceding one. However the focus here is on individual work steps, the way in which they are conducted, and the means by which the knowledge required to solve problems is developed. Central to this element is the nature of problem solving (involving both technical and managerial considerations) and the way in which testing and prototyping are used to validate progress to date, confirm the appropriateness of choices already made, and focus the project effort on the remaining tasks. This element, in combination with the preceding one of project management and leadership, largely determines the rate at which the project converges to a final, manufacturable solution ready for market introduction. We explore these issues in more detail in Chapters 7 and 10.

5. *Senior management review and control.* While senior managers do not directly perform specific tasks, their role in a project and the nature of their interaction with the project team (and project leader) is an important element of the overall framework. The way in which senior management reviews, evaluates, and modifies the project and its goals over time signals to those working on the project the degree to which responsibility has been delegated to them, and creates powerful incentives and motivation—some positive and some negative—during the course of the project. Seemingly routine patterns, such as the timing, frequency, and format of reviews, can have a significant impact on the overall effectiveness of the project.

6. *Real-time/midcourse corrections*. The ambiguity and uncertainty associated with any product or process development effort often makes feedback and revisions during the course of the project a necessity. This element deals with issues such as ongoing measurement and evaluation of project status, rescheduling, resequencing, and redefining the remaining tasks, resolving differences between problem solving in the lab and on the customer site, and determining when the organization is ready for production scale-up. Perhaps more subtle but also an important part of this element is the balance between early conflict resolution and subsequent adaptability, the relationship between unexpected early challenges and subsequent potential delays, and choices between deferring rescheduling to maintain motivation versus rescheduling early to maintain project credibility.

These six elements are like the components of a product. To work well, a product or development process needs components that function effectively. From the standpoint of development, this implies that the organization must have an effective way of defining products, must understand and appropriately deploy the mechanisms and tools for problem solving, and must understand and effectively deal with the issues involved in senior management review and control. All of this requires a depth of understanding of the individual elements. But like good components on a product, a good understanding of the elements is only part of the story. The elements must also fit well together in order to create a coherent system, and the system must be well matched to the development challenges it faces.

The experience of Medical Electronics Inc. (a manufacturer of medical instruments used in hospitals) in the development of the MEI 2010 illustrates the way the elements of the framework interact, and highlights the critical choices firms face in creating an effective development system. We have found the MEI case to be representative of the problems many firms confront in responding to the competitive imperatives for speed, productivity, and higher quality products. While there are always unique aspects in any case, the MEI experience provides a useful and relatively general context for our discussion of the principles that underlie effective development processes.[2]

The Framework for Development at Medical Electronics Incorporated

In January 1991, MEI introduced to the marketplace its portable, premature infant heart monitoring machine, the MEI 2010. While senior management was generally satisfied with the 2010 product, they were disappointed in the project management approach, particularly its inability to deliver the product on time and within budget. (The original date for market introduction had been the fall of 1989, fifteen months earlier than the actual introduction date. The overrun of the original budget had been $750,000.) This project provided an opportunity for management to use the basic elements of the development process framework to assess its approach and the connections between that approach and project results.

Background on the 2010 Portable Heart Monitoring Development Project

The development of the 2010, a unit with special capabilities for premature infant monitoring, brought together, in late 1984, several ideas that had been discussed in the organization over the preceding eighteen-to-twenty-month period. As one of the 2010 team members recalled, "This project had much more natural momentum than projects in diagnostics that MEI pursued during the same period. The organization knew how to deal with heart monitoring efforts—the main line of the business—much better than it knew how to deal with diagnostic products." While MEI's stated strategy at that time was to become a significant participant in diagnostics, a monitoring project like the 2010 seemed to go through the approval process with relative ease; in fact, if anything, the approval of the 2010 may have been too informal and too easy.

While the 2010 did not involve any radical new technologies, it was clear that it pushed the application software and graphics presentation toward more sophistication and complexity. It also involved the application of new sensor technology in the way in which sensors would be attached to the patient. Finally, both the electrical and mechanical requirements represented natural extensions of existing capabilities as the designers attempted to make this product more compact, portable, and usable in the hospital environment than existing MEI monitoring products.

A review of the stages of development used on the 2010 revealed five phases (see Exhibit 6–2 for a time line):

   I. Concept development
  II. Engineering prototyping
 III. Production prototyping
 IV. Market acceptance testing
  V. Market introduction

EXHIBIT 6–2
MEI 2010 Project Time Line (Actual and Original Plan)*

Actual Results

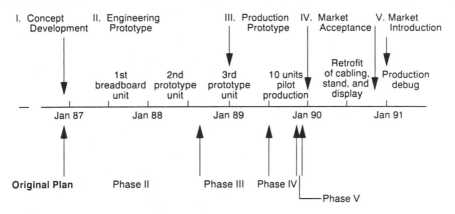

NOTE: Arrows indicate transition points between phases.

* This project time line outlines the planned and actual phases of the MEI 2010 project and the major prototype cycles. It makes clear that the project took longer than planned in each individual phase, making its market introduction over a year late.

These phases provide a convenient way of summarizing the history of the project. Interviews with the key functional heads, project participants, and senior management identified the salient developments.

Phase I—Concept Development. In the fall of 1984, there was no shortage of ideas regarding new product development opportunities and possible new features for existing MEI products. The issue was deciding which ideas and features to pursue, and through which projects. In the case of the 2010, the basic concept, focused on the premature infant segment, could be traced to a series of discussions between an electrical design engineer and a marketing specialist. However, several of the features (sensors, software, and data presentation graphics) came from other ideas that had been in the organization for many months, and in some cases even years. People recalled that there was a somewhat informal convergence process, during which time the ideas eventually coalesced to become the basic concept for the 2010 product. On this project the electrical design engineer involved in the original discussions became the champion within the design engineering group, convincing others that this project was a better and more challenging opportunity for the company to pursue than many of the other concepts on the drawing boards.

371

While there was ongoing discussion within marketing regarding the 2010 concept, the primary initial focus and emphasis came from the engineering disciplines. Once a marketing specialist grabbed the idea, however, it became much easier for the engineers to get it onto the "active list" of projects.

On the 2010, the transition from an idea or a concept to a specific project was rather fuzzy. The vice president of engineering recalled that at one of the executive staff meetings, he put the idea for such a product clearly on the table. As he explained the idea, the executive group warmed to it and saw the product's advantages and market growth opportunity. Within a relatively few weeks, the executive staff became solid backers of the 2010 portable heart monitoring machine targeted at the premature infant market.

A review of corporate records indicated that the project received formal budget approval (a head-count allocation for project management, a capital budget, an accounting reference number, and a target market introduction date of Fall 1989) in late 1986. While no formal written proposal could be located in early 1991, the project did appear in the 1987 business plan, prepared during the fall of 1986. By the spring of 1987, the project began to show up fairly regularly on the agenda of the monthly project reviews. (These sessions were held on the first Monday afternoon of each month and were attended by all executive staff members in town on that day—generally 80 percent of the senior management were in attendance.) Each of the "active projects" was reviewed by its project leader, in most cases a manager out of the function currently in charge of the project. (Generally project leadership passed from marketing during the formal concept approval phase to engineering during the second phase, to production during the third phase, and then back to marketing in the fourth and fifth phases.)

Phase II—Engineering Prototype. As recalled by the design engineering manager given responsibility for the 2010 project in this phase:

> We had already been doing some concept investigation and problem solving when the project received formal approval. However, within a couple of weeks of when the budget was put in place, I was appointed the engineering team leader and given three or four additional engineers who, during this phase, spent the bulk of their time on this project. I had responsibility for three other projects at the same time, but spent about 40 percent of my effort on the 2010.

In addition to responsibility for the engineering phase of four different projects, the engineering manager assigned to the 2010 also had his normal functional duties as head of the electrical engineering subgroup. Since all but one of the engineers largely dedicated to the project at this phase were electrical engineers, it was easy for him to manage them as part of his normal duties. One of the engineers, however, was a mechanical engineer, and the electrical engineering manager found working and communicating with that person somewhat more troublesome, since that mechanical engineer got his individual task assignments from the manager of the mechanical engineering subfunction.

Others in engineering recalled that the team working on the project (beyond the three or four largely dedicated engineers) was only loosely specified. This was partly a result of the basic structure of engineering at MEI, which grouped people by subfunction specialty (mechanical, electrical, software, sensors, and test), and partly because there were so many projects going on at the same time. When the 2010 moved into the engineering prototype phase, there were already fifteen to twenty projects being worked on by an engineering staff of approximately thirty-eight people spread across the five subfunctions.

By late 1987 the design engineering group had produced the first MEI prototype, albeit in a rough "breadboard" form. At that point the project became much more "real" because marketing could then "touch and feel" the concept. However, it was not until the spring of 1988—when the second engineering prototype was developed—that marketing had something solid enough to show to customers. Marketing then organized a customer focus group to help refine the desired features and the way in which they should be presented. As the product line manager for heart monitoring products recalled, "We would pass on comments and reactions to the engineers in an informal way, but since they still had numerous issues to work out before the completion of the engineering phase, we didn't really get all that involved."

Because of the strong functional and subfunctional organization at MEI, the first step in getting the work done in the engineering (or any other) phase was to decompose it into the tasks that could be done by a single function. Each of the subfunctions was then assumed to "know" how to do its assigned tasks, and project management did not seek to alter or influence those normal patterns of problem solving and task execution in any significant way.

In a very real sense, the 2010 project ebbed and flowed during this phase depending on the complexity of the issues that arose, what else the engineers were working on (competing projects), and the degree to which the monthly executive staff reviews shifted priorities on this and other projects. Fortunately the 2010 was considered relatively important throughout its duration, and did not face the major problems of rotating resources (other than the normal promotions for traditional career pathing) that many other projects did. However, 1987 and early 1988 were periods of growth for the company and a number of new people were being hired. When assigned to do engineering subtasks on the 2010, these new people often suggested new possibilities and ideas for exploration. As one senior engineer recalled, "On several occasions those new people went down paths that some of us could have told them would be futile. Unfortunately such explorations often lasted several months until the new person discovered the futility themselves, or until it happened to come to the attention of one of the more senior engineers on the project."

By late 1988, the 2010 had completed its third (or possibly fourth—it was difficult to tell) prototype cycle and was at a point where engineering felt they had validated the engineering design. At that point the project was "transferred" to production for their detailed definition of any production process changes that might be required in the factory.

Phase III—Production Prototype. In late 1988, manufacturing was brought into the process of development on the MEI 2010 in a serious way. While they had attended an occasional review session prior to that time, their policy was to wait for the validated engineering design before they began outlining production tasks, developing a detailed materials list, creating a vendor plan, and working jointly with engineering on factory test procedures. In early 1989, following a detailed review of the third engineering prototype, manufacturing outlined a work plan for this phase, the stated goal of which was "Produce a pilot batch of ten units and turn them over to quality assurance for market acceptance testing by 15 July 1989." Although the vice president of manufacturing took general responsibility for this third phase, there was one manufacturing engineer (an industrial engineer by training) who spent much of her time on the 2010 during this period. It was her effort that kept the project moving along.

Unfortunately, a number of changes in the vendor base, resulting from an ongoing vendor consolidation and improvement effort, as well as a number of requirements for tighter tolerances and improved process capabilities (much more demanding than those originally anticipated on the part of manufacturing) delayed pilot production until October 1989. The ten units produced in the pilot run consisted of only 75 percent "production vendor" supplied parts, because the remaining vendors were not able to produce the parts as quickly as needed. Thus a quarter of the parts in the ten pilot units were custom-built by local job shops and MEI's own production operations in order to get the pilot units done more quickly. The pilot units finally were turned over to quality assurance for the next phase in November 1989.

Phase IV—Market Acceptance. On the MEI 2010, as with any new MEI product, the market acceptance phase sought to validate the product and the ability of the user to achieve the desired performance in a consistent manner. This required a wide range of testing and approval processes, with the marketing manager overseeing those involving the customer, and the quality assurance (QA) manager overseeing those involving technical issues such as getting approval from the underwriter's lab (on electrical standards), the FCC (on electrical fields generated by the product), and often the FDA (on health efficacy issues). The quality assurance group also handled all clinical evaluation of the products. On the 2010, QA developed a market acceptance test plan during December of 1989. The ten units from the pilot production run were used to carry out this test plan, including life testing, government approval testing, and testing early prototypes with customers (i.e., beta site testing).

Because the project was already running late, the normal six to nine months allowed for execution of the market test plan was cut to four months. All market testing was to be completed by 1 May 1990. While there were no major delays in government approval over the next few months, the beta tests with customer sites revealed the need for some redesign of the stand on which the portable unit was mounted, the cabling used to connect some subelements of the product, and the data display device incorporated into the basic 2010 system. The first two changes were fairly minor, and by early April the parts had been redesigned, the material needed for the ten pilot units had been procured, and a retrofit had been made to each of the units.

The issue with the data display device was much more troublesome. Basically, customers found the display difficult to read and considered it of distinctly lower quality than the rest of the 2010 system. After considerable debate between marketing and engineering (because the higher quality alternative display device would raise material cost by $120 per unit and thus final system list price close to $500), it was decided in May 1989 that the higher priced display should be incorporated. This required procuring ten units of that display, adjusting the cabling, software, and other items required for it to interface smoothly with the rest of the system, and then getting customer reactions to the newly upgraded system. Work was rushed through but still not completed until October 1990.

By the fall of 1990, senior management was extremely anxious about market introduction of the 2010. While the original target introduction date had been fall 1989, in May 1990, when the handful of required changes had been identified by marketing and QA, management had set a firm target of September 1990 for introduction. Unfortunately, the delays with the display device made that unattainable. As a result the company did less testing of the 2010 on the customers' premises than originally planned. Quality assurance agreed reluctantly that they had originally set extremely high standards for product release with regard to government-mandated and functional performance requirements, and that the necessary standards had been met. However, no standards had been explored and developed thoroughly with regard to customer preferences for ease of use or the field service department's requirements for serviceability. In fact, the areas of testing that were cut back generally related to ease of use and serviceability issues.

Phase V—Market Introduction. By maintaining pressure during the redesigns of Phase IV (a time when senior management also made a few changes of its own to the design), the 2010 project received top priority. However, while the market introduction phase was normally planned to take a couple of months, for the 2010, it took from 1 November to 15 January, and even that was a real stretch. Manufacturing found that it had to go back and debug some of the materials coming from the 25 percent of the vendor base who had not participated on the pilot units. A stream of engineering change orders were still in-process in mid January 1991, but marketing and manufacturing, under pressure from senior management (who wanted to show shipped units of the product in the fiscal year ending 31 January 1991), approved shipment of the first five units on 15 January. These units went to some of the firm's best customers, who themselves were anxious to receive the product they had heard so much about.

Within a few weeks, however, MEI discovered that these "best customers" also turned out to be "heavy users" of the 2010, in part because its features were so superior to other infant heart monitoring products available in their hospitals. Though these early customers were extremely pleased with the features on the machine and its ability to meet their demanding functional requirements, they soon discovered that its ease of use was not nearly as great as they had anticipated. One problem not caught earlier was the stress put on the wheels of the unit's stand. It was discovered (through field failures) that when the units were pushed into an elevator misaligned with the hallway floor, the wheels tended to crack and break off. One reason this was not caught earlier was that, because the performance at the beta test sites was so outstanding, those customers had left the units in their prenatal intensive care wings and not moved them between floors. Within the first month after market introduction, the initial handful of units required almost a quarter of their wheels to be replaced. A "crash" redesign of the wheels was then instituted, but it took another few months before the problem was resolved and the new wheels installed. This put additional stress on field service, which, combined with its normal workload, fell far behind.

A number of other small problems (most of which could have been alleviated by more thorough testing) also emerged during the first quarter of 1991. These included: small bugs in the software, occasional failures of a connector (due to a vendor problem), and difficulty on the part of sales due to a lack of training on how to figure out exactly which options a specific customer would find most useful. Thus there were a number of additional demands placed on service, including the swapping of some options once a unit was in place in the field. In April 1991 senior management hoped that all of these problems were solidly behind them, but lamented the fact that their major competitor had recently introduced a premature infant monitoring device. Though MEI's engineers considered the competitor's features not nearly as good as those on the 2010, the competitor's product seemed much easier to use in practice than their own unit.

The Development Framework at MEI

Although some of the problems in the development of the MEI 2010 were peculiar to that product, many were rooted in the company's basic framework for new product development. Exhibit 6–3 summarizes the characteristics of MEI's development framework along the six dimensions developed earlier in the chapter. The exhibit also highlights the issues those characteristics raise for designing an effective development process.

The above summary of MEI's development framework underscores the difficulty this organization has in developing a product such as the 2010 where time is of the essence, engineers need to work new features and new technology into a coherent, integrated system, and where the product functions in a complex customer environment. All of this argues for a development framework that brings a broad, system perspective to the process and facilitates cross-functional integration. As the exhibit makes clear, however, MEI's process was narrow, functionally oriented, sequential, ad hoc, and largely undisciplined. Consider how these themes play out in each of the dimensions of the framework:

Project Definition. The tone for development at MEI is set at the very outset of the process. Project definition is not managed; it follows its "natural course." Actions to define a project are a response (reaction) to a mounting groundswell and set of pressures brought to bear by the external marketplace and competitors, and finally recognized by a sufficient number of MEI marketers, designers, and managers. The result is that project definition is slow, unsystematic and haphazard. It is ad hoc and responds to individual personalities and their preferences rather than strategic business purposes. Even at the point of formal project approval, the scope of the 2010 was still quite fuzzy. Although project performance objectives regarding market introduction date and approximate resource requirements had been set, no specific quality or perfor-

EXHIBIT 6–3

The Development Framework at Medical Electronics Inc.

Element of the Framework	MEI Characteristics	Issues
Pre-Project/Project Definition	Reactive process; ad hoc sequence of actions; stops and starts	Achieving focus, direction, and definition without missing opportunities or styling creativity
Project Organization	Engineering focus; part-time – job shop; frequent movement of people	Creating ownership and commitment on team; achieving continuity in the face of promotion and staffing needs; business as opposed to functional team
Project Leadership/ Management	Leadership shifts by phase; sequence of phases only loosely coordinated; baton passing	Building strong leadership across the phases; establishing tight communication linkages, clear interaction between phases
Prototype/Testing	Narrow focus on functional problems; sequential problem solving	Achieving integrated problem solving; using prototyping cycles to surface broader issues that cut across disciplines
Senior Management Review and Control	Monthly meeting; reactive fire fighting; late involvement; resource reallocation	Bringing senior management direction to bear early; developing the appropriate role during the project
Real-Time Adjustments	Narrow focus on immediate problems; informal, incomplete communication; problems handled through ad hoc changes to normal process	Creating discipline; capability for early resolution of conflicts; low-level, rapid problem solving

mance objectives for the resulting product were established at that point. Even the preliminary market introduction date was set based on senior management's sense of what the market "needed," without considering any detailed work plan of what could be delivered and when.

Project Organization and Staffing. In many respects, the 2010 project was initially an engineering effort, not a comprehensive business effort. In fact, it was not until late 1988—almost a year and a half after formal project approval—that other functions began to be involved actively on an ongoing basis. During the engineering and prototyping phase, a small group of electrical engineers worked on the design of the 2010 and its various subsystems. While the core group of engineers was largely full-time, many of the other subfunction specialties (mechanical engineering, software design, sensors, and test) shared their time on the 2010 with assignments on four or five other projects. They would work periodically on the 2010, pass their work on to others, and turn their attention to another project.

There was also a lack of continuity in project assignments. For example, a software engineer who might work on one piece of the 2010 development would not necessarily be the same software engineer who, a few months later, worked on another piece of the project. Stability and focus in project organization and staffing thus was secondary to the firm's traditional functional and subfunctional organization structure and to the career paths and promotion policies of the functional organization. While the project appeared to be a "team" on paper, people on those assignments were neither dedicated, co-located, nor equally focused on their efforts throughout the project's duration. In essence, the project's center of gravity moved from one function to another as it proceeded through the various phases.

As with project definition, the pattern of choices found at MEI in project organization and staffing are similar to those observed in many firms—projects are an exception to the normal functional organization, and are expected and forced to adapt and accommodate to the ongoing functional structure in many subtle but important ways. It is no surprise that while personal pride may lead individual contributors to exhibit a fair level of ownership and commitment in their activities on the project, there tends to be little "team commitment." Individual contributors consider themselves to have been very effective and successful if they perform their individual tasks well. They do not, to any significant extent, judge their success and contribution in terms of overall project success.

Project Management and Leadership. Leadership in the 2010 project (and in most MEI projects) followed the same pattern as the functional center of gravity. As the projects move forward, managers in engineering, manufacturing, and marketing "pass the baton" of responsibility for project supervision. Furthermore, managers have a normal set of functional duties (such as the head of the electrical engineering group responsible during Phase II on the 2010) and often supervise three or four projects at a time. Thus any project has to compete for the time and attention of the project manager on a day-to-day basis.

This pattern is a particular problem in marketing. The product marketing person, who has a leadership responsiblity in Phases I, IV, and V (definition, acceptance, and introduction), typically is not the same person throughout. The pattern of marketing career paths at MEI has been such that product managers are people on a "fast track" that involves going back and forth between sales and sales management, and marketing and product management, with at most twelve to eighteen months in each position. Since most projects—like the 2010—spend eighteen moths or more in Phases II and III combined, it is seldom the case that the same product market manager works on Phase I (product definition) and Phases IV and V (market acceptance and market introduction). With project definition as fuzzy as it is, this means that many of the refinements and redesign iterations in Phase IV can be driven largely by the product market manager's personal preferences and experiences, rather than fundamental strategic choices that were made in the product definition phase.

The shifting pattern of leadership is connected to the way MEI breaks the project into phases and how phase completion is recognized. Each phase has a functional orientation, and the criteria for deciding whether a phase is complete are relatively narrow. In the case of the 2010, senior management marks the completion of concept definition by creating a project account number, allocating resources in the annual plan, and adding the project to the "active list." The engineering and production prototype phases end when physical units meet certain minimum requirements. The completion of market acceptance comes with a sign-off on the design by quality assurance and product marketing. While these phases and their transition points are logical and appropriate at a macro level, they provide little guidance for the ongoing, day-to-day work being done on the project. Thus it is as though the project work goes on in the middle of a forest, and only occasionally (every six to eighteen months) does the project rise above that forest—at the time of one of those transitions—and become visible to other parts of the organization.

The concept of exercising consistent management and leadership across all of the activities required for project success is foreign to MEI's development process. Rather, there are a sequence of major phases, each of which is loosely coordinated and directed within itself, but never connected to other phases. Seldom are the issues, problems, and choices in one phase directly communicated, linked, and correlated to those in another; instead, the information transfer between phases tends to be a one-shot, batch exchange from those just completing the preceding phase to those who will take responsiblity for the next.

Problem Solving, Testing, and Prototyping. With each phase focused on a narrow objective and led by a different function, it is not surprising that testing, prototyping, and verification within each phase of the 2010 was focused largely on resolving that function's issues, not working to solve cross-functional issues. Thus the nature of problem solving during the project was to solve technical problems in the engineering phase; to solve manufacturing problems in the production phase; and to solve performance and use problems in the market acceptance phase. The early prototypes did not represent total solutions (cutting across functions) for the 2010 development effort, but rather represented functional solutions. Conceptually, the sequential nature of the phases assumed that the "downstream" functions would be able to solve their problems and issues within the set of constraints and choices specified by the

380

"upstream" functions. This was not always possible on the 2010. Many of the engineering redesigns required in the production prototype phase, and even more so in the market acceptance phase, required taking the project back through the original sequence of functions. However, with the time pressures that existed at that point, the tendency was to be very narrow and focused in those late cycles, rather than broad and integrative.

This functional decomposition approach to problem solving, testing, and prototyping is the one most commonly observed in engineering-driven firms. Unfortunately, it suffers in two major respects. First is that functional problem solving invariably proves to be suboptimal, requiring additional cycles late in the project when changes are costly and when expediency is likely to dictate compromises on performance and product quality that would not have been made had those same issues been raised and addressed much earlier. Thus the degree of integrity and integration in the final product or process suffers as a consequence.

The second problem is lost opportunity. Prototyping cycles offer a wonderful opportunity to bring together the various functions, determine the degree of progress made to date, and consider how alternative solutions might play together, at an intermediate stage. In essence, prototyping can be an important vehicle for cross-functional discussion, problem solving, and integration. However, all too often in the MEI case, the very structure of the phases and responsibility for them made it almost impossible for prototyping to be a major vehicle in achieving integration.

Senior Management Review and Control. At MEI, senior management's primary means of reviewing and controlling development projects was the monthly meeting where the executive staff would review all of the "active projects." With as many as fifteen to twenty projects on the active list, these monthly meetings tended to focus on the handful of projects that were already late in moving from one phase to another or had become bogged down in solving specific problems. In essence, management's role was after-the-fact tracking early in a project and then fire fighting, pressuring and shifting priorities later on. Such reactive demands consumed senior management's available "development attention" and prevented it from guiding and shaping proactively early on in individual projects when the leverage from such involvement would have been greatest (see Figure 2–3, Chapter 2), and when some of the the later problems could have been avoided.

The upshot of using a monthly meeting as the primary review mechanism is that senior management focuses on the wrong problems. But even the problems they do address suffer as a result. First, monthly reviews are only rarely associated with major events in the project itself.

Thus it is extremely difficult for senior management to assess just what progress had been made since the prior month, and whether or not the project is truly on track, unless it is in serious trouble. Senior management tries to manage against the calendar rather than against key events in the project itself. Furthermore, senior management does not (and cannot) take sufficient time in the monthly meetings to delve into the details of each project and connect what is happening currently with the issues likely to arise two, three, or even six months in the future as a consequence of current activities. Finally, as a result of these characteristics, the primary lever that senior management has for affecting on-going project performance and progress is resource allocation. But that creates a vicious cycle: senior management responds to problems by reprioritizing projects and moving key resources to the current crisis. Inevitably, this "robbing Peter to pay Paul" ensures that other projects subsequently will suffer the same fate because their key resources have been removed prematurely.

Real-Time/Midcourse Corrections. With a fuzzy project definition and limited cross-functional communication, unexpected problems occurred repeatedly and real-time adjustments in design and market plans became a significant proportion of the total development effort. The pattern for addressing such unanticipated issues on the 2010 reflected the approach to problem solving in general: postpone the cross-functional aspects until a subsequent phase and deal with the immediate issues from the perspective of the function in charge of the current phase. Subsequently, functions could claim: "I did my job. This problem is not my fault. While I'm willing to help out, it's not my responsibility." In essence, conflicts and difficult issues that arose within the function were addressed narrowly and those that involved downstream functions were postponed and left for later resolution. Late in the project, when conflicts and issues arose requiring input from upstream functions, little would happen until there was sufficient management awareness of the problem that upstream resources would be reprioritized and focused on the issue.

The structure of such real-time conflict resolution at MEI was further compounded by the tendency to communicate informally and often incompletely. Because the finished prototype or pilot unit was the primary means for information transfer between functions, the downstream group generally did not fully understand and appreciate the explorations, deliberations, and choices made by upstream groups. The converse was also true. Thus, even though marketing organized focus groups during the concept definition phase, many of the recommendations coming out of them fell on deaf ears during the engineering prototype and production pilot phases, only to resurface in the market acceptance phase.

Problems with real-time adjustments were compounded by time pressures. Projects at MEI tended to go longer than originally anticipated—and well beyond the date set originally by senior management—so that engineers and marketers found themselves under severe time deadlines in the final phases. This created pressure to cut corners and skip steps in order to avoid further delays. On the 2010, engineers hoped to make up lost time by using nonproduction vendor parts for a quarter of the items going into the pilot units. The reality, however, was that cutting this corner resulted in more expensive changes later on and a deterioration in the product's design and manufacturing quality and its market impact. As with much of the development process at MEI, real-time adjustments were characterized by an absence of discipline, an absence of early conflict resolution, and an absence of low level cross-functional problem solving.

Applying the Development Framework: Comparing Four Approaches

The MEI experience suggests several issues that firms confront in designing and implementing an effective development process. We present these issues in the third column of Exhibit 6–3. Like much of what we see in product and process development, some of the issues reflect conflicting requirements: the need for focus and direction and yet creativity; the need for strong functional expertise and yet tight integration across functions. Some issues, such as strong leadership across the phases, cut against the grain of the career paths, staffing patterns, and promotion practices of the "regular" organization. MEI tried to deal with these issues through the mechanisms in its development process, but had difficulty breaking out of its narrow, functional approach. Taken individually, the general mechanisms MEI used—the "active list," budgets, approvals, phases, a project team, prototyping, and monthly reviews—could be part of an effective process. The way MEI combined them to form an overall pattern and framework, however, was ineffective in meeting the need for speed, productivity, and quality.

But there are many firms that have confronted this problem and developed far more effective processes than the one we saw at MEI. In this part of the chapter we examine four approaches to effective development and compare them in terms of our six-dimension framework. The four development frameworks come from Kodak, GE, Motorola, and Lockheed and are briefly summarized in Exhibit 6–4, which is divided into two parts. We first provide an overview of the framework in each company, including a characterization of the dominant orientation of the framework, the primary mechanisms used, and an example of the

EXHIBIT 6–4

Representative Approaches to Project Management

A. Overview

	Kodak	General Electric	Motorola	Lockheed Skunkworks
Company's Characterization of the Process	Phases & Gates (Manufacturability Assurance Process — MAP)	Tollgate Process (see Figure 5–4)	Contract-Driven Cross-Functional Teams	Tiger Team
Dominant Characteristics	Strong functional orientation with discipline and focus in the process	Functional orientation, but cross-functional phases and a project team to achieve integration	Team focus with functional support and clear links to senior management	Fully dedicated team with control over resources and process
Key Mechanisms	Phases, gates; customer mission statement; gatekeepers	Tollgates; project manager; senior management review at milestones; cross-functional phases	Dedicated core team; general manager as project leader; the contract; senior management sponsor	Dedicated support resources; co-location; full budget authority; leader as CEO; small, hand-picked team
Major Phases in a Development Project	6 phases I. Customer mission/vision II. Technical demonstration III. Technical/operational feasibility IV. Capability demonstration V. Product/process design VI. Acceptance and production	10 phases (defined by reviews) I. Customer needs II. Concept III. Feasibility IV. Preliminary design V. Final design VI. Critical producibility VII. Market/field test VIII. Manufacturing feasibility IX. Market readiness X. Market introduction follow-up	4+ phases I. Product definition II. Contract development III. Development through manufacturing start-up (team defines subphases) IV. Program wrap-up (learning)	Nonstandard (team specifies major milestones and review procedures for those)
Dominant Type of Project	Manufacturing process; projects where technical advancement is paramount	Evolutions, enhancements, and incremental improvements; technical solutions important but balance across functions crucial; some emphasis on speed	Platform/next-generation; system solution crucial; environment turbulent; speed critical	Breakthrough projects; high risk; experimental efforts
Typical Project Duration	24–40 months	24–48 months	18–30 months	24–60 months

384

	Kodak	General Electric	Motorola	Lockheed Skunkworks
Primary Performance Drivers	a. Resource utilization b. Technical advancement	a. Risk management b. Resource utilization	a. System solution b. Speed	a. Technical performance b. Speed
B. *Basic Framework Elements*				
1. Project Definition	Ideas initiated from many sources; Initial funding can come from any function; "Definition" reflects funding source.	Initial phase is market need definition; Ideas initiated from many sources; Marketing must approve need/opportunity.	Phase I — "Blitz" product definition (7-day limit); Cross-functional; Colocated during definition.	Concept champion emerges (usually a technically trained general manager); Senior management agrees in principle on strategic opportunity; Team details the concept definition.
2. Project Organization and Staffing	Functions control their phase(s) of project; Functions assign people as needed; Work is done by a functional subgroup; Some overlap of R&D/engineering in Phase IV.	Representatives from each function assigned to the team at outset; Team members serve as functional liaisons; Detailed work done in the functions by staff assigned by the functional manager.	Job postings for cross-functional, dedicated/co-located core team; Part-time support groups; Core team responsible for development procedures (within broad corporate guidelines).	Project champion hand picks the team; Team relatively small, people have broad assignments; Most important support people also dedicated and co-located; Other support work subcontracted; Team develops own procedures without constraints.
3. Project Management and Leadership	Shifts from marketing (Phase I) to R&D (Phases II–IV) to engineering (Phases IV–V) to quality assurance and marketing (Phase VI); At phase transitions, a gatekeeper (upstream) releases project, and a stakeholder (downstream) accepts the project.	Program manager maintains schedule, follows up between reviews, facilitates transitions between functions; Functional managers direct the project work done by their people.	Full-time, general manager project head; Core team reports to project head; Project head is concept champion and allocates resources within the project.	Project leader is in charge — CEO of the effort; Does own hiring, training, and evaluation; Manages all aspects; Often creates an entire business unit.

Exhibit 6–4

Representative Approaches to Project Management (*continued*)

B. Basic Framework Elements (*continued*)	Kodak	General Electric	Motorola	Lockheed Skunkworks
4. Problem Solving, Testing, and Prototyping	Problem solving and prototyping done largely within the functions; Many specialized test and prototype groups used as subcontractors; Quality assurance does primary testing in Phases V–VI.	Problem solving done largely within single functions; Cross-functional issues raised in reviews and later prototypes; Testing and prototyping done by specialized support groups.	Cross-functional is dominant; Prototypes are project tests, not functional tests; Substantial testing to verify 10X progress.	Cross-functional, but early phases dominated by technical concerns; Emphasis on technical performance on critical dimensions; Engineers work directly with key customer(s) and do own prototypes.
5. Senior Management Review and Control	Senior functional manager does most reviews (their resources and funds); Senior, cross-functional advisory groups used on special issues (e.g., environmental) or to achieve special coordination (e.g., international).	Occurs at key reviews; Strict criteria defined to move to next phase; Emphasis on identifying and managing risks; Management "signs" approval at each tollgate.	Senior management as sponsor and coach; Reviews tied to key project events; Manage to team "contract"; Sponsor is focal point for others on executive staff.	Periodic one-on-one between project leader and corporate top manager; Limited formal reviews, but may hold "communication" exchanges; Senior management sets aggregate resource limits; Team is largely on its own.
6. Real Time/ Midcourse Corrections	Done primarily within single functions; Send projects back to an earlier phase if major problem identified later; Major transition from R&D to engineering (technical feasibility to commercialization).	Senior management involvement in conflict resolution; In concept, vary resources and time line in response to problems; Can halt project at any review if a serious problem.	Low-level problem solving by competent, core team members; Continual, extensive communication; Revise detailed plans periodically; Team changes tasks, their sequences, and groupings.	Do what is required for success; Creative, always trying new ways; Extensive discussions of options and next steps within the team.

market and technical environment where the framework is likely to be particularly effective. The second part of the exhibit summarizes the details of the framework along the six dimensions of the development process.

It should be noted that these processes are not all equally effective; we do not present them as models for all circumstances. Our purpose here is to illustrate the existing range of approaches and mechanisms for tackling the development process, both to show how choices made in the six dimensions combine to create a pattern of development, and to suggest some of the principles managers can apply in building an effective process.

Kodak: Functional Structure and Discipline

At Eastman Kodak Company the dominant approach for managing development projects, put into place in the late 1980s and early 1990s, is referred to as the Manufacturability Assurance Process (MAP).[3] The shorthand reference used internally is "phases and gates." Kodak's evolution to this approach has been driven in part by the firm's strong technical depth and by its expertise in chemically based manufacturing processes related to film production. However, the MAP approach, with its six distinctive phases, is also being used in such diverse product categories as microfilm equipment, copiers, cameras, and medical instruments.

The six phases (named in Exhibit 6–4) take a project through an initial customer mission/vision phase, into a sequence of technical demonstration and feasibility phases managed within the R&D group, and then into a set of commercialization phases that pass from engineering through production to quality assurance and market acceptance. Kodak's motivation for this approach was to shorten development times, improve the efficiency of development efforts, and ensure a smooth transition between various functional groups during the project. Basic performance drivers for Kodak development projects typically are resource utilization and technology advancement.

The development framework at Kodak resembles the system used at MEI: both have a strong functional orientation in project leadership and use a system of phases that is largely functional in focus and operation. But Kodak has introduced a set of mechanisms that give its process a different character. The key mechanisms include the customer mission statement, the use of gatekeepers and stakeholders, well-defined procedures, and senior cross-functional advisory groups. A customer mission statement, for example, lays out the critical unmet needs the customer faces, and how the new product (or process) will meet them. In developing a new coating for its film products, for example, Kodak

387

engineers focused on the customer's need for a much tougher coating (to eliminate scratches), yet one that would offer excellent clarity. This focus led to a clear mission statement: develop a new composition that will give the customer (the film division) a coating with exceptional toughness and clarity, leading to bright, sharp photographs with no scratches.

The process clearly emphasizes the need for technical depth in the projects, but the new mechanisms attempt to achieve integration through a customer focus, common procedures, shared concepts, and the testing process. While the Kodak process thus relies on strong functional groups for direction and focus, it also establishes a common philosophy and set of procedures that provide discipline and clarity. Consider the following differences in Kodak's approach (compared to MEI):

- The front end of the process is not fuzzy; there is a clear customer focus and clear project direction.
- The transition from one phase to another—and particularly the criteria for such a transition—is much clearer.
- The quality assurance group plays a strong integrative role in the last phases of the project and brings a market-based discipline to bear.
- Senior management reviews (done by functional managers) are substantive, rather than calendar-driven.

Compared to the haphazard, confused process at MEI, Kodak's process should operate much faster (because of fewer mistakes and less rework) and use fewer resources. In many ways, therefore, we can see MAP at Kodak as an evolutionary improvement on the basic functional structure in place at MEI. Indeed, it is likely that Kodak had projects similar to the 2010 before they instituted MAP. MAP has cleaned up the process and Kodak's experience has shown substantial improvement in performance.

While the Kodak framework is inherently better than the MEI framework, largely as a result of its discipline and structure, it also fits with Kodak's business and strategy. A process such as MAP, with its strong functional orientation, appears appropriate when the strategy emphasizes technical depth and excellent technical solutions are paramount.

GE: Coordinating and Linking the Functional Process

The dominant approach to product and process development at General Electric is called the "tollgate" process.[4] With an incredibly diverse set of businesses, manufacturing processes, technologies, and markets ad-

ExHIBIT 6–5

General Electric Tollgate Process

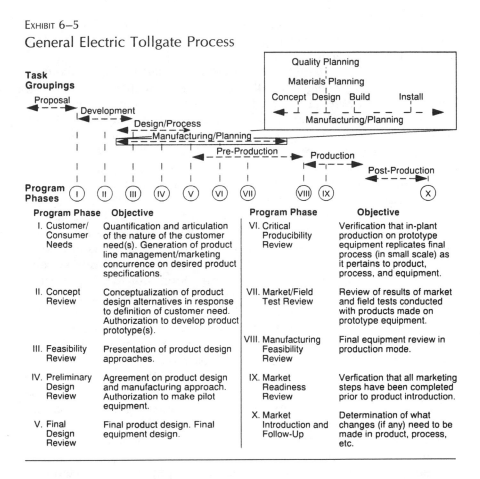

Program Phase	Objective	Program Phase	Objective
I. Customer/ Consumer Needs	Quantification and articulation of the nature of the customer need(s). Generation of product line management/marketing concurrence on desired product specifications.	VI. Critical Producibility Review	Verification that in-plant production on prototype equipment replicates final process (in small scale) as it pertains to product, process, and equipment.
II. Concept Review	Conceptualization of product design alternatives in response to definition of customer need. Authorization to develop product prototype(s).	VII. Market/Field Test Review	Review of results of market and field tests conducted with products made on prototype equipment.
III. Feasibility Review	Presentation of product design approaches.	VIII. Manufacturing Feasibility Review	Final equipment review in production mode.
IV. Preliminary Design Review	Agreement on product design and manufacturing approach. Authorization to make pilot equipment.	IX. Market Readiness Review	Verfication that all marketing steps have been completed prior to product introduction.
V. Final Design Review	Final product design. Final equipment design.	X. Market Introduction and Follow-Up	Determination of what changes (if any) need to be made in product, process, etc.

dressed by GE's divisions, the evolution to this particular approach in the mid to late 1980s was driven in part by senior management's need to control a wide range of development projects. While the bulk of the projects in most GE business units represent product line evolutions and incremental improvements, GE also wanted an approach that could be adapted to both breakthrough and platform projects.

A unique aspect of the GE tollgate approach is that its ten phases are the management review points during the development project. This is illustrated in Exhibit 6–5 where the sets of tasks are grouped together around seven themes, but the ten program phases are listed in terms of their management review purposes. The intent at GE was to create a review process with sufficiently small chunks so that the project would be unlikely to get very far off track between senior management reviews.

Additionally, as the word "tollgate" suggests, GE wanted an approach that would enable senior management to reevaluate projects and halt or redirect them as needed.

Projects to which the tollgate process is applied typically take from twenty-four to forty-eight months, depending on their scale and the type of project (incremental, platform, or breakthrough). In every case, however, the primary performance driver is the management of risk, followed by the secondary driver of maximizing resource utilization against major market opportunities.

The development process at GE shares a strong functional orientation with Kodak, but adds several elements. The phases at GE are more cross-functional in character, so that passing "tollgates" requires the involvement of several functions and applies broader criteria. Furthermore, the structure of the phases is such that there is some overlap in time, creating a need and forum for greater cross-functional interaction. Within the framework established by the tollgate system, work on the project gets done in the functions. But to achieve better interaction across functions GE has added integrative mechanisms in the way development is organized. A team of representatives from each function works under the direction of a program manager to enhance communication and coordination across functions. While the program manager's role is largely administrative, it does bring a cross-functional perspective into the process. In addition, the senior management review at each "tollgate" serves an integrative function. The reviews are closely linked to the natural progress of the project and thus are substantive in nature. Moreover, senior management involvement ensures that business (and therefore cross-functional) criteria are used in making decisions.

Like Kodak, Managing GE's diverse development efforts requires a common framework and language. Also like Kodak, much of the focus of GE's work relies on strong functional groups with depth of expertise. But GE has added more integrative mechanisms (a liaison team, program manager, cross-functional phases) and a more centralized, top management directed review process. These differences may reflect differences in environment and strategy. Historically GE often has undertaken very large projects (e.g., jet engines, plastics, turbine generators) with high technical and financial risks. A review process with close senior management involvement brings to bear an assessment of those risks, frequently, throughout the program. Compared to a process like MAP, GE's more coordinated and linked approach may be appropriate in markets, technologies, and strategies where technical solutions are crucial, but not paramount, and where other issues such as time-to-market or the fit between a technical solution and marketing strategy are more important. In such an environment the mechanisms GE employs may reduce the time required to solve problems and lead to solutions with more balance across functions.

Motorola: Cross-Functional Teams

Motorola's development framework is quite different from that followed at GE and Kodak. It is based on "contract-driven, cross-functional teams."[5] Essentially, a core cross-functional team is selected, dedicated, co-located, and put under the direction of a general manager who serves as a full-time project leader for the duration of the effort. Very early on, that core team develops a "contract" or detailed work plan, including resource requirements and anticipated performance results. Once agreed to by senior management, that contract is literally signed by both the core team members and senior management.

In the Motorola approach, there are four primary phases, but those phases cover a much broader set of activities and extended time line than do the project management phases in many other organizations. The first phase, product definition, is conducted with a cross-functional, highly focused effort. The second phase, contract development, is followed by the third and longest phase, development. This third phase covers product (or process) development from contract through manufacturing start-up. Within this phase there are several subphases, but their definitions are driven by the specifics of the individual project and are defined by the team as part of their work plan in the contract phase. The fourth phase, program wrap-up, focuses on what was learned during the project and the transfer of that learning to other parts of the Motorola organization. The dominant type of project handled at Motorola by this approach is the platform or next-generation project. Typically, goals that emerge from the first two phases represent a 10X performance improvement over the existing product or manufacturing process.

At Motorola, the typical duration of a development project is eighteen to thirty months. The impetus for this particular approach came largely from two factors. The first was a need for a "system solution" in platform or next-generation development efforts that effectively integrates across functions on a number of dimensions. Second, but close to it, was the need to speed the development process and, simultaneously, improve resource utilization.

The development framework at Motorola represents a fundamental shift in the traditional center of gravity—the functions—to a cross-functional team. Where Kodak and GE relied on the functions for basic development work, Motorola puts primary decision making and much (but not all) of the crucial detailed work in the team. In this setup, the team is where the action is, and the functions provide support to the team.

Consistent with the primary role of the team, leadership at the team level is much stronger and more direct than at GE, and there is much less central (corporate) direction on a day-to-day basis. The team defines its phases, working within corporate guidelines, and the team leader has broad responsibility for the effort. There are connections with senior management, but their role is much different than in the GE approach. Motorola has developed mechanisms—the contract and the senior management sponsor, for example—that give the team strategic direction, ongoing advice and coaching, and a forum for dealing with new issues. But the team leader functions as a general manager, and manages to the contract.

Motorola's framework places a premium on integration and is effective in situations where the "system solution" is what matters. In that sense, the team approach is likely to be used on platform projects where the creation of a new product or process architecture is central. In addition, the approach is likely to be more effective when markets are turbulent and fast action is essential. In those circumstances a focused team with a flexible process avoids the delays associated with coordinating across large functional groups. This is not to say that the functions are not important. Indeed, without the support of the functions and the depth of expertise the functions bring, the team would fail. But where the system is more important than specific technical solutions, and where the environment is dynamic, a more integrated development framework has advantages.

Lockheed's Skunkworks: The Autonomous Team

During World War II, Lockheed developed the "skunkworks" approach to aircraft development.[6] This approach focuses on radical or breakthrough projects, where the resultant product or manufacturing process is likely to create a whole new business or market opportunity. The essence of this approach is that a dedicated "tiger team" is formed and removed from the ongoing part of the business. That team is given complete responsibility, with no strings attached, for developing the new product or process.

Consistent with the Lockheed skunkworks approach is the notion that the major phases in the development effort should be specified by the team rather than some bureaucracy or standard set of procedures. Thus the team determines all the major milestones, and manages itself against those. Since projects undertaken as "breakthroughs" tend to involve substantial technical advancement, their duration can be fairly lengthy. At Lockheed, such skunkworks-managed projects take from twenty-four to sixty months. The primary performance driver typically is technical excellence on one or two factors of critical importance to the customer, with speed of development a close secondary driver of the effort.

Motorola's process has a strong team orientation, but the team is closely linked to the functions for support activities and part of the basic development work. At Lockheed, the team has direct control over most of the resources and decisions involved in the project, and the other dimensions of the development framework support the concept of an autonomous team. The team works within a set of guidelines on procedures (e.g, standards for testing) and has budget limits it must meet. But there are limited senior management reviews outside the team, and the team and its leadership have broad discretion on phases, practices, methods, and approaches.

Lockheed has implemented the autonomous team framework with mechanisms that reinforce team identification and the creation of a highly focused effort. The team contains the key resources required for the project, including support activities such as a model shop, and team members are handpicked by the team leader. The people involved in the project have broad skills and assignments, so that compared to other development approaches at Lockheed, the number of people involved is relatively small. All the people are co-located to ensure a high level of interaction and effective communication.

With its own budget and resources and with control over its procedures and process, the team can chart its own course and do what needs to be done to accomplish its mission. It does not have to be bound by precedent in other products or in existing systems, and is thus ideal for breakthrough projects where the intent is precisely to break new ground. It may also be effective in experimental situations or in advanced development where the objective is to explore new technical or commercial territory. But it is unlikely to be effective for platform projects that must connect to other products and processes or as the basic system of development for ongoing improvements and enhancements. Indeed, the skunkworks approach needs a larger organization and system to provide skills and resources.

Creating an Effective Development Process: Common Themes and Basic Principles

The four development frameworks presented in Exhibit 6–4 span a continuum that ranges from Kodak, with its strong functional leadership and phases on the left, to Lockheed's skunkworks, with its almost complete autonomy on the right. Along the spectrum, choices in the six

393

dimensions of the development process differ significantly and the mechanisms used to implement those choices are likewise quite different. They appear to be appropriate for quite different circumstances and have different implications for development performance. Yet a close look at these approaches suggests common themes and some basic principles that apply to all effective development processes. As a summary to the chapter and to set the stage for a more in-depth examination of certain aspects of the development process in subsequent chapters, we look briefly at five: customer focus, discipline, coherence, fit, and sharing the pattern.[7]

Customer Focus. A central challenge in any development process is to achieve integration across functions and yet obtain excellent solutions to functional problems. The frameworks in Exhibit 6–4 use several mechanisms to achieve integration, but the one that seems both common and most powerful is customer focus. A focus on the customer's requirements and *unmet* needs can be a powerful, unifying force. But bringing the customer into focus is a challenge. It requires an effort to understand and articulate what the *future* customer's requirements and unmet needs are (and will be). And it requires the capability to translate those needs into terms that everyone can understand and use in detailed actions and decisions.

Discipline. Most development processes—and those in place at Kodak, GE, Motorola, and Lockheed are no exception—are complex. They involve hundreds (even thousands) of decisions, many different people, competing interests, and multiple objectives. There are many approaches to coping with complexity, but the effective processes have discipline in common. The use of phases, clear criteria for moving forward, testing procedures, and prototyping are an effort to bring order and clarity to the process. Excessive rules, bureaucratic procedures and guidelines can, of course, stifle creativity, drain excitement, and bog down the project in a morass of red tape. Procedures, phases, and rules must be streamlined, appropriate, and adaptable. But discipline is crucial in achieving the rigor, thoroughness, and consistency that excellent development requires.

Coherence in Detail. No matter what its basic structure or focus, an effective development process must achieve a high level of coherence among its different elements. To be effective, for example, the approach to leadership must be consistent with and reinforce the way the project is staffed and organized. The mechanisms used to connect senior management to the project must reinforce the phases of development and the criteria for moving from one to another. This coherence across dimensions must pertain at the detail level; coherence in the large or at the level of principle is not enough. What matters is that small details, such as the timing and criteria for testing within a function for a particular component, match the overall phase of development and its milestone criteria. To take another example, the details of who gets selected for a project and the skills they have must match and respond to the approach to organization as well as problem solving in the framework.

Fit with the Mission. Each of the processes outlined in Exhibit 6–4 is better tuned to some environments than others. Establishing a fit between the process and the competitive, market, and technical imperatives that confront the project is essential to effectiveness. But establishing fit is not like plugging in a formula. Environments are complex and variable and firms continually need to monitor and adapt in those dimensions that are crucial to particular objectives. Take, for example, technical depth. If, as at Kodak, technical depth is crucial, the firm needs to understand what parts of its process drive technical excellence (e.g., testing procedures, particular skills and tools), and the implications that changes in the environment (e.g., new technology, new market requirements) may have for them. In addition, firms may face several environments and need more than one approach to development.

Sharing the Pattern. If the development framework is coherent, all of the dimensions work together to create a *pattern* of development—a model of how ideas are transformed into commercial products and processes. If articulated within the organization, the pattern becomes a shared language and framework for development. This is a crucial part of an effective development process. A common framework, especially if there is understanding about the way the elements work together to achieve results, offers direction and guidance in making the myriad of decisions that create products and processes. Things work faster and more efficiently because the framework helps people understand what must be done, when, and how. It also greatly facilitates the intensive communication at the heart of effective development.

Principles as Guidelines

We have argued that creating an effective development process is like building a great factory. Much of what goes into it is very specific to the particular product and process, markets and customers, and strategy. Our discussion suggests that dimensions common to the process provide senior managers a framework for making choices in the design of the process, and for improving the process over time (see Chapter 11 for additional discussion of this topic). Beyond the common dimensions, however, there are also basic principles that underlie effective performance no matter what kind of development process the firm uses.

These basic principles may serve as guideposts for senior managers as they move their organizations along the path toward truly outstanding development. Creating and nurturing a great development process involves many crucial details, but from time to time it is quite useful to ask: "Do we have a strong customer focus in our process?" "Do we have discipline and thoroughness in what we do?" "Do we have coherence in the details?" "Is there a good fit with the mission?" "Have we articulated and shared the pattern?" These questions are not easy to answer, but failing to ask them robs the development process of strong direction and leadership. To ask them well requires a grasp of development at the working level. In the next four chapters we examine in greater depth issues that are critical to making the detailed development process work effectively: integration across functions, leadership and organization, tools and methods for problem solving, and the prototyping process.

Study Questions

1. Consider the basic elements of the development framework outlined in Exhibit 6–1. What are the important interactions among these elements? For example, will the firm's approach to senior management review and control interact strongly with its approach to real-time/mid-course corrections? What are the sources of these interactions?
2. In explaining the performance of the MEI 2010 project, where would you place primary emphasis? Would it be on the way in which the project was organized, the front end of the process, or the role of senior management? What seems to be most important? Why?
3. Consider Exhibit 6–3. What is your evaluation of the underlying sources of the MEI characteristics listed in this table? What explains the pattern observed?
4. Compare the approaches to development depicted in Exhibit 6–4 for Kodak and Motorola. What are the strengths of the Kodak system? Would the Motorola approach work for Kodak? Why or why not? Would the Kodak process work at Motorola?
5. Approaches to development in an organization are among many business systems used by large organizations. How important is the fit and consistency across these systems? Why?
6. What are the key mechanisms used in the four companies depicted in Exhibit 6–4 for achieving customer focus? Are they appropriate given the context in which they work? Is one likely to be more effective than the other?

Campbell Soup Company

On 9 March 1988, Jim Elsner, vice president of engineering systems at Campbell Soup Company, sighed as he began to review John Gardner's report on the status of the Plastigon program. In January 1988, Elsner had asked Gardner to evaluate the status of engineering systems' Plastigon program and to develop his best plan for getting the Plastigon production line up and running as soon as possible. The Plastigon program was Campbell's first production-scale attempt at a microwavable soup, a product area that was considered key to Campbell's future success. Although the equipment for the line had been installed in Maxton, North Carolina, one of Campbell's five regional soup plants, over a year and a half earlier, it still was nowhere near ready to be turned over to production for regular operation.

Having been hired away from General Electric less than a year earlier, Elsner knew his boss was counting on him not only to resolve Plastigon's technical problems, but to strengthen Campbell's engineering effectiveness and efficiency. As Elsner saw it, the Plastigon program brought to light two broad issues that he and his technical group needed to address. One was the project management approach used within the engineering systems group. The Plastigon program clearly had suffered because of limits in the group's traditional approach. The second issue raised by Plastigon was what role engineering systems should take in Campbell's push into nontraditional packaging systems (such as nonmetal cans for microwavability). Elsner was not at all sure that the current organization structure and management practices of engineering systems, and its interaction and alignment with marketing and the plants, could support the variety and volume of projects already on the horizon.

This case was prepared by Geoffrey K. Gill under the supervision of Professor Steven C. Wheelwright; proprietary cost data have been disguised.

Campbell Soup Company

Headquartered in Camden, New Jersey, Campbell Soup Company was a diversified food processor known for its strong brands and product quality. Its 1987 sales of $4.5 billion (75% U.S. and Canada and 25% overseas) came from soup products (where Campbell's U.S. market share was approximately 60%), spaghetti products (the Franco-American and Prego lines), canned vegetable juices (primarily V8 and tomato juice), frozen dinners (through Le Menu, Swanson, and Mrs. Paul's), bakery products (Pepperidge Farm), and new enterprises (food service and Godiva Chocolates). With $1.6 billion of its 1987 revenues coming from soup products, Campbell dominated two of the three primary segments of that market—condensed soups (what Campbell people referred to as "red and white," from the color of their labels), and ready-to-serve soups (which Campbell addressed through its Chunky and Home Cookin' brands). The third segment was dry soup, which included instant dry soup and the rapidly growing Ramen Noodle subsegments. The U.S. division, under Herb Baum, was further subdivided into major product categories and a functionally organized U.S. manufacturing arm. (See Exhibit 1 for details.)

The food market and Campbell's competitive response changed rapidly during the 1980s. Consumers were demanding greater quality and freshness as well as convenience (through portion control and microwavability). Hence, Campbell's customer base—direct retailers (for example, supermarket chains) and distributors (who re-sold Campbell's products to independent stores)—was experiencing significant change. Convenience stores were increasing their share of the total food market, and supermarket chains were focusing on the periphery of their stores, where produce, dairy, baked goods, meat, and deli departments were gaining importance. Within the interior areas of food stores, private label and generic products were competing with branded products. In addition, Campbell was also witnessing sweeping changes among its competition, such as the consolidation of small competitors and the entry of foreign food processors into the U.S. market. Japanese firms recently had created a new market segment, dry ramen noodle "soups," suggesting a low-end Japanese entry strategy into food processing not unlike that observed in many other U.S. industries.

With Gordon McGovern, Campbell's chief executive officer, as a prime driver, the Campbell Soup Company took dramatic steps in response to these new challenges. In the 1980s, McGovern decentralized the U.S. business units and sales force into five regions to strengthen links with

EXHIBIT 1

1988 Corporate and U.S. Division Organization

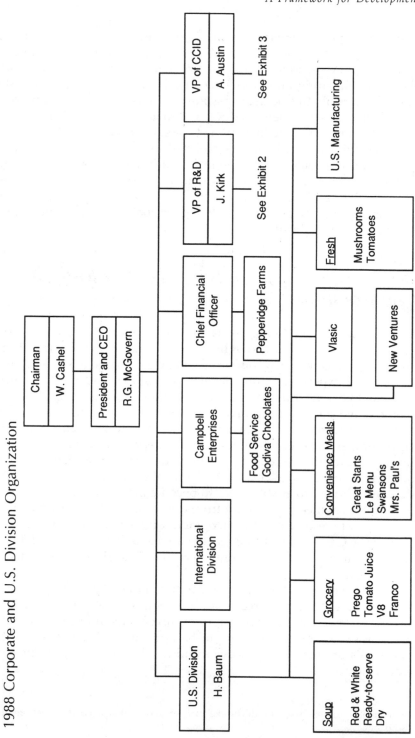

customers and consumers. Coming from a marketing and manufacturing background (he had been a plant manager, a marketing manager, and CEO of Pepperidge Farms), he pressed for development of world-class manufacturing and strong technical expertise, bringing in additional leadership and focusing resources. McGovern also championed Campbell's move into new products and markets—especially microwavable products. While the total market for such products in the U.S. was only $650 million in 1987, it was expected to be over $3 billion by 1992. Although Campbell's initial push in the early 1980s was into the frozen segment of this market (with Le Menu frozen dinners), McGovern felt strongly that developing microwavable shelf-stable soups[1] was not only a major opportunity but a necessity if Campbell were to retain its leadership of the soup business.

Developing and Applying Technology at Campbell

While Campbell Soup Company had always supported its business strategy of superior quality through strong technical competence, in the early 1980s McGovern saw opportunity and advantage in strengthening its technical expertise at three levels—in research and product microwavable, in engineering and packaging, and in the factories. McGovern strengthened the factories primarily through reorganizing into regional centers that could support the market regions, develop a critical mass of supporting engineering disciplines, and integrate a broad set of activities under each of five regional manufacturing vice presidents. By having more resources available to the regional manufacturing operations, McGovern hoped to enable them to become more self-sufficient and to require less engineering support from the corporate technical functions. The corporate research and development organization comprised three groups: the Campbell Institute for Research and Technology (CIRT) and two departments under the Containers and Capital Improvements Division (CCID).

McGovern charged the senior leadership of the corporate engineering functions to use the resources that had been released from the factory support tasks to achieve significant improvements in technical capabilities. Those improvements were to be applied to differentiate further Campbell's products and processes and to add significantly to its competitive advantage.

---

[1] Shelf-stable products were products like canned goods, that needed no refrigeration until opened.

Campbell Institute for Research and Technology (CIRT)

In 1983, Dr. Jim Kirk was recruited from the University of Florida to head the Campbell Institute for Research and Technology. At Florida, Kirk had run an extensive R&D program and was an accomplished researcher himself. At Campbell, CIRT was responsible for both long and short term research and product development, including process concept development. In early 1988, CIRT employed over 300 professionals, 30% of whom were Ph.D.s.

CIRT was divided into three primary operating departments: agricultural research, process R&D (microbiology and the pilot plant), and product development. (See Exhibit 2 for an organization chart.) The *agricultural research department* was directed primarily toward improving key ingredients, like tomatoes, and improving Campbell's farming operations, which included poultry and mushroom production—two critical inputs to its overall business. The *process R&D department* had responsibility for microbiology—researching the causes of food spoilage and improving product safety—and doing process development. Through its pilot plant section, CIRT did the initial work on process development before turning it over to engineering systems for scale-up and installation of full plant production lines. The *product development department* employed food engineers, scientists, and chefs to create new recipes and entirely new products. In addition, this department was expending considerable efforts in developing low-salt recipes as substitutes for existing products.

Containers and Capital Improvements Division (CCID)

In 1984, McGovern had hired Al Austin to head the Containers and Capital Improvements Division. Austin's experience included several decades in the packaging industry, working with a variety of marketing, sales, and engineering disciplines. Most recently, he had been a senior executive at a major packaging firm. The focus of CCID was on engineering and packaging development across a broad range of activities. These fell naturally into three departments: real estate, packaging, and engineering systems. (See Exhibit 3 for the 1988 organization chart.) *Real estate* was responsible for the acquisition of Campbell's real estate and plant facilities.

Austin brought in Dr. Mel Druin in 1985 to manage the second department, *packaging*, which developed packaging for all of Campbell's products. While most of the group's resources historically focused on metal can technology, the emphasis had shifted in recent years to plastic containers for microwavability and other non-metal packages. (Druin had been with Celanese, a plastics and synthetic fibers firm.) In early 1988, this group employed over 50 professionals.

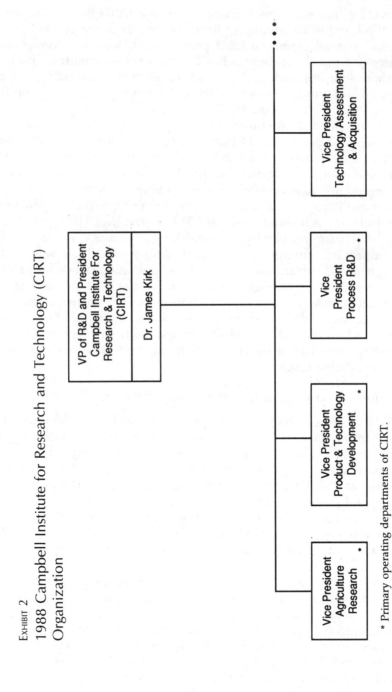

EXHIBIT 2
1988 Campbell Institute for Research and Technology (CIRT)
Organization

VP of R&D and President
Campbell Institute For
Research & Technology
(CIRT)

Dr. James Kirk

Vice President
Agriculture
Research *

Vice President
Product & Technology
Development *

Vice
President
Process R&D *

Vice President
Technology Assessment
& Acquisition

* Primary operating departments of CIRT.

Exhibit 3

1988 Containers and Capital Improvements Division (CCID) Organization

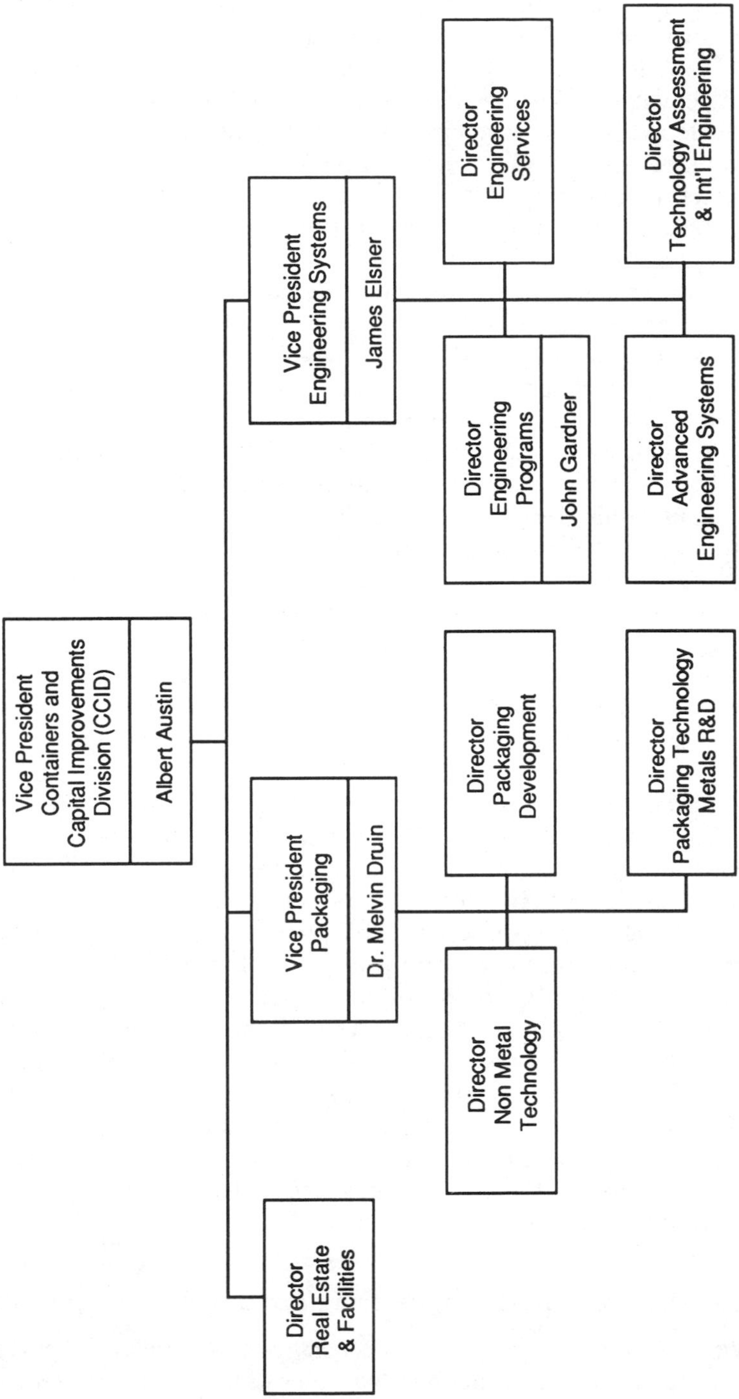

Vice President Containers and Capital Improvements Division (CCID)
Albert Austin

Vice President Packaging
Dr. Melvin Druin

Vice President Engineering Systems
James Elsner

Director Real Estate & Facilities

Director Packaging Development

Director Non Metal Technology

Director Packaging Technology Metals R&D

Director Engineering Programs
John Gardner

Director Engineering Services

Director Advanced Engineering Systems

Director Technology Assessment & Int'l Engineering

Engineering systems, under Jim Elsner, consisted of over 200 engineers and was responsible for developing advanced manufacturing processes for new food products and providing more traditional efficiency improvements in existing processes for all of Campbell's divisions. It also developed and/or purchased the plant equipment for new lines and provided special engineering support to the regional manufacturing plants. Engineering systems was viewed throughout the Campbell organization as a service group—responding to requests for support and initiatives from the line functions.

Within the engineering systems department, people were organized either by disciplines or by areas of project focus. For example, the advanced engineering systems group, which represented almost a third of Elsner's department, had subgroups that focused on advanced control systems (sensors and computerized manufacturing control), in-house equipment development, entirely new processes (working closely with CIRT), next-generation plant engineering, and advanced mechanical systems (filling, closing, sterilizing, etc.). The engineering services group provided traditional engineering services (drafting, civil, electrical, etc.) as well as environmental services.

Because of engineering systems' broad responsibilities, many diverse programs/projects were underway simultaneously (in early 1988, there were over 500). Programs (called projects if they were relatively small and could be handled largely within engineering) ranged from simple soup line extensions (taking two weeks of a single engineer's time), to long-term development efforts such as the development of new production processes or of an entirely new production line like Plastigon. Historically, the large number of simultaneous programs had meant that engineers typically divided their time among three or four projects or more during any given calendar period. Recently, Elsner had set up a special engineering programs group, which at this point included the effort Gardner was heading up in connection with Plastigon, and had responsibility for business unit liaisons and program prioritization.

The engineers in the containers and capital improvements division often worked closely with the professionals in CIRT, at senior as well as lower levels in the organization. As management liked to describe it, CIRT had primary responsibility for product, packaging had primary responsibility for the package, and engineering systems had primary responsibility for the production process. These three tasks were often referred to internally as P^3 (P-cubed).

The Management of Engineering Programs

With engineering systems as a centralized functional support group, a major management challenge was allocating that resource across a decentralized, diversified corporation. In 1988, the basic procedure had been in place for over a decade. The engineering systems department would first project aggregate demand for its services on an annual basis, and then use those projections during the budgeting cycle to negotiate modest increases to accommodate growing demands. Subsequently, those resources would be allocated on a program or project basis as individual opportunities were identified, reviewed, and approved.

A request for an engineering program or project could be initiated from anywhere within Campbell (see Exhibit 4). However, the primary sources (and those traditionally with a higher probability of success) were initiated either by the manufacturing plants or by the business units. Once a request was initiated, engineering systems would review its scope and technical content, and write a brief but formal proposal. Often there was little work done at this stage on design issues or feasibility of concepts, in part because so many of the projects were simply extensions or enhancements of an existing operating activity.

Once prepared, the brief proposal was sent to manufacturing engineering (a subgroup within Campbell US manufacturing) for review. Following predetermined guidelines, manufacturing engineering identified the organizational units that needed to give preliminary approval. This sign-off ensured that all the parties affected by the project agreed with the project's purpose and need, and were willing to support its eventual implementation. Next, resources were allocated by the appropriate engineering directors within Elsner's department. Any conflicting requests (such as for a scarce functional specialty or because of conflicting priorities) were resolved by the functional manager, if possible. If not, they were resolved by negotiating at the vice president level.

Each technical program or project within engineering systems or packaging was assigned a program coordinator. (A coordinator could have literally dozens of projects, but probably only one sizable program.) As a practical matter, if a project needed someone from packaging to do a week or two of work, the program coordinator would either talk directly with the desired engineer or with the manager of the appropriate packaging group. Generally speaking, the directors within packaging and engineering systems would determine and agree on priority, and the managers working for them would do the actual people selection and staff assignments for individual tasks and projects.

If a program could be handled primarily by engineering systems and/or packaging, then the program coordinator would take initial responsibility for the entire activity until it was handed over to one of the operating plants. If, however, a program required ongoing input from other groups—such as CIRT or marketing within a business unit, or even a manufacturing plant (because of transition issues)—then a program or project *task force* would be organized. This task force would have

Exhibit 4

Project (and Program) Request Flow Chart

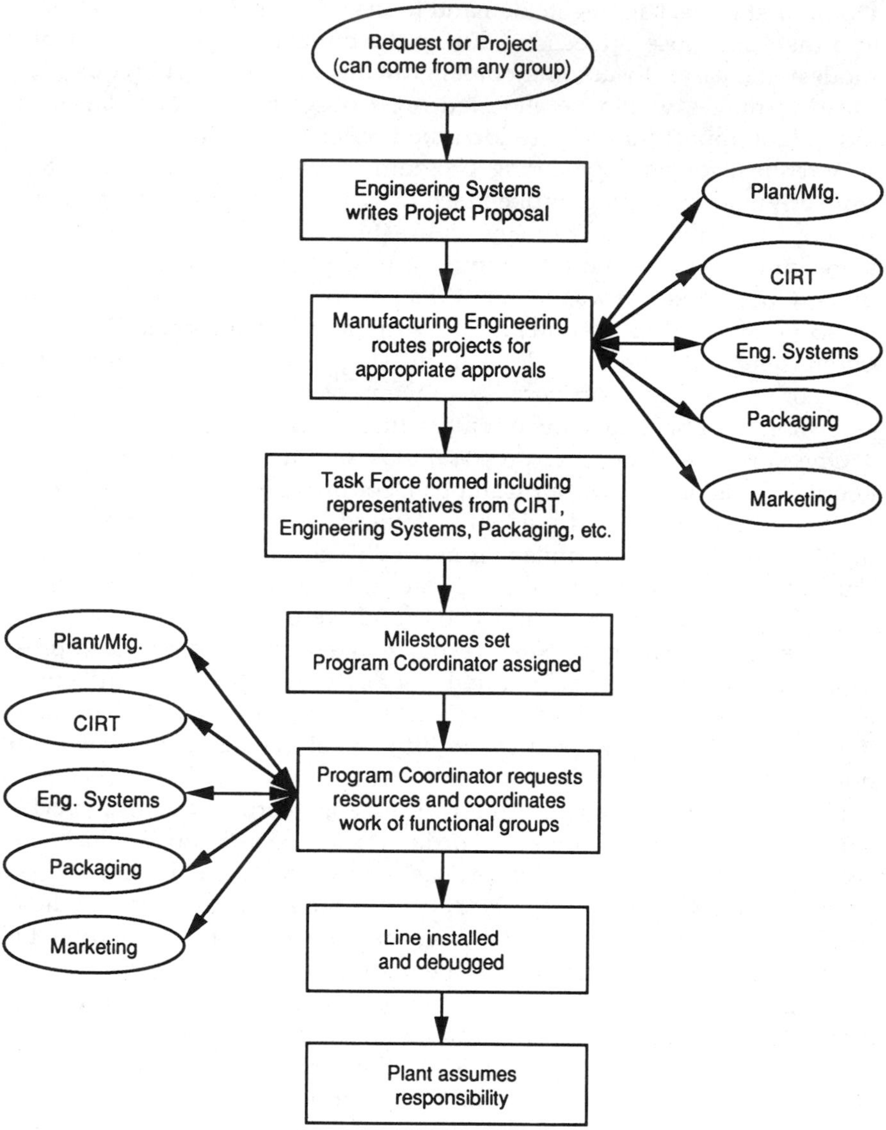

Request for Project
(can come from any group)

↓

Engineering Systems
writes Project Proposal

↓

Manufacturing Engineering
routes projects for
appropriate approvals

- Plant/Mfg.
- CIRT
- Eng. Systems
- Packaging
- Marketing

↓

Task Force formed including
representatives from CIRT,
Engineering Systems, Packaging, etc.

↓

Milestones set
Program Coordinator assigned

↓

Program Coordinator requests
resources and coordinates
work of functional groups

- Plant/Mfg.
- CIRT
- Eng. Systems
- Packaging
- Marketing

↓

Line installed
and debugged

↓

Plant assumes
responsibility

representatives from each of the primary organizational units involved and would meet weekly or biweekly to review the program and to make sure that technical inputs were provided and received.

Campbell had used task forces, particularly in the management of new product introductions, for a long time. The procedures, however, had become more complicated as the company grew and decentralized. As the marketing manager for red and white described it:

> We've had the task force concept for 30 or 40 years. Historically, these groups were small and centrally located because the company was small and more centralized. Thus everybody knew each other, and everybody could attend every meeting. Today, however, there are so many functional groups, which are so dispersed geographically, you need a score card to know who they are, and missing one of the weekly or biweekly meetings is no big deal.

When a task force was established, the leadership role generally fell to the person from the business unit (marketing), who was in some sense a customer for the new product development effort. As a practical matter, however, since those doing the bulk of the work did not report to that person, the day-to-day project leadership usually fell to a CIRT, engineering, or packaging coordinator and was passed to the manufacturing plant production line manager later on.

Pursuing Microwavable Soups[2]

In response to McGovern's mandate, several marketing groups within Campbell U.S. began exploring possible microwavable products and alternative packages. For the U.S. convenience meals group (see Exhibit 1), who had long been in the "TV dinner" business, this was simply another incremental step. Their efforts focused on developing microwavable entrées (under the Le Menu or Swanson brands) that could be prepared frozen and then cooked in the consumer's microwave oven. Since the product was stored in frozen form, the technical requirements for shelf stability were not nearly as great as they would be for a product stored at room temperature. In addition, the frozen dinners were high-value products whose ingredients were a significant proportion of their cost.

For the soup business units, microwavable shelf-stable products represented a much bigger step. In the early 1980s, the ready-to-serve (RTS) business unit responded by looking for the ideal container for such a

---

[2] Cost data in this section are representative of the industry, but have been disguised to protect the proprietary interests of Campbell Soup Company.

407

product. Focus groups and consumer surveys revealed that the container should have several characteristics: (1) the consumer should be able to eat the soup directly from the container; (2) the top of the container should be easy to open without a can opener; (3) the container should have handles so that it could be immediately removed by the consumer without danger of getting burned; and (4) the container should have an attractive, table-ready appearance.

In addition to the consumer requirements, there were a number of technical specifications. First, the container must be sealed air-tight so that the food would not go bad when stored on the shelf. Second, to be microwavable, the container could not be made of metal. Third, it had to withstand not only the heat of the microwave, but the heat of sterilization (the container and its soup had to be heated to 250° F for 40 minutes or longer during the production process). Finally, the container should not affect the taste and quality of the food.

While some market surveys indicated that consumers might pay up to twice as much (on a per-serving basis) for a microwavable soup, it was clear that there were significant economic constraints as well as technical and consumer preference considerations. A metal can line running at 600 units per minute resulted in fixed operating costs of $.10 per unit, while the same line running at a quarter of that speed (150 per minute) would incur fixed operating costs of $.40 per unit. Microwavable soup packaging costs tended to be much higher than those for conventional soup. The containers themselves were significantly more expensive, but another major differential lay in running the production line.

With the above issues in mind, the packaging group began to search for a company that could provide an appropriate container. The first effort (1983) resulted in a package that used a "scrapless forming process" (SFP). This package consisted of a plastic bowl covered with an all-plastic peel-off lid. As part of the SFP development, CIRT set up a small hand operated pilot line with 25 people packing 12 units per minute. It quickly became evident that the cost of the container and the eventual cost of the entire production process were going to be substantial. CIRT therefore developed a premium line of ready-to-serve soups called Cookbook Classics, with top-quality ingredients, for what was to be a premium-priced product.

The output of the SFP product line was test-marketed in six stores in the Camden, New Jersey, area. While the response to the Cookbook Classic product line was excellent and to a microwavable soup was quite positive, unfortunately, the seal on the SFP package was so strong that a knife with a serrated edge had to be included to "saw" the plastic lid off. It was decided that this seal was too difficult to open and defeated one of the major benefits of microwave packaging—convenience.

As the search continued and the packaging group identified several other possible containers, marketing conducted a consumer survey to evaluate various options and to determine the most suitable one. Because differences in price were not included in the survey, most customers chose the container with the most desirable attributes—the "Plastigon" bowl. This container was a brown plastic bowl, that looked like a crockpot, with a metal foil cover. The foil could be peeled off by hand before heating, and the two "ears" protruding from the top of the bowl enabled a consumer to remove the bowl from the microwave without getting burned. (See Exhibit 5 for a photograph of the Plastigon container.)

Although the initial cost of the Plastigon container was high (28¢ per bowl), the task force decided to go ahead with it. Preliminary market tests indicated that even at a premium price (99¢ retail per unit), a sizable market for the product existed (approximately 100 million units annually). To make this price profitable, it was expected that learning curve effects would cut the cost of the Plastigon bowl by a factor of two within a three-year period.

The Engineering Program to Support Plastigon

While engineering systems was an SFP task force member in 1983, the project had never really gotten out of the hands of CIRT, packaging, and

Exhibit 5

Plastigon Container

Description of container:
- Easy peel-off foil cover
- Two ears on sides allow consumer to pick up the bowl when hot without burning his or her fingers
- Attractive, table-ready appearance
- Container Cost: 28¢ per bowl
- 10 ounce size

the marketing group, and thus there had been only a small formal engineering project set up. When Plastigon emerged in late 1983 as the "ideal container," engineering systems established a major program and appointed John Dalton as coordinator to move that effort from its initial development in CIRT on through to a point where it could be transferred to a manufacturing plant. From the start, Austin and Elsner's predecessor recognized that this program would be a significant challenge. While engineering had worked with the frozen food groups on developing production lines for microwavable products, those were much simpler; they did not involve cooking and sterilization, and the seals did not need the same durability and reliability to maintain an airtight shelf-stable state.

The P^3 team had already developed a small-scale Plastigon prototype line in its laboratories in Camden, but much of the work on that line was done by hand, and CIRT had difficulty getting consistent results. Because the prototype line's technologies differed significantly from those proposed by engineering for the actual production line, the role of the pilot line was unclear, and eventually it was discontinued.

The Plastigon program began in earnest in late 1983 with Dalton and a small group from engineering systems directing the preliminary design of a production line process. (See Exhibit 6 for a program time line.) While no one remembered exactly how the decision was made, it was agreed that the production line should be a continuous process operation running at a rate of 200 units per minute. Although this rate was less than the 600 cans per minute of a typical metal can soup line, the goal was considered aggressive.

The line that engineering systems designed (see Exhibit 7) was very similar to a canned soup line, broken down into six sections:

1. blending, where the soup ingredients were mixed;
2. filling, where the bowls were filled with soup;
3. sealing, where the tops were placed on the bowls and sealed;
4. cooking, where the soup was cooked and sterilized;
5. incubation, where the bowls were tested for leaks; and
6. secondary packaging, where the bowls were individually boxed. (After secondary packaging, the bowls were placed in a case by hand.)

Each section was connected by a moving conveyor, making the line a continuous process. Despite the new shape of the containers, the conveyor system itself was fairly standard. But because each section of the line involved different technologies, different engineer(s) were assigned to them.

In late 1983, engineering systems put together a $10 million proposal to develop, acquire, install, and start up the Plastigon production line.

EXHIBIT 6

Plastigon Program Time Line

MANAGEMENT	TECHNOLOGY

1/83 SFP Pilot Line Setup

SFP Rejected
Ideal Attributes Determined by Focus Groups
Alternative Microwavable Packages Developed

RTS Business Unit Submits Request for Plastigon
Engineering Systems Writes Project
Project Submitted for Approval

Project Approved
Plastigon Task Force Formed   **1/84** Equipment Ordered for Maxton Line
J. Dalton from Engineering named Program
  Coordinator

Plastigon Pilot Line Set up in Camden by CIRT

1/85 Equipment Installation in Maxton, N.C. Started

Equipment Installation on Plastigon Line Complete

1/86

R. Winkler from Engineering Systems Replaces
  J. Dalton as Program Coordinator

1/87

Cooker Performs First Successful Processing of Soup

J. Elsner Hired as VP Engineering Systems   Line Runs Through Complete Cycle for First Time

J. Elsner Reviews Plastigon Program
J. Gardner Replaces R. Winkler   **1/88**

J. Gardner Proposes New Filling Equipment

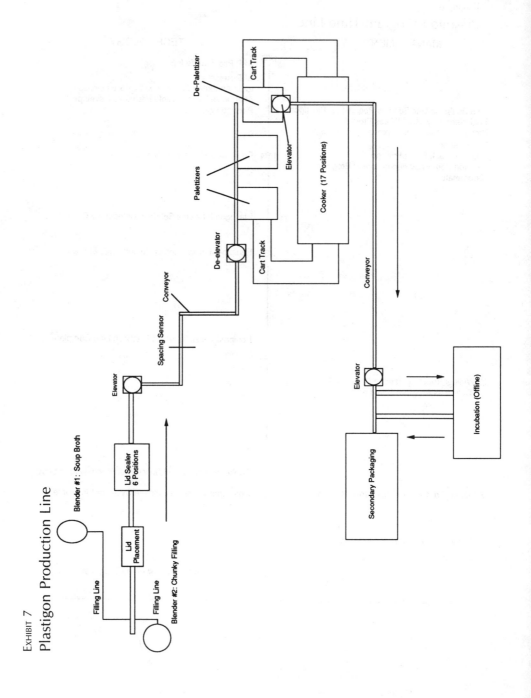

ExHIBIT 7
Plastigon Production Line

The proposal was approved by the Campbell Board of Directors early in 1984. At that point, each of the process engineers assigned to each section of the line was given a budget by the program coordinator and immediately began to work with vendors to develop the required equipment. In parallel, a pilot scale line was ordered for Camden to test out concepts. (Frequently Campbell developed production lines without first doing a pilot of that particular production process because of its extensive experience in manufacturing food products.)

The process engineers were quite familiar with equipment procurement. They specified the characteristics (capacity, tolerances, speed, etc.) of the equipment for their section and then sought out a vendor who could provide it. In retrospect, the equipment turned out to be sufficiently different from standard soup-making equipment that in many cases the vendor could not deliver exactly what was promised. Neither the vendor nor the Campbell engineers had adequately specified the equipment to anticipate this, however. Thus virtually every piece of equipment was "first of a kind."

After several discussions among senior management, it was decided in 1985 that the new Plastigon production line should be installed in the Maxton, North Carolina, plant, one of the five regional U.S. plants making soups and other canned products. Maxton was Campbell's most efficient plant, and had sufficient floor space to install the Plastigon line without expanding the building.

Over the next two and a half years, the equipment was ordered and delivered for each section of the line. When a piece of equipment arrived, the engineer(s) responsible for it would travel to Maxton to get the installation process started. Because of the large size of the equipment (the cooking chamber was a thick-walled, steel container 70' long and 15' in diameter), installation often involved major construction.

In early 1986, Bob Winkler became program coordinator for Plastigon, replacing Dalton. Winkler continued to hold regular task force meetings in Camden on a biweekly or monthly basis, and, by mid 1986, most of the equipment had been installed and the engineers were working to get each piece to run by itself without product. The engineers based in Camden, New Jersey, had to fly to Maxton to work on the equipment, sometimes as often as 30 times a year. Several of the engineers left the company or switched to other programs that required less travel.

Getting the Plastigon Line Up and Running

From mid 1986 through 1987, engineers from packaging and engineering systems worked to debug the line and get it running. In late 1986 packaging technology—non-metal R&D—was put into a single department, which provided some additional focus from the packaging side.

413

However, coordination between engineers from various groups was difficult because often the engineers were not at the plant at the same time. Even when some were present, they had their own tests to run and usually were not interested in running the line as a whole. Also, the engineers found themselves short of support staff to run the line because the plant did not want to devote operators and management time to something still in the "experimental" stage. As one of the engineers on the program recalled:

> For the first 18 months of the debug and start-up phase, no one at the plant was really committed to the line. In fact, as the time for turning on the production line drew closer, they actually wanted less and less to be involved. Their position was, "Wait until it's a proven process" and then we'll be ready to "accept" the line for our operation.

In part, the factory was following standard procedures by not getting involved too early. The general rule was that engineering systems and packaging took responsibility until the process had been "qualified," and then the plant took over. In addition, the Maxton plant was being stretched during this same period as it tried to run existing lines and also bring two-piece metal cans into full production. Finally, plant managers privately worried about the new lines' impact on their financial performance, since they were measured primarily on month-to-month operating results.

As the engineers sought to debug their individual sections and pieces of equipment and to begin running the line together, a number of important technical problems arose. Because the bowls had rounded bottoms and overhanging lips, they were more difficult to manage on the conveyor lines. The systems also had a large number of limit switches that checked to make sure that parts were within the required range. The cooker system alone had 150 limit switches. When one of the limit switches failed to make connection, that system would be shut down. This would cause a chain reaction that might set off 30 different alarms. The engineers would then have to track down the root causes of the failure and correct them.

By late 1987, most of the mechanical problems had been straightened out and testing began on bowls filled with water. This was done to ensure that no product manufactured with the test process was shipped to customers by mistake. (Campbell had strict regulations on the procedures used when running soup through a test process.)

When the bowls filled with water were sent through the cooker they became deformed. Solving this problem was especially difficult because the engineers had to evaluate degrees of "badness" to determine whether a change had improved matters or made them worse. Eventually, after exhausting all the relevant parameters, the engineers decided it was impossible to run the cooker at the rated speed. The cooker was slowed to half its original speed, and by completing tests on the full matrix of values of all variables, the engineers were able to determine a combination of those values where the bowls went through the cooker without deformation.

The cooker was then tested on pre-processed soup and finally on the actual soup. Because the thermal properties of the soup were different from water, several additional adjustments had to be made to the production process at each stage. While the cooker was being debugged, other parts of the line were also having difficulties. When the bowls were filled, soup splashed onto the rim. Although such splashing was common on metal can lines, on the Plastigon line, it prevented the metal foil lid from sealing properly. Even when the rims of the bowls were clean, the seals were often inadequate.

Within a few months of his arrival at Campbell, Elsner arranged for a review of the Plastigon project. As Elsner recalled:

> I knew the Plastigon program was in trouble, so I asked the engineering team to develop a *detailed* program plan for solving the problems. I then went down to Maxton, North Carolina, where they were working. When I got there, they had a single overhead slide with five or six bullet points. I asked them if that was their idea of a detailed plan. There was dead silence. I thought to myself, "Oh, no . . ." Finally, one of the old-timers spoke up. He said, "I know we look like idiots, but this is new to us. We've never had to do this before."

By January 1988, soup had been produced on the Plastigon line, but the line would rarely work for more than an hour at a time and large losses of product because of bad seals or other problems were common. It was at this point that Elsner replaced Winkler with Gardner, giving him full engineering responsibility for the Plastigon engineering program, and requesting that within six weeks he come back with his plan of action for completing the project. Gardner's background was well-suited to this assignment because of his extensive work with frozen foods, which had experienced similar problems. In fact, Gardner considered the Plastigon line "nothing more than a frozen food line with a sterilizer instead of a freezer."

Parallel Developments in Microwavable Products

During 1986 and 1987, interest in microwavable products both inside and outside Campbell had grown significantly. While this helped to build general knowledge about what options were viable, how consumers might respond to them, and some of their basic economics, it also had served to fuel direct competition for Plastigon as the microwavable soup solution for Campbell. (See Exhibit 8 for a comparison of the economics of several types of microwavable soups to a standard Chunky can of soup.)

Competitive Introductions

Since the Plastigon program had been initiated, several of Campbell's competitors had developed shelf-stable microwavable products. (See Exhibit 9.) Hormel, for example, had developed a line of nine entrées (chili, beef stew, etc.) in a microwavable container. Hormel's container was essentially a plastic can with a metal "pop" top. The top was a standard can top commonly used in peanut or potato chip cans with a

EXHIBIT 8

Comparisons of Economics of Different Containers

	Metal Can (Chunky Soup)	Plastigon	DRG	Brick Pack	Dry
Serving Size	10 oz.	9.5 oz.	7.5 oz.	8 oz.	10 oz.
Cost of Container	$0.07	$0.28	$0.25	$0.16	$0.27
Cost of Label/Secondary Packaging	$0.02	$0.06	$0.03	$0.00	$0.04
Ingredients	$0.15–0.25	$.015–0.25	$0.10–0.18	$0.07–0.10	$0.15–0.20
Fixed Operating Cost per Hour[a]	$3600	$3000	$2700	$2000	$1000
Theoretical Line Rates (Units/minute)	600/min	200/min	250/min	200/min	500/min
Actual Line Rate	600/min	50/min[b]	200/min[b]	200/min	500/min
Operating Cost per Unit[c]	$0.10	$1.00	$0.22	$0.17	$0.03
Total Cost per Unit	$0.34–0.44	$1.49–1.59	$0.60–0.68	$0.40–0.43	$0.49–0.54
Wholesale Price	$0.57	$0.85	$0.60	$0.45	$0.53
Suggested Retail Price	$0.65	$0.99	$0.70	$0.50	$0.60
Estimated Annual Unit Sales (Millions of $)	$195	$200	$140	$40	$20
Factory Investment (Millions of $)	$12	$10	$7	$8	$4

NOTE: All figures have been disguised.

[a] Operating cost per hour includes overhead, utilities, labor, and depreciation. These costs are largely independent of the number of units produced.

[b] There were some quality problems at these rates.

[c] Operating cost per unit is the operating cost per hour divided by the number of units (actual) produced in each hour.

Exhibit 9

Alternate Microwavable Containers

A. SFP Container:
- Saw top—difficult and messy to open
- No protection against burnt fingers
- Container Cost: 25¢ per bowl
- 10 ounce size

B. DRG Container:
- Easy-open "pop-top"
- Foam insulated walls to prevent burns
- Can-like top should be faster and easy to seal
- Container Cost: 25¢ per bowl
- 7.5 ounce size

Other Options:

C. Brick Pack
- Not yet microwavable
- Drinkable soups only
- Container Cost: 16¢ per container
- Highly convenient

D. Aseptic
- Technology of the future
- Not ready for production environment
- Better taste
- More convenient?

---

ring that could be pulled to open the can. The top was attached to the plastic can with a double seam. When the top was peeled off, the ring that sealed the top to the can remained. Despite this metal ring, the can was microwavable as long as the metal ring did not touch the edge of the microwave.

Both Chef Boyardee and Dial's Double-Tree food division also were involved in putting their products in a similar microwavable container. Chef Boyardee had test-marketed microwavable versions of some of its Italian products (for example, lasagna and ravioli), and Dial's Double-

417

Tree food division was test-marketing three product families (entrées, pastas, and soups) that could be put in the plastic can.

General Foods also had announced its intentions to serve the microwavable shelf-stable market with a line of entrées (for example, pepper steak and chicken) in a "tray" container. The plastic tray was covered with a metal foil that was heat-sealed during production in a manner similar to Plastigon (the foil had to be removed before heating in the microwave). The tray itself, however, was not made out of a "high barrier"[3] material, so the shelf life of the General Foods container was not nearly as long as Plastigon or other competitive products.

Although none of these products was out of the test market stage as of early 1988, and only Dial was involved with a soup product, they represented competitive threats to a Plastigon-type soup container. Furthermore, because of the relatively high value of an entrée (compared with soup), these products were less affected by the high costs of the packaging. A key result of these competitive actions was that the marketing people wanted to get to market fast with soup in a microwavable container. This pressure caused them to jump from one container or form of package to another.

Developments within Campbell

Because of the delays in getting the Plastigon production line up and running, some people in packaging and marketing were starting to question the original intent of "obtaining the ultimate solution for microwavable soups in one giant step." To many, the Hormel/Chef Boyardee/Dial containers seemed to offer an interim solution to the problem.

The red and white marketing group of Campbell U.S. in late 1986 initiated its own effort to develop a microwavable soup in a container that was essentially a minor modification of the Hormel package. This effort, supported by sub-efforts in CIRT, engineering systems, and packaging, was referred to as the DRG program (the name was taken from the material used in the container). Everyone agreed that the DRG container was a halfway step between a traditional can and the "ultimate" microwavable container (such as Plastigon) because the top was sealed with a standard double seal in a manner very similar to a metal can. However, it was also clear (given what competitors were doing) that DRG might offer red and white a way to get a microwavable soup to market even sooner than Plastigon would do so for the RTS business unit.

---

[3] A high barrier material did not allow the flow of oxygen through it. In this case, approximately 20 cc of oxygen passed through the tray per year compared to approximately 2–3 cc for a higher barrier material such as that used in the Plastigon container.

The DRG container had few of Plastigon's premium features—it had no easy-peel lid, it was not as attractive, and there were no special handles on the sides. Its economics were better, however (see Exhibit 8), and this product was expected to serve essentially the same market as Plastigon. Although DRG was to contain a ready-to-serve product, the red and white business unit was responsible for DRG because the product was to be taken from a red and white soup recipe and because they were the ones who initiated it.

While it was still too soon to tell what kind of start-up problems Campbell might have on the DRG production line, Elsner's engineers felt that because this container was more similar to a metal can, the problems probably could be solved within a few months. Assuming the problems were ironed out as expected, however, it still would be late 1988 before DRG would be sufficiently test-marketed and available in sufficient quantity and quality to permit a national roll-out.

Other Campbell Microwavable Efforts

Another product in development was a drinkable soup in a brick pack (the foil lined cardboard boxes often used for individual servings of juices). While this product used a well-understood technology, its market was somewhat different from Plastigon's market. Although both were convenience foods, the brick pack could contain only drinkable soups, and because it could not be microwaved in its present form (because of the foil liner), the soups had to be put into a mug to be microwaved. Efforts were underway to develop a microwavable plastic-lined brick pack; however, these were at least a year or two away from being commercially viable.

Packaging a dry soup in a microwavable bowl had also been suggested by one of the marketing groups. This product would allow the consumer to add water and then microwave the soup without having to find a container for the soup. Although dry soups were typically low-end, their convenience might make this type of product viable despite the package's high cost (27¢).

One of the most interesting technologies with promise for microwavable soup was aseptic packaging, where the soup was sterilized independently of the packaging and then added to a sterile package. This technology separated the cooking step from sterilization of the bowl. With aseptic packaging, the flavor of the soup could be improved significantly while eliminating one of the most erratic steps in the Plastigon production line process. Many people at Campbell felt that this technology was the "wave of the future." Unfortunately, because of several technical issues that remained, it looked like aseptic soup packaging was still several years away. This made it difficult to estimate the cost and market size for this technology.

In spite of these many options, and while all the technologies were useful, there were those within marketing who were not convinced. In the view of the marketing manager for red and white:

> Each of the new convenience technologies has slightly different consumer attributes and addresses a different market segment. The Plastigon product is a high-end product—almost a meal. DRG might be targeted as a snack or a meal for kids. The brick pack soups are more like a beverage than a soup. The advantage of the dry soups is that the consumer can just add hot water if the microwave is not available.
>
> While all of the technologies have attractive features, it is not clear that any of them is really necessary. A lot of the impetus to go into microwavable soups has come from McGovern rather than from solid market data. If you think about it, if we can just increase our market share in the red and white brand by one or two points, we would end up with more profit than from any reasonable sales projections for all these other segments.

Issues for Engineering Systems

In late February 1988, Elsner met with Gardner to discuss the status of the Plastigon engineering program. It was clear from Gardner's assessment that, while there had been many mistakes made along the way, the project was basically sound. Gardner was convinced that he and his engineering team could get the program on line and running over the next several months. Gardner had followed up with a memo outlining the major elements of his action plan for achieving that objective (see Exhibit 10).

As Elsner sat down to review Gardner's memo on 8 March, he reflected on what he had learned about the Plastigon program over the last several months.

> When I first saw that six-bullet slide, I got a sick feeling in the pit of my stomach. But I think we've come a long way since then, and I'm anxious to see what John wants to do. I want to make sure that John is on the right track, because the project is important. We not only have to get the line running well, but we've got to build momentum behind the product in other parts of the company.
>
> With all these projects going on in microwavable products, I've also got to make sure that we know where Plastigon fits in the overall scheme of things, and how we ought to be supporting these efforts. In a sense, the Plastigon program captures a lot of the issues that face engineering systems and Campbell as a whole in managing development. It's clear we've got to improve how we do individual programs and projects, but we've also got to do something

Exhibit 10
Action Plan

MEMORANDUM

To: J. Elsner
From: J. Gardner
Re: Near-Term Plan for Getting the Plastigon Line Up and Running
Date: 6 March 1988

Current Status

When I arrived at Maxton, the line was not running as a complete system. The eight engineers from engineering systems and the two from packaging were getting in each other's way. The engineering systems engineers wanted to run the line, but packaging would refuse to allow it because they were afraid of shipping bad product. This meant that engineering could not run tests on the whole system. Everyone was burned out.

As you know, I brought a couple of my own people down with me and we began to run the line. To get good seals, we've slowed down the sealing system and lowered the sealing temperature. With this new process, we get a good seal that a customer can open without too much effort. Because the sealer can only seal six bowls at a time, the reduced speed has limited the output of the line to 50 bowls per minute. We are currently trying to build the line up from there.

As we discussed in detail a few days ago, the current status of the Plastigon line is that we have run it for as much as four hours straight, but, in general, the line will not remain up for more than half an hour or so. I believe that it is possible to get the line running as a working production line within a six month time frame. I'm committed to making that happen.

The key problem with the effort so far is that the line has not been run enough as a complete system. The people down at Maxton have been trying to debug each of the parts of the system separately, but most of the problems involve two or more subsystems. We need to balance the line and then run it as a system, fixing problems as they come up. I see three steps to getting a working production line:

Equipment Changes

There are a couple of equipment changes that we need to make as soon as possible. The largest is that we need to replace the filling equipment. The current filling nozzles splash the soup onto the rim of the bowl which prevents a good seal from forming. To fix this problem, I would suggest using the FEMLO filling system which has been used for years on frozen lines. In addition, I plan to remove all the limit switches that are not directly related to product safety. Currently, there are over 200 limit switches on the line which get tripped any time something moves a little out of tolerance. Most of the time, the problem is not serious, is random, and would correct itself without intervention. By eliminating the unnecessary switches, we will be able to run the line consistently and deal only with the important problems. As we get those taken care of, we can then address refinements.

Once these equipment changes are implemented, we will try to get it running consistently, debugging the line as a system and fixing problems as they come up.

Engineering Team

We need to have a dedicated team down at Maxton for the next six months that can focus on getting the system running. I will detail my exact requirements within a week, but I would like to get at least a couple more engineers with frozen food experience. (These would be in addition to myself and the eight others I have already selected.) In addition to this team, I will need some support from the plant. In particular, I will need six machine operators and a plant production manager who should start to take over supervision of the day-to-day operations and get up to speed on how the line runs.

Long Term Development

In six months, we should have the system running consistently on one shift. We should be able to get some improvement in the system performance by making lots of small adjustments and we will probably be able to push the system to about 100 bowls/minute or possibly a little more by late summer. At that point, marketing is going to have to get involved and develop a roll-out plan, and we will have to add a second shift.

For improvement beyond 100 bowls per minute, we need to develop a better understanding of the process. We will start to build this knowledge base over the next six months. We should then look at bringing packaging technology back in to consider material changes and other options that will improve the performance of the system, especially its running speed. It may be that we have to rethink the entire concept of the line. The current, continuous system, while theoretically more efficient than a batch system, is not very flexible. We may not be able to adjust it sufficiently to obtain adequate efficiency.

---

about how we decide what the whole set of projects should be, and how we allocate resources in response to the many requests we receive. What we do about Plastigon could set a pattern for what we do with those larger issues.

Applied Materials

On July 15, 1986, Dan Maydan, corporate vice president of Applied Materials and president of the Applied Deposition Technology (ADT) Division, sat back in his chair mulling over his meeting earlier in the day with Jim Morgan, Applied's president and CEO. The two had discussed a competitor who was developing a product for the same marketplace as the 5000 system under development at ADT. Morgan and Maydan had just returned from a trade show where the competitor's offering had been displayed. Though it didn't necessarily appear closer to completion than the 5000, both men had heard strong and persistent rumors that in fact it was 10–12 months ahead of the 5000's schedule. This was a distinctly alarming possibility.

The carefully conceived and planned 5000 program was four months old and on track. Moreover, potential customers were highly enthusiastic about concept prototypes they had seen. But if a competitive offering were available so much earlier, who knew how they would react?

In their meeting Morgan and Maydan had explored accelerating the 5000 effort, the risks of which Maydan was now contemplating. To match the competitor's rumored schedule, the 5000 product development cycle would have to be cut from 20 months to 9. Obviously, if they succeeded, the company, Maydan, and his team would be elated. Equally obviously, should they fail, either by a significant delay in introduction or by delivering a disappointing product, disaster would ensue. Morgan had asked for Maydan's recommendations by the following afternoon.

This case was prepared by William Kennedy and Steven Zuckerman under the supervision of Professor Steven C. Wheelwright, and is an abridgement of Stanford Business School case S-PD-3.

423

Background

Industry Overview

Processing silicon wafers was the first step in the manufacture of integrated circuit (IC) chips and microprocessors. A wafer was a disc of semiconductor material (typically silicon), whose surface was subdivided into identical squares; upon each of these was constructed the circuitry for one chip. The circuitry was "built" in a precise series of steps, during which materials with different electrical characteristics were carefully deposited and removed. "Masks," like stencils used in silk screening, were placed over the wafer's surface, locally shielding it. After the portion of the wafer visible through the mask was bathed in ultraviolet light, which changed its chemical composition, material was removed from or added to the wafer's surface in the exposed areas. Completion of the circuits could require the addition (deposition) and removal (etching) of up to 10 different layers. After the circuits were complete, individual ICs were cut from the wafer and mounted on the hard plastic carriers that protected them from damage and allowed them to be mounted easily on a printed circuit board. The boards were then assembled into computers, televisions, radios, automobiles, etc.

One critical parameter for ICs was "device size," or the size of the individual transistors in the circuit. As the size of the individual parts of the circuit was reduced, more of them could be fitted onto a single chip, reducing cost and increasing computing capacity. The smaller devices, which were closer together, also worked faster, resulting in higher performance. The evolution of ICs had been accompanied by significant increases in the complexity and speed, i.e., bytes of memory per chip and computations per second. Improvements in the accuracy and precision of wafer fabrication equipment had been essential to the progress of IC technology.

Three primary technologies were used in transforming the surface of wafers into electrical circuits: deposition, etching (see Exhibit 1), and diffusion/implantation, whereby foreign molecules were forced into the wafer's surface. Chip manufacturers chose their process technology on the basis of the characteristics (size and complexity) of the chips they were planning to produce. Smaller circuit designs demanded more complicated process sequences and technology, which fueled the growth of the semiconductor fabrication equipment market. The worldwide market for semiconductor equipment of all types was expected to exceed $60 billion by 1989. The wafer processing equipment market, including the equipment technologies listed above, as well as over $1 billion in photolithographic masking machines, was expected to exceed $3 billion in 1986 and grow to $7 billion in 1989. (See Exhibits 2A and 2B.)

EXHIBIT 1

Wafer Fabrication Equipment Markets

Process Technologies

Deposition:

The deposition of material onto the surface of the chip could be achieved using a number of techniques. Most fell into one of two categories of Chemical Vapor Deposition (CVD): epitaxial and nonepitaxial. CVD technology involved various techniques for thin film deposition of conducting and insulating layers used to fabricate bipolar and MOS (Metal Oxide Semiconductor) devices. CVD techniques could be compared to simpler coating techniques, although it was important to remember that they involved extremely critical tolerances and difficult operating environments. Low- and mid-temperature *nonepitaxial CVD was like painting,* while *epitaxy was like veneering.* Epitaxial deposition involved depositing a very precise layer of material with a common crystalline grain alignment on top of the less consistent silicone wafer.

Etching:

Removal of materials from wafer surfaces, or etching, was performed using one of two primary technologies: wet and dry. Wet technologies were dominant in the early development of the industry, mainly because they were cheaper and easier to control than the dry technologies. Dry etching techniques, relying primarily on plasma physics, were developed later in response to the demands by chip designers for more precise and smaller circuit features. A plasma process utilized a partially ionized gas, with an equal number of positive and negative charged particles mixed with neutrally charged particles. The plasma, usually generated at low pressure using high intensity Radio Frequency (RF) power, eroded the surface of the wafer by attracting and bonding with molecules on the exposed surface.

Semiconductor manufacturers such as Texas Instruments and Intel in the United States and Hitachi and NEC in Japan also were demanding a higher level of automation in wafer fabrication equipment. Automation was being driven by the complexity and tighter tolerance requirements of the new chip designs and a continued emphasis on lower costs and shorter chip development time. The speed and efficiency of the wafer production, or "throughput," and the number of rejected chips per wafer, or "yield," could be increased if wafer handling and processing could be performed without potentially contaminating human contact.

Company History

Applied Materials was founded in 1967 to produce the specialized equipment used in semiconductor wafer fabrication. Its first products utilized chemical vapor deposition (CVD) technology. Through the early 1970s the company grew rapidly and expanded its position in the wafer fabrication (fab) market, controlling 6.5% in 1972. In the mid-1970s, the entire semiconductor industry suffered the effects of a severe recession; in 1975, Applied recorded a 45% sales decrease. To counter this down-

EXHIBIT 2A

Equipment Markets for Semiconductor Fabrication

Semiconductor fabrication
Equipment markets and leaders

1985 market

Equipment
- ⊕ Leaders, market share*
- ☐ Estimated worldwide sales** ($ millions)

Equipment
- Wafer processing
- Questor systems
- Assembly

Deposition

Chemical vapor
Advanced Semiconductor
25% Materials
15% TEL–Thermco
$250

Physical vapor
25% Varian
15% Materials Research
$300

Raw silicon and wafer making

Microlithography
(includes all alignment systems and spin/bake process equipment)
25% Perkin–Elmer
15% GCA
$1,140

Dry etching
30% Applied material
10% Tegal
$380

(includes factory management software and CAE systems)

Factory management systems
25% Calma (GE)
10% Schlumberger
$325

Diffusion furnaces
40% TEL–Thermco
25% Bruce
$225

Ion Implantation
30% Varian
30% Eaton
$420

Process diagnostics
(includes mask and wafer inspection systems)
15% KLA instruments
5% Nanometrics
$480

Epitaxy
35% Applied Materials
15% Gemini
$175

Dicing saws
55% Disco
25% General Signal
$50

Die bonders
30% Foton
20% General Signal
$125

Wire bonders
50% Kulicke & Soffa
25% Shinkawa
$220

Packaging
15% Yamada
10% Kras
$290

Automatic test
(includes VLSI, memory, linear and logic testers)
15% Avantest
15% Schlumberger
$1,070

*market share rounded to the nearest 5%

**worldwide sales are for fiscal 1985 and are rounded to the nearest $5 million

426

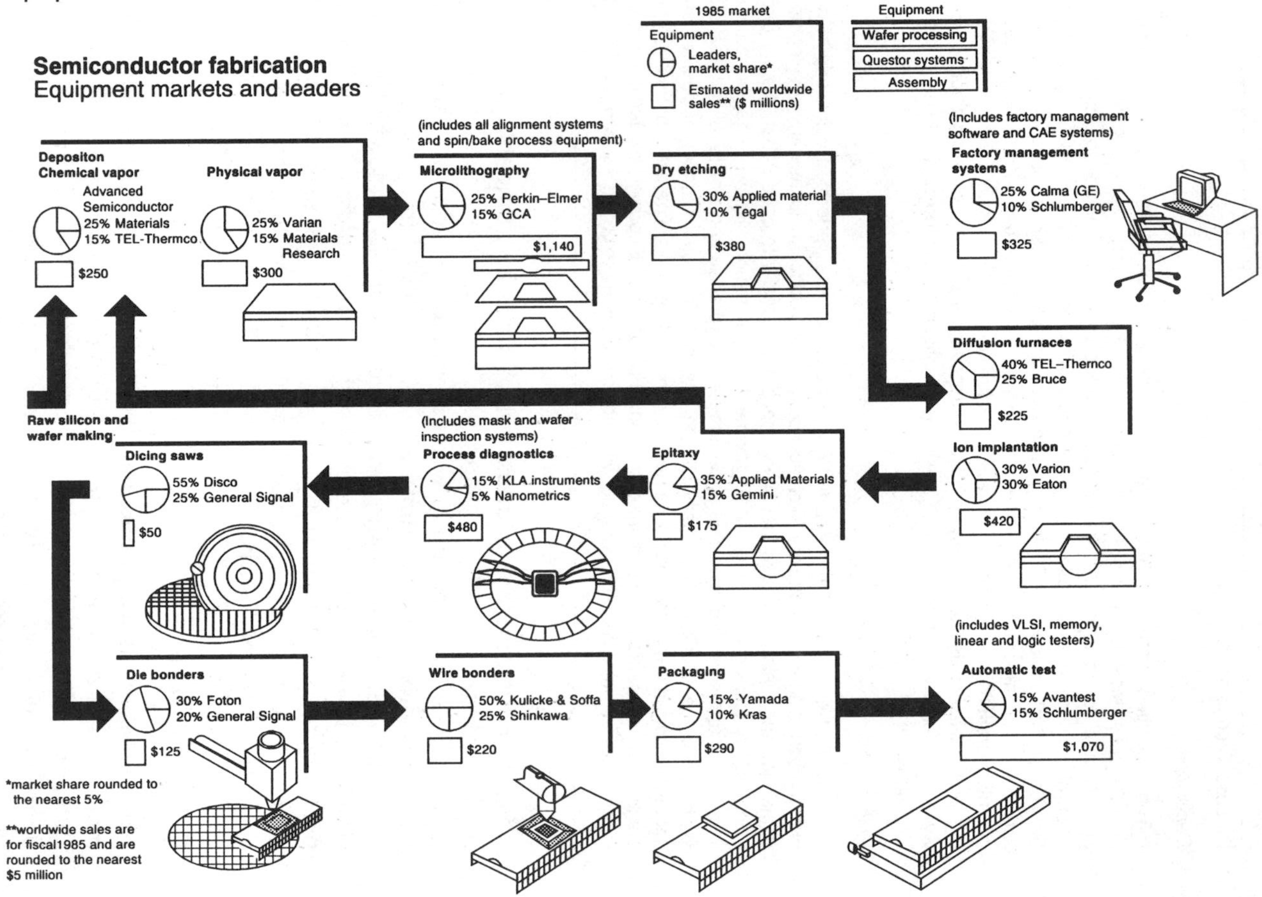

Exhibit 2B

Wafer Fabrication Equipment Markets (worldwide sales in $M)

	Actual					Projected	86–91
	1981	*1982*	*1983*	*1984*	*1985*	*1986*	*CAGR*
Microlithography &	*529.1*	*547.3*	*728.7*	*1227.4*	*1163.8*	*870.7*	*16.5%*
Mask Making							
Resist Processing	**80.9**	**74.4**	**92.3**	**196.1**	**209.6**	**142.8**	**19.2%**
Wafer Exposure	**398.7**	**413.6**	**567.7**	**955.4**	**869.9**	**655.2**	**16.2%**
Stepper	154.1	186.2	299.0	538.7	445.6	306.8	20.9%
Scanning Projection	163.0	141.7	166.8	267.1	266.5	195.0	9.2%
X-Ray	3.6	2.1	2.3	5.1	6.7	16.5	25.8%
Proximity	51.8	59.1	57.2	88.1	61.9	54.2	23.1%
Vector Scan E-Beam	23.5	22.7	34.6	50.4	84.6	78.9	21.1%
FIB	2.7	1.8	7.8	6.0	4.6	3.8	22.1%
Laser Beam	—	—	—	—	—	—	—
Mask Making	**49.5**	**59.3**	**68.7**	**75.9**	**84.3**	**75.0**	**13.7%**
Optical Pattern Gen.	5.8	7.3	9.1	6.0	5.4	4.2	5.2%
Raster Scan E-Beam	35.6	42.2	47.4	61.9	72.9	61.6	9.6%
Laser Beam	—	—	—	—	0.0	2.0	67.0%
Focused Ion Beam	—	—	—	—	0.0	1.0	35.7%
Photorepeaters	8.1	9.8	12.2	8.0	6.0	3.9	4.7%
Diffusion	*94.2*	*106.0*	*128.5*	*230.9*	*246.3*	*202.8*	*18.3%*
Furnaces	88.2	97.3	111.5	206.0	206.7	164.8	12.3%
Hi-Pox	5.2	5.6	9.9	16.4	19.1	17.3	33.7%
RTP	0.8	3.1	7.1	8.5	20.5	20.7	37.5%
Ion Implantation	*104.9*	*124.6*	*191.2*	*343.8*	*333.2*	*178.3*	*30.6%*
Medium Current	67.6	73.0	91.4	141.3	128.5	73.7	21.2%
High Current	36.8	49.0	96.8	198.2	199.3	97.5	34.2%
High Voltage	0.5	2.6	3.0	4.3	5.4	7.1	53.0%
Deposition	*324.8*	*364.3*	*450.6*	*690.6*	*762.5*	*683.6*	*15.3%*
CVD	**88.7**	**106.1**	**148.1**	**225.1**	**255.2**	**229.8**	**19.6%**
APCVD	17.4	15.3	22.3	28.2	36.7	31.3	6.4%
LBCVD	45.0	50.4	66.3	107.1	134.6	121.5	22.0%
PECVD	26.3	39.9	57.7	86.8	82.9	76.2	18.3%
Photo CVD	—	0.5	1.8	3.0	1.0	0.8	79.0%
PVD	**153.3**	**177.2**	**209.4**	**299.5**	**328.8**	**283.3**	**8.7%**
Sputtering	90.9	130.8	170.6	250.4	267.1	230.7	10.7%
E-Beam	62.4	46.4	38.8	49.1	61.7	52.6	− 3.1%
Epitaxy	**82.8**	**81.0**	**93.1**	**166.0**	**178.5**	**170.5**	**18.7%**
Horizontal	3.0	2.8	3.8	1.9	0.0	—	—%
Pancake	19.0	18.7	26.2	41.1	37.2	36.2	− 3.8%
Vertical	43.5	31.7	30.7	70.3	55.7	46.5	18.5%
MBE	16.9	24.7	25.3	40.4	59.1	59.1	26.5%
MCCVD	0.4	3.1	7.1	12.3	26.5	28.7	20.3%
Etch & Clean	*196.8*	*234.3*	*372.4*	*557.5*	*577.2*	*508.4*	*17.6%*
Dry Processing	**101.0**	**156.6**	**259.9**	**387.5**	**413.7**	**375.6**	**19.6%**
Dry Strip	9.0	9.8	17.6	23.4	34.6	41.0	22.3%
Dry Etch	86.4	139.2	232.8	349.3	360.0	317.2	19.6%
Ion Mills	5.6	7.6	9.5	14.8	19.1	17.4	13.0%
Wet Processing	**95.8**	**77.7**	**112.5**	**170.0**	**163.5**	**132.8**	**10.8%**
Wet Machines	15.8	19.9	44.6	61.3	70.5	62.5	21.2%
Workstations	68.3	47.6	55.6	95.0	78.2	60.0	− 5.1%
Apparatus	11.7	10.2	12.3	13.7	14.8	10.3	3.4%
Wafer Manufacturing	*43.1*	*49.8*	*73.5*	*109.4*	*101.7*	*76.0*	*7.6%*
Crystal Growing			**26.3**	**40.0**	**35.2**	**21.4**	**10.4%**
Crystal Machining			**47.2**	**69.4**	**66.5**	**54.6**	**6.4%**
ID Slicing			24.9	36.5	26.7	15.0	3.2%
OD Slicing			1.5	2.2	2.3	2.5	11.5%
Lapping			4.2	6.2	7.9	8.1	6.3%
Edge Grinding			1.5	3.6	8.7	13.0	9.0%
Polishing			10.0	14.6	15.7	12.6	6.3%
Other			5.1	6.3	5.2	3.4	5.3%
Total Wafer Process	1292.9	1426.3	1944.9	3159.6	3184.7	2519.8	17.6%

turn, a number of acquisitions and joint ventures, including the production of silicon, were attempted, but most proved unsuccessful.

In 1976, James C. Morgan was named president and chief executive officer. Confronted with mounting losses and a lack of engineering direction, Morgan returned the company's focus to its traditional area of expertise—wafer processing equipment utilizing CVD technology.

In 1978, Applied Materials released three new CVD products—the AMC 7600 Epitaxial Reactor and two non-epitaxial machines, the AMP 3300 Plasma Deposition System and the AMS 2000 Continuous Silox Reactor. Company sales volume increased by 17% in 1978 and 51% in 1979. Applied Materials renewed its leadership in CVD technology in 1979 when it released the AMC 7800 Reduced Pressure Epitaxial Reactor, which improved the process technology of the AMC 7600 machine. Epitaxial deposition grew in importance to Applied Materials as more and more chip designers/manufacturers utilized complementary metal oxide semiconductor (CMOS) technology, to which the epitaxial CVD process was particularly well suited. (CMOS devices used less power and generated less heat, two important functional criteria in chips.) Exhibits 3A and 3B outline Applied Materials' product offerings from 1976 through mid-1986; Exhibit 4 shows recent financial data; Exhibit 5 shows the semiconductor business cycle.

The 8100 Product Program

Program Start and Technology Acquisition

In the late 1970s the semiconductor fabrication industry was in dire need of equipment to facilitate volume production of very large scale integration (VLSI) devices, as feature size approached 3μm (.000003 meters) and accuracy became much more critical. The current state of the art in etching, high pressure plasma etching, used high pressures that caused undercutting, which eroded the sides of the masked wafer material. This undercutting limited the feature size and prevented VLSI designers from maximizing the performance of their chips (see Exhibit 6).

In 1979, Applied Materials, which had not marketed an etching machine for a number of years, established a research and development group whose charter included preliminary development of plasma etching technology, followed by its application in the design of a commercial machine. The team consisted of a number of Applied Materials' best engineers and managers, who were taken off other projects and product lines around the company and relocated to a separate building. However, the team had great difficulty developing a successful product,

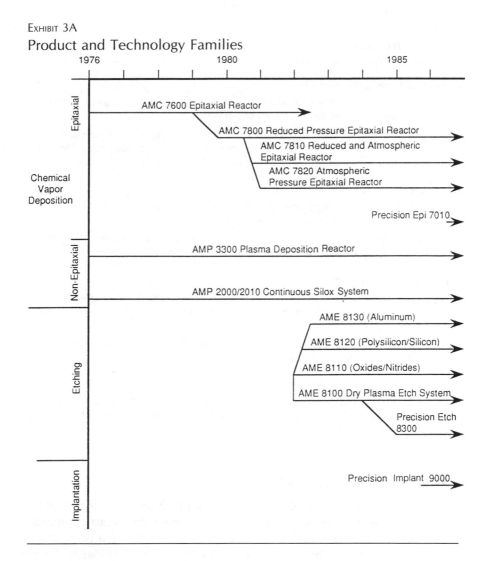

EXHIBIT 3A
Product and Technology Families

because unlike pure mechanical and electrical engineering systems, wafer fabrication processes were a combination of science and art.

Concurrently, scientists at Bell Laboratories had invented and successfully developed a new type of low-pressure etching machine. When members of the Applied Materials team visited Bell Labs, it became obvious that Bell engineers had a much clearer understanding of the art of controlling the new etch technology and that licensing the process from Bell was the best way for Applied Materials to accelerate its development program. Moreover, Bell could undoubtedly find a competitor to license it if Applied didn't.

EXHIBIT 3B
Current Products

Current Epitaxial CVD Products

AMC 7800 Series Epitaxial Reactors: Vertical "barrel" reactor using radiant heat for VLSI (Very Large Scale Integration) chip production.

Precision 7010 Epitaxial Reactor: Vertical "barrel" reactor using radiant and inductive heat for VLSI and CMOS (Complementary Metal Oxide Semiconductor) chip production. Features low process cost, low particulate levels, and full automation.

Current Non-Epitaxial CVD Products

AMP 3300 Plasma Deposition Reactor: Silicon Nitride plasma deposition, using a "dry" process and a vertical batch-loaded drum to hold the wafers.

AMS 2000/2100 Continuous Silox Systems: Conveyor belt "continuous" deposition system, using a gas spray to disperse the coating material.

Current Etching Products

AME 8100 Series Plasma Etching Systems: Dry etching using a hexagonal drum onto which batches of wafers are loaded for processing. Simple manual loading system.

Precision Etch 8300: Similar process to 8100, using a hexagonal drum, but with more sophisticated loading and control systems.

Current Implantation Products

Precision Implant 9000: Developed by an Applied Materials Division in England, this machine uses an ion beam to implant wafers. Wafers are processed in batches loaded on a rotating wheel.

8100 Product Development

Bell Labs' new hexagonal electrode (hexode) technology placed wafers on each side of the six edges of a hexagon during the production process. The team at Applied was given the task of designing a production machine, using the technology, to be called the AME 8100 Plasma Etching System. A handful of engineers who had implemented and developed the technology at Bell moved to Applied Materials, including Dan Maydan and David Wang. Shortly thereafter, they were joined by a former Bell associate, Sass Somekh. Maydan became the head of the 8100 development project, Wang assumed responsibility for technology, and Somekh oversaw engineering and operations.

The managers who had begun the development work at Applied remained to help manage the design and manufacturing implementation of the 8100. Mike Walk, a veteran of other Applied efforts, was heavily involved in the development of the process technology under David

Exhibit 4

Corporate Financial Summary ($000)

	1986	1985	1984	1983	1982
Net Sales	$149,261	$174,595	$168,400	$105,527	$ 90,830
Cost and Expenses					
Cost of Products Sold	$ 88,902	$ 94,210	$ 85,207	$ 64,128	$ 66,697
RD&E	24,621	31,519	21,219	16,436	14,689
M&S	18,297	16,836	12,412	9,171	10,047
G&A	13,514	15,927	15,923	9,723	9,534
Other	1,786	120	(919)	1,007	3,681
Total Costs & Expenses	$147,120	$158,612	$143,842	$100,474	$ 104,648
PBIT	$ 2,141	$ 15,983	$ 24,558	$ 5,053	$(13,818)
Provision for Taxes	899	6,713	11,054	2,000	(4,581)
Net Income (Loss)	$ 1,242	$ 9,270	$ 13,504	$ 3,053	$ (9,237)
EPS	$ .09	$ .71	$ 1.03	$ .25	$ (.93)
Order Backlog	$ 35,900	$ 47,833	$ 80,500	$ 38,254	$ 28,493
Working Capital	$ 71,782	$ 69,900	$ 65,614	$ 58,704	$ 34,263
LT-Debt	$ 19,615	$ 16,880	$ 18,573	$ 16,250	$ 16,226
Shareholders' Equity	$ 92,758	$ 86,426	$ 74,299	$ 61,553	$ 34,656
Shareholders' Equity/Share	$ 6.96	$ 6.57	$ 5.68	$ 4.99	$ 3.49
Total Assets	$154,138	$148,420	$139,464	$113,182	$ 74,037
Number of Employees	1,415	1,359	1,474	1,130	1,038
Capital Expenditures	$ 11,541	$ 12,930	$ 14,567	$ 7,825	$ 5,249

Wang. Under Sass Somekh, John Kingsley was responsible for the mechanical engineering functions of the 8100, while Ed Kaczorowski headed electrical engineering development. (See Exhibit 7 for an organization chart for the 8100 program.) The person largely responsible for the organization of the 8100 project was Bryant Campbel, who had previously been in charge of the program. He created the organizational structure and management philosophy for the development process.

Applied Materials' close contact with its customers revealed that the demand for low-pressure etching machines was a critical one and that its leading customers would accept the equipment in a very rough form. Campbel, and the rest of the project group, accepted Maydan's position that an uncomplicated product would be welcomed and that a more feature-laden version could be added later. Program veterans had a very clear image of what the customers needed, and therefore very few compromises had to be made. This commitment to the customers was reinforced by the inclusion of the marketing and customer support function in the 8100 development organization.

The Market Requirement Statement (MRS) was written by Maydan, Wang, Somekh, and other engineers. Applied Materials used the MRS

431

Exhibit 5

Semiconductor Business Cycle (year-to-year percent changes)

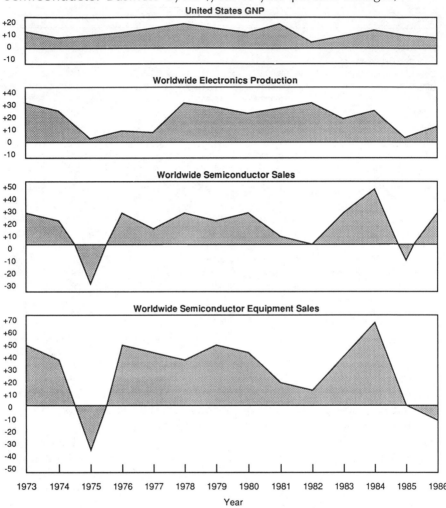

to state the fundamentals of a project, including definition of the objectives and target market for the product. It spelled out other product performance characteristics, the expected costs and selling prices, and a variety of other information. An MRS tended to vary from product to product within the company depending on the complexity and uncertainty of the project.

Maydan, Wang, and Somekh, who had spent their careers as research managers and exploratory engineers, were not accustomed to the con-

Exhibit 6

Etch Process Undercutting

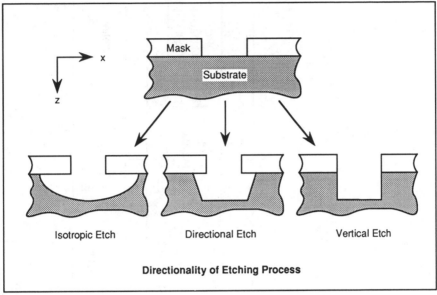

Directionality of Etching Process

---

straints inherent in the design of a commercial product. The prototype they made at Bell Labs had only a rudimentary control system. Its operation depended entirely on the skill of the operator, who had to activate the correct valves and switches at precise times in order to etch the wafer. Initially, Maydan felt that the first production machines should be released to customers with a very simple control system: just detailed instructions of how to set and run the process manually as they had learned to do. However, because the 8100 would be used in a volume manufacturing facility, it had to be possible to train production workers to operate the machine; their success at doing so could not depend on a detailed knowledge of the fundamental process technology. Bob Neilson, a software engineer who had developed a standard operating system for Applied products before being assigned to work on the 8100, grafted that system onto the new design. With it the fundamental process control steps needed on the 8100 could be programmed.

To ensure that the 8100 would be released quickly, the management team and others involved combined individual schedules to form detailed "activity networks," which helped coordinate the various functions and minimized the chances of missed or delayed activities (see Exhibit 8). Because everyone had a clear image of the final product,

Exhibit 7
Model 8100 Product Program Organization

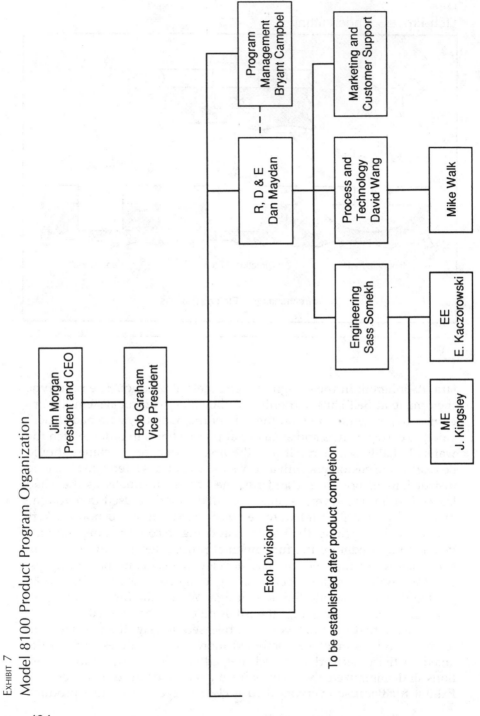

EXHIBIT 8
8100 Activity Network

September 1980
October
November
December
January 1981
February
March
April
May

Build process breadboard

Develop process

Customer demos

transfer process

Spec system

Design

Fabricate

Mech Assembly

Write Software

Software Simulator

Electrical Assembly

Software Test

Process Tests

Ship First System

Develop semi automatic loader concept

Design

Fabricate

test

Fabricate

test

Planned Staffing Table

	Engineers	Technicians/ drafters
process	4	3
mechanical	7	6
electrical	4	3
software	2	—

435

design compromises between the various functional groups were achieved with relative ease, and little time was wasted pursuing unusable concepts. In addition, a bonus system was created, so that when the various development steps were successfully completed, all team members would receive a cash payment of some significance.

8100 Introduction

The 8100 Plasma Etching System was introduced in May 1981, only nine months after Maydan and Wang arrived from Bell Labs with the hexode technology. To get the 8100 system to market as quickly as possible, Applied introduced a very basic design with the capability to process only one type of the four different materials to which the 8100 etch technology could be commercially applied: aluminum, oxide, single crystal silicon, and polysilicon. Because demand was highest for oxide etching, the oxide process was released first, with the others to follow as they were completed. The 8100 quickly captured more than 50% of the total market for dry plasma etching systems used for VLSI production. However, significant problems followed its introduction.

The development group was a separate organization from the division that would manufacture and sell the 8100, and there was little continuity in the transfer. Because manufacturing had not been involved with the development process, it needed significant help coming up to speed on the machine. Problems became so severe that tiger teams had to troubleshoot the numerous manufacturing problems. Ed Kaczorowski, who had been pivotal in the development of the electrical system, was transferred from the development group to head this effort.

Even though the 8100 was the only production-worthy tool on the market, it needed substantial engineering in the field during its first year. The development group was frequently called upon to solve problems with 8100 systems already installed at customer locations. By 1983 these problems had been worked out of both the installed base of systems and the manufacturing process. The 8100 was considered a very reliable piece of capital equipment and the only one on the market with the capability to process advanced devices.

The 8300 Product Program

With the 8100, wafers had to be loaded into the machine semimanually, which created frequent opportunities for contaminating dust particles to enter the process chamber. Because one particle of dust on the surface of a chip could ruin it, all wafer fabrication process machinery was located inside "clean rooms," which achieved particulate levels as low as 10 parts per million air molecules. Nevertheless, the particulate levels inside the processing chamber were best kept even lower than those in the clean room, which made it desirable to minimize the number of times the chamber had to be exposed to surrounding clean room air.

From the outset, a design "want" for the 8100 had been automated wafer handling, but this was not doable under the ambitious time schedule. Once the 8100 was completed, Applied's management decided that the next development effort for Maydan and his group would be "simply" an automated version of the 8100; the process chamber was to remain virtually unchanged, but the wafers would be handled automatically rather than manually. This development effort was called the 8300, because Applied intended to introduce it in 1983. (The 8100 effort had been introduced in 1981.)

By the time the 8300 program was started formally, many people in the development group who had worked on the 8100 had migrated into other Applied Materials divisions or to other companies. In fact, all four of the original Applied Materials managers involved in the 8100 project had left the group after that program was completed.

The 8300 project was to be under the direction of Maydan, Somekh, and Wang, with a new Research, Development, and Engineering group set up under Maydan. This team was given responsibility for developing the 8300; manufacturing and marketing were to be handled by a separate Etch Division (see Exhibit 9). Field problems on the 8100 distracted the engineers from concentrating on the new product, however, and the psychological lull that often followed the successful completion of a project drained enthusiasm. Because Applied's customers were very happy with the 8100, there was little external pull on the group to get the program moving quickly; the motivation had to come from within the organization. In place of the "can't lose" attitude that prevailed during work on the 8100 was a feeling that potential problems with the 8300 could hurt sales of the 8300 *and* the 8100. Thus, while Maydan was still getting used to managing a complete development program from the start, a certain conservatism pervaded the project.

Fundamentally, the 8300 was targeted to remedy shortcomings (missing features) in the 8100: the absence of a loadlock chamber,[1] automation, and the ability to handle an aluminum etch process. Because there was no comprehensive plan for the development project, progress review was done informally. At the start, the team was confident that the process knowledge that had been gained on the 8100 would translate

---

[1] The loadlock chamber was connected to the actual processing portion of the equipment; it sealed the cartridge and the wafer handler portion of the machine from the surrounding clean room air so the internal mechanisms of the machine could be kept purer than the external clean room environment.

EXHIBIT 9

Model 8300 Product Program Organization

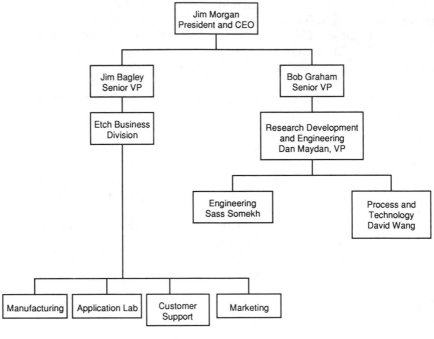

directly to the 8300. The different scale and configuration of the new process chamber, however, created a number of unforeseen problems. The "art" side of the technology was larger than the team had anticipated.

Moreover, the groups working on the various subassemblies communicated poorly. The engineering functions tended to concentrate on their own problems without considering effects on the other subsystems. Project review meetings were typically attended by large numbers of people. Veterans of the 8100 also were disappointed that there was no financial incentive plan. Finally, a significant economic recession in the semiconductor market affected the direction and motivation of the team.

From the beginning, the goal had been to produce a high-quality product that would be reliable when released. Maydan knew that the introduction difficulties experienced by the first 8100 customers would not be tolerated by 8300 customers, and made sure that as the design approached completion, it was reviewed thoroughly by the manufacturing and customer support groups. This led to a few major mid-course corrections. The first automation system developed was not satisfactory, and a significant portion had to be re-engineered. A prototype unit was presented to the Etch Division Field Engineering group, which noted that the machine was not serviceable because the physical layouts of the customer chip production facilities placed constraints on service access to the chemical and electrical systems of the machine. Back to the drawing board for the development team. Also, for the 8300, unlike the 8100, thorough reliability evaluations were conducted on all aspects of the completed design. These tests identified further modifications required before the product could be released to the field. When completed, the 8300 had required three prototype cycles rather than the single cycle envisioned in the original plan.

Commercial Release and Project Review

The first 8300 systems were shipped in December 1984. (See Exhibit 10 for a product description.) This was almost one year behind schedule. (See Exhibits 11A and 11B for planned and actual development schedules.) Though initial shipments of the 8300 were significantly late, the transfer to manufacturing had gone more smoothly than it had for the 8100, and there were few field problems even with the earliest systems. Parties inside and outside of the company gave the product excellent reviews,[2] although some criticism was directed at the efficiency of the product development process. In response, Maydan initiated a thorough review of the 8300 program with the objective of producing a set of "Product Development Guidelines."

As a start, he requested that everyone who had worked on the 8300 submit a list of "Reasons for Falling Behind Schedule." Those lists were compiled into a master list. (See Exhibit 12.) A similar list was compiled for another project that the company was just completing, and it was no surprise to anyone that the top three problems for each project were identical:

1. Unanticipated objectives were given higher priority than the original goals, which caused delays as work on various subprojects started and stopped.
2. Engineering specifications were incomplete or nonexistent when needed.
3. Magnitude of the work was underestimated at the beginning of the project.

---

[2] Commercially, both the 8100 and 8300 were very successful. By September 1986, their combined sales had reached approximately 1,000 units, with an average price of about $600,000 per unit.

439

Exhibit 10
Product Description of 8300

Precision Etch 8300: The New Technology

Clean Wafer Environment

- Fully automated cassette-to-cassette operation
- Sealed and filtered automated wafer handling system
- All wafer storage and transfer under vacuum
- Load lock pumped and vented through separate low-turbulence diffusers
- Process chamber always under vacuum
- Direct wafer load to hexode pedestal

Designed-in Clean Room Interface

- Airtight, flush-mount wall seal
- Flexible remote package location
- Minimum clean room equipment profile and operator activity
- Compatible with production line automation systems
- No maintenance required in clean room
- Particulate tested subsystems

Full Process Control

- Monitors for over 30 process parameters and machine status variables
- Two closed-loop end point controls: scanning laser and optical emission
- Menu-driven operator interface
- Password access control
- Full recipe editing and filing capability
- SECS II interface to host computer

Superior System Reliability

- Proven hexode technology
- Critical assemblies life-tested for 3–5 year equivalents
- Pretested modular subsystems
- Loader tested to high MTBF
- Modularity for short MTTR

Unequaled Etch Quality/Throughput

- Low-pressure RIE hexode process configuration
- 18 six-inch wafer load capacity
- Multi step process flexibility
- High-uniformity gas distribution system
- Etch uniformity ± 5%
- No particulate-generating assemblies
- Load lock for reduced overhead time

Low Maintenance Requirements

- No cold trap required
- Particle-tolerant pump system
- Process chamber vacuum-isolated to minimize cleaning
- Swing-out panels for easy access to all components
- Process controller for internal diagnostics and maintenance prompting
- Self-calibrating robotic handler

Exhɪʙɪᴛ 11A
8300 Planned Development Schedule

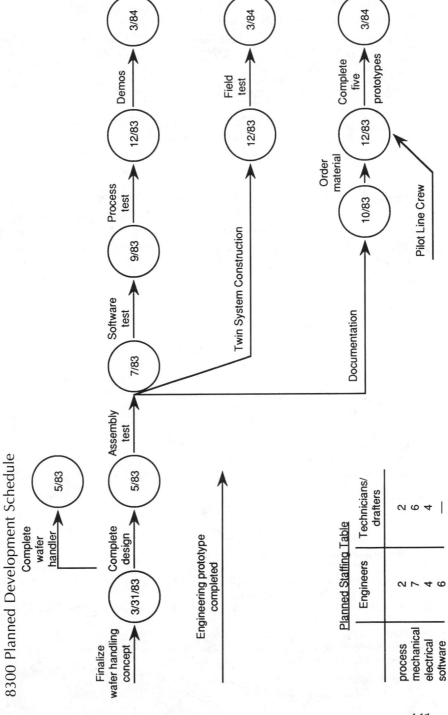

Planned Staffing Table		
	Engineers	Technicians/drafters
process	2	2
mechanical	7	6
electrical	4	4
software	6	—

441

ExHIBIT 11B
8300 Actual Development Schedule

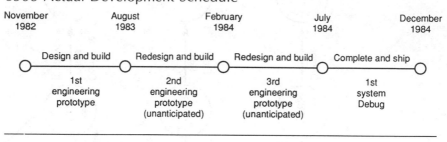

November 1982	August 1983	February 1984	July 1984	December 1984
Design and build	Redesign and build	Redesign and build	Complete and ship	
1st engineering prototype	2nd engineering prototype (unanticipated)	3rd engineering prototype (unanticipated)	1st system Debug	

These were considered symptoms of the larger problem of coordinating a development program on a product whose technology was changing very rapidly. When engineers saw new opportunities or unforeseen problems as a project progressed, they easily shifted resources—

ExHIBIT 12
Identified 8300 Project Problems

Reasons for Falling Behind Schedule (*not* in order of frequency):

1. Personnel changes cause confusion and lack of knowledge
2. Goal requires other groups or outside vendor commitments which are not met
3.* Unanticipated items are given higher priorities than original goals
4.* Magnitude of the work was underestimated
5. Poor communication between project members
6. Insufficient planning
7.* Specification not complete or nonexistent
8. Not enough time scheduled for testing
9. Schedule assumes 100% availability of an item with disregard to downtime and other usage
10. Unrealistic schedules
11. No commitment to schedule by implementor
12. Planning does not include vacation and possible illness
13. Planning does not allow for rework and design
14. Poor designs due to wrong technical choice
15. Too many design errors
16. Managers doing too much design work
17. Engineers do not know lead times
18. Goals become meaningless due to design changes requested by higher management
19. Lack of knowledge of materials
20. Things are put off until the last minute
21. Poor management
22. Lack of adequate resources—people and equipment

* Top three problems.

particularly people—to handle the latest crisis. This diffused the energy and direction of the team and forced the engineers to spend much of their time coming up to speed on a variety of projects in a short time frame.

Using the problem list as a starting point, Maydan directed his engineers to put together an ideal "product development process" so that the new program could be accomplished with less difficulty. The results included the following recommendations:

1. Programs should be comprised of five phases:
    a. Concept and Feasibility
    b. Engineering Program Planning
    c. Module/Subsystem Design and Prototype Construction
    d. Pre-Production
    e. Product Release
2. Each phase should have a distinct set of milestones to be met before the phase could be considered complete. For example, the Concept and Feasibility phase had two primary goals: to establish that (a) the product was needed and (b) it could be engineered.
3. A time flow chart, or "activity network," should be established during the planning phase. This chart should show not only what has to be done, but what each step would depend upon and how the sequence of steps would lead to progress.

This analysis of the product design process reflected Maydan's view of the relationship between research and development. He told Wang and Somekh that when someone was doing research, as they had done at Bell Labs, "the outcome could not be predicted." When someone was doing development, however, it was imperative that "the outcome could be predicted, and with a high degree of certainty." Maydan wanted to make sure that all of the future programs in this group were "development" programs.

The 5000 Program

Organizing the Program

In August 1985, Maydan met with Jim Morgan, the CEO, to discuss future plans for the 8300 development team. The knowledge that they had gained during the prolonged development of the 8300, as well as requests that a number of customers had made, led Maydan to conclude that there was significant potential for a new integrated machine that

443

incorporated both CVD and Etch processes in one "ultra clean" environment. He wanted to be sure, however, that he had management support to set up the team as he thought appropriate. He felt strongly that two things were required before he could begin:

1. The company had to be willing to let him organize a separate division to design, develop, procure materials, manufacture, and market the product. Corporate Sales and Field Service Groups, however, would still be used.
2. He had to be allowed to recruit some of the best people inside and outside the company, if necessary. He felt it important to get some young people who had not yet "tasted failure."

Morgan, who had a lot of faith in Maydan, Wang, and Somekh, agreed that formation of a separate division, to be called Applied Deposition Technology (ADT), was the best approach. He liked the concept of the new machine, to be called the 5000; it was considered revolutionary because it boasted the two chamber technologies (plasma etching and CVD), automated wafer handling, and very sophisticated integration. As with the 8100, the market seemed more than ready for such a product. Applied was particularly eager to introduce a new CVD system, a market they and other equipment manufacturers had neglected for quite some time. (See Exhibit 3.) The 5000 would introduce a significantly improved CVD process operating under significantly lower pressure than existing systems and offering significantly improved accuracy.

Both the 8100 and 8300 were designed to handle etch patterns ranging from a few microns down to the submicron level, while the etch version of the 5000 could do widths of 0.2 microns and depths of 10 microns. In addition, while the 8100 and 8300 were strong in metal etch and dielectric materials, the 5000 would initially handle polysilicon and eventually (through subsequent improvements) oxides. Thus, the 5000 would reach segments of the market not accessible to the 8100 and 8300. In a few applications where the 5000 would compete with the 8100 and 8300, it would be viewed as clearly superior to these older designs.

Unlike the 8100 and 8300, which had processed multiple wafers using a hexagonal electrode (hexode) with wafers on all six sides, the 5000 was to be a "single-wafer" machine, processing only one wafer at a time. This would guarantee a higher level of accuracy than had been possible previously. Single-wafer designs had three primary advantages over "batch" processors: (1) they were easier to operate and maintain; (2) performance did not depend on wafer load, and (3) process parameters could be controlled independently for each wafer, which gave customers a greater ability to control individual deposition and erosion parameters. A significant innovation, however, was the combination of two different types of process chambers in one machine. The 5000 was to have a core, where wafer cartridges were placed in a storage elevator and manipulated by a robot arm, surrounded by process chambers. The customer would be able to configure the 5000 with any desired combination of CVD and Etch process chambers. (See Exhibit 13 for initial product concepts and mockups.)

By having both CVD and Etch processes available inside the same ultra clean environment, the 5000 would also go a long way toward ensuring Applied's ability to provide its customers with extremely low levels of particulate contamination. The 8300 had been Applied's—and the industry's—first product with a stated particulate guarantee on the process, "generating fewer than .1 particles per square centimeter per wafer pass that is greater than 5 microns (.000005 meters) in size." The 5000 was expected to have even better performance.

5000 Product Development

Although the 5000 program did not officially begin until March 1986, concept and feasibility work started much earlier. Mechanical engineering had finished most of its work on the 8300 by late 1984, and by mid-1985, some effort had been focused on determining what the 5000 could and should be able to do.

In fall 1985, Maydan, Somekh, and Wang began to assemble the core team that would lead the development of the 5000. In addition to themselves, the team consisted of David Cheng (a specialist in mechanical design) and John White (a process chamber technology specialist). Using the recently completed Product Development Guidelines, the team assembled a detailed project plan, a fundamental aspect of which was the realization that integrating the various components would determine the project's success or failure. Because the product was to combine so many functions and have such a high degree of automation, Maydan was extremely concerned about communication between groups working on the different subassemblies; thus the project leaders decided that creating a sense of common mission and pride within ADT was vital.

The reputation of the project leaders attracted the best people from other Applied divisions, and recruiting the project team was completed in the first two months of 1986. A detailed MRS was also produced at this time that included product objectives, performance goals, estimates of market size, etc. and preliminary engineering information from the team's prior experiences. It also contained a brief plan for follow-up products.

On March 15, 1986, the 5000 development effort formally began with

EXHIBIT 13
5000 Product Configuration

A. Plan view of internal processing units and robot in loadlock chamber
   (each process chamber could be either Etch or CVD technology)

B. Prototype of robot and loadlock chamber

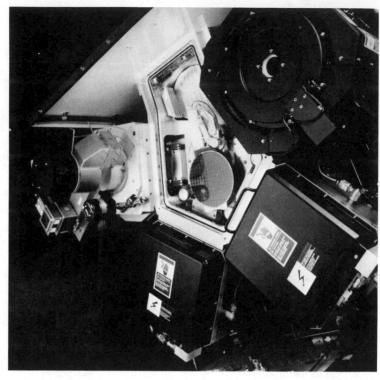

a kick-off meeting attended by all team members. Maydan stressed the importance of this product, the aggressive goals, and the commitment that would be required. He explained the project's two primary objectives:

1. Meeting all of the performance specifications and customer requirements in the MRS.
2. A short time to market—the goal was to start shipping production units in December 1987, just 20 months from official project start.

The prior experience of the engineers involved, as well as Applied Materials' consistent record of introducing outstanding products, convinced Maydan that the first objective would be met. He decided to concentrate, therefore, on achieving the second.

Because of the complexity of the 5000 design, it was clear that the project would have to be broken down into manageable units. The responsibility for developing the processes and the technology of the process chambers was given to Dave Wang; John White and Kam Law were to support him. The mechanical and electrical design areas, including the "wafer handler" that would transfer the wafer from the wafer cassette to the process chambers, were to be handled by Sass Somekh; David Cheng would be responsible for the wafer transfer. In addition, Wang would be responsible for Product Marketing, and Somekh would handle Materials and Manufacturing (see Exhibit 14).

All of these subassemblies and subtasks were interdependent. The safe way to develop the 5000 was to do each task in sequence: first the process technology, then the chambers, next the mechanical chassis, etc. This prolonged the development time, however, so it was decided to do all the tasks in parallel: each group would pursue its efforts concurrently, even if one group's final products were dependent upon another group's results, and each group had to be aware of what the others were doing. For example, work on process chambers and processes had to be started with concept feasibility. At the same time, the mechanical engineering group had to know the approximate dimensions and configuration of the chambers and the wafer handler so that they could scale the chassis. Work had to begin on the operating system and the fundamental control logic for these systems before prototype hardware was even built. Likewise, the prototype wafer handler had to be developed and tested using a crude approximation of the final software, a non-interactive system built around PCs, since the final system would not be running until the end of the integration phase (see Exhibit 15).

The integration phase of the schedule was designed to allow for a detailed design and construction of the complete mechanical and electrical aspects of the system, as well as the completion of the elaborate

447

EXHIBIT 14
Model 5000 Product Program Organization

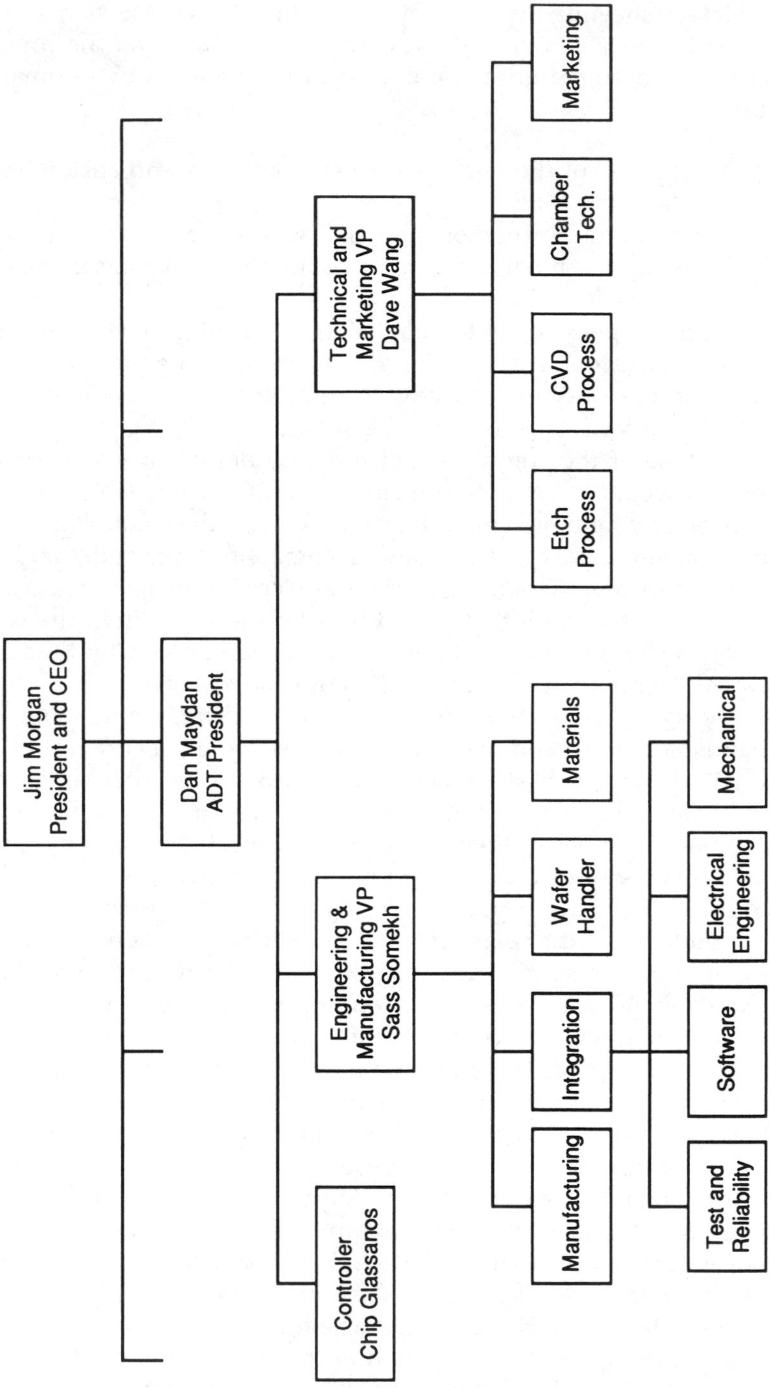

Exhibit 15
5000 Planned Activity Network

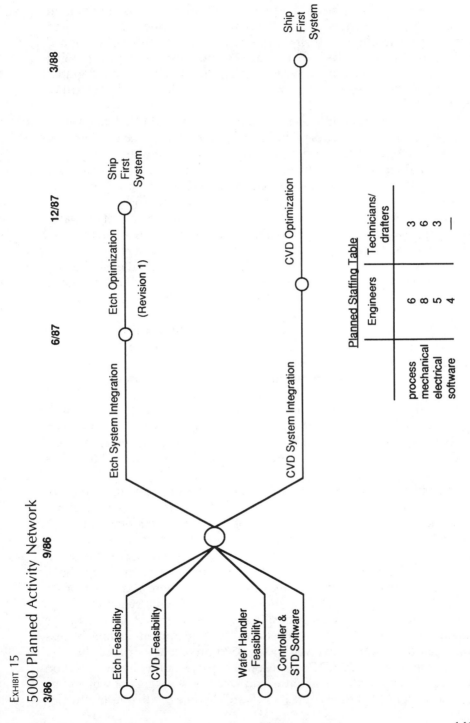

| 3/86 | 9/86 | 6/87 | 12/87 | 3/88 |

Etch Feasibility
CVD Feasibility
Wafer Handler Feasibility
Controller & STD Software

Etch System Integration
Etch Optimization
(Revision 1)
Ship First System

CVD System Integration
CVD Optimization
Ship First System

Planned Staffing Table

	Engineers	Technicians/drafters
process	6	3
mechanical	8	6
electrical	5	3
software	4	—

software and development of a plan for reliability testing. In addition, this period was intended to give the chamber and wafer handler designers a chance to optimize their design by coming up with a "Revision 1" as opposed to a "Revision 0" design. As shown in Exhibit 15, the Etch integration was scheduled to last nine months. The CVD integration was scheduled to take three months longer to avoid parallel critical paths.

Of particular importance were the optimization periods planned at the end of the integration phase. This six-month buffer had been planned to build in time for (1) any redesign needed as a result of reliability problems found late in the testing cycle, and (2) solving subtle system problems, particularly in the area of software and wafer handling, which were typically encountered after full system integration.

Each group had committed to well-defined task completion dates; individual work plans were combined to form "activity networks," which covered a 12' by 18' wall of the "war room," where all coordination meetings were held. At the root of all activities on the 500 was the basic assembly tree and system schematics. These broke the system down into approximately 70 basic modules, each assigned to a chief engineer.

A master project schedule identified the overall project activity with dates for the completion of and the interrelationships between the 70 basic modules. Chief engineers then generated individual activity networks for the design, procurement, build, test, and release of each module. Depending on the complexity of the particular activity, sometimes several different subactivity networks were needed for a single module. In all, these activities represented the selection, design, and integration of over 3,000 discreet components. Of these, 1,000 were custom-designed parts requiring detailed drawings. The remaining 2,000 were commercial parts to be selected and specified.

In addition to meetings within development groups and between each group and the three general managers of the project, regular meetings were held to ensure coordination among all the development groups. Every Tuesday at 3 P.M., the group heads met to discuss manufacturing issues; Wednesday's meeting covered technology, and Thursday's reviewed engineering issues. These were the only formal meetings held; everyone knew when they were scheduled, so there were no worries about irregularly scheduled meetings disrupting work schedules.

Informal, "hallway" communication was considered equally vital. The 5000 project would involve at most only 25 development engineers, less than half the number involved in the 8300 project at its peak. This size was made possible by ADT's focus on this project only, by the selection of team members whose strengths and weaknesses were known, and by the fact that most of the people had already worked with one another for a number of years. Further, the groups' interdependence created a strong sense of responsibility and commitment to the project.

The manufacturability and serviceability of the product received very close attention from the outset. An engineer from Field Service was included on the project team, and the designers were required to create clear documentation of their efforts so that a service manual could be assembled quickly. Key customers were identified, brought in early in the development phase to comment on prototype versions of the 5000 system, its capabilities, operating characteristics, etc., and asked to bring in sample wafers to be tested in the early process chamber prototypes. Numerous changes resulted from the feedback provided by these ac.ivities.

The 20-month effort before introduction was about the same as the original time frame for the 8300. Firm milestones were marked out for the development process, and it was decided that significant financial incentives would be paid if they were met. The incentive payments to the individual subassembly teams were dependent not only on their reaching relevant milestones but upon the performance of the project team as a whole. For example, if four out of the five teams reached their objectives, everyone would receive a smaller bonus, and all bonuses for the future milestones would be reduced. Reinforcing the financial incentives were the personal expectations of each of the team members, who knew that they had been chosen especially for this project; no one wanted to be the person who "screwed up."

In addition, management had articulated development process goals. For example, engineering change orders (ECOs) were not to affect more than 25% of the product components on the manufacture of the first five units (manufacturing prototypes), 10% for the next 10 units, and 0% once the full production was reached. Clear standards also existed for mean time before failure (MTBF) results and particle contamination levels in the system.

Progress to Date

By mid-July of 1986, the first four months of the program had gone extremely well; the members of the development team were confident that the first milestone—proof of feasibility—scheduled for September 15 would be reached by all of the small groups. The management of ADT was proving to be well balanced. Somekh provided the detailed organization, Wang the imagination, and Maydan the drive to go forward, and all three contributed technical expertise. Each was directly involved in the day-to-day work and played an active role in any decisions that had to be made. Somekh, in particular, gained much respect from the people in his organization by letting them go about their business until a conflict arose and then equitably resolving the problem. This fostered a feeling that it was OK to accept the middle ground of a dispute. Nontechnical disputes were severely frowned upon in the organization; the engineers felt that "conflict is an excuse for not getting things done."

One thing that the group had not foreseen was the excitement the 5000 generated with customers. When selected customers of the 8100 and 8300 were shown a prototype of the 5000 and invited to provide a sample wafer for testing, the response was extremely favorable. This further convinced the development team that they were on the right track but increased the pressure to get it to market quickly. There was also tremendous internal interest in the program; throughout Applied Materials, the 5000 was the "hot project."

The enthusiasm that fueled informal competition was evident in the ADT hallways. Team members shared the feeling that they were all in "slightly over their heads." Long hours were the norm, with 12 hours per day a minimum and 16 hours per day not at all unusual. The minimum number of official program reviews and presentations meant that most time was spent actually working on the prototypes. One of the engineers referred to the atmosphere as "Management by Brownian Motion"—high energy and activity in a focused environment.

Maydan's Dilemma

Dan Maydan knew he had a great program underway and that the 5000 would be an outstanding product. But could they compress the remaining 20 months of the planned program into 9 months?

The impetus for compressing the remaining steps came foremost from the rumors of the competitor's product being available possibly a year ahead of the 5000. Related to this was customers' enthusiasm for the 5000—the team had already witnessed that; but whether that enthusiasm would be easily transferred to a competitor's product was unknown. Maydan was also aware that Applied's corporate management was probably eager for a speed-up; the semiconductor equipment industry was in a slump and the 5000 clearly would be a big and needed boost to the whole firm. Finally, the project team itself might rise to the challenge. Early in July, both the Etch and CVD small groups had been able to define and detail the assembly trees for their respective process chambers (see Exhibits 16A and 16B). For the team members, that was a clear indicator that they were already somewhat ahead of schedule.

A number of concerns, however, ran through Maydan's mind, which he summarized in preparation for the meeting with Morgan:

Exhibit 16A

Etch Process Chamber Assembly Tree (July 1986)

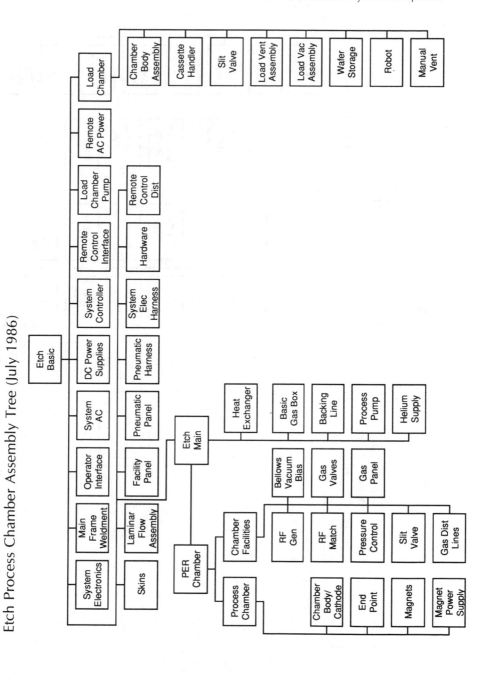

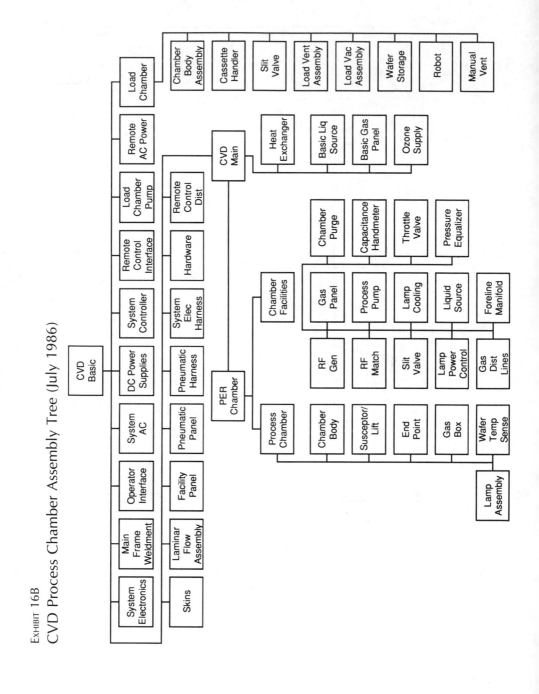

EXHIBIT 16B

CVD Process Chamber Assembly Tree (July 1986)

1. To accomplish an 11-month acceleration in the schedule would require taking on the following risks:

   a. Starting the parallel integration phases by 7/30 instead of 9/15, which meant starting integration a few weeks before feasibility had been completely signed off.
   b. The initial plan called for a 9-month period for Etch integration (see Exhibit 15) and 12 months for CVD. The dates and commitments for the Etch product were already established and there was no possibility of trading priorities between Etch and CVD. A decision to do these integrations in parallel 9-month efforts with equal priorities would mean more pressure on the development team. Adding more people would alleviate some of the pressure, but new people, previously unknown, would be a major risk in a critical schedule. (Adding more people from within Applied was not possible because of other existing priorities.)
   c. Accelerating the schedule by 11 months meant that the product had to be ready for shipment and announcement by the end of the 9-month integration period, which would do away with the "optimization" period. Thus, any problems found at the end of the period could cause damaging delays in actual product introduction and shipments. In addition, undetected product problems could result in costly field retrofits and schedule delays in manufacturing.

2. It wasn't clear how, if at all, the incentives should be changed if the schedule were accelerated. Arguably, since the team would be further improving the company's performance through early introduction, the incentives should be increased. However, since most of the additional risk fell upon the company and since the current incentive plan for the 5000 was already raising some questions about equity among other Applied Materials people, there were strong arguments not to change the incentive plan payments significantly, but simply to link the original target payments to the new dates.

   Following another line of reasoning, eventually the 5000 project needed to do everything on the activity network, but under acceleration would simply introduce the product sooner, leaving some of the tasks to be completed after introduction. In addition, the introduction might be staggered, such as introducing the CVD chamber version first, followed by the Etch chamber version a few months later. Under this type of scheme, a few incentives and their dates would be changed (to get a version of the 5000 to market 11 months sooner), but many of the dates and incentives would still be those set originally.

As he reread his notes, Maydan thought about a basic tenet of his management philosophy: Always take steps forward or back—never sideways. Thus, he knew he needed to recommend acting quickly either to change the schedule, shortening it dramatically, or put the issue to rest and stick to the original plan.

Cross-Functional Integration

Overview

Many elements are necessary to achieve success in new product or process development, including access to technology, understanding of customer requirements, expertise and knowledge in the key functions, and effective definition of key concepts. However, in and of themselves, these elements are insufficient for achieving outstanding development success. Cross-functional integration is essential for superior development performance along the dimensions of cost, time, and quality. The fact that the dominant structure in most organizations is functional, that peoples' experiences and careers are rooted in the functions, and that the vast majority of tasks needed in a development effort are defined and conducted in the functions adds to the challenge of attaining true integration.

Unfortunately, "cross-functional" is often limited to communication and coordination activity across the functions, with little or no impact on working level activities. The primary theme of the chapter is that effective cross-functional integration involves fundamental changes in how the detailed work is conducted. Picking up on the MEI 2010 development project outlined in Chapter 6, this chapter explores the integration between manufacturing and engineering and between engineering and marketing. Our purpose is to highlight the specificity and detailed level of action required to achieve cross-functional integration.

To aid in identifying necessary changes for realizing substantial improvements in cross-functional integration, we outline and discuss four modes of upstream/downstream interaction (see Exhibit 7–4). These modes range from sequential, one-way, batch communication (from the upstream to the downstream function), to overlapping, integrated, two-way exchanges between the upstream and downstream groups. Having identified the existing and desired modes of communication in a development setting, it is important to accurately assess the capabilities required to make the new mode a reality. We identify several such capabilities, ranging from downstream friendly solutions to quick problem solving, and from managing risk to coping with unexpected changes.

Finally, the chapter considers senior management's role in setting expectations and attitudes regarding integration, and altering incentives to support them. However, while senior management can do much to set the tone, all levels of the organization must understand the pervasiveness and depth of change required in a traditional functional organization to achieve the degree of cross-functional integration that will result in quantum leaps in efficiency, timeliness, and quality in development.

Product and process development create advantage in competition by delivering to the marketplace great products that attract customers and deliver exceptional quality and value. Great products and processes are much more than a clever design, novel technical solution, distinctive package, catchy promotion, or advanced equipment. Outstanding development requires effective action from all of the major functions in the business. From engineering one needs good designs, well-executed tests, and high-quality prototypes; from marketing, thoughtful product positioning, solid customer analysis, and well-thought-out product plans; from manufacturing, capable processes, precise cost estimates, and skillfull pilot production and ramp-up. But there is more than this. Great products and processes are achieved when all of these functional activities fit well together. They not only match in consistency, but they reinforce one another. In short, outstanding development requires integration across the functions. Furthermore, if new products and processes are to be developed rapidly and efficiently, the firm must develop the capability to achieve integration across the functions in a timely and effective way.

This chapter examines the principles that underlie effective cross-functional integration.[1] We begin with a look at the role of the functions in the development of the MEI 2010 described in Chapter 6. The MEI experience highlights the traditional functional activities in the traditional process, and makes clear where integrative activities were missing. We then illustrate what cross-functional integration means by looking at a framework for the interaction between engineering, manufacturing, and marketing during the development process. The final section of the chapter examines what it takes to achieve integration. We focus in particular on integration at the working level and the role of senior management in creating a context where effective integration will flourish.

The MEI Experience

The development of the 2010 portable premature infant heart monitor at MEI was dominated by the engineering function, but important and essential work was accomplished in marketing, manufacturing, quality assurance, and field service. These activities typically fell within the natural charter of the functional areas. Exhibit 7–1 lays out the major activities accomplished in the functional areas during the development of the 2010 product, arrayed according to the development process phases at MEI. Although a problem in the 2010 development project was the absence of clear phases, we have used the stated phases apparent in the sequence of development activities at MEI.

The 2010 began as a concept and was defined during concept development through interactions between design engineering and marketing. In order for the corporation to approve investment in the project, marketing and engineering combined to give definition to the concept, apply estimates of costs and investment, and develop projections of likely volumes, revenues, and profits. Approval by senior management triggered the design, construction, and testing of prototypes, as well as interaction with customers, as the organization moved to put ideas and concepts into practice. Once an engineering prototype was completed and verified, manufacturing moved in through the production prototype phase to define the process and develop the manufacturing system to be used in commercial production. This required identification of the process steps and their sequence, development of a bill of materials, selection of vendors, and ordering of tooling.

The production prototype phase culminated in the production of a small batch of the 2010 product. With pilot units in hand, quality assurance took the proposed product into customer tests while engineering handled redesign work that followed testing and customers' reactions to the product. As testing moved forward, manufacturing prepared to ramp up for volume production while marketing trained the sales force and developed promotional programs. Once the product was launched

Exhibit 7-1

Functional Activities in the MEI 2010 Development Process

Functions	Standard Phases of Development					
	Concept Development	Product Planning	Engineering Prototype	Production Prototype	Market Acceptance	Market Introduction
Engineering	Early discussions with marketing; take lead in developing and pushing product ideas; investigate ideas	Prepare budget and timetable	Build and test breadboard models; build complete prototype; validate design	Develop test procedures for in-process testing	Redesign product based on customer feedback	
Marketing	Provide input on customer needs and potential concepts; investigate concepts	Provide input to engineering on prices, volumes	Talk to customers; product focus groups to refine features			Develop literature on product; train sales force
Quality Assurance					Develop test plan; conduct customer tests	
Manufacturing		Make rough cost estimates		Develop materials list; define process; select vendors; develop tooling; produce pilot batch		Establish distribution; ramp up production to commercial volumes
Field Service						Train customer service representatives; support customers

into the market, field service supported customers in the use of the product.

Looking across the phases of development within each function in Exhibit 7–1, we find a set of activities that seems natural. Engineering puts ideas into hardware and software and conducts tests, marketing establishes linkages to the customer, and manufacturing makes the product. Each of these activities not only is essential to the development of the product and the process, but falls within the traditional definition of the function's role and mission in the organization. In spite of the fact that each function seems to have carried out its basic mission in this project, however, the project itself was problematic. Before arriving at a commercially viable product that met customer needs and operated effectively within the customer's system, the product had to undergo significant redesign. Moreover, it took the organization a long time to move from product concept to market introduction of a viable commercial product. Although the product itself delivered new features and performance that customers found attractive, the project failed to create the potential advantage that appeared so attractive at the outset of the project.

The outcome of the 2010 project suggests the need for a closer look at the activities accomplished in the development project as well as the timing and sequence of functional involvement. It is apparent, in retrospect, that some of what the functions did could have been done earlier and in a way that connected more closely to the work in other functions. Moreover, some activities that cut across functions simply did not get done. We examine what this means with two examples from the MEI project. The first deals with the relationship between engineering and manufacturing,[2] while the second focuses on the connection between marketing and engineering design.[3]

Engineering-Manufacturing Integration in the 2010 Project

When the MEI engineering organization set out to develop an infant heart monitor, the challenge was to take existing core concepts and technology and develop and package them in a new, smaller, lightweight, portable design. The product, as it emerged, was a design with a much smaller package and lower weight, but with many more features requiring new components, tighter tolerances, and more capable manufacturing processes. Though the design was built on the core technology and was eventually manufactured in an existing plant, manufacturing had to do a significant amount of process development in order to create the required design capabilities. The problem in all of this was that engineering did the design of the product at a time when manufacturing was neither focused on nor involved in the project. Likewise, manufacturing focused on the design and development of the process, including the flows of material, the sequence of processing steps, and the development of tools, *after* the engineers had established the product's basic architecture and implemented that architecture in hardware and software.

Because the design of the product and process were accomplished somewhat in isolation, the overall development of a completed design and manufacturing process was slow and required a great deal of rework, which ate up significant resources. Consider, for example, the selection of vendors. Choosing the vendors to work on the project began in late 1986, many months after product design had been launched. Assumptions made by designers about components and parts availability turned out to be inaccurate. Consolidation in the vendor base had occurred, eliminating some production facilities and components from the supply base. In addition, the design required and had assumed a certain level of process capability that vendors did not possess. All of these problems created a mismatch between the requirements of the design and the capabilities and availability of suppliers.

Achieving an integrated product and process design requires a very different approach. The focus of such an approach is to bring design choices into contact with process capabilities, and process capabilities into contact with design requirements early enough in the process that the two can influence and shape one another in a timely and effective way. In an integrated process, the solution to the vendor selection problem is apparent. The question of which vendors to use could have been examined early in the process as design needs and requirements emerged. Moreover, vendor qualification could have addressed at that early stage, much more directly and substantively, required process capabilities. Finally, the suppliers themselves could have been brought into the discussion at an early stage of the design process in order to obtain firsthand information and insight about potential problems and opportunities inherent in the choices the designers were making.

Solving the vendor selection problem involves doing things earlier, and doing things that cut across the traditional functions. Making that happen necessitates, in effect, what we call "cross-functional integration." Cross-functional integration requires in the first instance that the timing and substance of the activities in the various functions be coordinated. Integration, however, is more than mere coordination. Arriving at integrated solutions means that the actions taken in the functions support and reinforce one another. In the case of product design and process engineering, for example, integration across these two functions means that the design of the product comprehends and exploits the potential and capability inherent in the production process. It also means that the production process delivers the capability and performance required by the design. Achieving an integrated design clearly means doing old things earlier, but it also means doing a new set of things. For example, engineers in the MEI 2010 project had very little interaction or contact with manufacturing engineers on joint issues. In an integrated setup, designers communicate with manufacturing engineers on a variety of joint issues. This requires establishing a forum and context in which joint communication is effective: engineers must comprehend issues of manufacturability, foster skills in developing designs that are robust and exploit manufacturing capability, and be prepared to share designs. Likewise, manufacturing engineers must become oriented to customer satisfaction: they must comprehend issues of product performance and cost, and be prepared to deliver and develop manufacturing capability that will allow the design to achieve its objectives in the marketplace.

In order to make integrated design effective, therefore, the manufacturing organization must undertake process development and process planning up front in the project. In the case of the 2010, for example, had the manufacturing organization understood the implications of the design they could have developed the capability to hold tighter tolerances much earlier in the program. This requires that the manufacturing organization come to the table with a fairly deep understanding of its process capabilities and of the potential developments that lie ahead in its own planning.

Engineering-Marketing Integration at MEI

The interaction between engineering and marketing poses similar problems of timing, communication, and joint activity. In the 2010 project, marketing developed a good product concept in interaction with design engineering as far as the basic idea (a portable unit) and some of the features were concerned. Engineering did the design of the hardware and software, and marketing talked with customers and conducted clinics. The actual design that emerged from this process, however, did not fit well into the customer's system and did not deliver on all of the important features. While the basic concept was sound and the organization delivered many features that customers found attractive, the problems with the wheels, cart, and difficult-to-read display caused delay and rework and some damage to the perception of the product in the market.

Achieving an integrated solution implies that the design makes use of deep understanding and insight about the customer and the customer's potential use of the product. In this context, a particularly crucial problem is selecting which customer or customers to work with early in development. Some firms choose to work with "lead customers" who adopt new ideas early and help to push the state-of-the-art. Others choose a target customer whose requirements are judged to be representative of the broader market. Still others choose to work with customers to gain a broader perspective. The choice is important because the customer will influence the direction of the project. But the choice may also be critical because of what it means for the longer term relationship with the customer. If things work out well, the relationship may be strengthened. But the relationship may be hurt if, for example, the project leader decides that satisfying the customer's requests would take the project in the wrong direction. The customer may have idiosyncratic needs or may request something extreme that the team feels it cannot deliver within the project framework. Picking the right customer is thus critical.

With the right customer, getting deep insight is a matter of understanding the customer's system. In the case of the 2010, for example, this included knowing not only the needs of the customer's system, but also how the monitor functioned, how the hospital personnel interacted with it, and how they might have used it when it was portable. That insight came partly from marketers who knew the customer intimately, and partly from bringing the emerging product design into direct contact with potential customers.

Knowledge about the customer can help to guide engineering design, but it is also important that the design make use of and exploit the capabilities of the marketing organization in its relationships with customers. That includes its skills and resources in market research, promotion, distribution, customer sales, and support. But integration also means that marketing must develop the capabilities that the design requires.

While many of these activities occurred ultimately in the course of the 2010 project, they did not occur early enough to avoid difficult, expensive, and time-consuming rework and redesign. Thus, integration requires shifting the timing of a whole set of activities to earlier in the process. But, there is also a new set of activities required to support an integrated solution.

Marketers, for example, need to work with customers to develop insight that goes beyond product specifications.[4] They need to establish an understanding of the future customer's desired experience with the product. There may be much more here than simply identifying the right mix of technical specifications. Customers, for example, may care about aspects of the product that are not clearly identified or that may be difficult to articulate. Moreover, since the "customers" that will buy the product are in the future, marketing needs to identify underlying trends in customer requirements. All of this suggests that effective involvement of marketing in the early stages of product development requires marketing imagination.

Taking a broader view of the customer and the product is important, because it allows marketers and engineers to anticipate problems and opportunities early in development. But that will only occur if the concept development process focuses on system characteristics of the product. In the MEI 2010 case, for example, an integrated approach would have looked not just at the monitor, but at the customer interfaces, the cart it would travel on, and the procedures for using it. Engineers would be involved in that process to establish an architecture for the product as a system.

Engineers are also important in making it possible to confront the product architecture and the product concept with customer experience early in the process. The key is the construction of early system prototypes. In the heart monitor case, for example, such prototypes might capture some, but not all, of the functionality of the monitor, but could portray physically the package, the cart, the user interface, and the way the product will be used. Such prototypes could be the basis for early tests with customers, conducted jointly by marketing and engineering.

A Framework for Cross-Functional Integration

Achieving cross-functional integration changes what the functions do, when they do it, and how they get the work done. In order to illustrate the impact that integration has on the role of the functions in product development, we have laid out an example of development phases and functional activities in Exhibit 7–2. The table examines three of the major functions involved in development—engineering (with a focus on product design), marketing (including marketing research and sales), and manufacturing (including process development, manufacturing engineering, and plant operations). Within each function, we have identified the major activities in each of the phases of development.

The phases in Exhibit 7–2 are defined by critical milestones along the development path from initial concept to full commercial operation. The sequence begins with concept development and proceeds through product planning, detailed design and development, commercial preparation, and market introduction. We have divided the detailed design and development phase into two parts. The first focuses on verification of the product design and related process development, including design of tooling and equipment. The second phase focuses on verification of process design, with refinement of the product. This particular config-

Exhibit 7–2

Functional Activities Under Cross-Functional Integration

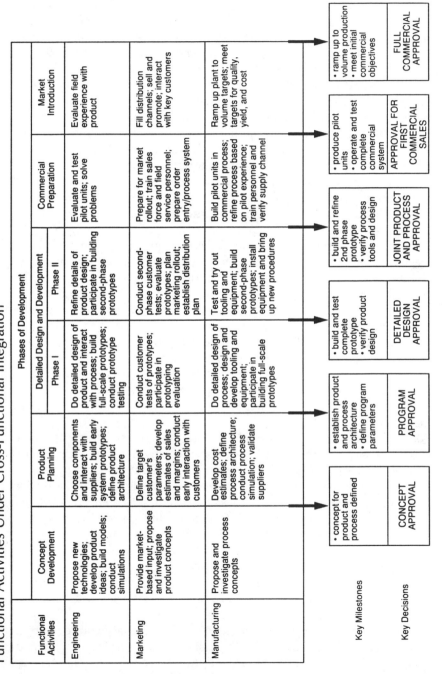

Functional Activities	Concept Development	Product Planning	Detailed Design and Development		Commercial Preparation	Market Introduction
			Phase I	Phase II		
Engineering	Propose new technologies; develop product ideas; build models; conduct simulations	Choose components and interact with suppliers; build early system prototypes; define product architecture	Do detailed design of product and interact with process; build full-scale prototypes; conduct prototype testing	Refine details of product design; participate in building second-phase prototypes	Evaluate and test pilot units; solve problems	Evaluate field experience with product
Marketing	Provide market-based input; propose and investigate product concepts	Define target customer's parameters; develop estimates of sales and margins; conduct early interaction with customers	Conduct customer tests of prototypes; participate in prototyping evaluation	Conduct second-phase customer tests; evaluate prototypes; plan marketing rollout; establish distribution plan	Prepare for market rollout; train sales force and field service personnel; prepare order entry/process system	Fill distribution channels; sell and promote; interact with key customers
Manufacturing	Propose and investigate process concepts	Develop cost estimates; define process architecture; conduct process simulation; validate suppliers	Do detailed design of process; design and develop tooling and equipment; participate in building full-scale prototypes	Test and try out tooling and equipment; build second-phase prototypes; install equipment and bring up new procedures	Build pilot units in commercial process; refine process based on pilot experience; train personnel and verify supply channel	Ramp up plant to volume targets; meet targets for quality, yield, and cost

Key Milestones

• concept for product and process defined	• establish product and process architecture; • define program parameters	• build and test complete prototype; • verify product design	• build and refine 2nd phase prototype; • verify process tools and design	• produce pilot units; • operate and test complete commercial system	• ramp up to volume production; • meet initial commercial objectives

Key Decisions

CONCEPT APPROVAL	PROGRAM APPROVAL	DETAILED DESIGN APPROVAL	JOINT PRODUCT AND PROCESS APPROVAL	APPROVAL FOR FIRST COMMERCIAL SALES	FULL COMMERCIAL APPROVAL

467

uration assumes that tooling and equipment development for the process requires somewhat longer lead time than the detailed design of the product. The product and the process are jointly designed, but the pattern of verification and testing (product first, process second) reflects the different lead times involved. The end result of the detailed design and development phase is joint product and process approval.

As laid out in Exhibit 7–2, development does not end with the first shipment from the commercial production process. Rather, we have added a market introduction phase, during which the manufacturing organization ramps up the production process to meet volume targets as well as targets for initial quality, yield, and cost. At the same time, marketing is involved in filling the distribution channels and establishing critical relationships with key customers. As we envision it here, the development process concludes when the organization has brought the design of the product, its marketing and distribution, and its manufacturing to the point of full commercial viability.

Compared to the highly segmented and sequential process used in the development of the MEI 2010, the much more integrated process in Exhibit 7–2 involves each of the functions in each of the phases. Thus, manufacturing not only plays its traditional role in preparing the product and the process for commercial production at the end of development, but is actively engaged in proposing concepts and investigating them at the very earliest stage of development. Similarly, marketing does not wait until full-scale engineering prototypes are complete to interact with customers and bring customer insight and information into the process. The net effect of these changes in the timing of activities is to pull forward in time the activity and involvement of the downstream functions.

But that is not all. It is evident that the greater integration across functions requires the addition of specific activities that support cross-functional work. For example, engineering builds very early system prototypes in order to support marketing's desire to develop richer customer insight early in the process. To complete the circle, engineers participate with marketing in interacting with customers in order to strengthen and deepen their understanding of the experience the product will create for future customers. Manufacturing establishes process concepts in the concept development phase and does process development and planning in collaboration with design engineers. Moreover, prototype testing and evaluation is a business process conducted jointly by all the functions involved in development.

The involvement of the functions in different phases of development is reinforced by the structure of decision making and the sequence of milestones envisioned in the development process. People from each function not only participate in the decision making at each milestone, but the milestones themselves focus attention on how the activity in each of the functions fits together with activity in the other functions. Thus, for example, the milestone at the conclusion of Phase I of detailed design and development is not an "engineering" milestone. Although attention focuses on the question of whether or not the product design captures the product concept, that question is framed in terms of marketing's activities in concept development and customer testing, manufacturing's activities in designing and developing the process, as well as the technical details of the design of the product itself. It is in effect an integrated milestone that looks at the progress of development from the standpoint of the emerging system, including engineering design, marketing, and manufacturing development.

Achieving Cross-Functional Integration

Not all development projects need deep, cross-functional integration. Where product designs are stable (or change only in a minor way), customer requirements are well defined, the interfaces between functions are clear and well established, and lifecycles and lead times are long, functional groups may develop new products effectively with a modest amount of coordination through procedures and the occasional meeting. But where markets and technologies are more dynamic and time is a more critical element of competition, deeper, more intensive cross-functional integration is crucial to effective development.

A starting point for achieving effective integration is the framework laid out in Exhibit 7–2. But simply devising and even implementing a framework of this kind does not ensure that the designs, tools, or market plans will be truly integrated. Cross-functional integration that really matters occurs when individual design engineers work together with individual marketers or process engineers to solve joint problems in development. Thus, to be truly effective, cross-functional integration must be much more than a scheme for linking in time the activities of the functions, and even more than adding new kinds of activities that support cross-functional interaction. True cross-functional integration occurs at the working level. It rests on a foundation of tight linkages in time and in communication between individuals and groups working on closely related problems.[5]

The extent to which problem solving is integrated in product development shows up most forcibly in relationships between individuals or engineering groups where the output of one is the input for the other—we will use here as an example the relationship between a design group responsible for the design of a plastic part and a process engineering group responsible for designing the mold that will be used in producing the part. The upstream group—in this case, the part designers—establishes the physical dimensions of the part, how it will interface with other parts within the system, the surface characteristics of the part, and the particular material to be used in its construction. All of these decisions—dimensions, tolerances, interfaces, surface characteristics, and materials—become inputs into production of the part. The mold designer's problem is to create a mold (or set of molds, particularly if the part is to be produced in volume) that will give the part its shape and surface characteristics, but will also be sufficiently durable, cost effective, and operational that the part can be manufactured in volume (can withstand repeated use, without breaking or sticking) reliably at low cost. How these two engineering groups work together determines the extent and effectiveness of integration in the design and development of the part and its associated mold.

Patterns of Communication

A critical element of the interaction between the upstream and the downstream group is the pattern of communication.[6] Four dimensions of the communication pattern—richness, frequency, direction, and timing—jointly determine its quality and effectiveness. Exhibit 7–3 presents the dimensions and their associated range of choice. The ends of the spectra in Exhibit 7–3 represent polar opposites in integration. On the left we have a pattern that is sparse, infrequent, one-way, and late. In this pattern, upstream engineers transmit information in formal documents that appear at the conclusion of a design process in finished form with little backup information about alternatives and no scope for feedback. In contrast, the pattern on the right is rich, frequent, reciprocal, and early. Here upstream engineers meet face to face with their downstream counterparts early in the design process and share preliminary ideas with sketches, models, and notes. Feedback is a natural part of this pattern. Whereas the first pattern is little and late, the second is early and often.

The choices firms make about communication between upstream and downstream groups play an important role in shaping the nature of cross-functional integration. But there are also choices about how to link the actual work in the two groups in time. The key issue is the extent to which work is done in parallel. Exhibit 7–4 puts the communication patterns together with different approaches to parallel activity to create four modes of upstream-downstream interaction.

The first panel depicts what we call the *serial mode* of interaction. This is a classic relationship in which the downstream group waits to begin its work until the upstream group has completely finished its design. The completed design is transmitted to the downstream group in a

EXHIBIT 7–3

Dimensions of Communication Between Upstream and Downstream Groups*

| Dimensions of Communication | | Range of Choice |

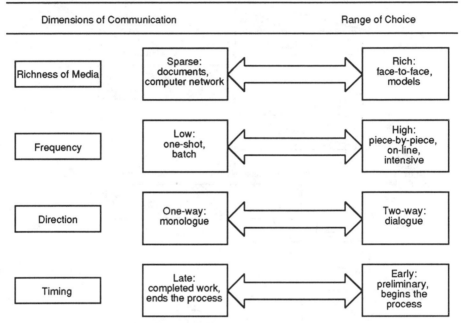

Richness of Media	Sparse: documents, computer network	⟺	Rich: face-to-face, models
Frequency	Low: one-shot, batch	⟺	High: piece-by-piece, on-line, intensive
Direction	One-way: monologue	⟺	Two-way: dialogue
Timing	Late: completed work, ends the process	⟺	Early: preliminary, begins the process

* This exhibit illustrates the range of choice firms have in determining the pattern of communication between upstream (for example, design) and downstream (for example, process) engineering groups. The boxes represent endpoints of a spectrum for each dimension of communication, while the arrows indicate the range of choice (for example, sparse to rich).

one-shot transmission of information. This one way "batch" style of communication may not convey all of the important nuances and background to the final design, nor does it necessarily comprehend the strengths and opportunities afforded by the downstream group. In that sense, the problem solving that lies behind the design of the product and that will produce the design of the mold is not integrated.

The second mode—what we call *"early start in the dark"*—links the upstream and downstream groups in time, but continues to employ a batch style of communication. This mode of interaction often occurs where the downstream group faces a deadline that it feels cannot be met without an early start on the project. But the upstream group communicates only at the end of its work, so the downstream group may be surprised by the design and may experience a period of confusion as it tries to adjust its work to the upstream design. While the net result may

471

EXHIBIT 7–4

Four Modes of Upstream-Downstream Interaction*

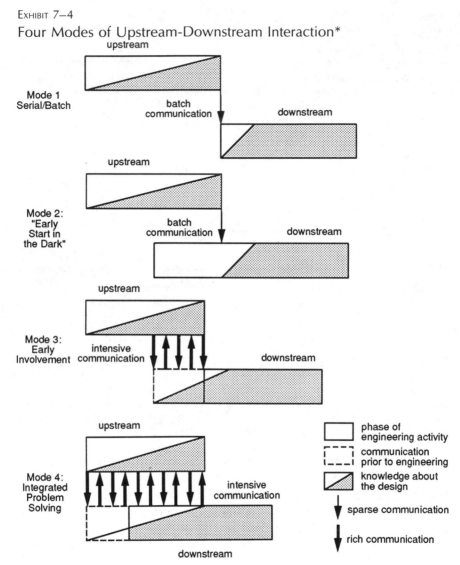

* Using the dimensions of communication in Exhibit 7–3, we define four modes of interaction between upstream and downstream groups. In Mode 1, communication is sparse, infrequent, one-way, and late; the information is serial and lengthy. Mode 2 maintains the pattern of communication, but moves up the starting point. Modes 3 and 4 make communication richer and more frequent (Mode 3) and starting much earlier (Mode 4).

472

be some reduction in overall lead time, the extent of the surprise and confusion can often be sufficient to make the actual process longer than the process in mode one. Although the downstream group works in parallel with the upstream group, and in this sense they are "concurrent," in actuality they operate without information and the problem solving cycles in the two organizations are not linked.

The third mode—what we call the *early involvement mode*—begins to move toward real integration. In this mode, the upstream and downstream players engage in an interactive pattern of communication. The upstream group, however, is still involved in the design of the part well before the downstream group begins its work. Thus, while the downstream group develops insight about the emerging design, and participates through feedback and interaction in the design process, it waits until the design is complete before undertaking problem solving in its own domain. The pattern of communication we envision here not only occurs earlier than it does in modes one and two, but involves two-way communication of preliminary, fragmentary information. For example, instead of waiting until the design is complete, engineers in the upstream group share preliminary analysis, alternative designs, and tentative proposals with their downstream colleagues. Similarly, the downstream group shares its views about capabilities of the downstream process, the constraints they face in designing the molds, and the relative merits of alternative concepts under discussion. Although they wait to begin work on the mold design until the part design is complete, the downstream group benefits from early involvement in two ways. First, the part design reflects a much better understanding of the issues confronting the process engineers than was true in either modes one or two. Second, the mold designers themselves have a much better sense of the issues and objectives embodied in the design. The net effect is that they are able to complete their work with fewer delays and downstream changes. In this sense, problem solving in the downstream and upstream groups is much more integrated.

The last mode in Exhibit 7–4—what we call *integrated problem solving*—links the upstream and downstream groups in time and in the pattern of communication. In this mode, downstream engineers not only participate in a preliminary and ongoing dialogue with their upstream counterparts, but use that information and insight to get a flying start on their own work. This changes the content of the downstream work in the early phases of upstream design, and is also likely to change fundamentally the content of communication between the two groups. Whereas in mode three the content of feedback from downstream engineers must rely on past practice, theoretical knowledge, and engineering judgment, under integrated problem solving that feedback will also reflect actual practice in attempting to implement the upstream design.

473

Communication that is rich, bilateral, and intense is an important, even essential, element of integrated problem solving. Where problem solving between upstream and downstream groups is intimately connected, the practice of "throwing the design (blueprints) over the wall"—inherent in mode one—will not support timely mutual adaptation of product and process design. What is needed to capture the nuance and detail important for joint problem solving is face-to-face discussion, direct observation, interaction with physical prototypes, and computer-based representations. Moreover, that intimate, rich pattern of communication must occur in a timely way so that action may be taken to avoid costly mistakes downstream. This does not mean the absence of conflict but rather the honest, open consideration of alternatives, and resolution based on data, analyses, and joint, creative problem solving. The essence of mutual adjustment is real time coordination between upstream and downstream groups. In this way design engineers take into account the preliminary results of process engineering problem solving in order to make products easier and less expensive to manufacture. Likewise, process engineers shape their problem-solving efforts in order to deliver the capabilities required by the upstream design. But this kind of mutual adjustment begins only after downstream problem solving has begun.

Capabilities and Relationships

Integrated problem solving relies on early action by the downstream group, dense, rich dialogue between upstream and downstream participants, and a style of problem solving that is broader and more comprehensive than one experiences in the more narrow functional focus inherent in mode one. Indeed, effective integration places heavy demands on the organization. The engineering process must link problem solving cycles in time; communication must be rich, precise, and intense; and the relationship between upstream and downstream groups must support and reinforce early and frequent exchange of constraints, ideas, and objectives. Moreover, because the problem solving across traditional functional boundaries occurs in real time, the capacity for quick and effective action is critical. Thus, effective integration relies on a specific set of capabilities, attitudes, and relationships.

Upstream Capabilities. From the perspective of the upstream engineering group, the challenge is to meet performance objectives in a way that complements downstream work and makes use of what the downstream can do. Making this happen requires skills and capabilities that go beyond the narrow technical ability to accomplish the upstream task. Three capabilities seem particularly important.

Downstream-friendly solutions. The first challenge is to create what we call "downstream-friendly" solutions. Upstream engineers must be knowledgeable about downstream constraints and capabilities. They must learn to use techniques for promoting early and continued communication with the downstream group, and to acquire relevant knowledge and experience from previous projects. A variety of methods have been developed in recent years, including design for manufacturability, value engineering, failure mode and effects analysis, and Taguchi Methods®, each of which is designed to enhance the upstream group's ability to predict the consequences of its actions and to devise solutions to its own problems that are downstream-friendly.

The objective here is not simply to make life easy for the downstream engineers. It is true that ignorance of downstream constraints hampers integrated problem solving, and may create very expensive and time-consuming engineering changes. It is also true, however, that excessive attention to downstream problems may hamper the commercial appeal of the design. Overemphasis on manufacturability or overreliance on simple parts may reduce downstream problems but render the product less attractive. Thus, downstream constraints must be carefully balanced with issues of design quality in order to maximize the total customer experience inherent in joint upstream-downstream solutions.

Error-free design. With an emphasis on creating downstream-friendly solutions, upstream engineers can have a substantial impact on the number of engineering changes and the time required to complete downstream work. But many such changes and much expensive time wasted are not due to lack of knowledge of downstream constraints or capabilities, but simply to outright mistakes. We have in mind things such as errors in copying documents, typing a "6" instead of a "9," sending a document to the wrong location, and so forth. Such minor details often have insidious consequences. In the first place, if not caught early, such errors require downstream engineering changes that are costly and time consuming, but add no value to the overall quality of the product. Second, such errors are often very difficult to track down once they have been propagated in the system. Third, they erode the mutual respect needed for groups to work as peers.

For all these reasons, error-free design is critical in achieving integrated problem solving. Designing it right the first time is a matter in the first instance of attention to detail, and discipline in the activities of individual engineers. But effective design reviews, testing, and engineering discipline can dramatically reduce or eliminate mistakes and errors.

Quick problem solving. Even where solutions are relatively friendly and careless mistakes have been eliminated, disagreements and conflict between upstream and downstream groups are inevitable in situations where the product is complex and customers are demanding. When differences arise, dealing with them effectively is enhanced by quick problem-solving capabilities in the upstream group. Faster design-build-test cycles in the upstream facilitate short feedback loops and quick mutual adjustment. When a problem arises downstream that requires upstream adjustment, the speed with which the upstream group can effect a new solution is critical in achieving responsive, fast action. Time is of the essence in this context. Since problem solving is mutual, getting to new alternatives quickly allows the downstream group to maintain its focus and complete its work in an integrated fashion. In organizations that have achieved integrated problem solving, there is a major difference between having a preliminary design done in two weeks rather than in four. In a slow organization those two weeks are not very important. In this case quick action supports integration.

Downstream Capabilities. Among downstream engineers, the challenge is to get a flying start on development before getting complete information. Moreover, that flying start must not create so many constraints on the design that it loses its appeal in the market. Moving fast, but moving effectively in the downstream depends on three capabilities.

Forecasting from upstream clues. In order to get a flying start, downstream engineers must start working on solving problems that have not been well defined. In that context, it is essential that downstream engineers develop the ability to forecast what the upstream group is likely to do. This requires that the downstream group develop skill in finding and using clues about upstream work. In combination with insight and understanding about previous patterns of upstream behavior, these clues become the basis for downstream action. For example, mold designers may know that the part designers are particularly worried about the strength of the part. They may also have learned from conversations with the part engineers that the alternative solutions include changes in the internal structure of the part. And given the way that the part designers have approached these issues in the past, the concern about strength means the part is likely to have internal ribs. These clues can therefore be the basis for initial mold design and planning.

Regular and close communication between downstream and upstream engineers is essential to finding clues and to using them effectively. But the downstream engineers need not be passive in this process. Once they discern a particular issue and a particular design direction, they may offer suggestions or counterproposals. If those suggestions are focused on helping the upstream engineers in solving their part design problems effectively—"if you want to go with small ribs, we can give you very tight tolerances that will cut down flash"—and are not simply expedients to make life in the downstream simple—"small ribs won't work; go with large ribs, they are easier to make"—the ideas from the downstream are much more likely to improve overall design and enhance the achievement of an integrated solution. Furthermore, active downstream involvement is likely to increase the quality of the clues and thus the forecasts they generate.

Managing risk. Getting off to a flying start based on a forecast of likely upstream action is a course fraught with risk. Downstream engineers must know how to make tradeoffs between the risk of a given change and the benefit of an early start. Moreover, they need to be skilled in managing the tradeoff so that the early start is made in a way that reduces risk. Take, for example, the case of process engineers trying to develop molds. Based on early clues from the part designers, and intensive discussion, mold engineers may identify sections of the part that are unlikely to undergo significant adjustment and change. Other sections of the part, however, may be less firm. This gives them the ability to begin mold design and construction by establishing the basic configuration and then using cutting margins (excess material that can be pared back once the final dimensions have been established) to allow a flying start. There is a significant amount of know-how involved in making such knife-edge tradeoffs. This implies that integration of problem solving requires significant skill in applying deliberate and detailed analysis and calculation in support of fast action.

Coping with unexpected changes. Even the best forecasters and the most clever downstream engineers will encounter unexpected changes in design. Given this fact of life, the downstream group needs to be flexible and skilled at quick diagnosis and quick remedy. Just as fast action in the upstream group facilitates mutual adaptation and integration, quick adjustment to unexpected changes on the part of the downstream group is essential to avoiding long delays and idle resources in development.

The ability to move quickly in reacting to unexpected changes relies on skill in problem diagnosis, and organizational capability in mobilizing resources and in focusing attention and effort on the important problems. But there is also the matter of raw engineering talent. It is one thing to get an organization to run tests quickly, build tools rapidly, and have decisions made promptly. But it is quite another to be able to size up a situation, identify a solution, and designate the appropriate test. Simply stated, downstream organizations that are fast and effective have many excellent engineers. Downstream (and upstream) groups that are slow have a few very good engineers and many others that only follow routine procedure and look up specifications in handbooks. While these groups may arrive at solutions given enough time, the name of the game in integrated problem solving is speed. In this case, there is no substitute for competence.

Attitudes Toward Integration

The effective deployment of upstream and downstream skills and capabilities in achieving integrated problem solving depends on fundamental attitudes that affect the relationship between upstream and downstream groups. People in the upstream group, for example, must be willing to share early preliminary information with their downstream colleagues. A perfectionist mentality, an attitude of "I won't give you anything now, because I know I'll have to change it later and I know that I will take the blame for it," is anathema to integrated problem solving. Likewise, people in the downstream must be willing to take risks based on their best forecast of the future. They must be comfortable in a very ambiguous environment. A "wait and see" attitude, an attitude of "don't talk to me until you are absolutely sure the design is done," may appear to minimize the risks of change, but is in fact a cultural obstacle to effective integration.

A sense of mutual trust and joint responsibility is essential to integrated problem solving. Once product engineers have worked hard to reduce unnecessary changes, they must trust the manufacturing process group's willingness and ability to cope with the changes that might emerge in the course of development. If process engineers trust product engineers to help them overcome manufacturing difficulties, they will be more willing and more capable to get a flying start.

Mutual trust hinges on mutual commitment to one another's success. Without such commitment engineers are less likely to expose themselves to the personal risks inherent in integrated problem solving. And there are risks. Integration requires that engineers in the upstream and downstream let their colleagues see what actually goes on in their respective departments. It exposes weaknesses and mistakes and makes clear the limits of their ability much more than does the sequential batch mode of operation.

Effective integration is also built on shared responsibility for the results of upstream-downstream collaboration. Where integrated problem solving prevails, the objective of the upstream group can not simply be a completed design, nor can the downstream group focus its attention solely on a well-conceived set of tools or processes. Both groups must recognize that the objective is a high-quality, low-cost part that fits well with other parts under development, that comes off the production line at commercial volume levels with the styling, surface finish, cost, and structural integrity to satisfy customer expectations, and that is available for the targeted market introduction. This is a very complex objective that neither the upstream nor the downstream group completely controls. In order to achieve the objective, therefore, there must be joint responsibility for joint output.

The Role of Senior Management

Our discussion thus far has focused on integrated problem solving at the level of individual work groups and engineers, and the role of the functional groups in the overall development process. We have argued that effective problem solving and cross-functional integration relies on individual skill, attitudes, and relationships across functional boundaries that facilitate intensive communication. Although the analysis has direct impact on the activities of functional managers and members of individual work groups, achieving integration across functions at each of these levels requires the support of, and focused action from, senior management.

Senior management establishes the context in which functional interaction and individual problem solving occur. In the first place, senior management may substantially shape the development process that establishes the sequence of functional activity, and the pattern and timing of functional involvement in development. By directly affecting what functional managers and functional specialists actually do in their daily work and in interaction with one another, senior management not only establishes a framework for integration, but can also lay out and communicate what the ideal pattern of involvement, interaction, and collaboration ought to be. Furthermore, senior management can put that pattern into effect in the day-to-day activities in which they participate directly. For example, how senior functional managers such as the vice presidents of manufacturing and engineering work together, the way they communicate with each other, and the degree of respect and trust that develops in their relationship have an important shaping influence on the members of their organizations and thus on the overall pattern of integration in the development process.

But senior management's role in building effective integration extends beyond establishing frameworks and patterns. Senior management also can have an important influence on the skills in the organization, the barriers to respect and trust that may exist between functions and work groups, and the tools, methods, and languages that are essential to effective cross-functional problem solving.

It is evident from our earlier discussion that effective integration requires a different set of skills than one finds in the traditional, sequential, functionally oriented development process. In an integrated set up, for example, an effective process engineer must not only be knowledgeable about equipment design, process layout, or tool design, but must also have an appreciation of product design and be oriented toward customer satisfaction. Moreover, that engineer must be skilled in quick problem diagnosis and problem solving. Senior management can play an important role in assuring the depth and quality of the skills and capabilities of its engineers by investing in education, training, and experience. All three are essential.

Education in the basic principles that underlie effective joint product-process design, for example, endows an engineer with knowledge and understanding that can be applied in a variety of different circumstances. *Training* in specific methods and procedures gives an engineer tools to use in solving specific kinds of problems. Finally, providing an engineer experience outside a specific discipline or function gives a much better feel for the nature of the problems that confront people in other functions, and also gives a better perspective on the way different functions interact.

Varied *experience* can also be an important element in senior management's attack on the barriers to respect, trust, and effective integration. One of the most important barriers to respect and trust is a simple lack of understanding of the nature of the work, processes, and constraints under which functional counterparts operate. Experience can help to build this imperative understanding.

Promotion and Compensation

Lack of understanding is only part of the problem. Organizations often create distance between functional groups through their policies on promotion and compensation, distance that is far greater than might arise naturally because of specialized expertise and focus. In a large industrial products company that we studied, for example, the sales organization had become the only route into general management. People with technical backgrounds and skills quickly learned to suppress those interests and move into sales if they wanted to move up in the organization. The effect was to create an implicit "second class" status for the engineering organization. Subsequent efforts to integrate marketing and engineering in order to improve development ran into serious problems.

Similar issues pertain to questions of compensation. In a semiconductor company that we studied we found wide differences in compensation practices between engineering and manufacturing. For example, a job in manufacturing engineering with the same level of responsibility (same number of direct reports, same budget authority, same degree of impact on competitive position) would often be rated two or three job grades below a comparable position in design engineering. Although due partly to extrinsic factors and widespread in other electronics firms, the message was clear: manufacturing engineering was not as important, nor populated by people as talented, as design engineering. It is not surprising that the company's initial efforts to encourage more effective interaction between design engineering and manufacturing were not successful. In fact, changing the compensation structure was a critical first step in achieving true cross-functional integration.

In addition to educating people and giving them cross-functional experience, and beyond breaking down barriers to trust and respect, senior management can influence the quality and effectiveness of cross-functional integration by investing in tools and methods that create a language in which different functional specialists can communicate and interact. We will have more to say about tools and methods in Chapter 9, but it is evident that investment in computer-based design and manufacturing systems, and in techniques and methods for design for manufacturability, or robust design, can not only facilitate more effective action within the function, but can provide a basis for more effective communication and functional integration. Electronic media, for example, have come to play an increasingly important role in the connection between product design and process development. Computer-aided design and computer-aided manufacturing (CAD-CAM) data representing a complex part, for example, enable much more accurate transmission of design information to mold engineers than traditional line drawings and models. This is partly because digital information (CAD-CAM), unlike analog information (drawings and models), is less subject to error accumulation through duplication, and partly because CAD-CAM can eliminate some of the steps required by the traditional approach and thereby reduce the length of the communication chain. Where such systems exist, and where both product designers and process engineers have been trained to use the system effectively, it can stimulate and enhance cross-functional interaction.

Study Questions

1. Based on the description of the MEI 2010 project in Chapters 6 and 7, what do you consider the dominant mode of upstream/downstream interaction at MEI (see Exhibit 7–4)? What resulting relationships and capabilities were exhibited on that project? How did these patterns contribute to the lack of integration on the 2010 effort?
2. Compare the functional activities chart for the MEI 2010 development process (Exhibit 7–1) with the comprehensive cross-functional integration activities chart in Exhibit 7–2. What are the most striking differences between the two charts? What objections do you think might be raised by engineering, marketing, and manufacturing if MEI's senior management were to push toward the cross-functional

integration implied by Exhibit 7–2? Why? How might those objections be addressed to encourage and facilitate such a transition?

3. In discussing the differences between Modes 1 and 4 of functional interaction, this chapter identifies several generic capabilities and skills that a Mode 1 organization would need to develop to effectively move into Mode 4. As an individual engineer involved in one or more development projects, how would you feel about moving from Mode 1 to Mode 4? If you were an individual contributor from manufacturing involved in a development project, how would you feel about such a move?

4. While not discussed in detail, interaction Modes 2 and 3 (Exhibit 7–4) appear to be much less attractive than Mode 4. Do you think Modes 2 and 3 are an improvement over Mode 1? Why or why not? Why might an organization move to Mode 2 or 3, but not push ahead to 4?

5. Compare the upstream and downstream capabilities required for effective cross-functional integration with those normally found in a strongly functional organization. What do you think largely functional upstream and downstream groups would find particularly difficult and challenging in developing those capabilities needed for cross-functional integration? Why?

6. As an organization moves towards effective cross-functional integration, what issues do you think might arise in support groups (for example, quality assurance, a test lab, or a prototype shop)? Among middle managers? Among external organizations (for example, suppliers and distributors)?

Plus Development Corporation (A)

Innovation starts with a belief; development transfers belief to evidence.
—JOEL HARRISON

In late September 1984 the Hardcard® product development had been underway for nearly six months. The miniaturized 10 megabyte hard disk drive that plugged into the slot of an IBM PC was like no other product on the market. The Plus development team had been working with its Japanese manufacturing counterpart, Japan Electro-Mechanical Corporation (JEMCO), to get the product on the market by June 1985. But the schedule had been gradually slipping as Plus and JEMCO engineers adjusted to each other's work style. Though there was daily progress, something would surely have to change to meet Hardcard's June target date.

Background

The inspiration for what eventually became Hardcard came from some customer conversations about what the ultimate low-cost disk drive subsystem would look like. James Patterson was the president of Quantum Corporation—makers of hard disk drives. He saw a solution which would be a "tin can surrounded by a few chips" which would be directly connected to the computer's motherboard (the main circuit board hold-

This case was prepared by Dr. Nan S. Langowitz under the supervision of Professor Steven C. Wheelwright.

483

ing the microprocessor). This solution would have to integrate some functions which were currently separate, such as the disk drive, the disk electronics, and the controller. And it would have to attach to the computer system without any cables.

Patterson shared this vision of the ultimate low cost disk drive with Quantum's senior managers, but there were some technical as well as marketing problems. On the technical side, the various hard disk drive components were too big to downsize a drive beyond the current size. Existing hard disk drives were generally larger than most personal computers. Also, the supporting electronics, in the form of integrated circuits, were not integrated enough to allow them to fit into a small space. (See Exhibit 1 for a description of hard disk drives and how they work.)

On the marketing side, there were not any clear standards for how small to shrink the disk drive and controller for the personal computer market. Since any downsizing would take many months and millions of dollars, it was very important that the resulting product fit the require-

---

EXHIBIT 1

How Disk Drives Work

A mass storage system, commonly called a disk drive, is comprised of three major elements: the disk, the disk drive, and the electronic controller. The combination of the disk and the disk drive is sometimes called the head disk assembly. The disk, also referred to as the "media," is where data are stored through the use of magnetics. In small capacity systems, two types of media are generally in use. Fixed, or rigid, media is a metal platter coated with a magnetic-sensitive coating. Floppy media is a plastic or mylar platter coated with magnetic-sensitive material. Data are stored in concentric rings on the disks. Hard disk drives use fixed media while "floppy" drives use floppy media.

The disk drive element has several subcomponents, including a magnetic head (containing an electromagnet), an actuator, an optical encoder, and a servo arm. The head serves to "read" or "write" data from or onto the media. "Writing" occurs when electric current passes through the head's electromagnet while the head is positioned above the spinning disk. A magnetic field is produced which orients the magnetic particles on the disk in a particular direction. In "reading," the head senses the magnetic orientation of the particles on the media and translates that pattern back into electric signals representing the data. The actuator controls the speed at which the head can "read" or "write," while the servo arm positions the heads in the appropriate position over the disk. The optical encoder serves to convert digital signals received from the computer through the electronic controller into analog signals which direct the servo arm and head. The disk drive also has a motor that rotates the disk, as well as a metal casting that holds the head disk assembly that serves as a base for the entire disk drive package.

The electronic controller functions as an intelligent interface between the head disk assembly and the computer. It interprets signals, defines data, responds to "seek" commands from the computer, and transmits data between the disk drive and the computer. The controller's electronics, a combination of integrated circuits, metal tracing (equivalent to wires), and discrete electronic components, are mounted on a printed circuit board, thus connecting all the electronic parts into a functional unit.

---

ments of a large number of computers. There were many historic examples of how companies had missed the market by downsizing to the wrong size, or using a nonstandard electrical interface between the disk drive and the computer.

Quantum's strategy to date had been to stay out of the personal computer market, which it saw as highly volatile. Quantum's focus was to provide hard disk storage to the minicomputer and technical work station segments of the computer market. This market segment had generally accepted standards for size and electrical interface, and Quantum had already established a successful niche for itself.

By 1983, the personal computer market was undergoing rapid change. Most significant was IBM's introduction of the IBM PC in 1981, followed by the IBM PC-XT in 1983. These products were beginning to establish standards for the fledgling personal computer segment of the market. For example, DOS (disk operating system) replaced CP/M (computer program for microcomputers), which had been used in Apple personal computers, as the standard operating system software for a personal computer. The addition of the PC-XT to IBM's personal computer line established the Winchester 5¼" hard disk drive as a standard technology for personal computers. Other hard disk drives could be installed instead of IBM's drive, but the installation of the disk drive, the controller, the cabling, and the electronic switch settings required some technical knowledge and hours of time. Additional standards established included plug-in cards (to add memory to the computer or to provide for communications capability by means of a modem), and the size of the slot for the plug-in cards.

IBM's entry into the personal computer segment created volume demand for personal computers and their standard components. Component technology—including electronics, integrated circuits, and peripherals—advanced at a rapid pace. One day in late 1983, when Quantum's manager of new product development opened up the case of an IBM XT, he suddenly recognized the feasibility of Patterson's idea. Joel Harrison's eyes followed the cable as it ran from the disk drive plug-in controller card to the separate hard disk drive at the front of the machine, and he realized that it didn't have to be that way. Why couldn't the controller and the drive reside on a single plug-in card, he wondered. Following up on the idea, Jim Patterson asked Stephen Berkley, then marketing vice president at Quantum, to put together a business plan for the development of hard disk technology for the personal computer marketplace.

In November 1983 four managers from Quantum started Plus Development Corporation, with Quantum owning 80% of the new venture. Berkley became president of Plus, Joel Harrison was vice president of engineering, Dave Brown was executive vice president of operations,

485

and Dale Hiatt, vice president of manufacturing and quality. (At Quantum, Brown and Hiatt had been vice president of engineering and vice president of manufacturing, respectively.) The hard-disk-on-a-card design, which ultimately became known as Hardcard, emerged as the most promising option of the various product possibilities considered by the Plus team during its original business planning. It was to be a 10 megabyte hard disk drive integrated onto a controller card that would slide into a single IBM PC card slot. The design would radically simplify the process of installing a Winchester disk drive into a personal computer, and reduce the time required from hours to minutes. The goal was to have Hardcard provide hard disk capability identical to that of an IBM PC-XT. Dale Hiatt said, "That is our focus. We live and die that focus."

The Microcomputer Mass Storage Market

The largest group of customers for hard disk drives in late 1983 were microcomputer producers such as IBM, Apple, and Hewlett-Packard. These original equipment manufacturers (OEMs) integrated disk drives, made by third-party producers such as Tandon, Seagate, or Shugart, into their own computer systems and then offered the entire package—perhaps computer system unit, monitor, and hard disk drive—for sale to end users. In 1983 OEMs purchased approximately 830,000 Winchester-type hard disk drives with up to 30 megabyte capacity. The price for these hard disks ranged from $500 to $650. Substantial markups of three to four times the OEM price occurred in the distribution channel until, for example, the retail price that the end-user customer paid for a 10 megabyte hard disk as part of a system might be $2,400. Two things seemed likely to affect the price to the end user. First, the high distribution channel margins provided incentive to disk drive manufacturers to offer their products directly to end users. Second, learning curves of 65–70% were common in disk drive manufacturing. Existing disk drive products had experienced an average price erosion of 20–40% per year.

As personal computers began to proliferate, a retail market developed for add-on hard disk drives. Add-on sales were made through retail computer stores, such as Computerland or Businessland, to individuals and small businesses who already owned a personal computer and wanted to expand its mass storage capability. Plus hoped to target this distribution channel and market niche. Hardcard would be aimed at customers who wanted to convert their existing IBM or IBM-compatible PC into an XT. (Exhibit 2 shows the growth of the U.S. installed base of IBM and IBM-compatible PCs from 1981 to 1984, and projection of the 1985 installed base of rigid [or hard] disks and PCs.)

Exhibit 2

IBM PCs and Compatible Systems and Rigid Disks Installed in the United States

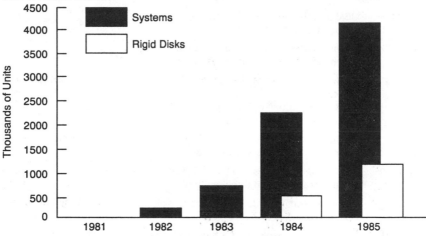

SOURCE: InfoCorp, *Segment Update: Mass Storage*, 7/12/85.

The Development of Hardcard

Armed with their business plan, the four Plus managers began to consider the details of how to manufacture Hardcard. They took a trip to Japan primarily to source components for heads, disks, and motors. A second reason for the trip was to better understand what was going on in Japan. The Plus managers saw computers as a maturing business and they foresaw a future similar to that of watches, calculators, and floppy disk drives—all industries which Japanese manufacturers had come to dominate. Plus expected that disk drives might soon go the same route; they felt they had to accept this reality. (Exhibit 3 provides a chronology of Japan's entry into and capture of the floppy disk drive industry.)

As the Plus managers visited with Japanese manufacturers and suppliers, they found two surprises. First, electronics companies in the video tape recorder business, such as Sony, JVC, and Sanyo, were expecting and fearing saturation in the video market. This fear was heightened by the recent entry of Korean manufacturers such as Samsung into the video business. Plus found that these Japanese electronics companies were rushing to get into the computer market. They all "were damn interested to talk to us," said Dave Brown, particularly because they had employment to sustain and money to invest. The Plus managers also discovered

487

EXHIBIT 3

Key Developments in Japanese Pursuit of Floppy Drives

Late 1960s– 1973:	IBM invents floppy technology. Shugart is founded.
1974–1977:	Many companies enter in this market. Technology license to Japanese companies.
1977–1981:	U.S. drive companies change from the U.S. to Japanese component vendors. Motor: Japan, Servo, Tamagawa, FDK, Oriental, Sanyo. Head: KEM, TDK, Tandon.
1979:	Tandon enters into floppy disk drive business and begins the manufacturing in India. Tandon offers lower price.
1979–1980:	Japanese companies into the U.S. floppy market. Teac, Alps, Hitachi, and others. Many fail and withdraw from the market.
1982 (early):	Tandon becomes a leader in floppy disk drive market. Sony announces micro floppy disk drive.
1982 (late):	Japanese companies come back to the U.S. market with half-height 5¼″ floppy disk drive.
1982–1983:	Japanese companies begin to use more LSI on floppy disk drive. They double production capacity to 12–15 million units/year; vertically integrated automation line or semiautomation with the utilization of outside subcontractors. U.S. companies have difficulty introducing new products. Japan becomes market share leader.

SOURCE: *Industry Note: Disk Drives for Small and Microcomputer Systems–1983*, Stanford University.

that the companies making electronics components, such as Kyocera, NEC, and Toshiba, sought the opportunity to forward integrate into computer products. These two findings made the new managers ask themselves, "How are we going to compete with these guys?" since it seemed clear they might jump into the computer products market soon.

The Japanese tour heightened Plus's awareness that the new company had a particular need to fill. Because Hardcard would be a retail distribution product, the Plus managers believed they would need an instant ramp-up to volume production. They wanted to be able to "flick a switch" and have production reach 5–10,000 per month, with high quality. Many of the Japanese companies they visited were capable of such a high-volume ramp, whereas Quantum, for example, took many months to achieve 500 disk drives per day—the equivalent of 10,000/ month. The Plus managers feared that any U.S. operation they set up would be unable to achieve instant ramp and volume; they knew the disk drive market would not allow them years to become as good as the Japanese manufacturers.

Choosing a Manufacturer

A tie-up with a Japanese company could offer Plus quality manufacturing and the achievement of instant ramp and volume. Because of close relationships generally existing between Japanese manufacturers and their suppliers, a Japanese connection might also allow Plus more flexibility for future product changes. On the downside, a Japanese tie-up meant a high investment of senior management time and probably some pressures due to cultural differences. There was also the more subjective issue of whether it was fair to American manufacturers for Plus to team up with a Japanese partner.

All the Plus managers except Joel Harrison had been involved with Japanese ventures before. They felt that they knew how to shop for a Japanese partner. Towards the end of their trip, the Plus managers met the senior management at JEMCO and toured its manufacturing facilities. A subsidiary of Japan Trading Corporation, JEMCO was solely a manufacturing company, receiving most of its product designs from Japan Trading's central laboratories, and manufacturing for private label or for Japan Trading. JEMCO had no marketing function of its own. The company had been tremendously successful in recent years; the Plus managers talked with many Japanese executives who considered JEMCO the premier electromechanical manufacturer in Japan. At JEMCO's video cassette recorder plant, an new VCR rolled off the production line every few seconds. Dave Brown's reaction was similar to the other Plus managers': "You feel insignificant. Their [JEMCO's] manufacturing expertise is beyond imagination, I've never seen anything like it in my life." Not only did JEMCO stand out in its manufacturing excellence, but Plus managers were confident that they could work well with JEMCO's executives, whose management style featured teamwork and open communication. On the other side, JEMCO had some incentive to work with Plus. It was interested in the opportunity to broaden its product offerings and manufacturing expertise by working with designs from companies other than Japan Trading.

The Plus managers left Japan quite excited about JEMCO. Nonetheless, they "had some gut-wrenching discussions," according to Brown, at home about whether to team up with a Japanese company. While the business reasons seemed clear, on an emotional level the managers were concerned about being unpatriotic and whether they were "copping out" on American manufacturers. They called in a consultant who eventually offered this analogy: "If you're going to build a fruit stand, don't build it in the middle of the freeway. Build it on the side." In other words, if the Plus managers believed that the Japanese would dominate the manufacturing of disk drives, they should act immediately to be in the best position once the stampede began. Brown acknowledged Japan's manufacturing expertise: "Why fight it? Our culture just isn't there." Berkley and Hiatt agreed. The process was set in motion to team up with JEMCO. Plus' expectation was that they would supply design and marketing expertise while JEMCO supplied manufacturing expertise.

The First Six Months

From the time Joel Harrison made his initial observation that a hard disk on a card might be possible, he had been tinkering with the design. By January 1984, when Bill Moon moved from Quantum and Richard Blackborow was hired from outside, more detailed Hardcard development was possible. Moon became the manager of mechanical engineering and Blackborow became Moon's counterpart in digital/VLSI (very large-scale integrated) circuit engineering. Harrison served as Hardcard's project manager. While Berkley, Brown, Harrison, and Hiatt were still in Japan, Moon and Blackborow began to refine the design.

Product Design Philosophy and Technical Choices

Hardcard would be Harrison's fifth hard disk drive in the last 10 years. Of the five designs he had contributed to, only two had the same size disk. Harrison thoroughly understood hard drive technology and was well-versed in the design adjustments required to build for a particular disk size. Yet it would surely be a challenge to miniaturize a drive to 3½" for Hardcard. Further, Hardcard was Harrison's first drive for the retail market. Plus hoped to introduce Hardcard in time for Christmas 1985; this seemed critical to retail success not only because of the home market, but also because much of the business market tended to spend late in the year to use up budgeted funds. In addition, Quantum was anxious to have Plus contribute to its own performance during calendar 1985.

Harrison recognized the vast difference between the retail and OEM disk drive markets. OEM customers frequently asked for product changes; they adapted to initial bugs and often demanded changes in features or functionality. In fact, the manufacturers came to rely on feedback from the field as they finalized a product's design. But in the retail world, customers were totally unforgiving. A manufacturer had only one chance to provide the right product. The focus for Hardcard, Harrison said, was therefore kept simple: "convert a PC into an XT on a single board." This simple target made it easier to determine whether a design proposal contributed to the goal and avoided the "creeping definitionalism" which Harrison had seen complicate and slow down other projects.

In addition to the simple focus, the Hardcard project was to involve only proven technologies and proven processes. This was similar to the approach taken at Quantum. Harrison believed that what he called "focused innovation" was required for success. In new product development, Harrison maintained that the number of items the design team had never done before should be limited to about five. In his experience, a limit on the number of innovative things allowed technological challenge while it prevented chaos. The Hardcard design had five major items which were new for the design team: (1) a thin motor—to be made by a vendor—which had to be mass producible; (2) new integrated VLSI circuits which would use state-of-the-art surface-mount technology— again, a vendor would be involved; (3) providing a controller function on the drive; (4) an integrated microprocessor which would manage the servo control, the interface to the computer, the disk drive control, and the drive controller—previously these functions had been uncoupled; and (5) a new, to Plus, encoding/decoding scheme. By limiting the number of new items, Harrison hoped to maximize the success of each one. For example, the most recent generation of encoder, already in use at Quantum, would not be included in Hardcard's design so as to improve the chances of success for the integrated microprocessor (4), and the new encoding scheme (5). Harrison commented: "This is an art. It's not the only way to do it."

Hardcard design involved two major subassemblies, the HDA (head/disk assembly) and the printed circuit (controller) board. (Exhibit 4 shows the final Hardcard design.) The mechanical engineers worked on the HDA, and the electrical/digital engineers were mainly responsible for the controller board. In January, the first mock-up was a "show and tell piece," according to Bill Moon. It was a block of aluminum with a disk that didn't even spin. From that point onward, Hardcard developers progressed from prototyping the mechanicals in metal and the electronics on printed circuit boards to creating working parts and designing the electronic circuitry into custom chips. Three chips were custom designed. (Plus had planned to design a fourth chip, but it turned out to be no cheaper than the circuitry it would have replaced, and it would have delayed the schedule.)

For the disk media, designers had to choose either metal oxide or thin film technology. Metal oxide was the standard for 8" and 5¼' disks and was thus already proven in the market. Thin film allowed more data to be stored on the same size disk, but with its lack of mass production history at the time it left many unknowns, such as what kind of corro-

EXHIBIT 4

The 10 Megabyte Hardcard

A. Hardcard—Shown with Exposed Head Disk Assembly

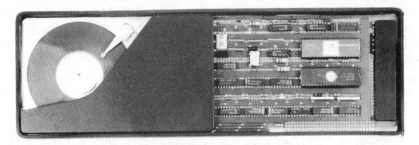

B. The Hardcard Being Inserted Into a PC Expansion Slot

SOURCE: Plus Development Corporation.

sion problems would occur. In fact, the rumor was the IBM had banned the use of thin film in its products. A key philosophy on Hardcard development was to minimize the risk of unknown technologies. Rather than use thin film, therefore, Plus designers used the electronic encod-

492

ing scheme "2,7" to take the stress out of the difficult task of storing 10 megabytes on a single 3½" disk. (In hard disks, the heads "write" by changing the magnetization of the media from north to south, or vice versa. When the heads "read" back from the disk, they get a signal from the direction changes, or flux transitions. What's important is how many changes occur per inch at the maximum frequency the heads try to read off the media—the closer the flux transitions are together, the more difficult it is to read. The 2,7 technique created a factor of 1.5 times fewer flux transitions per inch than the alternative coding technique MFM (modified frequency modulation). At the same flux density, therefore, 2,7 encoding allowed for more data storage.) The 2,7 technique required additional circuitry, which Plus designed. Harrison commented: "Nothing's ever free."

The Problem of Cultural Differences

Although the business agreement with JEMCO was not finalized until August 1984, a development schedule in early spring identified June 1985 as a target date for market introduction. JEMCO engineers, under the leadership of Toshihiro Utamoro, came to Plus in April 1984 to work with the twenty Plus engineers who were already on the project. The Plus engineers included mechanical, analog, and digital design engineers, as well as quality engineers. The JEMCO engineers, who were without their families, worked a long day at Plus, coming in at 8:15 A.M. and working until 8:00 P.M. They then went to English class from 8:00 until 11:00 P.M. Plus engineers generally worked similar hours (except no English classes), although if an individual engineer was finishing a particular piece of the project, he or she would work even longer. None of the Plus engineers spoke Japanese. A translator was on hand virtually every day. The Plus engineers were responsible for product design while the JEMCO engineers addressed manufacturability.

The JEMCO engineers were assigned to remain at Plus until the project was completed. There was also a Japan-based JEMCO manufacturing group that was an integral part of the design team. Phone calls went back and forth: the phone bill was equal to the travel bill. On the phone JEMCO could veto a design. Compromise solutions often evolved as a result of these calls. JEMCO was especially influential regarding the manufacturability of the mechanical HDA subassembly. (But not the digital/electronic controller board subassembly.) Digital design was an area in which JEMCO engineers had less experience. Most JEMCO products until this time were analog-based audio-visual consumer products.

During the initial period when engineers from both companies were learning to cooperate with each other, Plus held special classes so that the JEMCO engineers could learn about disk drive technology and applicable digital design theory. The styles of the two groups were very different. The JEMCO engineers could not describe in abstract terms how to design Hardcard for manufacturability; they preferred to see prototypes and then give concrete suggestions of what to change. The Plus engineers, on the other hand, tended to be contemplative before drawing—let alone prototyping. Once Plus learned that the JEMCO engineers were excellent at turning prototypes around quickly, Plus engineers began using more prototypes. The use of prototypes also helped communication. The JEMCO engineers were able to point to a part of the design to identify a problem, rather than having to describe the problem in English.

Achieving Manufacturability

Plus and JEMCO engineers spent the first three months almost entirely in design meetings. The JEMCO motto was "total cost down" and their target production yield was 99%. At first the Plus engineers thought they were wasting their time with all these meetings. They couldn't understand why the JEMCO engineers kept demanding so many details of how the design would work. The JEMCO engineers wanted to have specifications for everything—exactly how high, thick, or wide a piece would be. For the JEMCO engineers, "less than 10 mm" was not an acceptable specification. The Plus engineers were forced to specify exactly—"9.8 mm high." Before starting production, JEMCO engineers wanted to know for sure that the product could be made easily. The Plus engineers had difficulty adapting to JEMCO's approach. As Bill Moon said: "They live by specifications. The idea is that if every part meets specs, then every product assembled from those parts will work." The Plus engineers were used to the approach typical in U.S. companies, which was to do a design, make some mistakes, live with them, and learn for the next time. Gradually, the Plus engineers began to respect the different approach.

Frequently the JEMCO engineers called for design changes to enhance manufacturability, even if there was not a great cost savings to gain. For example, the actuator latch on the disk drive was redesigned so that it would lie against the metal curve of the disk inset in its relaxed position, allowing the disk to be easily inserted (or taken out for service). The new design saved only two yen or approximately one penny in labor cost per unit, but it made the product more "manufacturable."

The optical encoder was another example. There was a gap in the encoder between two pieces of etched glass which converted the light-emitting diode (LED) source into analog signals. As the gap changed the amplitude of the analog signals varied. The gap size had to be controlled in order to regulate the amplitudes. The servo mechanism used the converted analog signals to find the correct tracks (storage location) on the disk drive in order to read or write information. Quantum disk drives used this type of optical encoder design, and Plus had simply downsized it. The JEMCO engineers were concerned that the gap was too small to be able to volume produce within stringent tolerance requirements. They asked Plus to redesign the encoder to make the gap larger. After three months of re-design, the gap width was enlarged from $2/1000$ to $10/1000$ of an inch, satisfying the JEMCO engineers' request.

JEMCO engineers also called for the redesign of a metal plate guarding the disk drive. The original part was to be screwed into place during manufacture. JEMCO wanted each part to fit into place, regardless of screws, so that the production worker would not have to use any judgment in aligning the part. The JEMCO engineers did not like screws, and they maintained that glue was too hard to control. This redesign required two months.

Process Philosophy and Design

JEMCO designed the Hardcard production process during product design. JEMCO believed that the design of product parts and the design of the equipment which assembled those parts were inextricable. Plus senior managers had described JEMCO's automated VCR line to the Plus engineers, who then assumed that JEMCO would automate Hardcard production and therefore required simple parts. But JEMCO did not equate automation with simplicity. JEMCO's motivation to automate was not to increase quality but to increase volume. (Volume had to be at least 2,000 units per day before JEMCO would advocate automation.) Whether JEMCO automated or not, Plus gradually realized that JEMCO did not care whether the Hardcard had simple parts; what mattered was whether the parts would meet specifications and could be made simply, even if a complicated tool was required. JEMCO wanted a reliable process. JEMCO would often invent a new tool for making a single part. They were masters at designing and configuring such tools. For example, they built a machine to install the optical encoders, whereas Quantum did this by hand. JEMCO had a group of mechanical engineers devoted solely to making special assembly tools. It took some time for the Plus engineers to understand all this.

JEMCO's manufacturing philosophy also called for testing at every step of the production process. In a typical U.S. plant the head arm assembly might be inserted, then the drive motor mounted, with a test done afterward. If the head arm assembly failed in test, the drive motor would have to be removed in order to fix the head arm assembly. JEMCO preferred a different assembly sequence. The head arm assembly would be inserted and tested; if the head arm assembly passed, the drive motor

495

could then be inserted and tested. The point was to get rid of problems at each step so that "quality of the yield on the line is the quality in the field."

Bill Moon summed up the essence of JEMCO's manufacturing excellence: "One, prove the dimensions and tolerances that are required on each part up front. Two, create elaborate assembly tools. And three, check at every step of the process." Plus learned that JEMCO's approach to manufacturing had important implications not only for product development but also for vendor relations.

Vendor Management and the Single Source Philosophy

Plus managers were committed to the ideal of Plus as a small and entrepreneurial company, excellent at design and marketing, while relying heavily on vendors for manufacturing expertise. The managers felt that this could be achieved with the right people and organizational structure. Much depended on faith in human relationships. Plus looked at vendors in this way: "Do we need to put in resources? Maybe we don't—we can rely on their [an outside company's] work." Plus wanted to focus on adding value in its own areas of expertise, design and marketing, and to avoid trying to be the expert in everything. They sought to achieve this focus by forming strategic relationships with other vendors.

U.S. suppliers were selected by a team which included the Plus manager most directly involved, John Aubuchon, materials manager, Dale Hiatt, vice president of manufacturing, and Bob Lyells, manager of quality and reliability. The criteria for source evaluation were: (1) trust—the potential for a good working relationship, (2) quality/monitoring, (3) the supplier's process philosophy, (4) delivery capability and timing, (5) aggressive pricing, and (6) the use of technology to back up the supplier's claims. Components were characterized as critical if the manufacturer's sudden disappearance or failure would be a major problem, or if the particular design had never been done before—some of the ICs, for instance. Noncritical components were standard off-the-shelf parts. Plus visited and evaluated U.S. suppliers of both critical and noncritical components. Plus selected Japanese suppliers of critical components on JEMCO's recommendation. Plus relied on JEMCO's existing relationships for off-the-shelf parts sourced from Japan. Components such as the motor, off-the-shelf chips, and heads were sourced in Japan, while others, such as the media and custom-integrated circuits, were sourced in the United States.

Plus wanted vendors which were proven companies, with mature processes using proven technologies, an approach that JEMCO supported fully. John Aubuchon said, "Our objective was total cost down, without sacrificing the quality." Plus selected a single source for all critical items, following the theory that the best partnerships formed that way. Plus believed that having a single supplier did not necessarily increase the risk of calamity since in multisourced arrangements a company generally had one or two key suppliers anyway. They also stressed the difference between a *single* source—in which case other companies could make a part, if necessary, and a *sole* source—where that source was the only supplier capable of making a part. By avoiding sole sources Plus kept away from exclusive technologies, which fit with their focus on proven technologies.

As part of the single source philosophy, Plus tried to develop a partnership that recognized the vendor's business and processes. As Aubuchon explained, Plus "tried to manage that whole concept of the relationship . . . it was kind of holy." This approach extended to the U.S. export department and customs, as well. Plus managers looked at a vendor's process closely, tried to learn it inside and out, and to see if the vendor had control or if Plus could help them gain better control. Plus focused on the relationship and tried to develop mutual solutions. As Dale Hiatt said, Plus believed you "can't impose *your* solutions on *their* process." In pursuit of this mutuality, sometimes Plus (with the support of JEMCO) modified its specs.

Vendor Negotiations

Strong vendor relationships developed. Hiatt recalled, Plus "visited vendors of our vendors, three levels down" because you "can't afford somebody else's screw-up." They did their best to make sure that the vendors and JEMCO conducted up-front feasibility tests of all potential "show stoppers." On critical components such as the disk, motor and heads, Plus tried to get the vendors to indicate when a spec was especially difficult or expensive. Plus started by presenting the vendor with a budget: specifying a target price which might be 20–30% below the street price. Plus gave these target prices to all potential vendors, to someone as high up in the company as possible. At the same time that Plus presented their budget, they promised to single source the part— they shared their business plan without quite divulging the product— and offered to help the vendor in any way possible. (The only vendor Plus told about the whole product up front was the Japanese motor vendor; Plus needed them to understand the Hardcard design in order to say if it was possible.) Plus tried to avoid intense nose-to-nose negotiations with vendors, which Hiatt described as "demeaning to everyone." The emphasis in negotiations was to understand the vendor's process, and then either change the vendor's component or Hardcard, in order for the vendor to make money on the part.

Vendors usually gasped when they saw the budgeted prices. Plus would then ask them what Plus could do to help them meet that spec and price. For example, Plus designed Hardcard to take a "wide distribution" of components. The vendors would say what standard output was and Plus would design to use at least 90% of it. (Taking a wider distribution enhanced the vendors' yield so they could offer the component at a lower price to Plus.) With the media, for example, Plus could use electronics to "map out" errors on wide distribution media. The electronics would locate an error on the media, and "mark it" as "bad," so that Hardcard would be error-free and the bad spots on the media would be transparent to the customer. Another example illustrates Plus' willingness to work with a vendor. Plus visited the offshore assembly (chip packaging) facility of an integrated circuit supplier. Uncomfortable with how some things were done, Plus asked the supplier to source packages from elsewhere. The supplier preferred not to, so Plus designed and installed an auditing system for the supplier's facility.

Market Introduction: Push Ahead or Reschedule?

By September 1984 Hardcard development was well on its way, but there was much to be done to meet the target introduction date of June 1985. (See Exhibit 5 for the original engineering development schedule and Exhibit 6 for excerpts from Joel Harrison's July and August status reports.) Harrison called a meeting of the key managers. He identified two options: they could schedule a later introduction date, or they could

EXHIBIT 5
Plus Engineering Schedule—April 1984

5/30/84:	Select key technologies
6/30/84:	Breadbox of product operation
9/30/84:	3-board prototypes operation
12/30/84:	Design verification testing (DVT) complete
2/28/85:	Single-board VLSI prototypes operational
3/ /85:	Design transferred to factory for production
4/30/85:	Design maturity testing complete
6/ /85:	Production begins

SOURCE: Company documents.

Exhibit 6
Plus Engineering Status Reports

Schedule Status:

— The Hardcard Project is on schedule for June '85 production.
— The following milestones are behind schedule or have been rescheduled:

1. Mechanical Engineering Architecture based upon JEMCO input (was 7/13 now due 7/20). This is the critical path for mechanical engineering of Hardcard. The 7/20 date just keeps the prototypes on schedule.
2. Start Test Development has been rescheduled awaiting the hiring of our first test engineer (was 7/16 now 8/15).
3. The Hardcard Specification requirements are not well defined. This issue must be resolved before the specification can be finished.

— The Breadboard phase is complete. Several breadboard testing items have been delayed until DVT testing of the prototypes beginning in October.
— The following detailed schedules have been developed and are now being used in conjunction with the master schedule:

• Drive/Controller firmware development schedule
• Software development schedule including the PC BIOS and compatibility
• Three Digital VLSI Chip development schedules
• DVT prototype schedule and use plan

SOURCE: 7/16/84 Plus report.

---

push ahead and do a mop-up job once the product was in the market. "Okay, look," said Harrison, "you've all seen my status reports. We're falling behind. Making June is getting if-ier by the day, but if we cut some corners maybe we could still do it. I consider myself pretty good at schedule compression, but I've looked at every way I can imagine to resequence, regroup and double up—even sounding out JEMCO on steps they might compress—and it's just not possible without skipping some things and cutting a few corners."

"Yeah, well you know why we're behind, Joel," Bill Moon responded. "My guys have been in constant meetings with the JEMCO folks, and I don't need to tell you how many redesigns we've done for them. The amount of detail they want is driving us crazy. In fact one reason we have so many staffing positions open is that all this interaction with JEMCO has taken a lot of time and attention that had to come from somewhere."

Dale Hiatt spoke, "Now wait a minute. Isn't some of that detail important to getting this thing manufactured right? That's why we signed them up, isn't it? We're going to need an instant ramp. So, if it's detail they need, we'd better make sure we give it to them."

"So you're saying we should reschedule, Dale?" asked Harrison.

EXHIBIT 6 (*continued*)

Recruiting/Staffing:

— Recruiting needs focus!
— New Employees: new Mechanical Engineer and Digital Engineer start 8/20 and 8/1, respectively.
— Seven Present Openings: There are seven openings, two with candidates. Openings are for Digital Engineer, Mechanical Engineer, Diagnostic Programmer, Computer Scientist, Engineering Technicians (2), and Test Engineer.

Schedule Status:

— Hardcard Project is on schedule for June '85 production. *VLSI and Firmware/Software are the present critical paths.*
— The following milestones are behind schedule or have been rescheduled based upon the Engineering/Manufacturing Master Schedule:

  1. Start Test Development (was 7/16 now 8/1). The first test equipment meeting with the JEMCO will be held 8/1.
  2. The Hardcard Specification requirements are not well defined. This issue must be resolved before the specification can be finished.
  3. Software Quality/Reliability testing plans have not begun. Action will begin when our Quality/Reliability engineer starts.

— Motors from the vendors are the critical path for September mechanical prototypes. Commit dates have not yet been received.
— The Analog printed circuit board for September prototypes is being expedited to keep it on schedule. The Digital board is on schedule.
— Heads and disks are on schedule for September prototypes.
— Firmware is on schedule.

SOURCE: 7/30/84 Plus report.

"If that's what it'll take, I guess so. Yes," Hiatt answered. "But we need to hit the Christmas market. If there's a way to get it done on target, we need to think hard about it. We're riding on this one product."

"That's exactly it. We'd better get something out there soon," added Hank Chesbrough, product marketing manager. "This is going to be a terrific product. Just think of all those people waiting to upgrade their PCs to 10 megabytes. And we can be the ones to let them do it pain-free. Joel's got a staffing search on already. Why don't we just hire a few extra engineers? We're bound to recoup the $40K per hire if we hit the market right."

Bob Lyells was not convinced. As manager of quality and reliability, he did not look forward to mopping up after a sloppy ramp-up. "Not so fast, you guys. You know how Utamoro is. To hit the introduction target, I thought I heard Joel say we'd have to cut some corners. Utamoro would never knowingly agree to compromise the production yield, and his engineers are still going over the design with a fine tooth comb. JEMCO insists on solving all problems up front."

Exhibit 6 (*continued*)

Staffing/Recruiting:
— New Manager of Software Development began this week.
— Present Openings: Nine openings with one offer extended for Analog Technician and one other candidate. Offer made for Digital Engineer was turned down, priority of this position is reduced however. Positions open are: Software Technician, Mechanical Engineer, Diagnostic Programmer, Test Engineers (3), Engineering Technicians (2), and Digital Engineer.

Schedule Status:
— The DVT Plan is behind schedule. Recovery status by Friday.
— Mechanical Engineering parts for 100 prototype units may be late due to unplanned design iterations. Exact ME parts status will be available by Friday. Great effort will be made not to slip the schedule.
— Digital and Analog VLSI chips are on schedule.
— Product Design Specifications are late; Bob Couse is now responsible for Product Specs.
— Printed circuit boards are on schedule.
— There are technical problems with Start Stop Testing; the test conditions are not under control; the media has problems which may be due to the lubricant thickness.

SOURCE: 8/29/84 Plus report.

Moon said, "It's not even clear extra engineers would help, Hank. JEMCO needs three months for product transfer and maturity testing. Like Bob said, they need to know it'll work before they'll flip that switch in June. If we're gonna push ahead, we'd better figure out how we're going to solve JEMCO's requirements. Besides, most of JEMCO's interactions are primarily on the mechanical types of issues. We've got a whole raft of software tasks to do ourselves and those are already as compressed as possible."

Chesbrough chimed in again at this point. "Don't forget that we're responsible for marketing as well. In our marketing approach, we're trying to create a unique image for service and reliability. That means cultivating key dealers, building a distribution network, developing a training program for dealers, and establishing policies covering pricing, margins, promotion and service. If we're going to reschedule, we need at least 6–9 months warning if we're serious about creating a unique image and reputation in the market. We don't want to be late at the eleventh hour and have everyone conclude it was all just hype, that Plus is really just as unreliable and on the edge of being out of control as everyone else."

"Okay, so what's it gonna be?" Dave Brown asked. "I'm hearing arguments on both sides, but what we need is a commitment to get this project done, one way or the other."

Lehrer McGovern Bovis, Inc. (Abridged)

In November 1986, Peter Lehrer and Gene McGovern, co-founders of Lehrer McGovern Bovis, Inc. (LMB), one of the fastest growing firms in the construction industry, were on their way to the monthly senior management meeting. Several issues were on the agenda, but the key management challenge was to continue growth while maintaining quality. Peter Lehrer explained:

> When we started the business, we didn't have a grand design. We wanted challenging projects and the ability to enjoy what we do. We didn't set out to be the largest construction management firm in the industry, but the best. The critical issue for us now is, how big do we become?

LMB provided construction management services to investment builders and corporate clients. Hired for their construction expertise, they offered clients a range of project management services including construction supervision. They were most distinctive in their *phased*, or *"fast-track,"* approach, which integrated the design and construction phases, applied value engineering to reduce cost without compromising quality or performance, and substantially reduced overall project time.

Clients with construction needs typically chose one of three building methods for construction projects: (1) The traditional method of construction, *design-bid-build*, in which the client hired an architect to develop the building design and subsequently a general contractor to manage the physical construction; (2) The *design-build* method of con-

This case is based entirely on Lehrer McGovern Bovis, Inc. (687–089), prepared by Associate for Case Development Janet L. Simpson under the supervision of Professor David A. Garvin.

struction, in which one firm took total responsibility for both design and construction; and (3) The *phased*, or *fast-track*, method of construction, in which the client hired an architect and a construction manager concurrently so that the building was constructed as it was being designed.

For many years, the construction industry had been the largest industry and employer in the United States. In 1985, total new construction plans were valued at $206.6 billion, nearly 10% of the GNP. More than four million construction workers and three million people in related construction services depended on the core industry for their livelihood.

Despite its importance in the U.S. economy, the industry had been slow to invest in innovative methods, materials, and processes. In 1985, industry R&D expenditures averaged just 0.01% of sales, a figure comparable to the research dollars spent on razor blades. Only 3% of the firms in the industry owned computer-aided design systems. By contrast, the Japanese construction industry spent 3% of sales on R&D and was experimenting with robots for quality improvement. Barriers to innovation in the U.S. construction industry included its structure, the litigious nature of the business, and the traditional separation of design from construction. However, rising construction costs, schedule delays, and quality problems increasingly led clients to demand improvements in traditional building practices. This had fueled the growth of construction management (especially phased or fast-track) as a means for *managing* construction costs, not just *monitoring* them.

Alternative Building Methods

In most cases, the choice of building methods was determined by the complexity of the project, the repeatability of the project, the client's resources and past experiences, the client's corporate policies regarding construction contracts, and the value of time and innovation to the project.

The Traditional Design-Bid-Build Method of Construction

Historically, general contractors and the traditional method of construction were used for almost all large buildings (see Exhibit 1). In the *design phase*, a client retained the services of an architect and an engineering firm to develop the plans and specifications for the building. The architect was responsible for preparing a design which met the client's objectives in such areas as aesthetics, cost, and functionality. Engineers were responsible for determining the specifications of the building's systems. Specialization was the rule in the engineering function: an electrical engineer selected the building's electrical system, a civil engi-

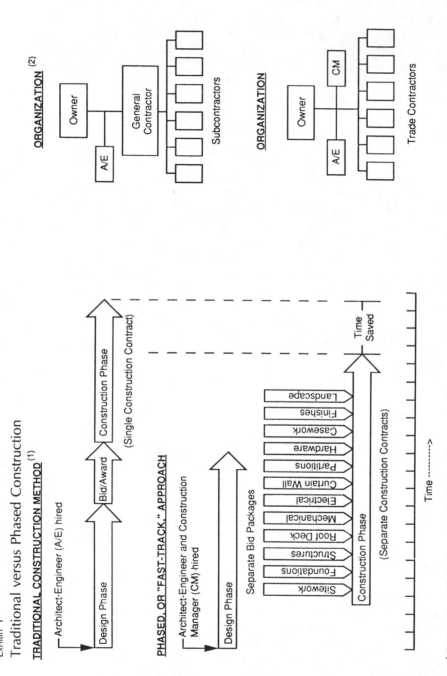

EXHIBIT 1

Traditional versus Phased Construction

[1] D. Barrie and B. Paulson, Jr., *Professional Construction Management*, 2nd edition (New York: McGraw-Hill Book Company, 1984), p. 37. Reprinted with permission.

[2] H. Newmark, "CM or GC? Untangling Pros and Cons of Building Methods," *Facilities and Design Management*, July/August 1982, pp. 48–49. Reprinted with permission.

neer selected the sewage and water system, and so forth. Between them, the architect and engineers determined which equipment, methods, and materials were most suitable for the project.

Following completion of the design, the *bid phase* distributed the entire package to several general contractors for competitive bidding. Each general contractor solicited bids from subcontractors, who would construct the building's components. The general contractor then collected these bids and submitted their own, all-inclusive bids to the client. The contract was awarded to the general contractor who submitted the lowest total bid.

Finally, the *construction phase* started after the client and general contractor had signed a fixed-price contract. Costs and schedule were monitored by the general contractor, who provided on-site supervision of construction (typically, general contractors provided 20% of the field staff, including superintendents and general foremen from their permanent organization). The general contractor assumed the financial risks of the project, and was liable for contracts negotiated with the subcontractors. Labor problems, material handling problems, and the complete logistics of the job were managed by the general contractor.

In the traditional design-bid-build approach, the activities of the architect, engineers, and general contractor were coordinated by either the architect or a project manager hired by the client for that purpose. Actual construction was coordinated by the general contractor, whose experience with methods and materials facilitated predictively sequencing the tasks of subcontractors. Despite its wide use, some clients were unhappy with this traditional arrangement. As Lehrer explained:

> On the surface, general contracting seems straightforward. Construction does not start until general contractors promise to deliver everything shown on the plans and specifications for a fixed price. In practice, however, companies frequently find that once the contract is signed, the general contractor's incentives are to maximize profits and minimize costs. They are not motivated to do anything to enhance the project that costs money. In fact, quality is often compromised to keep to schedule and budget.

The Design-Build Method of Construction

An alternative to the traditional method of construction had emerged when large general contractors began offering design services. The *design-build* method of construction offered clients an easier way to manage construction projects because it kept total responsibility for both design and construction in one firm. This method became the preferred approach for identical or related repeat projects—such as warehouses or cogeneration power plants—because it saved time over the traditional method and often had a lower first cost. In 1985, design-build contracts totaled $26 billion, and 25 of the top 40 contractors in the U.S. reported that they acted as design-build agents.

The design-build method had some disadvantages, particularly for an inexperienced client. The normal checks and balances between architect and general contractor were missing. In many cases, the firm used standard rather than customized designs to improve their profit margins. Cost cutting methods, such as value engineering, were often ignored.

The Overlapping Phased Construction Method

The third construction method, *phased* or *fast-track* construction, arose because of a new player in the industry, the construction manager. Fast-track was a scheduling process that overlapped traditionally sequential stages of design and construction. Its basic premise was that there was no reason to wait until all details of a building had been specified before starting construction. By overlapping the design and construction phases, the time period between concept and tenant occupancy was dramatically reduced.

This method of construction management had also emerged in response to clients needs for an agent with construction expertise to represent them in all phases of project execution. The fast-track firm provided a broad range of project management services, including procurement and logistics planning and proven cost-cutting methods such as value engineering. The construction manager typically was hired early in the design phase to assure constructability and to identify opportunities for cost reduction and schedule improvement as well as better methods for achieving the client's functional objectives. While the three phases of design-bid-build still occurred, the way in which they were handled differed significantly from the traditional, sequential approach.

During the *design phase*, the construction manager (the fast-track firm), the client, and an architect formed a team to develop the building design. The construction manager evaluated the proposed design's costs and time implications rather than its aesthetics. This information was given to the architect early in the design process, allowing the architect to maintain design integrity at least cost. Occasionally the construction manager's input resulted in major design changes. Mike Holloway, an assistant vice president at LMB, described one of the early projects he had managed:

> We were hired as the construction manager for a $21 million ABC-TV studio project on New York's West End Avenue. The client was under pressure to complete the project in nine months. Because of zoning restrictions on the

overall building height, the initial design decision was to drop the building 20 feet into the ground. As part of our evaluation, we took site borings and discovered that the site was solid rock dotted with concrete caves. To complicate matters, the site had once been a railroad, and tracks ran along the sides of the lot and underground. We determined the location of the rock and caves; we also located the old drawings of the rail yard in Penn Central's files; and from this information were able to quantify the cost of lowering the building 20 feet.

When we shared these numbers and their implications with the architect and engineers, they came up with a pyramid design which met the zoning requirements but only required excavating ten feet of rock. A general contractor would likely have gone through the same exercise once he received the bid documents from the architect. The difference would have been that at that point—perhaps four months into the project—the design already would have been fixed. The decision for the client would have been either to pay the extra $1 million to do the excavation or to go back to the drawing boards and revise the design. In all likelihood, the client would have missed the nine month deadline.

Using the fast-track method, the architect prepared the design documents in stages so that the construction manager could solicit bids (the *bid phase*) from subcontractors as quickly as possible. The construction manager was responsible for recommending subcontractors and negotiating final contracts for the client. The construction manager's responsibilities also included the procurement of materials for construction. By knowing early in the design process what materials were required, the construction manager could take advantage of market conditions to negotiate favorable prices. Early purchasing of items with long lead times, such as high-speed elevators (which could take as long as ten months to deliver), reduced delays during construction. Each day saved meant lower costs for the client.

In the *construction phase*, the approach of fast-track construction managers resulted in the building being designed, bid, and constructed in stages. Site clearing and grading, foundation, and structure were bid and construction was begun within a few months after the start of the basic design. Mechanical, electrical, and plumbing designs and contracts followed quickly, with details of architectural finish decided, designed, and bid while the core of the building was under construction. Shifting as much work as possible away from the site further collapsed overall development time.

Some critics argued that fast-track construction was risky because construction was completed as the design evolved and decisions and commitments were made based on incomplete drawings. They also argued that the architect had less design flexibility as the building progressed. Fast-track construction managers countered that their approach was no different than concurrent engineering in a manufacturing environment, and that better knowledge on the part of architects, engineers, and themselves substantially reduced those risks while improving the total solution to the client's needs (the resulting building) as well as getting it built faster and at lower cost.

Fast-track construction management firms generally charged for their services on a fixed-fee basis. LMB charged a fee equal to a project's expenses plus a percentage of the total cost of the project. Fees typically ranged from 2% to 5% of project costs. One senior LMB manager described the impact of that fee structure on client relationships:

> Because we work for a fixed fee, our interests are aligned with those of our clients. There is no incentive to increase project costs. The clients get what they are willing to pay for. If clients want changes, we tell them what their options are and what the cost implications will be. If they want to proceed with a change, we negotiate a fair and reasonable price in the market place. Our clients therefore have more control over cost and quality.

Unlike general contractors, fast-track construction managers did not guarantee budget or schedule. Slipped schedule and budget overruns were paid by the client, but at a major cost to the construction manager's reputation. As Lehrer observed:

> We compete on the basis of three items: reputation, first, qualification, second, and fees, third. If we can't deliver the job on time and on budget, we'll soon be out of business.

In 1985, the top 400 U.S. contractors recorded $136.1 billion in foreign and domestic contracts. Of these contracts, $81.7 billion were for traditional general contractor projects, $18 billion were for design-build contracts (managed by a single firm), and $36.4 billion were for construction management (fast-track) projects. The top construction managers were full-service firms who offered construction management services in all industry segments. As one LMB observer pointed out, "With both designers and general contractors offering construction management services, it's hard to pin down your competition."

The Company

In 1985, Lehrer McGovern Bovis ranked 17th among construction management firms. By mid 1986, the company employed 465 people in nine offices, eight in the U.S. and one in London. However, two-thirds of their employees worked in the New York office. Total 1985 revenues were $36.4 million, with almost 70% going to developers and the remainder split equally between corporate clients and restorations. After deducting project reimbursable expenses, total net fees were just over $10 million. In 1986, LMB projected total revenues of almost $56 million, with a disproportionate share of the growth coming from corporate clients and restorations. Total net fee revenues were projected to be almost $17 million in 1986.

LMB had first opened its doors in June 1979, when Peter Lehrer and Gene McGovern left their senior-level positions at Morse-Diesel, the nation's twelfth-largest construction management firm, to start a company of their own. Armed with their personal reputation and 32 years of construction expertise, within two weeks they had secured a contract to build a factory and an office building in northern New Jersey.

The firm's early strategy was to select projects that would attract immediate attention. In 1981, they accepted the challenge of removing a ten ton, 24 foot high statue from atop the old AT&T headquarters in Manhattan. The gold-leafed, bronze statue, nicknamed "Golden Boy," had crowned the building for 64 years; some experts believed that it could not be removed from its 30 story perch. LMB's crew started work on a Sunday afternoon, and by Monday morning "Golden Boy" was down. This unusual job brought the firm wide attention among builders and developers seeking construction management services, and new projects came quickly.

The firm's reputation was solidly established two years later when LMB won a 30 month contract to restore the Statue of Liberty. More than 25 firms submitted proposals to coordinate the activities of some 500 engineers, architects, contractors, and craft specialists. After an exhaustive screening process, LMB was awarded the job. As the construction manager, LMB selected the subcontractors and supervised rebuilding of the statue. "It was one big R&D project," a senior LMB manager explained. "No one was sure what to expect, as the Statue's iron frame had corroded and extensive structural problems required renovation."

The growth of LMB coincided with one of the most spectacular bull markets of New York City's real estate history. As construction flourished, developers demanded that buildings be erected quickly for early tenant occupancy. Fast-track construction, like that offered by LMB, met that need. Lehrer and McGovern also looked for opportunities to work for corporate clients. In 1981, they secured their first corporate project—a new General Foods headquarters in Rye, New York. Months of testing were required to make sure that the aluminum siding selected by the architect as the enclosure wall for the seven story building would be secure against wind and water. The architect later won the coveted Pritzker Prize in Architecture, and LMB greatly enhanced their standing among potential corporate clients.

Project Management at LMB

Through such efforts as the "Golden boy" project, the Statue of Liberty, and the General Foods headquarters, LMB earned a reputation for completing challenging projects on time and within budget. Management claimed that a major reason for these successes was their team approach to project management.

Construction projects at LMB were managed by *dedicated* project teams formed when the firm first received a request for a building proposal. That team was responsible for responding to the proposal, winning the contract, and then managing all facets of the construction project. At LMB, project managers—with support from the rest of the team—were totally responsible for the successful completion of the building.

Conceptually, project management at LMB could be divided into three stages: *winning the proposal,* when the team responded to a request for a proposal; *preconstruction activities,* when value engineering was done, bid packages were prepared, and construction logistics were planned; and *construction,* when the foundation was dug and the building was erected. Because of the fast-track approach used by LMB, the latter two stages—preconstruction activities and construction—overlapped considerably.

Winning the Proposal. The dedicated team assembled to respond to a building request typically included Lehrer and McGovern, a project executive (who supervised several projects simultaneously), a project manager (dedicated to that one project), an estimator, and a mechanical/electrical manager (who provided specific technical support concerning mechanical and electrical systems). The team worked through the proposal to evaluate the client's requirements and to identify opportunities for cost savings. The time investment at this stage was large as the team started formulating ideas for time and cost savings. This was viewed as a source of differentiation from competitors, and clients often responded to the LMB written proposal with "You've sent us a book; your competitors sent us three pieces of paper."

Once the written proposal was reviewed by the client, the project team prepared a client presentation. This presentation included a description of LMB's services and how they would approach the building's construction. Because seven or eight LMB people had already worked on preparation of the proposal, there was generally a strong chemistry between the LMB project team and the client at this presentation session. The company identified that high comfort level as an important key to winning the contract.

Preconstruction Activities. Once LMB was hired, the dedicated project team had to complete several tasks before construction could begin. The design was value engineered to reduce costs; bid packages were prepared and subcontractors hired; and construction logistics were planned.

The project team's first task was to scrutinize the design as it was being completed to identify opportunities for cost reduction or value enhancement. Value engineering was used to systematically evaluate alternatives in order to reduce costs without compromising quality or performance (see Exhibit 2).

Using value engineering techniques, the project manager isolated each building component, looking for ways to lower costs through newer, alternative construction materials and methods. The amount of time devoted to value engineering depended on the complexity of the project and its timetable. Typically, recommended changes might save a client $5 million in construction costs on a $50 million project, or 10% of the project cost.

Before value engineering was implemented, the LMB project team would meet with the client and architect to secure approval. LMB's recommendations were not always welcome by architects, whose concern for aesthetics sometimes clashed with the team's concern for cost and efficiency. "It's a polite professional battle," said one senior manager, "and one from which the client ultimately benefits." After the client, architect, and project team agreed on the design changes, the LMB team developed a final budget and construction schedule.

Among other items, the construction schedule included the dates when the architect would forward completed design documents to LMB. If the project were being constructed using the fast-track method, the architect would prepare the documents in stages so that the project team could solicit bids from subcontractors as quickly as possible. LMB's project manager would break the completed design documents into bid packages which were sent to subcontractors for pricing. These packages contained drawings, component specs, and a detailed scope of work for services the subcontractor was to provide. In most cases, several bids were solicited for each subcontract. These were reviewed by the project manager, and usually the lowest bidders were recommended to the client. Once the client approved these recommendations, the project manager negotiated contracts with individual subcontractors. To avoid change orders after construction started, LMB bid documents tended to be very detailed and left little room for negotiation.

While the project manager worked on the bid packages, the field staff prepared the construction site logistics plan. This plan described how the construction equipment and materials should be arranged on-site so that construction was as efficient as possible. Issues such as permits, power, water, sanitation facilities, and site conditions were addressed at this time. Through such planning, construction would be able to start as soon as the first subcontractors were hired.

EXHIBIT 2

Value Engineering in the Construction Industry[1]

Value engineering is a technique used to reduce the costs associated with a product without compromising quality or performance. Historically, there was little incentive for architects and contractors to use value engineering to reduce construction costs. Obsolete building codes often bound them to past construction practices. Moreover, architects and contractors seldom wanted to take the financial risks associated with new materials or methods.

Value Engineering Methodology

A five-step approach was normally used. First, the construction manager quantified the cost of each building component. Design specifications were reviewed on a system-by-system basis, with the foundation and structural components evaluated first, and then the curtain wall, mechanical and electrical systems, plumbing, and so forth. Those components which appeared to be out of line with historical costs or the construction manager's experience were isolated for further study.

The construction management team then defined the primary function of the component; that is, what the component did. The team brainstormed alternate materials that could provide the same function for lower cost. Consideration was given to new materials or process technology, modification of the client's needs, and feedback from field experience. The most promising alternatives were then evaluated on the basis of cost and how well they met the project's requirements. Because a design change might improve initial construction costs while increasing the long term maintenance costs of a building, the impact of a component change on the total cost of designing, building, operating, and maintaining the facility (the life-cycle cost) was also determined.

Finally, recommendations for change were documented and presented to the architect and client for approval.

Value Engineering at LMB

The following example illustrates a value engineering exercise completed for one of LMB's construction projects.

LMB was awarded a contract for a new corporate headquarters. The building complex had three low-rise buildings connected by atriums, bridges, and tunnels. Most building space was devoted to offices, but there were a number of highly finished common areas including a cafeteria, executive dining rooms, a large auditorium, a multi-media center, a health club, and medical facilities.

LMB's initial cost estimate was $89.50/sq. ft. for the 690,000 square-foot facility. Value engineered changes reduced construction costs to $79.89/sq. ft., a $6.63 million savings. Changes in four major systems contributed most of the cost savings:

[1] For a complete description of the value engineering technique, see the *Note on Value Analysis*, HBS Case Services 9–687–066.

System	Components	Savings
Structural (Evaluated 4 roof and 20 office bay designs. Selected designs which satisfied customer requirements for least cost.)	Structural steel for the roof and office bays	$1,586,761
Site work (Modified paving materials, reduced number of light poles, changed lamps.)	Roadway and parking paving, exterior lighting	$ 868,952
Curtain wall (Reviewed suggestions for cost savings from seven curtain wall contractors. Successful bidder met design intent with cost savings.)	Exterior and interior walls of the building	$ 430,000
Finishes (Evaluated and revised materials used for partitions, acoustical ceilings, flooring, and door finishes.)	Partitions, ceilings, flooring, doors	$1,967,035

Total Savings: $4,852,000

Construction. During a building's construction phase, the project manager remained in-house, negotiating subcontractor contracts for the client and purchasing any additional materials needed for the job. The physical construction of the project was managed by a field superintendent and assistants under the supervision of Eric McGovern, the general superintendent (and son of Gene McGovern).

Construction started as soon as the foundation subcontractor had been hired. While the foundation was being dug, the field superintendent completed the site logistics plan, preparing and posting the equipment time and work schedules, determining how the construction crews would be sequenced, and scheduling material deliveries. When the foundation was partially completed, the field superintendent held the first of many coordination meetings with subcontractors. As Jim Abadie, a field superintendent, described these meetings:

> We don't wait for the architect and engineers to initiate meetings with subcontractors. Before the first floor is poured, I pull the subcontractors into a coordinating meeting, lock the door, and don't let them leave until they map out the first floor. We work off of the drawings and try to make it all fit. We decide where everything goes and how the work should be coordinated. These meetings are repeated for every floor.

During the construction phase, the field superintendent, the assistant for the site, Eric McGovern, the project executive, and the project manager hold weekly status meetings. The project manager in turn schedules weekly meetings with the client and architect to keep them informed of progress. Construction costs and schedule are monitored by the project manager.

The proper sequencing of people, materials, and equipment (managing the site) was essential to meeting tight construction schedules. Work crews had to be closely scheduled so that they did not interfere with one another but had a minimum of idle time. The proper placement of materials and machines could sharply reduce unnecessary delays and wasted motions. Great skill was required to do this effectively. One senior LMB manager described the job of field superintendent as "master chess player." Not only did the field superintendent have to stay several moves ahead, but through such actions as moving the scaffolding up on schedule, the project team put pressure on subcontractors to finish their work quickly on the lower floors.

Overall, LMB's managers attributed much of their firm's success to their dedicated team approach to construction management. Decisions were made by the project team, and the team felt very much in charge of its own destiny. As a result, everybody became an innovator and an entrepreneur. This was in sharp contrast with many of LMB's larger competitors, who had a more departmentalized approach to construction management. Such firms would tend to specialize, and had a separate proposal team, a preconstruction department, a purchasing department, and a construction department. Although competitors gained some economies of scale through such specialization, LMB project managers felt that their team approach provided better client service and tighter project control.

Project Support

People. All of LMB's project teams were staffed with experienced construction managers. They also drew informally on the expertise of Lehrer, McGovern, and other senior managers. In the early years, Lehrer McGovern had hired experienced project managers and field staff—often people with whom they had previously done business. Once the supply of experienced people was exhausted, they began actively recruiting young engineering talent on college campuses. Gene McGovern interviewed all engineering applicants, looking for "confidence, ambition, a strong work ethic . . . the right attitude." Furthermore, McGovern explained the absence of a personnel department "because personnel people tend to hire people like themselves."

Training. Most training at LMB was done informally—"hands on"—under the guidance of project teams. A training program for new college graduates, however, was being formalized in 1986. During their first two years with LMB, all new hires would split their time between the field and the office, working as assistants either to field superintendents or project managers.

Appraisal/Awards. In their first two years, new employees were evaluated every six months and annually thereafter. One of the rewards for a job well done was the satisfaction of seeing a project completed and the opportunity for another challenge. In a firm with only three senior managers over forty years of age, it was not uncommon to find young engineers managing major projects. The creation of regional profit centers in 1984 provided additional incentives. These centers gave experienced managers the opportunity to be entrepreneurial. A bonus system was established to reward profit centers for strong performance, with a bonus pool based on a formula that included the profit center's profitability goal, set during the budgeting process, plus its increase in profitability over the past year.

Support Services. The dedicated project teams at LMB were backed by support services in marketing, estimating, scheduling, and accounting. The New York headquarters had a full complement of support groups, including legal and computer services. The regional profit centers formed support staffs as soon as their size warranted; until then, they used the resources available in New York.

Project managers were responsible for monitoring costs and schedules for clients. Initial budgets prepared with estimators were the basic mechanism for project control. These budgets segregated work by trade so that actual costs could be easily monitored during construction. Scheduling software packages were also available, but many preferred to prepare schedules manually and have them enhanced by the scheduling department before client presentations.

Lehrer, McGovern, and the profit centers met monthly to discuss strategic and operations issues. As explained by Lehrer in 1986, "We're a close-knit group. We have the same philosophical viewpoint about work, the desire to succeed, and entrepreneurial spirit. We don't have a business plan on paper; it's in our heads."

Growth Issues

In 1986, LMB's senior management had made two key strategic decisions. The first was to merge the company with Bovis International Limited, a London-based construction management firm. This merger was not expected to significantly affect operations at LMB. The motivation was primarily financial, and included better access to projects in the New York area that were financed by foreign sources.

The second strategic decision, prompted by changing market conditions, was to shift from the firm's traditional markets of commercial and restoration projects to the construction of corporate facilities and institutions such as hospitals, colleges, and universities. This shift in client mix was expected to have an impact on operations because of the size of corporate projects and client's reporting needs. One project manager explained:

> The technical skills required are the same for all clients. But corporate clients are more bureaucratic than developers. You have to work through the hierarchy to get changes approved. Corporate procedures must be followed and reports filed. Corporate project managers want support when they report to their superiors; that requires the creation of an audit trail.

Changing market conditions also meant that other construction firms would be pursuing these same clients. Competition was expected to be intense. As one LMB manager expressed it, "Fee structures might be hurt, but it's important to keep our people busy. We don't want to lose them."

One of the pressures accompanying growth that had been identified by senior management at LMB was the pressure for specialization in order to achieve the benefits of larger scale. Project managers who had recently supervised corporate client projects had already identified LMB's need for better systems for scheduling, cost control, and document control. In addition, technical support—such as mechanical and electrical expertise—might best be centralized and used as needed by individual project teams.

In addition to the issues of specialization accompanying growth, issues of staffing, bonuses, and equity were also being raised. It clearly was not feasible for Lehrer and McGovern to be on every project in the future, but it was unclear as to what organizational model would make best use of their time. Would they be best served with a corporate structure with several support departments—as typically found in large construction firms—or would they be better served by autonomous operating units, each headed by a largely autonomous "clone" of Lehrer or McGovern? This latter structure raised all sorts of issues with regard to control, reputation, and consistency across regional profit centers. With an increasing number of corporate clients whose reach was national and international, this consistency seemed particularly important.

Finally, the issue of incentives and bonuses had recently been called into question. Toward the end of 1986, the Edison, New Jersey profit center had encountered an issue of how to reward profit centers equitably. The Edison profit center had an extremely profitable year, with revenues increasing from $100,000 in 1985 to $1.5 million in 1986. Clearly the profitability formula could not be used to determine their bonus pool. It was complicated by the fact that one project credited to the Edison office was a new office building in Queens, New York. Although the building fell geographically within the jurisdiction of the New York profit center, the client had specifically requested that a senior manager in the Edison office manage the project. That was done, and all project revenues were credited to the New Jersey profit center, although the full-time support of six members of the New York staff was used on the project. The New York office felt they should share in some of those revenues, besides having their costs covered by the Edison office for the project.

Looking to the future, McGovern saw the firm's ability to manage growth without compromising quality as a key management challenge. He was equally concerned with keeping the firm energized:

> When you look at other companies in this business, you see a lot of lethargy and stale thinking. There are few companies our size, and few companies where the principals are deeply involved in the firm's operations. We continually have to prove ourselves; I hope it stays that way.

CHAPTER **8**

Organizing and Leading Project Teams

Overview

In development project management, achieving an effective team requires more than simply naming members to a core team and designating a project head. Years of experience and ingrained systems create both physical and organizational distance for those involved in a development effort. Yet the likelihood of achieving outstanding new products and processes is greatly enhanced when teams are used to make fundamental alterations in the ways in which detailed work is done during the project. In this chapter we describe four types of development teams—functional, lightweight, heavyweight, and autonomous. These teams represent a continuum ranging from a loosely linked set of vertical organizational functions to an independent, fully integrated team that cuts horizontally across functions. Perhaps the easiest way to distinguish a vertical from a horizontal form in practice is to consider where primary, full-time project contributors look for guidance, evaluation, and rewards. If they look to senior functional managers, then the dominant form is vertical; if to the team leader, then horizontal.

Building on the primary theme of Chapter 7, this chapter illustrates how teams may facilitate cross-functional integration by changing how work is done within a traditionally functional organization. An important theme in this chapter is the importance of leadership in making teams effective. Because of their power in developing major new products quickly and efficiently, we focus the discussion on heavyweight teams and heavyweight leaders. A crucial element in the success of heavyweight teams is the development of core team members and leaders with the organizational skills to make the heavyweight concept a reality. Critical skills include the ability to take initiative and develop nontraditional solutions to problems that arise.

Motorola is one of a handful of firms that has selected the heavyweight team structure as its primary development approach. As illustrated by the Bandit pager project conducted in the late 1980s, their heavyweight team efforts include six primary elements or characteristics: (1) a project charter, (2) a contract book, (3) a co-located core team, (4) heavyweight leadership, (5) broad team member responsibilities, and (6) an executive sponsor. These elements provide a useful starting point for any organization considering a move to heavyweight development teams.

A final theme in this chapter is that the approach chosen for organizing and leading individual projects must fit the setting and specifics of each individual project, as well as the organizational capabilities available. To paraphrase, "one size *does not* fit all." There is no one best team structure or form of project leadership that applies to all firms, nor is there a single form and structure that applies to all projects in a single firm. Thus, a key senior management responsibility is to develop multiple approaches and the organization's skill at determining which should be applied in any specific situation.

CHAPTER *8*

*E*ffective product and process development requires both that all of the organizational groups involved develop and bring to bear the appropriate specialized capabilities, and that the efforts of all of these groups be appropriately integrated. For most young, small organizations, particularly those still in the start-up phase, the organization structure and the role of the project manager are not burning issues, although certainly product and process development are of critical importance. The entire organization finds itself focused on a single major development project, and the CEO or some other senior executive exercises strong project leadership. Furthermore, the various functional managers naturally take broad responsibility not only for their parts of the project but for the successful outcome of the entire effort. Thus while a number of issues—involving cross-functional problem solving, refining product and process specifications, and integrating product performance with customer needs—challenge the organization, only modest amounts of their energy gets spent on how best to organize the project and direct its execution.

In large, mature firms that over time have established strong functional groups (especially in engineering, but also in marketing and manufacturing) with extensive specialization, have large numbers of people, and have a number of ongoing operating concerns as well as development project concerns, the challenge of organizing and leading product and process development efforts is increased dramatically. In such firms, development projects become the exception for the ongoing operating organization rather than representing their primary focus of attention. Even for those on the project, years of experience and the establishment of a broad range of systems—covering everything from career paths to performance evaluation, and from reporting relationships to breadth of job definitions—create both physical and organizational distance between individual contributors and among organizational subfunctions. Often this is complicated further by organization structures in marketing that are based on product families and market segments, organization structures in engineering based on functional disciplines and technical focus, and organization structures in manufacturing operations that are a mix between functional and product market. The result is that in large, mature organizations, team organization and the leadership of development efforts is a major challenge. This is accentuated as organizations find their traditionally stable markets and competitive environments challenged by new entrants, new technologies, and rapidly changing customer demands.

It is no surprise in such an environment that, by 1990, the concept of "teams"—especially cross-functional teams—had become almost a fad in the management literature.[1] However, as organizations experimented with such teams, they discovered that success with a cross-functional team required much more than simply "naming" the team and setting up a regular schedule of team meetings. In fact, many firms who had adopted the team solution found their managers increasingly stretched, with less time for substantive work, and projects taking just as long—if not longer—for completion. This was in sharp contrast to a handful of firms in different industries who apparently had discovered the "keys to success" in making such teams work effectively.

Some of the most dramatic stories in the popular press relating to fast-cycle turnaround and time-based competitive advantage have attributed success to effective team organizations and project leadership. Particularly compelling has been the work of Clark and Fujimoto[2] in the world auto industry. In a nutshell, their findings suggest that the best firms in the auto industry have cut traditional new car development cycle times significantly; in the process, they have delivered better products and, in many cases, more than doubled the productivity of critical development engineering resources. These leading firms in the auto industry seem to have developed a much more effective way to organize and lead development projects than their slower, less efficient rivals.

The focus of this chapter is on the range of organizational options for directing development projects and their associated options for project leadership. We begin by outlining four types of project organization structures and their primary differences. This includes consideration of the differences in the roles and responsibilities of the project leader as well as those of individual team members, and their relationship with the traditional functional groups and with senior executives. The section also explores the evolution of organizations over time, an understanding of which helps explain the pervasive yet subtle nature of the patterns that influence team structures and their effectiveness.

The subsequent section focuses on a type of organization structure and leadership—heavyweight project teams—that seems particularly promising in today's environment, yet is strikingly absent in many mature organizations. The nature of such heavyweight teams and the dimensions along which they differ from their much more prevalent counterparts, "lightweight" teams, is also explored. The intent in this section is to illustrate how such heavyweight project teams and their project leaders function, and thus some of the things that an organization must do to create and utilize such a capability. While such teams are powerful in certain settings, they are not without their own unique issues and challenges, and those are the focus of the final portion of this section.

Next, we turn attention to the need for firms to match their required types of projects (a topic discussed in Chapter 4) with the appropriate project organization structure and leadership mode. Using a number of examples, this segment develops the idea that organizations, while needing a "dominant mode" for product and process development, also need alternate modes for other less frequent, yet essential, types of projects.

We conclude the chapter by exploring some of the approaches that firms have found effective in building a range of team capabilities. These vary from how to improve existing approaches to creating credible new approaches, to making sure that multiple approaches to development can coexist and be strengthened in the organization over the longer term. We hope that by the end of the chapter the reader will conclude—as we have—that this is indeed a high-leverage aspect of project execution, and that while it has no simple answers, there are several principles that can be pursued to significant advantage.

Project Organization and Leadership

Our work has identified four dominant structures around which project activities can be organized. Each has an associated project leadership role. The result is a range of options for managing development projects, each with its own unique strengths and weaknesses. The four basic types of development team structures are illustrated in Exhibit 8–1.[3]

Exhibit 8–1

Types of Development Teams*

1. Functional Team Structure

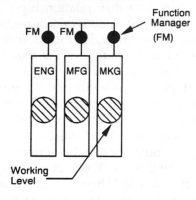

2. Lightweight Team Structure

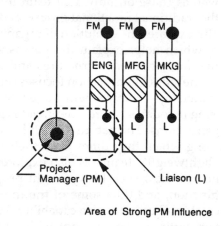

3. Heavyweight Team Structure

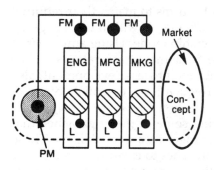

4. Autonomous Team Structure

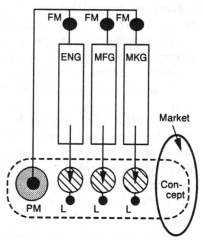

* This exhibit depicts four levels of teams: functional, where the work is completed in the function and coordinated by functional managers; lightweight, where a coordinator works through liaison representatives but has little influence over the work; heavyweight, where a strong leader exerts direct, integrating influence across all functions; and autonomous, where a heavyweight team is removed from the function, dedicated to a single project, and co-located.

Functional Team Structure. The upper left-hand corner depicts the traditional functional organization found in larger, more mature firms. People are grouped together principally by discipline, each working under the direction of a specialized subfunction manager and a senior functional manager. Within each engineering discipline, for example, specific engineers specialize in various aspects of the product or process under development. Representative groupings would include industrial, maintenance, and manufacturing process engineering under the subcategory of manufacturing engineering, and electrical, mechanical, software, and test engineering under the subcategory of R&D or design engineering.

The work of the different subfunctions and functions is to coordinate ideas through a set of detailed specifications agreed to by all parties at the start of the project, and by occasional meetings where issues that cut across groups are discussed. Over time, primary responsibility for the project passes sequentially—although often not smoothly—from one function to the next. This might be thought of as shifting the center of gravity in the project as time passes. The transfer of project responsibility from one function to the next is sometimes referred to as "the hand-off," or, less euphemistically, but probably more accurately, as "throwing it over the wall."

This organization structure has a number of major strengths as well as weaknesses. One strength is that those managers who control the resources also control performance of the project tasks that need to occur in their area. Thus the traditional wisdom of aligning responsibility and authority tends to be followed here. The rub is that to make it work, the set of tasks must be subdivided at the outset of the project, requiring a decomposition of the entire development activity into a set of separable, somewhat independent tasks. Unfortunately, on most development efforts, not all required activities are known at the outset, nor can they all be easily and realistically subdivided into separable pieces. The primary weakness of this approach thus shows up in limited coordination and integration.

Another major strength of this approach is that most career paths are functional in nature until one reaches a general management level in the firm. This mode of project organization ensures that the work done on a project is judged, evaluated, and rewarded by the same subfunction and functional managers who make the decisions about career paths. The associated disadvantage is that individual contributions to a development project tend to be judged largely independently of overall project success. The traditional tenet cited is that individuals cannot be evaluated fairly on outcomes over which they have little or no control. But as a practical matter, that often means that no one directly involved in the details of the project is responsible for the project results finally achieved.

A third primary strength of the functional project organization is that it ensures that specialized expertise is brought to bear on the key technical issues. With such an organization in a company such as an auto manufacturer, the same person or small group of people literally can be responsible for the design of every windshield wiper or door lock over a wide range of development efforts. Thus the functions and subfunctions capture the benefits of prior experience and become the keepers of the organization's depth of knowledge while ensuring that it is systematically applied over time and across projects. The disadvantage is that every development project will differ somewhat in its objectives and performance requirements, and it is unlikely that specialists developing a single component—such as a windshield wiper or door lock—will do so very differently on one project than on another. Their tendency will be to design what they consider the "best" component or subsystem, where best is defined by technical parameters in the areas of their expertise rather than by overall system characteristics or specific customer requirements dictated by the market for which this development effort is aimed.

Lightweight Team Structure. The second approach, outlined in Exhibit 8–1 in the upper right-hand quadrant, is called the lightweight project team approach. Like the functional structure, those assigned to the team reside physically in their functional areas, but each functional organization designates a liaison person to "represent" it on a project coordinating committee. These liaison representatives work with a "lightweight project manager," usually a design engineer or product marketing manager, who has responsibility for coordinating the activities of the different functions. In most cases, the lightweight project team represents a fairly minor modification to the traditional functional team. In fact, it usually occurs as an add-on to a traditional functional organization, with the liaison person having that functional liaison role added to his or her other duties. The position of lightweight project manager, however, does tend to be a type of overall coordination assignment not present in the traditional functional team structure.

The project manager in this approach is a "lightweight" in two important respects. First, he or she is generally a middle- or junior-level person who, although having considerable expertise, usually has little status or influence in the organization. Often these people have spent a handful of years in one of the functions, and this assignment is seen as a "broadening experience," a chance for them to move out of that function. Second, although they are responsible for informing and coordinating the activities of the functional organizations, the key resources (including engineers on the project) remain under the control of their respective functional managers. Lightweight project managers do not have power to reassign people or reallocate resources. Much of their time is spent confirming schedules, updating time lines, and expediting across groups. Typically such project leaders spend no more than 25 percent of their time on a single project.

The primary strengths and weaknesses of the lightweight project team are those stated previously for the functional project structure. In addition, however, there is now at least one person who, over the course of the project, looks across functions and seeks to make certain that individual tasks—especially those on the critical path—get done in a timely fashion, and that everyone is kept aware of potential cross-functional issues and what is going on elsewhere on this particular project. Thus improved communication and coordination are the added strengths expected by an organization that moves from a functional to a lightweight team structure.

The weakness is the fact that the project manager is "lightweight." The power still resides with the subfunction and functional managers; as a consequence, expectations for improved efficiency, speed, and project quality from moving to the lightweight team structure are seldom met. Lightweight project leaders find themselves tolerated at best, and often ignored and even preempted. This can easily become a "no-win" situation for the individual thus assigned.

Heavyweight Team Structure. The third approach, outlined in the lower left of Exhibit 8–1, is the heavyweight project team. In contrast to the lightweight setup, the heavyweight project manager has direct access to and responsibility for the work of all those involved in the project. Such project leaders are "heavyweights" in two respects. First, they are senior managers within the organization. In some organizations they are at the same level or even outrank the functional managers. As a result, not only do they have expertise and experience, they also wield significant organizational clout. Second, heavyweight project leaders have primary influence over the people working on the development effort and supervise their work directly through key functional people on the core teams. Often, the core group of people are dedicated and physically co-located with that heavyweight project leader. However, the longer-term career development of individual contributors continues to rest with their functional managers rather than the project leader because they are not assigned to a project team on a permanent basis.

There are a number of dimensions—in addition to stature within the organization and resource control—along which lightweight project managers differ. Several of these are summarized in Exhibit 8–2. Each is shown along a continuum, suggesting that the difference between light-

EXHIBIT 8–2

Project Manager Profile*

	Lightweight (limited)			Heavyweight (extensive)

Span of coordination responsibilities	⊢————————————————————————⊣	
Duration of responsibilities	⊢————————————————————————⊣	
Responsible for specs, cost, layout, components	⊢————————————————————————⊣	
Working level contact with engineers	⊢————————————————————————⊣	
Direct contact with customers	⊢————————————————————————⊣	
Multilingual/multidiscipline skills	⊢————————————————————————⊣	
Role in conflict resolution	⊢————————————————————————⊣	
Marketing imagination/concept champion	⊢————————————————————————⊣	
Influence in:		
engineering	⊢————————————————————————⊣	
marketing	⊢————————————————————————⊣	
manufacturing	⊢————————————————————————⊣	

* Project managers take on a variety of roles and responsibilities, eleven of which are depicted here. How much of a heavyweight (versus lightweight) project manager role occurs on a specific project is determined by how extensive a role the project manager takes in each of these areas.

---

weight and heavyweight team structures is more one of degree than an all-or-none issue. By presenting these dimensions of difference on a continuum, it also is easy to have teams and their project managers assess their own position relative to "degree" of lightweight versus heavyweight characteristics.

The heavyweight team structure has a number of advantages and strengths, but also an associated set of weaknesses. Because this team structure is observed much less frequently in practice and yet seems to have tremendous potential for a wide range of organizations, it will be discussed in detail in the next section. We will leave our discussion of strengths and weaknesses to the conclusion of that in-depth exploration.

Autonomous Team Structure. The fourth form of project structure, outlined in the lower right-hand portion of Exhibit 8–1, is the autonomous team structure, often referred to as the "tiger team." Under this structure, individuals from the different fuctional areas are formally assigned, dedicated, and co-located to the project team. The project leader is a heavyweight in the organization and is given full control over the resources contributed by the different functional groups. Furthermore, that project leader becomes the sole evaluator of the contribution made by individual team members.

In essence, the autonomous team is given a "clean sheet of paper" with regards to the development project and all of its aspects and details. Typically, such tiger teams are not required to follow existing organizational practices and procedures, but are allowed to create their own. This includes establishing incentives and rewards as well as norms for behavior. However, they understand that as a team they will be held fully accountable for the final results of the project. If the project does not succeed as planned, the responsibility will be theirs and no one else's.

The fundamental strength of the autonomous team structure is focus. Everything that the individual team members and the team leader do is concentrated on making the project successful. Because of their focus, tiger teams tend to do well at rapid, efficient new product and new process development. They handle cross-functional integration in a particularly effective manner. This often may be due in part to their being able to attract and select team participants much more freely than the other project structures.

The countering disadvantage is that they take little or nothing as "given"; thus, they are likely to expand the bounds of their project definition and tackle redesign of the entire product and its components and subassemblies rather than looking for opportunities to utilize existing materials, designs, and organizational relationships. Their solutions tend to be unique, making it more difficult to fold the resulting product and process—and, in many cases, the team members themselves—back into the traditional organization upon project completion. As a consequence, such tiger teams often become the birthplace of new business units or they experience unusually high turnover following project completion.

Senior managers often become nervous at the prospects of a tiger team because they are asked to delegate much more responsibility and control to the team and its project leader than under any of the other organization structures. Unless clear guidelines have been established in advance, it is extremely difficult during the project for senior managers to make mid-course corrections or exercise substantial influence without destroying the team. More than one team has "gotten away" from senior management and created major problems.

The Evolution of Development Organization

Because of the wide range of situations in which firms find themselves, it is not surprising that different organizations tend to gravitate toward one particular team structure as their dominant mode for doing development projects. While that dominant mode may evolve over time, at any point in time the procedures and systems in place in the organization encourage all projects to follow that same mode with only minor variations. Sometimes exceptions will be allowed when a project clearly requires something different than the dominant mode, but those will be viewed as exceptions.

It is interesting in this regard to refer back to the framework and six basic elements of project management discussed in Chapter 5. In that chapter, the project management approaches of four different firms—Kodak, General Electric, Motorola, and Lockheed Skunkworks—were described. Each of those is an example of one of the four types of development structures summarized in Exhibit 8–1. The Kodak MAP process is an effective form of the functional structure. The GE system of tollgates, with a heavy dose of senior management review and control, is a fairly effective form of the lightweight, or perhaps middleweight, team. The Motorola cross-functional contract approach is a particularly effective implementation of the heavyweight team. Finally, the skunkworks set-up at Lockheed is a clear illustration of the tiger or autonomous team. The history of each of these firms, their competitive environment, and their particular strategies have resulted in each choosing a different dominant mode for conducting its development activities. These patterns of choice and evolution can be generalized, and help to explain practices currently observed in a variety of firms and industries.

As discussed at the outset of this chapter, start-up firms typically focus their entire organization on a single development project. The characteristics of that environment and the mode in which they carry out development efforts are reflective of those described above for the autonomous or tiger team structure. In essence, the entire organization is on the team, and because of their small size, they are physically co-located and dedicated to this activity. Furthermore, because these organizations are new, those doing the work are given extensive leeway to define performance evaluation and reward systems and to create procedures and approaches that they think will be most effective in that development environment. They fully understand that if the primary project does not succeed, they will pay the consequences and will have no one to blame but themselves.

As a start-up firm grows and completes its initial handful of projects, it invariably faces the issue of how to balance operating needs (selling, producing, distributing, and servicing previously designed products using previously designed processes) with the need for ongoing product and process development efforts. The initial solution often is one that closely resembles a move toward a heavyweight team structure. Because the next development project (often a next-generation platform project) is so important, a strong functional or general manager is put in charge of it and the firm adjusts its fledgling functional organization to balance that heavyweight team. While the transition is not always smooth as different managers learn to share power and coexist, the organization is usually small enough that senior people quickly recognize when the balance needs to shift one way or the other, and take appropriate action. The result often is a successful sequence of major development efforts over a period of half a dozen or more years.

Depending on the maximum volume that a single platform product (and its related derivatives) can support, at some point the organization faces increasing pressure to develop multiple projects that will be done concurrently and in support of multiple product lines. For many firms this is a traumatic period, and in today's world it is often avoided by the single-product, five-to-ten-year-old organization selling out (being acquired) by a much larger, multiple-product line firm.

Whether or not the firm remains independent as it moves to multiple product lines, invariably a functional organization begins to dominate. After all, the functions have responsibility for sustaining the existing activities of the firm (which account for an increasingly large portion of the resources and influence on performance results), and it seems natural to divide up development responsibility among those functions. The result is an organization whose primary approach to development is the functional team structure. Over time, that structure and its associated project manager approach handles an increasing number of projects, a large portion of which are sustaining or derivative in nature. In fact, when major (platform) or breakthrough projects are called for, they are likely to be viewed as "development engineering projects" as opposed to true business projects. If the firm has continued to follow a competitive strategy of technical distinctiveness and superior features in its product performance, it seems natural that the functional team structure be applied in development.

For projects that are incremental and sustaining in nature, the functional structure is a comfortable approach, because the stable environment and the limited amount of change involved in such projects makes it relatively easy to subdivide tasks and to pass the project successfully from one function to another. Thus firms that have come to dominate their market—and often its associated technologies—may, for years and even decades, find the functional team structure very satisfactory for handling development efforts. However, if the rates of change in technology, competitive positions, and customer requirements accelerate, that functional team structure may be found wanting.

Mature organizations whose environments have shifted in recent years increasingly sense that their traditional functional structure is too slow, too costly, and not sufficiently customer-focused to compete with smaller, nimbler organizations who use tiger and heavyweight team structures to develop whole new product offerings and platforms. Not wanting to upset all of their existing procedures or discard what have been major strengths in their traditional functional team structure, they choose naturally to add lightweight project managers and liaisons in hopes of becoming faster, less costly, and more on target in their efforts. If they do find themselves imminently threatened on a substantial product line, they may complement this lightweight team structure with an occasional tiger team. However, for the majority of their development projects, they are anxious to make the lightweight team structure work, thereby overcoming some of the weaknesses of their traditional approach while maintaining its major strengths.

Depending on the evolution and duration of these higher rates of change, such mature organizations may find that creating a heavyweight team structure capability is the only way to effectively compete against their most focused, effective competitors. Furthermore, because the lightweight-heavyweight difference represents a continuum, they are able to move in that direction at whatever pace they find most appropriate. From our experience, this natural evolution helps explain the trends that can be observed in a wide range of industries with regard to approaches to project management.

The challenge for any single firm is to make sure that its dominant mode matches its environment and its strategic imperatives, and that the firm develops capabilities that allow it to apply alternative modes when those are deemed most appropriate for particular projects. To make the organization and leadership characteristics of their dominant approach fully effective also requires two other things. First is making sure that the types and mix or projects undertaken (a major topic discussed in Chapter 4) are indeed appropriate for their environment, and that the mix matches what they have selected as their dominant team structure. This was what happened at Motorola when they developed their cross-functional, contract team approach in the late 1980s. Prior to that time their approach had been largely functional, adding some lightweight project managers to help speed development efforts. During the mid 1980s, they discovered that next-generation platform projects were the key to their longer-term success, and that such projects required that a heavyweight team structure be developed and applied throughout the corporation.

The second thing an organization must do is make sure that its human resource selection, training, and development policies, as well as its organizational systems, provide the mix of skills in the quantities needed by the overall development strategy. As stated repeatedly in earlier chapters, development projects represent not only the application of those skills and abilities and the capturing of their value in the marketplace, but also the further enhancement and expansion of those development capabilities so that they will be available for future projects.

The Heavyweight Team Structure

In many popular and academic discussions of reducing time-to-market, or making major changes in design quality or development productivity, cross-functional, heavyweight teams often are an important part of the proposed solution. Teams offer improved communication, stronger identification with and commitment to the project, and a focus for cross-functional problem solving. The evidence suggests that when managed effectively, heavyweight teams can indeed bring significant advantage in improved development. Consider the experience of Motorola in developing its Bandit line of pagers.

The Bandit Pager: An Example of a Heavyweight Team

An excellent example of an effective heavyweight team structure was that used by the Motorola Communications Sector on the development of its "Bandit" pager.[4] The project charter was to develop an automated, onshore, profitable production operation for its high-volume Bravo pager line. (This is the belt-worn pager that Motorola sold from the mid 1980s into the early 1990s.) The core team on the Motorola Bandit project consisted of a heavyweight project leader and eight other individuals. These individuals, who were dedicated and co-located, represented industrial engineering, robotics, process engineering, procurement, and product design/Computer Integrated Manufacturing (CIM). The need for these functions was dictated by the nature of the Bandit platform automation project and its focus on manufacturing technology with a minimal change in product technology. In addition, a human resource person and an accounting/finance person were also part of the core team. The human resource person was particularly active early on as subteam positions were defined and jobs posted throughout Motorola's Communications Sector. Additionally, the human resource person played an important role as training and development of operating support people were needed later on. The accounting/finance person was invaluable in "costing out" different options and performing detailed

533

analysis of options and choices identified during the course of the project.

An eighth member of the core team was a Hewlett Packard employee. Hewlett Packard was chosen as the vendor for the "software backplane," providing an HP 3000 computer and the integrated software communication network that linked individual automated workstations together, downloaded controls and instructions during production operations, and captured quality and other operating performance data. Because of the importance of HP support to the success of the overall project, it was felt essential that they be represented on the core team.

Not only was this core team co-located, it was housed in a corner of the existing engineering/manufacturing facility used by Motorola Telecommunications in Boynton Beach, Florida. The team chose to enclose in glass the area where the automated production line was to be set up so that others in the factory would be able to track the progress on this project and, hopefully, be more willing to offer suggestions and adopt the lessons learned from it in their own production and engineering environments. The team chose to call their project "Bandit" to indicate their willingness to take ideas from literally anywhere.

The heavyweight project leader, Scott Shamlin, was described by team members as "a crusader," "a renegade," and "a workaholic." Shamlin became the champion for the Bandit effort. He was a hands-on manager with several years of experience in operations, and played a major role in stimulating and facilitating communication across functions. Moreover, he helped to articulate a vision of the Bandit line, and to infuse it into the detailed work of the project team. His goal was to make sure the new manufacturing process worked for the pager line, but would also provide real insight for many other production lines in Motorola's Communications Sector.

On the Motorola Bandit project, a contract book was created and signed early on by the core team members and senior management. The contract book provided the blueprint and work plan for the team's efforts. Initially, the team's executive sponsor—although not formally identified as such—was George Fisher, the Sector Executive. He made the original investment proposal to the board of directors and was an early champion and supporter, as well as direct supervisor in selecting the project leader and helping get the team underway. Subsequently, the vice president and general manager of the Paging Products division filled the role of executive sponsor.

Throughout the project, the heavyweight team took responsibility for the substance of its work, the means by which that work was accomplished, and the results that it provided. The overall results of the project were extremely satisfying to the team and to Motorola. The project was completed in eighteen months as per the contract book, and that represented about half the time of a normal project of such magnitude. In addition, the automated production operation was up and running with process tolerances of five sigma (referring to the degree of precision achieved by the manufacturing processes) at the completion of that eighteen-month period. Ongoing production verified that the cost objectives (substantially reduced direct costs and improved profit margins) had indeed been met, and product reliability was even higher than the standards already achieved on the offshore versions of the Bravo product. Finally, a variety of lessons were successfully transferred to other parts of the sector's operations, and additional heavyweight teams have proven the viability and robustness of the approach in Motorola's business and further refined its effectiveness as the dominant mode throughout the corporation.

The Challenge of Heavyweight Teams

Motorola's experience with the Bandit underscores the potential power available in the use of heavyweight teams. But the experience also makes clear that there is more to creating an effective heavyweight team capability than selecting a leader and forming a team. By their very nature—product (or process) focused, strong, independent leadership, broad skills and cross-functional perspective, clear mission—heavyweight teams create potential conflict with the functional organization and raise questions about the nature of senior management's influence and control. And even the advantages of the team approach bring with them potential disadvantages that may hurt development performance if not recognized and addressed.

Take, for example, the advantages of ownership and commitment. One of the most striking advantages of the heavyweight team is the ownership and commitment that arise among core team members, enabling tough issues to be addressed and major challenges to be overcome in a timely and effective fashion. Identifying with the product and creating a sense of esprit de corps motivates team members to extend themselves and do what needs to be done to help the team succeed. But such teams sometimes expand the definition of their role and the scope of the project, and get carried away with themselves and their abilities. We have seen heavyweight teams become autonomous tiger teams and go off on a tangent because senior executives gave insufficient direction and the bounds of the team were only vaguely specified at the outset. Even if the team stays focused, the rest of the organization may see themselves as "second class." Although the core team may not make that distinction explicit, it happens because the team has responsibilities and authority beyond those commonly given to functional team members. Thus, such projects can inadvertently become the "haves" and

535

other, smaller projects the "have-nots" with regard to key resources and management attention.

Support activities are particularly vulnerable to an excess of ownership and commitment. Often the heavyweight team will want to have the same control over secondary support activities as it does over the primary tasks performed by dedicated team members. When the heavyweight team has to wait for prototypes to be constructed, analytical tests to be performed, or quality assurance procedures to be conducted, their natural response is to "demand" top priority with the support organization or to be allowed to go outside and subcontract to independent groups. While these may sometimes be the appropriate choices, establishing make-buy guidelines and clear priorities that can be applied to all projects—perhaps changing service levels provided by support groups (rather than maintaining the traditional emphasis on resource utilization)—or having support groups provide capacity and advisory technical services but letting team members do more of the actual task work in those support areas may be other needed changes. Whatever the particular actions the organization takes, the challenge is to achieve a balance between the needs of the individual project and the needs of the broader organization.

Much the same is true of the advantage the heavyweight team brings in the integration and integrity it provides through a system solution to a set of customer needs. Getting all of the components and subsystems to complement one another and to address effectively the fundamental requirements of the core customer segment can result in a winning platform product and/or process. The team achieves an effective system design by using generalist skills applied by broadly trained team members, with fewer specialists and, on occasion, less depth in individual component solutions and technical problem solving.

But the lack of depth may disclose a disadvantage. Some of the individual components or subassemblies may not attain the same level of technical excellence they would under a more traditional functional team structure. For instance, in the case of an automobile, generalists often can develop a windshield wiper system that is extremely complementary and integrated with the total car system and its core concept. But they also may embed in their windshield wiper design some potential weaknesses or flaws that might have been caught by a functional team of specialists who had designed a long series of windshield wipers. To counter this potential disadvantage, many organizations have found that more testing of completed units is required to discover such possible flaws, and that review of components and subassemblies by expert specialists may be very worthwhile. In some cases, the quality assurance function has expanded its role to make sure sufficient technical specialists review designs at appropriate points so that such weaknesses can be minimized.

Managing the Challenges of Heavyweight Teams

Problems with depth in technical solutions and allocations of support resources suggest the tension that exists between heavyweight teams and the functional groups where much of the work gets done. The problem with the teams exceeding their bounds reflects in part how teams manage themselves, in part how boundaries are set, and in part the ongoing relationship between the team and senior management. Dealing with these issues requires the development of mechanisms and practices that reinforce the basic thrust of the team—ownership, focus, system architecture, integrity—and yet improve the team's ability to take advantage of the strengths of the supporting functional organization—technical depth, consistency across projects, senior management direction. We have grouped the mechanisms and problems into six categories of management action: the project charter, the contract, staffing, leadership, team responsibility, and the executive sponsor.

The Project Charter. A heavyweight project team needs a clear mission. One way to capture that mission in a concise way is in an explicit, measurable project charter. Such a charter sets broad performance objectives and usually is articulated even before the core team is selected; thus, joining the core team includes accepting the charter established by senior management. A typical charter for a heavyweight project would be the following;

> "The resulting product will be selected and ramped by Company XYZ during Quarter 4 of calendar year 1991, at a minimum of a 20% gross margin."

This charter is representative of an industrial products firm whose product goes into a system sold by its customers. Company XYZ is the leading customer for a certain family of products, and this project is focused on developing the next-generation platform offering in that family.

The argument for this team charter is that if the heavyweight program results in that platform product being chosen by the leading customer in the segment by a certain date and at a certain gross margin, it will have demonstrated that the next-generation platform is not only viable, but likely to be very successful over the next three to five years. Projects and settings for which such a charter might be appropriate would include a microprocessor being developed for a new computer system, a diesel engine being developed for the heavy equipment industry, or a certain type of slitting and folding piece of equipment being developed for the newspaper printing press industry. Even in a medical diagnostics business with hundreds of customers, a charter that sets a goal of "capturing 30 percent of market purchases in the second twelve months during which the product is offered" sets a clear charter for the team. The objective is to have a clear project charter that will set appropriate expectations as to the nature of success for that effort.

The Contract Book. A charter lays out the mission in broad terms. The contract book defines, in detail, the basic plan to achieve the stated goal. Creating a contract book occurs at the outset, as soon as the core team and heavyweight project leader have been designated and given the project charter by senior management. While it can take a variety of forms, the concept is that the team develops its own detailed work plan by which it will conduct the project, it estimates the resources that will be required, and it outlines the results that will be achieved. The contract book thus elaborates on how the team plans to achieve the chartered performance, and what resources it will require. The table of contents of a typical heavyweight team contract book is shown in Exhibit 8–3. Such documents range from twenty-five to a hundred pages, depending on the complexity of the project and level of detail desired by the team and senior management before proceeding. A common practice following negotiation and acceptance of this contract between the team and senior management is for the individuals from both groups to sign the contract book as an indication of their commitment to honor the plan and achieve those results.

The core team may take anywhere from a long week to a few months to create and complete the contract book. The duration depends on the experience of the team, the expectations of senior management, and the level of detail being pursued. As indicated in Chapter 6, Motorola, after several years of experience, decided that a maximum of seven days should be allowed for this activity. Having watched other heavyweight teams—particularly in organizations with no prior experience in using such a structure—take up to several months, we can appreciate why Motorola has nicknamed this the "blitz phase" and decided that the time allowed should be kept to a minimum.

Staffing. As suggested in Exhibit 8–1, a heavyweight team includes a group of core cross-functional team members who are dedicated (and usually physically co-located) for the duration of the development effort. Typically there is one core team member from each primary function of the organization; for instance, in several electronics firms we have observed core teams consisting of six functional participants—design engineering, marketing, quality assurance, manufacturing, finance, and

EXHIBIT 8–3

Heavyweight Team Contract Book—Major Sections*

- Executive Summary

- Business Plan and Purposes

- Development Plan

  – Schedule
  – Materials
  – Resources

- Product Design Plan

- Quality Plan

- Manufacturing Plan

- Project Deliverables

- Performance Measurement and Incentives

* The contract book for a heavyweight team contains detailed plans and objectives for the project, including the time table, resource requirements, and product performance specifications. Often this twenty-five- to one-hundred-page document is signed by the six to eight core team members and senior management.

---

human resources. Individually, core team members represent their functions and provide leadership for their function's inputs to the project. Collectively, they constitute a management team that works under the direction of the heavyweight project manager and takes responsibility for managing the overall development effort.

While frequently there are other participants—especially from design engineering early on and manufacturing later on—who may be dedicated to such a heavyweight team for several months, those participants usually are not made part of the core team that provides guidance and overall direction for the effort. However, they may well be co-located and, over time, develop the same level of ownership and commitment to the project as those on the core team. The primary difference is that the core team members help manage the total project and the coordination and integration of individual functional efforts, whereas other dedicated team members work primarily within a single function or subfunction.

The question is often raised as to whether these dedicated team members—who may be working full-time on the project for several months—are actually part of the core team. Different firms choose to handle this issue in different ways, but those with considerable experience tend to distinguish between core and other dedicated (and often

539

co-located) team members. The difference between the two groups is one of management responsibility for the core group that is not shared equally by the others. Also, it is primarily the half a dozen members of the core group who will be dedicated throughout the duration of the project, with other subfunctional contributors having a portion of their time reassigned to other projects before this heavyweight project is fully completed.

Additionally, whether physical co-location is essential is often questioned in such teams. We have seen it work both ways. Given the complexity of development projects, and especially the uncertainty and ambiguity often associated with major projects like those assigned to heavyweight teams, physical co-location has several advantages over even the best of on-line communication approaches. With physical co-location, real-time problems that arise are much more likely to be addressed effectively with all of the functions represented and present than when they are separate and must either wait for a periodic meeting or use remote communication links to open up cross-functional discussions.

A final issue often raised is whether an individual can be a core team member on more than one heavyweight team at the same time. If the rule for a core team member is that 80 percent or more of his or her time must be spent on the heavyweight project, then the answer to this question is no. Frequently, however, a choice must be made between someone being on two core teams—for example, from the finance or human resource function—or putting a different individual on one of those teams who has neither the experience nor stature to be a full peer with the other core team members. In the majority of cases we have seen, experienced organizations opt to put the same person on two teams to ensure the peer relationship and level of contribution required, even though it means having one person on two teams and with two desks. They then work diligently to develop other people in the function so that multiple team assignments will not be necessary in the future.

Sometimes multiple assignments will also be justified on the basis that a function such as finance does not need a full-time person on a project. In most instances, however, there are a variety of potential value-adding tasks that are broader than finance's traditional contribution. A person largely dedicated to the core team will search for those opportunities and the project will be better because of it. The risk of allowing core team members to be assigned to multiple projects is that they will not be available when their inputs are most needed, nor will they be as committed to project success as their peers. They become secondary core team members, and the full potential of the heavyweight team structure fails to be realized.

Project Leadership. Heavyweight teams require a distinctive style of leadership.[5] A number of differences between lightweight and heavyweight project managers were highlighted in Exhibit 8–2. Three of those are particularly distinctive. First, heavyweight project leaders manage, lead, and evaluate other members of the core team. They are also the persons to whom the core team reports throughout the project's duration. Another distinctive aspect of heavyweight team leaders is that, rather than being neutral or a facilitator with regard to substantive issues requiring problem solving and conflict resolution, they are concept champions. That is, they see themselves as championing the basic core concept around which the platform product and/or process is being shaped. They make sure that those who work on subtasks of the project understand the core concept. Thus they play a central role in ensuring the system integrity of the final product and/or process.

Finally, the heavyweight project manager carries out his or her role in a very different fashion than the lightweight project manager. Most lightweights spend the bulk of their time working at a desk, with paper. They revise schedules, get frequent updates, and encourage people to meet previously agreed upon deadlines. The heavyweight project manager spends little time at a desk, is out talking to project contributors, and makes sure that decisions are made and implemented whenever and wherever needed. Some of the ways in which the heavyweight project manager achieves project results are highlighted by the five roles illustrated in Exhibit 8–4 for a heavyweight project manager on a platform development project in the auto industry.

The *first role* of the heavyweight project manager is to provide for the team a direct interpretation of the market and customer needs. This involves gathering market data directly from customers, dealers, and industry shows, as well as through systematic study and contact with the firm's marketing organization. A *second role* is to become a multilingual translator, not just taking marketing information to the various functions involved in the project, but being fluent in the language of each of those functions and making sure the translation and communication going on among the functions—particularly between customer needs and product specifications—are done effectively.

A *third role* is the direct engineering manager, orchestrating, directing, and coordinating the various engineering subfunctions. Because of the size of auto development programs and the number of types of engineering disciplines that must be brought to bear, it is essential in a heavyweight structure that the project manager be able to work directly with each of those engineering subfunctions on a day-to-day basis and ensure that their work will indeed integrate and support that of others and serve to execute effectively the chosen product concept.

A *fourth role* is best described as staying in motion: out of the office

EXHIBIT 8—4

The Heavyweight Project Manager

Role	Description
Direct Market Interpreter	Gathers firsthand information from customers, distributor visits, industry shows; has own marketing budget, market study team, direct contact and discussions with customers
Multilingual Translator	Fluency in language of customers, engineers, marketers, stylists; translator between customer experience/requirements and engineering specifications
"Direct" Engineering Manager	Orchestra conductor, evangelist of conceptual integrity and coordinator of component development; direct eye-to-eye discussions with working-level engineers; shows up in drafting room, looks over engineers' shoulders
Program Manager "in motion"	Out of the office, not too many meetings, not too much paperwork, face-to-face communication, conflict resolution manager
Concept Infuser	Concept guardian, confronts conflicts, not only reacts but implements own philosophy; ultimate decision maker, coordination of details and creation of harmony

conducting face-to-face sessions, and highlighting and resolving potential conflicts as soon as possible. A *final role* is that of concept champion. Here the heavyweight project manager becomes the guardian of the concept and not only reacts and responds to the interests of others, but also sees that the choices made are consistent and in harmony with the basic concept. This requires a careful blend of communication and teaching skills so that individual contributors and their groups understand the core concept, and then sufficient concept and conflict resolution skills to ensure that tough issues are raised and addressed in a timely fashion.

It should be apparent from this description that heavyweight project managers earn the respect and right to carry out these roles based on prior experience, carefully developed skills, and status earned over time, rather than simply being endowed through a designation on the part of senior management. A qualified leader who can play those roles as a heavyweight project manager is a prerequisite to an effective heavyweight team structure.

Team Member Responsibilities. People who serve on a heavyweight team have responsibilities that extend beyond their usual functional assign-

Exhibit 8–5
Responsibilities of Heavyweight Core Team Members*
Functional Hat Accountabilities

• Ensuring functional expertise on the project
• Representing the functional perspective on the project
• Ensuring that subobjectives are met that depend on their function
• Ensuring that functional issues impacting the team are raised proactively within the team

Team Hat Accountabilities

• Sharing responsibility for team results
• Reconstituting tasks and content
• Establishing reporting and other organizational relationships
• Participating in monitoring and improving team performance
• Sharing responsibility for ensuring effective team processes
• Examining issues from an executive point of view
  (answering the question, "Is this the appropriate business response for the company?")
• Understanding, recognizing, and responsibly challenging the boundaries of the project
  and team process

  * The six to eight core team members of a heavyweight development team have two types of responsibility. One is that of representing their function and ensuring that the project tasks associated with their function are completed as planned. The other is that of helping to manage the team's activities and ensuring that the commitments made in the contract book are met.

---

ment. As illustrated in Exhibit 8–5, these are of two primary types. Functional hat responsibilities are those accepted by the individual core team member as a representative of their function. For example, the core team member from marketing is responsible for ensuring that appropriate marketing expertise is brought to bear on the project, that a marketing perspective is provided on all key issues of the project, that project subobjectives dependent on the marketing function are met in a timely fashion, and that marketing issues that impact other functions are raised proactively within the team. Each core team member wears a functional hat which makes him or her the focal point and manager responsible for a function that delivers its unique contribution to the overall project.

But each core team member also wears a team hat. In addition to representing his or her function, each core team member accepts responsibility for overall team results. In this role, the core team shares responsibility with the heavyweight project manager for the development procedures followed by the team, and for the overall results that those procedures deliver. The core team is accountable for the success of the project, and can blame no one but itself if it fails to manage the project, execute the tasks, and deliver the performance agreed upon at the outset.

543

What is unique in the core team members' responsibilities is not so much their accountability for tasks in their own function, but the fact that they are responsible for how those tasks are subdivided, organized, and accomplished. Unlike the traditional functional team structure, which takes as given the subdivision of tasks and the means by which those tasks will be conducted and completed, the core heavyweight team is given the power and responsibility to change the substance of those tasks when doing so will improve the performance of the project. Since this is a role that core team members do not play under a lightweight or functional team structure, it is often the most difficult for them to accept fully and learn to apply. It is essential, however, if the heavyweight team is to realize its full potential. Often core team members came to view these new skills as a major contribution to their career and its development.

The Executive Sponsor. With so much more accountability delegated to the project team, it is not surprising that establishing effective relationships with senior management requires special mechanisms. The need is for senior management to retain the ability to guide the project and its leader, while empowering the team to lead and act. The definition of such a person is an executive sponsor. This sponsor takes on the role of coach and mentor for the heavyweight project leader and core team, and seeks to maintain close, ongoing contact with the team's efforts. Typically such a sponsor might be the vice president of engineering, marketing, or manufacturing for the business unit. In addition to serving as a coach for the team, the executive sponsor serves as a liaison through which other members of the executive staff must work in interfacing with the team. If other members of senior management have concerns or inputs to voice or need current information on project status, communication takes place through the executive sponsor. This reduces the number of mixed signals received by the team and clarifies for the organization the reporting and evaluation relationship between the team and senior management. It also increases the burden on the assigned executive sponsor to set appropriate limits and bounds on the team so that organizational surprises are avoided.

Often the executive sponsor and team find it useful to identify and distinguish those areas where the team clearly has decision-making power and control and need not check with their executive sponsor before moving ahead from areas where other organizational concerns require review. In one electronics firm that has used heavyweight teams for some time, one of the early meetings between the executive sponsor and the core team focuses on generating a list of areas where the executive sponsor expects to provide oversight and be consulted because those areas are of great concern to the entire executive staff and represent areas where team actions may well raise policy issues for the larger organization. In this firm, areas over which the executive staff want to maintain some control include:

- Resource commitment—head count, fixed costs, expenses outside the approved project plan
- Pricing for major customers and major accounts
- Potential slips in major milestone dates (the executive sponsor wants early warning and recovery plans)
- Plans for the transition from development project to operating status
- Thorough reviews at major milestones or every three months, whichever occurs sooner
- Review of incentive rewards that have company-wide implications for consistency and equity
- Cross-project issues such as resource optimization, prioritization, and balance.

Identifying these areas of potential concern at the outset can help the executive sponsor and the core team better carry out their assigned responsibilities. It also helps other executives feel more comfortable working through the executive sponsor when they have concerns, since they know these "boundary issues" have been articulated and are jointly understood.

The Necessity of Fundamental Change

Compared to a traditional functional organization, creating a team that is "heavy," a team with effective leadership, strong problem-solving skills and, the ability to integrate across functions, requires basic changes in the way development works. But it also requires change in the fundamental behavior of engineers, designers, and marketers in their day-to-day work. A comparison of two development teams, each working in the computer industry, illustrates the depth of change required to realize fully the power of the heavyweight team.

The two teams, A and B, launched the development of a small computer system, each aimed at a different market at about the same time. Both teams had market introduction targets within the next twelve months. By chance, both products were to use an identical, custom-designed microprocessor chip in addition to other unique and standard chips.

The situation[6] illustrating the nature of the challenge in creating an effective heavyweight team structure where none had existed previously arose when each team sent this identical, custom-designed chip—call it "supercontroller"—to the vendor for pilot production. Initially, the vendor quoted a twenty-week turnaround to both teams. At the time of the quote, the supercontroller chip was already on the critical path for Team B, with a planned turnaround of eleven weeks. Thus, every week saved on that chip would save one week in the overall project schedule. Furthermore, Team B already was anticipating that it would be late in meeting its initial market introduction target date. When the twenty-week vendor lead time issue first came up in a Team B meeting, Jim, the core team member from engineering, reported that they were working on accelerating the delivery date, but that the vendor was a large company known for its slowness. Suggestions from other core team members on how to accelerate the delivery were politely rebuffed, including one suggestion to have a senior executive contact their counterpart at the vendor. While Team B's Company did considerable business with the chip vendor, Jim did not consider that suggestion promising.

For Team A, the original quote of a twenty-week turnaround still left a little slack, and thus initially the supercontroller chip was not on the critical path. Within a couple of weeks, however, other changes in the activities and schedule put this chip on Team A's critical path, and the issue received immediate attention. When raised at the team's weekly meeting, Fred, the core team member from manufacturing, stated that he thought the turnaround time quoted was too long and that he would try to reduce it. At the next meeting of Team A, Fred brought some good news: through discussions with the vendor, he had been able to get a commitment that pulled in the delivery of the supercontroller chip by eleven weeks! That is, rather than the original twenty-week quote, the vendor was now willing to assure a nine-week cycle. Furthermore, Fred thought that the quote might be reduced even further by a phone call from one of the company's senior manufacturing executives to a contact of his at the vendor. Jim and Fred clearly had different approaches to solving the same problem. But what makes this episode so instructive is that Teams A and B (and Jim and Fred) were in the same company. Not only were they in the same company, but the company had developed a structure for project management, including guidelines on roles and responsibilities of team members. Thus, Jim and Fred worked in the same basic system. But their approaches were very different. Consider what happened shortly after Jim obtained the new commitment from the vendor.

Two days later, Team B held one of its regular team meetings. The supercontroller chip again came up during the status review, and no change from the original schedule was identified. Since the finance person, Ann, served on both teams and had been present at Team A's meeting, she told Team B that Team A had reduced the cycle time from twenty to nine weeks. Jim responded that the core team was aware that Team A had made such efforts, but that the information concerning nine weeks was not correct, and that the original twenty-week delivery date still held. Furthermore, Jim indicated that Fred's efforts (on behalf of Team A) had caused some disruption internally, and in the future it was important that Team A not take such initiatives before coordinating with Team B. Jim stated that this was particularly true when an outside vendor was involved, and closed the topic by saying that a meeting to clear up the situation would be held that afternoon with Fred from Team A and Team B's engineering and purchasing people.

The next afternoon there was a Team A meeting which Ann attended. At that meeting Fred confirmed the accelerated delivery schedule for the supercontroller chip. Eleven weeks had indeed been clipped out of the schedule to the benefit of both Teams A and B. At a subsequent Team B meeting, Jim confirmed the new schedule for Team B. Curious about the differences in perspective, Ann decided to learn more about this situation. On the one hand, Team A had identified an obstacle and removed it from its path; Team B had identified an identical obstacle and failed to move it at all.

In a follow-up discussion with Ann, Fred pointed out that the Team B person negotiating with the vendor was the engineering manager responsible for development of the supercontroller chip. That manager knew the chip's technical requirements, but had little experience dealing with chip vendors. (He had long been a specialist in circuit design.) Without that experience, he had a hard time pushing back against the vendor's "standard line." Fred's manufacturing experience with several chip vendors enabled him to calibrate the vendor's dates against his best-case experience and extract an earlier commitment.

Fred's experience, therefore, told him that the vendor's initial commitment did not make sense. But there was more. Fred had also bought into the team's charter, and the long lead time on the supercontroller chip stood in the way of the team's success. So, Fred went after it and figured out how to get it off the critical path. In contrast, Jim—who had worked in the traditional functional organization for many years—saw vendor relations on a pilot build as his job, but did not see getting the vendor to shorten the cycle time as his responsibility, or even within the range of his authority. He was more concerned with avoiding conflict and not disturbing the water than with achieving the overarching goal of the team.

It is interesting to note that in the case of Team B, engineering raised the issue, and, while unwilling to take aggressive steps to resolve it, also blocked the resolution of the issue on the part of others. In Team A, however, while the issue came up initially through engineering, it was Fred in manufacturing who proactively went after it. In the case of Team B, getting a prototype chip returned from a vendor was still being treated as an "engineering responsibility," whereas in the case of Team A, it was treated as a "team responsibility." Since Fred was the person best qualified to attack that issue, he did so.

Both Team A and Team B had a charter, a contract, a co-located core team staffed with generalists, a project leader, articulated responsibilities, and an executive sponsor. Yet Jim's and Fred's understanding of what these things meant for them personally and for the team at the detailed, working level was quite different. While the teams had been through similar training and team start-up processes, Jim apparently saw the new approach as a different organizational framework within which work would get done as before. Fred seemed to see it as an opportunity to work in a different way—to take responsibility for reconfiguring tasks, drawing skills, and resources, where required, for getting the job done in the best way possible.

Although both teams were "heavyweight" in theory, Fred's team was much "heavier" in its operation and impact. Heaviness, then, is not just a matter of structure and mechanism, but of attitudes and behavior. Firms that try to create heavyweight teams without making the deep changes needed to realize the power in the team's structure will find the team approach problematic. Those intent on using teams for platform projects and willing to make the basic changes we have discussed here, will enjoy the advantages of focus, integration and effectiveness.

Building Capability for Multiple Approaches

Not all projects that firms undertake require the creation of a dedicated cross-functional heavyweight team. Heavyweight teams may be highly effective for platforms or next-generation development, but they approach overkill for those projects so small that only a few engineers need to work on the project. Others may require a significant technical advance, or involve the creation of a whole new business. Indeed, we can easily imagine a situation in which the firm would need capability in all four of the project organization types that we have discussed in this chapter.

But creating a portfolio of approaches is complicated by the tendency for development organizations to adopt a dominant orientation or a standard approach to leadership and organization. That dominant orientation in firms determines what is easy and likely to work, and what is hard and likely to be less effective. It thus determines the range of approaches and projects the firm can hope to apply and carry out.

In the four models of development organization we presented in this chapter, two represent a dominant orientation—the functional structure, and the heavyweight team. Firms whose basic systems, skills, practices, and mechanisms are functional, for example, will find it relatively easy to implement lightweight teams. The lightweight setup is largely functional with an overlay of light coordination. Moving to a heavyweight team, however, is much more difficult, and is unlikely to be fully successful if the functional structure remains the dominant orientation. Like Jim and Team A, a functional orientation runs deep and affects behavior in subtle ways, ways that make a heavyweight structure difficult. Without basic changes in systems, practices, attitudes, and behaviors, attempts to add a heavyweight team capability in what is essentially a functional organization may create a "middleweight" approach, but are unlikely to build a true heavyweight team.

In contrast, firms that have teams as their dominant orientation and have built their systems, training efforts, communication structures, and patterns of leadership around heavyweight teams, will find it relatively easy to implement autonomous tiger teams. And unlike the functional structure, they will find it possible to work a lightweight and functional approach as well. Because the heavyweight team has a functional organization carrying out detailed work and support activities, carrying out lightweight projects or even functional projects involves adjustments in the standard approach (e.g., teams are not dedicated or co-located, task structure is defined by function rather than team) instead of adding new activities or capabilities that conflict with the established system. Of course, the lightweight teams are likely to be somewhat "heavier" than if the dominant orientation were functional. But that may have positive consequences as well.

The experience of Chaparral Steel illustrates the challenge and the advantages of building capability for several approaches to development.[7] Located in Midlothian, Texas, thirty miles south of Dallas, by the early 1990s Chaparral was producing well over a million tons per year of steel products used in forging (high alloy) and construction (structural) products. Using an electric furnace, a continuous caster, and a rolling mill to convert steel scrap into various milled products, Chaparral had continued to improve its performance through a variety of product and process development efforts. Chaparral defined three types of projects: major advanced development, platform, and incremental. Projects of the first type might require an expenditure of $3–$5 million over a period of three to five years, but would provide a breakthrough product or process. Platform projects might require $500,000 to $1 million in development expenses and take twelve to twenty-four months to execute. Incremental projects typically incurred development expenditures of $100,000–$200,000 dollars, lasted a couple of months, and provided very quick payback. At any point in time, the organization might have forty or fifty development projects underway, of which no more than a couple would be major advanced development efforts, perhaps three to five would be platform efforts, and the remainder would be incremental efforts.

Because of the cost competitiveness of their industry and the operating demands required for profitable products and processes, Chaparral conducts all of its development efforts on its factory floor and staffs them primarily with line people. However, the team structure and project leadership used for each of the three types varies considerably. The incremental projects are almost all done by functional subgroups with a lightweight project manager. However, with so many projects going on and projects being so common, everyone understands the role of the lightweight project manager and wants to be supportive: they know, at some point, they will be one of those lightweight project managers and will desire the same kind of treatment. Thus the support and cooperation provided to lightweight project managers tends to be substantially greater than in many traditional functional organizations. The platform projects are headed up by heavyweight project managers who have probably been a department manager and, following completion of the platform effort, will go back to being a department manager. The advanced development projects are put under the direction of one of seven general foreman who report directly to the vice president of manufacturing (or one of the other vice presidents). These major projects start as advanced development efforts; once technical feasibility is proven they quickly become breakthrough projects, but with little or no change in team composition.

For Chaparral, this mix of approaches has served it well in satisfying the range of development opportunities and challenges faced in their business. Depending on the mix of technical depth, coordination and integration of known tasks, the level of system integration, and the degree of breakthrough and new thinking required, Chaparral can pick a team structure, a project manager, and an overall management approach that makes sense for the situation. Expectations have been established over more than a decade and thus procedures and approaches—as well as their governing principles—are well known throughout the organization.

It thus appears that the central choice is whether the firm wants the capability to run effective heavyweight teams in its development portfolio. If so, it must create the heavyweight team as its dominant orientation. With a functional orientation, the firm's effective capabilities will range from a functional structure to "middleweight" systems. Tiger teams could also exist as a wholly independent, separate activity. With heavyweight teams as the dominant orientation, the firm's capabilities could range from the tiger team to the functional structure, although steps then must be taken to ensure that the team orientation does not limit the depth of technical skill developed in the functional organization.

Study Questions

1. Of the four types of development teams summarized in Exhibit 8–1, what type most accurately characterizes the MEI 2010 effort? What were the strengths and weaknesses of that approach for the 2010? Is there another type of development team that you think would have been more appropriate? Which one? Why?
2. If an organization has been using the lightweight team structure for a few years, what do you think they would find particularly difficult about a move to a heavyweight team structure? For example, what would such a move mean for the functional heads? For senior management? For the project leader? For core team members?
3. If an organization has recently gone from a functional to a lightweight team structure, why might they tend to jump to an autonomous team on major projects, rather than pursuing the heavyweight option? What are the pros and cons of using the autonomous team structure on a project ideally suited for a heavyweight structure?
4. This chapter outlines six elements used by Motorola and others in implementing heavyweight teams—a project charter, a contract book, dedicated co-located staffing, a heavyweight leader, broad team member responsibilities, and an executive sponsor. If any one of these six elements were dropped, what would the impact be? Why?
5. What risks do you think senior management would most need to guard against when moving from a lightweight to a heavyweight structure? Use the Motorola Bandit pager example to illustrate the specifics of those risks and their potential impact.
6. The illustration of the integrated circuit needed by Teams A and B at the computer firm suggests the fundamental changes required in individual behavior to make heavyweight teams fully effective. Do you think senior management should have gotten involved to avoid those problems? Why or why not? To make sure that both teams solved the problem quickly and efficiently? Using that situation as an example, what guidelines might you suggest for achieving the proper balance between top management direction and individual team initiative and responsibility?
7. What do you think would be the challenges in developing two different structures and modes for conducting development projects within a single organization? What might management do to ensure that both become established and remain viable?

Quantum Corporation: Business and Product Teams

The April 1991 announcement of Quantum Corporation's fiscal 1991 financial performance capped a remarkable five years for the Milpitas, California-based manufacturer of rigid disk drives. Quantum had logged $878 million in revenues—up 627% over its 1987 level—and net earnings had shot up from $9 to $74 million, boosting it from ninth to third place among the world's independent disk drive manufacturers. "I think our decision in 1989 to manage through business teams was a key to this growth," reflected Dave Brown, Quantum's vice chairman and chief operating officer. "The major questions now are whether we have enough people in the company who have the talent and training to staff the number of teams we'll need in the future, and what the relationships among the teams ought to be."

Company Background

Quantum Corporation was founded in 1980 to manufacture and market a four-model product line of 10-, 20-, 30-, and 40-megabyte (Mb) 8-inch Winchester disk drives for minicomputer manufacturers such as DEC, and makers of sophisticated multiuser word processor systems such as Xerox and Wang. Quantum's first products were well received, and sales reached $119 million by 1985. But a 1985 decision to integrate the

---

This case was prepared by doctoral candidate Clayton Christensen; selected data about Quantum Corporation's products, employees, and markets are disguised to protect information which is proprietary to the company.

Copyright © 1992 by the President and Fellows of Harvard College. Harvard Business School Case 692–023.

technologies further—especially the disk drive controller and the system interface—led to the launch of a line of lower cost (and subsequently lower priced) drives targeted at the rapidly growing multiuser micro-computer and workstation market. This strategy moved Quantum to-ward new customers, higher unit volumes, and smaller form-factor, or diameter (5.25-inch) drives, and proved disastrous. Quantum was late to market with its new designs, and its product employed a nonstand-ard interface not readily accepted by most PC manufacturers. As a re-sult, sales and profits tumbled as its initial 8-inch products aged.

The company was saved from total failure, however, by a subsidiary firm, Plus Development Corporation, whose Hardcard® product—a 3.5-inch hard disk drive (initially with a capacity of 10 Mb)—was sold di-rectly to PC owners through computer retailers and direct-mail marketers. Matsushita Kotobuki Electronics Industries, Ltd. (MKE), a leading manufacturer of video cassette recorders, produced Hardcard in one of its plants in southern Japan. Plus's rapidly growing revenues in the 1985–1988 period offset the evaporating sales of the original Quan-tum OEM (original equipment manufacturer) business. (See Exhibit 1.)

In 1988, Quantum bought the 20% of Plus's shares it did not already own, and two Plus executives, Steve Berkley and Dave Brown, became Quantum's new chairman/CEO and president/COO, respectively. Plus was kept a wholly owned, independently managed subsidiary. The bal-ance of Quantum's business, consisting of sales, to original equipment computer manufacturers, became known internally as "Quantum OEM."

Quantum's new management team saw the opportunity to build upon Plus's technological experience in 3.5-inch disk drive design by devel-oping a new family of small form-factor, high-capacity products for the rapidly growing OEM market for engineering workstations and high-end desktop personal computers. In late 1988, Quantum announced it would stop developing and manufacturing all 5.25-inch products and replace them with 3.5-inch disk drives of comparable capacities. Quan-tum also decided to phase out its Puerto Rico manufacturing operations and source the majority of its drives from MKE. The results were dra-matic. Whereas two-thirds of Quantum's 1988 revenues (and all of its OEM sales) had come from 5.25-inch products, in 1989 it derived 100% of its revenues from 3.5-inch products. The company continued this strong momentum in fiscal 1990 and 1991.

Preparations for Continued Growth

Between 1988 and 1991, senior management launched three initiatives to reinforce Quantum's OEM momentum in the face of factors which they

EXHIBIT 1

Selected Financial Data, Fiscal Years Ending March 31, 1982 to 1991 ($ in millions)

	1982	1983	1984	1985	1986	1987	1988	1989	1990	1991
Summary Income Statement:										
Quantum Revenues	$13.7	$41.8	$67.1	$120.3	$121.2	$ 47.8	$120.5	—	—	—
Plus Development Revenues						73.0	66.0	—	—	—
Total Reported Revenues	13.7	41.8	67.1	120.3	121.2	120.8	186.5	$208.0	$446.3	$887.7
Gross Margins	3.3	18.3	26.0	46.6	48.3	41.5	38.5	59.8	131.7	215.9
Operating Profit	.2	11.9	15.8	28.8	21.5	6.8	(11.9)	12.4	67.8	108.3
Profit After Tax	.2	7.8	10.7	21.0	22.2	8.8	(3.2)	12.9	47.2	73.9
Summary Balance Sheet										
Cash		20.8	18.7	47.0	78.0	65.6	59.1	50.9	79.3	139.6
Total Assets		56.6	74.8	99.5	107.2	137.3	141.7	157.0	243.2	497.5
Long-term Debt		0	0	0	0	0	0	0	0	0
Total Liabilities		8.1	14.5	17.1	20.3	29.2	27.7	56.9	89.6	259.2
Equity		48.5	57.9	82.4	86.9	108.1	114.0	100.1	153.6	238.3

believed would characterize the disk drive industry in the 1990s: shortened lead times, stiffer competition, and slower market growth. Dave Brown played a leadership role as the organization pursued all three.

The first initiative was to reduce the time required to define, engineer, and produce new products in volume. As strong competitors' product lines overlapped across a broadened range of the capacity spectrum, Brown felt it would be increasingly difficult to sustain an enduring competitive advantage around performance-differentiated products. Although he was confident that the Quantum/MKE design engineering and manufacturing teams could continue to offer the best price/performance products in the industry, the period during which a new Quantum product could retain a performance edge before being leapfrogged by a competitor was shortening dramatically.

Quantum's OEM customers were accelerating their own development cycles, and the time during which they would evaluate and select the disk drive for a new computer system was also becoming increasingly short—opening and closing within a few months. Being even a few weeks late in product development could cost tens of millions of dollars in lost revenues and lower margins on whatever sales Quantum could make on a late product. From the industry's early days, disk drive prices had been falling about 5% per quarter. "The price will decline on you whether your product is in the market, in the factory getting the production bugs worked out, or in the development lab waiting for a new chip to come in from a vendor," reflected a Quantum marketing manager. This effectively meant that if Quantum could shave three months off its time-to-market cycle, not only could it garner revenues and profits from each product for an additional three months, but its average price realization over the life of each product would increase 5% as well.

The second initiative was to broaden the product line and provide customers with both follow-on generation product plans and currently competitive products. In addition to expanding the number of models targeted to the single-user PC and workstation markets from 10 to 27, Quantum in 1989 initiated development of a high-capacity family of drives for multiuser workstations and file servers. An additional program to develop smaller, lower-cost 2.5-inch drives targeted at the rapidly emerging notebook computer market was launched in 1990.

The third initiative was to push decision making lower into the company, and to begin managing critical programs through a team approach. Brown could remember sitting in an executive staff[1] meeting in late 1987 and asking why they were not shipping a particular product.

---

[1] "The Quantum OEM executive staff consisted of COO Dave Brown and the vice presidents of each of the company's functions: Engineering, Marketing, Operations, Quality, Finances, and Human Resources.

To get at the answer, he had to start wading through all the details about whether enough components had been ordered, enough capacity put in place, the right forecasts provided, and so on. After that discussion, he realized management was part of the problem. "We were trying to manage details we weren't knowledgeable about. We had a bandwidth problem—the executive staff just didn't have enough time or brain capacity to keep making all the key decisions. To maintain our growth, we had to push decision-making down into the organization, to the levels where the most informed people were."

Quantum had tried team-level coordination before. In 1985, the company promoted an experienced manager and charged him to manage development of a key family of 5.25-inch drives by coordinating the work of functional employees. In retrospect, the attempt failed at least in part because the project was extremely ambitious technically, and in part because the project leader had a hub-and-spoke management style—all information and decision-making flowed through him. In 1988, the company hired from outside a senior manager with program management experience and gave him a similar charge on a development project. As one executive recalled, that attempt failed because, "The project manager didn't understand the business well enough to be able to make the right decisions. Even though he ostensibly had the authority to make key decisions, he didn't have the knowledge or credibility to make them—so the decisions kept getting bumped up to the executive staff anyway."

On Quantum's next major product development program, Impala, two functional managers, Mike Spencer from Marketing and Bill Benson from Engineering, assumed ad hoc responsibility for managing the development effort. No one assigned these two managers to work together closely, nor did they ask permission to alter the way their functions interacted; they simply went ahead and did it. Spencer and Benson were wildly successful. Quantum announced 40- and 80-Mb Impala models in February 1988, and the line generated revenues of $320 million in the next 18 months.

Initiating Formal Product Teams at Quantum OEM

In summer 1989, Brown established an explicit product team system within Quantum OEM to manage the definition, design, manufacturing, and marketing of all new products. Although the Impala line of 3.5-inch drives was Quantum's major product, a follow-on generation of 60- and 120-Mb drives, code-named Cheetah and built upon the same product architecture as Impala, had been under development since early 1988. A second product family under development, code-named Aerostar, was a line of 100- and 150-Mb drives targeted at the multiuser engineering workstation and file server markets. Brown established the Cheetah and Aerostar Teams to oversee these efforts. A third team, code-named Wolverine, was created in early 1990 to manage the development and launch of Quantum's 2.5-inch products, in 40- and 80-Mb models, for the notebook computer market. Exhibit 2 charts the development and market introduction times for each of these products.

The product teams' charter was to work in a coordinated way to address *market* needs. To ensure that no important details would fall through the cracks in the team management system, Brown carefully delineated which issues were the responsibility of the product teams, the functional organizations, and the executive staff. Teams were responsible for the definition, development, and introduction of new products; for the revenues and gross margins generated by the products; and for the inventories required to support the revenues. Furthermore, product planning was to become a continuous process, rather than an occasional, event-triggered exercise, within the teams. The product teams also were responsible for achieving Quantum OEM's Fast Cycle Time objective: to slash development time from 18 months on average to 12 months. Product team leaders, because they had critical general managerial responsibilities, came to be viewed within the company as key "heavyweight" employees.

Functional VPs, on the other hand, were charged with managing ongoing functional activities and expenses, providing effective career paths and skill-building programs, and executing the plans and staffing the programs initiated by the teams. For example, the marketing and sales groups represented Quantum's entire product line to customers, hired and developed qualified people, and staffed and supported the product development teams. The objective was to use teams to coordinate internal operations to meet market needs, but to have the teams be largely invisible to customers. Likewise, Quantum OEM's VP-Engineering (and VP-Manufacturing) was responsible for allocating engineering (manufacturing) personnel to the various teams' development projects, to ensure that projects were supported responsively, and to provide specialized services as needed.

Guidelines for Teams

The OEM executive staff established several principles for staffing, managing, and evaluating the product teams.

1. *Care in Selecting Team Members.* The executive staff chose initial team members carefully. Brown used two questions to determine whether

Exhibit 2

Exhibit 2

Product Development (1988–1992)—Teams, Products, and Markets

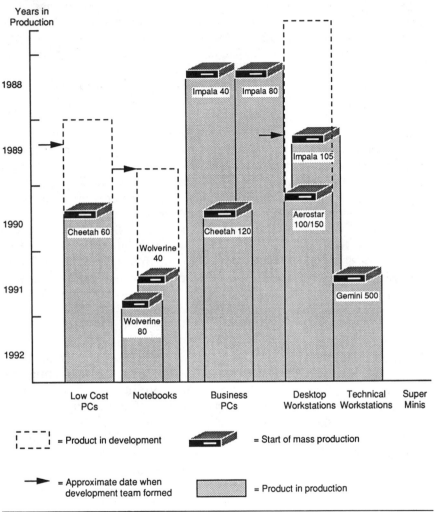

someone could successfully serve on a product team: "Would the executive staff trust this person to run this business?" and "Can he or she think like a general manager?" Such questions implied that the pool from which team members would be drawn comprised directors or managers in one of the functional organizations, one or two levels below the functional vice presidents on the executive staff. Although Quantum employees were known throughout the industry to have above-average capability, Brown was able to identify only about 14 people in the 450-person organization in 1989 whom he felt were capable of succeeding in the team management structure. Of them, four had to be relieved of team responsibilities within six months because they proved not to have the aptitude required.

Teams originally were to consist of a core group of six members, one from each function. The core team members were *collectively* responsible for the general management of their project; they were explicitly charged *not* merely to represent their functional point of view. In general, the team member from engineering was to be the leader of the team during the initial phases of the program. As the product approached its commercial launch, the marketing member assumed team leadership duties. A member of the executive staff was also assigned to each team as a sponsor and coach, to assist in communicating with and getting decisions from the executive staff, when necessary.

Core team members generally were to spend about 75% of their time on the team's work and the remainder on other functional responsibilities. As the work load demanded it, other members could also be drawn from the functions and added to the teams, on a less-than-full-time basis. In practice, team leaders found it awkward to distinguish between core and other temporary, non-core members, many of whom made invaluable contributions to the team. Over time the term "core" was gradually dropped.

2. Performance Evaluations. All Quantum employees were eligible for a profit-sharing bonus that had been running about 5% of salary, but core team members could be awarded significant additional compensation, depending on personal, team, and company performance. Performance was assessed and weighted on three dimensions:

Performance Dimension	Weight	Performance Assessed By:
1. Achievement of team objectives	25%	Executive staff
2. Individual contribution to team	25%	Ratings by team leader and executive staff sponsor with input from peers
3. Competence in dealing with functional responsibilities	50%	Functional manager

3. Co-location. Insofar as possible, the six core team members were to be housed together in work areas called Bump Spaces, where the layout forced frequent informal encounters. Initially, only Wolverine members were co-located because many of the people were new and space was being added. In addition, those who were to be dedicated to the team for several months (usually a dozen or more engineers) were also to be moved to the team's Bump space. By early 1991, the value of co-location was fully accepted and all new teams were co-located, even if it meant substantial rearrangement to free up the needed space.

4. *Process as Product.* Developing a *process* for managing the development and launch of new products with fast cycle times—and not just the development of the physical products themselves—was an important goal of the team approach. Although Dave Brown conceded that the first team might be relatively inefficient and that each new team would have to go through its own learning cycle, he hoped subsequent teams would benefit from the processes developed by predecessor teams, while not feeling constrained by them. To nurture effective team management processes, a facilitator—either a consultant or a specially-trained Quantum employee—met with each team in its weekly meeting. The facilitator's role was to pull team discussions back from tangential discussions, to ensure that no member's defensiveness blocked the team's progress on an issue, and to keep discussions moving on an agreed-upon timetable. At each meeting's end, the team took 10 minutes to evaluate the meeting's effectiveness in results achieved and process employed, and the members offered ideas to improve future meetings.

Product Teams' Performance

Although Quantum's teams ostensibly were to operate along the same guidelines, their performance differed substantially.

Cheetah/Lightning Team

Formed just as the Cheetah product was ramping up to mass production, Cheetah was Quantum's most successful team. The Cheetah was a close technological relative of the successful Hardcard/Impala product series, employing the same optically encoded, closed-loop servo architecture for positioning the read-write heads as had been used on the earlier products.[2] Thanks in part to the coordinated leadership of the product team and to customers' booming sales of personal computers and engineering workstations. Cheetah generated over 30% of Quantum's total sales revenues in calendar year 1990, despite Cheetah products' having been on allocation (capacity constrained) for much of the year.

---

[2] Optical encoders beamed light through grids on glass plates that extended from the head assembly. By measuring the alignment of the grids to a fixed reference point on the base of the drive, this system closed the feedback loop to the actuator that controlled head positioning.

Spencer found that in managing the Cheetah Team after the transition to mass production in early 1990, his team tasks had become very much those of the general operating manager: determining customer priority, forecasting manufacturing requirements, controlling the size and location of inventories, and reevaluating pricing strategies. At the same time, knowing Cheetah's life expectancy probably would not exceed 18 months, Spencer and others saw the need to initiate next-generation product development efforts, targeted at future needs in the same markets Impala and Cheetah had addressed so effectively.

To simultaneously manage the revenues and gross margins of Impala and Cheetah, and yet provide sufficient team depth to staff the Wolverine project, the executive staff restructured and put Mike Spencer in charge of the Lightning *Business* Team. The purpose of the business team was to manage a *family* of product lines, each of which was in a different stage of development. Two new product teams were established to manage the development and launch of follow-on products using the basic Cheetah architecture: products code-named Gazelle and Bobcat. Since Cheetah was now fully in production, the operations management responsibilities of the old Cheetah product team were passed to a Lightning *operations* team. This meant that general management responsibility for the product line as an operating business rested with the *operation team* (and above it, the business team), rather than an individual.

Although it made little sense to Quantum's managers to draw team organization charts when their structures were changing so regularly, this reorganization essentially resulted in a two-tier team structure. Members of the business team were responsible for the success of its product teams and its operations team. The product teams were responsible for products from conception to mass production, at which time responsibility shifted to the operations team.

At the time he was put in charge of the Lightning *Business* Team, Spencer was fresh from successfully leading the Impala team. He was asked to infuse a similar everybody-take-charge culture into the integrated business effort as well as its subprojects. He was aided in this by the fact that many Cheetah Team members also had previously shared crossfunctional team management experiences on the Impala program.

Recognizing the need to "seed" Lightning's subsidiary operating and product teams with personnel experienced in team management, Spencer assigned a core member of the original Cheetah product team to serve simultaneously as a member of the Lightning Business Team and as leader of an operations or product team. The operations team had its own crossfunctional core group of six members, but the product teams, especially during their early stages, were staffed by three members, from engineering, marketing, and operations functions only. To make it clear that manufacturing, marketing, and other issues needed to be integrated with product engineering decisions, even at the earliest stages, Spencer avoided labeling the new product teams as development teams.

Even though its task was much more complex than the original Cheetah Team's charter had been, the Lightning Team proved to be a successful manager of the broader effort. Cheetah customers were happy with the product and its pricing, MKE was producing it with high yields, and gross margins were attractive. The first of the follow-on products, Gazelle, was introduced in mid–1991, only four months late from its aggressive 12-month time-to-market plan.

The Aerostar Team

In contrast to the Cheetah/Lightning Team, the Aerostar product team's history was characterized by frustration and conflict. Introduced in September 1990, Aerostar's product line was several months late to market, overran its budget, and was unable to garner the margins management had targeted when initiating the development effort.

The Aerostar Team's product design was technically ambitious. At 100 and 150 Mb, Aerostar was the largest-capacity 3.5-inch drive Quantum had ever attempted; at 18 ms access time, it was by far the fastest. In addition, rather than employ the type of off-disk optical encoder technology used in the Hardcard, Impala, and Cheetah drives, Aerostar had special codes embedded on each disk surface that helped the heads self-adjust to stay precisely over the track on which they were reading or writing data. Whereas IBM had long used this positioning technique in its drives, this technology was new to Quantum. Finally, the Aerostar Team attempted a broader interface[3] development effort than had ever been attempted at Quantum. In addition to the AT interface, which linked the drives to IBM and compatible computers, the Aerostar program called for simultaneous development of an ESDI interface for complex systems employing multiple disk drives. By offering multiple interfaces, Quantum hoped to gain flexibility in addressing the markets for sophisticated file servers and multiuser workstations—segments in which it had not recently competed.

---

[3] The drive's interface was the logic circuitry that allowed the drive to communicate with the computer's operating system. Until about 1984, interface circuitry was installed on a separate circuit board in the computer and typically was provided by a third-party company, other than the drive manufacturer. By the late 1980s, most drives were sold with interfaces embedded within the drive housing. Hence, at the time Quantum initiated interface development for Aerostar, few independent disk drive manufacturers had extensive experience in interface development. The three primary types of embedded interfaces were the Small Computer System Interface (SCSI), used primarily on Apple computers; the AT interface for IBM and compatible equipment; and the Enhanced Small Device Interface (ESDI), a circuit used primarily with large, multiunit systems.

As a conscious strategic move, Quantum management decided to manufacture Aerostar itself. This required significant investment in advanced manufacturing processes and equipment, and start-up of that operating system on a technically demanding product. It also required establishing additional relationships between design engineering and manufacturing so the Aerostar product and process choices would be fully compatible. Building these new capabilities while developing the Aerostar product added another dimension of risk and complexity to the team's tasks.

Many, however, felt the decisions made in staffing the Aerostar Team contributed to the program's woes. "We learned that we needed three or four people on a team with the personality to energize the team—and that those key people need to respect one another," reflected one early member. The team's first leader, in fact, had accepted his team assignment reluctantly. As the functional engineering manager charged with Aerostar's design, he resented the diversions team management required, feeling that resolving product engineering design crises was a more pressing target for his managerial energies.

In response to the team's struggle to meet its time-to-market mandate, the executive staff kept trying to find a combination of people who could solve Aerostar's problems—but to no avail. The Aerostar core team had 4 sponsors, 4 leaders, and 16 members in its first 18 months. But it seemed that the modest commitment, low morale, and lack of interfunctional respect that characterized the team's culture in its early months persisted in the group, regardless of the personalities who occupied the offices in Aerostar's Bump space.

After months of delay and intense involvement of the executive staff, Aerostar was finally introduced to the market. Because it represented an important strategic thrust into a new market segment, the executive staff determined not to let Aerostar's belated launch taint the entire initiative. They therefore began development of an additional product built on Aerostar's basic architecture, code-named Gemini. To manage the operational issues associated with Aerostar after its introduction and to oversee launch of Gemini and additional products, a Business Team/Product Team structure similar to that of the Lightning Team was instituted, and the umbrella team was labeled the Apollo Business Team.

The Wolverine Team—A More Detailed Look

Whereas the Cheetah and Aerostar Teams had been formed around products that were well into the development process, the Wolverine Team—first as a product team and later as a business team—was created to manage the development and launch of a completely new product—a 2.5-inch drive for notebook computers—and was to be sold in 40- and 80-Mb versions.

Wolverine, a mid–1989 Bill Benson brainchild, started to move toward full product development status in October 1989, when Larry Peterson, a development manager who had worked on typewriter design at SCM, was hired specifically to be the initial leader of the Wolverine Team.[4] After Benson and Peterson worked four months to refine the product concept more thoroughly, a full team was recruited in January 1990 to manage the effort. Although none of the original Wolverine Team had prior crossfunctional team experience, the group coalesced relatively quickly under Peterson's leadership into an effective organization.

The Wolverine core team met every Monday afternoon from 1:30 to 4:30. "That is where the decisions get made," noted Peterson. "If you want to contribute, you've got to be there." It was not unusual for team members to fly back from Japan to be at a key team meeting.

As one of its first actions, the Wolverine Team assigned priorities to its objectives: (1) minimize time to market; (2) create intrinsically low-cost 40- and 80-Mb drive designs which could also be manufactured at low costs; (3) minimize power consumption (an important factor for battery-powered notebook applications); and (4) achieve the fastest possible access performance (the time required to retrieve and transmit a block of data from the drive to the computer).

These priorities guided the team in making several difficult choices in design technology. For example, developing a unique ASIC[5] controller chip might provide the Wolverine product with an extra performance cushion to compensate for possible performance-limiting compromises made in later design phases. However, the priority given to time-to-market over high performance led the team to select the ASIC that had been developed for the Cheetah product.

The time-to-market priority also encouraged the team to explore ways to regroup and restructure critical development activities. Quantum engineers thought of a typical product design effort as a sequence of Design, Fabrication, Assembly and Test cycles (DFAT), through which the team iterated three or four times before product introduction. Historically, these DFAT iterations had been conducted serially, with each iteration averaging 3 to 4 months:

$$D_1 \, F_1 \, A_1 \, T_1 \longrightarrow D_2 \, F_2 \, A_2 \, T_2 \longrightarrow D_3 \, F_3 \, A_3 \, T_3 \longrightarrow \text{Mass Production}$$

The design steps were the exclusive responsibility of Quantum. Component fabrication was the responsibility of MKE and of third-party sup-

---

[4] Peterson's newness to the disk drive world was not unique on the Wolverine Team. Gregg James, the Quality representative, joined the team from Freightliner, a manufacturer of Class–8 trucks.

[5] ASIC is an acronym for Application-Specific Integrated Circuit.

pliers. Assembly (also called "pre-production builds") was done at MKE. Units made in the preproduction builds were tested by Quantum and MKE engineers independently, and results were shared and discussed.

To accelerate time to market, Peterson's team attempted to overlap the test and design stages, hoping to reduce the time for each iteration from 3 or 4 months to 2 months, as follows:

$$D_1 \quad F_1 \quad A_1 \quad T_1$$
$$D_2 \quad F_2 \quad A_2 \quad T_2$$
$$D_3 \quad F_3 \quad A_3 \quad T_3 \longrightarrow \text{Mass Production}$$

This overlapping plan meant that many of the problems uncovered in the tests of A_1 units were not known to the design team when D_2 began, and the second DFAT cycle's purpose became primarily manufacturing learning, rather than design improvement. The design phase of the third cycle, therefore, needed to catch and correct a larger proportion of the design problems than under the prior serial structure.

Peterson found, as did the original Aerostar team leader, that managing the Wolverine Business Team *and* his 30-person product engineering function was an overpowering task. He was relieved, therefore, when in May 1990, the executive staff decided to install one of its own, VP-Marketing Mark Quinn, as full-time Wolverine Business Team leader. Quinn's title was changed to VP-Portable Storage Products, and Mike Spencer became corporate OEM marketing vice president.

The Wolverine Team's overlapping DFAT strategy made it more important than ever that details not be overlooked as critical information passed between functions. To ensure smooth coordination with MKE and component suppliers based in the United States and Japan, Quinn invited Kurt Jackson, an experienced Lightning operations team member with functional responsibility under the VP-Operations for the Quantum-MKE relationship, to join the Wolverine Team. As iterations of drawings for the design emerged from the team, engineers would electronically transfer them to MKE for manufacturability[6] evaluation. MKE would then transmit the drawings that same day to its parts suppliers to permit them to start tooling design and longer-range equipment and capacity planning.

Engineering-marketing interactions within the Wolverine Team often centered around allocation of preproduction models. Marketing had an insatiable appetite for early prototypes to give to key customers for early

[6] Manufacturability evaluation proceeded in two stages at MKE. The first was a "repeatability" evaluation, which included an analysis of tolerances actually required and achievable on the parts. The second was an analysis of processes and design modifications, which would reduce the cost of fabricating and assembling the parts.

evaluation and design into their systems. But engineering also needed preproduction models for testing in the DFAT cycle. Wolverine Team meetings provided a forum where, with functional representatives taking a general manager's perspective for revenues and gross margins, such demands for preproduction models could be granted priorities and managed.

To understand whether the posture taken by the functional members represented the viewpoints of functional or general management when such issues were addressed, the casewriter characterized all comments made at a typical team meeting. The results, summarized in Exhibit 3, show that the executive staff seemed to have succeeded in selecting members from the functional groups "who could think like a general manager." Team members were frequently vocal about issues that had little impact on their functions and, on occasion, advocated positions that were in the team's, but not their function's, interest.

As they approached Wolverine's launch, team members uniformly felt that what they had learned the first time around would make their performance on follow-on development programs much stronger. A partial listing of lessons learned, prepared for team discussion by Larry Peterson, is included as Exhibit 4. Like the Lightning and Apollo Teams, the Wolverine Team eventually became a business team, establishing product teams to manage specific product lines. (Exhibit 5 characterizes the composition of these teams in mid–1990.)

The Teams' Impact on Quantum's Performance

Although team management had not yet had its full desired impact on Quantum's fast cycle time objective (see Exhibit 6), Dave Brown and others felt this would improve as more people became experienced in core team management. Moreover, management felt that the team management system had brought additional valuable benefits to Quantum.

One important benefit was that Quantum's product planning was better integrated into the company's strategy. Whereas historically, product development was often initiated by resource availability (i.e., "We have four engineers freeing up on this project next week, so we'd better start working on another product"), continuous business team-level product planning had become the trigger for product development initiatives.

The team system also had taught the executive staff to delegate important decisions. "Team management has given us a model of how to empower people," Brown reflected. "It has also taught us the value of specificity—how to delegate big, important pieces of responsibility into

EXHIBIT 3

Sources of Input on Issues Discussed at a Representative Wolverine Team Business Meeting

Importance	Topic/Subject Addressed (A) or Decision Made (D)	Engineering	Marketing	Mfg./MKE[a]	Quality	Finance	Human Res.	Team Leader
Recurrent	Get to market quickly (A)	X		X	x			x
2	Get good preproduction samples into key customers' hands quickly (D)	X	x	X				
1	Design Wolverine's next product to the specification of Quantum's largest corporate customer, even though it was not the largest potential customer in the market segment where Wolverine was targeted (D)	X	O	X	O	O		O
2	Allocate fewer (mainly defective) preproduction samples to engineering for testing (D)	x	x					
2	Pressure MKE to use a new thin-film head supplier who seems more capable than MKE's preferred long-standing supplier (A)	x		X	x			
3	Determine priorities of potential customers (A)		x	x				
4	Define format and agenda for off-site strategic planning meeting (D)	x	X	X	X	x	x	X
3	How to get test results from preproduction builds faster (D)	X		x	X			
2	Discuss design/engineering progress (A)	X		x	x			
4	Discuss schedule conflict at MKE for preprocuction builds between Wolverine and Gazelle Teams (A)							X

Legend:

Importance refers to the amount of time spent in the meeting considering the topic and the sense of urgency members conveyed about the issue. 1 = most important; 4 = least important.

Those issues that required decisions to be made in the meeting are denoted by (D), and those that were addressed without requiring a decision are denoted by (A).

X indicates that an individual strongly supported a position that was consistent with the team's final decision or direction.

x indicates that an individual weakly supported a position or direction that the team eventually decided upon.

O indicates than an individual strongly opposed the position or direction that the team finally decided upon.

o indicates that an individual weakly opposed the team's final decision or sense of direction.

[a]The manufacturing representative in the meeting was a Quantum employee, who was responsible for the quantum-MKE interface.

567

EXHIBIT 4

Wolverine Team Lessons Learned: Key Points of Fast Cycle Leverage

Do Again:

Spend time on up-front architecting; *no specification changes.*

> Actions for next go-around:
>> Get critical mass of resources available for early focus on architecture.
>> Define architecture and get functional and team buy-in.
>> Implement formal process on spec. changes.

Get MKE input on mechanical design early.

> Actions for next go-around:
>> Get Mike to send mechanical engineers to Quantum for a residence period.
>> Ensure connection of MKE mechanical engineers with MKE's vendor base to get early design feedback prior to tooling start.

Co-locate offices and development labs; heads/media engineering groups; test, process and continuous engineering groups, etc.

> Actions for next go-around:
>> Ensure building layout plans are optimized to preserve as much as possible the present environment.
>> Brainstorm ways of adapting new facilities to maximize co-location benefits.

Do Differently:

Buy a dedicated spin stand with a *drive's* read channel already installed.
> Actions for next go-around:
>> Reverse decision to cancel purchase of spin stand. Add to the approved capital budget.

Make better use of modeling; bring finite element analysis capability in-house.
> Actions for next go-around:
>> Hire consultant to review needs and recommend software.
>> Purchase software.
>> Train engineers and run sample test case for practice.

Use designers/draftspeople for CAD input and operation. Free mechanical engineers to do more testing.
> Actions for next go-around:
>> Screen, interview, & hire.

Influence work done in advanced product engineering so that they develop "building blocks," which can leverage future development projects.

---

the organization. It has taught us a *process* for managing the company, now that things are more complex. Our key people have started thinking like general managers. They care less about whom they work for and more about getting done what needs to be done. The boundaries between the functions are beginning to blur."

EXHIBIT 5

Team Management Structure, June 1991

	Functional Areas						
	Engineering	Operations	Marketing	Quality	Finance	Human Resources	Strategy & Planning
Lightning Business Team	X	X	X	X	X	X	
Cheetah Operations Team	X	X	X	X	X	X	
Gazelle Product Team	X	X	X				
Bobcat Product Team	X	X	X				
Apollo Business Team	X	X	X	X	X	X	
Aerostar Operations Team	X	X	X	X	X	X	
Gemini Product Team	X	X	X				
Wolverine Business Team	X	X	X	X	X	X	
Wolverine Product Team	X	X	X	X	X	X	
Mongoose Product Team	X	X	X				

(Left margin label: Executive Staff Sponsors)

Support	Director, Advanced Engineering						Director, Strategy & Planning
	Other Functional Directors	Other Functional Directors	Other Functional Directors	Other Functional Directors	Other Functional Directors	Other Functional Directors	
	Other Functional Managers	Other Functional Managers	Other Functional Managers	Other Functional Managers	Other Functional Managers	Other Functional Managers	

NOTE: X indicates where a member of a function serves as a member of a team.

Although several executive staff members had wondered whether adopting a division organization might have been a simpler way of organizing, most felt teams gave the company the flexibility it needed to organize and reorganize around shifting markets. In Brown's view, "In order to maintain our growth we need to compete in a broader range of market segments than we did in the past. Segments appear and disappear rapidly, and customers in each segment have somewhat different

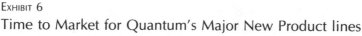

EXHIBIT 6

Time to Market for Quantum's Major New Product lines

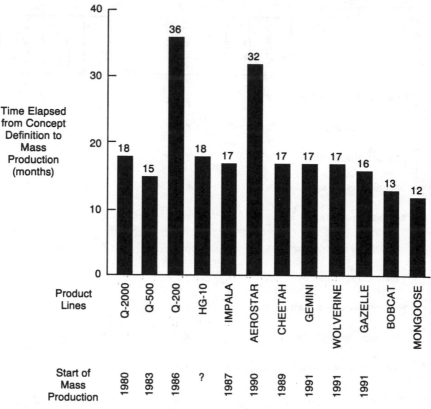

needs. Top management continually has to ask, 'What do we focus on?' We have to keep looking for new ways of organizing to get the right decisions made by the people best qualified to make them."

Individual team members also felt the team experience had augmented their managerial skills. One member's enthusiasm was not unusual: "Sometimes I leave those team meetings thinking, 'Wow! I can personally affect this business!' It's really exhilarating. Team management gives you a better understanding of the over-all problem set—you see how it all fits together. It is great general management training."

Kurt Jackson, who had served on the Lightning and Wolverine teams, claimed, "If I were to leave Quantum (which I'm not planning to do) I'd write 'Crossfunctional Team Management Experience' across the top of my resume. It's really been valuable."

The personal benefits to the *managers* involved in the team system

570

could, however, be somewhat asymmetrical. Mark Quinn, who opted to leave his position as VP-Marketing to assume leadership of the Wolverine Team, reflected that "It was a tough situation for a while. Previously, I had 60 people in my organization. I had been used to asking people to do things and having it get done. Now I'm responsible for the success of this business, but I don't really have direct authority. It would be a lot easier to get the job done if I had power to 'hire and fire,' rather than just 'influence and persuade.' " Initially, other team members had a hard time adjusting to Quinn's assertive leadership style as well. Quinn recalled that the group "eventually developed a norm that when I got too 'directive,' a team member would yell 'Boss!' I then would back off and try to get the job done through 'influence.' "

Another executive staff member mused that "the team system is great for the team members. It gives them major responsibilities, a great learning opportunity, and visibility—it puts them on the fast track. For the executive staff, however, it means less authority, no additional financial rewards—and you still get your ass kicked when things go wrong." One functional vice president, in fact, had been reassigned when he proved unable to adjust to the new role the team system demanded.

Problems in Quantum's Team Management System

Even in the more successful teams, managers found that the team structure itself could exacerbate problems. Mark Quinn described one issue:

> Last week, I learned that a group of engineers (working under the supervision of the functional engineering VP in pursuit of a Wolverine Team objective) was late on a key milestone. I stepped in and resolved the bottleneck. This particular issue had just fallen through the crack. Since the team has primary responsibility for getting Wolverine to market, I think the engineering vice president watched it less closely than he would have if his own neck had been the only one on the block. And since I'm not directly managing the engineering effort, I probably learned about this problem several weeks later than a closely involved functional manager would have.

An Apollo core team member reinforced this point. "When the team's involved, functional managers seem to feel that the team will take care of it. They feel less responsible for getting the job done. And from the team's perspective, we really don't have the competence to tell whether the functional groups are getting their jobs done well or not."

When the Wolverine Business Team established an additional product team, called Mongoose, to manage the development and introduction of the next-generation product, all of the core business team members' schedules were already so stretched with the launch of the initial Wolverine product that Quinn could not expect any of them to serve simultaneously as members of the Wolverine Business Team and to lead a new product team, as Mike Spencer had done in the Lightning Business Team. The Wolverine Team therefore staffed the Mongoose Team with the best people it could find, but there was concern that the Mongoose Team members' lack of stature and team experience might make the team less effective. Quinn reflected:

> Folks will sit in those meetings and say, "I'm only a quality specialist. I can't say what we ought to do." It's hard getting these product teams to work—to get individual members to drive the decisions and progress of the group. They tend to think of themselves as functional people with circumscribed authority, rather than as general managers with shared responsibility for this business. I think the executives in Quantum understand this team concept very well. But the people farther down in the organization really don't.

"Do you know what the key is?" queried another manager. "It's the people. Give me the pick of the best five or six people, and we'll have a *great* team. With the right group of people who understand the business and have the confidence to run it, you don't need a boss to give orders. As a group, they'll just go after the objectives we set for the business. But how do you empower people—I hate to use that word, but it's exactly what we're trying to do—when they don't want power, or aren't experienced in using it?"

In Quantum's rapid growth environment, the shortage of experienced team members was a critical issue for management to resolve. "It would be great if they could all turn out like the Lightning Team," one manager reflected. "But that takes *people*. Where are they going to come from? From my experience on the Aerostar Team, I am sure the project would have gone better in a simple functional organization. I think having *no* team is better than having an ineffective team."

One incident affecting the Cheetah and Aerostar Teams illustrated the people-specific nature of Quantum's experience with teams. Both teams had decided to use the same new ASIC in the controllers embedded in their respective products. The ASIC vendor informed an Aerostar Team member that it would be 14 weeks late in delivering its first prototypes. Because procuring and testing the ASIC was on the team's critical time path, the chip's delayed delivery forced the team to adjust its entire schedule, pushing its time-to-market back by a couple of months. A few weeks later, the Cheetah Team also became aware (from the vendor, not the Aerostar Team) of its intention to deliver the ASIC chip 14 weeks behind schedule. Within three days, the Cheetah Team member charged with component procurement had renegotiated the ASIC delivery delay down from 14 to 2 weeks, for the Cheetah *and* the Aerostar projects.

Reflecting on this incident, VP-Operations Claude Quichaud commented, "Fast cycle time is not a system. It requires fundamental behavioral change at the individual level, everywhere in the company. It's also a simplification to think of time-to-market as only an issue of product design. You can have very fast development programs feeding into a very slow company."

Key Issues

As Dave Brown reviewed the experience and concerns regarding the impact team management was having at Quantum, three issues stood out:

1. *Team management*: Would the business and product team management process *really* be instrumental in molding Quantum into the fast cycle time leader that Brown felt was imperative? In his more skeptical moments, he worried that all that had been demonstrated to date was that teams worked well when the technical challenges were not excessive and when team members were experienced and took initiative. Many of the products Quantum was contemplating for the future were technically more complex than those in the Impala-Cheetah sequence, and Brown felt they had already promoted all of the employees who had the requisite experience to be part of a successful team. Under such conditions, could they forge ahead with team management with the confidence that it would succeed?
2. *How to train*: How should Quantum train more people to be strong team contributors? In the past, new employees typically had been brought into the functions, and then the best people in the functions had been selected to work on the teams. Should Quantum continue this process, possibly asking functionally trained employees first to cut their team teeth on small projects before being assigned to larger business teams? Or should it hire people specifically for their team management capability and make a product or operations team their initial assignment, as had been done with Larry Peterson and the initial Wolverine Team? And had he and the executive staff been right in establishing team membership as the "fast track" at Quantum OEM?
3. *How to operate next time*: It seemed, as Brown examined the information summarized in Exhibits 4 and 5, that team management as a *process* was working well. People seemed to be thinking as general, rather than functional, managers. But did he, or anyone else at Quantum, have the right model in mind for how teams ought to work the next time around? How could management define an improvement path for team performance and the company's team capabilities?

As competitive time-to-market pressures intensified, as new market segments in the computer industry continually redefined the boundaries of Quantum's markets and the sources of future growth, and as disk drive technology accelerated, Brown could see no good alternative to managing through Quantum's kind of team structure. Whether this team structure could *succeed*, however, given the limited number of employees with the depth in multiple functions and the general management breadth and experience needed to staff teams faced with increasingly complex tasks, was the critical question.

Corning Glass Works: The Z-Glass Project

After several highly successful years, 1977 had been difficult at Corning Glass Works' Harrisburg plant. In July 1977 the yields and productivity of the Z-Glass process began a long decline, and the entire plant organization was working overtime trying to correct the problem. Morale plummeted as yields continued to decline throughout the summer and fall. In December 1977 a team of engineers from the corporate manufacturing and engineering (M&E) staff were assigned to the plant; the group's charter was to focus on long-term process improvement while the line organization concentrated on day-to-day operations.

On the morning of March 24, 1978, Eric Davidson, leader of the M&E project team at Harrisburg, sat in his office and reflected on the group's first three months at the plant. The project had not gone well, and Davidson knew that his team members were discouraged. The technical problems they faced were difficult enough, but apparently the line organization had resisted almost everything the M&E team had attempted. In addition to conflicts over responsibility and authority, deep disagreements arose concerning the sources of the problems and how best to solve them. Cooperation was almost nonexistent, and tense relationships developed in some departments between team and line personnel. Davidson favored an immediate change in the project's direction.

Sifting through the comments and memos from his team, he recalled David Leibson, vice president of manufacturing and engineering, saying to him shortly after he accepted the Harrisburg assignment: "Eric, this is the M&E group's first major turnaround project, and the first real project of any kind in the Industrial Products Division. I picked you for this job, because you're the kind of guy who gets things done. This is a key one for our group and I think a big one for the company. In situations like this, you either win big, or you lose big. There's very little middle ground."

Corning Glass Works in the 1970s

During the late 1960s and early 1970s Corning Glass Works was a corporation in transition. Long a leader in the development of glass and ceramic products for industrial and commercial uses, Corning had entered several consumer goods markets during the 1960s. Under the direction of Lee Waterman, president from 1962–1971, Corning developed a strong marketing emphasis to accompany several new consumer products.

Although the public's perception of Corning in the 1960s was no doubt dominated by its well-known Pyrex and Ovenware cooking products and Pyroceram dinnerware, its most successful consumer product was actually TV tube casings. Utilizing an innovative glass-forming process, Corning entered the market for TV tube funnels and front plates in 1958 and soon attained a strong market position. Throughout the mid-to-late 1960s growth in TV at Corning was rapid, and the profits at the TV division constituted the backbone of the income statement.

During the heyday of TV, Corning's organization was decentralized. The operating divisions had considerable control over marketing and manufacturing decisions, and corporate staffs in these areas were relatively small. Only in research and development did corporate staff personnel influence the company's direction. The Technical Staffs Division was responsible for all research and development activities, as well as for manufacturing engineering. New products were regarded as the lifeblood of the corporation, and the director of new product development, Harvey Blackburn, had built a creative and energetic staff. This staff developed the glass-forming process that made TV tube production possible, and the corporation looked to this group when growth in the TV division and other consumer products began to slow in the late 1960s.

Changes in TV and Corporate Reorganization

The critical year for the TV division was 1968. Until then sales and profits had grown rapidly, and Corning had carved out a substantial share of the market. In 1968, however, RCA (a major Corning customer) opened a plant in Ohio to produce glass funnels and front plates. Several of the engineering and management personnel at the new RCA plant were former Corning employees. RCA's decision to integrate backward into glass production had a noticeable effect on the performance of Corning's TV division. Although the business remained profitable, over the next three years growth slowed and Corning's market share declined.

Slower growth in TV in the 1969–1972 period coincided with reduced profitability in other consumer products as costs for labor and basic materials escalated sharply. These developments resulted in weaker corporate financial performance and prompted a reevaluation of the company's basic direction.

These deliberations created a reemphasis of the technical competence of the company in new product development and a focus on process excellence and productivity. A major step in the new approach to operations and production was the establishment of M&E at the corporate level. This reorganization brought together staff specialists in processes, systems, and equipment under the direction of Leibson, who was promoted from director of manufacturing at the TV division to a corporate vice president.

Shortly after the M&E Division was formed, Thomas MacAvoy, the general manager of the Electronics Division and the former director of Physical Research on Corning's technical staff, was named president of the company. MacAvoy was the first Corning president in recent times with a technical background; he had a Ph.D. in chemistry and a strong record in research and development. An internal staff memorandum summed up the issues facing Corning under MacAvoy:

> Our analysis of productivity growth at Corning from 1960–1970 shows that we performed no better than the average for other glass products manufacturers (2%–4% per year) and in the last two years have actually been below average. With prices on the increase, improved productivity growth is imperative. At the same time, we have to improve our ability to exploit new products. It appears that research output has, if anything, increased in the last few years (Z-Glass is a prime example), but we have to do a much better job of transferring products from the lab into production.

Manufacturing and Engineering Division

Much of the responsibility for improved productivity and the transfer of technology (either product or process) from research to production fell to the new and untried M&E Division. Because of the company's historical preference for a small, relatively inactive manufacturing staff, building the M&E group into a strong and effective organization was a considerable challenge. Remembering the early days, Leibson reflected on his approach:

> I tried to do two things in the first year: (1) attract people with very strong technical skills in the basic processes and disciplines in use at Corning; and (2) establish a working relationship with the manufacturing people in the operating divisions. I think the thing that made the difference in that first year was the solid support we got from Tom MacAvoy. It was made clear to all of the division general managers that productivity growth and cost reduction were top priorities.

From 1972 to 1977 engineers from the M&E Division participated in numerous projects throughout Corning involving the installation of new equipment and process changes. A typical project might require 4 or 5 M&E engineers to work with a plant organization to install an innovative conveyor system, possibly designed by the M&E Division. The installation project might last 3 to 4 months and the M&E team would normally serve as consultants thereafter.

In addition to equipment projects and internal consulting, the M&E group participated in the transfer of products from R&D to production. After laboratory development and prototype testing, new products were assigned to an M&E product team that designed any new equipment required, and engineered and implemented the new process. Leibson believed that successful transfer required people who appreciated both the development process and the problems of production. In many respects M&E product teams served as mediators and translators; especially in the first few projects, their primary task was to establish credibility with the R&D group and with the manufacturing people in the operating divisions.

By 1976 M&E had conducted projects and helped to transfer new products in most of Corning's divisions, although its role in Industrial Products remained limited. The manufacturing organization in that division had been relatively strong and independent, but Leibson felt that the reputation and expertise of his staff was increasing and that opportunities for collaboration were not far off. He also felt that M&E was ready to take on a completely new responsibility—a turnaround project. Occasionally parts of a production process, even whole plants, would experience a deterioration in performance, sometimes lasting for several months with serious competitive consequences. Leibson maintained that a concentrated application of engineering expertise could significantly shorten the turnaround time and could have a measurable impact on overall corporate productivity.

The Z-Glass Project

The opportunity for M&E involvement in a major turnaround effort, and for collaboration with the Industrial Products Division came in late 1977. Since June of that year, yields on the Z-Glass process at the division's Harrisburg plant had declined sharply (see Figure A). Substantial effort by the plant organization failed to change the downward plunge in yields and in October, Oliver Williams, director of manufacturing for Industrial Products, met with Leibson to establish an M&E project at Harrisburg.

Williams, a chemical engineer with an MBA from N.Y.U., had been named director of manufacturing in November 1976, after 18 years in various engineering and operations positions at Corning. He felt that the product's importance (corporate expectations for Z-Glass were great) coupled with the seriousness of the problem warranted strong measures. Williams and Leibson agreed that an M&E project team would work in the plant under the general supervision of a review board composed of Leib-

FIGURE A

Overall Yield, 1973–1977'

%Overall Yield

son, Williams, Martin Abramson, head of process engineering in the M&E Division, and Bill Chenevert, head of M&E's equipment development group (see Figure B for an organization chart). The team's charter was to increase yields, define and document the process, and train the operating people (see Exhibit 1). A budget, the team's size, specific goals, and a timetable were to be developed in the first month of the team's operation.

Although the plant manager and his staff had not participated in the decision to bring in the M&E team, Williams and Leibson agreed that their involvement and support were essential. A decision was made to allocate all M&E charges to the Industrial Products Division to relieve the plant of the extra overhead. Moreover, M&E specialists assigned to the project would be at the plant full-time.

Since this was M&E's first turnaround project, Leibson personally selected the team leader and key project engineers. He easily found people willing to work on the project. Everyone in the M&E group realized that turnarounds were the next major activity for the group and that those working on the first team would be breaking new ground. Leibson chose Eric Davidson to lead the Harrisburg project. He was 32 years old with a master's degree in mechanical engineering from Cornell and six years of experience at Corning. Davidson had completed several projects in the M&E Division, including one in France, and had also worked as an assistant plant manager. A close friend and colleague

FIGURE B
Organization Chart

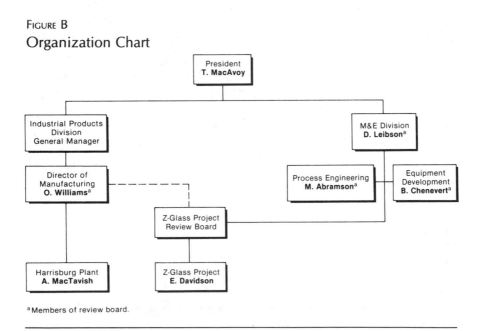

[a] Members of review board.

EXHIBIT 1

Memorandum on Team Charter

To: Harrisburg Project Team
From: E. Davidson
Date: November 24, 1977
Re: Team Charter

The charter of the project team is yield improvement as a top priority, definition and documentation of the process, and operator training. Enclosed is a copy of the proposed Process Definition and Documentation Program; it will serve as the framework for process diagnosis and control. Its main elements are as follows:

Priority

1	Define best known *operating setpoint* for each major variable.
2	Establish auditing system to track variables daily with built-in feedback loop.
3	Develop and implement *process troubleshooting* guides.
4	Write and implement *Operating Procedures.*
5	*Train* operating personnel in procedure usage.
6	*Audit* operating procedures on random frequency.
7	Write and implement *Machine Specification Procedures.*

Your comments on the program are encouraged.

---

commented on Davidson's reputation: "To say that Eric is on the fast track is a bit of an understatement. He has been given one challenging assignment after another and has been very successful. The word around M&E is that if you have a tough problem you want solved, just give it to Eric and get out of the way."

Working under Leibson's direction, Davidson spent the first two weeks meeting with the plant management and selecting members of the M&E team. At the outset, he chose four specialists to work on the first phase of the project—data collection and problem definition:

Richard Grebwell: 35 years old, an expert in statistical process analysis with 10 years at Corning. Although Grebwell was considered a bit eccentric by some, his characteristically brilliant use of statistical analysis was vital to the project.

Jennifer Rigby: 28 years old, with a master's degree in industrial engineering from the University of Texas. She had worked in the Harrisburg plant for six months on her first assignment at Corning.

Arthur Hopkins: 40 years old, a mechanical engineer with 12 years at Corning. Hopkins had worked with Davidson on the French project and was, in Davidson's words, "a wizard with equipment."

Frank Arnoldus: 37 years old, a chemist with Corning for six years, he also had worked on the French project and had earned Davidson's admiration for his ability to solve processing problems.

For the first two or three weeks Davidson planned to use the small group to identify problems and then expand the team as specific tasks and subprojects were established. Focusing his objectives on the long term, he explained:

> I'm after increases in yields as soon as we can get them, but what I'm really shooting for is permanent improvements in the process. To do that we've got to define the process and document its operation. My whole approach is based on the idea of *receivership*: whatever solutions we come up with have to be received, or accepted, by the plant organization. And I mean really accepted; they have to *own* the changes. That's why I will be taking a team approach—each project we do will have two coleaders, one from M&E (the transferrer) and one from the plant (the receiver).

After a brief period to get acquainted and develop a plan, Davidson and his M&E team began working in the plant on December 10, 1977.

Z-Glass: Product and Process

Z-Glass was Corning's code name for a multilayered, compression-molded glass product that was exceptionally strong and impact-resistant for its weight. Its durability and hardness, combined with its low weight and competitive cost, made it an attractive substitute for ceramic and plastic products used in the construction and auto industries. Introduced in 1973, Z-Glass products were an immediate success. From 1973 to 1977 production capacity grew 35% to 40% annually yet failed to meet demand (see Exhibit 2). Many people thought that the array of products was only the beginning of Z-Glass applications.

To Corning's knowledge, no other company in the world had yet developed the capability to make a product like Z-Glass and if one did, presumably it would have to license the technology from Corning. In fact, much of this technology was still an art form because numerous characteristics of most Z-Glass products were not completely explainable in known glass technology: people knew what it could do and roughly why it could do it, but were still utilizing trial-and-error methods to perfect existing products and develop new ones.

Blackburn and his staff developed Z-Glass during the early 1970s. The product was literally Blackburn's baby. He not only conceived the idea but, typical of the way Corning operated before the M&E Division was created, he and his staff solved numerous technical problems, built all

Exhibit 2

Harrisburg Plant—Sales by Product Line, 1973–1978
(numbers in thousands)

	Z1		Z4[a]		Z10		Z35		Z12[b]		Total	
	Pieces	$	Pieces	$	Pieces	$	Pieces	$	Pieces	$	Pieces	$
1973	—	—	—	—	119	$2,220.1	495	$5,217.8	—	—	614	$ 7,437.9
1974	—	—	—	—	232	4,315.2	549	6,313.5	—	—	781	10,628.7
1975	384	$ 5,161.5	—	—	239	4,983.2	552	6,513.6	—	—	1,175	16,658.3
1976	784	11,514.2	45	$ 552.3	268	5,831.9	591	7,541.7	82	$1,213.2	1,770	26,653.3
1977	803	12,005.0	407	5,372.4	264	6,087.6	671	8,689.5	534	8,410.5	2,679	40,565.0
1978[c]	171	2,565.1	35	493.5	145	1,957.5	250	2,975.2	61	988.3	662	8,979.6

[a] Introduced in early 1975.

[b] Introduced in late 1976.

[c] Data for 1978 cover reporting periods 1–3 (i.e., first 12 weeks of 1978). Note that because of seasonal factors it is not possible to arrive at an accurate indication of annual output of a particular product by multiplying the 1978 (1–3) results by 13/3.

the machinery and equipment needed for prototype production, and even worked in the plant during start-up. Furthermore, Blackburn had championed the product in discussions with top management. Several times when the project faltered, his reputation and skills of persuasion obtained the necessary funding. When yields began to fall in 1977, engineers at Harrisburg had consulted Blackburn when necessary; he still felt responsible for the product and intimately knew its nuances and subtleties.

The Process

Making Z-Glass products consisted of three main steps: melting, molding, and finishing, which were linked and had to be carried out in a fixed time sequence. The process required precise control over the composition and thicknesses of the various glass layers, as well as careful timing and monitoring during the molding and finishing operations. Maintaining this precision in a high-volume environment required continuous, tight controls as well as a feel for the process.

Melting

The first step was the preparation of the different types of molten glass that composed the various layers. These mixtures were prepared in separate electrically heated vats, designed and built by Corning. Each vat was carefully monitored to insure that the ingredients of the glass were in correct proportion, evenly distributed throughout the vat, and at the appropriate temperature.

The base layer was poured continuously onto a narrow (2 to 3 feet) moving strip. The other layers were poured on top of each other at precisely controlled intervals so that when the layered strip arrived at the molding stage each layer of the multilayered glass sandwich was at the proper temperature and thickness for molding. Minor (and, at the beginning of process development, almost unmeasurable) deviations from the recipe could lead to major problems, often requiring ad hoc solutions utilizing the unprogrammable skill of the operators and technicians.

Some problems were clearly identifiable with the melting operation. For example, the existence of *blisters* (tiny bubbles in one or more of the glass layers), *stones* (unmelted bits of sand), and *streaks* (imperfectly melted or mixed ingredients) were visible and obvious indicators of problems. Separation of the different layers, either after the molding or after the finishing operations, often could also be traced to improper execution during melting. But when the glass sandwich did not mold properly, there was usually some question as to which operation was at fault.

A process engineer explained the difficulty of melting control:

> The secret to avoiding problems at the melting state is maintaining its stability. Sometimes it's easy to tell when something has gone wrong there, but more often you don't find out until something goes wrong at a later stage. And usually it takes a long time to determine whether you've really solved the problem or are simply treating a symptom of a larger problem. It's tough to keep on top of what is gong on in each of those melting vats because it's largely a chemical operation.

Despite the difficulty of maintaining control over the melting operation and of correcting it when problems developed, Corning had been able to achieve yields as high as 95% at this stage of the process.

Molding

In contrast to melting, molding was basically a physical operation: rectangles of the soft glass sandwich were cut off the moving strip and moved onto a series of separated conveyor belts. Each slab was inserted between the jaws of a compression-molding device that contained several molds for the particular parts being produced. After the parts were stamped out, they continued down the conveyor line while the glass trim was discarded. Depending on the product mix, several conveyors might pool their contents before the parts entered the finishing stage.

Despite the apparent simplicity of this process (problems could be detected quickly and usually corrected quickly), so many different problems arose and so many different variables could be manipulated that it was generally considered to be even more difficult to control this stage than the melting stage. Typical problems included the basic dimensional specifications of the product, its edge configuration, and buckling and flattening after molding. These problems, together with machine downtime associated both with correcting problems and changing the product mix, made it difficult to achieve more than 80% efficiency (good output to rated machine capacity) during this stage.

Finishing

The finishing operation consisted of heat treating the molded objects, then applying one of several possible coatings. Heat treating stabilized the internal tensions generated by the molding operation and appeared to improve the lamination between the various layers of the glass sandwich. Since it required a precise sequence of temperatures and their duration, this operation occurred as the objects passed on conveyor belts through long ovens. Cracks or layer separation occurred infrequently, sometimes caused by the heat-treating operation.

The application of coatings, however, was more of a job-shop operation and could be done off-line. There were numerous coatings that could be applied, from the practical (improving the reflective, insulating, or electrical conducting properties of the surface) to the ornamental. Sometimes decals were also applied either in place of or in addition to a coating. The selection of coatings was steadily increasing, and one process engineer characterized the operation as "a continual bother: lots of new processes and equipment, lots of short runs but a necessity to maintain high speeds." The seldom-attained target yield was 95%.

The unique characteristics of the three stages made overall control and fine-tuning of the total process quite difficult. The backgrounds and skills of the hot-end workers varied considerably from those at the cold end, and involved entirely separate branches of engineering. When problems arose, many went undetected for some time, and often only appeared during destructive testing of parts after they had completed the process. Then it was often difficult to isolate which part of the process was at fault, because there appeared to be a high degree of interrelation among them. And, finally, once a problem and its cause were identified, it sometimes took a long period of trial-and-error fiddling until people could be convinced that it was indeed corrected.

The Harrisburg Plant

The decision to put Z-Glass into the Harrisburg plant had been based on its availability. Built in 1958 and long devoted to the production of headlights and other auto products, the plant had operated at excess capacity for several years in the late 1960s. In 1972 headlight production was consolidated in the Farwell, Ohio, plant while Harrisburg was set up for Z-Glass production. Several of the production foremen and manufacturing staff members were transferred to Farwell and replaced by individuals who had been involved in Z-Glass prototype production. (Table A contains a profit and loss statement for the Harrisburg plant in 1975–1976.)

The Harrisburg plant manager was Andrew MacTavish, a 54-year-old Scotsman. He came to the United States shortly after World War II and began working at Corning as a helper on a shipping crew at the old main plant. Over the years, MacTavish had worked his way up through various supervisory positions to production superintendent and finally to plant manager. He was a large man with a ruddy complexion and a booming voice. Although his temper was notorious, most people who

TABLE A

Harrisburg Plant—Profit and Loss Statement, 1976–1977
($ thousands)

	1976	1977
Sales[a]	$26,653.3	$40,565.0
Direct expenses		
Materials	9,947.2	16,214.2
Labor	3,714.3	6,194.7
Gross profit	12,991.8	18,156.1
Manufacturing overhead		
Fixed[b]	6,582.6	11,106.9
Variable[c]	1,429.3	2,114.4
Plant administrative expenses	1,784.5	2,715.2
Plant profit	3,195.4	2,219.6

[a] Capacity utilization (on a nominal sales basis) was 92% in 1976 and 84% in 1977.

[b] Included depreciation, insurance, taxes, maintenance, utilities, and supervision.

[c] Included fringe benefits, indirect labor, tools, and supplies.

had worked with him felt that some of his tirades were more than a little calculated. Whatever peoples' perceptions of his personality might be, there was no question who was in charge at Harrisburg.

In mid–1977 MacTavish had been at Harrisburg for six years. From the beginning he had developed a reputation as a champion of the little people as he called them. He wore what the workers wore, and spent two to three hours each day on the factory floor talking with foremen, supervisors, and production workers. If he had a philosophy of plant operations, it was to keep management as close to the people as possible and to rely on the experience, judgment, and skill of his workers in solving problems.

The Harrisburg plant was organized along department lines, with a production superintendent responsible for three general foremen who managed the melting, forming, and finishing departments. Ron Lewis, production superintendent, had come to the plant in 1975 after eight years at Corning. He was quietly efficient and had a good rapport with the foremen and supervisors. Besides Lewis, three other managers reported to MacTavish: Al Midgely, director of maintenance and engineering, Arnie Haggstrom, director of production planning and inventory control, and Royce Ferguson, head of personnel.

By June 1977 the management group at the Harrisburg plant had worked together for two years and had established what MacTavish thought was a solid organization. He commented to a visitor in May 1977:

587

I've seen a lot of plant organizations in my time, but this one has worked better than any of them. When we sit down in staff meetings every morning everyone is on top of their situation and we've learned to get to the heart of our problems quickly. With the different personalities around here you'd think it would be a dog fight, but these people really work together.

Of all the managers on his staff, MacTavish worked most closely with Midgely. Midgely, 46 years old, came to the plant with MacTavish, had a B.S. in mechanical engineering, and was regarded as a genius when it came to equipment. "He can build or fix anything," MacTavish claimed. Midgely was devoted to MacTavish: "Ten years ago, Andy MacTavish saved my life. I had some family problems after I lost my job at Bausch and Lomb, but Andy gave me a chance and helped me pick up the pieces. Everything I have I owe to him." Several people in the Harrisburg plant gratefully acknowledged MacTavish's willingness to help his people.

M&E Project at Harrisburg

Davidson's top priority in the first two weeks of the project was to define the problem. Overall yields had declined, but no one had analyzed available information to identify the major causes. The M&E group believed that the plant organization had spent its time on fire fighting during the past six months with little overall direction. Grebwell analyzed the historical data collected by the production control department. Other team members spent this time familiarizing themselves with the process, meeting with their counterparts in the plant organization, and meeting together to compare notes and develop hypotheses about what was going on.

One problem surfaced immediately: the relative inexperience of the department supervisors. As MacTavish explained to them, four of the six supervisors had been in the plant less than nine months. The people they replaced had been with the Z-Glass process since its prototype days. MacTavish felt that part of the explanation for the decline in yields was the departure of experts. He expressed confidence in the new people and indicated that they were rapidly becoming quite knowledgeable.

Grebwell's preliminary statistical work (see Exhibit 3) pointed to the molding department as the primary source of defects, with melting the second major source. The team identified four areas for immediate attention: overall downtime, trim settings, glass adhesion, and layer separation. As Grebwell's work proceeded, other projects in other departments were identified and staff members were added to the team. By mid-January it was evident that the overall project would have to

EXHIBIT 3
Grebwell's Memorandum on Preliminary Statistics

To: M&E Project Team
From: R. Grebwell
Re: Yield Report for December 1977

Below are data on yields in period 13 (provided by the production control department) along with notes based on preliminary observations. Rejects are based on 100% inspection. Note that selecting a reason for rejection is based on the concept of "principal cause"; if more than one defect is present, the inspector must designate one as the primary reason for rejection.

Harrisburg Plant
Yield Report Period 13, 1977

I. Melting

	Good Output as a % of Scheduled Capacity[a]					Downtime[b] as a % of Total Scheduled Time
	Z1	Z4	Z10	Z35	Z12	
Glass	70.4	65.4	72.3	73.5	66.9	—
Equipment Downtime	—	—	—	—	—	10.3

II. Molding and Finishing

	% Rejected by Product, Reason, and Department[c]					Downtime as a % of Total Scheduled Time
	Z1	Z4	Z10	Z35	Z12	
A. Molding						
Trim[d]	6.4	12.8	4.1	3.4	10.2	—
Structural	3.7	6.2	1.7	2.8	5.7	—
Adhesion	4.5	8.3	2.5	3.1	8.5	—
downtime	—	—	—	—	—	15.2
					24.4	
B. Finishing						
Cracks	0.8	4.2	0.3	1.2	3.6	
Separation	2.6	3.8	1.5	2.2	4.4	
Coatings	1.9	2.4	0.6	1.7	2.1	
Downtime						12.6

III. Summary[e]

	Good Output as a % of Scheduled Capacity					Total
	Z1	Z4	Z10	Z35	Z12	
Melting	70.4	65.4	72.3	73.5	66.9	—
Molding	72.4	61.6	77.8	76.9	64.1	—

589

Finishing	82.8	78.3	85.3	82.9	78.6	—
Overall	42.2	31.5	48.0	46.9	33.7	40.7

[a] This is overall yield and includes the effects of glass defects as well as downtime.

[b] No data are available on equipment downtime by product; the overall figure is applied to each product.

[c] The data are presented by department. They indicate the percentage of *department* output rejected and the principal reason for rejection. Total overall process yield (good output as a % of rated capacity) depends on both product defects and downtime.

[d] The reasons for rejection break down as follows:

Molding

Trim: This is basically two things—dimensions and edge configuration. It looks to me like the biggest problem is with the edges. The most common cause of defects in the runs I have watched is that the settings drift out of line. Apparently this depends on where the settings are established, how they are adjusted and the quality of the glass.

Structural: Pieces are rejected if they buckle or if the surface has indentations. This one is a real mystery—it could be a problem with the equipment (not right specs) or the operating procedures. Without some testing it's hard to tell. One possibility we need to check is whether the temperature of the incoming glass is a factor.

Adhesion: If compression ratios are too low or if the glass temperature is not "just right" or the glass has stones, then the glass adheres to the surface of the molds. The operators check the ratios, but the ideal range is marked on the gauges with little bits of tape, and I suspect the margin of error is pretty large.

Finishing

Cracks: Pieces sometimes develop cracks after heat treating. The principal suspect is consistency of temperature and flame zone. It is very hard to tell whether this is due to poor initial settings or changes in flames once the process starts. Inconsistencies in the material may be another source of cracks.

Layer
Separation: Layer separation seems to be caused by same factors as cracks.

Coatings: This is almost entirely a problem of operator error—handling damage, poor settings on the equipment, inattention to equipment going out of spec, and so forth.

[e] There are four steps to calculating overall yield:
1. For a given product in a given department, add up reject rates by reason and subtract from 1;
2. Then multiply by (1 − % downtime) to get department yield for that product (e.g., molding yield for Z12 = (1 − .244) (1 − .152) = .641);
3. Multiply department yields to get overall yield by product (e.g., yield for Z12 = .669 × .641 × .786 =.337);
4. To get overall yield, take a weighted average of product yields, with share in total output (on a total pieces basis) as weights; in period 13 these weights were Z1 = .3, Z4 = .15, Z10 = .10, Z35 = .25, and Z12 = .2.

encompass activities throughout the plant. It was decided that the only way to measure performance equitably was to use overall yield improvement. A timetable for improved yields was established and approved by the review board in late January 1978.

Davidson commented on the first six weeks of the project:

> Our initial reception in the plant was lukewarm. People were a little wary of us at first, but we did establish a pretty good relationship with Ron Lewis and some of the people in the production control group. I was confident that with time we could work together with MacTavish and people in other departments, but I wasn't as confident that the problems themselves could be solved. My objective was to obtain long-term improvements by defining and documenting the process, but when I arrived I found an inadequate data base and a process more complex than anyone had imagined.

Davidson encountered resistance to the very idea of process documentation. The view of MacTavish and others in the plant was aptly summarized by Blackburn, who appeared in Harrisburg off and on throughout the first three months of the M&E project. On one such visit he took Davidson into a conference room to converse:

BLACKBURN: [after drawing on the blackboard] Do you know what this is? This is a corral and inside the corral is a bucking bronco. Now what do you suppose this is?

DAVIDSON: It looks like a cowboy with a book in his hand.

BLACKBURN: That's right, sonny, it's a greenhorn cowboy trying to learn how to ride a bucking bronco by reading a book. And that's just what you are trying to do with all your talk about documentation. And you'll end right where that greenhorn is going to end up—flat on your face.

Conflict Emerges

Following the review board's acceptance of the proposed timetable, Davidson intended to create subproject teams, with an M&E specialist and a plant representative as coleaders. Despite Blackburn's lecture, Davidson pressed ahead with plans for process definition and documentation. A key element of the program was the development of instrumentation to collect information on the critical operating variables (glass temperature, machine speeds, timing, and so forth). Beginning in early January, Arnoldus had spent three weeks quietly observing the process, asking questions of the operators, and working on the development of instruments. He had decided to debug and confirm the systems on one production line (there were five separate lines in the plant) before transferring the instruments to other lines.

591

The instrumentation project was scheduled to begin on February 1, with the installation of sensors to monitor glass temperature in the molding process. No plant representative for the project had been designated by that time, however, and Davidson postponed the installation. A series of meetings between Davidson and MacTavish followed, but not until two days before the next review board meeting on February 23 were plant representatives for each subproject chosen. Even then, things did not go smoothly. Arnoldus described his experience:

> I didn't want to impose the instrumentation program on the people; I wanted them to understand that it was a tool to help them do their jobs better. But I had a terrible time getting Hank Gordel (the coleader of the project team) to even talk to me. He claimed he was swamped with other things. The thing of it is, he *was* busy. The plant engineering group had several projects of their own going, and those people were working 15 hours a day. But I knew there was more to it than that when I started hearing people refer to the M&E team as *spies.* After a while, people stopped talking to me and even avoided me in elevators and the cafeteria.

The other subprojects suffered a similar fate. The only team to make any progress was the group working on materials control. Ron Lewis thought the program was a good one and supported it; he had appointed one of his better supervisors to be coleader. In the other areas of the plant, however, little was accomplished. Attempts to deal informally (lunch, drinks after work) with people in the plant organization failed, and Davidson's meetings with MacTavish and his requests for support were fruitless. Indeed, MacTavish viewed the M&E team as part of the problem. He forcefully expressed himself in a meeting with Davidson in late March 1978:

> I've said right from the beginning that this yield problem is basically a people problem. My experienced production people were promoted out from under me, and it has taken a few months for the new people to get up to speed. But this kind of thing is not going to happen again. I've been working on a supervisor backup training program that will give me some bench strength.
>
> I'm not saying we don't have problems. I know there are problems with the process, but the way to solve them is to get good people and give them some room. What this process needs now is some stability. Last year two new products were introduced, and this year I've got you and your engineers out there with your experiments and your projects, fiddling around with my equipment and bothering my people.
>
> And then there's Blackburn. He blows in here with some crazy idea and goes right out there on the floor, and gets the operators to let him try out his latest scheme. The best thing for this plant right now would be for all of you to just get out and let us get this place turned around.
>
> I am convinced we can do it. In fact, we've already been doing it. You've

seen the data for the last 12 weeks. Yields have been increasing steadily and we're now above the average for last year. While you people have been making plans and writing memos, we've been solving the problem. [Data from the preliminary yield report are presented in Figure C and Table B.]

Resolving the Crisis

Davidson sat at his desk in the Harrisburg plant on March 24, 1978, and reviewed the events of the last three months. He realized that he also had been guilty of excessive fire fighting, and had not taken the time to

FIGURE C

Yields and Downtime, 1976–1978

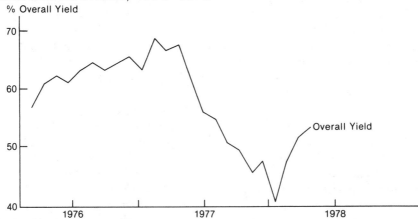

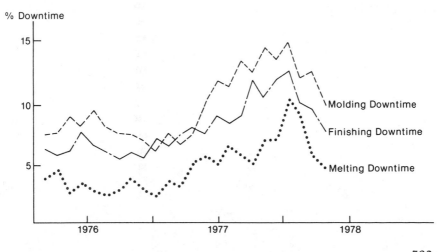

TABLE B

Harrisburg Plant—Summary of Yields, Period 3, 1978

Department	Product Lines					Total
	Z1	Z4	Z10	Z35	Z12	
Melting	74.6	69.3	76.6	77.9	70.9	—
Molding	79.7	71.3	83.5	83.8	72.4	—
Finishing	85.8	83.7	88.7	87.6	84.9	—
Overall	51.0	41.4	56.7	57.2	43.6	53.4

step back from the situation and plot out a course of action. The situation demanded careful thought.

He was genuinely puzzled by the recent improvement in yield performance; since the M&E team had done very little beyond data analysis the improvement must have come from elsewhere. All his training and experience supported the concept of definition and documentation, but he had never encountered such a complex process. Perhaps MacTavish was right, but he just couldn't bring himself to believe that.

Several options came to mind as he thought of ways to resolve the crisis; none of them were appealing. He could go to Leibson and Williams and ask, perhaps demand, that MacTavish be replaced with someone more supportive. He could continue to try to build alliances with supporters in the plant (there were a few such people) and get a foothold in the organization. Or he could develop a new approach to the problem (perhaps new people) and attempt to win over MacTavish. Davidson knew that his handling of this situation could have important consequences for the M&E Division, for the company, and for the careers of several people, his included.

Tools and Methods

Overview

At the heart of effective product and process development lies effective problem solving. In this chapter we examine tools and methods for problem solving. In reading the chapter, it is important to understand the central role of design-build-test cycles in solving problems in department. To understand the nature of each phase of a design-build-test cycle and the way in which a sequence of cycles forms the backbone of a development effort, the chapter focuses on a specific example— designing the gear system for an automatic film rewinder. In working through the example we illustrate each step of the cycle: the *design phase*, in which the developer frames the problem and establishes goals for the problem-solving process; the *build phase*, in which the developer builds working models of design alternatives; and the *test phase*, in which these models are analyzed and evaluated as input for the next design-build-test cycle.

To illustrate the problem solving required at the front end of a development effort, we apply a structured methodology known as quality function deployment (QFD) and its associated "house of quality" to the design of the automatic film rewinder gear system. QFD provides a set of formal procedures for identifying critical customer attributes and creating strong linkages between those attributes and key design parameters. An important theme in this discussion is QFD as a framework for problem solving. The specific techniques are less important than the general approach that focuses on translating customer experience into implications for engineering design.

A second structured methodology, particularly relevant in areas where engineering and manufacturing must arrive at integrated solutions, is design for manufacturability (DFM). Like QFD, DFM is a category of methodologies that includes a wide variety of individual tools and techniques. We examine two in detail in this chapter—design rules and design for producibility. Design rules express the boundaries within which the manufacturing process operates, in terms of the issues that confront product designers. By observing and adhering to those rules, product designers can have confidence that their choices will be manufacturable. Design for producibility is a technique that looks at specific process constraints and, utilizing a "house of producibility," seeks to consider a full range of manufacturing process parameters, linking them to product design parameters and subsequent manufacturing system performance. The basic intent of DFM is to provide a comprehensive and integrated system solution for the entire organization, not just a brilliant design for design engineering.

The final class of tools we examine is computer-based software such as computer-aided design/computer-aided manufacturing (CAD/CAM) and computer-aided engineering (CAE). These software systems combine graphics, databases, and problem-solving methods within a consistent framework. While it is widely agreed that the most advanced forms of these systems have the potential to transform an organization's approach to development, an important theme in this chapter is that tools and systems need the right context to be effective. A fragmented organization with parochial philosophies and substantial barriers to communication can frustrate the most clever and powerful system. The appendix reviews four generations of computer-based design systems, indicating their key characteristics and limitations. Using the gear design problem as an example, we illustrate the power of a fourth-generation system and highlight some of the opportunities and challenges associated with advanced software tools.

CHAPTER 9

A fundamental challenge in developing a new product or process is to combine engineering detail—specific dimensions, parts parameters, materials, and components—into a coherent whole. What attracts and delights customers in a new product, and what is compelling in a new process, is system performance. As we have argued thus far in this book, achieving superior performance in a new product or process demands getting the strategy right, laying out an effective aggregate plan, creating an overall process that effectively integrates the functions, and creating communications processes, skills, and capabilities that support effective cross-functional interaction. All of these things are crucial, but in the final analysis, when we search for an understanding of truly outstanding development, we must eventually get down to the working level where individual designers, marketers, and engineers work together to make detailed decisions and solve specific problems. The magic in an outstanding product or a superior process is in the details. Thus, detailed problem solving is at the core of outstanding development.

Effective problem solving and the methods and tools used to accomplish it are the focus of Chapters 9 and 10. Problems may arise in any phase of development and concern all the functions. Thus, we are interested in understanding how individuals, work groups, and organizations carry out problem solving in product and process engineering, marketing, field service, and manufacturing. In this context a "problem" occurs when developers encounter a gap between the current design (or plan, process, or prototype) and customer requirements. In the development of the MEI 2010, discussed in Chapter 6, engineers encountered a screen problem on the monitor's display device. Through testing and interaction with customers it became apparent that nurses experienced a glare that obscured information and made the display difficult to read. The nurses' experience signaled the existence of a problem, but did not define it precisely enough to allow immediate solution. Excessive glare could be the result of an inappropriate display angle, inappropriate materials, absence of control in the manufacturing process, or any number of underlying causes. When confronted by this gap between customer needs and product performance, the development team faces a number of ways of meeting customer expectations. Although there may be a team member responsible for the display, solving excessive glare is likely to involve issues that extend beyond that narrow functional domain. Thus, the problem cuts across disciplines and perhaps even functions.

How the development team takes action to close the gap—the way it frames and defines the problem, generates alternatives, organizes and conducts tasks, and implements solutions—detemines the speed, efficiency, and effectiveness of problem solving. Where such problems are critical to overall system performance, drive program lead time, involve significant resources, or have decisive influence on a customer's perception of the product or process as a whole, the effectiveness of problem solving at the detailed local level can have a powerful influence on the overall performance of the development process. Effective problem solving at the working level is not a sufficient condition for overall success, but in our experience, it is a critical and necessary part of an outstanding development process.

The remainder of this chapter is divided into three parts. We first lay out a framework for thinking about problem solving at the detailed level. Using what we call the "design-build-test" cycle, we identify activities that seem to be crucial in solving problems and suggest some of the problems and pitfalls that often accompany traditional methods. In the second part of the chapter we study examples of formal approaches to problem solving. These "structured methodologies"—in particular, quality function deployment (QFD) and design for manufacturability (DFM)—have been developed to deal with the challenge of solving detailed problems that cut across traditional disciplines, departments, and functions. We then turn to an examination of new computer-based systems and methods. The computer has the potential to change in fundamental ways the nature of development, including the modes of solving detailed problems. Our focus in this section of the chapter is on systems that facilitate communication, manage large-scale databases, and provide a means for capturing knowledge generated through the problem-solving process. We conclude with observations and discussion of the implications of such computer systems for management.

Although our focus is on activities that occur at a very detailed level in the development process, our perspective in this chapter remains that of the general manager. We have argued in previous chapters that the role of the general manager is to build capability and create effective processes in the organization. It is our view that carrying out that role requires an in-depth understanding of the problem solving process at the working level. General managers need to understand the process not only because changes in it often provide significant leverage for improving development, but also because such an understanding can be an important guide in making investment decisions about processes and capabilities. Furthermore, deep understanding may be useful as general managers make specific decisions about specific projects. With a framework for thinking about detailed problem solving and an understanding of modern methods and systems, general managers will be in a much better position to evaluate the potential and progress of specific products or processes under development.

A Framework: The Design-Build Test Cycle

The essence of product and process development problems may be defined as a performance gap between current practice or designs and the desired target. Whether it is a component within a system or a single part, whether it is a new process layout in the plant or a new piece of equipment, the fundamental problem is to design and develop something that will close the gap between current performance and the requirements of the new product or process. If the old system or existing design already meets requirements, then the design problem is trivial. But where a gap exists, developers must search for new concepts that will deliver the desired level of performance.

Consider, for example, the problem of developing a gear system for the automatic film rewinder in a new camera.[1] Exhibit 9–1 illustrates the placement of the gear system in a simple schematic diagram of the automatic rewinder in a new camera design. In this example, a company that we shall call New West Photo has launched a project to develop a new product to compete in the compact, easy-to-use, 35 mm camera market. The designers have determined that the new camera must have an improved automatic rewind system. The rewinder performs two functions: it advances the film one position after each shot, and it rewinds the film when the roll is finished. The rewinder is powered by a battery which drives an electric motor connected to a film roller

Exhibit 9–1

The Gear System in an Auto Rewinder for a 35 mm Camera

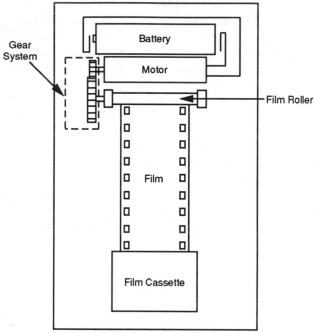

NOTE: The gear system is drawn with two gears for illustration only. The number of gears is a design parameter and designs with more than two gears are possible.

by the gear system. After preliminary testing of an initial design, it became clear that the design was too noisy, bulky, and expensive. Thus, the design problem in this example is to develop a gear system for a rewinder that takes less space and is less noisy and less expensive.

From the standpoint of the gear system, the new design involves establishing a fit between two very different aspects of the system. The first is what we will call "design parameters." These are the decisions under the control of the designers or engineers. Typical design parameters in a gear system include the diameter of the gears, the profiles of the gear teeth, gear thickness, and the manufacturing tolerances associated with each. Other design parameters include the number of gears, the materials used in the gears, and the types of lubrication.

The second aspect of the system is "customer attributes," or customer requirements. From a customer's perspective, the gear system is important because of its impact on the performance of the film rewind system. Framed in these terms, customers care about speed (wait time), sound,

EXHIBIT 9–2

Selected Design Parameters for Gears and Customer Attributes
in a Film Rewind System

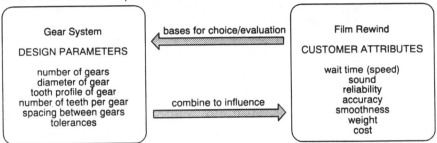

NOTE: Design parameters create a gear system that influences attributes of the film
rewind system that customers care about. These attributes are, in turn, the basis for
evaluation and choice of design parameters.

---

reliability, size, and cost. These attributes are only a part of a broad set
that customers evaluate when deciding whether to buy a specific camera, and are the attributes most directly connected to the performance of
the gear system. Since performance is influenced by design parameters,
they are closely linked to customer attributes. But there is not a one-to-
one correspondence between a specific design parameter and a specific
customer attribute. Indeed, for the most part, a given customer attribute
is determined or influenced by several design parameters. Furthermore,
customer requirements reflect the performance of the system as a whole.
As long as the gear system is sufficiently quiet, customers do not care
whether it is because the gear is intrinsically quiet or because the camera
case muffles the noise effectively. However, while both approaches may
satisfy a customer's desire for a quiet camera, they have very different
implications for cost and weight. Thus, the example of noise illustrates
problems of tradeoffs in design. Design parameters often interact in
ways that impose choices on designers. An important challenge of design, therefore, is to select design parameters that strike an effective
balance among competing customer attributes.[2]

Exhibit 9–2 lays out the basic relationship between design parameters
and customer attributes, using our gear design example. System design
parameters for the gear system include the number of gears, the diameter and tooth profile for each gear (and hence the number of teeth and
spacing between gears), and associated manufacturing tolerances. These
design parameters influence important customer attributes of the rewind system such as wait time (the time a photographer must wait
between photographs or at the end of a roll), sound (it is important to

maintain a balance—some sound is necessary to indicate to the customer that the mechanism is working, but too much "noise" disturbs the photographer's subjects and may be unpleasant to the photographer), reliability, accuracy, smoothness, weight, and cost. These attributes are the basis for customer evaluation of a particular film rewind system, and therefore become the basis for choice and evaluation of alternative gear design parameters.

The Design-Build-Test Cycle

Striking an effective balance among customer attributes and closing the gap in performance is the focus of problem solving in development.[3] Solving problems is a learning process. No matter how much an engineer, a marketer, or a manufacturer may know about a given problem, there are always unique aspects of any new system that must be understood before an effective design may be developed. Except for the easiest of problems, developers are unlikely to come up with a complete, effective design in a single iteration. Instead, developers go through several iterations, learning a little more about the problem and alternative solutions each time, as they converge to a final design and complete, detailed specifications.

Each iteration or problem-solving cycle consists of three phases illustrated in Exhibit 9–3. In the *design phase*, a developer frames the problem and establishes goals for the problem-solving process. Problem framing is crucial, since the apparent gaps in performance that we observe are often caused by underlying conditions that are difficult to observe and characterize. A problem with noise, for example, may be caused by the type of material, gear width, tooth profile, gear train alignment, or a variety of other design parameters, including the precision of the manufacturing process. But the frame we put on a problem also depends on how we define the objectives. In the case of noise, for example, it may be apparent because of customer feedback that the old design had undesirable noise characteristics. A clear objective of the new system could be, therefore, to reduce noise below a given threshold level. A deeper understanding of the problem, however, may suggest that customers like to hear the rewind system working. Thus, the objective may not be simply to reduce noise below some threshold, but rather to create the right kind of sound—a sound that is distinct but soft and nonabrasive.

Once the developer has framed the problem, the next step in the design phase is to generate alternatives. Based on the developer's understanding of the relationship between design parameters and customer attributes, several alternative designs for physical models may be appropriate. The purpose of the alternative designs may be to explore the relationship between design parameters and specific customer at-

ExHIBIT 9–3

The Design-Build-Test Cycle in Problem Solving*

Phases of Problem Solving

DESIGN	BUILD	TEST

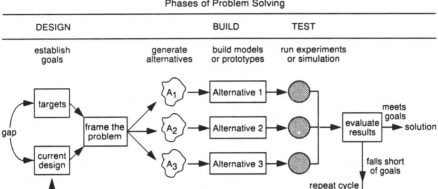

* The diagram illustates the design-build-test cycle. Goals are set, problems framed, alternatives developed, models or prototypes built, and tests conducted. If the test reveals a solution, the process stops. If no solution is found or the goals are not yet reached, the cycle is repeated. Note that repeating the cycle may involve revising the goals. Later cycles are often of shorter duration than earlier cycles.

tributes. If the particular design cycle under discussion comes at a later stage of development, the purpose of the alternative designs may be to refine an established concept.

In the second, or *build phase* of the problem-solving cycle, the developer builds working models of the design alternatives. The purpose of the second phase is to put alternative designs into a form that allows for testing. Depending upon what a developer is trying to learn, the working models may take several forms. At an early stage of gear development, for example, a developer may implement alternatives electronically in a computer-aided design (CAD) workstation, using the computer to display graphically and visually the gears' characteristics. For some purposes it may be useful to take the build phase one step further, creating alternatives using easy-to-work with materials such as plastic or soft metals. While computer simulation may provide sufficient information to arrive at effective solutions, later-stage testing and development may require the building of physical prototypes using materials and production processes that are reasonably close to those used in a commercial process.

In the third or *test phase* of the problem-solving cycle, working models, prototypes, or computer-generated images are tested. Depending upon the purposes of the particular problem-solving cycle, the tests may focus on a particular dimension or may involve full-scale system evaluation. In the case of gear noise, for example, an early testing scheme may examine the decibel level generated by alternative designs. Such a test could be run in a testing laboratory and the results used to generate an understanding of the connection between different design parameters and the overall noise level. Subsequently, given designs may be implemented with prototype parts and tested with potential customers.

Although conducting tests appears relatively straightforward, in practice getting good information out of the testing phase requires very careful forethought and skilled execution of a test plan. In a laboratory setting, test engineers worry about things such as accuracy, precision, and the ability to calibrate measurements. In addition, tests are subject to noise, or random variation caused by fluctuations in the environment that have not been accounted for or controlled. In order to cope with noise from vibration, temperature, humidity, and even stray magnetic fields, engineers often repeat tests several times to identify the amount of noise in the testing process. Even when engineers have well-designed procedures to deal with noise and have established instruments and processes to ensure accurate and precise measurement, there is still the problem of fidelity. Fidelity refers to the extent to which the test being conducted reflects the actual case of interest. With respect to gears in the film rewind system, the issue is whether a laboratory test of decibel levels reflects the way customers will perceive noise in the use of the camera. Yet even when the test moves into the field, the issue of fidelity continues to come into play. For example, developers must be concerned that the customers involved in the field tests are representative of the customers they are trying to reach, and that the conditions under which the tests are conducted effectively represent the mode in which the camera actually will be used.

A single design-build-test cycle generates insight and information about the connection between specific design parameters and customer attributes. That information becomes the basis for a new design-build-test cycle and the process continues until developers arrive at a solution—a design—that meets the requirements. Thus, the effectiveness of problem solving in development depends not only on the speed, productivity, and quality of each individual step in the cycle, but also on the number of cycles required to achieve a solution. The number of cycles depends directly on the extent to which activities at each of the problem-solving steps are linked and integrated. However, the number of cycles and their length also depends on the processes and procedures established by management and thus can be viewed as critical development decisions.

While it is important that individual activities in problem solving—the design of alternatives, building of prototypes and conducting of tests—be carried out effectively, performance in problem solving depends on establishing effective connections between these activities. If the tests conducted are not planned with a clear understanding of design objectives and the nature of the problem being solved, then the information developed may be only partially useful in the hands of the designers. If the prototypes or models built do not reflect design intent, they likewise will fail to deliver powerful information in the problem-solving process. The absence of close connections in the different steps of problem solving leads to multiple reiterations and extra cycles, and thus longer development times and lower productivity.

The issue of connectedness between problem-solving cycles also arises in the relationship between the individual part or component and the larger system in which it is embedded. In the case of the film rewinder, for example, problem solving around the gear system must be connected not only to the design of the new rewinder, but to manufacturing and vendor process development as well. Moreover, establishing targets for the design of the gear system is connected to choices about customer attributes and thus to problem solving going on in marketing. Each of these problem-solving cycles must be linked if the overall system is to be coherent. It is not enough to do a good job designing a gear system; the solutions developed must be consistent with solutions developed in manufacturing or marketing. Thus, effective problem solving at the working level is a matter of skill and capability in carrying out individual tasks in individual design-build-test cycles, as well as a matter of effectively linking and integrating problem-solving cycles in closely related areas.

Structured Methodologies for Effective Problem Solving

The challenge in effective problem solving is both to execute individual elements of the cycle (and individual cycles) rapidly and well, and to link individual cycles so that solutions are coherent. As pressure for improved performance in lead time, cost, and quality has increased, firms have adopted a variety of methods to improve problem solving. At first glance many of these methods appear to be little more than applied common sense—plan your work, think before you act, consider the consequences, and do it right the first time. While common sense is an all-too-rare commodity, there is more to structured methods than a straightforward application of what everyone already knows. The difficulty is in finding a method and logic that works where people, information, objectives, and capabilities interact in a complex system. Indeed, for people intimately familiar with detailed problem solving in traditional development processes, the ebb and flow of problem formulation and solution within and across functions and departments often has an illogical, surreal quality to it. Consider the following vignettes drawn from a project to develop a gear system for a new camera:

Developing the Auto Rewind System

Bob Hancock, a design engineer in the gear design department, read through Beth Lardner's report on the new camera project. Lardner, the project liaison engineer for gear design, had summarized a recent design meeting:

> The critical design issues for us are clearly cost, reliability, and speed of rewind. The targets are aggressive, but within our reach. [Hancock smiled when he read that line.] I have enclosed marketing's specifications and the project timing plan.

As he read through the specifications, Hancock noted that most of what marketing wanted conformed to the standard specifications for gears used in the gear design department. There would be some problems in meeting both the speed and cost objectives, but he had some ideas to try out. And there were some new requirements for sound. The marketing group was asking for "sound that is quiet, but effective." While that sounded pretty vague, Lardner's notes in the margin indicated that noise below 60 decibels was the target.

(*Three months later.*) Bob Hancock could not believe his eyes. Beth Lardner's latest report on the design of the rewind system called for another redesign to improve sound. This was the fifth iteration on the specifications and the project was already five weeks behind and slipping. After the first two iterations it had become clear that somebody in marketing really cared about sound. Hancock's tests had shown that meeting the noise requirement was likely to create problems in cost (his design called for more teeth per gear and higher precision in machining). But that was not all. Even after the design met the decibel target, marketing's feedback was that the sound wasn't "crisp" enough.

(*Nine months later.*) Ellen Gaither, an engineer in the gear engineering department, looked over the latest report from the test department on the new gear system for the auto rewinder. The gears had failed life testing again! Ellen walked down the hall and put the report in front of her supervisor, Randy Etheridge, stating:

> Randy, this is really weird. The redesign of the gear teeth we put into prototype last month should have worked. All of our tests indicated that we had solved the failure problem. And now this! There must be something funny going on in processing. We keep getting these process notification reports that tell us our designs are not feasible because of tolerances, but the plant should be able to handle this. There's got to be something else going on, but Jankowski (liaison engineer for gear engineering) doesn't seem to be able to get any data out of process engineering.

While Gaither was talking to Etheridge, another conversation was going on in process engineering between Rod McQuarrie (process engineer) and Eddie Robertson (gear machining supervisor):

> Robertson: I told you that new design wouldn't work. We just can't hold the tolerances on that drive gear without taking a hit on our costs. We must have sent through five or six process notification sheets on that design. You've got to get the engineers to change their approach.
>
> McQuarrie: Yeah, I know. But I'm not sure that the tolerances are behind this life test problem. We've got to work on the tolerances to hit our cost target, but I think something else is going on in this reliability problem.

Structured Methods

The problem-solving attempts depicted in these vignettes are characteristic of organizations that rely on highly specialized engineers working in an environment in which communication occurs through formal documents and intermediaries, with few common methods and limited language to facilitate cross-functional problem solving. Hancock goes through cycles of redesign because the relative importance of different attributes is vague, and because new requirements for sound are difficult to translate into terms with which he can work. Gaither and McQuarrie both think "something else is going on," but they have been playing engineering "Ping-pong," throwing the problem back and forth with little headway and limited resolution.

Indeed, the root cause of the life-testing problem was a change in the metal being used in the gears (a change made by the supplier and unknown to either department) and a control problem in one of the heat treating processes in the plant. The patterns of communications in use (formal documents, indirect through intermediaries) and the absence of a shared framework and language made it very difficult (and thus time consuming and expensive) for people in gear engineering and process engineering to arrive at a common formulation of the problem and thus an effective solution.[4]

Structured methodologies—formal procedures with structured tasks, and explicit representations of issues and choices—for design and development have been formulated to deal with these problems. In this section, we illustrate two commonly used methodologies. Although both of these methods have application throughout the development process, we apply them to a very specific phase of development. The first, quality function deployment, we apply to the early stages of development where targets are set and the basic product or process architecture is established. The second, design for manufacturability, we apply to the later phases of development, where detailed engineering linking product and process design is the focus of development effort. In both cases, we use our gear design problem to illustrate the methodology. Our intent here is not to provide a detailed treatment of each method. Rather, we use a very simple example to illustrate the nature of the methodology and its potential role in creating effective problem solving at the working level.

Quality Function Deployment

Quality function deployment, or QFD, is a method used to identify critical customer attributes and to create a specific link between customer attributes and design parameters.[5] The method uses matrices to organize information and to help marketers and design engineers answer three primary questions: What attributes are critical to our customers? What design parameters are important in driving those customer attributes? What should the design parameter targets be for the new design?

The organizing framework for the QFD process is a planning tool called the "house of quality." Each step in the QFD process involves building up an element of the house of quality. Exhibit 9–4 lays out a simplified house of quality for our gear system design problem. Working as a team, design engineers and marketers *first establish critical customer attributes for the product*. These attributes become the rows of the central matrix of the house of quality. Customer attributes may be expressed in terms that customers use in describing their use and perceptions of the product. Working together, the team may also group various attributes to create a broader category that simplifies the planning and analysis. In our example, we have singled out six attributes for analysis: speed, quiet operation, crisp and accurate sound, cost, size, and reliability. The team also establishes weightings that represent the relative importance of the different attributes from the customer's perspective. Using percentages (the complete set of weightings adds up to 100 percent), we have indicated that of the six attributes, our target customers (sophisticated amateur photographers) place most emphasis on speed and reliability, although taken together the two dimensions of sound are relatively important.

Once customer requirements have been identified, in the *second* step the team establishes *the critical design parameters that drive system performance*. These parameters describe the part or product in measurable terms and should be directly linked to customer attributes. The selected design parameters form the columns of the central matrix. Exhibit 9–4 presents four parameters: number of teeth, lubricant, tooth thickness, and manufacturing precision.

The *third* step in the QFD process is *to fill in the body of the central matrix*.

Exhibit 9–4

The "House of Quality" for a Gear Design Problem at New West Photo*

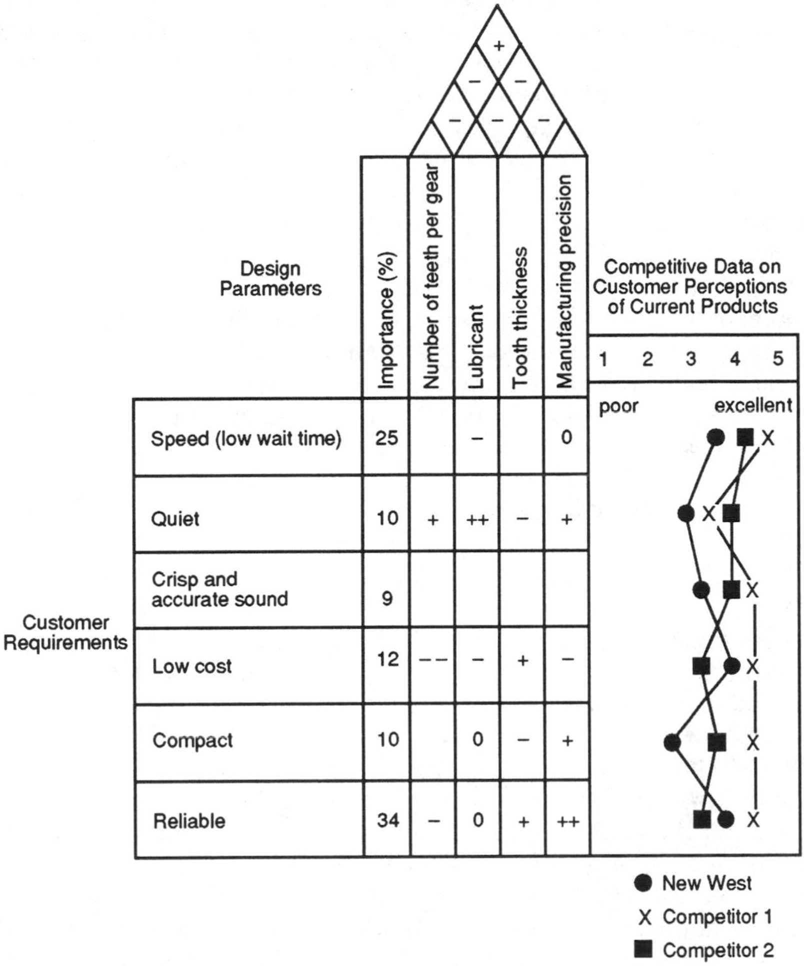

Customer Requirements / Design Parameters	Importance (%)	Number of teeth per gear	Lubricant	Tooth thickness	Manufacturing precision	Competitive Data on Customer Perceptions of Current Products
Speed (low wait time)	25		−		0	
Quiet	10	+	++	−	+	
Crisp and accurate sound	9					
Low cost	12	− −	−	+	−	
Compact	10	0	−		+	
Reliable	34	−	0	+	++	

● New West
X Competitor 1
■ Competitor 2

* The "house of quality" relates primary customer requirements to the major design parameters about which the development team will make design choices. The right-hand side shows customer perceptions of existing competitive products, while the top portion shows the interrelationship of the design parameters.

Each cell in the matrix represents a potential link between a design parameter and a customer attribute. This "relationship matrix" indicates both the direction and the strength of the relationship. Numbers or symbols may be used to establish the character of the relationship. Depending upon the extent of engineering knowledge, the team may be able to assign very specific values to the relationship. For other relationships, where less information is available, the value may be only qualitative in nature. In the gear design problem, for example, we have used simple pluses and minuses to indicate the nature and strength of the relationships. Increasing the number of teeth per gear, for example, reduces gear noise and thus has a positive impact on the customer attribute "quiet." However, increasing the number of teeth requires better tooling and more machining time. As a result, increasing the number of teeth may increase the cost and have a negative impact on the customer attribute "low cost." Such an evaluation of the relationship between design parameters and customer attributes evolves through an interactive process based on engineering experience, information from customers, and data from statistical analysis or designed experiments.

Two additional types of information complete the house of quality. The *fourth* step focuses on *customer perceptions of the company's existing product compared to its competitors*. The company's relative position on each customer attribute provides insight both as to where problems in the market may exist, and where opportunities for potential advantage may lie. New West Photo's existing designs are perceived as relatively low cost, and their automatic rewind systems are relatively slow, noisy, and bulky. In contrast, Competitor 1 has an edge in both cost and performance.

The *fifth* and last piece of analysis in the house of quality is the interrelationship or *interaction between design parameters*. In order to establish these interactions, the house of quality builds two diagonals—up and to the left, and up and to the right—growing out of each column of the matrix. The cells of this "roof matrix" indicate the strength and direction of interrelationships among design parameters. The negative sign in the cell connecting lubricants and number of teeth indicates that increasing the value of one (e.g., using lubricants to reduce noise) tends to decrease the value of the others (e.g., with a better lubricant, the design engineer can tolerate fewer teeth per gear) in engineering design. The roof matrix thus makes clear important tradeoffs that may exist in selecting design parameters, and may identify opportunities for improvements that add important second- or third-order consequences. A new lubricant, for example, may improve smoothness and reduce noise, therefore allowing for a gear design with less precise manufacturing requirements and lower cost.

When the analysis behind the house of quality is complete, the development team has a summary of critical customer attributes, the design parameters most closely connected to them, the pattern of interactions among those design parameters, and potential opportunities for improving competitive position. But until the house of quality is actually used—until the team establishes targets for critical design parameters, and thus customer attributes—the house of quality is only a summary of information. The QFD process creates a framework within which the issues may be examined in a fruitful and effective way, but hard choices must still be made.

Consider, for example, the problem of sound in the gear system. The house of quality suggests that overall noise level performance is not competitive; the current auto rewind system is too noisy. Moreover, the sound that the auto rewind creates is less "crisp" and "accurate" than competitors' products. Since the sound has a relatively high importance, it is clearly a problem area and an item for focus in the early-stage design process. The most important design parameters for sound are the tooth profiles in the gears and type of lubricant used. (Though other design parameters may have some influence, these two are clearly the most critical.) As far as "crisp" and "accurate" are concerned, however, the cells in the relationship matrix are blank. The implication is that while a crisp and accurate sound is an important attribute from the customer's standpoint, there is little engineering knowledge about the design parameters that drive it.

Before proceeding to establish targets, therefore, it is necessary to investigate the underlying sources of a crisp and accurate sound through discussions with customers and perhaps through experiments involving different camera designs (especially competitive modes that come close to the desired sound). Such experimental evidence may help characterize the customer attribute (e.g., crisp and accurate may be driven by a particular pattern of high frequency sounds) and identify the parameters that influence it. We may find, for example, that the number of gears used in the system as well as the diameter and tooth profiles of each gear are the major factors behind a crisp and accurate sound, although other parameters may have some influence. We may also find however, that design parameters not on the list are important—for example, harmonics in the gear train caused by poor gear-train alignment. Important at this stage of the development process is to use relatively inexpensive experiments to identify the requirements and underlying design parameters. This is far more effective than going through a series of preliminary design iterations that provide little insight into the underlying issues.

In addition to getting a crisp and accurate sound, the noise in the gear system must be reduced. If we focus on the two most important drivers of noise—tooth profile and lubricants—we can use the house of quality to identify the important issues that must be examined in setting targets for those parameters. Improving the tooth profile, for example, is likely to affect manufacturing costs and tooth thickness (to retain strength), and therefore space. A change in the lubricant system could bear some of the burden in reducing noise, but that may also increase cost. At this (early) stage in the design process, the team may weigh costs and benefits and set targets for the lubricant and tooth profile that reduce noise, even at the expense of some additional cost. But the team may also decide that this is an area worth further investigation during the detailed design phase (e.g., looking at additional alternatives or running special experiments to increase knowledge about the sources of gear noise). This may be a tough issue, but it is much better to address it early and within a common framework than to address it late from different perspectives and on a random trial-and-error basis.

QFD has power because it provides a common language and framework within which design engineers and marketers may fruitfully interact. The house of quality makes interrelationships and inherent design choices explicit. It gives precision to the conversations and discussions that go on in identifying design objectives and critical design parameters. By clarifying a very complex and ambiguous situation, the house of quality facilitates early consideration of difficult issues and helps to identify gaps in engineering and marketing knowledge. But QFD, and the "house of quality" in particular, is a tool to be used with focus and flexibility. It needs to be adapted to fit the circumstances of particular products and processes, and it needs to be used where it will have the most value. Many users of QFD have horror stories about design teams that literally fill up wall after wall with matrices so complicated that no one understands them. The organization's time and energy is absorbed in the minutiae of nuts and bolts and no one concentrates on those design parameters that are most crucial in driving customer attributes or in doing the experiments that will provide real insight.

Once an organization has developed some experience with QFD as a process, it becomes apparent that the formal methodology—the specific matrices and the filling in of cells, columns, and rows—is less important than the underlying philosophy and framework for analysis, discussion, and experimentation. Moreover, QFD can be a way to build and store knowledge crucial to the design and development of particular products or processes. Thus, to have its most significant impact, QFD needs to be managed as a framework for communications and analysis, and as a methodology for building and summarizing knowledge about the linkages between design parameters and customer attributes.

Yet even where QFD is understood and used effectively, outstanding firms do not rely on formal procedure or mechanisms by themselves.

QFD is a useful framework. But there really is no substitute for engineers who understand customers, or for marketing specialists who understand the basic technology of the product. Thus, while formal methods like QFD have an important role to play, they are at their most powerful when used in a development organization where engineers interact directly with customers and have experience in dealing with issues of marketing, and where marketing specialists are comfortable with the technology and have experience interacting with engineers on technical problems. In this, as in so much of development, there is no substitute for competence and understanding the territory of one's functional counterpart.

Design for Manufacturability

In the early phases of development—when attention focuses on establishing overall objectives, laying out product architecture, and setting target design parameters—a methodology like QFD provides a useful framework for cross-functional integration. Much of the analysis and discussion may focus on design engineering and marketing, but manufacturing issues arise at the earliest phases of this process and may be incorporated quite easily in the QFD framework. As development proceeds through detailed engineering, manufacturing issues become acute as engineers begin to establish specific processing requirements and build prototypes. In a traditional, sequential setup (like the one at New West Photo in which Rod McQuarrie and Ellen Gaither found themselves involved), manufacturing issues arise directly only after parts engineers have established basic design parameters and built and tested prototypes for functionality. In order to bring issues of manufacturability into the design process earlier, many firms have implemented "design for manufacturability" (DFM) methods. Like QFD, DFM is a summary category that includes a wide variety of methods.[6] Here we examine two kinds of DFM methods—design rules and design for producibility—and then apply them to our gear system design problem.

Design Rules. The idea that product (or manufacturing process) design needs to comprehend the constraints and capabilities in the downstream manufacturing process has been recognized since the earliest days of mass production. Henry Ford's famous dictum, "any color as long as it's black," illustrates a rule that expresses a process constraint for product designers. Today, design rules are used in a variety of industries ranging from semiconductors to specialty chemicals, and from structural steel to consumer appliances. In essence, design rules express the boundaries within which the manufacturing process operates in terms of the issues confronting product designers. In the case of the new gear

EXHIBIT 9–5

Design Rules for Fabricated-Assembled Products*

Rule	Intended Impact on Performance
Minimize the number of parts in a design	Simplify assembly; reduce direct labor; reduce material handling and inventory costs
Minimize the number of part numbers (use common parts)	Reduce material handling and inventory costs; improve economies of scale (increase volume through commonality)
Eliminate adjustments	Reduce assembly errors; allow automation; increase capacity and throughput
Eliminate fasteners	Simplify assembly; reduce direct labor cost; reduce squeaks and rattles; improve durability; allow automation
Eliminate jigs and fixtures	Reduce line changeover cost; lower required investment

* Design rules provide directional guidance for designers across a variety of dimensions. Product developers often must choose among conflicting guidelines and determine how far to push in pursuing a given guideline.

system, design rules might be expressed in terms of allowable gear size, tolerances on machining dimensions, production volumes, material types, surface finish characteristics, aging and heat treating requirements, and other processing characteristics that determine critical design parameters. The basic idea behind design rules is to establish an envelope within which the manufacturing process is capable of meeting design requirements. Manufacturing engineers send a message to product designers which says, "if you design within this envelope, our manufacturing process can meet your requirements for volume, cost, quality, and product performance."

If the rules are up to date and accurate, and if product designers have a process for comparing their designs against the rules, design rules can be quite useful in highlighting potential problems early in the design process and identifying high leverage areas for process development. Indeed, one of the outcomes of a design rule process can be choices by the firm to invest in expanding the boundaries of the envelope.

Some firms have expanded the notion of design rules to include principles of design whose application will improve manufacturing performance. Exhibit 9–5 provides examples of such "rules of thumb" for a fabricated, assembled product. These rules reflect experience in which overhead costs (of material handling or inventory tracking, for example) are driven by the number of parts in the total manufacturing system. They also reflect problems with quality where a product design requires careful adjustment of components or subassemblies, or where assembly involves fasteners (e.g., screws, nuts, and bolts) that are difficult to control and are often the source of reliability problems. The rule "eliminate jigs and fixtures" is intended to lower the cost of production line changeovers and reduce the investment required for a new product. Where a product requires parts positioning for transport or assembly, process engineers often use jigs and fixtures to hold the piece in place. If there are many different models or many different products produced in the same assembly facility, an important part of the cost and time for changeover from one product to another is associated with changing jigs and fixtures. A "jigless" design, therefore, may make the assembly process much more flexible.

Experience has shown that the application of such design rules of thumb can have an extraordinary impact on manufacturing cost and productivity. NCR, for example, has shown that application of design for manufacturability concepts like those articulated in Exhibit 9–5 can result in significant reductions in assembly time, the number of parts required in its products, the number of tools and fasteners required, and the number of suppliers involved in the production system. In the NCR 2760—an electronic cash register—DFM methodology resulted in major savings over the predecessor product: a 75 percent reduction in assembly time, 85 percent fewer parts, 65 percent fewer suppliers, no tools required for assembly, no fasteners in the design, and 75 percent less direct labor time (resulting in design lifetime direct labor savings estimated at over $1 million).[7]

Design for Producibility. Rules of thumb like "minimize the number of parts" have often produced dramatic results, particularly in contexts where previous designs have been highly complex and difficult to manufacture. But experience in a number of industries suggests the need to broaden the principles of DFM to encompass a more comprehensive notion of manufacturing system performance. More modern applications of the DFM principle—such as Boothroyd's design-for-assembly concepts—typically focus on an individual part and consider ways to simplify it, combine it with others to reduce the total number of parts, or modify it for easier assembly. Most of these DFM methods are designed to reduce direct labor and manufacturing overhead costs or to improve in-plant quality. But there are other dimensions of manufacturing performance that may suffer as a result of applying traditional DFM rules of thumb.

Take, for example, lead time in product development. Application of the rule "minimize the number of parts" often results in designers combining several simple parts into one complex part. This has the effect of reducing assembly time, inventory carrying costs, and costs associated with managing specific part numbers, and in general makes the product easier to assemble at a lower cost. But it also requires a very complex mold for production. If the new part is on the critical path of the development project, the complexity of the mold may increase development lead time significantly. In a competitive market, increased lead time means that revenues will occur further in the future, and may be smaller because of the loss of early potential customers. Exhibit 9–6 summarizes examples developed by Karl Ulrich that illustrate the impact of alternative designs on overall manufacturing system performance, including the cost associated with lead time. These examples suggest that where parts are on the critical path, application of the rule of thumb that calls for minimizing the number of parts may be very expensive.

The solution to this dilemma is not to abandon DFM principles; rather, it is to embed issues of the number of parts, the choice of fasteners, and other issues associated with traditional DFM rules in a much more comprehensive analysis of manufacturing system performance. This requires methods to evaluate the implications of differences in lead time associated with alternative designs. It may also require rethinking the way that a particular process fits into the overall manufacturing system. The interaction between specific parts and products and the manufacturing system is evident in the issue of manufacturing flexibility.

Take, for example, the situation in which a firm like New West Photo manufactures many different camera models in the same plant. Given increasingly fragmented markets and the need to offer specialized products that meet the requirements and demands of increasingly diversified customers, the plant needs the capability to produce a high variety of products at low cost. Moreover, it needs to be able to respond effectively to shifts in the product mix that occur from time to time in unexpected ways. In this context, flexibility with respect to variety and responsiveness to shifts in product mix are important dimensions of manufacturing performance.

The design of the product may have an important influence on the flexibility actually achieved in manufacturing, but improving system flexibility is unlikely to occur by focusing on the design of a single part or even a single camera. What is required is an approach to design that comprehends the product family as a whole. Dan Whitney has described an approach to modularized design that he calls the "combinatorial method":

EXHIBIT 9–6

Impact on Manufacturing Performance (Lifetime Cost) of Alternative Designs for Fasteners in a High-Volume Camera Cover*

	Basic Parameters		Lifetime Impact on Cost if Design Shifts from Option 1 to Option 2 (000s of $)
	Option 1: Snap Fit Camera cover is assembled to camera base with snap fit plastic fasteners molded into cover	Option 2: Screws Camera cover is assembled to camera base with four screws	
Material Cost	included in molding cost	screws add 8¢/unit	+254
Labor Cost	easy to assemble	additional assembly time of 15 seconds	+204
Capital Cost	more complex molds	lower tooling costs	−41
System Cost	fewer parts; less material handling	four new parts; one new vendor	+487
Time Cost	longer lead time on molds	simpler mold design and shorter lead time	−2,598
		Total (negative implies net benefit)	−1,694

NOTE: Cost changes are based on an activity cost model developed by Karl Ulrich and his associates. They assume 4 million units produced over the life of the camera, and use prices and cost estimates from experience at Polaroid. For additional information, see K. Ulrich et al., "A Framework for Including the Value of Time in Design-for-Manufacturing Decision Making," M.I.T. Working Paper #3243-9-MSA, February 1991.

* The design matrix identifies the relationship between the manufacturing process design parameters and the product design parameters. The performance matrix shows the relationship between the process design parameters and the performance parameters of the manufacturing process.

The combinatorial method, carried out by marketing and engineering team members, divides a product into generic parts or subassemblies, and identifies the necessary variations of each. The product is then designed to permit any combination of variations of these basic parts to go together physically and functionally. (If there are six basic parts and three varieties of each, for example, the company can build 3^6 or 729 different models.)[8]

When designers and marketers use this kind of methodology to develop a new platform product, they develop not only a specific product, but an architecture for an entire family of products. In the case of our gear design problem, a firm using modular design would not design a new automatic rewind system every time it brought out a new version of a particular camera. Instead, the project to develop the platform product would include an effort to develop a new rewinder and a new gear system that designers would use in several future versions of that product. Engineers working on the platform would design the rewinder to fit a given space constraint and would establish interfaces (how the parts fit together physically, how control is achieved, how the users interact with the rewinder) to guide future development efforts. Future versions of the platform product might incorporate improvements in the rewinder and the gear system, but these improvements would occur within the framework established by the platform product. When subsequent development focuses on introduction of a new member of the family, designers work within the architecture of parts, interfaces, and subassemblies established by the basic platform product. Although adjustments may be required to meet specific requirements, these must be examined within the context of the basic architecture and with respect to their implications for overall system performance.

Implementing DFM. Thus far our discussion of DFM has moved from a relatively narrow definition of specific design rules to a much broader concept of producibility. We have broadened and deepened the scope of DFM in two ways. First, we have redefined performance to include total manufacturing system behavior, including the role of time and flexibility. Second, we have broadened the focus of design itself to include the architecture of a family of products, including the modular design of parts and components and the establishment of interfaces. In all of this analysis, the basic thrust is very similar—to create designs that comprehend the constraints and opportunities in the manufacturing system broadly defined.

Framed in these terms, implementation of a DFM methodology involves: (1) establishing the envelope for the existing process; (2) identifying important connections between design choices and manufacturing system performance; and (3) establishing key dimensions of the product architecture and its impact on the overall manufacturing system. To do this, developers require a design process that structures thinking and establishes critical relationships. Such a process may involve design checklists used by all engineers, procedures for calculating manufacturing system costs (and other dimensions of performance), or creating access to a library of established parts that are consistent with product architecture and capable of providing required functionality (e.g., the engineer does not need to specify a different electric motor for every new camera design).

One can image such a set of procedures as a static, one-way process in which design engineers take the existing manufacturing process as given and design around those constraints. For firms with unwieldy designs, such a static approach to DFM may have significant benefits. Moreover, for some products—particularly derivative products or products that extend an established design—such an approach may be highly effective. But for platform products that represent a new generation of technology or a new segment of the market, such an approach may miss crucial opportunities to change the manufacturing process in order to enhance the performance of the product and manufacturing system. To exploit its full potential, DFM has to be an interactive, integrative process in which product and process engineers create a joint product-process design. In such a setting, product design choices comprehend key process restraints, but the process itself may also change (through process development and investment) to enhance capability and provide what the emerging design requires.

Exhibit 9–7 lays out one approach to integrating detailed product and process design in what we shall call the "house of producibility" (or, perhaps more accurately, the duplex of producibility).[9] Using our gear system example we have developed two matrices: a design matrix that links product and process design parameters; and a manufacturing performance matrix that connects process design parameters to manufacturing system performance. In the design matrix, process-oriented product design parameters make up the columns of the matrix, while process design parameters create the rows. In the performance matrix, the process parameters become the columns, while the dimensions of manufacturing system performance make up the rows.

In the design matrix, the numbers in the cells indicate the direction and strength of the relationship between choices in gear design and gear processing (i.e., 1 = modest effort, 5 = strong impact). For example, an increase in the number of gears moderately increases the number of tools, makes material handling more complex, and increases the number of assembly operations. A narrowing of the tolerances on tooth profile increases required precision, and will change the metal removal sequence significantly. We have used qualitative symbols to represent these linkages in the design matrix, but engineers may be able to express these relationships more precisely. The relationships rest on knowledge about the existing process, but may also draw on theoretical knowledge in order to allow for new process ideas. For example, new methods for metal removal (e.g., laser machining) might change the way a product design parameter affects the process design. Such a new process might increase the range of metal removal capability, thus reducing the com-

Exhibit 9–7

The "House of Producibility" for a Gear Design Problem at New West Photo

DESIGN MATRIX

Product Design Parameters

Process Design Parameters	number of gears	tooth profile tolerances	material strength
number and complexity of tools	+2	+3	+2
complexity of metal removal sequence		+4	
material handling	+3		
number of heat treating steps	+2		+4
precision	0	+5	
number of assembly operations	+5		

PERFORMANCE MATRIX

Process Design Parameters

Manufacturing Performance Parameters	importance	complexity of tools	metal removal complexity	material handling	heat treating	precision	assembly operations
labor cost	10		+2		+2	+2	+5
system cost	15	+3	+3	+5	+2	+4	+4
reliability	35	?	-3	0		+3	-3
lead time	15	+5	0	0		+2	0
flexibility	5	-3	0	-3		+2	-2
material cost	20	+2	+3		-2	+1	+2

plexity of the metal removal sequence required for any given product design. The implication is that the new process would change the sensitivity of the process to design changes and would be incorporated into the design (and performance) matrix by changing the relationships recorded in the appropriate cells.

The performance matrix links changes in the gear manufacturing process to manufacturing system performance. Here we have adopted a broad definition of performance to include time-to-market, flexibility, and total system cost. In this context, the process design parameters are drivers of manufacturing system performance. The cells in the matrix indicate the sensitivity of different performance dimensions to changes in process design, with the same relative ratings used in the design matrix. Increasing the complexity of tooling, for example, has a substantial impact on lead time (assuming the part in question is on the critical path), reduces flexibility (because of changeover costs) and adds to overall system cost because of increased maintenance.

As it stands in Exhibit 9–7, the house of producibility helps engineers clarify the implications of their design choices for manufacturing system performance. But we need not take the empty cells (which may indicate absence of knowledge) or the relative sensitivity of performance to process design as fixed. The framework allows individuals from different functions to identify opportunities for increasing knowledge and introducing new processes.

Both the design and performance matrices embody DFM principles in the parameters used for analysis as well as in the linkages between them. The gear design parameters used in the design matrix, for example, are "process-oriented" parameters. They include not only dimensions critical to gear performance from the customer's standpoint, but also aspects of gear design that are important from the standpoint of the production process. Likewise, linkages established between parameters and manufacturing systems performance may be based on DFM rules of thumb, as well as on more systematic analysis that one typically finds in a variety of DFM methodologies. Although the cells of the performance matrix as portrayed in Exhibit 9–7 are qualitative in character, detailed calculations of cost—or of any other manufacturing performance dimension—could be used to give the linkage a quantitative basis.

As we saw in our discussion of the house of quality, the most important aspect of an effective problem-solving process is neither the matrix itself nor the other formal tools used to organize knowledge and information. Indeed, a variety of other formats may prove highly useful, including network diagrams that provide a more graphic depiction of the critical interrelationships among the parameters. Moreover, we could elaborate the design and performance matrices—add a "roof" to them, add competitive information on manufacturing performance for perspective, or summarize quantitatively the relative importance of different dimensions of performance. Other refinements, such as quantitative targets for process parameters or indications of the relative significance of different design parameters, could also be developed.

Whether in simple or complex form, the point of the matrices remains the same: to facilitate integration of product and process design and to bring issues of producibility (broadly defined) to the center of the development process. The critical issues here are exactly those we found in the earlier QFD analysis: language, framework, communication, discipline, and focus. Indeed, there is a fundamental unity in the substance and process of the various methodologies we have examined in this section of the chapter. Whether we are looking at design targets or issues of producibility, the methods focus attention on customer requirements (in the field or in the plant), linkages between design parameters and performance, and the tradeoffs among them. Moreover, the process behind the substance—the systematic listing of dimensions and parameters, establishing qualitative and quantitative estimates of critical linkages, assessing their relative importance, and structuring choices around the evidence derived from these analyses—not only provides a useful way to organize and use knowledge, but also creates a new framework for cross-functional interaction. As we have noted before, such methods are not a substitute for design engineers who are knowledgeable and oriented toward manufacturing system performance, or manufacturing engineers who are sensitive to customer needs. These tools and methods complement and make those integrative skills even more effective.

The tools and methods do change the nature of the development process. The focus in applying them, therefore, should not be just to do old things better. This is a new set of activities and interactions; a new way to frame and solve problems. Structured methods are not a panacea, but they have a role to play in making working-level problem solving more effective. They create a common framework and language and, if applied well, raise important tradeoffs and conflicts early, thus saving valuable time and resources. They make holes in the organization's knowledge about critical relationships apparent and provide a basis for capturing and using knowledge important in making choices about design.

Computer-Based Systems

In the Appendix to this chapter we examine developments in advanced computer systems that may have a profound influence on the nature of the development process. Computer-aided design and manufacturing systems are in widespread use today. Advanced systems, involving sophisticated database capability, electronic interchange of data, and intelligent support for group interaction, are under development. Such systems have the potential to greatly improve problem solving processes. The computer system itself, however, is not a panacea. Commercial hardware and software systems are unlikely to be a source of competitive advantage; instead, advantage will lie in an organization's ability to develop proprietary software and coherently integrate software, hardware, and "humanware" into an effective system. Human creativity, face-to-face contact, and interpersonal communication will continue to be an integral, essential aspect of product and process development. What will be different is the context in which face-to-face communication and human creativity have their application.

The kinds of systems we have outlined in the Appendix combine graphics, databases, and problem-solving methods, and may afford development groups rapid access to data, drawings, models, and analysis—all within a consistent framework. Today, data on customer experience, manufacturing processes, and alternative designs often are organized in incompatible formats, processed in very different computer systems, and managed by different organizations. New systems will create open access to common databases and provide a consistent framework within which designers, process engineers, and marketers may probe the underlying sources of the problems they confront. The problem-solving group will still employ face-to-face communication, but the conversations are likely to be very different. Communication will be faster and occur within a new (informed) framework, possibly using new media. These new systems in effect may provide a new "language" that will allow difficult functional groups with their own "dialects" to develop shared understanding.

Observations and Implications for Management

It is clear that advanced computer-based systems have the potential for significant impact. It is also clear that a fragmented organization with parochial philosophies and substantial barriers to communication will frustrate even the most clever and powerful computer system. In this respect, automating information and communications in the development process has much in common with the automation of manufacturing processes. Companies have learned, often by sad experience, that automation in manufacturing is most powerful and effective when applied in a manufacturing process that is well-characterized, capable, and in control. Many firms have seen automation as the means by which they would achieve a well-characterized, capable, in-control process. But these companies have learned that attempts to automate a manufacturing process that is not in control only serves to highlight and underscore much more sharply the inherent weaknesses, absence of understanding, and gaps of knowledge in the process.

An analogous outcome is likely in the application of advanced computer-based systems for design and development. Organizations that have broken down barriers to communication across functions, implemented a development process that integrates functional activities, developed a facility for and capability in structured methods for problem solving, and cultivated an organizational structure and approach to leadership that complements and reinforces cross-functional integration are likely to find advanced computer-based systems not only easier to implement but much more powerful in their effects on the speed, efficiency, and quality of problem solving. Of course, some organizations may see the implementation of such a computer-based system as the catalyst that will spur an organization to greater integration. In either case, it is important to understand that effective implementation of such systems requires significant change from the traditional, sequential, parochial development organization.

Appendix to Chapter 9

Structured methods can play an important role in moving an organization toward effective problem solving. They provide a framework for cross-functional interaction and a common language that marketers and design and manufacturing engineers can use to create a shared understanding of their joint problems in development. But even where structured methods are deeply ingrained in the organization, the speed, efficiency, and quality of problem solving will depend on how rapidly and efficiently the organization can access the right data, how quickly the information moves from one source of knowledge to another, how well the organization uses the data it has to establish critical relationships and linkages, and how effectively the organization captures what it learns from experience. In effect, the challenge of quickly and efficiently moving complex data and storing and accessing knowledge in complex systems offers significant additional opportunity for improvements in problem solving.

In short, information systems that harness the power of the computer to store, manipulate, process, and communicate information across different functional groups and projects have the potential to play a crucial role in improving the effectiveness of problem solving at the working level. The amount of information (and in manual systems; the amount of paper) required to solve even moderately complex problems effectively can be daunting. A variety of studies have shown that in electromechanical products, such as home appliances, computers, or consumer electronics, engineers spend as little as a half to a third of their time doing real engineering.[1] The rest of their time is spent filling out forms, attending meetings, tracking down data, and traveling to the next activity. This is true even in organizations where computer-based systems are in use. Indeed, it appears that the application of the computer to the problems of design and development has focused primarily on automating existing engineering tasks. Much less progress has been made in using computer systems to integrate problem solving.

Computers, of course, have had a major impact in some settings, particularly in applications like drafting and in industries like semiconductor design where many of the design problems can be represented in two dimensions. Furthermore, recent developments in computer-aided engineering (CAE) systems allow engineers to simulate the performance of designs electronically and thus provide the means for faster, lower-cost analysis. By building engineering equations into the software, CAE systems can aid engineers in the selection of design parameters. In designing something like a gear system, an advanced CAE system will evaluate the merits of the gear design based on theoretical equations and previous experience. Advanced systems may also embody something of an "expert system" which may suggest alternative design concepts based on input provided by the design engineer.

All of these applications of computer-based tools are useful and important. By giving engineers rapid feedback on the potential performance of their designs, these tools can improve initial design quality and substitute, at least in part, for expensive physical model building and prototype construction. For very complex systems, prototypes are likely to continue to be necessary, but their quality can be increased and the number of prototypes required can be substantially reduced with the application of the new computer-based tools. Tools that automate existing design tasks, however, fall short of the potential in the computer, and in information technology in general, to change fundamentally the way problem solving (particularly across functional groups) gets done. What is needed is a system that not only provides tools for analysis and design, but also changes the way people in different functions communicate, cope with large-scale, complex data, and capture and store knowledge. To illustrate what such systems might look like, what they might accomplish, and what the challenges in their design and implementation might be, we consider how systems might be applied to our gear design problem.

Four Generations of Computer-Based Design Systems

Exhibit A–1 lays out four generations of competitor-based systems that take us progressively from automating existing tasks to creating a fully

EXHIBIT A–1

Four Generation of Computer-Based Design and Development Systems

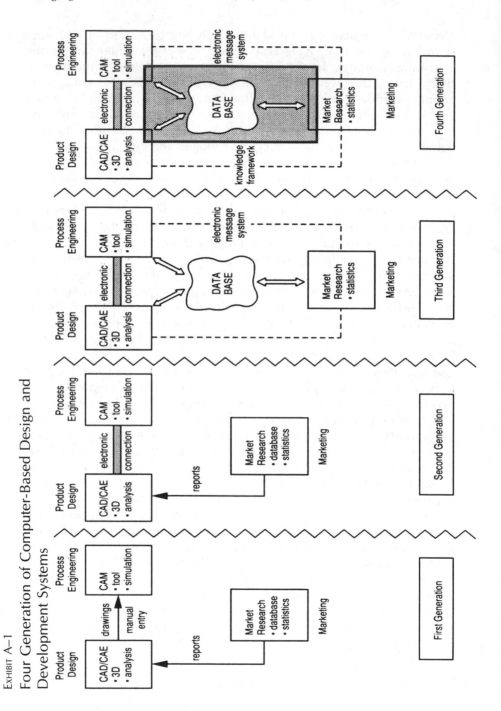

integrated system for managing the design process and the information, data, and knowledge that underlie it. In first generation systems, gear designers work with CAD software that allows them to draw alternative gear designs in three dimensions on their computer screens. The system has embedded in it analytical routines that help a design engineer examine the behavior of the gear system under design consideration. The gear designer's counterpart in process engineering uses a CAM system that programs the machining process for the gears. The CAM system also has some simulation capability that allows the process engineer to explore alternative metal removal sequences (such as heat treating steps using alternative materials). Finally, the marketing specialist uses a workstation with access to a customer database that includes data on sales by model, warranty experience, customer complaints, and other information received from customers through the field sales and service organization. The marketing specialist can also access a market research database that has information based on customer surveys, as well as the result of special studies conducted on specific products.

These systems are powerful in executing individual tasks such as selecting gear design parameters, establishing processing sequences, or identifying attractive feature sets for products. However, connecting these individual activities within a first-generation system is complex and time consuming. A design from the CAD system is printed out on a plotter and manually transferred to process engineering. (In fact, the drawings are transported manually through the internal mail system. They actually move around on little carts.) Once recognized by process engineering, the dimensions from the drawings as well as other important specifications are entered manually into the CAM system. Similarly, the marketing specialist does analysis on the workstation and then prepares reports and memos. These reports are circulated in the marketing organization and, after review and approval, are transmitted to design engineering. (They typically are not sent to process engineering.)

Compared to the traditional system without computers, this first generation system has a number of significant advantages. Design engineers consider many more alternatives quickly and efficiently, process engineers are able to execute a process plan for new designs much more quickly than before, and marketing specialists have greatly increased the amount of analysis that they accomplish for a given program. Even with these advantages, however, problem solving across departments can be cumbersome and difficult. There are lags in the flow of information, and designers, process engineers, and marketers work with different kinds of data and make very different assumptions about the nature of the problems they face.

The second-generation system depicted in Exhibit A–1 attempts to deal with some of these problems. In the second-generation system, interfaces are developed and communication links established so that gear design information may be transmitted electronically directly to the CAM system. Creating such an integrating CAD-CAM system eliminates a great deal of paperwork, avoids errors associated with translation from computer systems to paper, and reduces the amount of time required to complete a design. Design information moves across the network in digital format, allowing process and design engineers to work with the identical design. Marketing specialists, however, are still working with reports and memos, and the CAD-CAM linkage applies to the current design but captures neither previous experience nor alternatives considered on the current design.

The third-generation system focuses on the issues just cited. This system links the databases in design, engineering, and marketing, establishing a common interface among them. The combined database tracks historical experience with gear design and provides tools that allow engineers and marketers to analyze the data and establish important interrelationships, and allows engineers in different functions to keep track of design changes and maintain consistent information about development status. The third-generation system also provides a facility for sending and receiving messages, such as "post-it" notes attached to drawings and other documents. This allows the participants in development to communicate with each other about current design problems. The final element of the third-generation system is a local archive that allows a design engineer, for example, to store notes, test results, and important messages pertaining to particular issues in the design.

The fourth-generation system takes integration across product and process design and marketing an important step further. Where the third-generation system established a common database, the focus of the fourth-generation system may use a network diagram to structure the relationship between design parameters and customer attributes. Using common software and a common interface (everyone's workstation has access to the same software and the screens everyone sees are the same, even in real time), the system allows design engineers, process engineers, and marketers working together as a team to define important parameters, attributes, and connections. The system also provides access to supporting data, analysis, and information that lie behind a particular relationship.

An example of an Advanced Computer-Based Design System

In order to illustrate a fourth-generation system, we have applied a system developed by Salzberg and Watkins to the gear design problem.[3] This system uses a network structure to organize information about

Exhibit A–2

Sample Screen for Advanced Computer-Based Design System: Databases Related to Gear Machining

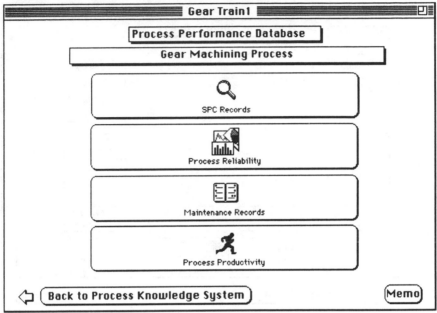

NOTE: From a system developed by Steven Salzberg and Michael Watkins. See Salzberg and Watkins, "Managing Information for Concurrent Engineering: Challenges and Barriers," *Research in Engineering Design*, 2 (1990), pp. 35–52.

attributes and parameters, and provides clear connections between the choices engineers and marketers must make and underlying supporting analyses and data. Exhibits A–2 to A–6 are examples of the screens that engineers might use when working with the system. Exhibit A–2, for example, shows a screen that allows an engineer to select among different databases related to the gear machining process. Some of these databases contain statistical data while others include graphs or digitized drawings. By selecting the process productivity database, an engineer can access a process flow diagram which indicates the sequence of operations required to process a gear (see Exhibit A–3). The screen in Exhibit A–3 provides further access to information on problem histories associated with a given step in the process, process performance data, and engineering drawings for this process.

Exhibit A–4 presents a network diagram connecting customer attributes to gear design parameters. The system allows engineers to cre-

EXHIBIT A–3

Sample Screen for Advanced Computer-Based Design System: The Gear Machining Process

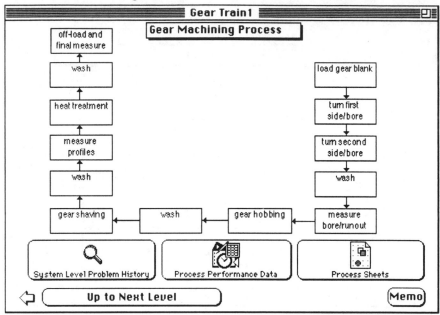

NOTE: From a system developed by Steven Salzberg and Michael Watkins. See Salzberg and Watkins, "Managing Information for Concurrent Engineering: Challenges and Barriers," *Research in Engineering Design*, 2 (1990), pp. 35–52.

ate their own diagrams and establish connections between attributes and parameters. Each parameter entered in the network diagram is connected to a variety of other databases. An engineer interested in gear spacing, for example, could easily pull up detailed drawings of that parameter in the system. Such a detailed drawing is illustrated in Exhibit A–5. The screen includes not only a schematic of alternative gear designs, but also a description of the particular parameter and access to further information related to this design aspect. Thus, an engineer working on gear design can easily access information, drawings, process reliability data, and other information relevant to the selection of a specific design parameter. The same access to underlying data and information would be available for customer attributes. Exhibit A–6 summarizes detailed information about customer attributes compared to competitor experience. This screen provides competitive information as well as data reflecting customer experience in the field.

Eхнівіт A–4

Sample Screen for Advanced Computer-Based Design System:
Network Diagram Connecting Design Parameters and
Customer Attributes

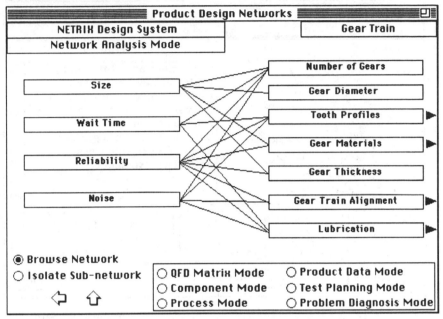

NOTE: From a system developed by Steven Salzberg and Michael Watkins. See Salzberg and Watkins, "Managing Information for Concurrent Engineering: Challenges and Barriers," *Research in Engineering Design*, 2 (1990), pp. 35–52.

The network diagrams and the connections to the databases and analytical tools become the framework within which the team jointly develops its knowledge about the design. In effect, the fourth generation system provides a more complete and electronic format for the kind of structured methodology we depicted earlier in discussing QFD and DFM. By joining the databases, analytical tools, and critical relationship diagrams in one system, the fourth-generation system shortens feedback loops drastically, makes access to data easier and more consistent, and enhances the ability of development team members to communicate and collaborate. Moreover, because the results of analysis and problem solving are captured and stored in computer memory, the fourth-generation system facilitates organizational learning. With the ease of appending notes, comments, and test results, the system becomes a framework within which the design team can communicate, manage complex data, and create and store knowledge about design and development.

EXHIBIT A–5

Sample Screen for Advanced Computer-Based Design System:
Detailed Drawing of Tooth Profile

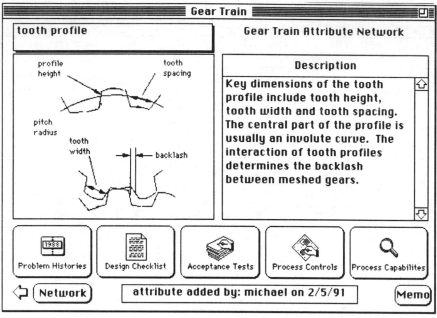

NOTE: From a system developed by Steven Salzberg and Michael Watkins. See Salzberg
and Watkins, "Managing Information for Concurrent Engineering: Challenges and
Barriers," *Research in Engineering Design*, 2 (1990), pp. 35–52.

One can, of course, imagine further generations of computer systems.
Systems may be developed, for example, that provide intelligent support
to the design team. By intelligent support, we mean the ability to discern
patterns in the actions of the human design team—patterns that indicate
the design teams are overlooking certain important issues or pursuing
alternatives that experience has proven problematic. Such an intelligent
system could track the pattern and flag inconsistencies, oversights, or impending problems. Furthermore, such systems could aid designers by
suggesting design alternatives based on information about desired customer attributes or process performance. Such fifth-generation systems
are not a substitute for human intelligence and creativity; rather, they use
the power of the computer for computation, memory, and high-speed
processing to complement and enhance the power of the human mind.

First- and second-generation computer systems are widely used, and
a number of firms have begun to implement third-generation systems.

EXHIBIT A–6

Sample Screen for Advanced Computer-Based Design System:
Detailed Customer Attributes and Competitor Comparisons

System Quality								
Netrix Product Design Data				**New West**		**Gear Train**		
Competitor Comparison				**Competitor 1**				

Attribute	! [1]	Best in Class			TGW [2]		TGR [3]	
		own	comp	diff	own	comp	own	comp
low wait time	22	3.5	5	–1.5	4	5	3	4.5
quiet	10	3	4	–1	3	5	3	4.5
crisp	11	3	4.5	–1.5	4	3	2.5	4
low cost	16	4	4.5	–.5	4.5	4.5	3.5	4.5
compact	13	2	4.5	–2.5	3	4	2.5	4
reliable	22	5	4	+1	5	3.5	4.5	3

Change Attributes

[1] Relative importance
[2] Things gone wrong
[3] Things gone right

NOTE: From a system developed by Steven Salzberg and Michael Watkins. See Salzberg and Watkins, "Managing Information for Concurrent Engineering: Challenges and Barriers," *Research in Engineering Design*, 2 (1990), pp. 35–52.

Companies such as Intergraph and Computervision have developed commercial software designed to provide third-generation capability. Fourth-generation systems, however, represent the frontier of computer-based system development for product and process design. They are an active focus of ongoing development, and some firms have developed prototypes and begun to implement custom versions of such design systems.

Study Questions

1. Using the gear system as an illustration (see Exhibit 9–2), outline how the choice of design parameters and customer attributes made by the

633

development team affects the quality, speed, and efficiency with which a final design is achieved. In this particular case, what are two or three additional design parameters and customer attributes that might usefully be included? Are there any drawbacks to including them?

2. What skills are essential for each of the three phases of the design-build-test cycle of problem solving? Where do such skills typically reside in an organization? How does the distribution of those skills add to the challenge of achieving integrated solutions in development?

3. How does the type of team (see Exhibit 8–1) impact the nature of problem solving? For what kind of problem solving do you think each type of team would be best suited? Why?

4. The house of quality is an organizing framework for relating design parameters to customer requirements. For the gear design problem (summarized in Exhibit 9–4), what conclusions would you draw from those QFD results with regard to key relationships, their importance, and their impact on development choices?

5. How might design rules, like those shown in Exhibit 9–5, be embedded and used by a computer system (e.g., CAD/CAM)? What would be the advantages and disadvantages of such a computerized set of design rules?

6. If design for producibility issues had not been fully considered in prior generations of gear design, what difficulties in manufacturing would likely have resulted? How might the structured approach known as design for producibility help eliminate those problems?

7. What are the major differences between each of the four generations of computer systems outlined in the appendix? What advantages and disadvantages might accrue to a firm by going straight to the fourth-generation system, versus those accruing to a firm that passes progressively from one generation to the next?

Design for Manufacturability at Midwest Industries

After 45 years at Midwest Industries, Gary Thurlow, Senior Technical Planning Manager, was looking forward to his retirement on April 1, 1990, only one month from now. Today, however, Thurlow was absorbed by plans for a smooth transition for his successor. Roger Myers, Director of Technical Planning and Thurlow's boss, had already selected an engineer from the Memphis plant to take over Thurlow's role as the corporate "champion" for Design for Manufacturability (DFM).

As a member of the corporate staff, Thurlow had spent the past six years developing and promoting the use of DFM throughout the corporation. He was reviewing the efforts toward DFM that had taken place to assess the lessons learned to date, where DFM should go from here, and how best his successor could facilitate that.

Midwest Industries Corporation

Midwest Industries Corporation's stated mission was to "create value for our stakeholders." In 1990, Midwest Industries, whose world headquarters was in Chicago, Illinois, was in the business of developing, manufacturing, marketing, installing, and servicing retail and self-service vending equipment worldwide. In 1989, Midwest Industries' net income was $275 million on revenue of $4.0 billion.

Midwest Industries was highly decentralized and multinational, with

This case was prepared by Research Associate Sherri L. Goodman under the supervision of Professor W. Bruce Chew.

18 worldwide autonomous business units. Each unit had a vocational charter, with responsibility for identifying market opportunities, engineering and manufacturing the product, and marketing the product through Midwest Industries' captive worldwide sales network and/or outside channels. The divisions within each business unit were treated as profit centers.

Originally named Vending Services Inc., Midwest Industries had pioneered the use of mechanical vending machines in retailing and dominated that market for over half a century. As electronics began to replace mechanics as the basis for vending machines and other retailing systems, Midwest Industries, with a huge investment in mechanical parts production, was slow to respond. When it did convert to electronics, it did so rapidly, at some pain to the organization.

The changing and increasing competitive pressures of the 1970s led management to stress technology, engineering creativity, and speed of product development by instituting such engineering performance measures as the number of drawings released to manufacturing per week. Unfortunately, this move encouraged engineers to design for function against time, turning out drawings with little regard for how the product would be manufactured.

Recognizing the increasing need for new manufacturing skills, processes, and quality, a separate corporate staff organization for manufacturing was created in 1983. Before then, manufacturing was not considered an important element of corporate strategy. By summer 1985, this staff organization was beginning to implement the six-part operations strategy described below. In 1989, staff personnel were reorganized, integrating quality assurance into the manufacturing organization to form Manufacturing & Quality Assurance. Exhibit 1 shows the corporate organization in 1990.

Operations Strategy

In 1985 the corporate manufacturing staff group created a manufacturing operations strategy comprising six major elements: people; quality environment; just-in-time; supply line management; computer integrated manufacturing; design for manufacturability (DFM).

A central element of operations strategy was the belief that the very core of excellence in Midwest Industries lay in the recruitment and development of people.

In pursuing a *quality environment*, the staff's objectives were to achieve higher quality, lower product cost, and improve response to customers.

The *just-in-time* (JIT) concepts originated with a four-stage program to reduce by 72%, the corporation's on-hand inventory by the end of 1988:

EXHIBIT 1

Corporate Organization Chart, 1990

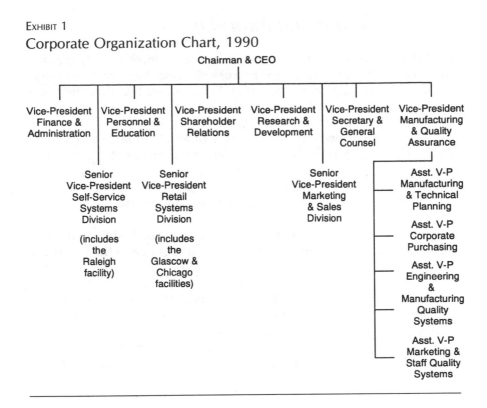

(1) Inventory Reduction—reduce safety stock and improve point-of-use scheduling; (2) JIT Methods—introduce "Kanban," manufacturing cells, cross-training, and better supplier relationships; (3) JIT/TQC—use Total Quality Control to facilitate root cause problem resolution; and (4) External Influence—expand JIT/TQC to affect customers and suppliers.

The key to the *supply line management* strategy was early supplier involvement (ESI) in the early stages of product and process planning to maximize the supplier's performance and value added to the product. To accomplish this, improving supplier relationships was emphasized.

The drive toward computer integrated manufacturing (CIM) focused on total systems integration to create a completely automated, integrated, and paperless factory. Efforts began by developing and using interconnect technologies and standards to facilitate communications among dissimilar computers. Once the computers were linked successfully, the focus would move toward sharing and managing data among the various software programs running on the network.

The sixth element of Midwest Industries' operations strategy was *design for manufacturability* (DFM).

Design for Manufacturability

At Midwest Industries, DFM was defined as "a methodology that addresses *early* in the development process *all* those things that can *impact* production and customer satisfaction." However, this definition was not fully developed until about 18 months after DFM was made part of the corporation's operations strategy.

Prior to the introduction of DFM, new products were developed in a traditional, serial process, i.e., the product management group would define the product, then pass it to the engineering group for product design, and after the design was completed, it was "passed over the wall" to the manufacturing group for process design and actual production.

Establishing the corporate manufacturing function had riveted attention and resources to manufacturability problems due to the increasing influx of new, more complex designs. Gary Thurlow was given the responsibility for helping the divisions address these producibility issues by educating them about DFM benefits. According to Thurlow, the objective was to achieve "*best in class* product and process designs *prior* to production prototyping and production."

Manufacturing & Quality Assurance segmented the DFM process into four dimensions: development process, software tools, design guidelines, and skills.

Development Process

Thurlow, as well as articles written on DFM, stressed that a key factor in the methodology's success was effective interaction in crossfunctional teams, allowing for product and process designs to be done in parallel. He felt that involving suppliers early in the development process was also essential.

Software Tools

Thurlow promoted computer-aided engineering (CAE) and computer-aided design (CAD) systems through training seminars, corporate funding of pilot programs, and personal promotion at the plant level. These software tools expedited mechanical designing by providing quick 3-D solid modeling. This modeling allowed a designer to visualize and change easily a design via a computer screen, reducing the need for time-consuming physical prototyping. These systems also expedited the required calculations for such things as structural and thermal analyses. Electrical designers could use the systems to develop schematic diagrams and simulate the actual performance of circuits, once again reducing the need for extensive prototyping. Using CAE/CAD for product designs enabled an electronic link to computer-aided manufacturing (CAM) systems.

Corporate staff strongly advocated CAD software utilizing the Boothroyd & Dewhurst Design For Assembly method. Through a series of interactive questions, this software sought to quantify the assembly time cost for a proposed product design and forecast the minimum number of parts to achieve the product function.

Design Guidelines

In DFM, engineers developed and followed guidelines to reduce the complexity of product manufacturing. For example, designers should select standard components from their library of preferred purchased components, rather than from a multitude of catalog sources. Likewise, designers should follow guidelines delineating existing, characterized manufacturing capabilities so that new designs adhered to required manufacturing process capabilities.

Skills

Thurlow believed that to be effective, personnel needed to be educated in the "art" of practical product and process design; science and engineering skills could be hired, but "art" skills had to be developed on-the-job. To promote such learning Thurlow wanted to lessen the traditional specialization of skills by function both to increase skill breadth and enhance the collaborative process needed for DFM.

When DFM was named a specific element of corporate operations strategy, Thurlow began looking for a site for a DFM pilot project. He reached agreement with the Raleigh, North Carolina, facility to try a full-fledged DFM project, which started up in January 1986.

The Raleigh Facility

The Raleigh facility was the headquarters of the Self-Service Systems Division, formed in 1989, which engineered and manufactured automatic currency changers, customer-activated retail service machines, and peripheral and support devices.

In the early 1970s, Midwest Industries had several plants in Raleigh and over 6,000 employees; by the early 1980s, only one facility remained, with about 1,000 employees and annual revenues of about $25 million. At this point, Midwest Industries' automated currency changer product line was transferred to Raleigh from another U.S. plant, a move that spurred tremendous growth: by 1990, the Raleigh plant had grown to 1,300 employees and expected sales of over $300 million.

Raleigh's DFM Decision

Ron Jenkins, an engineering manager at Raleigh, sowed the first seeds of DFM at the facility after attending an international conference on DFM with Gary Thurlow in mid–1985.

Around this time, engineering entailed redesigning the interchangeable coin cassette, essentially an aluminum box used to store and secure coins for delivery and placement into automated currency changers. About the size of a large shoe box, the cassette contained many features, such as internal adjustments for different sizes of coins, spring-loaded plates to keep the coins compressed and secure as they were dispensed, and a tamper indicator.

The cassette contained 241 separate parts that required approximately 76 minutes to assemble. In addition, the aluminum material used for the enclosure made it vulnerable to damage in the field. Raleigh engineers discovered that delivery personnel who transported the cassettes between the vendors and their currency changing machines might throw the cassettes into the back of their trucks, step on them to reach something else, or drop them to the ground from the back of a truck. Although the enclosure was strong enough to securely contain the money, it would become disfigured and damaged during this rough handling to the point that the cassette would not function properly in an automated currency changer. This problem was a major source of irritation and expense to the vendors and became a significant customer service liability to Midwest Industries.

In their decision to redesign the cassette, engineering settled on five design objectives: low cost (reduce by 50%), more robust, lightweight, simpler mechanisms and improved appearance.

Since Ron Jenkins had worked on the original cassette design, he took responsibility for the cassette redesign project with the additional objective of using DFM. He planned to (1) form an engineering/manufacturing dedicated team; (2) apply DFM rules; and (3) maximize use of CAD/CAE tools for design and for mold-flow and stress analyses.

Raleigh management supported the DFM project for two reasons. First, product volume, both current and projected, had created an impending shortage of manufacturing floor space. It was thought that DFM could help reduce assembly times, thereby increasing plant throughput; and, it would reduce the number of parts necessary, freeing up some parts storeroom space for production activities. Second, tremendous growth had introduced many newly hired "green" design engineers with no manufacturing experience or expertise, who would benefit from appropriate training.

Raleigh's Pilot

In January 1986, the official DFM team was organized, consisting of a design engineer, a manufacturing engineer, a quality assurance engineer, and a purchasing specialist. The three engineers were expected to work full time on this project until its scheduled completion in 18 months. The team leader was the design engineer, who coincidentally had worked as a manufacturing engineer many years earlier. Jenkins was responsible for the team and its results.

The team planned a design approach aimed at (1) efficient assembly; (2) minimum part count; (3) maximum use of plastic moldings; and (4) maximum use of cost-effective automatic assembly. They planned on a daily volume of 80 cassettes, growing at 13% annually.

After completing its third prototype in November, 1986—seven months before their final deadline—the team turned to designing and producing the hard tooling required for the prototype's complex, molded plastic box. Eight months later, the vendor delivered the first 200 fully-molded boxes. When subjected to the impact resistance test, (10 six-foot drops onto a concrete floor), the plastic boxes, made up of a number of separate plastic pieces glued together to simulate the single-piece plastic box, failed.

Raleigh then began making design adjustments, getting the hard tooling changed, molding new samples, and testing their impact resistance. During this process, the team enlisted the help of people knowledgeable about complex injection molding: consultants from their plastics supplier, scientists from a local university, their tool designer, their tool maker, and their molder to try and improve the robustness of the cassette.

Meanwhile, Raleigh's general manager was becoming impatient. One day while watching the cassette boxes' drop test, he exclaimed, "That's not good enough! I want these boxes to be able to survive this!" and threw one over his shoulder across the room. The box crashed against the back wall of the lab and fell to the floor in pieces. From that point on, the team adopted an informal "The G.M.'s Over-the-Shoulder Test" for all future impact testing.

The final cassette design was released in April 1988, and 80 new cassettes were sent to two vending service companies for testing in their automated currency changers. The trial cassettes were 100% successful through mid-June, when the team approved the design for full-scale production. The first shipments to customers were made in July, reaching full production by the beginning of September. This 10-week ramp-up in manufacturing was uncommonly quick and problem-free for a new product in Raleigh.

Raleigh management viewed the DFM cassette team as a great success. Parts for the cassette were reduced from 241 to 101, and assembly time from 76 minutes to 17 minutes, resulting in a significant product cost reduction, that was magnified by the unexpected jump in demand and production, from 80 per day to 400 per day in mid–1989. However, these cost savings did not result from one primary goal of the project—using automatic assembly equipment, which could not be fully justified because the final design was so simple to assemble. Subsequent increases in production capacity came from adding line workers to assemble the cassettes manually.

Team members cited several keys to their success: the small, multidisciplinary team approach to the design; team members being dedicated resources throughout the project; having one manager/leader with responsibility for the project; and most importantly, support from top management.

Management's biggest complaint about the project was that what was originally scheduled to be an 18-month project turned into a 30-month design marathon. Early in the project, management encouraged the team by saying the new cassette would save the plant thousands of dollars per day of production. After the team missed its original deadline, management said the delays were costing the plant thousands of dollars per day.

Raleigh After the Pilot

Nonetheless, Raleigh management was enthusiastic about the potential of early involvement by manufacturing engineering, purchasing, and quality assurance in the design process, although they decided that the large number of products precluded the use of dedicated teams. Instead, management reassigned seven "line" manufacturing engineers to "staff" positions reporting to the Advanced Manufacturing Group, which had previously dealt with the development and implementation of advanced processes; each manufacturing engineer was assigned a specific product module (e.g., coin dispenser, currency reader, frame, enclosure) and was now co-located with the design engineers working on the same module.

Likewise, six materials engineers from the early supplier involvement (ESI) group were also moved to design and assigned to specific modules. Their input was considered crucial since Raleigh purchased two-thirds of its metal parts and one-fourth of its printed circuit boards.

In contrast, although the design quality assurance engineers monitored the development of specific products, they were not located in the design engineering area. Management felt that design quality assurance needed to be separated to help maintain objectivity about the designs. According to the manager of Design Quality Assurance, "we used to be inspection-oriented; now we act as a pseudo-customer to designers."

No formal procedure ensured that manufacturing engineers, ESI engineers, or quality assurance were involved in the design process until the prototype was released, when a formal design review was held, as it had been in the past. Management felt that interaction between functional areas should be spontaneous and, therefore, need not be institutionalized.

Three new communication devices were designed to promote DFM at Raleigh. GRIT (Get it Right the 1st Time) was a computer database of design problems. Anyone could enter a design concern, which had to be addressed via the database by the engineer responsible for that part. Only the person who entered the problem could remove it from the database to ensure that the problem had been satisfactorily handled. A weekly GRIT database summary (see Exhibit 2) was presented to the General Manager's staff.

The other new communication devices were a DFM newsletter (sent to all engineers, buyers, and managers in the plant), and a manual of design guidelines that was developed by Advanced Manufacturing staff and distributed to other Raleigh engineers. Some examples of the guidelines are shown in Exhibit 3.

While some of the design engineers consulted the guidelines fairly regularly, many never took the manual off the shelf or accessed the guidelines through the CAD database. GRIT was deemed a good idea, but some design engineers felt that the database was too often used to air grievances or pet peeves that were not truly design problems. One design engineer commented, "When push comes to shove, the designer has final say on the design."

Following the DFM pilot, Raleigh completed two other major DFM-based product redesigns. On the first, the designers' attempt to minimize the number of parts resulted in parts so complex that one manager described them as "origami in metal . . . We went about 80% of the way using the Boothroyd-Dewhurst design-for-assembly guidelines, when we should have gone only about 60%."

In the second redesign, the coin dispenser module's part count was reduced from over 700 to roughly 500, but the resulting design was still difficult to manufacture. Some team members felt this project's gains had been limited by the sheer size of their team (about 50 engineers) and the late involvement of Advanced Manufacturing. Designers also blamed the manufacturing personnel: "Some of them come in like gangbusters to 'correct all of the design mistakes.' "

Raleigh's director of operations believed that the key to future DFM

EXHIBIT 2
Raleigh Sample GRIT Report
Date: February 5, 1990

No.	Module Resp.	Problem Description/Reporter	Latest Response/Fix Due	Date/From
38	Shutter JB	Review strength of baseplate to ensure shutter alignment to fascia; eliminate thin sections across various areas. Life test to eval deflection through cyclical use of fascia (open/close) Reptr: ADVM Reporter ATM-MH	This part redesigned. Thin sextons eliminated where possible. Life test to be arranged. Fix due 10/11/89. Status: E4	1/16/90 From Norrie
41	Shutter JB	Reduce clearances between shutter bar and solenoid plunger to reduce risk of wear on solenoid plunger. Possibly hem edge of bar to double material thickness. Life test reqd in operational orientation. Reptr: ATM-MH	Spacers to be added (Ref D Christie). Still see no reason why hemming is unsuitable, reducing parts count. Fix due 10/11/89. Status: E2	1/11/90 From DC
42	Shutter JB	Pivot arm-review plating spec and lubrication requirement. Objective is for no lubricant to be added during assembly. Reptr: ADVM Reporter ATM-MH	Plating is zinc phosphate which is generally used on moving parts in contact with other parts. Testing will show if lubricant is needed. Fix due 10/11/89. Status: E4	1/16/90 From Norrie
43	Shutter JB	Life test required to show areas of high wear rate on part. Reptr: ADVM Reporter ATM-MH	Agree life test necessary. Some testing has shown wear in certain areas. Fix due 10/11/89. Status: E4	1/16/90 From Norrie
46	Shutter JB	Spring (shutter)-check spring extension on drawing. Life test required. Spring should have closed ends to prevent tangling. Reptr: ADVM Reporter ATM-MH	Spring design to be reviewed. Fix due 10/11/89. Status: E2	1/11/90 From DC
47	Shutter JB	Spring (shutter)-check maximum cycle capability is within func reqd spec. Environmental test reqd to evaluate effects of corrosion. Reptr: ADVM Reporter ATM-MH	Spring design to be reviewed. Fix due 10/11/89. Status: E2	1/11/90 From DC

EXHIBIT 3

Sample Raleigh Guidelines

7) *Simplify part handling.* Avoid parts that nest, tangle, stick together, or that are slippery, flexible, sticky, sharp, delicate, very small, very large, or very heavy. Use parts that are easy to grip, maneuver, and manipulate.

Design Out Tangling

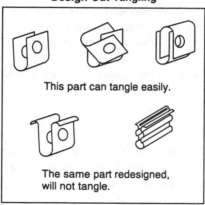

This part can tangle easily.

The same part redesigned, will not tangle.

Design Out Part Nesting

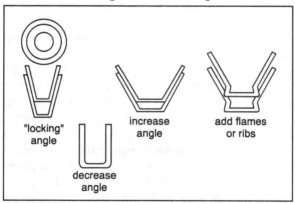

"locking" angle

increase angle

add flames or ribs

decrease angle

efforts was daily implementation by the engineers: "We [managers] provide the strategy and direction—they [engineers] must implement. We prove to them we mean it by such things as sending them to 4-week training courses."

The director of engineering agreed: "If the design engineers are not self-motivated to use DFM, I'm dead." Managers outside of engineering felt that "the way it [DFM] drives itself is through success." All concurred with the manager who said, "It all comes down to attitude."

The Coventry Facility

The Coventry, England facility, an engineering and manufacturing unit of the Retail Systems Division, designed and manufactured Midwest Industries' PINNACLE family of retailing workstations and its UNIX System V-based operating system.

The primary technical challenge in Coventry's product lines were the electronics, which could make up as much as 90% of total variable manufacturing costs. Although only about 10 wholly new printed circuit boards (PCB) were designed each quarter, approximately 50 board designs were released from the designers per quarter, including board upgrades and needed revisions.

Origins of DFM

In early 1985, Tina Townsend of Coventry's Advanced Manufacturing Technology group had a clean-up effort to improve the manufacturability, reliability, and appearance of Coventry's assembled PCBs. Previously, many minor redesigns of PCBs were made by simply adding jumper wires between electronic components, the simplest procedure for the design engineers, but not for manufacturing. Jumper wires had to be soldered in place after the boards passed through their automatic assembly processes. Not only was this time consuming, it introduced greater possibilities for errors and quality problems and made the PCB look like a patchwork quilt.

Townsend's team included representatives from the purchasing, production planning, manufacturing, and PCB layout design departments. They evaluated their existing PCB assemblies on defect rates, production volumes, prototype leadtimes, and engineering risks to determine which PCBs to attack first.

The PCBs being redesigned were made using standard "thru-hole technology," i.e., wire leads of the electronic components were inserted through pre-drilled holes on the PCBs and soldered in place on the back of the board. During late 1984 and early 1985 the Advanced Manufacturing Technology group was experimenting with "surface-mount technology" (SMT), which differed from thru-hole technology in that the leads of SMT components were soldered on the surface of the PCB, rather than inserted through holes in the board. SMT allowed smaller components to be placed closer together, resulting in more functionality and speed on the same size PCB. Through 1985 and 1986 the Advanced Manufacturing Technology group worked hard to qualify a reliable production process for this new SMT technology.

When the clean-up team was asked to design-in some SMT components while working to design-out jumpers, they recognized the need for some design guidelines to ensure manufacturability of the new PCB designs with SMT. During 1986, the team drafted some basic "rules-of-thumb" such as the orientation of components on the boards and the spacing required between components. Meanwhile, several Coventry managers attended several DFM seminars and discovered that although their own efforts were not labeled "DFM" at the time, they were basically the first steps in that process. Subsequently, DFM terminology was used at Coventry.

The BN5 Board Crisis

A major new product introduction for the PINNACLE family of retailing workstations necessitated a new, complex PCB assembly, called the "BN5 board." In mid–1985 engineering began to design substantial SMT into the BN5, which by the beginning of 1987, was released to manufacturing for production process development. Full scale production was scheduled to be up and running by mid–1987 to meet customer deliveries. Manufacturing yields, however, reached only 20–30% on good days, a situation that took everyone by surprise.

When Coventry was unable to meet its shipments in mid–1987, some customers grew impatient and canceled their orders; others substituted a similar, existing PINNACLE product. No only did plant revenue drop severely, the unexpected surge of orders for the older product created a whiplash effect. Manufacturing couldn't adjust inventory and production capacity quickly enough to compensate for the sudden increase in demand. Thus, manufacturing was unable either to produce the new BN5 board in the quantities demanded, or to satisfy the demand for its nearest substitute.

Management soon recognized that no matter how good the BN5 board design had looked on paper, it was worthless unless it could be reliably manufactured. Indeed, John Grossman, the director of operations during the crisis, had been in charge of design engineering during the development of the BN5 board and now was experiencing first-hand what it was like to have to manufacture a product he had helped design. Then general manager Hubert Webster had also worked in both manufacturing and design engineering at Coventry. Thus, management quickly changed the charter of design engineering from "design a superior product" to "design a superior product that we can manufacture."

Instituting DFM at Coventry

Prior to the BN5 board crisis, engineering and manufacturing formally interacted only at the customary design review meetings, where two engineers each from Advanced Manufacturing, Design Engineering, and Quality Assurance were to approve product designs throughout all stages of the design process. Historically, the manufacturing engineers had never actively participated in these meetings believing they had no meaningful power or influence in design decisions. With management's newfound emphasis on manufacturability, the role of manufacturing engineers in design review meetings took on great importance.

At the time of the BN5 crisis, Coventry had at least three different sets of independently developed and often contradictory design guidelines, including those of the PCB clean-up team. A manufacturing engineer in Advanced Manufacturing Technology began consolidating the various ad hoc design guidelines into one comprehensive, consistent set. He and Tina Townsend consulted people in quality assurance, engineering, manufacturing, and purchasing, and by the end of 1987, guidelines had been agreed upon, documented, published, and distributed to all involved in the design process. Moreover, a management system was instituted to *enforce* adherence to the guidelines in the design process. Every violated guideline was noted as an exception and posted on a chart for management to review each week.

The weekly design review meetings now became a forum for negotiation among the departments about what should be in the guidelines. By mid–1989, the original consolidated set had been revised numerous times and become relatively comprehensive and stable. As Townsend later noted, "The guidelines were developed practically, not scientifically."

Although design review meetings were effective in resolving technical issues of designing and manufacturing PCB assemblies, it was less clear how decisions about cost trade-offs were made. For example, during a clean-up revision of a PCB, manufacturing requested that epoxy plugs be added to the board to minimize short-circuits and rework during manufacture. Since this addition did not affect PCB technical specifications or performance, engineering and quality assurance readily agreed to the request. The team members simply made a judgment call that improved board yields would justify the additional $10 cost of the epoxy plugs per PCB.

A designer who worked for Townsend ensured that the meetings were scheduled, attended them all, and distributed their results to its members and management (see Exhibit 4). He also managed the technical relationships with suppliers whenever design questions arose. An example of these efforts is shown in Exhibit 5.

The difference between the old design review process and the current one was attributed to top management's support, which was demonstrated by performance evaluations based on department-determined quality measures. For example, PCB board designers were evaluated on

EXHIBIT 4
Coventry—Design Review Results

MFG./ENG. DESIGN REVIEW RESULTS

D. Pardue
X6889

BOARD: RP II BASEBOARD (H1130–3610–02–36)
PT. NO.: 530–0031194 Rev. A
New Design: X Cleanup Pass:
MFG. DESIGN REVIEW — 12/13/89

+ 1. Move the 4 fiducials, top and bottom sides, within the specified placement zone in the guidelines. Make sure that at least 3 fiducials form a 90 degree angle and are located on the same planes. See page 8 of the guidelines.

#* 2. Rotate one of the two test coupons 90 degrees so that one is horizontal and one is vertical.

+ 3. The tooling holes on the board should be .125 dia. They are specified as .106 dia. Guidelines state that .125 dia. and .158 are standard sizes.

+ 4. Change the tolerance on the board thickness from +/− .007 to +/− .008 to agree with the guidelines.

+ 5. The bottom side placement of capacitors has some components that are at staggered locations. These components must have a minimum distance between them of .250, or they should be placed in line with each other.
See components: C246, C335, C300, C235, C35.
Check the remainder of bottom placement for this requirement.

6. Does the large submodule have mechanical support devices along the top edge to support it?

* 7. If the fine pitch device, U3, is not used on this pass of the layout, leave it off the solder cream mask.
When U3 is used the solder cream mask opening size needs to be .012 × .085″.

Attendance: D. Denney, M. Demos, K. Pomeroy, T. Finn, D. Pardue

ENG. DESIGN REVIEW — 12/14/89

1. Fiducials will be placed according to guidelines.
2. One test coupon will be rotated.
3. Tooling holes of .125 dia. will be added.
4. Tolerance on the thickness of the board will be changed.
5. Component placement will be checked and changed to conform to the guidelines.
6. Large submodule is supported along the top by the bulkhead.
7. U3 will have electrical connections and may be used on this artwork pass. Solder cream will need to be present on this pass.

Attendance: P. McMahon, T. Inman, B. Taylor, D. Pardue

EXCEPTIONS (+)	ENHANCEMENTS (*)	GUIDELINE CHG (#)
Eng. 2	Eng. 1	1
Mfg. 2	Mfg. 1	

Unresolved (>)		Unresolved (>)		
Distribution	G. Biehl	Engineer	: T. Inman, B. Taylor	
	M. Crockett	Designer	: P. McMahon	
	T. DeFelice	Mechanical	: D. Wong	
	M. Demos	T. Finn		C. Wall
	D. Denney	R. Kraynick		M. Wilson
	M. Ezekiel	T. Sellers		

EXHIBIT 5

Coventry—Vendor Inquiry Form

Index No.: 109

EPT—VENDOR INQUIRY FORM

Date: November 9, 1989
Board Name :
Part No.   :
PCB Vendor :
Vendor Rep :
Phone No. :

SUBJECT: Immersion Tin/Lead Plating for Fine Pitch Parts (TAB)

Hadco, Doug Haney, Regional Sales Manager

> Hadco does not have a process to do Immersion Tin/Lead plating. This is an electroless process. They can supply bare copper or hot air leveled surface treatments. Their experience has been that their horizontal–hot air leveling process is capable of producing an acceptable surface for very fine pitch parts. If required to produce product with immersion tin/lead for fine pitch parts and hot air leveled surface for standard SMT parts, additional process steps would be required. These additional steps would add cost to the product.

Zycon, John Young, Technical Support

> We are the third inquiry that Zycon has received this month concerning immersion tin/lead plating. Zycon currently does not have a process developed to supply this for TAB technology. They are working with a customer and producing six builds of 25 pieces each using different solder thickness. At this time Zycon is not sure exactly what position they will take with this requirement. They will know more when these test boards are complete.
>
> Their engineering department has pointed out several concerns.
> 1. With immersion tin/lead there are more organic containments and the shelf life is greatly reduced.
> 2. There tend to be spikes or slivers of solder on the edges, which could cause shorting. This is related to the composition of the solder having not gone through a reflow process.
>
> John is sending me a copy of their early concerns and pending plans for the testing of this. John said he is sure that Zycon will be able to deliver the services for the TAB technology as soon as the industry decides exactly what is needed.

Tektronix, Donna Hodgson, Senior Sales Engineer

> At this time Tektronic does not have the capability to offer immersion tin/lead plating. Donna believes that their new hot air leveling equipment will be able to deliver the flatness required for TAB. She is to get back with flatness data.

650

their performance toward their goal of minimizing the number of requested exceptions to design guidelines. Manufacturing engineers established a similar goal of minimizing the number of requested exceptions to ensure a designer's manufacturability. Every department kept exhibits posted near their workplace to display their weekly progress reports. Exhibit 4, bottom, shows how the metrics were tracked.

Every Friday key managers toured each department to review its progress toward performance quality measures. Once a department met its quality goal for several weeks, management gave it a party at work. This signalled that the department either had to raise its goal or revise its quality metric.

In 1988, management further demonstrated its commitment to DFM by investing nearly $5 million in new CAE/CAD equipment.

Coventry's Plans for the Future

After two years of iterative negotiations the PCB design guidelines had become relatively stable, as the lead designer stated: "The design guidelines should be the designers' Bible now." In addition, people in mechanical design were developing guidelines of their own, and Advanced Manufacturing Technology was working to draw up better economic measures and spreadsheet models to guide manufacturing and design tradeoffs. These activities, however, did not appear to be high priority concerns of Coventry's management.

Management did plan to encourage people to move around among the different departments and functions at Midwest Industries-Coventry, believing that their successes in DFM were greatly enhanced by such a rotation policy. John Grossman specifically cited his management experiences in both engineering and operations as key to his ardent support of DFM.

The Chicago Facility

In 1990, the Chicago, Illinois facility, part of the Retail Systems Division, engineered and manufactured modular retail sales and administration workstations, integrated point-of-sale terminals, and retailing terminal system peripherals and software/tools.

In the early 1970s, this facility had built the automated currency changer transferred to the Raleigh facility in the late 1970s, but by the late 1980s, the division had become primarily a retailing systems integration manufacturer. The approximately 350 employees at Chicago in 1989 generated intracorporate revenues of $56 million.

DFA Origins at Chicago

Manufacturing & Quality Assurance began promoting DFA software in mid–1986, after a series of workshops taught the Boothroyd & Dewhurst Design for Assembly process to the Engineering, Manufacturing, Purchasing and Quality Assurance departments. DFM had become a specific element of Chicago's strategy at the beginning of 1987. Largely through the work of Danny Doyle, manager of Development and Engineering Services, manufacturing and purchasing became involved early in the design of the model 55 retail workstation. Beyond the model 55, however, progress toward integrating DFM concepts into the operation practices was slow. At the end of the second quarter of 1988, senior management, concerned about diminishing margins, insisted that Chicago "get on the ball" with DFM to make some significant cost improvements.

A DFM steering committee, composed of all of the plant directors and some engineering managers, was formed and quickly selected the new model A22 receipt printer on which to focus and implement their DFM efforts. Although the model A22 had already progressed through its conceptual and preliminary design stages, it was the only significant product currently available in the development pipeline.

Doyle stated DFM's strategic objective:

> Establish comprehensive practices for the product development environment which will assure world class quality products that are significantly more reliable, more manufacturable, and design stable before first production.

Development of the Model A22

The model A22 was a redesign of the model A20, which was introduced in 1983 and held a declining worldwide market share of 15–20% in 1990. The new model A22 required greater functionality, speed, ease of use, reliability, and efficiency in retail counter space use than the model A20.

The model A22 DFM working team consisted of 15 representatives, from manufacturing, test engineering, financial printer development engineering, peripherals development engineering, development engineering services, purchasing, industrial design, customer services, product evaluation engineering, supply line management, quality, product management, safety engineering, materials engineering, technical publications, and ESI engineering.

The steering committee created a new DFM engineering position, filled by David Hawkins, the DFM engineer working for Danny Doyle in the development engineering services department. He served as the facilitator and/or leader of the model A22 DFM working team, and eventually became regarded as the "DFM champion." He coordinated the weekly team meetings, writing and distributing the meeting minutes and action list, and hounding team members for active participation.

Among the team's many goals, purchasing was interested in minimizing the number of bought-outside parts and their cost; manufacturing also wanted a reduced parts count, as well as minimize the number of assembly adjustments, increase the ease of assembly, and achieve low direct labor content; design engineering needed to fulfill the product requirements with a functional design as quickly as possible; quality assurance wanted greater reliability than the previous model; customer service also wanted greater reliability, as well as improved serviceability.

A key factor in obtaining the participation of the design engineers on the project was the printer's engineering development manager, who supported the DFM working team. Although she did not attend all meetings, her willingness to let the team tackle and attempt to solve issues was encouraging to participants. Most team members, however, felt that engineers were used to designing things their own way and were not always receptive to one-on-one comments from their peers in other functional departments. "With 40 years of experience, I don't need to consult with manufacturing to find out what they can make," was a representative comment from one engineer.

Moreover, no one on the team had official authority to settle disputes. The meeting leader, usually David Hawkins, often would simply document conflicts in the minutes.

When it was chartered by the DFM steering committee, the team was told that any conflicts that could not be settled within the team would be referred to the steering committee for resolution. The steering committee would sometimes simply push the issue back down to the team for a decision; at other times the committee vetoed decisions made by the team. After almost a year of weekly working meetings, the steering committee had effectively disbanded and no longer served a regular role in the DFM process. Further, even at team meetings where issues were resolved, it was unclear whether the "best" decision for the product had been made or merely a compromise among members had been reached. This situation spawned the term "Design for Mediocrity" around the engineering departments.

Many team members also complained that too many issues were addressed by too many people in each meeting, and in so much technical detail that not all of the team could understand. Moreover, some representatives from smaller areas, such as technical publications or customer services, would often sit through many meetings without ever confronting an issue related to their function. These factors contributed to waning meeting attendance as the project wore on.

Nevertheless, the people involved with DFM at the plant considered the model A22 program a success. At the beginning, the steering committee had set goals to make the model A22 with 50% fewer parts, 40% less assembly time and space, and for 15% less cost than the existing model A20. By February, 1990, one month before actual manufacturing production, they had met or nearly met all of these goals.

However, since a primary impetus for DFM had been achieving product cost reductions and corresponding improvements in operating margins, division management viewed the 13% cost reduction the team realized as a disappointment; almost all the DFM literature claimed that a 50% cost reduction could be achieved.

The Move to DFX

Shortly after the model A22 team began, it was dealing with issues far beyond the scope of manufacturability, including product reliability, serviceability, testability, durability, and ease of use. As a result, the term DFX (Design for Excellence) was adopted for all future DFM-type work.

In December 1988, a DFX steering committee and working team were established for all new workstation developments. However, this team had not progressed as far as the model A22 team during its first year of operation. According to the workstation design engineering manager, because workstations were primarily technically complex PCBs in a plastic enclosure, the team's efforts were focused on PCB redesigns. He believed that this type of electronic product did not lend itself as readily to the application of mechanical DFM rules such as "minimize fasteners."

Chicago's DFM efforts thus far had been on designing *new* products, not improving existing ones. Cost reductions for existing products were pursued by cost reduction teams, but DFM served no formal role in them. Some managers argued that DFM should be an ongoing process, regardless of a product's position in its life cycle, but others felt that DFM teams should work on specific projects, and disband at project completion.

Thurlow's Concern: A DFM Plateau

Midwest Industries was pleased with its overall DFM progress: the plants had achieved results significant enough to be written up favorably in national business magazines. Pilot projects had been adopted throughout the organization, and lead plants had moved on to subsequent DFM projects. However, Manufacturing & Quality Assurance was concerned that DFM efforts appeared to have plateaued. Application was on an ad hoc basis; Coventry had not implemented DFM on mechanical assemblies; Chicago didn't use DFM on existing products. Designs were better, but Thurlow's goal of significantly changing Midwest Industries' approach to design had not yet come to pass. He noted:

> We, as an organization, are still talking about 5% and 10% improvements. In the future we should be expecting 50–100% percent improvements.
>
> I think we need a broader scope for DFM. People have been focusing on producibility issues, particularly design for assembly. We want to design for excellence—design for competitiveness. I believe that in order to design our products through the customer's eyes we're going to need fundamental changes—changes in the way we define our up-front product requirements; changes in how people work together; changes in how people are managed; changes in how people are measured and rewarded; and finally, a change in infrastructure that supports a crossfunctional team approach to the development process.
>
> Our success with DFM has gotten the company's attention. The challenge for the next person who holds my job is to use that attention to transform the way we design products. We need to identify the lessons of our past DFM experience and develop a vision for Design for Competitiveness. The trick then will be to get the divisions on board in this decentralized company.

Prototype Test Cycles

Overview

In most development projects, the prototyping process represents the project's central design-build-test cycles. Prototyping cycles become reference points for the organization to monitor and validate its progress, and for individual functional groups to demonstrate the efficacy of proposed solutions. Thus the sequence of prototyping cycles (including the final cycle, frequently referred to as pilot production) forms the backbone and paces the flow of development activities, often with numerous secondary and tertiary design-build-test cycles connected to it. Understanding the form and sequence of an organization's prototype test cycles is an important building block in identifying opportunities for significantly improving the development approach.

In this chapter we examine two quite different prototyping philosophies. The more common, which we refer to as the traditional approach, treats early cycles as the domain of designers and later cycles as the domain of manufacturing. Responsibility shifts as the project progresses which, in turn, results in dramatic differences in the focus of individual prototyping cycles, the people involved in them, and the tests conducted on the resulting designs. In contrast, periodic prototyping (see the comparison summarized in Exhibit 10–3) envisions a cross-functional development team owning all the primary prototyping cycles, conducting each cycle as a complete test of all aspects of the design at that point in time, and producing a substantial number of prototype units so that all functions can test them as they deem appropriate.

In performance these two approaches are quite different. A key theme in the chapter is the power of the periodic approach, particularly with regard to the rate at which the organization learns, the way in which the development effort converges to a final solution, and the degree of cross-functional integration realized. Periodic prototyping appears to be an opportunity for a wide range of firms to markedly improve their development processes.

While the choice of the underlying prototyping philosophy is an important one, there are also several dimensions of "best practice" that would be relevant and useful in most firms. These include finding ways to reduce the cost of prototypes, improving the quality of prototyping procedures, rationalizing the timing and sequence of prototyping cycles, and capturing and applying the knowledge gained from each individual cycle. Unfortunately, few organizations focus attention on what they consider a "support" activity and thus the disparity between best and common practice is often dramatic.

As with teams in Chapter 8, a primary theme in this chapter is the leverage available from matching the type of prototyping process with the type of project. We describe three models of prototyping—a rapid response to engineering, an integrated system solution (periodic), and an early replication of manufacturing—in some detail, and discuss the ways in which they match project types—breakthrough (technical), platform (new architecture), and incremental (stable architecture). Most firms adopt a single model and apply it to all of their development efforts. While the advantages of doing so are often recognized, the disadvantages, which can be significant, are not. An important implication of this chapter is that prototyping is a largely untapped area which requires management attention if its full potential is to be realized.

CHAPTER 10

*T*raditionally, managers have treated prototyping as a technical tool to be used by engineers responsible for the progress of technical activities and related development efforts. The natural flow and focus of traditional prototyping has generally progressed as illustrated in Exhibit 10–1: from overall concept to detailed component engineering and finally to producible units made by the operating system. That is, an initial concept prototype tends to be a rough cut done at the system level, and the final pilot production prototype also is at the system level, albeit in a finished form. In between, the prototypes are done at the component or subsystem level and deal with the detailed technical choices being considered and evaluated at that stage of development.

The premise regarding prototyping in this chapter is considerably different. It is that prototyping—the build and test activities of each design-build test cycle—is a key management tool for guiding development projects. It is not just a technical tool. Instead of getting extensively involved only in the final state (pilot production) of prototyping—much like the pattern depicted in Exhibit 2–1 of Chapter 2—managers can and should be involved in each cycle. Even more importantly, management can use prototyping cycles to guide and pace development projects and to assess their progress, pinpoint unresolved issues, and focus resources and attention. Senior managers, functional heads, and project leaders who do not understand and fully utilize the power of

Exhibit 10–1

Traditional Path of Design-Build-Test Cycles*

Progression of Prototyping Cycles

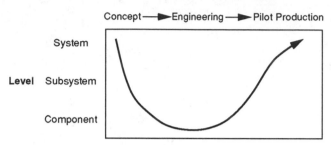

Concept ➤ Engineering ➤ Pilot Production

* Traditionally, the initial design-build-test cycle is done at the system level as a prototype of the concept. The next few cycles are then done primarily by engineering at the component level and eventually at the subsystem level. The final prototyping is done at the system level, usually as a pilot production design-build-test cycle.

prototyping unintentionally handicap their efforts to achieve rapid, effective, and productive development results.

Prototyping is a common activity that is of high leverage because of the central role it plays in the basic building blocks of development projects—the sequence of design-build-test cycles. Prototypes answer questions about customer reactions, industrial design, durability, fit and finish, and manufacturing cost. Furthermore, prototypes can take many forms—simulation (such as CAD modeling, finite element analysis, or heat transfer approximations), breadboards and mockups (such as styrofoam block models or parts made through stereolithography, and functional products (such as a first-unit circuit board, engineering-built engines, and pre-production washing machines). In each case, however, the basic cycle consists of taking the current thinking regarding the design, building a prototype that embodies the key aspects of that thinking, and then testing that prototype to determine where additional design refinements are and are not needed.

Prototyping in Major Appliance Development Projects

Data gathered from three firms in the major appliance industry in the mid 1980s illustrate the nature of the sequence of prototyping cycles and the management leverage inherent in them. These data, and the design-build-test cycles they reflect, are summarized in Exhibit 10–2.

Perhaps the most striking difference among the development efforts of these major appliance firms is that a major new product development

EXHIBIT 10–2

Prototype Cycles and Design Timetables (in Months): Major Appliances*

Event/Activity	Companies A & B Prototyping Cycles	Company A	Company B	Company C	Company C Prototyping Cycles
Pre-feasibility scoping		1-3	2-6	3	
Drawing for feasibility, sample		1-2	1-2	1	Cycle (1)
Build sample		1-2	1	1	
Test sample	Cycle (1)	2-5	2	3	
Drawings for design geometry		design		2	
Build design geometry		frozen		2	Cycle (2)
Test design geometry				3	
Complete drawings for issue		2	2	1	
Build evaluation models				2	Cycle (3)
Test evaluation models (drawing release)				3	
Tool release			2		
Tooling time	Cycle (2)	2-4	2-3	6	Cycle (4)
Inspect samples				2	
Prepare and conduct pre-pilot run				1	
Testing of product		1	1	2	
Prepare and conduct pilot run	Cycle (3)			1	Cycle (5)
Prepare for production		2-3	1	3	
Total Development Project Cycle Time		12-22 months	14-20 months	36 months	

* For these three firms, the development process involves a similar sequence of tasks. However, at Companies A and B, these are grouped into three prototyping (design-build-test) cycles, while at Company C, these are grouped into five prototyping cycles. One result is that Companies A and B develop products in twenty-two months or less, while Company C requires thirty-six months.

---

effort takes twelve to twenty-two months and fourteen to twenty months at Companies A and B, respectively, whereas at Company C, it takes thirty-six months. Looking at where that total time is spent reveals a very different pattern for the two faster firms than for Company C. The source of that difference is reflected in the number and duration of the design-build-test cycles needed by each firm.

At Companies A and B, a major development effort requires three primary prototyping cycles. Each consists of articulating current thinking and detail regarding the design, preparing one or more prototypes of that design, and then testing and evaluating those units, thus setting the stage for the subsequent cycle. The initial cycle for Companies A and B consists of taking the product concept, preparing sample drawings, building and testing a prototype unit based on those drawings, and completing the final drawings. While there are undoubtedly some small subcycles, the allocation of calendar time suggests they must be relatively minor if this first cycle takes from seven to fourteen months. Subsequently, these two companies do a second cycle which takes three to six months and involves preparing tooling for the factory, producing samples from that tooling, assembling units from such sample parts (as part of a pre-pilot production run), and complete testing of the resulting units. Finally, these firms engage in a third cycle of one to three months—the pilot production run—where revisions from the second cycle are incorporated into the final product and process designs, and the entire system is tested by building pilot production units. Customers evaluate those units, final revisions are made, and plans for volume production of the new product are approved. Market rollout and production ramp-up then follow.

In stark contrast, Company C engages in five separate design-build-test cycles. The first cycle, planned to take ten months, is analogous to the first cycle at Companies A and B, but ends without completion of a fully functional prototype unit. A second cycle of six months is required to refine the design geometry, tolerances, and physical relationship of the subassemblies. The results of those two cycles then are combined into a third cycle, which takes five months and builds a handful of final engineering models that can be tested and evaluated. The output of that third cycle is a set of final revisions to the engineering drawings.

Company C's fourth cycle is analogous to the second cycle at Companies A and B, but requires eleven months versus the three to six required by the other two firms. The aim at all three companies is to procure and test the tooling and to plan out a pre-pilot production run. The prototypes built during the pre-pilot run are then tested thoroughly, and final revisions are made to the design of the product and its manufacturing process. Finally, Company C engages in a fifth prototyping and test cycle—pilot production—that is analogous to the third cycle pursued at Companies A and B. However, Company C requires four months rather than the one to three months required by Companies A and B.

It is instructive to contrast the substantive differences between Companies A and B and Company C. One difference is that activity and cycle durations in the first two firms generally are anticipated to vary from project to project, whereas Company C anticipates that the planned duration of each cycle will be the same on every project. An even more striking difference is Company C's sequence of five design-build-test cycles. Companies A and B have compressed the time from concept to pre-production, while Company C has subdivided project steps to reduce complexity and "level of concurrency." Their intent has been to reduce what they perceive as the risks of costly mistakes. However, Company C, like Companies A and B, would claim that it is pushing hard to reduce its product development cycle time. So why does it use five cycles instead of three?

One response might be for Company C to drop steps and do prototypes like its faster competitors, but that is likely to be a recipe for disaster. The real explanation for the number and duration of these cycles at Company C lies in how rapidly their organization solves problems, learns, and converges to a final design. Because of poor communications, a narrow technical focus, and an excessively segmented process, Company C needs five cycles to reach a final design that can be produced in volume, while Companies A and B need only three. Furthermore, because of the way Company C handles the sequence of individual activities and the way they structure and manage the project, they also need more time to complete each cycle. If management arbitrarily were to cut that time or eliminate one or two cycles, many issues would go unresolved, leading to serious problems in production and the field.

Conceptually, any development project can be thought of (and usually is, at least implicitly) as a sequence of design-build-test cycles. Within each cycle, the prototype serves as a focal point for problem solving, testing communications, and conflict resolution. Furthermore, it forces specificity in design, provides feedback about the choices made thus far, and highlights remaining unresolved issues. By creating a physical embodiment of the design's current state, engineers are able to study critical issues of functionality, marketing can test and explore customer needs and reactions, and manufacturing can determine the feasibility and options it has for producing the product in volume.

But in spite of prototyping's substantial potential and leverage, Company C treats it as a technical and tactical concern. Even after reviewing the data in Exhibit 10-2, management at Company C did not conceive of prototyping as a management tool. They did not grasp the nature of the process and its potential role in making development work more effectively. The same seems to hold true even for industries where new product development is the basis of competition, and the speed of development and resulting product performance are the focus of the firm's stated strategy. For example, in the engineering workstation segment of the computer industry, where firms such as Sun Microsystems, Sony, Hewlett Packard, Apollo (now HP-Apollo), and IBM compete for a large, growing market, recent studies reveal differences in the number and duration of such cycles even greater than in major appliances—from as few as three cycles with durations as short as 100 days each, to as many as eleven cycles with durations as long as 200 days each.[1] Furthermore, the variety of ways in which prototyping cycles are managed and linked to the product development effort itself are as numerous as the number of firms in the industry.

Prototyping and Management Leverage

Our argument—of which we hope to convince the reader by the end of this chapter—is that prototyping and its role in design-build-test cycles is a core element of development and a major area of opportunity for managements seeking to improve the effectiveness and efficiency of their development process.[2] Increasing the rate and amount of learning that occurs in each cycle and then linking cycles in a sequence that is effective both technically and managerially permits an organization to shorten the duration and number of cycles needed to develop high-quality products and manufacturing processes and get to market significantly faster than competitors. That is exactly what Companies A and B in the major appliance industry had done by the mid 1980s, and what leading firms in the workstation industry were pursuing a few years later. By the early 1990s, firms in a range of industries increasingly viewed prototyping as an area of major opportunity in their efforts to improve product and process development capability.

The remainder of this chapter is organized into three sections. We first examine the basic elements of prototyping and its traditional role in technical problem solving. We illustrate the traditional approach in the left panel of Exhibit 10–3. In this approach there are four cycles—concept, design verification, engineering verification, and pilot production. It is important that management understand the traditional, technical role both as a reference point in planning improvements and because the use of prototyping as an important management tool is *in addition to* its technical purposes, not as a substitute for them. We conclude that section with a review of "best practice" procedures than can significantly enhance prototyping's contribution to technical problem solving.

The subsequent section focuses on the opportunity to restructure significantly the sequence, number, and duration of prototyping cycles into what we refer to as a periodic pattern of prototyping. The periodic approach is depicted in the right panel of Exhibit 10–3. In this approach, there are four main stages, but, within the second and third stage, there are shorter prototyping cycles that occur at regular intervals. This approach appears particularly promising for platform or next-generation product or manufacturing process projects carried out by a cross-

Exhibit 10–3

Contrasting Approaches to Prototyping Cycles*

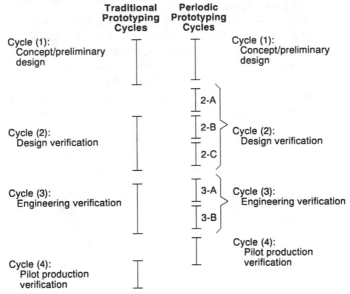

* In many engineering intensive industries, product development tasks are grouped into four phases or cycles, each with its own prototyping cycle. Adopting a pattern of periodic prototyping does not replace those four phases, but does add several shorter, more integrated prototyping cycles. This can lead to higher quality products and shorter overall development time.

functional team. The approach and its benefits are illustrated using Motorola's highly successful "Bandit" pager project.

The final section then looks at the opportunity and benefits accruing when management matches the prototyping approach used with the type of development project. We suggest that rather than using a single approach to prototyping, varying the approach to match the needs of different types of projects can enhance both its technical and managerial roles and contribute significantly to the competitive success of individual development projects.

The Traditional Approach to Prototyping

The goal of new product and process development is to create a product and/or process that provides customers with the form and functionality they require. Superior products are distinctive and exceed customer

Exhibit 10–4
Automotive Product Development Prototyping*

A. Primary Prototyping Cycles

Cycle	Focus of Testing and Refinement
Stage 0 – Architectural	Basic layout and aesthetics
Stage 1 – Subsystem	Subsystem characteristics
Stage 2 – System	System characteristics
Stage 3 – Verification	Confirm system characteristics
Stage 4 – Pilot	Production system
Stage 5 – Production Start-Up	Volume ramp-up of production

B. Cost and Representativeness of Different Types of Prototypes

	CAD Model	Clay Model	Engineering Prototype	Pilot Production
Cost:				
Cost	Low	Low	Medium	High
Time	Low	Low	Medium	High
Representativeness:				
Form	Medium	High	High	High
Fit	Low	Medium	High	High
Function	Low	Low	High	High
Materials	Low	Low	High	High
Process	Low	Low	Low/Medium	High

* For automotive companies, there are up to six prototyping cycles in new car development, each with a different focus and purpose. There are also different types of prototypes that can be developed, each with its own advantages and disadvantages.

---

expectations in ways that are difficult for competitors to match. Meeting this goal requires outstanding design quality—a design that provides what the customer needs and wants—and superb manufacturability—a product that uses process capabilities efficiently and reliably to meet the final design specifications. The purpose of prototyping is to demonstrate to the organization that the design has outstanding quality and high levels of manufacturability. In addition, early prototyping cycles indicate how far development has progressed toward this goal and what is still required to reach it.

The auto industry provides a useful example of a traditional approach to prototyping. The various forms of primary design-build-test cycles used in the auto industry are summarized in the top portion of Exhibit 10–4.[3] The development cycles progress from architecture or product concept, through subsystem and system evaluation and verification, on to pilot production system verification, and eventually to production start-up. The evolution is from a basic product concept, its aesthetics, and shape, through the design engineering of specifications that provide product functionality. Much of the product design is verified as a total system in Stage 3, following which attention and responsibility shifts toward the production system that will build the car, and eventually to the factory floor where volume production will take place. Since different prototype cycles have different purposes, different functions traditionally have taken responsibility for each one: early cycles have been the responsibility and domain of industrial designers and body engineers; middle cycles, the responsibility of various subsystem quality assurance engineers; and final cycles, the responsibility of manufacturing process engineers and factory operations.

Not only does the locus of responsibility shift for various prototype cycles; the cost and time to create and form prototypes shifts as well. As illustrated in the bottom portion of Exhibit 10–4, initial prototypes of components and subsystems in today's environment are computer-aided design (CAD) models, while the early exterior prototypes are made of clay or other formable materials like plastic. These are then followed by engineering-built subsystem and system prototypes. Eventually complete automobiles are constructed on a pilot production line, and finally, on the factory floor using operating systems. As indicated, the early physical prototype forms tend to be low cost and can be constructed fairly quickly. Later forms of auto prototypes become much more expensive and take longer to create.

If cost and time to develop were the only considerations, prototypes would be built in the cheapest and fastest way possible. There is another dimension of primary interest in new product and process development efforts, however: fidelity or representativeness—the degrees to which the prototype represents what the customer eventually will receive in the manufactured product, and what manufacturing operations eventually will produce with their production processes. The bottom of Exhibit 10–4 suggests a number of subdimensions of representativeness that apply in the development of automobile prototypes. These include form, fit, function, materials, and process. The most representative prototype is one produced on the production floor to the final design specs; the least representative is the clay or CAD model. However, each has its role and place in a development effort.

Linking Development Phases and Prototype Cycles

Prototypes play an important role in the testing of the design and thus in the progress of the project. They provide critical information about

Exhibit 10–5

Workstation Product Development Prototyping*

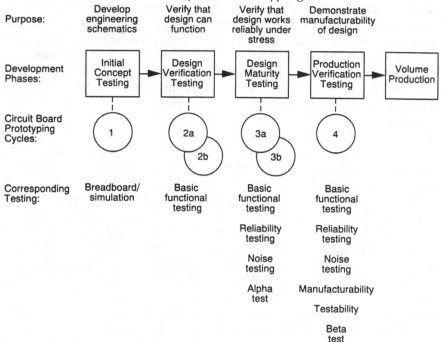

Purpose:	Develop engineering schematics	Verify that design can function	Verify that design works reliably under stress	Demonstrate manufacturability of design
Development Phases:	Initial Concept Testing	Design Verification Testing	Design Maturity Testing	Production Verification Testing	Volume Production
Circuit Board Prototyping Cycles:	1	2a / 2b	3a / 3b	4
Corresponding Testing:	Breadboard/ simulation	Basic functional testing	Basic functional testing	Basic functional testing
			Reliability testing	Reliability testing
			Noise testing	Noise testing
			Alpha test	Manufacturability
				Testability
				Beta test

* In the development of a new engineering workstation, there are four primary types of prototyping cycles, each with its own purposes and set of related tests. Often, a complex development project will require two or more cycles of types 2 and 3 to ensure completion of the tasks in that phase before moving on to the next phase.

---

the design and its potential to meet project objectives. How firms connect prototyping to the major phases of development, therefore, is a crucial dimension of the development process. We present these connections for the engineering workstation industry in Exhibit 10–5. Like development in much of the computer and electronic equipment industry, workstation development is generally organized into four phases. Each phase is completed when certain requirements, embedded in "testing hurdles," have been met. Initial concept development ends when a breadboard model or simulated version demonstrates feasibility of the basic product and its core concepts. Design verification ends when a prototype unit demonstrates the functionality required for the product to meet the performance requirements in its intended competitive segment. Design maturity ends when the prototype from that phase works reliably under stress and conditions beginning to approach those representative of the customer's environment. Finally, product verification ends when the prototype from that phase not only demonstrates functionality in a representative customer setting, but also passes tests related to manufacturability and testability. Completion of the last phase signals that the product is ready for volume production.

Much like the sequence of prototype/test cycles used in a traditional automotive development project, workstation firms generally shift primary responsibility and involvement from engineering to manufacturing as the project progresses. It is not until design maturity testing that manufacturing plays a significant role in developing the prototypes. Engineering builds early prototypes exclusively or exercises direct control. By the production verification phase, the full responsibility for prototyping rests with production; design engineers usually are anxious to get on to another project. That prototype cycle is not of major interest or concern to them.

Issues and Choices in Prototyping: Improving the Traditional Model Through "Best Practice"

In its traditional form, prototyping is technically driven, managed by different functions in different phases, and focused primarily on design evaluation and verification. If done well, this form of prototyping has important strengths, including close ties between the type of prototype, the phase of development, and the function most knowledgeable and interested in prototyping performance. But this passing of responsibility may have the effect of limiting communications and understanding across functions. Later we shall offer a different model of prototyping that may deal with some of the problems found in the traditional approach. Even within the traditional framework, however, firms face a range of choices that influence the effectiveness of the prototyping process, and present important opportunities for improvement.

Evidence from a variety of industries suggests four "best practices" that apply to any firm and any prototyping cycle:

Low-Cost Prototypes. As illustrated in Exhibit 10–4, the progression from inexpensive, simple models and prototypes to complex, expensive ones generally is correlated inversely with the representatives that those prototypes have to the customer situation in which the product and/or process will be applied. Typically, simple industrial design models (showing form and shape), computer-aided engineering (CAE) models, and simulation models are considerably less expensive to construct than pilot production units. Making better use of these classes of models and seeking ways to improve their representatives can strengthen significantly prototyping's contribution to development efforts. Actions as simple as choosing outside providers of prototyping services who have equipment comparable to that in one's own factory can help in this regard.

Prototyping Process Quality. Studies of prototyping practice invariably reveal many simple but costly mistakes in both building and testing prototypes that never should have occurred. Whether it is misreading a drawing, reversing an overlay, or failing to check a material before using it, making sure that the prototyping process is a "quality process" can improve significantly the reliability and learning that occur in each cycle. Similarly, improving the response time in prototyping—what is often referred to as rapid prototyping—can also be extremely beneficial. Shorter, more accurate feedback cycles provide better, more usable information to those waiting for the results of prototyping.

This is especially true in early phases where the prototype represents "current thinking" and where that thinking continues to progress, even while the prototype is being constructed and tested. The faster such cycles can be completed, the more valuable and timely will be the information provided to development engineers. While this may seem obvious, speed is not always so highly valued. In one setting development engineers joked about "birth dates" for prototype units—it took more than a full year to construct and test units from a single prototyping cycle.

Timing and Sequence. Experience has taught most firms not to overlap individual prototype cycles. When cycles are overlapped, people lose track of the status of the project, which problems have been solved, and which should be given top priority in the current cycle. Ensuring that testing is completed following the production of prototypes and getting closure on each learning cycle is an important practice. Then, waiting to start the build portion of the next cycle until appropriate amounts of additional design have been completed ensures that each cycle provides the maximum progress.

Building Knowledge. Using prototypes to capture and enhance the knowledge regarding prototyping and the principles of effective design-build-test cycles provides real leverage to an organization. This practice includes continually improving the quality, speed, and efficiency of the prototyping process, and strengthening prototyping's representativeness and its ability to capture critical problems at each stage of development. Systematic study of the types of problems that can and should be solved in each cycle during the development effort can help identify better ways to plan those cycles and realize their full potential.

Dimensions of Choice in Prototyping

These four areas of practice apply to any development effort, but there are other dimensions of the traditional prototyping process where choice may depend on the type of product and the objectives of the project. Even here, however, recognizing these dimensions and making choices explicit may improve the performance of prototyping. In order to make the choices and their implications clear, Exhibit 10–6 lists several dimensions of the prototyping process and defines a particular set of choices for the standard, traditional prototyping model, a revised version of the traditional model, and an alternative model that we shall call periodic prototyping.

Our discussion of the traditional prototyping system has concentrated on the first three dimensions in Exhibit 10–6: the driving force, focus, and control over prototyping. The traditional model is technical, focused on design intent and largely controlled by engineering until the later phases. What we have called the revised version preserves the basic thrust of the traditional model, but adds a focus on customers and a drive for commercial performance. This implies that the criteria engineers use in the revised model will be broader and more customer-focused.

The last four dimensions define important issues in the way prototyping is structured, and the two models illustrate the range of choices firms face. Who builds the prototypes, for instance, is an issue of great import in the project. For example, in rapidly changing markets where speed is crucial, it is not unusual for engineers responsible for early phases of product development to press hard for the freedom to subcontract the construction of early prototype units. Their argument, often relevant in larger firms, is that the in-house "specialists" in prototyping tend to focus on asset utilization at the expense of fast feedback on prototypes. When construction is subcontracted, design engineering has the flexibility to decide how much it is willing to pay for fast cycles.

The "who builds" issue is particularly important in the middle phases of the traditional prototyping models. These prototype build and test cycles are controlled by engineering, but provide an important opportunity for manufacturing learning and input. In the engineering workstation industry cited earlier (see Exhibit 10–5), this usually arises in the design maturity test (DMT) phase of prototyping. There are very different choices for building prototypes in that cycle. These are shown in Exhibit 10–7. One is to leave it under the control of engineering, but outsource to a prototype supplier who will meet engineering's service requirements. Another is to have it done by a specialized group located in engineering—typically called a "model shop"—which will meet engineering's service requirements and yet benefit from the scale and prox-

Exhibit 10–6

Dimensions of Prototyping: Three Models*

DIMENSIONS	MODELS		
	Standard Traditional	Revised Traditional	Periodic
Driving Force	Technical performance	Technical/commercial performance	System performance/cross-functional integration
Focus	Evaluate design intent	Design intent/customer satisfaction	Superior system solution
Control of Cycles			
Early	Engineering	Engineering	Heavyweight team
Middle	Engineering	Engineering	Heavyweight team
Late	Manufacturing	Manufacturing	Heavyweight team
Responsibility for Building			
Early	Subcontracted	Engineering model shop	Engineering model shop
Middle	Engineering model shop	Model shop in manufacturing	Manufacturing/production line
Late	Plant	Plant	Commercial production line
Role/Involvement of Customers	Limited to testing in late phases	Early: evaluation of mock-ups Late: system evaluation	Early: customer test of prototypes Late: extensive customer field tests
Test Criteria	Early: functionality by component Late: system functionality	Early: functionality/fidelity Late: system functionality/fidelity	Product: system functionality Process: system functionality
Link to Management Milestones	Limited; milestone reviews based on calendar	Milestones tied to prototype phases	Prototype cycles are the management milestones

* Most firms have a dominant model for how they conduct their prototyping cycles, established by a set of choices they make regarding several important dimensions. Three quite different models observed in practice are the standard traditional, the revised traditional, and the periodic.

Prototyping Choices in the Mid-Phase of Workstation Development Projects*

DVT: Design Verification Testing
DMT: Design Maturity Testing
PVT: Production Verification Testing

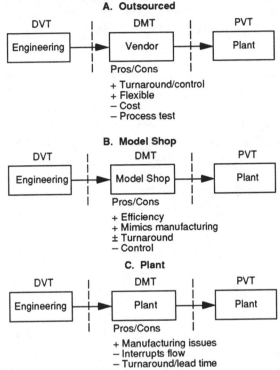

A. Outsourced

DVT | DMT | PVT

Engineering → Vendor → Plant

Pros/Cons

+ Turnaround/control
+ Flexible
− Cost
− Process test

B. Model Shop

DVT | DMT | PVT

Engineering → Model Shop → Plant

Pros/Cons

+ Efficiency
+ Mimics manufacturing
± Turnaround
− Control

C. Plant

DVT | DMT | PVT

Engineering → Plant → Plant

Pros/Cons

+ Manufacturing issues
− Interrupts flow
− Turnaround/lead time

* In the development of a new engineering workstation, the middle phase of design maturity testing may be carried out in three quite different locations, each with its own approach, mode of operation, and pros and cons: outsourced (by a specialized subcontractor), the model shop (by a specialist group in engineering or production), or the plant (by the regular production staff).

---

imity advantages available from doing many prototype cycles on different projects. Still another option is to have prototypes built in the factory. This ensures early involvement and consideration of manufacturing issues, but is likely to raise howls from engineering if they experience longer response times and get feedback (test results) on a set of manufacturability issues that they may not have considered the primary concern for that phase.

Under the traditional model in Exhibit 10–6, the firm has subcontracted early prototypes, done the middle phase in an engineering model shop, and the late prototypes in the plant. The revised model brings early prototypes in-house, does the middle phase in a model shop located in manufacturing, and does the prototypes in the plant. This set-up emphasizes manufacturability and capturing prototype knowledge inside the firm. As a general rule, in-house groups do not move quickly. Thus, an additional action we have seen a handful of firms take is to change the performance dimensions used to measure specialized prototyping groups to reflect "service level objectives" rather than primarily asset utilization objectives.

Since the primary focus of the traditional model is technical functionality, customers play a small role until the late phases of development. The role of customers, however, is an important choice. Often the engineers responsible for early prototype build and test cycles are so focused on technical issues that they see little need to provide units for marketing to test prototypes with customers. Often engineers view themselves as good judges of customer reactions. That may be true in some products, but where customers may have input that is relevant to choices being made in the early cycles, attractive options exists for involving them directly. These include having development engineers talk with customers, having marketing run focus groups with early prototypes, and producing additional prototype units in a subcycle (but without slowing down or hindering the main prototyping cycle) and getting customer comments that can feed back into development one cycle later.

We have added customer tests of early mock-ups under the revised model of Exhibit 10–6. Involving customers at this stage, however, requires some care and considerable skill. When the Coca Cola Company ran early tests of its New Coke with customers, the results suggested strong support for the new product.[4] But the tests only focused on taste, and the testers never asked: "How would you feel about this new product if it were to *replace* Coke?" The remarkable protests that took Coca-Cola by surprise when it replaced Old Coke with New Coke (and led to the reintroduction of "Classic" Coke) suggests the dangers of ill-conceived early customer involvement in development.

The question of appropriate tests and test criteria goes beyond customer involvement. Typically the connection between a prototype unit and its testing focuses on specific functionalities the organization feels must be resolved in that phase of development. However, it is important that testing explicitly address the *representativeness* of that prototype to the final environment in which it will be applied. Two examples help to illustrate this. In one, a piece of equipment (part of a process development project) was tested extensively in the supplier's plant as part of an early prototype cycle. Though the equipment planned for the customer's plant appeared identical, the supplier's environment sufficiently constrained the testing done that it turned out not to be representative of the commercial environment. In another case, an early prototype component was adjusted by its builder so that it would work in the system-level prototype. The adjustments could not be replicated by standard production equipment, however. Though the prototype builder thought he was doing exactly what was needed so testing could be done on the subsystem, the testing did not raise explicitly the issue of whether similar units with those tolerances could be produced on the factory floor. A major redesign subsequently was required when the initial design—which had worked in the prototype—could not be made in the factory.

Test procedure choices must not only consider what is needed in that particular phase, but also capture important issues of representativeness for the entire project. Some organizations have found that creating "test strategies" that span the duration of the development project, not just individual phases, is one way to get at this. Others have sought to have specialized groups (for example, quality assurance) do the bulk of the testing in hopes that the group's cumulative experience will ensure that representativeness issues are addressed early and appropriately. The broader criteria for testing—including fidelity—that we have added in the revised model of Exhibit 10–6 is consistent with the commercial focus of that model and its deeper involvement with customers.

The final dimension of choice shown in Exhibit 10–6 is the link between completion of prototyping cycles and management milestone reviews during the project. As indicated in Chapter 6, some firms choose to link milestone reviews almost exclusively to completion of a prototype build and test cycle while others—like our traditional model in Exhibit 10–6—schedule milestone reviews based on the calendar (for example, every three months) rather than waiting for completion of a particular prototyping cycle. Though most would agree that reviews connected to a prototyping cycle tend to be more objective and thorough with regard to work actually accomplished and what remains to be done, when a given cycle is running late (by weeks or even months, as is sometimes the case) or when it has been several months since a cycle was completed, a milestone review that is not tied to completion of a prototyping cycle is called for. Alternatively, when a project appears to be in trouble, an additional prototyping cycle might be inserted to refocus the effort and provide senior management with a reference point for a midcourse assessment and review.

Consequences of the Traditional Approach

The results of applying best practice principles and thoughtful planning to the traditional cycles can result in significant leverage and improvement in the overall development effort. The revised model in Exhibit 10–6, for example, is likely to avoid some of the late changes caused by potential mismatches between the design and the manufacturing process inherent in the traditional model. Further, the broadening of criteria for testing may uncover potential problems with customer acceptance and reliability in the field that the traditional prototyping cycles would miss. In the right environment—manufacturability is important and the product must fit in a customer's system—the revised model may be a substantial improvement. However, the very nature of the traditional approach to prototyping—with its shifting of responsibility from one function to another and its primary emphasis on its technical role—has important consequences for management at the project, functional, and senior levels of the organization.

First, it reinforces and legitimizes the separation of design engineering and manufacturing process engineering and limits the overlap between these two functions. When design engineers are responsible for a prototype build and test cycle, their focus is primarily on design feasibility (and the ability of the product to meet customer requirements, usually as stated by marketing). When manufacturing is responsible for the cycle, their focus is on resource utilization and manufacturability. Thus, under the traditional model—whether standard or revised—early prototyping cycles differ from later ones in primary emphasis and their focus of attention, as well as in who has primary responsibility for them. This shifting focus also affects learning. Because the prototypes generally are built by different people in early and later cycles, there can be substantial information and potential learning generated on early (or later) cycles that fails to get transferred and utilized later on (or on subsequent projects). While some information gets transferred from one cycle to another in the physical prototype units, it is much less than is available and much less than might be transferred under a different system.

The functional, somewhat fragmented nature of responsibility in the traditional model also affects how the product is tested. In the traditional model, it is not until late in the product development effort that a prototype build and test cycle occurs where the entire organization's contributions are brought together and tested as a system. Early prototype cycles are, by their design, tests of only subparts of the final product and/or manufacturing system. As a result, cross-functional issues tend not to get highlighted or raised until late in the development effort. Because of the cost and time required for prototyping, particularly in early phases, and because only a subpart (a single function) of the organization tests and evaluates early prototypes, relatively few units get constructed in early cycles. It is not until pilot production that most firms build a substantial number of prototype units. This means that prototype units may be a scarce resource early on and will tend to be "hoarded" by the function who manages the cycle that created them. Thus even if marketing and manufacturing could get a head start on certain system issues using early prototypes, they may not be able to get their hands on them. Furthermore, the testing that is done on early units tends to be narrow, aimed at resolving specific functional issues. It is not until late in the development effort that system-wide testing and exploration of subtle interactions with the customer's environment tend to be explored fully. At that point, most organizations are anxious to move toward market introduction, and the temptation is to underinvest in broad testing of the full product with intended customers.

Prototyping: A Managerial Perspective

Even with thoughtful adjustment and attention to speed, quality, and building knowledge, the traditional prototyping model has inherent limitations. Particularly where cross-functional integration is crucial and the system is central to customer choice and competition, the traditional model will fail to deliver all the leverage and power that prototyping can provide. Capturing that power, however, requires a basic rethinking of the model of prototyping. A starting point for that alternative approach is the recognition that prototyping can play crucial *managerial* roles in development, in addition to its more traditional, technical roles. Prototyping seems particularly well suited to four roles in development management:

Feedback and Learning. Prototypes create insight about a variety of dimensions of the product, ranging from such factors as form, style, and feel, to functionality, performance, and interactions with the customer's environment and existing support systems. As a result of that feedback individual functions as well as the broader organization can learn the degree to which choices made thus far are likely to achieve the intended results, what refinements still need to be made, and what work remains for project completion. While much of this learning is technical in nature, some is commercial and can play a significant role in helping to assess what skills are critical, defining the opportunities and need for integration, and suggesting choices that can provide superior advantage over competitors.

Communication and Information Sharing. The physical object represented by the prototype becomes the vehicle by which different contributors can focus and articulate their concerns and issues, and reach agreement on the best ways to resolve conflicts and solve problems. Because even simple prototypes can convey substantial amounts of information, they serve as a bridge between individuals and groups with very different backgrounds, experiences, and interests. Thus management can use prototypes to gauge, share, and extend organizational knowledge.

Outside Evaluation. Prototypes make possible an "in-process" look and assessment on the part of suppliers and customers. They give management the basis for assessing progress to date and making plans to integrate the firm's needs and development efforts with its suppliers and customers. A not inconsequential aspect of this role is providing credibility in the marketplace. The prototype tells customers that the development effort is, in fact, progressing and deserving of the customer's attention. Management can use prototypes to help set expectations and influence behavior on the part of anticipated customers. In addition, prototypes can be used with suppliers, the financial community, and even others within the firm. We have seen early prototypes shared with employees to generate enthusiasm and excitement well beyond those directly involved, and with senior management to get their support for key development strategies.

Establishing, Pacing, and Monitoring the Development Schedule. Since the number, duration, and frequency of prototyping cycles are closely linked to the critical path of the development project, managing those cycles is often the best way to manage the rate of convergence and the cycle time of the overall development effort. Companies A and B in the appliance example of Exhibit 10–2 had used prototyping in this role to improve dramatically their product development performance. Management systematically had recombined and grouped functional tasks into three design-build-test cycles (versus the five cycles at Company C), ensured that each cycle achieved its knowledge-building goals, and instilled the discipline needed to complete those cycles as planned.

Periodic Prototyping—An Approach for Platform Projects

The managerial roles that prototypes might play are particularly important in platform projects. By its nature, a platform lays down the architecture for a whole family of products and thus confronts the organization with a range of system issues. Moreover, the complexity and extent of performance improvement of a platform effort is likely to create important cross-functional issues. In that context, an approach to prototyping that fulfills the technical role, but exploits managerial potential more than the traditional model, could be of substantial value.

One approach that meets these criteria is called "periodic prototyping." Its basic characteristics are presented in Exhibit 10–6. We have seen it used by a handful of firms on major platform projects with a heavyweight team. In addition, periodic prototyping appears best suited for medium- to high-volume products where functional integration and system performance are likely to be key determinants of success in the marketplace and where the cost of prototypes is relatively small. Next-generation platform efforts on products ranging from computers to disk drives, and from medical devices to home appliances, would be candidates for this approach; commercial aircraft or turbine generators would not. What is different in periodic prototyping is that integration is a concern throughout all cycles, even the early ones, and prototyping is done on a calendar basis rather than a phase completion basis. The goal is to balance the technical and managerial roles of prototyping as effectively as possible. An example is perhaps the best way to illustrate the fundamental characteristics of periodic prototyping.

The Motorola Bandit pager project, referenced in Chapter 8, utilized periodic prototyping. As illustrated in Exhibit 10–8, the prototyping schedule set up by the cross-functional heavyweight team started with an initial demonstration breadboard unit built in the lab. The first design-build-test cycle was conducted by the development engineering function, as it traditionally would have been. The next five cycles, however, were done using a periodic approach. The team set a date on which each of the prototype builds would occur, and then stuck to that date whether or not each function had completed all of its tasks originally planned as prerequisites to that cycle.

Prototype build #1, scheduled for 10 January 1987, was conducted on that date with the participation of the entire cross-functional team. This early cycle, as well as every subsequent cycle, involved the integrated effort of all project participants. Obviously, at the time of each cycle, some functions were further along in their project tasks than were others. As shown at the bottom of Exhibit 10–8, for prototype build #1, the traditional pager factory provided the front end activities required for that prototyping cycle (development of the printed circuit boards), and the back end of the cycle (assembly and test) was done manually in the Bandit factory area. (The new production line was still under construction.) Though eventually the entire cycle would be conducted on the Bandit pager production line with highly automated robotics linked through computer-integrated manufacturing software, the intent was to build full units with everyone involved even in the first full prototype cycle.

The subsequent cycles (#2 through pilot) also involved all of the functions and were done in the factory. Increasingly, those cycles were done with the equipment and systems that would finally be used on an ongoing operating basis. If for some reason a function, like factory software, had not completed all of its planned steps prior to a scheduled

Exhibit 10–8

Periodic Prototyping—Motorola Bandit Pager*

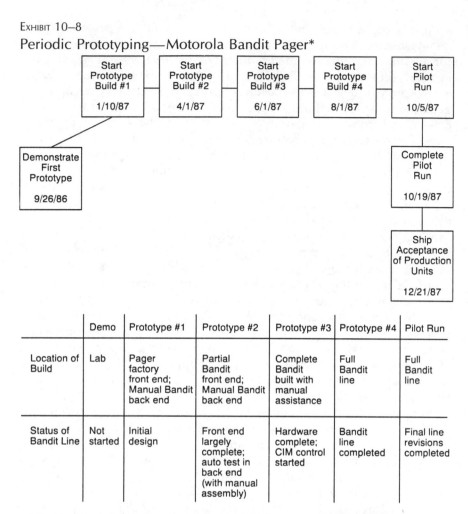

	Demo	Prototype #1	Prototype #2	Prototype #3	Prototype #4	Pilot Run
Location of Build	Lab	Pager factory front end; Manual Bandit back end	Partial Bandit front end; Manual Bandit back end	Complete Bandit built with manual assistance	Full Bandit line	Full Bandit line
Status of Bandit Line	Not started	Initial design	Front end largely complete; auto test in back end (with manual assembly)	Hardware complete; CIM control started	Bandit line completed	Final line revisions completed

* On the Motorola Bandit project, after the initial prototype build, subsequent prototyping cycles were done periodically (generally every two months.) This facilitated the regular testing of progress on all aspects of the system design and allowed the design-build-test cycles to be used as an integrating mechanism on a periodic basis throughout the project.

prototype build date, such as the phase 2 build scheduled for 1 April, the cycle would not be delayed. Instead, the prototyping schedule would proceed as planned, but the factory software group would have to fill in manually, as required. In addition, the software group would be expected to document what was incomplete, the corrective actions to be taken, and the expected status by the next build (#3 scheduled for 1

June). This approach places substantial pressure on all project participants to meet their commitments, but also provides objective feedback
on their real status, motivates them to get back on track, and ensures
them of receiving the "help" needed from others.

Characteristics of Periodic Prototyping

The Motorola Bandit project highlights several important differences
between the periodic prototyping model and the traditional model. With
the periodic approach, prototyping is done on a regular schedule (for
example, every other month), and that schedule is adhered to whether
or not all anticipated tasks have been completed. Each function goes
with what it has and fills in on an ad hoc basis as required. Thus functions continue to be responsible for completion of their individual tasks
and activities as part of the prototyping cycle, but know others on the
project are depending on them.

Once the prototyping schedule has been specified, it is relatively easy
for each of the functions to state what tasks they plan to have completed
by each prototype build date. This stimulates the functional groups to
think about restructuring and regrouping tasks and then resequencing
and altering the timing traditionally followed. Initially, they may move
as many tasks as possible into earlier prototype build cycles. Over time
they may be even more creative, finding ways to further "front load"
early cycles and eventually dropping late cycles that no longer are
needed. Thus, periodic prototyping leads to innovative solutions to task
planning issues.

Because every function is involved in every prototyping cycle (with
the possible exception of the first one), each cycle provides a set of
physical activities that brings together all the key players (periodically)
to communicate the status of their portion of the project's tasks and to
see the status of counterpart activities on the project. Each prototype
build becomes an opportunity for regrouping and recalibrating. The
amount of information exchanged and the detailed problem-solving focus that occurs in each cycle is substantially greater than under the
traditional pattern. Cross-functional exchanges are especially strengthened.

Given their cross-functional nature, prototyping cycles become timely
review points for senior management as well as the core team. The focus
of those reviews is product-driven and objective, because both the status
of each individual function's activities (based on what they have to do
manually or on an ad hoc basis to complete the cycle) and how cross-
functional issues are being raised and resolved are clear. The result of
each cycle is shared understanding of what needs to happen in the next
cycle to make substantial progress.

Shared understanding and learning for the project as a whole is also increased because of the number of units produced. In each cycle, many more units are produced than those needed for a single function; every function ends up with units it can test, evaluate, and study as a result of even the early cycles. Functions that traditionally only had units for testing late in the development project now have units much sooner, and the quality assurance function can initiate its activities—including life testing and customer evaluations—with the first cycle. The result is much more thorough testing across a broad range of variables. This is particularly valuable in next-generation platform efforts that target an improved system solution for the marketplace.

Not only does learning increase within the project, but, over time, an organization using periodic prototyping can more easily and systematically improve its development capabilities. Since project pacing and momentum are controlled and reflected in the progress that occurs over a sequence of design-build-test cycles, and since cycles are now on a regular calendar and every cycle involves all the key functions, it is much easier to track progress and identify problem areas. When done on multiple projects, the organization can examine systematically what tasks, if moved to an earlier cycle, would have the most leverage. Eventually, as sufficient learning is moved to earlier cycles, the number of cycles may be reduced.

Prerequisites for Periodic Prototyping

Periodic prototyping has significant advantages, but it requires particular organizational capability and a particular development process. It requires, for example, that all of the functions with key roles at some point during the development effort be involved throughout the project's duration. Thus heavyweight teams, with their cross-functional emphasis, are a natural for the periodic approach. The team must be given authority and responsibility to plan the organizing, sequencing, and timing of individual tasks on a project. Since this "goes with the territory" of heavyweight project teams, it is much easier in that environment than it would be in the traditional functional environment, where the functions have control of individual project tasks, their sequence, and their form of execution.

Because the firm builds many more prototype units in the periodic model, prototype units must be sufficiently inexpensive that the approach is feasible. However, prototypes do not have to be "cheap." Organizations that have adopted periodic prototyping have found that spending an additional $500,000 on prototyping units and materials (over that spent under the traditional approach) is money well spent. We've seen products that range in value from a few cents per unit to a few thousand dollars per unit developed with this periodic approach.

Support groups have a particularly crucial role to play. Groups such as the model shop and quality assurance or analytical testing must have the capacity to meet the requirements associated with the periodic prototyping schedule. Once familiar with the approach, scheduling support resources tends to be easier under periodic prototyping than under the conventional approach. This is because the prototyping schedule is locked in early and adhered to. Thus support groups can plan their resource requirements knowing the schedule will be followed. A major problem in the traditional approach to prototyping is that support groups often discover at the last minute that a project needs their help, and they are unable to balance and coordinate demands across multiple projects.

Periodic prototyping seems best suited to platform projects where there is substantial payoff from achieving a better system solution. In a breakthrough project where the leverage is in excelling on a single, groundbreaking feature or technical component, forcing adherence to preset dates for prototype build cycles and forcing early cycles to incorporate inputs from all the functions may complicate the project unnecessarily and make it too complex to be managed realistically. Thus periodic prototyping is not the answer in every situation, but in many, it holds significant promise.

Matching Prototyping and Development Project Requirements

Under the right conditions, periodic prototyping is an attractive, appropriate model for design-build-test cycles. But a different set of factors may make a well-conceived traditional approach to prototyping attractive and appropriate. Even within these two broad models, however, a number of variables associated with different types of projects determine what pattern of prototyping choices will be most effective. A key opportunity for management is to match the details of the design-build-test cycles with the requirements of each specific development project. Making that match requires an understanding of the characteristics of different prototyping patterns and the decisions that determine them.

Our discussion thus far has identified three critical characteristics of the project's environment that determine the appropriate dominant orientation of the prototyping process. While these characteristics may be present to different degrees in any project, we shall focus here on relatively "pure" types of projects in order to illustrate the key relationships. The three characteristics are:

1. The relative importance of advanced, innovative technical developments in driving superior product performance
2. The relative importance of a balanced, total system solution to customer choice
3. The relative importance of manufacturability (i.e., manufacturing cost and reliability) in competition and customer decisions

When one of these characteristics dominates a project's environment, the pattern of prototyping must adapt to that basic thrust. Consider the following three projects and their associated prototyping patterns.

Technical Breakthrough (advanced semiconductor manufacturing equipment). In this project, achieving superior technical performance is the name of the game. Prototyping thus focuses on rapid service and quick turnaround to provide engineers with timely and effective feedback. Because the product pushes the state of the art, design specifications are not frozen, but remain somewhat flexible until customers have had a chance to test early versions. Control of prototypes remains with engineering until very late in the program and issues of manufacturability receive less concern than product performance. Finally, the criteria for testing are related to technical performance, and representativeness becomes a factor only in later cycles.

Platform System (next-generation microwave oven). In this project the crucial issue is product architecture and the behavior of the product as a complete system. An effective design requires the integration of physical dimensions, ergonomics, software, sensors, aesthetics, ease of use, safety, and issues of reliability. Prototyping focuses on team learning and representativeness. Control over prototypes and prototyping rests with the heavyweight team doing the platform project, and testing criteria pertain to the performance of the system. Specifications are established relatively early in the program, but are broadly defined to allow for adaptation in later, derivative versions of the product.

Incremental Refinement (new version of desktop printer with improved reliability and lower cost). In this project cost and reliability are paramount. The new product is based on an established platform so that the basic architecture is unchanged. What matters is a major improvement in manufacturability. Prototyping focuses on early involvement and input from manufacturing. The quality of prototypes, particularly their representativeness, is the primary performance dimension used to evaluate the prototyping activity. Specifications are frozen early, since the basic product is well established and the target market is well known. While design engineers play a critical role in this project (e.g., changing the design to make it more reliable), control over prototypes passes to manufacturing relatively early in order to give issues of cost and reliability high priority.

These descriptions underscore the different patterns of prototyping appropriate for different kinds of projects. Exhibit 10–9 summarizes the patterns and indicates the problems that may arise when projects and the mode of prototyping are mismatched.

The first prototyping model—rapid response to engineering—is well suited to the technical breakthrough project run by an autonomous team. We assume that the rapid response mode uses best practice in quality, in using cost-effective processes and materials, and in tying prototypes to project milestones. But in its control, organization, focus and testing criteria, the rapid response to engineering model is dedicated to the support of technical innovation. Using a modified version of the traditional model with its emphasis on technical performance, the rapid response mode provides early feedback, flexible scheduling, quick response to the needs of design engineers, and a focus on achieving significant advances in the state of the art of technical performance.

While the rapid response mode is effective in technical breakthrough projects, it has serious limits when applied to platform projects or incremental improvements. A glance down the first column of Exhibit 10–9 indicates the central problem—lack of balance and integration. A more appropriate mode for platform projects is the integrated system model, a variation of periodic prototyping described above. Here representativeness is the crucial criterion, and the organization reflects the emphasis on balance across functions and the performance of the system as a whole. All functions participate in each stage of prototyping, and the heavyweight team controls the focus, criteria, and evaluation of prototyping. Because of the importance of the total system, the team places less emphasis on narrow technical criteria in specific components, and more on how specific component designs interact with and influence other elements of the product. In this setup the focus of prototyping is convergence to a system design and integration across functions.

Of course, one can imagine platform projects where technical excellence in a narrow sense is more important than we have indicated. In that circumstance, managers would need to adjust the mode of prototyping, particularly in the early stages, to give more weight to technical problem solving. Depending on the nature of the problems and the technology, this might involve creating a staged process in which the team adds advanced engineering prototypes to its schedule in the early stages of development. Subsequent stages might then move to a system focus.

The last mode of prototyping—replicate manufacturing early—is well suited to incremental improvement projects where issues of manufacturability are central. Given a stable architecture and an established

Exhibit 10–9

Matching Three Models of Prototyping and Three Types of Projects*

Models of Prototyping: Dominant Orientation

PROJECT TYPE	Model I	Model II (periodic prototyping)	Model III
	Rapid Response to Engineering	Integrated System Solution	Replicate Manufacturing Early
	• rapid turnaround • flexible specs • engineering control • technical focus	• team learning • specs established early • team control • system integration	• prototype quality • established specs • manufacturing control • manufacturability
Breakthrough (technical)	– creative, innovative results – fast response enhances feedback – manufacturing in late performance and features – easily overcome problems with manufacturing	– system focus causes technical compromise – complexity and uncertainty slow down technical work – constraints of system limit innovation	– slow turnaround; late introductions – engineers out of loop – performance suffers, leading to many late engineering changes
Platform (new architecture)	– technical focus skews architecture, hurts balance – system performance suffers in field leading to design revisions	– system focus achieves clear interfaces, integration – team learning leads to early design convergence – team control facilitates communication, eliminates late design changes	– manufacturing focus hurts design balance – performance inadequate, leading to late design revisions
Incremental (stable architecture)	– lack early manufacturing involvement – late revisions required for manufacturability	– team approach is overkill; complicates project – system focus leads to late revisions because of technical (processing) problems	– early involvement solves problems in design – smooth ramp-up – enhanced reliability and cost performance

* The type of development project—breakthrough, platform, or incremental— determines the most appropriate model of prototyping. However, since most firms use the same model of prototyping for all their development projects, it is useful to recognize the implications of each model for the various types of development projects.

market, design changes focus on making the product easier to make and more reliable in operation. In some respects, this mode is the manufacturing version of the traditional model—manufacturability criteria top the agenda, the prototypes are built by manufacturing, and manufacturing controls the focus, direction, and evaluation of prototypes. Representativeness, particularly the fit with the volume production process, is the principal criterion for evaluation.

Such an approach, as the third column in Exhibit 10–9 suggests, is not effective for a technical breakthrough project. Issues of manufacturability may be important even there, but a prototyping process that focuses on those issues may not yield the quick, rapid insights design engineers need to make significant advances in the state of the art. Replicating manufacturing early is also less effective in a platform project because of issues of balance. However, if the platform has a high manufacturability content, early manufacturing involvement and emphasis—even more than we would get in an integrated system approach—may be important.

Matching the mode of prototyping, particularly the focus, criteria, control, and pattern of functional involvement, can play an important role in improving development performance. No matter what the type of project, there are certain practices and characteristics (such as quality, timeliness, efficient use of materials and processes) that contribute to superior performance. But dimensions of control, involvement, and criteria represent crucial choices that drive the behavior of the prototyping system. The concepts we have developed here provide managers with a framework for systematic evaluation of existing patterns, their drivers, and their impact on development. With a close look at the set of projects, and the needs of specific projects, managers can develop new patterns of prototyping that better match project requirements. Prototyping represents a significant tool for managing development projects, and changing the prototyping process represents an important tool for improving development performance.

Study Questions

1. Exhibit 10–2 summarizes the prototyping patterns for three competing major appliance firms. If you were a manager in Company C and had these data, how might you respond? What should be your objective with regard to your cycles? How much that best be pursued?
2. Most elements of best practice for prototyping explored in this chapter go unaddressed by the majority of firms. Why? How might an organization focus its efforts to consistently achieve best practice in prototyping?

687

3. What objections do you think an organization being introduced to the concept of periodic prototyping might raise? How would you address those objections? How broadly do you think periodic prototyping can be applied (in what range of firms and situations)?

4. In Chapter 6, the concept of the development funnel was defined and applied. Suppose that same concept were applied in contrasting the traditional and periodic approaches to prototyping. If each prototyping cycle represents its own funnel, how might you graphically connect the funnels to represent the convergence process under traditional prototyping? Under periodic prototyping?

5. Exhibit 10–9 summarizes three different models of prototyping. Which functions in an organization do you think would prefer each model? How would you make the appropriate model for a given project type attractive to all the participants in the project?

6. A theme running throughout this chapter is that prototyping is an underutilized vehicle for improving product development capability. Why haven't many firms taken advantage of prototyping's potential? If senior management thought prototyping were important, how might they get their organization to respond?

Sony Corporation: Workstation Division

In July 1989, Dr. Toshi T. Doi, general manger of Sony's Workstation Division, was reviewing a proposal to split hardware design engineering into two separate departments. Isao Yamazaki, manager of the hardware design engineering department, had proposed the split to help alleviate the pressures of extremely rapid growth while maintaining past strengths in product development, and to make workstation designs more manufacturable.

In just over three years since its founding, the Workstation Division had grown to annual sales of approximately 6,200 units, giving it the largest share in Japan's workstation market. Furthermore, sales were expected to double again in 1989.

This rapid growth created stress in all areas of the division, including the hardware design engineering department. Yet because Sony's development cycle had traditionally been much shorter than that of most competitors, Doi wanted to avoid any changes that might have an adverse effect. An efficient product development effort was crucial in an industry where life cycles were measured in months rather than years. Any decision on Yamazaki's proposal would have to take that fact into account.

Sony Corporation History

The Tokyo Telecommunications Engineer Company (later renamed Sony) was founded in 1945 immediately after the end of World War II by

This case was prepared by Geoffrey K. Gill under the supervision of Professor Steven C. Wheelright and with input from doctoral candidate David Ellison.

Masaru Ibuka, who was soon joined by his friend (and later chairman), Akio Morita. During its first four decades, Sony concentrated almost solely on consumer electronics, introducing a wide range of products, starting with the first Japanese tape recorder and continuing with the world's first transistor radio, the Trinitron color TV, the Walkman line of portable radios and tape recorders, and the Camcorder video camera. Because of such products, Sony Corporation had become a recognized leader in the consumer electronics field, with 1988 worldwide sales of more than $16 billion.

Throughout this growth period, Sony relied on innovative products that created new markets. As Morita explained the firm's philosophy: "We don't believe in doing market research for a new product unknown to the public. So we never do any. We are the experts." During the 1970s, one of the most promising new products to be developed at Sony was the Betamax VCR. Unfortunately, several of Sony's competitors adopted the VHS standard and, after a long and costly battle, Sony admitted defeat by introducing a VHS model in 1988.

The Betamax disaster forced Sony to rethink its strategy in several ways. The company began to pay more attention to expanding its markets in existing lines in addition to developing totally new products. For example, it entered low end markets for equipment such as Walkmans. It also started cooperating more with competitors, developing standards for products such as compact disks. Perhaps the most fundamental shift was a move away from total dependence on consumer electronics. When Norio Ohga became president in 1982, he set a goal of 50% of sales from nonconsumer products.

The Workstation Division

One side effect of Sony's preoccupation with the video business was that its computer business had been largely ignored. Although Sony had some success in the computer game market, its first entrants in the computer market were 8-bit machines (the SMC–70 and SMC–777, introduced in 1982 and 1984, respectively), which failed quickly in competition with 16-bit MS-DOS systems (e.g., the IBM PC). Sony considered developing a 16-bit microcomputer but it soon abandoned the idea because that market had already matured.

When Doi took charge of the project to develop a new computer in 1984, he recruited 11 top-flight engineers to form the team. Doi established three basic guidelines for the development: (1) the computer should be 32 bit; (2) it should be multipurpose; and (3) the project should be completed as soon as possible. The engineers, however, decided that they wanted to design a machine (an engineering workstation) that would help them in their own engineering work rather than a multipurpose machine. Doi approved their plan, but he required that it be finished in six months.

The initial development effort, named the IKKI project, began to move quickly. The hardware prototype was completed in three months, and the operating system was installed three months later—meeting the aggressive schedule set by Doi. This speed was in sharp contrast to the two years of development typical for a project of this kind at Sony. As Doi recalled the development period:

> . . . [the design team] had little consciousness of producing a marketable product . . . they first wanted to create a computer they could use themselves . . . I decided that what the Sony engineers wanted was probably what other engineers also wanted, and went ahead. . . . [W]e showed this machine to Mr. Koichi Kishida from SRA (Software Research Associates), which had brought Unix to Japan, and he was elated. . . . The developers at Sony created something they themselves wanted and a developer from another company was elated. This was very simple and no market research was necessary.[1]

Despite its technical success, the computer division (which was focused primarily on optical disks and game computers) was slow to proceed with the IKKI project. It was reluctant to terminate any of its other projects to squeeze out enough money to pursue IKKI as a new business. When the computer division proposed a market introduction of 1988, Doi felt that date was unacceptable and he persuaded Ohga to let him develop the workstation business as an in-house venture.

Developing a business was a challenge to Doi, who had been primarily a manager of R&D. He had to implement prototyping for commercialization, develop standard operating procedures, recruit dealers and applications software vendors, and create promotional materials. Doi saw the new venture as very much in the tradition of the "original Sony"—a small and dynamic venture business, whereas the "current Sony" was an established organization suffering from bureaucratic stagnancy and a lack of entrepreneurial spirit.

The new workstation computer, called NEWS℗ (NEtWork Station), was introduced in October 1986 at the Tokyo Data Show. It was a remarkable success, generating over 1000 inquiries at the show. In a few months, investment in the new venture was fully recovered. Since that time, Sony's workstation sales had doubled each year.

In June 1987, all the computer-related divisions were incorporated into one internal venture, including Workstation, CD-ROM Development and Home Interactive (which worked with game computers and portable work processors), which became the Super Micro Group.

---

[1] From *The Computer* magazine, June 1988.

Current Workstation Products

At the highest level, workstations were systems consisting of several different components. Although the exact configuration varied somewhat, a typical workstation had a main system unit (including the mother board), a cathode ray tube (CRT) display, a keyboard, a hard disk drive for permanent storage that could be accessed at any time, a floppy disk drive to allow data to be carried from one computer to another, and a network interface that allowed the workstation to communicate with other computers on a local area network (LAN). The heart of the workstation was the main system unit; the other components were called peripherals.

The primary component of the main system unit was the mother board. This printed circuit board (PCB) typically contained the electronics required to perform all major functions of the computer: the central processor unit (CPU), the random access memory (RAM), the bus control logic, and the read only memory (ROM), as well as some peripheral control functions such as a network controller. These terms are explained further in Appendix I.

Sony's workstation product line was segmented into three categories and marketed under the NEWS™ trademark (see Exhibit 1). The low end, the Series 700, had developed from the original IKKI workstation[2] which was based on the 68020 chip and did not have a hard disk. The mid-range, the Series 1500 and Series 1700, were based on a single 68030 microprocessor and did have hard disk capabilities. The high end, Series 1800 and 1900, also were based on the 68030 but had a special dual processor architecture in which a second 68030 handled all the input/output (I/O) tasks. This architecture increased the processing speeds by about 25% over the mid-range products. Although the Workstation Division was still small (with approximately $140 million of Sony's $16 billion in sales), by July 1989, it was the company's most profitable division.

Each computer within a given series used the same basic mother board and differed from other offerings in the same series only by the peripheral devices that were attached. For example, the 1550 workstation, the initial offering in the 1500 series, had a black and white display, whereas the 1560, a subsequent line extension, had color. (See Exhibit 2 for a description of the 1500 Series and optional peripherals.)

The workstation product strategy had not been based on leadership in either price or performance (see Exhibit 3); its systems were in the middle to upper range in both categories. The performance leaders were Sun Microsystems and Hewlett-Packard/Apollo, both of which had recently introduced a workstation based on a RISC (Reduced Instruction

---

[2] The IKKI workstation was marketed as the 800 Series, which was soon to be phased out.

EXHIBIT 1

Product Line

The NEWS family of Sony workstations not only offers compact high performance but also leads the way in network computing. The Open Distributed Processing capability of these workstations helps build a heterogeneous, easily expandable network of shared resources. The dual-processor architecture demonstrates its power in I/O-intensive applications, delivering a constant CPU processing speed regardless of I/O loads and application programs. Furthermore, the NEWS family encompasses a wide range of products to meet the diversified needs of software engineers and technical professionals.

Open Distributed Processing

The NEWS workstations allow networking of various machines from different manufacturers, as well as efficient file sharing and distributed processing among these machines.

The key to this networking flexibility is the adoption of the latest version of the industry standards or defacto standards. All NEWS workstations use Sony's implementation of UNIX 4.3BSD, NFS Rel. 3.2 and X Window System Ver. 11, combined with CGI graphics libraries and a number of languages such as C, Fortran 77, Franz Lisp and Pascal. Network interfacing is based on the standard IEEE802.3 Ethernet and TCP/IP and XNS protocols.

Dual Processors

The NEWS/1800 and 1900 Series of workstations feature Sony's unique dual-processor architecture. They use two MC68030's—one for the main processor and the other as a dedicated I/O processor. Equipped with a 256K byte static RAM and a real-time multitask monitor, the I/O processor handles all I/O processing (except the VME bus) and direct memory access, freeing the CPU power to run applications.

This means that the processing speed of the main processor can be maintained despite the increase in I/O loads caused by color graphics, network communications and disk access. The dual-processor NEWS can perform much faster in actual applications than single-processor workstations with the same MIPS value.

High-Speed X Window System

Established as the industry standard, the X Window System is one of the most important human interfaces available for workstation users. With this in mind, Sony has placed a high priority on the implementing of the X Window software on NEWS workstations. In addition to the software, the X Window System used in NEWS workstations owes its speed to specifically designed display boards which make possible high-speed bitblt (bit boundary block transfer) and raster operation. Furthermore, a dedicated high-speed bus is employed between the CPU and the display board, in order to maintain the high performance of the CPU during window operations. This combination of software and hardware found in NEWS workstations has resulted in one of the fastest and most reliable X Window Systems in the industry.

Versatile Product Lines

NEWS workstations come in a variety of configurations: deskside file servers, desktop power machines, cost-effective disk-based workstations, and color/monochrome diskless nodes. The wide line-up enables installation of the right machine for the right job, making it possible to achieve maximum efficiency at minimum network cost. Taking advantage of over 40 years of experience as a total electronics manufacturer, Sony also offers a wide selections of option units including high-resolution display monitors and an ultra-capacity MO disk drive unit.

Model	700 Series			1500 Series			1700 Series			1800 Series		1900 Series	
	NWS-711(UC)	NWS-712(EK)	NWS-721	NWS-1510(EK)	NWS-1530(EK)	NWS-1580(EK)	NWS-1720	NWS-1750(UC)	NWS-1750(EK)	NWS-1830	NWS-1850	NWS-1930(UC)	NWS-1930(EK)
CPU	MC68020 (16.67MHz)	MC68020 (20MHz)		MC68030 (25MHz)									
I/O Processor	—									MC68030 (25MHz)			
Floating-Point Coprocessor	MC68881 (16.67MHz)	MC68881 (20MHz)		MC68882 (25MHz)									
Main Memory	4MB	4MB (expandble to 8MB)		4MB (expandable to 16MB)			4MB (expandable to 32MB)		8MB (expandable to 32MB)	16MB (expandable to 32MB)			
Cache Memory	—			16KB						64KB			
Streamer	—						125MB			—		125MB	
3.5" FDD (formatted)	—			1.44MB									
Hard Disk (formatted)	—			40MB		170MB	156MB		286MB	156MB	286MB	286MB × 1 (expandable to ×4)	286MB × 2 (expandable to ×4)
Power Requirements	AC100-120V	AC220-240V	AC100-120V or AC220-240V	AC220-240V			AC100-120V or AC220-240V	AC100-120V	AC220-240V	AC100-120V or AC220-240V		AC120V	AC220-240V
Standard Software	•Operating System: NEWS-OS (UNIX 4.3BSD+X Window System Ver. 11+NFS Rel. 3.2) •Communications: TCP/IP, XNS •Languages: C, Fortran 77, Franz Lisp, Pascal •Graphics: CGI												

- •UNIX is a registered trademark of AT&T in the USA and other countries.
- •NFS is a product created and developed by Sun Microsystems, Inc. and is a trademark of Sun Microsystems, Inc.
- •X Window is a trademark of MIT.
- •Ethernet and XNS are trademarks of Xerox Corporation.
- •The MIPS value is determined in comparison with the performance of VAX 11/780 measured using the Dhrystone program. VAX is a registered trademark

of Digital Equipment Corporation.
- •NEWS is a trademark of Sony Corporation for their Workstation.
- •UC models are available in the areas with AC100—120V, while EK models are available for the areas with AC220—240V. Those models with no suffix are designed for use in both areas.
- •The NWS-1510/1530 are installed with part of NEWS operating system.

EXHIBIT 2
1500 Series and Optional Peripherals

1500 Series
The Perfect Low-Cost Choice for Any Network

NWS-1510(EK)

System Connection

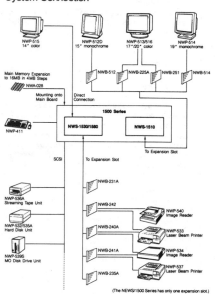

(The NEWS/1500 Series has only one expansion slot.)

The NEWS/1500 Series is an ideal way to reduce the network cost without affecting its efficiency. Based on the 25MHz MC68030 CPU and the 25MHz MC68882 floating-point coprocessor, the 1500 Series packs 3.9 MIPS processing power in a unit that's smaller than a personal computer. It is priced in the range of diskless machines but has its own local disk, making it possible to start up faster and operate faster.

The NEWS/1500 Series consists of three models, all featuring the extremely compact dimensions of 355 × 341 × 110mm. The NWS-1530(EK)/1580(EK) are equipped with a high-resolution color bitmap interface board. Up to 256 colors from a 16.7 million color palette can be displayed at once on the 1024 × 768 dot NWP-515 14" (13" viewable) color display designed specially to match these machines. The bitblt (bit boundary block transfer) function is implemented in hardware to realize a high-speed, multi-window display.

The NWS-1510(EK) has no display interface and thus can be connected to any color or monochrome display of your choice using the appropriate bitmap interface board.

The capacity of the main memory is 4M bytes for all models and is expandable in 4M byte steps to a maximum of 16M bytes with the use of the optional NWA-028 expansion RAM kits.

The capacity of the internal hard disk is 170M bytes for the NWS-1580(EK) and 40M bytes for the NWS-1530(EK) and 1510(EK). The SCSI bus enables the addition of external storage options.

The RS232C ports accept up to two personal computers, modems and printers. There is also a parallel interface for connection to a Centronics compatible unit.

Specifications

Model Name	NWS-1510(EK)	NWS-1530(EK)	NWS-1580(EK)
CPU	MC68030 (25MHz)		
Floating-Point Coprocessor	MC68882 (25MHz)		
MIPS	3.9		
Main Memory	4MB (expandable in 4MB steps to 16MB with NWA-028)		
Hard Disk	40MB (formatted)		170MB (formatted)
3.5" FDD	1.44MB (formatted)		
Standard Interfaces	Ethernet, SCSI RS232C (×2), Centronics Parallel	Ethernet, SCSI, RS232C (×2), Centronics Parallel, Color Bitmap Display	
Expansion Slot	1		
Power Requirements	AC220—240V		
Power Consumption	330VA (220V)		
Dimensions	355(W) × 341(D) × 110(H)mm (14 × 13½ × 4⅜")		
Weight	10kg (22 lb 1 oz)		
Operating System	NEWS-OS (UNIX 4.3BSD + X Window System Ver. 11 + NFS Rel. 3.2)		
Communications	TCP/IP, XNS		
Languages	C, Fortran 77, Franz Lisp, Pascal		
Graphics	CGI		

NOTE: Because of limited internal storage capacity, the NWS-1510(EK)/1530(EK) are installed with part of the NEWS operating system.

EXHIBIT 3
Sony and Sun Microsystems Product Introductions

First Product to Use New Microprocessor

| | Sun Microsystems | | Sony | |
Microprocessor	Product	Date	Product	Date
68000	Sun-2	11/83	—	—
68010	Sun–2/160	11/84	—	—
68020	Sun–3	9/85	800 Series	1/87
68030	Sun–3/60	7/87	1800 Series	9/88
RISC	Sun–4	7/87	?	?

Set Chip) microprocessor. While Sony was researching a RISC-based workstation, it was not yet ready to organize a product development effort whose output would be a marketable product.

Because the Workstation Division felt that it lacked the marketing power to create entirely new markets, it concentrated on creating a competitive workstation by making use of Sony's capabilities in manufacturing the other technologies such as optical disks and video to exploit niches. It concentrated also on the Japanese market where U.S. workstation firms were at a disadvantage because of the complexity of the characters in the Japanese language.

Although Sony's strategy had worked in the early stages of its entry into the workstation market, to grow further it had to expand its traditional role to become more of a leader. In particular, the U.S. market was more competitive because Sun and HP/Apollo did not have to face the difficulties of the Japanese language in the U.S. (See Exhibit 4 for a comparison of Sony and U.S. workstations.) On the other hand, Sony management felt that manufacturing expertise and costs would become more important as the industry matured, and Sony's size and experience in electronics manufacturing would give it a competitive advantage.

New Product Development in the Workstation Division

The division's development process had evolved somewhat since Doi had assembled 11 maverick engineers and given them free rein. In 1989, the development process had three stages: (1) basic architecture specification, (2) product design, and (3) first lot production. During each phase, a different group (or groups) had primary responsibility for the

Exhibit 4

Comparison of the 1500 with Competitors' Workstations

	Sony	Sun	HP/Apollo
Model	1520	3/80	DN 2500
CPU	68030/25 MHz	68030/20 MHz	68030/20 MHz
Coprocessor	68881	68882	68882
MIPS	3.9	3.0	4.0
Amount of Main Memory	4–16 MB	4–16 MB	4–16 MB
Hard Disk	40 MB	104 MB	100 MB
Floppy Drive	3.5" 1.44 MB	3.5" 1.44 MB	5.25" 1.2 MB
Standard Interfaces	Ethernet, SCSI, RS232C, Centronics	Ethernet, SCSI, RS432	Ethernet, Tokenring, RS232C
Operating System	NEWS-OS (UNIX 4.3BSD + X Window System Ver. 11 + NFS 3.2)	Sun OS 4.1 (UNIX 4.3BSD + System V, NeWS, SunView, NFS)	Domain/OS (Aegis UNIX System V, 4.3BSD NFS, X Window DM)
Display	15" Monochrome (816X1024)	16" Monochrome (1280x1024)	15" Monochrome (1024X800)
Price	$7,860	$8,720	$5,420
Date of Introduction	December 1988	January 1988	Announced (to be introduced in Dec. 89)

development effort, although their responsibilities tended to overlap for a considerable amount of time and people were transferred across groups as projects moved through the process. (See Exhibit 5 for the organization of the SuperMicro Group and Exhibit 6 for a flow chart of how the process was intended to work.)

The basic architecture stage occurred before a specific product was targeted. The R&D department would examine new and existing technologies to determine the basic hardware and software on which Sony should develop its line. The R&D department would then study the technologies it had chosen by developing a prototype workstation based on the new technology. While this prototype was not directly connected to a particular product line, it gave R&D engineers "hands-on" experience with the new technology. With this experience, they would develop a basic architecture for the workstations which would form the core or platform projects in the product line.

The R&D group was continually working on the basic technologies that would be used in the top-of-the-line next generation systems. For exam-

EXHIBIT 5

Workstation Division Organization Chart

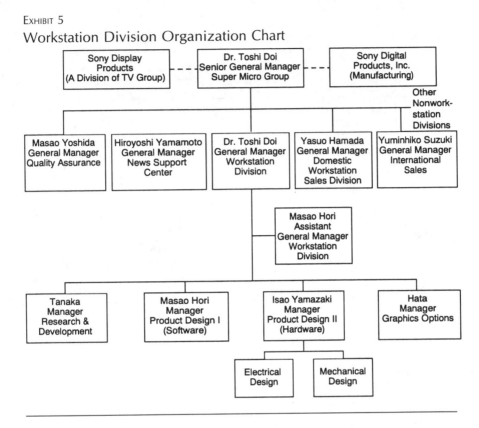

ple, after studying the 68020, several engineers were transferred from R&D to the two design engineering groups to lead the design effort when the time came to develop an actual product. The R&D group then studied the 68030 chip and later a RISC microprocessor from MIPS Computer Systems Inc. for the division's next generation products (see Exhibit 7).

The second stage in the development process was the actual product design effort, which started with the generation of a New Product Plan (NPP). While one person was assigned to write the NPP, it was a collaborative effort by people in the Planning, R&D, and Design Engineering departments. The primary author could be a member of any of the relevant departments, although normally he or she was in the hardware design engineering department. The NPP included a description of the proposed product, a brief competitive analysis, cost and schedule projections, and a summary of other relevant business and technical data (see Exhibit 8).

After the NPP was formulated (and approved by Doi), two design engineering groups became involved. Most product-specific work was done

EXHIBIT 6

Flow Chart of Prototyping in the Development Process

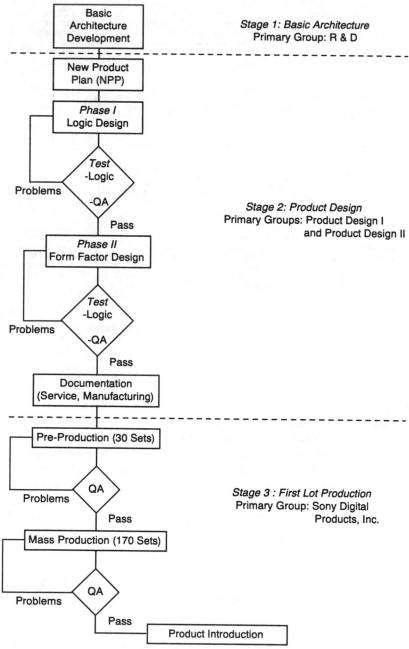

Stage 1: Basic Architecture
Primary Group: R & D

Stage 2: Product Design
Primary Groups: Product Design I
and Product Design II

Stage 3 : First Lot Production
Primary Group: Sony Digital
Products, Inc.

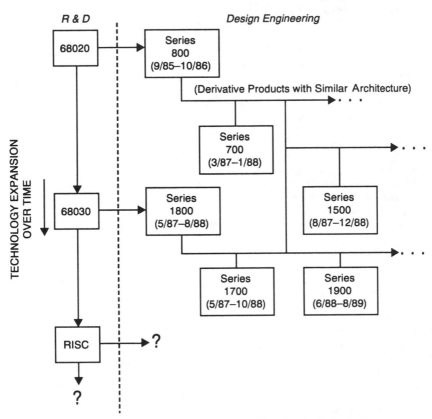

Exhibit 7

Transfer of Products from R&D to Design, and Product Families

**PRODUCT LINE EXPANSION
OVER TIME** ——▶

Dates in parentheses are the NPP to Product Introduction

by the hardware design engineering department managed by Isao Yamazaki (Design Engineering II). The majority of the software development effort was based on the Unix kernel and the creation of the low level
routines that made up the operating system. Relatively little effort was
devoted to applications programs (e.g., a spreadsheet or word processing
program), although some work was done on applications that would be
common across the entire NEWS™ product line. A very small subset of
hardware-dependent software (e.g., the operating system) was developed by five or six software engineers from Masao Hori's department
(Design Engineering I), which employed a total of 25 software engineers.

EXHIBIT 8

New Product Plan (NPP) Data Requirements

1. Product Concepts and Main Features
2. Competitors' Products
3. Sales and Distribution Channel
4. Target Market Segments
5. Target Price Points
   a. List
   b. FOB
6. Competitors' Prices
7. Cost of Material
8. Production Cost
9. Maintenance Information
   a. Technical
   b. Warrantee Length
   c. Special Services (Periodic Maintenance, etc.)
10. Applicable Safety Regulations (UL, CSA, FCC, etc.)
11. Other Regulations (EMI, EBU, etc.)
12. Manufacturing Plants to Be Used
13. Product Lifecycle
14. Estimated Sales
    a. Monthly
    b. By Geographic Region
    c. Market Share
15. System Concept
    a. Monitor
    b. Computer
    c. How to connect to peripherals, network, etc.
16. Accessories (Power Cords, etc.)
17. Anticipated Product Line Evolution
18. Approvals
    a. Planner
    b. Plant Manager
    c. Design Leader
    d. Design Manager
    e. Senior Manager
    f. Accounting Manager
    g. Department Manager
    h. General Manager

The software design engineering department's primary task was porting[3] Unix and Sony's application programs to the new computer.

The hardware development task—designing the main system board

---

[3] Porting Software was the technical term for modifying a software program so that it would run on a different type of system. Unix was highly modularized in order to ease the porting task; applications programs that ran under Unix tended to need very little, if any, modification to run under Unix on a different computer.

for the computer—was divided into two phases, each of which culminated in building and validating a prototype. In Phase I, the system's format of the board was specified to fit into the overall system design a (e.g., to make sure the board would physically fit into the housing) and logic was designed and checked. Toward the end of this phase, the few sample boards were built and tested. In Phase II, several prototype printed circuit boards (PCBs) with the final format were produced, tested, and debugged.

The R&D group and both design engineering groups were located in two adjacent buildings in the Shinagawa section of Tokyo. Each of the three departments had one large room where everyone (including the manager) worked. There were no partitions or doors and because this arrangement kept the manager well informed, Sony did not rely very much on formal project reviews. However, each department had one or two rooms that could be used for meetings so that the rest of the group would not be disturbed.

The third and final stage of new product development was first lot production, for which the manufacturing division, Sony Digital Products Inc., had primary responsibility. This division, a wholly owned subsidiary of the Sony Group, produced CD players, optical disks and other digital products for several Sony divisions. Its plant was located in the mountains, four hours (by train) from Tokyo.

Project Management in the Workstation Division

At Sony, a project manager was assigned after the NPP approval. Based on merit and availability rather than seniority, this assignment did not confer special status on the project manager—at least not permanently. An engineer who served as manager on one project might be a regular member on the next. Often the project manager was a member of the R&D department who was transferred to a design engineering department when an NPP for the area in which he or she had been working was written, and the project was sent to design engineering for development. This procedure was adopted to make the transfer of knowledge from R&D to design engineering as quick and effective as possible.

The project manager was in fact more of a senior engineer than a manager. Because the teams were so small (typically three or four hardware engineers), the need for many of the traditional management tasks, such as coordinating within the team, essentially disappeared. The engineers typically had to split their time among two or three projects, although they were generally assigned only one major project (such as a new workstation) at a time. The major project tended to take about 70% of an engineer's time with the other 30% divided up among smaller projects. In general, the major project took precedence over the minor ones, although there were occasional conflicts over priority (which were settled by Yamazaki).

Doi felt strongly that senior management's role in a project should be to build a team, establish broad objectives, and then leave it alone. He believed managers should remain outside the project, perform miscellaneous tasks for it, and remove any obstacles to it. High-level managers also had a role in developing strategy and monitoring the project, but not in the day-to-day operations of the project.

Doi's management approach was successful in part because of the skills and abilities of the engineers in the Workstation Division. Although the division had grown from the original 11 to over 100 engineers in 1989, the original 11 still formed the technical core for the division. The newer engineers had been brought in from a variety of sources. While some had been hired straight out of college, many had been transferred from other Sony divisions, and some had even been hired away from other companies. This diverse mix had given the engineering function a breadth and depth of experience unusual in a Japanese company.

The 1550 Project (August 1987 to December 1988)

One of the division's recent major development projects had been the 1550, a general purpose workstation positioned in the middle of the Sony line. Although every project had some unique aspects, the 1550 development was fairly typical of an initial offering in a next generation product series. (A time line is shown in Exhibit 9.)

The first stage, specification of the basic architecture and concepts, typically was done by the R&D department for "core" products. For the 1550, however, the basic architecture was well understood because the division had developed several computers based on the same microprocessor chip. Therefore the project began directly with an NPP written in August 1987 by a senior hardware engineer, Takashi Yoshida.

Because he had written the NPP, Yoshida was the logical choice to manage the second stage of the development effort on the 1550. Joining Yoshida for the project team were three other electrical engineers, who worked on designing the mother board while one software engineer (from Hori's group) was responsible for the product-specific programming to be included in the ROM on the board. An overview of workstation technology is found in Appendix II.

Phase I

The first task in any development effort was creating a detailed design of the logic for the mother board. The logic design determined how the

Exhibit 9
Time Line of the 1550 Project

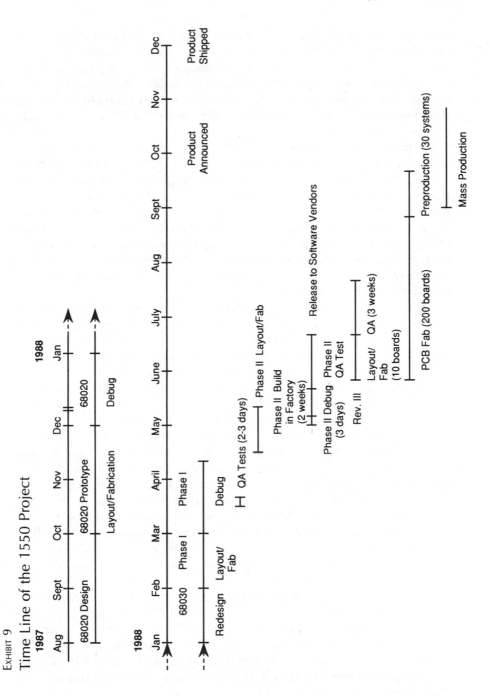

computer would function, although the details of the PCB (e.g., dimensions, number of layers, and routing of wires) were left until later. The logic functions were determined by choosing the components (e.g., chips, resistors, and capacitors) and specifying how they would be connected. The final output of this task was a set of schematics (engineering drawings) that showed each of the components and the wires connecting them.

Because wires on the same layer of a PCB could not cross one another (such crossing would cause a short circuit), specifying the logic of how all the chips were to be connected did not complete the design. The position of the chips, the number of layers, and the physical routing of the connecting wires on the PCB also had to be determined. Because of the many connections necessary and the desire to minimize the number of layers on the PCB, this process was quite complex. When there was no way to connect one point to another without crossing a wire, a new layer had to be added, even though doing so increased the board's production cost considerably.

After the schematics were completed, a layout was developed so a first prototype could be built. Because of the Workstation Division's small size, it did not have the resources either to develop the layout or to fabricate the prototype PCB in-house. Instead, the schematics were sent to one of several outside vendors who developed the detailed board layout. This process generally took four to five weeks the first time it was done. Subsequently, when changes were made to a previous design, much of the layout stayed the same and the time for developing the remainder was reduced to as little as two to three weeks.

After the board layout was completed, it was sent to a vendor who would fabricate a batch of boards. Often the same vendor would do both the layout and fabrication, but sometimes a different subcontractor would be used. Fabrication took an additional two to three weeks; typically, a batch of ten prototype boards would be made in Phase I.

Thus, the total time required from the time the schematics were finished until the prototype board was returned was usually about six to eight weeks. During this waiting period, the engineers were able to catch up on their smaller projects.

For the 1550 project, the NPP called for the system to be based on a 68020 microprocessor, and by mid-October 1987, Yoshida and his project team had developed a set of schematics for the main board. The board was then sent to Oki, an outside vendor who not only developed its layout but also fabricated it. By early December, the 10 units of the Phase I prototype had been made and Yoshida's small team of engineers had started their debugging procedures.

It took about one month for the first prototype board of the 1550 to be 90% debugged. However, further work was terminated when management decided that, because Sun Microsystems had just introduced a competing machine based on the 68030, a newer and more powerful microprocessor, the 1550 should be based on the 68030 instead of the 68020. Although the 68030 was very similar to the 68020, much of the design did have to be redone. The primary difference between the chips was that the 68030 contained its own memory management unit,[4] making the memory management unit designed for the 68020 irrelevant and an unnecessary cost for the 1550.

Phase I on the 1550 therefore needed to be repeated, and the first several weeks of 1988 were spent redesigning the mother board to use the 68030. The new schematics were then sent to Oki, and six weeks later 10 revised prototype PCBs were delivered to Sony. Next, the hardware design engineers hand-inserted the chips into the boards and started the low-level hardware checks, which included testing the data and address buses to ensure the voltage levels were in the required range, and testing that the clock and reset waveforms had the right shape. Software to drive a monitor was then placed in ROM so that a CRT could be connected to the serial port[5] on the board. Because of the similarity with the 68020 version of the 1550, the "terminal driver" software needed only slight modifications from the previous version. By the end of the first week, the engineers were able to test memory by typing commands from a keyboard.

After the low-level tests were completed, the more complicated tasks of debugging the various interfaces (e.g., interfaces to disk controllers, networks, and displays) began. The software to test these interfaces was written on three levels: the top-level shell, the middle-level controller, and the low-level device drivers. Usually, when altering the basic architecture of the interface, higher level code did require modifications. When modifying the software from an existing workstation, however, only the device drivers needed to be changed. Thus, modifying the 1550's software structure to work on the new system could be done quickly. For example, although the test code for the disk controller contained approximately 4,000 lines of assembly language, adapting it to the new system took only two to three days.

Debugging the various interfaces for the 1550 mother board took ap-

---

[4] A memory management unit was the electronics that controlled a high speed memory cache. A cache, a high speed memory bank for frequently accessed data, was used because the microprocessor was much faster than main memory. This dual memory system allowed the computer to utilize low-speed memory without much loss in performance yet without the extremely high cost of using very high speed memory exclusively.

[5] A serial port was one of several interfaces to external devices on a computer. It allowed the computer to communicate with devices that sent and received data in a serial fashion (e.g., terminals, plotters, and some printers).

proximately one month, during which several software engineers worked closely with the hardware engineers. Once the system was debugged (by the end of April 1988), the software people who were converting application software were given several of the debugged boards on which to continue their work. Three of the remaining boards were given to the quality assurance division (which performed QA for the entire SuperMicro Group) to test for electromagnetic interference (EMI) and to complete other Phase I tests. The final form factor (e.g., size and shape) of the board also was determined during the final portion of Phase I. This task was performed in conjunction with an outside vendor who was designing the box into which the mother board and all the other electronics were to be placed. Once these tasks were completed, the electrical engineers then spent a couple of days documenting changes in the circuits before returning the updated schematics back to Oki for layout and manufacture of the Phase II prototype boards.

The purpose of Phase I was to ensure that the logic of the design worked properly. If the problems with the PCB design were excessive, another Phase I prototype cycle would be performed. Fortunately, on the 1550 project the problems were not that severe, and in most cases only one Phase I prototyping cycle was necessary. After the Phase I debugging was completed, the components with long lead times were ordered and a date was set for first lot production. (Most of the long lead items were semiconductor devices that had to be ordered three or four months in advance.)

Phase II

In Phase II, the size and shape of the PCBs were adjusted to meet the form factor requirements that had just been established at the end of Phase I. Phase II also provided an opportunity for the manufacturing division (Sony Digital Products, Inc.) to start learning about the new product and preparing its manufacturing processes.

Because the 1550 was the first computer in the 1500 series, 100 boards were ordered in the Phase II prototype cycle so that third-party software vendors could be given beta-test systems to use in developing their applications. Oki finished the 100 boards by mid-June, having taken approximately six weeks to redo the layout and fabricate the boards. Five boards were sent directly to the hardware engineering team, and the remaining 95 were sent directly to the Sony Digital Products factory, where the chips were inserted using the automatic chip insertion machines. Normally, the hardware engineers would have debugged and corrected the prototype boards before sending the batch to the factory. In this instance, however, the switch from the 68020 to the 68030 had delayed the project several weeks and the capacity had been scheduled months in advance—making it impossible to delay or reschedule.

This schedule put a great deal of pressure on the engineers to debug the Phase II prototype board quickly, because any cuts of connecting wires (i.e., electrical paths) had to be made before the chips were inserted. Adding jumper wires—additional connections—was done afterwards. On the 1550, the hardware and software people had only three days in which to debug the prototype mother boards before the factory inserted the chips.

There were usually very few logic bugs at this point because they had been removed in Phase I, but noise and EMI problems could appear. Noise problems occurred when chips could not react fast enough to handle the speed at which the computer was run. EMI problems occurred when the computer's internal signals emitted radio waves that interfered with other equipment (such as TV and radio receivers).

Fortunately, in the 1550 project, there were no noise or EMI problems and only a couple of minor logic errors. Through a great deal of effort, the hardware team managed to find the problems, which were solved by one cut and two jumpers. Sony Digital Products was then able to begin production of the batch of prototype boards on schedule.

While the hardware design engineers were debugging the system, several manufacturing people had been present to learn about the system and to help wherever possible. After the boards were debugged, the engineers went to the factory with the manufacturing people to help with the production of the 985 prototype boards. The engineers remained at the factory for a week, of which three days were spent making the logic changes to the PCBs and an additional day was spent inserting and soldering some special components.

Approximately 70% of the boards worked after the first pass through production, that is, at the end of the fourth day. The engineers remained through much of the night to determine the problems with the other 30%. Most of the problems involved soldering- and manufacturing-related issues and by the next morning 90% of the boards were working. The boards were assembled into complete systems the next day, and on day six, the remaining boards were fixed and completed.

Several of the completed systems were sent to quality assurance for special tests: EMI, UL, FCC, and other environmental concerns. The Phase II QA tests were more extensive than in Phase I and included testing under extreme conditions of temperature, humidity, and vibration, and with wide voltage swings (+/–10%).

The other systems were distributed with the majority (approximately 50) going to software vendors, who were writing third-party application software. The balance was divided among the two design engineering groups and the R&D department, with a few systems sent to marketing for customer presentations.

First Lot Production

After returning from the Sony Digital Products plant, the hardware engineers documented the Phase II design changes and sent them to Oki, which was to do a final layout for the boards in anticipation of first lot production. Because the changes were so small, Oki was able to build 10 of these "Prototype III" boards in three weeks (including one week for layout). These boards were used by the project team to ensure that all the changes had been made properly before the first lot production boards were built. By the second week in August, following Sony's companywide vacation week (August 1 to 7), the Prototype III systems had passed QA tests. The remaining 200 boards for the first lot production were then ordered from Oki.

After the Prototype III boards passed QA's tests, the hardware engineers expanded the system's documentation, writing maintenance manuals, test procedures for manufacturing, and other instructions. Throughout this period, the engineers also had to help maintain the prototype systems that had been sent to the software houses.

The first lot production of the 1550 was scheduled to start in the third week of October at which time the hardware design engineers returned to the factory for a couple of weeks to help with ramp-up and testing, and to troubleshoot any problems. The first lot production was done in two phases. The first batch, pre-production, sent 30 systems through the production line.

Because of the large number of products manufactured at Sony Digital Products, the plant operation was extremely flexible. There were 10 lines for automatic chip insertion as well as a couple of manual insertion lines for especially difficult insertion tasks. The plant automatically inserted over 90% of the chips onto approximately 2,500 PCBs a day. About 600 different PCBs, all made by subcontractors, were run through the various insertion lines in a typical month. In addition to the traditional chip insertion machines, a new Sony-designed machine for placing surface mount chips had recently been installed.

After the chips were inserted into the PCBs, the boards passed through wave soldering twice to improve the soldering's quality and yield. (Most problems with PCBs could be traced to bad solders.) The boards and other components then were assembled into the final system. Although the plant had several traditional assembly lines (with conveyor belts and each worker performing a precisely defined task), workstation volumes were too small for an assembly line to be efficient.

The workstations were therefore assembled off-line by two workers, each of whom did half the tasks.

After the 30 pre-production systems were completed, they were tested intensively and again debugged. At this time, any remaining systematic errors were found and corrected and then the balance of the first lot production units were produced. In the 1550 project, no major problems were found and the factory continued producing the remaining systems. The product was announced at the end of October, and shipments started on December 21, 1988.

Yamazaki considered the development process at the Workstation Division quite successful. He attributed its success to several factors: very little time was wasted passing project responsibility from group to group; the project teams tended to be small groups of very expert engineers who took the development of a new computer from the NPP all the way through to manufacturing; the project team was typically formed around either an R&D person who had worked on the system's basic concept or a person who had experience with a similar system; and this same team eventually ended up on the manufacturing plant floor, helping to ramp-up production.

Comparing Workstation Development Processes

From what Doi knew about similar PCB-based product development efforts at different Sony divisions as well as at other companies, the Workstation Division's development effort was very efficient. Its usual development cycle time was 12 months, while product development cycles at other workstation companies usually lasted 18 to 24 months.

In the number of prototyping cycles, Sony's advantage was even more obvious: competitors typically went through 6 to 8 (although there was a wide variation from about 4 to 12 depending on the company and the project). Sony's development process typically required only two to four cycles.

Although Sony had far fewer prototyping cycles on average, the time for each cycle tended to be about the same as at other companies—approximately two months. The time at Sony, however, was spent very differently. In general, other companies did their own board layout with automated CAD/CAM systems. Sony had placed little emphasis on CAD/CAM tools and instead subcontracted the layout task to a variety of small firms that specialized in PCB layout design.

Most companies in the workstation business did focus on getting the prototypes back quickly. Often these companies would go to a board prototyping house that, for an extra free, might be able to fabricate the boards in a week. When the boards returned from the prototyping vendor, the chips would be inserted by an internal model shop. Because these tasks were handled by groups other than hardware or software design, the design engineers at other companies were able to focus exclusively on their primary design tasks.

There were also differences in the philosophy of developing new workstations. Most companies divided the development process into three phases: Engineering Verification Test (EVT), Design Verification Test (DVT), and Production Verification Test (PVT). The EVT stage verified that the board logic worked properly; the DVT stage verified that the board worked in its final size and shape; and the PVT stage verified that the factory's fabrication process could produce that board in volume and on specification.

Sony's development process consisted of Phase I, which was essentially EVT, but then seemed to combine DVT and PVT stages into the Phase II prototyping step. In Phase II, not only was the board reduced to its final size and shape, but the factory was involved in inserting the chips and assembling the board into complete systems. While there was an element of testing in the first lot production stage, the primary purpose was to produce systems that were sold to customers.

Yamazaki's Proposal

Although the development process at the Workstation Division was efficient, changes were needed. The principal problem was that too much was required of the hardware design engineers. Small teams were more efficient but they required that each engineer be able to handle the complete range of design tasks, from high-level architecture down to minor details. Furthermore, because the same engineer dealt with all the issues—from logic design to manufacturability—the procedure required a great breadth of knowledge. Thus the engineer's skills and knowledge had to be both broad and deep. Even the current, experienced engineers had trouble with these requirements; getting new engineers with this combination of skills appeared almost impossible. New engineers would have to be trained, and that could take years.

The current system also required an almost superhuman effort by hardware engineers, who typically worked 60–70 hours a week, and even more during a crisis. Yamazaki was afraid that some of them would burn out after only a few years at such a pace.

Another problem with the current procedure was that the designs were not optimized for manufacturability. Because hardware design engineers were unfamiliar with all of the manufacturing concerns, they often missed simple redesigns that could make manufacturing far more efficient. For example, the size of a hole could be changed slightly to allow easier insertion of a component, or the orientations of the components altered to better fit the capabilities of the particular insertion machines used by Sony Digital Products. Even when these problems were brought to the attention of the design engineers, they lacked time to go back and fix them.

Masao Hori, the assistant general manger of the Workstation Division, stated the problem succinctly:

> The current process is not so bad, because it is very quick. It is very difficult to separate technology into neat little steps and for this reason it takes time to transfer technology. Because the workstation market is so competitive there is no time to do this transfer. On the other hand, design engineering does not have enough manpower or expertise to support manufacturing properly, especially as our product line and the number of development projects continue to grow.

Yamazaki's proposal involved adding a Manufacturing Engineering Section (MES) between the hardware design engineering department and manufacturing (at Sony Digital Products, Inc.). This new section would have five responsibilities: (1) representing manufacturability issues and concerns early in the development process; (2) supporting manufacturing during ramp-up; (3) doing follow-up engineering and redesigns necessary after first lot production; (4) developing minor upgrades, extensions, and enhancements to the product; and (5) supporting field service and providing analysis of recurrent problems in the field.

MES would get involved with a development project in Phase II, playing a support role in building and testing the prototypes and preparing design documentation. By first lot production they would take over primary responsibility for supporting manufacturing. Given MES involvement, the design engineers would have to spend less time supervising prototyping and less time at the factory during first lot production. In some instances, MES could probably itself handle the manufacturing support required during first lot production.

After production introduction, MES would perform any redesigns requested by manufacturing (for example, a chip from a certain vendor might have too high a defect rate and a small redesign might be necessary to switch to a different vendor). Under the current system, these tasks were delayed or not completed at all because the hardware design engineering department was overloaded.

MES would also design small upgrades to existing systems. For example, for the 1500 Series, MES would perform the minor redesigns of the mother board needed so it could interface with a high resolution graphics display.

Support of field service was another area in which MES would fill an important gap. In addition to pure technical support when field service could not solve a problem, MES could analyze the different types of failures and determine their root causes. They could then redesign the product to prevent similar failures in the future.

By transferring tasks to MES, design engineering's workload would be significantly reduced, and the remaining tasks would be completed in a more timely fashion. The hardware design engineering department would also be able to spend more time designing new systems, thus reducing the development cycle. Furthermore, the design engineers could become more specialized because MES would handle most of the manufacturing issues.

Because the tasks proposed for MES involved only minor adjustments in existing design and manufacturing knowledge, the MES engineers would not require the same breadth of knowledge as the design engineers. They would not be required to design the architecture of the workstations or even do major design tasks. Hiring relatively young, less experienced engineers for MES would be much easier than hiring the type of people currently required for the hardware design department. Furthermore, because design would become more focused, even hardware engineers would be easier to find.

Yamazaki proposed that the new section be located in Tokyo, near the hardware design engineering department, and report to him. It would eventually need 10 engineers, but the section could be started with fewer (a minimum of five) because it would have responsibility for only a limited number of products. Of course, as it took responsibility for more and more products, the staffing would have to be increased.

Although Doi understood and agreed with many of Yamazaki's points, he was worried about the effects on Sony's development process of implementing the proposal. He did not want the Workstation Division to fall into the big-company mode like the rest of Sony, yet he knew that growth necessitated some changes. If he merely tried to add engineers to the current structure, those engineers would probably begin to specialize anyway.

Appendix I   Selected Workstation Terminology

The CPU (central processor unit) formed the "brains" of the computer, interpreting the software commands and controlling all the other components of the computer. At the heart of the CPU was a microprocessor, a single chip for arithmetic, input and output data, and similar operations. In 1989, most workstations used a microprocessor from the Motorola 68000™ family (the 68000, 68020, 68030, etc.). There was, however, a distinct trend toward using Reduced Instruction Set Chips (RISC). Although the RISC microprocessors had many fewer functions, they were optimized for speed, thus improving the total system performance.

The RAM (random access memory) consisted of all the memory chips that provided fast, temporary storage for data that the computer used while running. Because data in RAM were lost if the power were turned off, workstations needed permanent storage as well, and that was provided by the hard disk(s). Data were stored magnetically on disks and remained even when the power was turned off. However, being mechanical devices, hard disks were much slower than RAM.

The ROM (read only memory), like RAM, was a collection of chips that provided memory. Unlike RAM, however, ROM could not be altered after the chips were fabricated and programmed. Furthermore, ROM did not lose its data when the power was shut off. For this reason, ROM was used as a place to store a small "kernel" of software that the computer used when it was first turned on.

The CPU communicated with these devices, as well as with peripherals, through the bus. The bus, like a telephone junction box, was a collection of wires that ran through the computer system. Two buses existed: the address bus and the data bus. The address bus contained the signal from the CPU that determined which device should respond. The data bus carried information (data) to be communicated. To make sure that the signals were sent and received properly, some chips (the bus controller) performed logic functions to test for data validity.

Appendix II   Workstation Technology (1989)

All the chips to be included in a workstation were located on a PCB. The circuit board was a sheet of plastic on which alternating layers of wires and insulation were placed. Within the same layer, spaces were left between wires so that they did not short-circuit the electrical signal. The wires could cross between layers because wire layers were separated by insulation. (The green insulation gave the boards their green appearance.) Because the wires on each layer were laid down using a printing process, the cost of a board was related directly to the number of layers. The manufacturing process also became more difficult when more layers were added, further increasing the cost, complicating the debugging process, and making it more difficult to achieve consistently high quality. There was, therefore, a great incentive to reduce the number of layers.

Historically, once a board was fabricated and appropriate holes were created, chips were inserted into those holes and soldered on the bottom side. While this could be done by hand, using an automatic chip insertion machine was much more efficient. After the chips were inserted, they had to be soldered into place. Again, this could be done by hand, but a more efficient method was wave soldering: the protruding "legs" of the chips that had been pushed all the way through the board were passed over a "river" of molten solder. This technique uniformly soldered all the chips on a board at one time.

A newer method for attaching chips to a board was called surface mount. In this method, the chips were connected only to the surface of the board, without going through holes. Soldering by hand was much more difficult and sometimes impossible with surface mount chips. Because surface mount reduced the size of a board by three-quarters or more, the electronics industry was adopting this technology quite quickly.

Mistakes found in the design of a PCB usually could be corrected by hand; if a new connection were needed, a short wire could be handsoldered onto the board, connecting the two points desired. Such a hand-soldered wire was called a jumper. If an extra connection between two components had to be made, the wire often could be cut by finding a space on the board where no other wires crossed the offending wire and then cutting through the layers until the connection was broken. Because these hand fixes were difficult, time consuming, and not fully reliable, all such design problems normally were corrected before regular volume production began.

Another problem often occurring in workstations was noise from the signals changing so rapidly. Noise had two manifestations. The first was "external" noise or electromagnetic interference: the wires in the computer started acting like little antennae, producing radio signals that could disrupt nearby television and radio reception. In the United States, the amount of EMI permitted was regulated by government agencies such as the FCC. The second, "internal" noise, was caused when some of the chips did not respond fast enough to the signals they received, resulting in misread data. So, computers that worked perfectly when run slowly, sometimes failed when operated more quickly. Because many things affected the ability of the chips to respond quickly (e.g., temperature, strength of the signal), these problems were often sporadic and very difficult to find. Much QA testing during product development focused on discovering such problems before the product was deliver to customers.

Bendix Automation Group (B): A Case of Integrating New Technologies—The Weidemann Quantum 2000

In March 1983 the Warner & Swasey Wiedemann division introduced its new punch press, the Quantum 2000, at the Westec Machine Tool Show in Los Angeles. It was an immediate success. The show alone generated nine new orders and, by July, 19 orders had been booked. One Group executive saw the Quantum 2000 as "the beginning of the end of the erosion of our market share." Other people within the Group pointed to the development of the Quantum 2000 as illustrating the kind of cooperative effort between a division and the Research Center that would be required to achieve successful product innovation in the future.

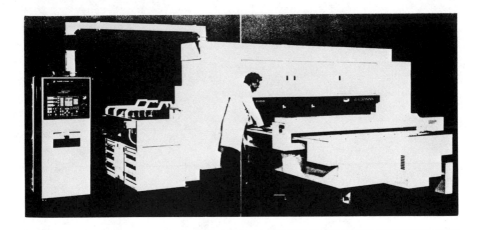

This case was prepared by Marcie Tyre, Instructor, under the supervision of Professor Richard S. Rosenbloom.

Background: The Wiedemann Division

The Wiedemann division had long been a leading punch press manufacturer. In 1958, it was the first company to offer a numerically controlled (NC) punch press, and it later introduced computer numerically controlled (CNC) models. Competing CNC machines were introduced in the early 1960s, and between 1964 and 1974 Wiedemann's market share fell from 100 percent to less than 50 percent. Still, margins remained extremely attractive since Wiedemann, as the acknowledged leader in the field, could virtually set punch press prices. However, in the mid–1970s Japanese competition began to make itself felt. By 1987, it was clear that Japanese and European competitors were catching up or had caught up. The Japanese company Amada introduced its Coma and Pega turret punch press models at that time, and quickly gained dominant market share.

Wiedemann's competing entry in the turret press market was called the Wiedematic W-Line (Exhibit 1). Introduced in 1972, it had been among the fastest CNC punch presses then available and was considered a successful product line. However, the W-Line had proven unreliable in the field until two to three years after its introduction. Also, while the Wiedemann division continued to generate an attractive flow of cash to its parent, Warner & Swasey, its market share was declining steadily (Exhibit 2).

Origin of the Quantum 2000

In 1978, a year and a half before the purchase of Warner & Swasey by Bendix, Wiedemann management took stock of its declining market share, and decided they must act. They defined three possible responses:

1. Bring out an interim machine, targeted for introduction in 1980. The design would embody improvements over the W-Line but remain essentially conventional, like the Japanese Pega.
2. Stick with the most recent member of the W-Line, which had been fairly successful in the market, and upgrade it.
3. Develop a radically new concept that would be the basis of Wiedemann's competitive thrust in the 1980s.

Wiedemann management soon realized that, with the resources available, they could not undertake two major projects simultaneously. Further, it was not clear that the first option was a viable one. After working

717

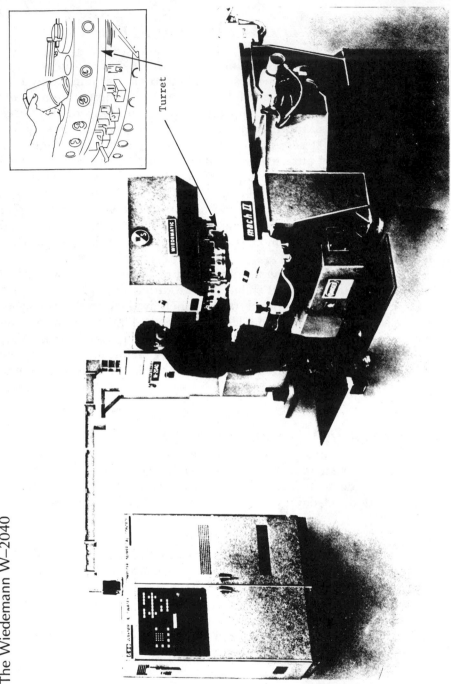

EXHIBIT 1
The Wiedemann W–2040

EXHIBIT 2

EXHIBIT 2
Market Share Trends—Bendix Shipments
U.S. Consumption-Based

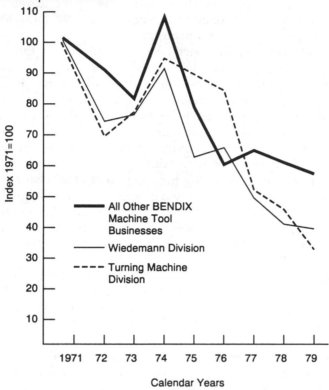

Legend:
- **All Other BENDIX Machine Tool Businesses**
- — Wiedemann Division
- - - - Turning Machine Division

Index 1971=100

Calendar Years

SOURCE: Company documents.

on specifications for an interim punch press design, engineers began to doubt whether Wiedemann could implement the design at a competitive price. They decided instead to go for broke: try to develop a fundamentally superior product, and try to do it quickly enough to stop Amada.

Wiedemann's director of engineering, Joe Basko, and its director of marketing, Brad Peck, identified the first challenge facing them as the definition of a target. In order to get the project off the ground, they would have to define what the new machine should be able to do. Therefore, Basko, Peck, and their staffs designed a questionnaire and distributed it to the broad range of small- and medium-lot metal part fabricators who made up Wiedemann's customer base. Results showed that customer concern centered on tool change time and frequency.

In most machines, tool change time and frequency was determined by the configuration of the turret, then the dominant method of holding and positioning tools (Exhibit 1). The Turret concept had been introduced by Wiedemann in the 1930s. The basic principle was that a variety of tools could be stored inside the punch press on the turret, a sort of lazy Susan which would rotate to present any one of these tools into punching position for a given operation.

The total efficiency of the machine was a function of three factors. First, the operating rate was determined by how fast the workpiece could be positioned under the punching head and how rapidly the head could deliver successive punches. Second, tool change time was determined by the difficulty of disengaging the turret and of taking tools out of toolholders and replacing them with new tools. Finally, the frequency of tool changes was largely determined by the number of tools that could be stored in the turret at any one time.

In order to minimize operating time lost due to tool changes, punch press manufacturers in the 1970s were designing increasingly large capacity turrets. The W–2040, Wiedemann's smallest machine in 1978, had a turret with spaces for 24 tools. Amada's comparable product, the Pega, had topped this by introducing a turret with two levels and spaces for 56 tools.

The challenge to Wiedemann was to come up with a punch press concept that would be faster than existing offerings in terms of both tool changes and operating rates. Given the keenly competitive nature of the market, the new machine would also have to be at least cost competitive.

Therefore, Joe Basko and his team approached the Research Center, then under the direction of Jack Hubbard. Engineers at Research, they hoped, would be able to help them develop some of the concepts on which the new machine would be based and to act as a sounding board for their own ideas. They found that many people who had been or were still at Research, including Hubbard, were dissatisfied with the fact that the Center had drifted away from concept development in order to provide engineering support to operating divisions. They wanted to get into something new, and welcomed Wiedemann's challenge.

"We asked for their participation on the project," explained Basko, "and we got it. And not because we picked the best people to work with us, but because we picked the right people." Basko himself had worked at Research before coming to Wiedemann. In fact, he had worked on an extensive testing program on the W-Line when Wiedemann had needed Research help to solve reliability problems that had developed in the field. The project had been a success, and helped to forge a link between Wiedemann and the Research Center. Some of the people who were asked to work on the Quantum 2000 project had in fact worked under Basko on the earlier project.

Just as important, according to Basko, was picking the right people from Wiedemann's engineering staff to make up the other half of the team. They tended to be new and innovative people—for some, this was their first experience designing a CNC punch press. They were not afraid to entertain new ideas. Finally, the interaction between the two groups included a helpful competitive element. Both wanted to be first to come up with a new idea.

In retrospect, however, it was not easy to reconstruct the origins of each of the ideas behind the finished product, or to point to the individual contributions of the members of the project team. One of the consequences of the successful development of the Quantum was that both the Research Center and the division felt proud of their individual contributions and, in both cases, felt some right to claim ownership. As Randy Thompson, a Research Center manager, explained.

> Cooperative research can be a problem. Call it "not invented here" or anything else, it's a problem. An idea is not a working product—people have to make it work. But if their heart and soul is not in it first, they'll wreck it. In this case, we let the division build their heart into it—or, rather, they built their heart into it themselves. That's why it was successful. Our letting go was key to its survival. The consequence is that I'm not sure how well we can define the process of exactly how the people involved worked on it.

One of the advantages of working with the Research Center was that researchers would sometimes be in a position to ask the basic questions that can be overlooked by division engineers who live with existing products. On the other hand, as one of the researchers who worked on the project explained, "We can interject some thoughts, some ideas, and even some strong suggestions. But the commitment to the idea has to come from the profit center. They're the ones who take the financial risk. . . . They decided which ideas they would accept, which they would reject—and they came up with the overall machine design."

Development of the Quantum 2000 Concept

To start with, Wiedemann used the Research Center to help them do technological forecasting and to generate technological alternatives to conventional ways of putting holes and shapes into a sheet of metal. Traditional hardened punch and die tooling, laser, plasma-arc, and electron beam technology were all considered. Gradually alternatives were ruled out as traditional hardened punch and die tooling emerged as still the fastest, cheapest, most reliable technology available then, and into the near future. "We decided to bet on it," explained Basko, "to be the technology of the next 5–10 years."

Next, Wiedemann and Research looked together for new machine concepts using the conventional punch and die approach. One of the basic questions they had to explore was, what really determines the productivity of a punch press? Tool changing appeared to be key, so the group generated and evaluated alternative methods for holding and storing tools. There were two existing alternatives: the conventional turret, and the automatic tool changer. The team worked on developing and improving on those ideas, but simultaneously began to look in a different direction. Instead of loading more tools on a turret, they tried loading fewer tools into the machine at any one time but making the tool change process easier and more efficient. They arrived at the idea of using rectangular cartridges, each of which held only 12 tools compared to 24 in a round turret. The cartridges would simply slide in and out for tool changes—a cartridge takes about one minute to change compared to an average of five minutes per tool or two hours for a complete change of a 24-station turret. Further, extra cartridges could be stored inside the machine. This cartridge could be unloaded, its magazine of tools changed, and reloaded into the machine without interrupting the run (Exhibit 3).

The productivity of the Quantum 2000 would be further enhanced by equipping it on an optional basis with two punching heads. This innovation would allow simultaneous punching of an identical pattern on two narrow pieces or a repeating pattern on one wide piece.

The team also considered alternatives to conventional methods of driving the punch and die tooling, of positioning the piece, and of building support structures for the machine. Some projects were carried out at Research, some at Wiedemann's engineering lab. "But even when Research's ideas proved not to be cost effective," says Basko, citing the twin tool changers that the Research team suggested, "they triggered our thinking." Out of the interplay came ideas for a simpler, more reliable mechanism to drive the right tool at the right time; a simple and cheap gravity-driven automatic unload feature (Exhibit 4), and a new structural support system that allowed the machine to be installed without special foundations or even level flooring.

Design and Engineering—A Joint Effort

Even before the concepts around which the quantum would be designed were settled on, Wiedemann began planning for the manufacturability of the new machine. Introduction of the Quantum 2000 had been scheduled for early 1983—in time, the marketing people hoped, to benefit

EXHIBIT 3

The Wiedemann Quantum 2000 Cartridge Tool Holder

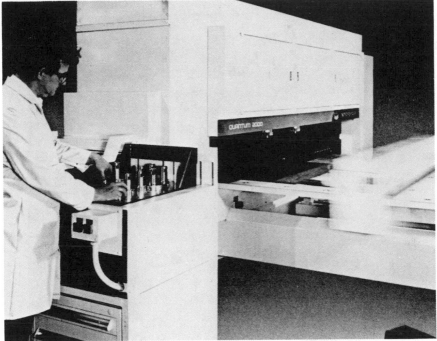

Tool changing on the Quantum 2000. Punch and die alignment can be preset and checked off line, then loaded into the machine. Above, tools are changed in one cartridge while the press is in operation.

from a projected upturn in orders. Competitive pressures dictated that the machine be reliable at introduction. Further, it had to be produced at a cost low enough to allow it to be priced at the level of Amada's Pega.

Therefore, in 1980 a joint manufacturing-engineering team was set up to work on design of the Quantum. John Wake, then the new director of the Research Center, had suggested a structure for the team. It included two industrial engineering managers, the manager of design engineering, a project engineer and a design engineer. Later, the director of manufacturing was added to the team. The team included members of the original design team and, like the design team, included people who had never before designed a punch press. They spent several months in an off-site hotel, refining design concepts, doing cost analyses and deciding on manufacturing methods. Their goal was to design a machine that could be delivered at the lowest possible cost, but that retained the advanced features the market seemed to demand.

EXHIBIT 4

The Wiedemann Quantum 2000 Automatic Unload Feature

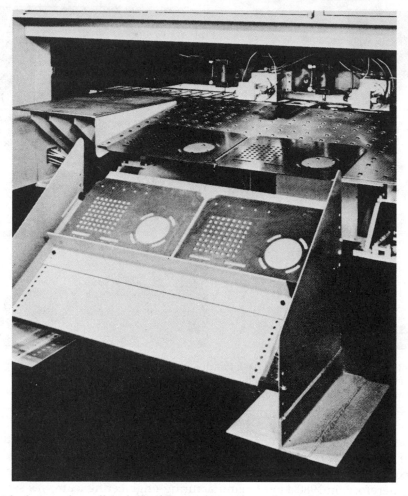

Finished pieces drop off the back of the machine. Above, the machine is operating with two punching heads and is stamping two pieces simultaneously.

According to Joe Basko, ''It was a difficult switch. Before, design engineers would design a machine, and then industrial engineers had to figure out from the drawings how to make it. Now, they were being asked to consider whether this was the way we wanted to make it. They had never disagreed with anything Engineering Design had said before, and they had never had to manage the optimization of costs. But it became a real team effort. The industrial engineer is frequently a customer for machine tools himself. He helps set the requirements for the machines he buys. So he is able to bring an outside viewpoint on market needs, and a manufacturing viewpoint on why we do certain things."

Managers at Wiedemann agree that one of the most positive outcomes of their approach to conceptualizing and designing the Quantum was that the use of teams built a genuinely integrated effort across functions and between facilities.

Testing the Design

The designs that came out of the work of the joint manufacturing-engineering team were then tested by Research engineers. The Research Center had been building capabilities in modern analytical techniques, such as stress testing via finite element analysis.[1] Joe Basko, as manager of the Research Center's Advanced Design department during the mid–1970s, had been part of that effort. Since 1975, FEA had been used successfully on work with several divisions, including problem solving on the W-Line for Wiedemann. These experiences had convinced the divisions involved of the usefulness of testing new concepts at as early a stage as possible.

One example of the kind of cooperation that developed involved an alternate machine concept that was conceived by Research. Feasibility studies, simulation, and analysis were all performed at the Research Center. The idea was then further developed at Wiedemann, where a breadboard model was built and preliminary testing performed, before the idea was finally rejected. In other cases, advanced testing, including breadboard model and life-cycle tests of subsystems and of the entire machine were performed at Research based on designs from Wiedemann engineers.

The Quantum team at Wiedemann viewed Research's analytical capabilities as critical to the project. The more thorough the testing at the early stages, the more certain they could be that their design was sound, in terms of both the productivity it offered customers and the manufacturability of the machine.

The original plan had called for six months of field testing with a prototype machine before the Quantum would be put into production. But by late 1982 it was clear that Wiedemann could not stick to the original plan and still begin filling orders on schedule. Therefore, the engineering, marketing, and manufacturing managers decided to raise

---

[1] Finite Element Analysis (FEA) is a computer-assisted technique that allows the user to model and analyze the dynamic reactions of a part or structure before building a prototype.

the stakes: they would begin releasing orders for parts and materials before the first prototype was built, and start shipping orders before the Quantum field testing was complete.

Two factors made the risks involved tolerable to Wiedemann. One was the involvement of Wiedemann's manufacturing team from the early phases of the project. The other was the series of analytical efforts and prototype testing performed at Research. The result was that the project team had confidence that the design would work.

The Next Step: Dealing with Change

Just four months after introduction of the Quantum 2000, the development project was considered a success. Not only had it resulted in a new product which was generating enthusiastic customer response; perhaps more important, the project illustrated an integrated effort between the Research Center and an operating division. During conversations with Joe Basko and other team members at Wiedemann, several questions were raised as to how to maintain and benefit from that integration, given some of the changes that the Automation Group and the Wiedemann division were facing.

One of the changes that was causing some concern was John Wake's redirection of the Research Center from primarily providing short-term engineering support to concentrating on long-term technological thrusts. As the Research Center continued to develop its skills in computer simulation techniques and finite element analysis, for example, Wake planned to apply these skills to research into new FMS concepts. However, explained Joe Basko, "to the extent that Research stops being willing to do structural analyses of divisions' new products, the divisions will be hurt."

Like Basko, most divisional directors of engineering applauded Wake's efforts to develop the technological competences that Bendix would need in the future. But they worried about the concomitant loss of immediate support. Joe Basko argued for a gradual decrease in the project hours that would be allocated for divisional support over the next 5 years. Working with his liaison engineer at Research, Basko managed to increase the amount of computer-aided engineering and testing he could expect from Research during the following year relative to the plan announced by Research. "It is necessary to have interplay and guidance from the divisions to keep the work at Research useful," he explained. "It's also a way for us to gather new concepts, such as in FMS. And it helps to maintain a good relationship between the Research engineer and the Wiedemann engineer. We need to know what tools are there, and how and when to use them."

Another challenge was Wiedemann's movement towards less in-house manufacturing. Traditionally, the division had bought more than 50% of its cost of goods sold from the outside, yet it maintained an almost fully integrated manufacturing capability. This meant significant investment in large, expensive machine tools. However, given the cost competition that Wiedemann was facing and Fred Searby's attention to return on investment measures, this approach was no longer feasible. According to Noel Ashworth, who had been at Wiedemann as general manager since the inception of the Quantum project, "We had to sit down and figure out what it is that this division does that really adds value." In the assessment of Ashworth and his functional managers, if Wiedemann was to continue to sell automated sheet metal stamping systems, then it needed to be strong in engineering and in marketing. Engineering expertise was necessary in machine tool conceptual design, electrical and control engineering and software development. Strong marketing skills were required in order to understand customer needs, improve distribution capabilities, and provide specific technical sales support to the general Group-level sales force. The division concluded, however, that manufacturing was not their main mission, and that there-fore they could not afford to remain fully integrated. Instead, Wiede-mann was to discontinue almost all machining and subassembly functions, and retain only final assembly, test, and demonstration and staging. "We believe that we can be competitive with anyone in the world on final assembly," explained Ashworth. "And it's important that both our own people and our customers be able to touch the iron and see the full system put together here."

The change was being initiated with the Quantum 2000. As stated in a New Product Analysis statement from early 1981, "A major objective in (the Quantum 2000) centers on exploring alternate manufacturing methods that will potentially reduce or eliminate our dependency on large horizontal boring machines. Grouting[2] concepts currently being adopted by the Turning Machine Division promise to meet this objec-tive." While Wiedemann engineers were working on adapting the grout-ing techniques to form pieces of the Quantum frame, models then going into production were to use conventional machining.

Meanwhile Frank Wedge, Wiedemann's director of manufacturing, was putting together a team to find outside sources for the machining they needed. "There is a high degree of anxiety," explained Wedge. "It's very hard to make the floor people and even the supervisors un-derstand that margins have shrunk, and that therefore we have got to restructure operations. The willingness to integrate is rare. I doubt if

---

[2] Grouting is a bonding technique for producing precision machine elements with little or no precision machining.

there are two other people in this manufacturing group who believe that all of our machining can be successfully outsourced." Wedge predicted that the hardest part of outsourcing would be finding subcontractors who had the capacity or were willing to make the investment in horizontal boring that was now done in-house. It was a cyclical business, and no one could afford to let the large investment sit idle. And the very success of the Quantum 2000 to date exacerbated the difficulty—the more the order backlog rose, the greater the amount of work that would have to be shifted to outside sources.

All of these concerns put pressure on the production of the first Quantum machines, scheduled for delivery in September 1983. The lead time from release of parts to shipping the product had been squeezed from the normal 11 months to 6. "All the little problems become a lot more serious in that time frame," said Wedge. "There is lots of frustration, and lots of disgruntlement."

The Future

While work was continuing on the Quantum project, Noel Ashworth was quick to point out the need to look beyond the Quantum 2000. "We need to be thinking *now* about what we will be introducing in 5 years."

Until then new introductions would be enhancements of the Quantum 2000 concept. New technologies being developed, such as laser cutting, could be added to the current generation. Automated loading and tool changing options were under development and were already being quoted. A possible next step would be to make the current Quantum 2000 into a machining cell with automatic material handling and control via distributed numerical control. "The market is dragging this machine into FMS concepts," explained Ashworth. He estimated that within ten years at least 50% of Wiedemann's volume would be in unmanned machines.

On the other hand, Ashworth pointed out that Wiedemann must also be thinking about the next generation of hole-making machines. "The real problem," said Basko, "is how to predict what the needs and problems will be in five to seven years. It's harder to start with a clean slate—define the problems, see what will be of benefit to the user, and redesign our approach." Most current efforts were directed at enlarging and improving the Quantum 2000, while the timing and resources that would be required to develop the next generation of machines were beginning to be sketched out.

One thing that was known about the next generation was that it would have to be developed faster than previous machines had been. The Quantum took five years from preliminary thoughts to finished product. As it turned out, the product was well-timed in being introduced just as orders began to turn up after a long recession. But economic conditions were not expected to give Wiedemann the luxury of time again.

According to Basko, the amount of time the project took was partly related to the amount of risk the company was willing to take. A great deal of time on the Quantum project was spent examining whether the concepts were indeed the right ones to be developing. Once this was decided, management at various levels had to be educated and, given the turnover in management during that period, reeducated.

There was some consensus, however, that part of the problem lay in the fact that designing and engineering tended to happen much too slowly. Said Ashworth, "We need to invest much more in people, in skills, and in outside services." The hardware, software, and systems capabilities of the in-house engineering staff had to be augmented. As a first step, introducing CAD was seen as one way of reducing lead times. Some services, such as software development, could be purchased from outside vendors. Increased cooperation with Warner & Swasey's 50/50 joint venture in Japan, Murata W&S, was also seen as a way of leveraging engineering capability. For instance, Murata had for the last year and a half been working on the detail design, prototype testing, and production of a downsized turret punch press. Wiedemann, with help from the Research Center, had designed the specifications, but realized that the small press market was too small to support development and manufacture in both countries. They preferred to concentrate their efforts on the Quantum 2000.

Finally, continued and increased collaboration with the Research Center was seen as key to helping to cut lead times on major projects. Joe Basko was convinced that, without collaboration in concept formulation and in testing, the Quantum would have taken much longer than it did to put into production.

It did not necessarily follow, however, that new product development in the Automation Group should follow the Quantum model. "The model," said Basko, "is teamwork, and maybe the types of services that Research can provide. But I'm not sure that the same kind of interaction would work for every situation. Operations people tend to shy away from Research as being too academic. I'm not sure we could have used them so well if I had not come out of Research. The guy who worked directly under me on the testing of the W-Line was really eager to participate. They were eager to do something new. We were able to find the right people to help us."

DW

729

Learning from Development Projects

Overview

For a firm seeking to improve its development capability, no task seems more challenging than learning from individual development projects. The dominant organization structure in most firms is functional; as a result, it is within those functions that firms typically seek to capture and share learning. Unfortunately, with no major organizational unit having broad responsibility for development, no single group is responsible for capturing development learning. In fact, the concept of learning across development projects is one that most firms have never explicitly discussed or addressed. Yet those same firms would agree that they can only improve as fast as they can learn. Thus this chapter examines a theme of apparent importance, but for which little collective wisdom and experience exist.

Every development effort can identify a series of things that have gone wrong. The challenge is to turn those errors into organizational learning. For those involved in development, individual learning by doing does occur—ensuring that individuals are unlikely to make the same mistake again. But without organizational learning, others who encounter similar problems, but lack that prior experience, will not be so fortunate. In reading the chapter it is important to understand that organizational learning entails getting individual insights and understanding refined, captured, and shared broadly across the organization. Functions naturally do this for their areas of responsibility, but not for the broad, cross-functional activities so essential to successful development.

To illustrate the process of systematic learning, we use the example of shaft roundness in a compressor at a company we call HVAC. The example outlines five crucial themes or steps in systematic organizational learning: (a) viewing learning as a team process, (b) creating a model of the development process, (c) gathering and analyzing data regarding specific problems, (d) searching for patterns in the results, and (e) pursuing those patterns to their root causes. This requires the commitment of energies and talent far beyond what most firms expend on identifying, analyzing, and eliminating the causes of development problems. Far too often the development team, under time pressure and resource constraints, glosses over potential problems; even when finding a solution to their specific needs, they seldom pursue root causes and their elimination. Significant commitment is necessary to identify the appropriate dimensions of change to be used in eliminating root causes and to prevent similar problems from recurring in the future.

A central theme in the chapter is the power of the project audit. A number of firms have found a project audit conducted by a cross-functional team useful in learning from development projects. An audit is not a witch hunt, but rather, a thorough, focused effort to identify opportunities for learning that emphasizes understanding the project's setting and background, evaluating pre-project activities, project team staffing and management, prototyping and test cycles, and assessing the way in which senior management reviews and controls projects. The firm must capture insights by changing the procedures, systems, people, and philosophies that govern the development process. Audits can be done fairly quickly and serve not only to foster organizational learning, but to aid the development and training of people on the audit team in subsequent development projects.

*I*n the new industrial competition, both survival and advantage depend upon the ability to sustain improvements in product development performance. In a world of intense international competition, where customers are sophisticated and demanding and technologies are diverse and dramatic in their effects, those who stand still in product and process development will neither prosper nor survive. The ability to sustain significant improvements in development over long periods of time rests on the capability to learn from experience. What is crucial in improving development is insight and understanding about how the organization works in practice. Studies that benchmark the best practice among competitors or that generate new concepts and frameworks may prove valuable in establishing perspective, but solving the problems that limit performance requires a detailed understanding of the root causes of those problems as they play out in the specific circumstances of the organization's development process. Thus, learning from experience is crucial.

In the context of product and process development, learning from experience means learning from development projects. But organizational learning is not a natural outcome of development projects, even in successful development efforts. There seem to be two fundamental problems. The first is that the performance that matters is often a result of complex interactions within the overall development system. Moreover, the connection between cause and effect may be separated significantly in time and place. In some instances, for example, the outcomes of interest are only evident at the conclusion of the project. Thus, while symptoms and potential causes may be observed by individuals at various points along the development path, systematic investigation requires observation of the outcomes, followed by an analysis that looks back to find the underlying causes. The second problem, however is that natural incentives in the organization favor pressing forward to the next project. Without concerted effort and focused attention on learning from the project that has just been completed, it is unlikely that engineers, marketers, or manufacturers will naturally devote time and energy to yesterday's problems. Most companies learn very little from their development experience. Those that do understand the power in improvement have developed tools and methods to help people—individually and collectively—gain insight and understanding and focus energy and attention on the problem of learning.

In this chapter, we identify the challenges that projects pose to the organizations trying to learn from them, suggest tools and methods that may be useful in meeting those challenges, and apply the ideas to specific examples. We first develop a framework for thinking about learning in a complex, ambiguous, and often confusing project environment. The framework identifies what can be learned from projects, and the general methods that seem most effective in generating insight and understanding. We then focus on the problem of capturing insight and learning and using it to change the development process. Here we examine the role of procedures, specific methods and tools, the development process itself, and specific principles that can be used to guide decisions in development. The next section of the chapter illustrates the application of the framework in what we call the project audit. The audit is a procedure for systematically developing data on the project's characteristics and performance, and conducting an analysis of the underlying sources (i.e., the causes) of the performance one observes. In addition to describing what an audit is, we present an example—taken from an actual audit—that lays out what one can learn from an audit and how the audit can be used to identify specific changes in the organization that will improve performance.

A Framework for Learning

Development projects are complex, with activity going on in many different locations, involving many different people and extended periods of time. Moreover, the outcomes we are interested in are often ambiguous—they are the result of complex interactions that may be poorly characterized and not well understood. But development does have a pattern. There is a specific sequence of activities, each of which is designed to influence the character of the product or process, and each of which determines in some way development performance. There are plans that lead to designs, designs that lead to prototypes, and prototypes that are tested, piloted, and introduced. And there are critical events that seem to have a direct impact on project performance. In order to learn from development projects, therefore, we need to understand this sequence of activities and critical events. Understanding may yield leverage over the development process and create insight into what must be changed in order to seek improvement. To learn from events or sequences of activities, one needs a structure—a way to frame the problems observed. Events, activities, and their outcomes do not come neatly packaged with cause and effect well defined. Consider the following examples of critical events or activities:

- The tooling on a pump housing for a new medical instrument is delivered two months late. The tool is on the critical path of the program, and thus delays the new product significantly.
- A new piece of process equipment fails to meet quality targets during commercial ramp-up of a new production process. The process is supposed to produce perfectly round shafts for a new compressor. The shafts produced during prototype meet the specifications, but those produced during commercial ramp-up do not.
- A consumer products company discovers that its next-generation shampoo has achieved superior performance, but is far more costly than expected. Originally intended to be positioned just below premium brands in performance, but at a much lower price, the new shampoo must be either reformulated or repositioned as a "me-too" premium product.
- The doors on a new sports sedan fail water leak tests during pilot manufacturing. The sedan uses a door design similar to the design on the last three models developed by the company. Those models also failed the water leak test during pilot. The problem of water leaks with this door design was well known at the outset of the sports sedan project, but was left unresolved until pilot manufacturing.

Each of the events described above created problems for the development organization. Solving those problems required additional resources and time, and, in some cases, affected the quality of performance. Getting at the root causes of these problems could, therefore, lay the foundation for substantial improvement in development performance. But the potential for learning is not limited to things gone wrong. Consider the following examples where things went right:

- A new flexible manufacturing system experiences very rapid development (less than two years, when the average for such systems is four years) and performs at a very high level of reliability (85–90 percent) in the first few months of implementation.
- A new portable table for use in hospitals achieves dramatic market penetration in the first year of introduction. Customers report levels of satisfaction with the product that exceed competitive offerings and the prior generation by a significant amount.
- A new household appliance completes manufacturing ramp-up smoothly and in record time. The number of engineering changes introduced after completion of prototype testing is far below the normal levels achieved in previous projects.

Episodes where things go wrong (or, sometimes, right) are the raw material for learning. In Exhibit 11–1 we have presented five categories of such "critical events" and provided examples of the kinds of observations that lie behind them and issues for potential learning. What makes an event critical is its connection to an aspect of the development process that drives performance. While the event itself may be a symptom, pursuing it can lead to a deeper understanding of the forces that influence the speed, quality, and productivity of development.

Consider, for example, the first category in Exhibit 11–1—recurring problems. Here the immediate observation might involve a quality problem like the water leak that shows up in several designs. Learning, in this instance, could (and should) focus on how to solve the particular quality problem, but its recurrence suggests a basic issue with the way the organization deals with these kinds of problems. The challenge for learning, therefore, is to uncover the more fundamental source of the reoccurrence, so that once found and solved a quality problem does not reoccur. Similar observations apply to problems in the other categories in Exhibit 11–1: specific activities like carrying out a market research clinic, or conducting a product test, as well as working-level linkages, design-build-test cycles, and decision-making processes.

Individual Versus Organizational Learning

Getting at the fundamental sources of problems in the development process, however, is unlikely to occur naturally. Because the development process is so complex and involves so many different people in different groups, and because the issues cut across groups, departments, functions, and organizations, learning is likely to require careful, systematic effort.[1] Of course, some learning will occur naturally. For example, individual engineers routinely learn how to use new methods and tools—a CAD system or a testing device, for example. Engineers who

Exhibit 11-1

The Focus of Learning: Five Categories of Critical Events in
Development Projects*

Category	Nature of Observations	Issues for Learning
1. Recurring problems linked to critical performance dimensions	• Persistent quality problems with design • Engineering changes at pilot for problems that could have been uncovered long before	• Does the organization capture solutions and make them permanent? • Discipline and methodology in engineering
2. Crucial individual activities/tasks and associated capabilities	• Time to complete key tasks (e.g., testing) • Quality of tasks	• Do we measure/track the right information about tasks? • Do we have the skills needed?
3. Working-level linkages (e.g., engineering – manufacturing)	• Timing of downstream (e.g., manufacturing) involvement • Degree of influence exerted by upstream and downstream on problem solving in the other group	• Do we have a process and framework for integration? • Do we have the skills, attitudes, and values that drive integration?
4. Design-build-test cycles	• Speed of the cycle/number of cycles • Quality of solutions	• Do we have the right people involved in design-build-test cycles? • Do we have the right tools, supporting resources, and skills?
5. Processes for making decisions and allocating resources	• Time required to decide/number of reiterations • Resource constraints/problems	• Are the right people involved at the right time with the right information? • Do we have too many projects? Do we have an aggregate project plan?

* Critical to improving product development capabilities is recognizing the primary areas of activity that can be altered. Through systematic observation and subsequent modification of these fundamental activities, an organization can focus its efforts and increase its rate of learning.

take on new jobs learn what is expected of them and how to do the work from their colleagues in the department. And both new and experienced people add to their repertoire of problem solutions when they encounter and solve new problems in their work.

This kind of "learning by doing" requires that engineers pay attention to the task at hand, draw inferences about cause-and-effect relationships, and develop ways of remembering what they learn. Where these conditions exist, individual learning about specific tasks may occur naturally as a by-product of doing the work. Thus, without any explicit action on the part of management, individual know-how will increase. Moreover, there may even be some transfer of that know-how within the work groups of which engineers are a part. Through the use of stories, rules of thumb, changes in procedures or methods, or other modes of communication, what one engineer learns may be shared with others working on the same or closely related tasks. Thus, for example, a gear design engineer may learn how to use a new stress analysis on a CAD system, and through this identify a way to pinpoint potential problems in design prior to prototyping. When incorporated in a story about how this tool allowed the engineer to spot a latent design problem much earlier than ever before, the know-how becomes transferable to other engineers who may use the tool to solve similar problems.

But the kinds of learning of specific interest in this chapter—about the behavior of the development system; about tasks and capabilities that cut across functional boundaries; about critical linkages at the working level between different disciplines, functions, and departments; and about complex decision and resource allocation processes—are unlikely to occur simply through "learning by doing." In this case, the "doers" tend to focus on the completion of specific tasks and activities over which they have control. But at the level of the development system, where many elements come together and interact and where the patterns of cause-and-effect relationships may be complex, there is no guarantee that the doers at the working level will observe the important interactions, let alone be able to draw complex inferences about them. Take, for example, the problem of unresolved issues showing up very late in a development program. The problem might be a leak in an automobile door seal that is observed by test engineers working on prototypes (in reality, the potential sources of the leak—and even potential solutions to the problem—are many and varied). If we look beyond the specific technical sources—which might involve the design of the rubber gasket around the door, the design of the body opening, the design of dies, or the sheet metal forming processes—we need to understand how a problem that surfaced early in the program could have remained unresolved all the way through the prototyping process. This deeper question focuses on the organizational processes and involves many different departments and many different individuals. Learning about that kind of problem will require systematic effort.

The effort to learn about development system performance in a given project, and in particular about organizational processes that drive performance, must be not only systematic but also tenacious. Such learning is not easy. The problems are broad-based and often ill-defined. The data one might want to use to understand the problem and draw inferences about its sources do not come in nice neat packages. Moreover, gaining insight and improved understanding about how the development process works is only part of the solution. The organization must also determine how to change the process in order to improve its performance.

The Shaft Roundness Problem at HVAC

But systematic learning about the development process is possible. Indeed, there seem to be a small number of common denominators in successful efforts to learn from development projects. Consider the following case:

> When Mark Shaw came to work on the morning of 15 October 1991, a problem with the drive shaft in the new compressor was the last thing he expected. Shaw was the project leader for a new-generation compressor at HVAC, Inc. The project was an aggressive attempt by HVAC to bring to market a new compressor design that was more compact, efficient, and quieter in operation, and that sold for half the cost of its predecessor. Shaw led a team of ten people, drawn from the different engineering disciplines within HVAC as well as from marketing, manufacturing, and finance. The team had developed a strong working relationship and the project had moved along well. The first pilot production units were scheduled for completion at the end of October. All indications were that the project was on schedule to meet its target introduction date.
>
> When Shaw came to work that crisp autumn morning, he found a serious problem awaiting him. Kelly Fortunado, a test engineer on the team, had left the following E-mail message: "Mark: We've got a problem. The first five pilot production drive shafts we tested did not meet the specifications for roundness. This is a crucial parameter. Without it, we can not meet the performance targets in the design."
>
> After talking to Fortunado on the phone, Shaw called a meeting of the project team. The problem was troubling because months earlier the team had thoroughly tested all of the prototype units for drive

shaft roundness. Every single one had met specification. The team brainstormed on possible causes of the problem and laid out several for investigation. They checked and rechecked the tooling, machine settings, tool programming, drawings, and material specifications. They conducted experimental runs of drive shafts and subjected them to rigorous testing. This work revealed the fundamental dilemma: all of the parameters in pilot production that they could identify were identical to those employed during prototyping when the drive shafts met specification. Yet all of the drive shafts produced during the pilot production runs failed to meet the specification for roundness.

After a week of intensive effort, Shaw concluded that the problem must lie in the prototyping process. Consequently, the team went back and examined the prototype shafts. They reviewed the prototype testing data, and confirmed the earlier results—all of the prototype shafts met the specification for roundness. The team then pursued the process specification used during prototype production. In searching for answers, they discovered all the production of the prototype drive shafts had been subcontracted to an outside machine shop. Shaw, along with two other members of the team, visited the prototype machine shop and discussed the prototype work with the shop supervisor. They reviewed the processes used to machine drive shafts and interviewed all of the personnel in the machine shop involved in prototype production. Shaw and his colleagues determined that the machine shop had used the specific procedures and a machining sequence identical to the one employed in pilot production. At the same time, three other members of the team conducted interviews with the materials suppliers and with test engineers involved in prototyping. This work failed to uncover a solution; it appeared that the prototyping process had been identical to the pilot production process.

Still not satisfied with the results of their work, Shaw made another visit to the prototype machine shop. He met with the machinist who had worked most closely on the drive shaft job. After reviewing yet again the procedures used, the machine settings, and the machinist's memory of the performance of the job, Shaw was left with no explanation of the problem. Disheartened, he prepared to leave. One last time, Shaw asked the machinist: "Is there anything you can remember about this job that might help us?" The machinist shook his head; Shaw started to leave. The machinist suddenly said, "Hey, wait a minute! There was one thing. What did you guys do about that fixture problem?" In that brief question, Shaw had an answer to this problem. The machinist continued, "I took a look at the specifications on that shaft, but there was no way I could see to meet them with the kind of fixturing you had suggested. I figured out a way to modify the fixtures so I could meet the specification on the shaft. The way you had planned those fixtures, I don't think you could ever get round parts out of the process."

Shaw's investigation uncovered the fact that the machinist in the prototype shop had changed the fixtures in the machining process in order to obtain in-spec parts, but that change had never been incorporated into the process specifications. Furthermore, the machinist had never told anyone about the changes he had made. He assumed his job was to make good parts, which it was—in part. Shaw took the information from the machinist back to his manufacturing plant where the changes were introduced rapidly. The new fixturing solved the roundness problem, and the pilot production runs were carried out without further significant difficulty.

Shaw's conversation with the machinist in the prototype shop revealed several important dimensions of the roundness problem. First, the conversation revealed a solution for the immediate problem. It also revealed where the development team's assumptions had gone wrong. The team had assumed that the process specifications, in particular the design of the fixturing, used during the pilot run were identical to those used during prototype production. This turned out to be a false assumption. It was also apparent that the development systems in place failed to uncover this discrepancy. There was no mechanism for ensuring that the prototype process was completely representative of the commercial production system. Furthermore, as the team pursed the issue, they learned that the practice of subcontracting prototype part production created a potential barrier to the transfer of insight and information about the prototype parts and their associated production processes to the commercial production system. There was, indeed, nothing in the system that linked the insight of the machinist about fixturing and tooling to subsequent changes in process specifications. Finally, the machinist who worked on the prototype part did not comprehend fully the role that he played in the development process. He did understand that part of his role was to produce parts that met the design intent. But he did not know that the changes he made in fixtures and tooling should be communicated to the process engineers in order to ensure that the parts could be made round in the commerical process.

This episode could, of course, be nothing more than an idiosyncratic fluke event. But on reflection, and in comparison with other programs and processes with which they were familiar, the development team determined that the gaps they had observed in the case of the prototype drive shaft—involving linkages between prototype production and the commercial production system—were not idiosyncratic or isolated incidents. The gaps they uncovered in their search for an understanding of the roundness problem were part of a pattern of organizational practice, structure, and capability that applied to all of the parts, components, and subsystems developed at HVAC.

Themes in Systematic Organizational Learning

The HVAC case illustrates five crucial themes in successful systematic learning about the process.[2]

Learning as a Team Process. Learning goes on inside the heads of individuals. In order to create the kind of shared understanding essential to implementation of new concepts of development, however, learning must be pursued and occur within the context of the development team. Team members bring different perspectives and different capabilities, and will read evidence in different ways. This can be a powerful and important source of insight and understanding. In effect, the kind of learning that is most crucial is learning that cuts across the narrow, functionally oriented tasks in development and concentrates on the behavior of the development system. It therefore is important that the organizational processes used to learn match the learning objectives. The team process for learning is thus critical to generating insight that cuts across narrow departmental, discipline, or functional lines.

A Model of the Process. At HVAC, the search for insight about the source of the roundness problem did not occur in a random or haphazard fashion. It was guided by a model of how the development process ought to work. They understood both the technical determinants of the performance they sought (the role of process specifications, material quality, operator training, and product design) as well as the organizational processes designed to carry out the specific technical tasks. No matter what the specific issue or problem that may prompt the search for improved learning and understanding, a framework—some kind of shared model of the development process—is an important starting point for identifying potential improvement opportunities. Such models may include descriptions of the development process like those laid out in Chapter 6, some kind of funnel diagram such as that discussed in Chapter 5, or perhaps a description of the development strategy that captures current understanding of the key process dimensions and areas of leverage, including critical linkages, tasks, and important processes.

Data and Analyses. The HVAC team sought understanding of the roundness problem through data and analyses. Through experimental runs of the production plant machining process, they determined that the roundness problem was systematic. They developed and reviewed data on prototype testing of the shafts in order to pinpoint potential sources of the problem. Their conclusions were based on neither impressions nor the most recent events that they could recall, but instead were rooted in the facts of the matter. That is not to say that judgment and intuition played no part; indeed, the instincts and intuitions of the engineers and managers involved played an important role in searching out potential sources of the problem and in pursuing a range of avenues and potential leads. Such intuition and judgment are essential in learning about the development process. But where our interest centers on performance and where determinants of performance are likely to be complex, it is crucial to observe the actual activities, linkages, and decisions, and to connect them to measured criteria for evaluation.

Search for Patterns. The episodes that trigger a search for new understanding may not be representative of underlying process tendencies. They may be strongly affected by random events or idiosyncratic developments. Moreover, for any given observed outcome (like the roundness problem), there may be many different competing explanations. What is required is evidence that what appears to drive the results is in fact fundamental. We need a sense that the explanation is not only logical but also characteristic of the way the organization works. The roundness problem could have reflected nothing more than a machinist who forgot to include process specification changes in the supporting documents with the prototype parts. But as the HVAC team compared its experience with other examples of prototype part production, they recognized a pattern. This was not an isolated incident, but a recurrent theme in the relationship between prototype production and the commerical pilot operation. Indeed, the team had only to look within its own experience to identify other parts where a similar lack of knowledge and information transfer had also occurred.

Root Causes. In any problem, like the roundness of the shaft, there are numerous proximate causes that a search for understanding may uncover. Following a process that resembles peeling an onion, the team moved from recognizing that the problem had occurred to identifying the potential sources (such as failure on the part of the operators in the commercial production process to follow specifications, failure of the material supplier to deliver material according to specification, incorrect machine settings, or incorrect product design). None of these proved useful in explaining the existence of the roundness problem. They then pursued the next step, which lay in the apparent gap between the prototype testing results and the results of the pilot production run. This led them to the prototype machine shop and eventually to an understanding of the actions of the machinist in changing the tooling and fixturing. The search for understanding yielded a solution to the roundness problem. But the team didn't stop there. They sought a deeper understanding of the root causes of the problem, which in this case involved both a machinist who did not understand the full purposes of the prototyping process and a development process that failed to create effective communication links between either prototype production and design engineering, or prototype production and the commercial pilot production line. Thus, the search for understanding involves not only establishing patterns that are characteristic, but also pursuing understanding to its most fundamental or root level. Continually pushing this search deeper is important because it ensures that the solution developed solves the immediate problem and prevents future recurrences, as well as yields insights of a broader and more lasting nature. A search for root causes will uncover opportunities for changing the development process in ways that will make for fundamental and continuous improvement in performance.

Capturing Insight and Learning to Change the Development Process

Given a framework to guide the search for patterns and data analyses to explain the critical events we observe, the pursuit of root causes yields insight into opportunities for improvement. But it is one thing to be able to recognize, as Shaw did at HVAC, that a change in the way prototype parts get produced could improve the development process, and quite another to capture that learning and deploy it in practice. Capturing and using learning requires change in the way development gets done. In Exhibit 11–2 we have identified five areas of focus for capturing learning. Each of these areas—procedures, tools and methods, process, structure, and principles—provides a way for the organization to "remember" what it learns from development projects. These areas of focus play two important roles. They are the mechanism through which managers introduce new capability and improve performance in development. But they are also the vehicle that managers use to capture and store what the organization learns about development over time.

In addition to defining the five areas of focus, Exhibit 11–2 also provides examples of changes in each that are related to one of the examples of critical events referred to earlier in the chapter. In the case of the round drive shaft problem at HVAC, for instance, what the development team learned about the prototype process could be captured through a change in the development procedures. The example we use in the table is to make production part suppliers, including the in-house

EXHIBIT 11–2

Capturing Learning from Development Projects*

Areas of Focus	Types of Changes to Capture Learning	Examples
Procedures	Changing the specific, detailed sequence of activities or rules that developers follow	Case: the round drive shafts Change: make production parts suppliers (including in-house factory) responsible for the quality of prototype parts
Tools/Methods	Teaching engineers and developers new skills in using specific tools and methods	Case: the shampoo that is too expensive Change: introduce QFD tools to engineering and marketing
Process	Changing the broad sequence of activities and phases that structure development	Case: the production tools delivered late Change: add a phase/activity — advanced tooling release — to the prototype and tool building process
Structure	Changing the formal organization, the locus of responsibility, and the geographic location of development activities	Case: the recurring water leaks Change: create a "door design team" composed of product and process engineers and locate members in same area
Principles	Adding to the set of ideas and values used to guide decisions in development	Case: the new FMS system developed in record time Change: a new concept — a small team of skilled generalists is far more effective at basic design and system architecture than a larger team of specialists

* In order to capture the learning available from individual development projects, attention must be focused on specific subareas and opportunities for change must be identified and pursued, as illustrated here.

manufacturing organization, responsible for the quality of prototype parts. This *change in procedure* would require the production part suppliers to establish criteria for judging the prototype parts with the development team, and would involve testing and analysis of prototype parts to ensure not only that the parts met design intent, but that the manufacturing process used to make them was representative of the commercial process.

Adding to developmental procedures, as we have done in this example, is not the only kind of change to procedures that the development organization may use to capture learning. In certain circumstances it may be important to eliminate procedures and streamline the development process in order to make it work much more effectively. In the case of the late delivery of tools, for example, it is often the case that the procedures used to approve and implement engineering changes slow down the tooling process to such an extent that long delays are commonplace. Thus, in this circumstance, one of the ways to capture that insight is to eliminate many of the levels of approval required for an engineering change. Streamlining the engineering change process thus can have substantial positive impact on the performance of the tooling design and development cycle.

The second area of focus—*tools and methods*—is important in those circumstances where the opportunity for improvement requires new capability. In the case of the shampoo that was too expensive, the search for patterns and root causes revealed that engineers and marketing personnel had little basis for communication. They did not speak each other's language. Moreover, even had they tried, there was no forum in which they could communicate effectively. One approach to capturing that insight, therefore, is to introduce the methodology and tools associated with quality function deployment (QFD) to both the engineering and marketing organizations. These tools can be customized and tailored to fit the requirements and circumstances of the particular development process in question, and can be used to capture the learning that grows out of development projects. If for example, the problem lay in the appropriate selection of the target competitor (as it did in the shampoo case—the engineers targeted the high-price, best in-class competitor), the QFD methodology can be adapted to add a competitive analysis to the main house of quality. The kind of tool and methodology, thus, becomes a vehicle to focus attention on the areas of weakness in the organization, as well as an opportunity for substantial improvement.

Introducing a methodology like QFD cannot, of course, occur in isolation. Indeed, depending upon the nature of the development process in the shampoo manufacturer, introduction of QFD methods may require a change in the sequence of activities or the phases of development. Such a change falls into the third area of focus in Exhibit 11–2—

changes in process. Whereas in previous projects, marketing may have determined the specifications for the new shampoo product and passed them to engineering for technical development, in the new QFD setup, there is an added phase and set of activities at the front end of the process. Likewise, in the case of the late tool delivery problem, one approach to improving the speed of tool development would be to enhance overlapping between product designers and tooling engineers by adding a phase or activity in the development process called advanced tooling release. This would be a decision point within the prototyping process that would precede final release of the design, but would represent a point at which the design was far enough along that authorization could be given to the tooling engineers to begin tooling design and procurement. Putting such an activity in the middle of the prototyping process requires that product designers and tooling engineers focus very early on the critical issues involved in the design and associated tools. Thus, changing the process captures insight about the importance of overlapping and, in addition, stimulates the development of required capabilities to make overlapping work.

Enhancing integration across functions is often one of the key opportunities for improving product development that surfaces as organizations learn about their development process. Changes in the development process are but one of the important determinants of the degree of integration. Another is the basic *structure* of the development organization itself. As noted in Exhibit 11–2, structure includes both the formal organization as well as the locus of responsibility and the geographic location of activities. These structural elements influence the nature of interaction across functions, the quality of decision making, and the intensity of completeness of communication. In the case of the recurring water leaks in automobile doors, for example, it became apparent through further analysis that the technical problems behind the leaks reflected important gaps in the way the manufacturing and design engineering organizations worked together. Process engineers, for example, had critical pieces of information about the performance of different design alternatives that were stored in databases inaccessible to product designers.

Moreover, individual process engineers were themselves unaware of the historical performances of alternative designs. In addition, there were critical dimensions of the design itself that were not obvious to either product designers or process engineers, because the two organizations had interacted only through formal documents and had never developed close working relationships. One way to capture these insights was to create a "door design" team, composed of both product and process engineers, that was co-located in an area of the engineering organization in which the members could interact on a daily basis. Such a change in structure would facilitate close personal interaction and enhance the quality and effectiveness of communication. It would need to be supplemented and supported by other changes in procedures, tools, and methods, allowing product and process engineers to more effectively integrate problem solving in their individual tasks. But a change in structure would provide an important organizational framework in which the new tools, methods, and procedures could be applied.

The last area of focus is the *principles* that the organization uses to guide decision-making and development activities. These principles include concepts, ideas, and values that provide more fundamental guidance in situations that may be unfamiliar. One way to capture learning in the organization is to crystallize the learning into a principle or concept that can be communicated easily and used in the future when confronting analogous decisions.

For example, in the case of the new flexible manufacturing system (FMS) developed in a very short period of time, the organization learned something about the composition of the development team. Prior FMS development projects had been accomplish by teams of specialists that were relatively large in number and were composed of individuals who brought deep but narrow expertise to the problem. In the new approach, the team was composed of a much smaller number of highly capable generalists who focused on establishing the basic design of the system, including its information architecture, basic machinery specifications, and the logic that provided system control. This high-level design team was then supplemented by a small number of specialists that were able to work within the established framework to implement the design through detailed work and decisions. The organization learned that such an approach was far more effective than its previous methodology. The learning here applied to both the procedures in the organization and the organizational structure used on FMS projects. But it also uncovered an apparent principle that the organization could apply very broadly in subsequent programs: a small team of skilled generalists is far more effective at basic design and system architecture development for a new system project than a larger team of specialists.

Taken together, the five areas of focus we have outlined in Exhibit 11–2 establish the framework for development in the organization. Capturing learning requires coming back, full circle, to this fundamental framework that guides development in the organization. The framework is where the learning process starts. Armed with that framework the organization may interpret critical events that raise questions about its current procedures, tools and methods, processes, and the structures and principles it uses to guide development. These questions and problems become devices for focusing the organization's attention on potential opportunities for learning and thus for improvement. Systematically exploring the underlying sources of both the problems and the things that went right yields insight into ways that the organization may change in order to improve itself. Those changes, however, focus on the basic framework for development. Learning does not end with recognition of cause-and-effect relationships, or with insight into the behavior of the organization. In order to be effective, it must also extend to the introduction of change into the organization—capturing the insight and incorporating it into behaviors (that is, into the way the organization does development). These changes become integral aspects of the revised framework for subsequent development projects, as the learning cycle begins again.[3]

The Project Audit: A Framework for Learning

In the previous sections of this chapter, we have identified what an organization can expect to learn from development projects and the methods that seem most fruitful in both generating and permanently capturing insight and understanding. We have argued that learning about the behavior of the development system requires a conscious, focused effort on the part of managers, engineers, designers, marketers, and manufacturers within the firm. But that effort to learn itself requires structure and organization to give it energy and coherence.

We have found the project audit—a systematic project review conducted by a cross-functional team—to be particularly useful in organizing and managing the search for understanding and insight from specific projects. In this sense, a project audit is conducted not to make sure that development has proceeded according to established rules and regulations; rather, its purpose is to help the organization learn from its experience. In effect, the audit becomes a learning project conducted by a project leader and involving individuals from the key functions represented in development. This cross-functional team reviews the project, conducts interviews with participants at all levels, and gathers data about project execution and performance. The learning logic described earlier in this chapter (developing a model for perspective, collecting data, searching for patterns, and identifying root causes) is then applied to these data and insights to identify all critical themes that seem to drive the development process and its performance. Through discussion among its members, and analysis and synthesis of insights and observations, the team develops recommendations for change that will help to capture the learning they have developed.

749

Exhibit 11–3 presents a set of sample questions that might structure and guide the conduct of the project audit. We have used these questions in a number of different firms and industries, and have found them useful in organizing the effort to collect the essential pieces of data and information. The questions are built around the specific categories of things to be learned from development projects, as identified in Exhibit 11–1: recurring problems linked to critical performance dimensions, individual tasks and activities, important linkages at the working level, design-build-test cycles, and processes for making decisions and allocating resources. Of course, the degree of emphasis placed in any one category, the particular questions asked, and the focus of the audit must be adapted and tailored to fit the needs and requirements of the individual situation.

The questions are a starting point for collecting data and developing insight. Once information has been collected, the team must share its observations and begin to analyze and synthesize the data. At this audit stage the team begins to search for patterns in its findings. These patterns then become the basis for a deeper search for root causes, and ultimately for recommendations for changes in fundamental aspects of the development process. The following condensed description of an actual project audit illustrates how an audit works, possible kinds of analysis and synthesis, and resulting insights.

The ABC-4 Computer Project Audit

The ABC-4, a high-performance portable computer developed by Omega Systems, was introduced into the market in October 1990. The ABC-4 grew out of advanced development work that had been done on a portable computer for the Department of Defense. The initial project proposal was formally approved in early 1988, the preliminary set of product drawings was released in December 1988, prototype units were developed and tested at beta sites during the first half of 1990, the product was announced in the summer of 1990, and initial shipments began in October.

Although portable computers represented a relatively small fraction of the total revenues of Omega Systems, the ABC-4 was regarded by the organization as a relatively important project. Market share in portable computers had fallen somewhat during the 1988–1989 time period, and Omega's position as the technical and performance leader had begun to slip. Several additional aspects of the context in which the ABC-4 was developed are important in understanding the outcomes of the project.

- During the course of the project, both the engineering function and the business unit (portable computer systems) underwent significant reorganization.

Exhibit 11–3
Framing the Project Audit: Sample Questions*
Background
- What was the motivation for the project? Why was it done at this particular time?
- What was the product strategy? Where was the greatest emphasis placed? What were the goals of the project?

Pre-Project Activities
- How many alternatives did the firm consider at the concept stage, and how, in this instance, did the particular project we are studying emerge as a development project?
- What were the sources of the ideas?
- How did the firm lay the foundation for the project in terms of establishing business and functional strategies, and how were those strategies used in the decision making/selection process?
- What does the development strategy look like?

Project Team
- Which functions within the business formally assigned people to the project on a full-time basis?
- Which functions had people assigned part-time?
- What was the basic project organization structure (e.g., purely functional, lightweight project manager, heavyweight project manager without dedicated resources, a full-scale project team with heavyweight manager, and dedicated team members from all functions)?

Project Management
- Was there a project manager – some individual who had the title of project manager or who was responsible for the project?
- If so, what was the role of the project manager? What degree of influence did she or he have over working-level decisions in marketing, engineering, and manufacturing?
- If there was no project manager, how was leadership exerted?
- What were the formal phases of development and the milestones that the project had to meet? When did they occur?
- Who was responsible for decision making and resource allocation in the project? What were the roles of functional managers, the project leader, and senior management?
- When conflicts arose in the project, how were they resolved? What kinds of conflicts were most difficult to resolve? What was the role of senior management in conflicts?

Senior Management Review and Control
- What was senior management's role in the project at different phases?
- What criteria did senior management use in reviewing the project?
- How were objectives set and defined? Using what kind of information?

Exhibit 11–3 (cont.)
Prototype and Test

- How was prototyping used in development?
- How many prototype cycles were there? How many prototypes were produced in each cycle?
- How was the prototype process organized (e.g., was it done by suppliers or in-house)?
- What tests were conducted? By whom?

* The project audit seeks to identify and explain—after a development effort has been completed—the connection between its management and execution and the results achieved. Six major areas for investigation and the types of questions that can be addressed in each are outlined here.

- Several concurrent development projects competed for resources during the ABC-4 project. One project, Ranger 5, was among the largest ever undertaken by the organization, and was easily an order of magnitude larger than the ABC-4 project.
- Restructuring of manufacturing at Omega Systems resulted in the closing of several plants and the shift to more outsourcing for key components. This change caught the ABC-4 project team by surprise.
- The engineering organization introduced a new engineering change notice procedure during the course of the project. The new procedure was not well understood and resulted in long turnaround cycles on changes to parts and components.

Overall, the performance of the ABC-4 project was mixed. The product itself was well received by customers but, because of its relatively late entry into the market, faced an uphill battle in a very competitive segment. The project was late according to both its own internal schedules and competitive projects. In addition, management judged the development cost to be problematic. The challenge for the project audit team was to understand the sources of problems in lead time and productivity, as well as the success of the design and development effort in producing a product judged by most customers to be outstanding. The portable computer systems division wanted to offer equally attractive products in the future, but ones that were more rapidly and efficiently developed.

A project audit team was formed, led by Marcia Karas and consisting of one member each from design engineering, process development, manufacturing operations, marketing, field service, and finance. Though the team had not been involved in developing ABC-4, members were familiar with the general performance of the effort. As the team probed the performance of the ABC-4 project, they concentrated on a set of critical events. Analysis of these key events led to an assessment of strengths and weaknesses in the six dimensions of the development process that were discussed in Chapter 6 (see Exhibit 11–4), and summarized below in an excerpt from a memo by the audit team to senior management.

> In contrast to the concerns often expressed about the ABC-4 by senior management, we found a considerable number of strengths in the way this program was organized and carried out. However, most of the strengths we uncovered were in the front end of the development process. For example, the project team was highly dedicated, was responsible for design from the very outset of the project, and was led by a very committed and talented leader who not only coordinated activity but also championed the product concept. Additionally, the product concept itself was well defined and clearly articulated so that all team members shared a common view of overall program objectives.
>
> At the same time, however, we uncovered a significant number of weaknesses in the way the program was organized and managed. Initially, because many critical events occurred late in the program, we focused our attention on activities that occurred in the later stages of development, such as prototyping and testing. As we probed the sources of problems, such as difficulty in manufacturing ramp-up, however, we uncovered problems that extended all the way back to pre-project activities. In the early stages of product planning, for example, senior management set ambitious targets for functionality and reliability, but also summarily removed three months from the normal development cycle. This strong emphasis on schedule was reinforced repeatedly during the senior management review process. As a result, the project became schedule driven to the point that the team chose to skip key tests and push ahead before critical predecessor work was complete.

The lack of team involvement in setting objectives and the challenge posed by an aggressive schedule, on top of aggressive performance goals, interacted with two other aspects of project structure to create significant problems downstream. First, senior management and the project team each seemed to regard the ABC-4 as a design engineering rather than a business project. Both groups tended to underestimate non-design tasks and developed insufficient skill and capability in downstream (e.g., manufacturing) and support (e.g., vendor selection) activities. These were precisely the areas where problems began to surface after the team had skipped tests and other critical activities. Second, the project was managed in a relatively informal way. This had important advantages in day-to-day interactions within the team, but created problems for integrating the activities of various functions. There was, in fact, no development process or structure that laid out the sequence of activities or critical milestones that needed to be accomplished. As a result, it was difficult to tell where the project was at any given time.

753

Exhibit 11–4

Strengths and Weaknesses in the Development of the ABC-4 Portable Computer*

Project Dimensions	Strengths	Weaknesses	Key Events
Pre-Project Activities	Complete concept definition; early manufacturing involvement	Top down setting of goals without team involvement; no product line strategy; management and team mismatch – team focus on performance, management on cost	Great product, but late; expensive redesign in late stages
Project Team	Dedicated core team responsible for design; strong commitment and high level of expertise	Lack of integration of new people; insufficient skill in manufacturing; inability to deliver bad news	Delays in completing prototype tasks; problems in manufacturing ramp-up
Project Management	Project leader who coordinated and championed the concept from the outset	No development process or structure; design project not a business project (underestimated non-design tasks)	Details "slipped through the cracks"; problems in manufacturing ramp-up
Senior Management Review and Control	Regular senior management reviews; willingness to support change by team	Schedule-driven development (released drawings even though design not finished); stretch targets without recognizing risks	Initial reliability problems in the field
Prototype/Test	Strong engineering/manufacturing collaboration	Skipped key tests/tested too early; no pilot production run; confusion in prototype cycles	Problems in manufacturing ramp-up; redesign late in program; in-field reliability problems
Real-Time Adjustments	Willingness to commit resources to deal with problems	Pushing ahead before tasks complete; assumed time lost early could be made up later; no measurement system to determine project status	Problems in manufacturing ramp-up; reliability problems in the field

* As the result of a systematic audit of the ABC-4 portable computer project, this exhibit shows the audit team's conclusions regarding project strengths and weaknesses in each of the six areas examined. These can then serve as a basis for making systematic changes in the development process (see Exhibit 11–5).

The upshot of these developments was that several problems remained undetected in the early stages of design and throughout the prototyping process. They became obvious only when the product had reached the customer's hands. In addition, the decision to skip pilot production (made largely because the ABC-4 was thought to be very similar to its predecessor, the ABC-3) meant that many design problems surfaced in manufacturing ramp-up: though the basic architecture of the ABC-4 was quite similar to that of the ABC-3, several new components and subsystems had been introduced and their interaction with carryover parts was important, yet not fully tested.

The audit team's review of the strengths and weaknesses in the management and organization of the ABC-4 development project suggests several critical themes that may have more general application. Although it is relatively easy to point to specific activities that may have led to a problem, it is perhaps more useful to consider a broader pattern by focusing on a small number of critical ideas that grew out of the team's analysis. The audit team included five of these ideas in its memo to senior management.

Cutting cycle times on individual tasks. Senior management cut the time for primary task completion in the ABC-4 project (e.g., allowing six rather than eight months for prototype development). However, there was no corresponding change in support activity cycle times, nor was there a reconceptualization of the overall structure of activities that underlay the completion of those tasks. Failure to rethink the basic nature of the tasks involved and restructure the activity network meant that the only way to accomplish primary tasks in less time was postponing or skipping what were regarded as second- or third-order activities. This had a decidedly negative impact on the project. The basic concept here is that while tasks can be prioritized (e.g., design tasks as first order, testing tasks as second order, and vendor selection as third order), the full set of tasks is important to the project and its overall cycle time.

Integrating art and science. Reducing weight and cost while increasing performance made the ABC-4 (a highly engineered product) much more dependent on science than previous generations. In consequence, the assumption that many of the old parts (and production processes) could be used without change was simply invalid. Additionally, though each of the new parts was relatively straightforward, their closer interaction increased the complexity of the product exponentially. Efforts to advance the science on several elements of a product while sticking with former art on other elements (particularly where those elements are embedded and integral in the overall system) may well push the art beyond its limits.

Internal and external fit—strategy and the customer system. The strategy and position of the business called for improved performance and high reliability at market introduction (Omega needed to catch up, but had a strong market franchise). Senior management emphasized time and cost while engineering focused on speed and features. This internal gap, or mismatch, was accompanied by an external gap: the failure to consider all aspects of the customer system (especially service and reliability) in the development process. These gaps required multiple engineering changes and redesign after market introduction.

The need for a structured process. Creating a development organization and a project management system that are robust, replicable, and successful requires a structure for the development process that everyone understands and follows. This includes clearly defined stages with understood milestones that mark completion, and separable prototype cycles of design-build-test where each can be shortened and still result in maximum learning. Finally, the structure needs to provide adequate testing of three types: components, total system (finished product), and customer use. These tests should not be viewed as hurdles or gates, but as opportunities to build the experience and knowledge needed for subsequent stages.

Measuring/calibrating project status. The ability to assess and measure the status of a development project is crucial to its effective management. The ABC-4 suffered from unrealistic judgments about the amount of work remaining to be done. These judgments were, in part, driven by the absence of good measurements of project status. It is particularly crucial to measure status relative to work that remains to be done rather than only against progress to date. An accurate, detailed activity network provides the framework for determining the remaining work to be completed.

Recommendations for Action

The audit team learned much about the development process at Omega Systems, and uncovered some important opportunities for improving time to market as well as development productivity. Exhibit 11–5 presents the team's recommendations for each of the major dimensions of development, and groups them under the five kinds of changes outlined earlier in this chapter: procedures, tools/methods, the development process, organization structure, and basic development principles. The thrust of the recommendations was to make adjustments across the board, in all aspects of development, in order to change the overall pattern. Thus, recommendations that seemed systematic to the organization were highlighted. While there were many things in the ABC-4 that were special cases, Exhibit 11–5 presents those recommendations with the greatest leverage. Collectively, they had the potential to change the basic pattern of development.

A central focus of the recommendations is the role of senior management—not only in changing the senior management review process, but in introducing a new development process and in communicating fundamental principles. The audit team put forth three aspects which summarize the basic approach:

Exhibit 11–5

Recommendations for Change in the ABC-4 Audit*

Project Dimensions	Procedures	Tools/Methods	Process	Structure	Principles
Pre-Project Activities	Set objectives using a contract book as part of the first stage of the project	Develop maps for product generations; develop tools for customer system evaluation	Define pre-project stage (key activities)	Involve manufacturing and service people in concept development	Planning can pre-empt subsequent problems and aid in concept convergence
Project Team	New members added to team must be trained and certified	Link career expectations to project completions	Project leader must do much of the training	Use a dedicated core team with multiple functions to manage major projects	Teams need a balance of experience and youth
Project Management	Develop an activity network for each project	Introduce an activity network capability	Establish formal stages of the development process	Select project leader at outset; role includes coordination and concept leadership	Product development is a <u>business</u> project, not just an engineering project
Senior Management Review	Set forth competitive imperatives clearly before the project is launched	Establish a method for calibrating the status of the project (work remaining to be done)	Review thoroughly at major milestones (at least every 3 months)	Set up a senior staff mentor/coach/sponsor	Review and control against key milestones (task completion), not just schedule
Test and Prototype	All mechanical systems will be piloted before commercial release	Introduce new method for evaluating the tradeoffs between new and carryover parts	Establish clear design-build-test cycles for prototyping	Develop a test strategy that covers components, systems, and subsystems	Solve problems early
Real Time Adjustments	Regenerate activity network after major changes	Use PERT system linked to formal development stages	Establish a process for responding to new developments (maintain focus, avoid fire fighting)	Compare planned schedule against tasks remaining	Fix problems before moving forward

* Based on an audit of the ABC-4 portable computer project, a number of improvements in the development process were identified. For each of the six areas examined, changes in procedures, tools/methods, process, structure, and principles were identified and implemented, improving significantly the development efforts on subsequent projects.

Essentially, the front end of the development process and the organizational structure have been relatively solid in the past and remain quite strong. However, changes must be introduced in both areas to bring the downstream organizations (manufacturing and service) into the development process in a central way and to provide stronger, more direct links to basic business strategy.

Integration at the working level is fairly good. Engineers and manufacturing people work well together. There is a weaker relationship between engineering and marketing, and this needs attention. More importantly, however, Omega Systems must create a different context for development within which integration at the working level can take place. There really isn't a clear development process at Omega Systems. We don't need a bunch of manuals with detailed procedures. What is required is a systematic, shared process that provides an overall framework.

While the introduction of a new structure and principles is important, it is also crucial to upgrade people's skills and give them better tools with which to work. The problems are not just structure and process; there is a real need for capability in areas such as customer system analysis, activity network design, and project measurement.

In summary, the above-mentioned changes in the basic development system will allow Omega Systems to proceed more rapidly and efficiently in development, but will also preserve the organization's strengths in product design, product concept development, teamwork, and collaboration.

Conclusions and Implications

Learning from development projects is one of the most difficult things that an organization can do.[4] It requires focused effort and attention, and the willingness to make hard choices. When a firm seeks competitive advantage through its development capability, the object is to become better at designing and developing new products and processes. It is not to succeed just on a particular project, but continually to build and improve the organization's procedures, processes, leadership skills, and tools and methods in order to do things faster, more efficiently, and with higher quality.

The project audit of the ABC-4 implies that being good at learning from development projects requires many of the same skills and capabilities that being good at development itself requires. Because what we want to learn cuts across individuals, work groups, and functions to encompass the development system as a whole, and because the phenomena that we are examining are themselves complex and often ambiguous, learning needs to be organized, managed, and directed by leaders with skill, tenacity, and perspective. In this sense, a project audit (which is a primary organizing framework that we advocate for learning about development projects) is every bit as much a project—with all of the attendant requirements for leadership, collaboration across functions, clarity of process and objectives, and effective tools and methods—as the development of a new product or process.

Of course, this does not imply that individuals, small work groups, or even functions should go about their business and not pay attention to learning opportunities. Important learning must occur at each of these levels in the organization. Indeed, a development organization populated by individuals, work groups, and functions that pay attention to their experience and learn to improve their operation will be in a much better position to implement a structured learning process about the development system as a whole. Thus, from senior management's perspective, the important mission is to foster an environment in which learning takes place at each of the levels we have discussed, and to create the capability to learn about specific development projects through a process built of several elements, such as the development audit.

Although learning to learn through the development experience is not easy, making the commitment and pursuing it vigorously can have significant payoffs. Indeed, learning from projects is an important element in the organization's overall approach to improving its development capabilities. Precisely because learning and sustained improvement are inherently difficult, they provide—when done effectively—a source of competitive advantage. One need only recall the experience of Northern and Southern Electronics outlined in the first chapter of this book to recognize the power of sustained improvement in development capability. But learning from projects is only one element, albeit a crucial and vital one, in the overall problem of building development capability over a long period of time. We examine the rest of the story in the concluding chapter of this book.

Study Questions

1. Based on your experience and the reading of this chapter, what do you see as the major similarities and differences between individual and organizational learning? What makes organizational learning so difficult? What makes it especially difficult with regard to development capabilities?
2. Identify a cross-functional organizational unit (team, business, division, or firm) that you think learns well as an organization. What evidence illustrates its abilities at organizational learning? What has it done that contributes significantly to those learning capabilities?
3. What do you see as the potential role of tools such as CAD/CAM and CAE in contributing to organizational learning about development?

What would be most important for an organization to consider in developing and applying such tools if one of its primary objectives were to maximize organizational learning?

4. The example of the shaft roundness problem at HVAC illustrates five crucial activities in successful development learning: learning as a team process, providing a model of the process, effective data gathering and analyses, a guided search for patterns, and pursuit of root causes. Using an organization that you know (perhaps one of the case studies included in this book), consider which of these five themes that organization would find most challenging to apply. Why is this the case? What would help it to be more effective in applying these themes?

5. Conduct a project audit using the guidelines provided in this chapter. (This might be of a project described in a case such as Sun Microsystems or Campbell Soup Company.) What key conclusions can you draw from this audit? What recommendations for action would you make to management?

6. Most firms do not conduct audits of development projects. Why? How might an organization overcome hindrances and stumbling blocks to make project audits a standard tool for learning and improving development capabilities?

Motorola, Inc.:
Bandit Pager Project
(Abridged)

The Bandit project demonstrated several important points. First, we proved that building an automated factory was worthwhile, financially. Second, with adequate resources and clear goals, ambitious targets can be achieved. Finally, you can't overplan the project. On Bandit, there were clear milestones defined for each prototype cycle, and each station on the production line had someone in charge who knew what had to be done. Managers did not have to get involved in those details. (Laura Saucier, staff industrial engineer.)

From June 1986 to December 1987, the Bandit project had developed and implemented a fully automated line for manufacturing Motorola's Bravo pagers. Now, in October 1989, the Bandit line was near its goal of producing almost half of all the Bravo series pagers, the remainder being made in the company's Puerto Rico and Singapore plants. Further, not only did the Bandit line pagers hold the highest quality record in Motorola's history, the project's $8–$10 million investment had already been paid back in cost—and quality—savings.

Buoyed by these results, the Paging Products Division was embarking on a new project, dubbed Son-of-Bandit, which would emphasize product, not just process, technology. The division's vice president and general manager, Merle Gilmore, was aware that Son-of-Bandit posed significant challenges:

The Bandit program was a tremendous success, showing once and for all that American manufacturing can compete with off-shore production. The challenge now is to take what we have learned on Bandit and apply these lessons to the next generation of pagers and throughout the rest of the company.

This case, based in part on Motorola Inc.: Bandit Pager Project (690–043) and in part on published material, was prepared by Research Associate Geoffrey K. Gill under the supervision of Professor Steven C. Wheelwright.

Motorola Company Background

Motorola, one of the world's largest electronics companies with 1988 annual sales of $8.25 billion, was founded in 1928. Initially, the company produced car radios, moving into military electronics during World War II and then semiconductors in 1952. The company also entered the consumer electronics field, becoming the number-three producer of color TV sets in 1965 and introducing the first U.S.-made all-transistorized TV set in 1967 (the Quasar line). In 1974, Motorola exited consumer electronics completely because of foreign competitive pressures, selling its color TV business to Matsushita of Japan.

Foreign competition continued unabated through the 1970s, and by the early 1980s Motorola was leading the charge for protection against Japanese semiconductor manufacturers. Robert Galvin, Motorola's chairman, felt that the Japanese were employing unfair trade practices by dumping chips to gain market share.

During the mid–1980s, Motorola management familiarized themselves with Japanese manufacturing quality and defect level standards. Although the Japanese unfair trade practices remained a focal point, management reexamined their firm's own quality, defect level standards, and manufacturing process. A formal "benchmarking project" ended in 1986 with a report made to Motorola president and CEO, Bill Weisz. Bruce Piltch, director of manufacturing operations for the Paging Division, recalled:

> The report compared Motorola performance to worldwide state-of-the-art, function by function. It was a cold slap in the face. We had been lulled into complacency, reading newspaper accounts about how good we were. It was a real education. Not only did we discover that we weren't so hot, but we also came to realize that things were getting worse instead of better.

According to Piltch, what motivated Project Bandit was foreign competition: "We needed to make sure that we would have the skills we'd need to participate in the business in the future." It was clear that Motorola's manufacturing capabilities had to be improved, and emphasizing manufacturing excellence became a corporate strategy, a major thrust of which was a companywide drive to obtain six-sigma quality levels in all its manufacturing operations (see Exhibit 1).

The Paging Products Division

During the 1980s, Motorola was structured in six major business segments and a New Enterprises organization. The Paging Products Division was part of the Communications Sector, the largest of the six,

EXHIBIT 1

Six-sigma concept

WHY 6-SIGMA?

Consider a product—its performance is determined by the margin between the actual characteristic values of design requirements and its parts. These characteristics are produced by factory processes and at the suppliers.

Every process attempts to reproduce its characteristic values identically from unit to unit, but variations occur. Processes that use real-time feedback have a small variation but other processes may have a large variation.

Variation of the process is measured in standard deviations (sigma) from the mean. Normal process variation is considered to be ±3-sigma.

Under normal conditions, about 2,700 parts per million will be outside the normal variation. This, by itself, does not appear disconcerting. But a product containing 1,500 parts will have 4.05 defects per unit. This would result in fewer than two units

out of every hundred going through the entire manufacturing process without a defect.

Thus, we can see that for a product to be built virtually defect-free, it must be designed to accept characteristics that are significantly more than ±3-sigma from the mean.

It can be shown that a design that can accept twice the normal variation of the process, ±6-sigma, can be expected to have no more than 3.4 ppm defective for each characteristic, even if the process mean were to shift by as much as ±1.5-sigma.

In the same case, for a product containing 1,500 parts, we would now expect only 0.0051 defect per unit. This would mean that 995 units out of 1,000 would go through the enire manufacturing process without a defect.

The goal is to design a product that will accept maximum variation and processes that produce minimum variation, ultimately reaching zero defects. Motorola's 1992 step toward this objective is to achieve ±6-sigma capability.

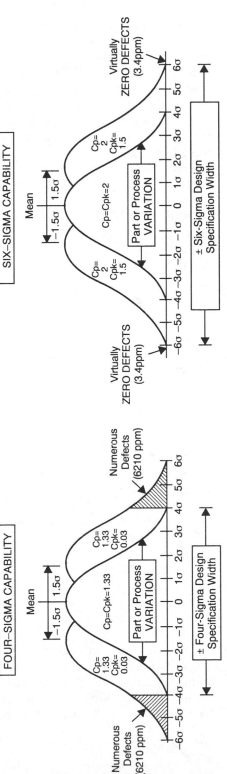

SOURCE: J. Wolak (May 1987). "Motorola Revisited." *Quality*, 5, pp. 18–23. Reprinted with permission.

averaging $3.2 billion in sales annually. Other products in the Communication Sector included portable and mobile FM two-way radio communication systems, microwave communication systems, and portable data terminals.

Motorola sold its pager to carriers (like Metro Media and Bell South) who owned an infrastructure system. These carriers in turn leased or sold the pagers to end users. In addition to the cost of the pager, the end user paid a monthly service charge to be connected to the system. Motorola's pagers varied in size, type of paging (numeric, alpha-numeric, voice, tone-only), and range.

The Paging Products Division, like the rest of Motorola, was under extreme pressure from Japanese competitors. Moreover, from 1979 to 1989, all other U.S. manufacturers of pagers (including RCA, GE, Bell & Howell, Harris, and Stromberg Carlson) dropped out of the market. Edward Holland, a staff engineer in the Advanced Manufacturing Technology/Robotics Group, recalled that period:

> Motorola was always a product-oriented company. We made sales by having the best product with the most features before anyone else. During the early 1980s, we began to discover that having the best product was not enough— people could copy us very quickly. One obvious answer was to increase our quality level by improving the manufacturing process using robotics and automation. The Robotics Group, started with half a dozen people, was a strategic move in that direction. We began by automating small parts of the process with robots—developing small islands of automation. At that point it was more learning than anything. It was reasonably successful and we gained some credibility.

Upper management, as a result of their tours of Japanese facilities during this period, was also convinced that Motorola would have to automate in order to compete. Likewise, the Paging Products Division decided that automation and design for manufacturability were necessary for it to remain competitive.

In February 1986, top technical people from the Paging Products Division met offsite with some people from the Advanced Manufacturing Technologies/Robotics Group to develop an approach for designing a totally automated line. Said Holland: "It was really a bunch of smart people locked up in a hotel room for a week to hash out a project plan." They developed an approach based on the Bravo product (see Exhibit 2), which was in pilot production under the code name Jstar at the time.

The Jstar pager was selected because it was mechanically more conducive to automation than other designs. Also, because Bravo was to be a high volume product in the middle of Motorola's pager line, its automation could take full advantage of any economies of scale. Finally, the Jstar Bravo was being started up in conventional plants in Puerto Rico

Exhibit 2

Bravo Pager Product Description

On the Go? Stay in touch with the BRAVO Numeric Display Pager!

When your lifestyle demands that you be on the move, the BRAVO Numeric Display Pager will help you keep important lines of communication open. It actually displays phone numbers or coded information so that you can make more efficient use of your time!

Compact, easy to use

Motorola knows that convenience is essential when it comes to pagers. That's why we designed the BRAVO Numeric Display Pager!

The BRAVO pager is equipped with a sturdy belt clip so that you can affix it to your pocket, belt, or purse. It's easy to remove the clip so you can also slip the pager into your pocket or briefcase. We even have an optional lanyard that can be used with or without the clip.

Return calls at your convenience

Don't panic if you can't answer your messages immediately upon receiving them! At times like these you'll appreciate the BRAVO pager's memory. It can hold up to five messages in memory so that you can return calls when it's best for you. The most recent messages stay in memory, pushing the oldest ones out. Each message can include not only the phone number but other important information such as extension, caller identification number or degree of urgency. When you read your messages, you can freeze the numbers on the display so that you can write them down. Duplicate messages won't take up valuable memory space. The pager scans each message so that duplicates will not be entered into memory more than once.

Should you choose, you can save up to three important numbers for future reference by protecting them. These numbers cannot be overwritten by other messages and will stay in memory until you remove their protection or turn your pager off.

This pager offers you a variety of alerts

During standard operation, the pager will beep for several seconds (or until reset) when a page is received. However, you can set the pager to emit only a single discreet beep if you prefer. If you need privacy, or don't want to disturb others, two options are available: You can choose to have the discreet beep removed leaving only the flashing message light; or you can choose our VIBRA-PAGE option which alerts you by means of a gentle vibration. The latter is great for places where silence is important such as conferences, hospitals, quiet zones, as well as in high noise environments, such as construction sites, manufacturing plants, and airports, where a beep tone might not be heard. Whether you choose the beep tone or silent alert, a red light will also flash to indicate that you have a message.

The display tells it all

The 12-digit liquid crystal display tells you more than just your messages. At a glance you can see whether your pager is on, what type of alert it is set to, how many new messages you have to read, and if your battery is starting to run low. There is even a built-in light for use when viewing the display in low light environments. All of this information helps to make the BRAVO Numeric Display Pager a valuable communication and business tool.

BRAVO pagers manufactured by:

 MOTOROLA

1301 East Algonquin Road
Schaumburg, Illinois 60196
(312) 397-1000

Specifications subject to change without notice. Ⓜ, Motorola, BRAVO, and VIBRA-PAGE are trademarks of Motorola, Inc.

Best of all—Motorola reliability

At Motorola, providing quality products is a commitment we make to all our customers. Part of the process of building reliable pagers is the extensive testing that's done during the design and production phases. Our accelerated life test (ALT) program is one such example. For the BRAVO Numeric Display Pager, this testing simulates five years of field stress in a few weeks, enabling us to design out potential problems. The result is pagers that stand up to the most demanding situations, when used as instructed under normal conditions.

Try one today! We think you'll agree that using a Motorola pager is the best choice you can make.

Shown actual size.

and Singapore, which provided a safety net if the automated factory failed or was late.

From the beginning it was clear that this project had strategic significance. Chris Galvin, then general manager of the Paging Division (and son of Robert Galvin), felt that Motorola needed to develop new skills to survive in the competitive paging market, and Operation Bandit, as the Bravo automation project came to be known, was a way to learn them.

The project also was consistent with Motorola's new strategic emphasis on manufacturing; it would raise the level of expectations for U.S. manufacturing and prove that it was not necessary to go off-shore to obtain low cost, as the Jstar version had done.

George Fisher, then the assistant general manager of the Communications Sector (and later CEO), personally made the funding request presentation to the Motorola board of directors to get approval for Operation Bandit.

Operation Bandit

Philosophy

The original plan for Bandit called for the development and implementation of a fully automated pager line for the Bravo pager within 18 months. The schedule for the project was tied to a December 1987 target date for shipping product from the line; all the other dates were determined by that end date. Bruce Piltch, director of manufacturing operations for the Pager Division, assumed the role of project manager. Although Motorola had a history of schedule slippage on some past projects, Piltch was determined to hold this one to its schedule.

Piltch was a highly driven and persuasive leader, whom team members described as a "crusader," a "renegade," and a "workaholic." His philosophy of project management fit his personality. As he described it:

> America is best at crisis management—our culture is oriented toward crisis management, tactics, emotional involvement, instant gratification. That's how we put a man on the moon. We take advantage of that in managing our teams—if you don't have a crisis, create a few.
>
> Project Bandit had this same kind of feeling. We were in a crisis most of the time anyway, but we had to foment a few crises as well. And you would not believe the output you can get out of a team of U.S. engineers—phenomenal increases in productivity—100 percent or more.[1]

Piltch did not agree with the standard Motorola methods for managing and evaluating a project; he felt that project performance was measured only subjectively, by how one interpreted the fine print. He therefore introduced a "contract book" containing agreements between

---

[1] From "This Bandit is Not a Thief: A Case Study of Advanced Manufacturing at the Paging Products Division of Motorola, Inc.," by Thomas W. Schlie, Associate Professor of Business Administration, Illinois Institute of Technology, 1989, p. 21.

the development team and management. The book set out clear financial and technical benchmarks against which the project was to be evaluated. It also laid out the method by which those goals were to be
achieved.

While the content of the contract book mostly resembled Motorola's
existing standard operating procedures, its implementation differed.
With the standard operating procedures, each group set its own goals
more or less independently. Because these goals often conflicted, when
the project fell short in some area, responsibility for the shortcoming
was difficult to ascribe. With the contract book, all the relevant groups
agreed to a single document; responsibility was clearly stated and
shared.

To meet their timetable, Piltch felt they should develop as few new
technologies as possible. Indeed, the project was named Operation Bandit to emphasize the importance of eliminating the "Not Invented Here"
(NIH) syndrome. Outside the entrance to the project area a sign read:
Please don't leave the area without leaving us a good idea. George Keller, the
engineering manager for Bandit, recalled the philosophy of the project:

> NIH would have killed us, given the chance. In the past we rewarded the
> designer who came up with the newest, the greatest, the latest thing. We
> should have been looking for the designer who took something that basically
> worked and optimized it.[2]

Piltch elaborated:

> Our biggest problem has been cultural—thinking that only Motorola had or
> could develop the best technology. The Japanese are much less myopic in this
> regard. They view the problem as a clean sheet opportunity and are willing
> to take ideas and technology from anywhere. That was part of our mission in
> doing the benchmarking—to raise expectations at Motorola of what could be
> done, and foster a clean-sheet mentality that would welcome ideas and tech-
> nology from all sources.[3]

Staffing

The project was staffed using Motorola's Internal Opportunity System,
where job openings were posted so that anyone who was interested
could apply. Despite the project's ambitious goals, its visibility enabled
Piltch to attract large numbers of applicants. Because of the multidisci-

[2] From "How They Brought Home the Prize: A Visit to Motorola's Bandit Plant," *Manufacturing Systems*, April 1989, p. 27.
[3] From "This Bandit is Not a Thief," p. 21.

plinary nature of the project, it turned out to be somewhat difficult to free up people who had the necessary qualifications, however.

The team comprised about 25 engineers from different engineering disciplines: robotics, industrial engineering, manufacturing, mechanical, electrical, tooling, and test systems (see Exhibit 3). Eventually, an accountant was assigned to the team, because Piltch recognized that with a totally automated production line, most of the standard accounting measures would have to be altered. Since the product was a redesign of the Jstar pager with no change that affected the customer, marketing was not involved day-to-day on the team.

All team members were moved to an office area adjacent to the Bandit production line and the division's main assembly area. The walls enclosing the Bandit area had large glass windows, which had been installed partly so that the factory workers did not feel that management was trying to hide its automation efforts, and partly so that the Bandit team would feel that it could not hide its mistakes.

The Bandit team worked fairly autonomously. As one team member put it: "we were all a team in one room with no red tape. . . ." The testing department provided some specialized support, performing Accelerated Life Tests (ALT) on the prototypes for the team. Part of the Computer Integrated Manufacturing (CIM) system was also developed outside the team. The higher-level CIM system was the responsibility of a member of the Material Control Systems (MCS) Department. Bandit also entered into a joint development contract with Hewlett-Packard to

Exhibit 3
Bandit Project Team Organization (Late 1986)

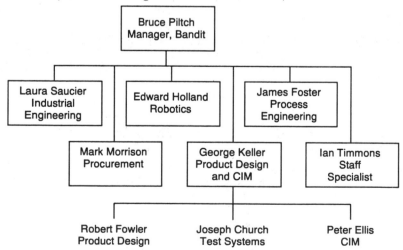

768

help develop a software backplane to link all the cell controllers. Although other major computer firms also bid on the job, HP was selected because it was willing to work as a partner with Motorola.

Suppliers

The Bandit team started to screen suppliers very early on to make sure only those who could meet the six-sigma quality goal were selected. They started with a list of 300 eligible suppliers and reduced that to 60 based on Motorola's prior experience with them. Bandit team members visited these 60, examining their manufacturing processes, and the 22 best were ultimately selected. Mark Morrison, procurement manager for component and product quality, commented on supplier relationships:

> In searching for ways to make dramatic improvements in our operations, we discovered we needed to develop better working relationships with our suppliers. This was evidenced by the fact that outgoing quality was maintained by screening out at least one order of magnitude defective materials in the production process.
>
> We found that this was not necessarily due to problems with our suppliers, but rather outdated and cumbersome Motorola systems. Our specifications were outdated and poorly written; our ordering system was confusing and we put too much emphasis on price rather than value. We also found that we had too many suppliers—several hundred too many.
>
> I concentrated my efforts on electrical components like transducers first . . . but I should have looked first at the mechanical parts, like the plastic housing for the pagers. It took longer to get the mechanical parts suppliers up to our requirements—to get their tooling improved—than it did the electrical, and we ran into a time crunch with them on Bandit.[4]

Keller elaborated on what happened when he and others went to talk to suppliers about improving the quality of their product:

> We went out to talk to them, but they also talked to us and the poor quality of our component specs was their biggest gripe. They showed us stacks of paper for a single part, and we couldn't even understand everything. So we entered into a major effort with our Bandit suppliers to rewrite all the specs—make them short, simple, easy to understand.

Piltch (as quoted in *Manufacturing Engineering*, April 1989) also recalled this aspect of the problem:

> We would ask to see the blueprints we had sent them, and the blueprints were antiquated or contradictory—they were a real mess. . . . We had to

---

[4] Ibid., pp. 48–50.

scrap the entire process we had been using to describe to our suppliers what we wanted. . . . That procedure took us close to four months and a great deal of very precious engineering resources. Once components were defined and goals were established, suppliers were sought.

Design/Redesign

Several internal components and subassemblies of the Bravo pager had to be redesigned for assembly by the automated line. This redesign involved mainly small changes to the geometry of components to provide flat surfaces that the robots could grab when placing the component. For the customer, division management decided that the pager itself had to be functionally equivalent and visually identical to the Jstar Bravo pager. Because the new design had to take into account both manufacturability and quality issues, the team tried to be conservative in their choices.

The design of the printed circuit board that carried and integrated all the electrical components (e.g., chips, resistors, and capacitors) was a good example of the kind of tradeoffs that were made. Originally, to make the assembly of the printed circuit board easier, the board was designed so that all the components could be placed from one side. But because only one side would be used, the components had to be tightly packed and the traces (wires) that connected them could be only 2 mils wide.

Keller realized that getting six-sigma quality out of this state-of-the-art board design would be impossible and insisted that it be redesigned to have components on both sides; this change would make the spacing less critical and allow standard chips to be used. He explained:

> I found myself becoming a process designer also. Prior to this experience, we used to go through endless negotiations with the process engineers, kind of formally with memos and position papers. With Bandit, there were 30 minutes of screaming and yelling at each other, and then we would reach a compromise.
>
> It worked the other way too, the process engineers, becoming involved in the product. The process engineers kept pushing for one, single-sided printed circuit board, but we finally convinced them that the board density would be too great. So we had the choice of two boards or one board on both sides, and we chose the latter approach. That choice meant 90 extra feet of conveyor and $200,000 more for equipment—two more robots, another oven, and so forth.

Redesigning Bravo to meet Motorola's six-sigma quality goal was also an exacting process, explained one engineer:

> So with electrical components, we would take capacitors, for example, and measure them, calculate the means, and design them so that tuning adjust-

ments on the Bandit Bravo could meet six-sigma requirements. On the mechanical side, we measured hundreds of the plastic housing units, developed tolerance requirements, and worked with our vendor so he could hold dimensional tolerances within .002" and also meet six-sigma standards."[5]

The production line was built up from automated cells like those used in conventional production lines. These were modified slightly to fit into the fully automated Bandit line. The engineers started with the beginning of the line and added cells one by one until the line was completed. By January 1987, the date of the first prototype build, the line was completed, although not debugged.

Subsequently, the project revolved around four major prototype cycles and a pilot production run, whose dates remained tied to the December 1987 goal. Prior to each cycle, the design was temporarily frozen. The line, as it existed at that point, was used to produce all prototype units (see Exhibit 4). This approach to prototyping cycles, referred to as *periodic prototyping*, differed dramatically from that used traditionally by Motorola and others. Under the traditional approach, early prototypes tested engineering feasibility, functionality, and design, and later cycles tested manufacturing processes. Furthermore, a given prototype cycle occurred after a set of tasks was completed (which, if late, delayed prototyping), not at scheduled intervals.

With periodic prototyping, the entire set of cross-functional efforts was evaluated in each cycle according to a preset schedule. Thus each cycle was a test of how all functions and elements of the system were progressing, not just a subpart. Because the dates were preset for every few months, they provided a recurring focal point for assessing the status of each part of the project and helped direct efforts needed to get back on track by the next prototyping date. Also, because each cycle produced 50 to 100 units, every group had a number of units they could test and work with between prototyping cycles.

Although Bandit was the first project at Motorola to use periodic prototyping, all the prototype dates were met within one or two days. While not all of the planned technical progress had been made prior to each cycle, any shortcomings were generally made up within a few days and *always* by the next prototyping cycle. When the computer system was down, the engineers built the prototypes by hand. In the first two prototyping cycles, the full line was not completed, so the prototype units were only partially built on the line. By the third cycle, however, complete units were assembled on the line. In addition to the prototype cycles, project milestones were also reviewed quarterly with Chris Galvin. For most of these reviews George Fisher was also present. On

[5] Ibid., p. 24.

EXHIBIT 4

Bandit Prototype Schedule

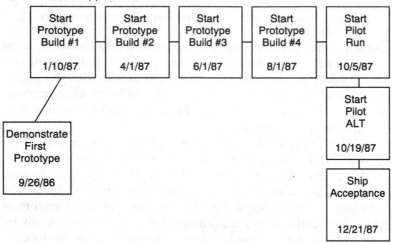

	Demo	Prototype #1	Prototype #2	Prototype #3	Prototype #4
Location of Build	Lab	Pager Factory Front End Manual Bandit Back End	Partial Bandit Front End Manual Bandit Back End	Complete Bandit Build with Manual Assistance	Full Bandit Line
Status of Bandit Line	Not Started	Initial Design	Front End Largely Complete AutoTest in Back End (with Manual Assembly)	Hardware Complete CIM Control Started	Bandit Line Completed

the whole these reviews were regarded positively because of the increased visibility they gave the project.

Robert Fowler, product design manager, contrasted the Bandit development process to its predecessor:

> In the old system, the design engineers would do two or three prototype runs and then it would be transferred to manufacturing and they would try to get all the problems out in one pilot run (which would often turn into two or three pilot runs). On Bandit, we scheduled periodic prototype cycles and manufacturing was involved in every one of them.

This approach to prototyping had several advantages. Since everyone had to be ready for the prototype build, no excuses were accepted for delay. It also greatly facilitated communication among all the groups. Furthermore, by running the prototypes down the Bandit line, we were able to build many more units at each cycle, which enabled widespread distribution of the prototype units for testing. In most projects, the model shop would build only a few prototype units because it was too expensive to build very many. Because of the availability of Bandit prototype units and because of the high priority of the Bandit project, we were able to do an Accelerated Life Test (ALT) at each prototype cycle.

By doing the ALT, we discovered several problems that were caused by interaction of the process and product design. For example, we found that over time the pagers' frequency drifted from the set point. On investigating, we determined that it occurred because of the short cycle time on the Bandit line; the pagers were still warm from the soldering oven when they were tuned. As they cooled down, the frequency tended to drift. To fix this problem, we had to change the material in the PCB and change the design of the oscillator. If the prototypes had not been built on the line and then put through an ALT, we would not have found this problem until much later, and the schedule would have been severely impacted.

By December 1987, the line was up and running and had passed the required benchmark—five-sigma quality performance on a batch of 1,000 units. While the final goal was six-sigma quality, signoff was tied to reaching demonstrated five-sigma quality.

The Bandit Line

The result of Operation Bandit was a fully automated factory that was driven by individual customer orders. The order, placed by a salesperson (or even directly by the customer) into the pager order system on the corporate IBM mainframe, could contain any number of pagers in any one of 21 million possible feature combinations. Order data were then passed to the Communications Sector's Material Control System (MCS), which generated a bill of materials and a shop order. These data were then transferred to a Stratus computer that prioritized, scheduled, and assigned serial numbers to the order. The Stratus also performed plantwide CIM tasks such as production line summary reporting. The order was then sent to the Bandit line controller, which instructed the line to build the required pagers. (See Exhibits 5 and 6.)

The Bandit production line was a true lot-size-of-one, flexible production facility. All the production line functions were completely automated with the exception of component material handling, which was purposely not automated because to do so was far more costly than the benefits justified.

The U-shaped Bandit line was about 450 feet long, with 34 work

EXHIBIT 5
Bandit Factory Layout

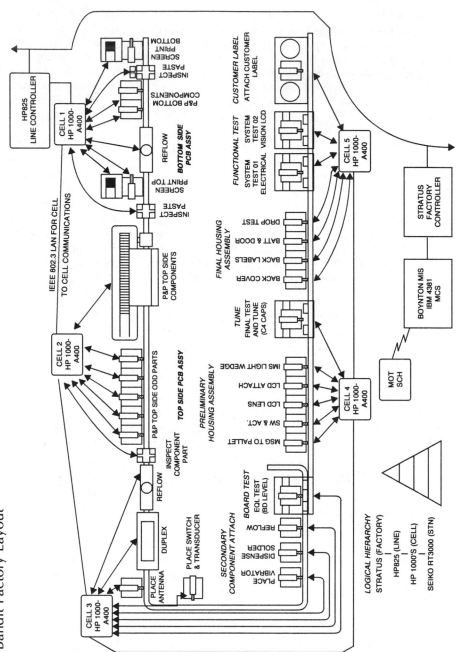

Exhibit 6
Close up of a Bandit Line Robot Cell

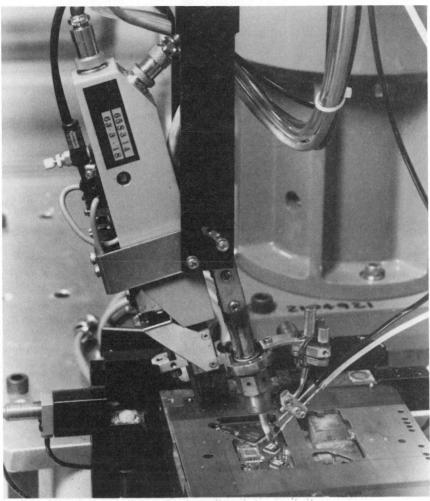

Automated soldering robot performs its operations on the Bravo circuit board with a high degree of consistency . . . another step toward six-sigma quality.

stations connected by conveyors. Each work station had a status light. If the light was green, all was normal; if yellow, the work station had detected an anomaly but was still functioning; if red, the work station was down (non-functional). The line was staffed each shift by approximately 12 workers who corrected the problems that caused the red and yellow lights, kept the machines supplied with materials, and performed maintenance tasks on the machines. They were supported by a shift supervisor and two engineers.

Early Bandit Production (December 1987 to October 1989)

During the year and a half of production that followed the project's official completion, conflicts arose between meeting production goals and experimenting to enhance the operation of the line. For example, to pick up components some of the robots used "grippers" that required adjustments every few days. To eliminate this problem, the engineers wanted to switch to a different kind of gripper but doing so would have cost several hours of production and so the change was postponed.

Recalled Richard Spira, Bandit production manager (as of March 1989):

> One thing we learned after the project was officially completed is we had to get the engineering people off the production line. They were constantly trying to optimize the system. When I took over, my charge was to concentrate on producing pagers. Once the engineers were off the line, the biggest problem I had was we could never get satistically significant trends because of robot downtime. Achieving five-sigma quality day in and day out is a world apart from briefly demonstrating five-sigma quality. We learned that one key was the preventative maintenance (PM) schedule. We started with the standard PM schedule used on robots elsewhere in the plant but still had problems. It turned out that we had to rewrite the PM schedule just for Bandit because the Bandit robots are used very differently. In the rest of the factory, robots may move in a 10 or 20 degree arc, but on the Bandit line they move a full 180 degrees.
>
> We also had problems with slow morning startups, after being shut down at night. The first step in solving this problem turned out to be easy—I just put in a third shift. My motto has become "The Factory Never Stops." Having solved these problems, we are now concentrating on throughput, some minor equipment capability modifications, and continuously improving the line's performance.

Other problems cropped up as well. Despite early vendor involvement, obtaining a continuous supply of high quality components was difficult. When production started to ramp up, not all the vendors consistently met the production and quality demands. The Bandit team had to help them solve their problems.

The CIM system also had several startup difficulties. Increasing production volume generated much heavier processing loads and an additional cell controller computer had to be added to the line. A great deal of work also was done on the CIM system to integrate it more fully with the corporate MIS systems for order entry and material requisitions. Noted Bruce Keller:

Probably the most impressive technology to come out of Bandit was the CIM system. We don't know of anyone else in the U.S. that has developed a factory running on lot sizes of one based on actual customer orders in a totally automated environment. We also are able to do real time statistical process control that gives the workers immediate feedback on how everything is going. These real time data will be extremely important as we push toward six-sigma quality, because to obtain six-sigma we not only have to identify problems quickly, but must track trends in order to anticipate problems and avoid them. We can never get to six-sigma quality without anticipating problems in this manner.

Peter Ellis, CIM engineer on Bandit, added:

The software connection of all the different elements of the CIM system was the most challenging part of the Bandit project, and the newest to the company. A major problem was communication between the different groups. Although the CIM group was brought in early, we spent most of the early period worrying about the overall architecture of the system, not working on the detailed level of how to communicate with robots. As a result, when we tried to integrate with the robotics, we did not know what to expect and CIM was often the bottleneck.

Piltch and other managers felt, however, that the absence of difficulties would have signaled that they had not attempted enough. Although the Bandit project met its required five-sigma performance during a production run in December 1987, it did not reach that level of performance on a day-to-day basis for another eighteen months. However, by August 1989, the Bandit line had stabilized at five-sigma quality, was producing substantial volume, and was considered a great success throughout Motorola. Albert Cameron, strategic marketing manager, explained:

The Bandit production line has finally given us the ability to ramp up quickly to meet demand. The pager business is very seasonal and, even though it is growing about 20% per year, there is a big spurt in demand in the second quarter followed by a sharp *decline* after the summer. Every year we have problems getting enough pagers out in the second quarter, and so we risk losing market share. In 1989, the Bandit line provided the flexibility to enable us to meet demand much more effectively—reducing our second quarter delivery problems dramatically.

While I know the product line marketing manager would have liked to have had more input on Bandit, the team had to concentrate on getting the job done.

One marketing manager voiced a different opinion, however:

The Bandit people thought that because they were not changing any of the customer features, they did not have to involve marketing. However, they ended up making some decisions to simplify their tasks that caused me considerable grief. For example, they decided to use a five-spot crystal which limited the type of pagers they could produce to only high-band pagers. When they made that decision, the bulk of market was high-band. Since then, however, the market has shifted to 900 Mhz pagers and I've had to tell half of my customers that they can't get a Bandit Bravo—they can only get a Jstar Bravo. The customers get real upset when they hear this—in part because the Bandit people sent out brochures explaining how good the Bandit line is and how high the quality is. I didn't even see one of these brochures until a customer showed it to me!

Nevertheless, the Bandit line received considerable attention from the business press, and some industry analysts felt Bandit's success was influential in the decision to award Motorola the first Malcolm Baldrige National Quality Award in 1988. Furthermore, senior corporate management saw periodic projects such as Bandit—involving significant jumps in product and/or process performance every two to four years—as a primary source of improvement in competitive advantage. By late 1989 several Motorola divisions, with top management's encouragement, were pursuing major "home run" projects using an approach very similar to that used by the Pager Division on Bandit.

Beyond Bandit

By October 1989, most of the startup problems had been ironed out and Merle Gilmore, vice president and general manager of the Paging Division, was concerned with optimizing the payback on the Bandit investment. Both direct and indirect returns from Bandit were important. Line utilization on Bandit had to be as high as possible to maximize the direct return; yet everyone felt that the line could be made more efficient with experimentation and further process development. Furthermore, the Bandit line's flexibility made it very attractive for prototyping and even initial production of other products. All but the final assembly of pilot production on Motorola's new wristwatch pager was done on the Bandit line, for example. Such "external" demands for the line were often in direct conflict with obtaining the optimum line utilization.

In addition, having two internal designs for the Bravo pager itself had intrinsic difficulties because two separate product lines had to be maintained. Any change in one had to be made in the other. For example, one of Motorola's customers had trouble with water leakage and the Jstar pager had to be redesigned slightly. The customer also insisted that the Bandit version be redesigned even though it was not clear that the Bandit pager had the leakage problem. Such problems required substantially more support effort.

Nonetheless, from the beginning, Chris Galvin had told Piltch that the success of the Bandit line was only half the job. The other half was to transfer the knowledge gained in the Bandit operation throughout the division and the company. It was clear that given the rate of change in most of Motorola's businesses, top management saw the bulk of the company's performance improvement coming from significant projects such as Bandit, with tuning and refining taking place between such projects. Thus, one obvious successor to the legacy of Bandit was the next generation Bravo pager, appropriately nicknamed "Son-of-Bandit," a project directed at improving the product while supporting some further gains in the productivity of the process.

Son-of-Bandit Issues

Pagers were differentiated by a variety of features, e.g., size, battery life, number of messages stored in memory, message display (type, readability, etc.), and ability to lock and delete messages. Motorola's product development strategy had been to compete aggressively on such features. By continually changing the customers' view of what the standard pager should consist of, Motorola dominated the pager business. Over time, marketing developed a series of guidelines for new product specifications: (1) smaller is better; (2) pagers should be more attractive physically; (3) features customers accept remain unchanged (so the end user need not learn how to use a pager with each generation); and (4) being alert for "gotchas." A marketing manager explained the last-named guideline:

> A gotcha is when a competitor designs in a feature that customers feel is superior, and you don't have it in your pager. For example, NEC developed a display that would automatically light when the surrounding lighting is low. On our display, you have to push a button to light the display. Many customers feel NEC's display is superior because of that feature, and we have lost some sales because of it. Of course, gotchas work both ways, and we try to design in our own.

Historically, marketing obtained most of its feedback by discussing with big carriers what they would like in the next generation pager. Marketing then developed specifications for the new product and passed them on to product development. If product development had problems with the specifications, they would meet with marketing and hammer out a compromise.

Because of the pager market's rapid growth, however, pagers were becoming more of a consumer business. To adapt, marketing initiated a drive to identify the end users and which market segments had high or low penetration, so Motorola could focus its marketing (and some product development) effort on certain segments with high growth potential. The results of this effort were not expected until the end of 1990, when the Son-of-Bandit development would be well underway.

For his part, while he hoped that Son-of-Bandit would learn from the Bandit project, Gilmore felt that it was important not to copy the Bandit process blindly. There were significant differences in the goals of the two projects: Bandit had been a big push in *process* technology and the Son-of-Bandit had to concentrate on pushing the *product* technology. There were also the question of whether Son-of-Bandit should have only a single, fully automated production process or retain the combined automated/conventional approach used in Bravo.

Gilmore felt that many of the reasons for the success of Operation Bandit had been understood, but he wanted to make sure these lessons were disseminated and applied effectively throughout the division and company.

Associated Instruments Corporation: Analytic Instruments Division

On October 1, 1985, Bob Hoffenberger, division manager for Associated Instruments Corporation's Analytic Instruments Division, felt considerable dismay as he studied the latest marketing projections for the model 77000 mass spectrometer. The 77000 was the division's hot development effort, which was scheduled to begin customer shipments in late 1986. The annual volume projections for the 77000 had been drifting steadily downward over the past few months, while the projected sales price had risen to cover increases in the projected cost of goods sold as the product's design evolved. Those cost increase had resulted from improved features added to the basic product and changes to make it more reliable.

Both division management and the design team had deemed each individual improvement a necessity, given the high priority assigned to product performance and product reliability. Yet, at a higher price than originally planned, the 77000 might fail to capture the market position envisioned when corporate approved the product development effort. By falling short of key strategic and profit goals outlined for it by management, the 77000 threatened to disrupt the smooth execution of the five-year business strategy the division had embarked on in 1983.

Hoffenberger knew that corporate management would be expecting a

Portions of the field work for this case were conducted by Sandeep Dugal, Research Assistant, Stanford University, under the supervision of Professor Steven C. Wheelwright. Selected data have been disguised to protect the proprietary interests of the firm.

review and update on the 77000 project within the next week. From a passing comment made by the CEO, he knew corporate was aware of the increasing price (cost) and decreasing volume projections. He felt he should do his homework and take a position before his next review meeting, rather than wait for questions that he was not prepared to answer.

Corporate Background

The Associated Instruments Corporation (AIC) was a $200+ million designer, manufacturer, and marketer of precision instruments for construction firms, chemical laboratories, university research facilities, and other institutions. (See Exhibit 1 for financial statements.) The Analytic Instruments Division, one of six divisions within the company, manufactured high-quality, high-priced, fully featured mass spectrometers and related instruments. The company traditionally had been a technology leader. Recently, however, each division increasingly had been required to compete on the basis of price as the performance of competitors' equipment had improved and as industry product standards had emerged. This was particularly true in the Analytic Instruments Division, where the rate of technological change in mass spectrometry had slowed markedly. With the maturing of its base technology, the Analytic Instruments Division could no longer expect customers to pay the 25%–50% premium for its equipment they had been willing to pay in the past. Thus, part of the repositioning of AIC and its divisions involved changing priorities and building the capability to develop cost-effective yet highly featured and highly reliable products. The 77000 effort was the Analytic Instruments Division's first attempt to address this new reality and operationalize this new strategy.

Mass Spectrometers and the Mass Spectrometry Industry

Mass spectrometers were powerful analytic instruments used to isolate and identify the chemical compounds or elements in a sample. Mass spectrometers were designed to work in conjunction with several pieces of associated equipment including powerful small computers, liquid and gas chromatographs, and various detector devices. Customers were moving toward more systems, although in the mid–1980s, stand-alone units still represented almost 50% of the market. (The building blocks for a mass spectrometer system were offered individually by the Ana-

Exhibit 1

AIC Corporate Financial Statements
(Fiscal year ending 8/31/85; in 000s)

Corporate Assets		Corporate Liabilities and Equity	
Current Assets		Current Liabilities	
Cash	$ 11,050	Accounts Payable	$ 15,944
Accounts Receivable	34,190	Other Accrued Liabilities	53,567
Inventories	64,760	Total Current Liabilities	69,511
Deferred Tax Benefit	4,372		
Prepaid Expenses	1,511	Long-Term Debt & Equity	
Total Current Assets	$ 115,883	Long-Term Debt	37,030
		Deferred Taxes	7,807
Property, Plant, & Equipment		Deferred Employee Benefits	9,296
Land, Buildings, &		Common Stock	28,154
Improvements	60,122	Retained Earnings	33,184
Machinery & Equipment	43,666	Translation Adjustments	5,118
Less: Depreciation	(29,671)		
Net Property, Plant,		Stockholder's Equity	66,456
& Equipment	74,117	Total	$ 190,000
Total	$ 190,000		

Corporate Profit and Loss	
Net Revenues	$ 201,070
Cost & Expenses	
Costs of Goods Sold	116,977
Research & Development	18,629
Selling, General, &	
Administrative	48,941
Interest, net	4,101
Income Before Taxes	12,422
Provision for Income Taxes	5,590
Net Income	$ 6,832

lytic Instruments Division or in combination, linked through the division's proprietary software network.)

In a mass spectrometer system, small quantities of the sample to be analyzed were vaporized in a low-pressure chamber. Molecules were analyzed using one of several techniques, such as electron impact or field ionization. When chemical compounds were ionized, for example, they formed unique mass/charge combinations, each of which created a different signal when accelerated using electric and magnetic fields. The nature of each element was determined by this unique "fingerprint," and the quantity was determined by the intensity of the signal. By the mid–1980s, the output of most mass spectrometers was fed directly to a small computer which used a database and sophisticated software to automatically analyze and identify the nature and quantity of the compounds in the sample.

Customers for mass spectrometers included independent chemical laboratories, such as test houses, or chemical analysis laboratories—often part of large companies—that needed to determine the composition of a sample for research, quality, or environmental protection purposes. In addition, mass spectrometers were increasingly used on production lines to monitor the chemical composition of products, by-products, and wastes. Oil, pharmaceutical, and chemical companies were some of the biggest users of mass spectrometers. Although the market had been maturing during the early 1980s, it was expected to continue to grow at 15%–20% per year as environmental protection concerns required more companies to determine the quantity of certain compounds.

In addition to AIC, three U.S. firms competed in the mass spectrometer industry: Hewlett-Packard, Varian Associates, and Finnigan Corporation. All four companies were California-based. In addition, competitors from Japan, Germany, and Great Britain held viable positions in this worldwide market. (U.S. industry sales, as well as AIC's Analytic Instruments Division's market share, are shown in Exhibit 2).

Mass spectrometers currently were priced in the $3,000–$10,000 range, but prices had been falling 10%–20% per year. When purchased with

EXHIBIT 2

Industry and Division Sales of Mass Spectrometers

| | | Analytic Instruments Division | |
Year	U.S. Industry Sales (000s)*	U.S. Sales (000s)	U.S. Market Share**
1986 (est.)	$158,000	$19,000	12.0%
1985 (est.)	126,000	17,800	14.1
1984	106,022	16,221	15.3
1983	92,871	14,952	16.1
1982	87,623	14,721	16.8
1981	96,100	17,298	18.0
1980	82,500	14,190	17.2

* U.S. sales were thought to represent about half of the total worldwide market.

** Although data were sketchy, Associated's Analytic Instruments Division thought its worldwide market share was about the same as its U.S. market share. The 1986 estimates do *not* include any sales of the 77000.

SOURCE: Division estimates.

784

peripherals like small computers, gas chromatographs, and software networks, they were part of a much more expensive system, priced in the $25,000–$120,000 range. Virtually all of the major competitors sold their products as individual instruments or modules, as well as complete systems.

New equipment manufacturers' warranties in the mid–1980s ranged from 90 to 180 days. Most customers subsequently purchased a service contract that was renewable every twelve months and priced annually at 4%–10% of the original unit price. Purchase decisions were based not only on reliability and price but also on the availability of such special features as automatic loading, versatile software, faster speeds, user-friendliness, and easy-to-read displays.

The Analytic Instruments Division of AIC had a reputation for being relatively high priced in comparison with its competitors but offering the latest in features and system capabilities. The Division's sales force focused on sophisticated customers in research and analytical laboratories who valued performance and advanced features. As illustrated by the market share figures in Exhibit 2, the division had done extremely well with its third-generation mass spectrometer family, introduced in 1980. However, by 1984, that offering was being challenged effectively by competitors and the division expected its market position to continue to slip until the introduction of the fourth-generation 77000 in late 1986.

Analytic Instruments Division, 1983–1985

The Analytic Instruments Division historically had designed most of its products in house but purchased many of the parts and subassemblies such a high-precision mechanical components and displays. As a result of the emphasis on technology leadership and the latest features, engineering design teams generally had functioned quite autonomously, with only minimal input from other functions. According to one division executive, "'In those days, manufacturing was just trying to keep up, . . . and marketing and sales were seen as necessary evils."

In the early 1980s, the Analytic Instruments Division found itself under increasing competitive pressure on all aspects of the product—features, price, reliability, and follow-on service. For example, dead-on-arrival (DOA) rates were very high (5%–15%) and the company's European subsidiary had made it a habit to reinspect every unit it received from the Analytic Instruments Division before shipping to its final customers. By late 1983, declines in market share, margins, and growth had become apparent throughout the division, and a general sense of gloom permeated most of the planning meetings in those days.

It was at this time that Bob Hoffenberger was appointed division general manager. Hoffenberger, who had come from the sales and marketing function of a strong competitor, was viewed as very bright and capable. Young and aggressive, Hoffenberger set out to develop a strategy to improve the division's competitive position and profitability. In line with the general strategy being supported by the corporate offices of AIC, Hoffenberger's long-range plan consisted of three steps or phases:

1. Cut costs to "trim the fat";
2. Upgrade manufacturing's role and capability to compete in a cost-competitive environment, and develop (in parallel) a new fourth-generation family of products; and
3. Based on the success of the new product family, expand the sales force and enhance the field support group.

This entire plan was to be accomplished in a three- to four-year span and staged so that the division could remain profitable throughout that period. Under this plan, the sales force would be upgraded as the fourth-generation effort neared market introduction, but it would not be expanded until it actually had new products to sell. In turn, the design of the new product was to be done using largely existing resources (but with more marketing and manufacturing input), and the manufacturing improvements were to be largely a self-directed, self-funded effort. While this plan would stretch the division's resources significantly, it was one that everyone agreed was absolutely necessary and one to which people were willing to make a commitment.

Under Hoffenberger's strategy, the 77000 product development effort played a central role. It was not only the logical next generation for product development, as well as for the overall strategy, but it was to provide the basis for profitably expanding the sales and field service organization and regaining the type of market leadership position the division had enjoyed in 1981.

The 77000 New Product Development Effort

Discussions of a possible fourth-generation produce began in earnest in June of 1983. As a part of those discussions, the basic procedure to be used for product development was reviewed and revised. It was agreed that product development should be a business effort and should be initiated by completing three major steps:

1. Writing a feasibility proposal (referred to as a *job order*).

2. Preparing a detailed marketing-driven *product plan.*
3. Obtaining *corporate approval* of a formal new product development proposal.

During the feasibility stage (in 1983), approximately $50,000 was allocated to the study and exploration of competitors' products and features that might be included in this fourth-generation mass spectrometer effort. The *job order* was to include a brief summary of the product's unique features and its estimated cost and development schedule. The *product plan* was then to be developed by the marketing group, focusing on the market opportunity and the market needs. It was to be a comprehensive and fairly lengthy document that covered in competitive, financial, and technical terms the major aspects of the effort and its intended results. This document was to be combined with the formal product development proposal and "'signed off" by several senior managers before *corporate approval* of major funding for the development effort. The official start date of the project was the date on which this corporate approval was given.

Historically, product development at the Analytic Instruments Division had been treated rather informally, and had been largely under the control of the engineering group. Often development steps had been omitted or circumvented because the engineering group did not perceive them as necessary or useful or because senior management was imposing pressure on the schedule, unaware of the difficulties caused by resulting shortcuts.

However, Hoffenberger had persuaded corporate management to agree not only that the 77000 was essential to the division's strategy, but that it should be used as an opportunity to establish a new mode for the division's product development efforts.

In June of 1983, the feasibility job order was prepared and approved, and Bill Lind, a 10-year veteran of the division's engineering group, was appointed project manager. (Lind had worked on the third-generation product family, was extremely well respected by both his technical colleagues and division management, and was regarded as someone who could work closely with the other functions.) Lind and a half-time employee spent the next nine months refining the project proposal, researching the concepts behind the new product, and working with marketing to define the market needs and opportunities. Lind focused on reducing cost, perhaps by half. A variety of ideas for cost reductions were gathered and evaluated by talking with manufacturing, marketing, customers, and field service, and by studying competitors' products. In addition, Lind determined that the product had to be significantly more reliable (greater up-time and significantly fewer dead-on-arrivals), and needed to correct or eliminate minor irritants (such as noise or unnecessarily hard-to-use features) that had prompted customer complaints.

By mid–1984, it was clear to everyone in the division that the 77000 was feasible, that it had a good shot at delivering on its primary objectives, and that it was absolutely necessary to the division's overall strategy. At this point, additional resources were committed, even though the formal new product development proposal was not yet completed and approved. (The final approval was obtained in early November of 1984.) Exhibit 3 summarizes several of the project parameters incorporated in that formal proposal and outlines the staffing that was approved and on-board as of November 1, 1984.

As had been the practice in the division in the past, the initial development project for the 77000 family was to concentrate on designing, manufacturing, and introducing the platform or core product offering. This was to be the fully-featured model 77000. Subsequently (usually 6 to 8 months later), additional models and options would be developed and offered, including a stripped-down (low cost) version and special modules aimed at specific subsegments of the market. While everyone was aware of these natural follow-ons, they were not detailed extensively in the initial job order, product plan, and corporate approval. Rather, the initial approval and resources related directly to the core product, in this case the 77000.

By the fall of 1984, Lind and his team had identified a number of potential sources of cost savings on the 77000. Those included (1) greatly reducing the number of parts to be assembled into the final unit, (2) giving the vendors more complete responsibility for the design, quality, reliability, and cost of the components or subassemblies they supplied, and (3) getting the division's own manufacturing operation up and going with Just-in-Time. In addition, the design team discussed the possibility of changing to injection-molded plastic for some of the key parts, rather than using the much higher variable-cost, machined parts made from sand castings. While plastic molding would add substantial tooling fixed costs, the team felt that the increased reliability and the significantly lower variable costs of these injection-molded parts would be much more in keeping with the goals for the fourth-generation product. In addition, the team decided that the five circuit boards in the third-generation product could be reduced to a single board. Finally, a number of minor changes, such as purchasing the switches, fan, and other items with connecting cables trimmed to length and ready for final assembly, would further improve the cost picture on the 77000.

To build solid reliability into the product, the pump design—a major source of field failure and probably the most important subassembly from a reliability point of view—was given special attention. By December of 1984, pump design had been completed, and 10 units had been built. Beginning on January 1, 1985, these units were to be run contin-

EXHIBIT 3

Initial Research and Development 77000 Project Proposal (11/1/84)

A. Key Project Parameters

1. Schedule (as planned, 11/1/84)

Event/Task	Date
Complete 1st Engineering Breadboard Assembly	08/01/84
Breadboard Review	10/16/84
Interface Freeze (for networking into a system)	11/15/84
Completion of 1st Engineering Prototype Parts	03/15/85
Completion of 1st Prototype Engineering Evaluation	06/15/85
Completion of 2nd Prototype Parts (Fabricated in Engineering)	08/15/85
Completion of 2nd Prototype Parts (Assembly & Final Test in Manufacturing)	09/15/85
Release Package Tooling	08/15/85
Prototype Review	11/15/85
Engineering Buyoff Complete	12/15/85
1st Pilot Run Tested	04/15/86
1st Production Run (Customer Shipment)	07/15/86
Manufacturing Buyoff Complete	10/15/86

2. Project Investment

Design Engineering Expenses (Excluding Labor)	$1,925,000
Engineering Labor	842,000
Other Direct Project	126,000
Total	$2,893,000

3. Annual Volume Projections

1986 (Startup, 07/15/86)	250
1987	1,700
1988	2,000
1989	2,100

4. 77000 Product Price/Cost-of-Goods-Sold (COGS)

Average Annual Unit Sales	2,000
Average Price/Unit	$4,500
COGS-Factory Cost	
Material	645
Component Labor	22
Direct Factory Labor	138
Overhead (Including Tooling)	803
Total COGS	$1,608

B. Project Staffing (core group as of 11/1/84)

1 - Software Eng.	1 - Mechanical Drafting	½ - Purchasing
2 - Mechanical Eng.	1 - PCB Layout	¼ - Marketing
2 - Electrical Eng.	½ - Lab Technician	¼ - QA
1½ - Chemist	1 - Manufacturing Eng.	1 - Project Manager (Lind-Engineering)

789

uously, 24 hours a day, seven days a week, for a entire year to verify and improve (as needed) their reliability.

Although initially cost had been the driving force for Lind and his design team, features became the central focus of their efforts in 1985. Lind and members of his team had visited a number of customers in late 1984 and determined that while cost was extremely important, features had to at least match (and because of the division's historical reputation, should in many cases exceed) those of competitors.

The design team made fairly good progress during the last quarter of 1984 and the first quarter of 1985. By the middle of 1985, the purchasing department was actively involved in the design effort, seeking and establishing relationships with qualified vendors. One of the goals in the product development effort was to decrease significantly the number of vendors, to increase their range of responsibility, and to select vendors on the basis of reliability and lifetime cost, not just initial component prices. All key vendors were visited by a team consisting of three members of the product development team—a design engineer, a manufacturing engineer, and a representative from purchasing. Each vendor was evaluated by the three individually as well as collectively, and any individual team member could veto approval of a particular vendor.

During the spring of 1985, as the development team sought to refine and close in on the remaining open issues of the design, it became clear that some difficult tradeoffs and choices still had to be made. A low cost display device had been selected for the 77000 in early 1985, but there was a nagging feeling that it was not consistent with the division's traditional quality image, nor would it match the performance of competitor's products upon introduction. However, its cost was low enough to enable the 77000 to meet its primary factory cost objectives. A much better, more costly alternative display had been identified, but because of its significantly higher cost, no one on the project team wanted to champion its adoption.

In addition, a number of other small enhancements and features were identified, each representing only five or ten dollars in additional cost of goods sold, but all of which would further enhance the 77000. About this time (March 1985), the division's marketing vice president left to join another firm, and that position was empty for almost five months.

In August, a new vice president of marketing, Fred Taylor, was brought in from one of the other divisions at AIC. Within a couple of weeks, Taylor realized that the 77000 development effort was losing momentum. His investigations indicated that some tough choices needed to be made and enthusiasm rekindled. With Hoffenberger's approval, he spent the first 10 days of September doing an in-depth review of the 77000 development effort. Lind and his team welcomed this review because they saw the need for more marketing input and Taylor had a strong reputation throughout the corporation.

Reassessment and Mid-Course Adjustment

After reviewing the 77000 project in detail, Taylor joined with Lind, Hoffenberger, and Jean Smith, the division's vice president of manufacturing, for an all-day offsite meeting. The group reached several conclusions that day. First, each of the small enhancements and features that had already been added to the design was appropriate and could be provided without significantly increasing the factory cost. (Manufacturing's discovery of several small incremental improvements in their process would provide savings about equal to the costs added by these features.) In fact, Taylor's investigations indicated that conflict resolution had worked well on these small issues—the knowledgeable functions had surfaced issues and options early, worked out balanced solutions, and pursued those effectively.

A second conclusion was that the much more attractive fluorescent display should be adopted in place of the cheaper unit selected in early 1985. Taylor's questioning had found virtually unanimous agreement in the division on this point, but because there was no way to offset the additional factory cost of $150 per unit, no one had wanted to make the decision to adopt it. Basically, the team had waited for someone more senior to act. However, without a marketing vice president to push for resolution and with Hoffenberger tied up in several other pressing division issues, the team simply had opted to live with its initial selection of the cheaper display unit. While Hoffenberger, Lind, Taylor, and Smith agreed and committed to the fluorescent display, they also charged Taylor with pulling together the data needed to evaluate its impact on price and volume, and to suggest ways to compensate for that.

A third conclusion was that the project schedule had slipped a couple of months, in part because the fluorescent display device issue had not been resolved as rapidly as it should have. Lind was charged with developing a revised project schedule that detailed the remaining steps to market introduction and manufacturing buyoff. Because of the importance of this project to the division and its entire strategy, Hoffenberger, with the group's concurrence, decided that he should play a more active role and have the entire development team report directly to him for the duration of the project.

Following this meeting, the marketing group—with appropriate input from engineering and manufacturing—actively pursued their assign-

791

ment regarding the impact and modifications required by the higher priced, higher quality fluorescent display. They concluded that one way to build volume was to pull forward the development of the stripped-down, low-cost 77100 model, and ready it for introduction at the same time the 77000 was introduced. Because the 77000 and 77100 were to be a product family, the division's strength and reputation were in premium quality, a consistent image was important, and the 77100 was to be a stripped-down (defeatured) version, not an inferior quality version, they concluded that the more expensive display would need to be used in the 77100, as in the 77000. Their analysis also showed that in order to realize the margin goals needed for the division to maintain its profitability and meet its overall strategic commitments to the corporation, the additional $150 in cost of goods sold would translate into $600 added to the selling price. This addition to the price would have a significant impact on the product's anticipated sales volume.

At this point Taylor went back to the original marketing input to the product development effort (contained in the product plan) and updated the volume/price projections for the 77000. As shown in Exhibit 4, Taylor and his people determined that at a price of $4,500 per unit for the full-featured 77000 and $2,800 per unit for the stripped-down 77100, the division could expect to be selling 2,000 units a year by 1988.

While the division had always had a stripped-down version of its core product, that version had been viewed primarily as a line extension to be sold to good, solid customers who had applications that were extremely price-sensitive, rather than as a major source of revenue. In fact, the Analytic Instruments Division's sales force did not sell into the really price-sensitive market segment. The stripped-down 77100 was to have a very limited set of features so that it would not cannibalize the fully featured 77000. In addition, it was to be priced where it could make some contribution and yet be competitive with the really low-cost offerings of some of the low-end companies in the marketplace.

Originally, the direct factory costs had been targeted at $1,608 for the fully featured 77000 unit, assuming production volumes of 2,000 units per year. When eventually introduced, the stripped-down 77100 would have far fewer software features as well as limited capabilities for flow control of the sample being tested, but would be produced on the same production line as the 77000. Eliminating these options on the 77100 would save only $80 or roughly 5% in factory costs. With the cost increase of the fluorescent display, factory cost would rise $150 to $1,758 on the 77000 and $1,678 on the 77100, assuming combined volumes of 2,000 units per year.

Taylor and his team determined that if the price of the fully featured 77000 were raised to $5,100 (as needed to maintain margin percentages and cover the additional cost of the fluorescent display), sales volume of

EXHIBIT 4

Volume/Price Projections for the 77000 (as of 10/1/85)

	Price per Unit (77000)				
	$4,000	$4,500	$5,000	$5,100	$5,500
Annual Sales Volume (1988)*					
Featured Unit (77000)	2,000	1,800	1,600	1,500	1,300
Stripped-Down Unit (77100)	100	200	250	250	250
Total Volume	2,100	2,000	1,850	1,750	1,550
Projected 77000 COGS** (Direct Factory Cost)	$1,560	$1,608	$1,730	$1,755	$1,910

Tooling Options:	As Originally Planned***	Lower-Volume Option
Initial Investment (One-time charge)	$160,000	$57,000
Variable Cost (per unit produced)	$86.50/unit	$101.00/unit
Production Process	More automated Tighter tolerances Extra 10% MTBF	Modest automation Meets specifications Meets MTBF goal

* Assumes both versions are offered and the stripped-down version is pushed with traditional AIC customers for their price-sensitive applications. The stripped-down version would be priced at about $2,800. This price was viewed by marketing as the maximum possible to still be considered competitive with low end competitors in 1988.

** Each of these costs *would increase by $150* with the addition of the higher cost fluorescent display.

*** The projected COGS shown above includes the cost of this tooling option.

the 77000 would drop significantly, although the stripped-down 77100 volume would increase slightly because of the bigger price gap between the two units. However, the total combined annual volume would drop to 1,750 (versus 2,000), and this drop would have major implications for the division's overall performance.

As Smith and her manufacturing team explored the options for additional cost cutting to offset some of the cost of the higher quality fluorescent display, it became clear that the significant opportunities for manufacturing cost reductions (switching to a single printed circuit board, changing to vendor parts that were fully tested and ready for final assembly, and changing to fewer parts from more reliable vendors) already had been incorporated. The best that manufacturing felt it could do using the fluorescent display was a factor cost of $1,758 for the 77000 (at 2,000 total units per year).

In late September 1985, manufacturing pulled together additional information on the tooling options associated with the injection-molded parts in the new product. As originally planned, there would be a fixed cost of $160,000 for tooling, and the parts coming from that tooling would have a variable cost of $86.50 per mass spectrometer produced. Smith's group suggested that those fixed costs could be lowered substantially by changing to a less automated, more manual, injection-molded part.

Manufacturing estimated that this lower-volume option would have one-time fixed tooling costs of $57,000 and a variable cost per mass spectrometer produced of $101. However, manufacturing was quick to point out that this lower-volume option, while meeting the specifications, would not hold tolerances as tight as the higher-volume option. In addition, while it would meet the mean-time-between-failures (MTBF) goal for the 77000, manufacturing was confident that the higher fixed-cost option would exceed that goal by at least 10%. (These numbers are summarized in Exhibit 4.)

The analysis of the schedule done by Lind and the development team showed that indeed the project was a couple of months behind its original plan. However, test results from the prototype pumps that had been running continuously for almost nine months indicated even higher reliability than originally planned. Based on the test results Lind estimated that product reliability was likely to be twice that experienced with the third-generation product. Lind was confident that the revised schedule his team has just completed was realistic and would deliver on the project's primary objectives. (See Exhibit 5.)

Hoffenberger's Decision

On October 1, 1985, as Hoffenberger reviewed the available data (including some estimates he had put together with Taylor's help—see Exhibit 6) and the inputs he had received from manufacturing, marketing, design, and the entire development team, he realized that he needed to commit to a detailed action plan. His choices (as he, Lind, Taylor, and Smith had outlined them on the preceding afternoon) appeared to be as follows:

1a. Stay with the existing plan and level of tooling and parts automation, and then, after introducing the 77000, pursue an aggressive cost-reduction effort to refine the design, develop the 77100, help key vendors, and further improve the division's own manufacturing processes. This option was attractive in that it minimized disruption to the current product development project, would initiate customer

Exhibit 5
Revised Product Development Schedule (10/1/85)

Events/Tasks	Date
Prototype Parts in Manufacturing	11/12/85
Packaging & Die Cast Tooling Release	11/19/85
8 Prototype Units Completed (Assembly through Final Test)	12/10/85
Start Prototype Evaluations (Marketing, Engineering, QA, Field Service, and Manufacturing)	12/10/85
Inputs to Technical Publications Completed	01/15/86
All Long Lead Time Items on Order	02/01/86
Review of Prototype Evaluations	02/11/86
Engineering Design Buyoff (Complete)	03/11/86
Pilot Run Parts In-House	05/20/86
Pilot Run Completed (Including Shop-Floor Testing)	07/22/86
QA Evaluation of Pilot Run Units Completed	10/02/86
1st Production Run Completed (Customer Shipment)	10/08/86
Manufacturing Buyoff	01/15/87

shipments in October of 1986, and yet subsequently developed a cost-reduction capability, which he felt was essential to the company and to his division. Committing to this option would make it highly likely that this capability would be developed because market and business strategy pressures would demand it. Hoffenberger was aware that Lind and his development team favored this option.

1b. While sticking with the basic plan, he could accept the reality of the numbers (Exhibit 4) and switch now to smaller-volume, less-automated, lower-cost tooling. This would be the safe thing to do, and there would be substantial opportunity after the 77000 was introduced to work on refinements and cost reductions. This choice would ensure that the division could meet its margin targets, and although it would fall somewhat short of its revenue targets, he knew there were a number of other potential products that the reenergized division had identified recently that might fill that revenue shortfall. His own inclination was to take this route, because he knew the division was already extremely stretched and he wanted to be certain that the 77000 was a success. His division controller and the corporate planner were likely to be strong supporters of this option as well.

2. A second major option that had surfaced recently seemed intriguing. The division had solicited a proposal from an outside engineering consulting firm to perform a value engineering review of the 77000 project early in 1986. This review would be aimed at refining the

795

EXHIBIT 6

Additional Data Collected by Hoffenberger During September 1985

A. Cost of further delays in the 77000 introduction
   1. Market Share (Hoffenberger's and Taylor's estimates)
      a. By late 1986, during each month when the third-generation product was available but the fourth (the 77000) was not, the division's market share would slip by 0.2% per month (2.4% per year).
      b. Once the fourth-generation product (77000) was available, the division should see its market share gain 0.5% per month (6.0% per year) for the first year. During the second year of 77000 availability, the division should gain additional market share of 2%–3% to put it at about 20% share of market. (This assumed the division's share of market was still 10%+ at the time of 77000 introduction.)
   2. Margins (Marketing's and Manufacturing's estimates)
      a. During 1986, the third-generation product was expected to deliver gross margins (Revenue − Factory Cost) of 50% on average revenues of $6,600 per unit. The pre-tax contribution margin (after manufacturing, marketing, and selling costs but before depreciation, interest and G&A costs) was expected to be 25%.
      b. Within six months of introduction (and at a price of $5,100), the 77000 was expected to have a gross margin of 60%–65% and a pre-tax contribution margin of about 40%. (At a price of $2,800, the 77100 was expected to have a gross margin of 35% and a pre-tax contribution margin of 15%.)

B. Cost of Warranty and Service
   1. For the third-generation product, introduced in 1980, the following pattern had emerged:

	Full cost as % of initial price	Price charged to customer
months 1–3 (under full warranty)	2%	0%*
months 4–27 (under full service contract)	2%	4%
months 28–39 (under full service contract)	2%	4%
months 40–51(under full service contract)	3%	6%
months 52–63 (under full service contract)	4% (est.)	8%

   * included in purchase price

   2. For the fourth-generation product (both the 77000 and the 77100), the warranty and service dollar costs per unit were expected to be no more than half of those experienced on the third generation and might be considerably less than that. The division would be in a much better position to estimate these costs on the 77000 in February of 1986, following the full evaluation of the initial 8 prototypes. (See Exhibit 5.)

design, scrutinizing each component and subassembly for cost reduction opportunities, and linking the various cost elements of the product to the value those elements provided in the marketplace.

Although such value engineering was new to Associated Instruments, Hoffenberger was aware that it had been used extensively by other firms. A few more months of in-house work would be required before the consulting engineering firm could make a definitive proposal, but preliminary discussions suggested that such a value engineering review would (a) add three months to the development schedule (delaying product introduction until January 1987), (b) shave about 10% off the factory cost of goods sold (assuming this would be a normal project), and (c) cost approximately $90,000 (the price charged by the consulting firm).

This option not only would reduce factory costs and teach his management team much about value engineering, but, by adding another short prototype cycle to the development, would ensure that the reliability and performance of the 77000 would be the best possible when it was introduced. Hoffenberger had contacted a sufficient number of the consulting firm's prior clients to feel comfortable with the firm's claims regarding improvements in factory cost, product performance, and market introduction.

3. Finally, he could accelerate development of the 77100, the stripped-down version, so that it could be introduced simultaneously with the fully featured 77000. The objective in doing so would be to obtain a significant chunk of business at the low end, in addition to the fully featured business. Relying as much on his own experience and gut feel as anything, he felt that the stripped-down version might be able to sell 400 or 500 units if it were promoted appropriately, and that it might even add another 100 to 200 units of annual sales to the 77000 version just because it would be so exciting to the marketplace. Thus, even at $5,100 for the fully featured version, if the division pursued this option, it might well realize sales of 2,100 units a year by 1988.

While this option would clearly delay the project another two or three months (until January of 1987), he had a number of ideas for how it might be pursued. From a marketing perspective, if advertised appropriately it could give the salesforce a tremendous boost at introduction and provide them access to a much wider customer base, especially if the warranty period were lengthened significantly. For manufacturing, it could add needed volume to cover fixed tooling costs, but also provide the ongoing discipline to reduce costs even further since almost a quarter of the volume would be at the low end. Finally, it would give him an opportunity to make his mark on the division and particularly its new product development effort. For Hoffenberger, this option was the most exciting personally, although probably the most risky and the least well developed of the four.

As Hoffenberger reviewed these options, he also reflected on the new product development process that had brought the fourth-generation product to this point. He wondered if it were as much an improvement as he had originally thought. If it were, why had it taken so long to resolve the fluorescent display issue? Obviously the month of September 1985 had been a period of reopening the development funnel. Was that appropriate? Even now, he wondered if he had handled it well. Finally, the very fact that marketing had been able to go several months without executive input to the project suggested some shortcomings in how they viewed their role. After preparation of the initial product plan, was volume, price, and profit analysis the appropriate extent for marketing's input?

Building Development Capability

Overview

Firms that consistently and aggressively build development capability do so on a foundation of learning across projects, creating new tools and techniques, periodically reviewing their development approaches (including prototyping), continually refocusing the attention of critical development resources, and, perhaps most importantly, developing outstanding capabilities in their people. Such firms view development capability as a dynamic advantage that management must constantly renew and enhance through personal attention and effort. Development capabilities then become a distinctive strength, resulting in products and processes that delight customers and disarm competitors. Unfortunately, while firms find it in vogue to espouse such a perspective, relatively few have figured out how to turn it into reality. We examine this problem in this chapter.

An important theme in this chapter is the need to match the approach to building capability to the situation facing the firm. There are many possible starting points for an organization intent on increasing the rate at which it builds and applies distinctive development capabilities. Four have proven to be particularly powerful in practice. One, *creating a development strategy*, is illustrated in this chapter using the experience of

Physio Control, a manufacturer of cardiovascular defibrillators and heart monitors. This approach includes setting specific development goals, identifying available resources, creating an aggregate set of projects to which those resources can be efficiently applies, and managing resources across a portfolio of projects on an ongoing basis. An alternative starting point is to make *fundamental changes in the organization's development process*, as illustrated by Ford Motor Company's effort to restructure the sequence of activities and redefine the development phases and milestones used to characterize phase completion—creating what Ford refers to as their new "concept to customer" approach.

A third starting point for building development capability, *creating building block skills and tools*, has been used by the Eastman Kodak division charged with developing and supporting a family of single-use, 35 mm cameras. Efforts of this type often focus on creating new skills in engineering, tooling, manufacturing, and marketing, and linking those, as Kodak did, using a CAD system. The fourth starting point that has been particularly successful is the *demonstration project*. (This was Motorola's approach on the Bandit pager project described in Chapter 10.) Using Hewlett-Packard's Vancouver Division's application of an innovative technology in a low-cost, high-quality product—inkjet printing in the DeskJet—this chapter gives a detailed illustration of the fourth approach. The essence of this approach is to use an important development effort as a focal point to "demonstrate" the types of changes needed to significantly improve development capabilities and performance.

Selecting which approach to use as a starting point in any particular situation involves understanding the settings where each approach has proved most successful (see Exhibit 12–1). However, whichever approach is used at the outset, all four inevitably become part of a larger process of dynamic organizational change as the firm creates difficult-to-copy strategic capabilities. The path followed by organizations that achieve success in this effort is typically characterized by evolutionary, incremental, consistent, and persistent improvements in performance on one project after another. To help an organization focus its energy on achieving such potential, the four primary approaches are often complemented by activities such as competitive benchmarking, projects focused on improving specific aspects of development, and project audits. Recognizing that new skills and knowledge must pervade all of these efforts is paramount. After putting in place a systematic plan incorporating these and other elements, it is leadership that makes the difference between average results and outstanding results.

*T*he capability to develop new products and processes rapidly and efficiently is a powerful source of competitive advantage. Our discussion of Northern and Southern Electronics in Chapter 1 underscores the importance of product and process development in every strategy and business. Of course, its relative importance depends on the particular circumstance, strategy, market, and technical environment. But a development capability that matches that environment can create a significant edge in the marketplace.

Such capability, however, is not a static characteristic of the outstanding organization. Indeed, in order to be a source of sustainable advantage, development capability must be continually expanded, upgraded, and improved. Thus, it is not enough to be good at development at a particular point in time. What is required is to be both good now and getting better all the time. That means that no matter what the position of the firm—whether the firm is an industry leader, a close second, or under significant competitive pressure because of gaps between its capabilities and those of its rivals—the ability to build development capability at a rapid rate is crucial to long-term competitive success.

One of the reasons development capability is so powerful and valuable is because building it is exceedingly difficult. The vast majority of organizations that we have studied do not improve significantly and continuously their development performance over time. Building development capability takes determination, persistence, and careful attention to those aspects of the development process that are most crucial in a given organizational situation. Those that succeed make significant investments of resources, managerial time and attention, and organizational energy. The key to effecting real change is to change the total pattern of development—the development strategy and process, the basic organizational structure and leadership, particular skills and tools, and the systems that provide the context in which development takes place.[1] Even if a whole new pattern is not required, substantial refinement and alignment of parts of that pattern may be needed.

Since firms are in many different competitive positions and face different problems and opportunities, numerous approaches to changing the pattern of development seem to work. But, behind them all are a set of common principles that appear to govern success. In this chapter, we examine four different approaches to building development capability and present specific examples of each. The examples give content to the approaches, but they also suggest the particular challenges associated with each approach. We then step back in order to identify the common themes that characterize successful building of this capability. Our intent here is to develop a set of principles that managers can use in launching and guiding efforts to improve the development of new products and processes. The chapter concludes with observations about the importance of managerial leadership in building a competitive advantage in development capability.

Four Approaches to Building Capability

The development process touches so much of what a company does that changing it often seems a daunting challenge. Indeed, efforts that start out intending to change the company's entire pattern of development in one fell swoop are likely to fail. Firms that succeed in building capability do so by finding a starting point—some aspect of the pattern of development that provides a useful vehicle through which to introduce change into the organization. In some cases, simply refining and upgrading what is fundamentally a sound approach is the appropriate starting point. In other cases, more radical change—such as establishing a whole new approach—is appropriate. In this section of the chapter, we present four different approaches to building a development capability. These represent a range of starting points and strategies for changing the pattern of development. The examples we use illustrate the interaction of approach and the firm's situation, and the challenges involved in each approach, and provide the context for identifying the common themes that characterize successful strategies for change.[2] Whatever combination of these four is pursued, sustained learning is the goal, and inevitably that requires a systematic, managed process of improvement. It simply does not happen by chance or good fortune.

Creating A Development Strategy

In organizations with complex product lines, heavy demands for improved product or process performance, and the need to effectively launch and execute multiple development projects with shorter lead times, a useful starting point for building the required capability is often the creation of a development strategy. Physio Control, a manufacturer of cardiovascular defibrillators and heart monitors used in emergency rooms, has used the creation of a development strategy as a starting point for its efforts to improve new product capability over the last few years. Based on its innovative technology, strong reputation for high quality, and strong customer service and support, Physio Control, by the mid 1950s, had established a strong market position in emergency unit defribrillators and emergency room heart monitors. That position, however, came under attack from aggressive small competitors who took advantage of regulatory and technology changes to open new product niches. Legislation in many states, for example, required a defibrillator in all emergency vehicles, thus creating a new product category—the lightweight, small, convenient defibrillator. In addition, changes in electronics technology, software, display devices, and batteries all combined to create new opportunities for products with superior power, space, weight, and communication characteristics.

The thrust of competition and of changes in the environment created a significant requirement for new products at Physio Control. The number of models in production doubled from eight to sixteen between 1985 and 1990. Over that same period, estimated product production life shrank from fourteen years to five years or less. Furthermore, because of growing customer demands and the development of new technologies, the new products under development were more complex and sophisticated than ever before.

The challenge at Physio Control, therefore, was to cope with an exploding product diversity while at the same time meeting requirements for increased responsiveness and improved productivity. Analysis of the situation by the vice president of R&D and the senior management group suggested that the proliferation of new product development projects overlaid on the existing system for development created significant bottlenecks in key support groups and a scramble for resources among competing project teams. Although there were several possible avenues for pursuing improvement and change in the development system, the senior management group saw development strategy—particularly the creation of an engineering and development capacity plan—as a critical first step in their efforts to improve performance.

The process the senior management group used to create a development strategy involved data collection and analysis completed under the direction of the relevant functional heads (the directors of R&D, manufacturing, and marketing) and discussion and synthesis among the senior management group itself. In effect, the senior management group chose to take line responsibility for the development strategy. They did not want the creation of this strategy to be perceived among themselves or in the organization as a "staff activity."

In a day-long meeting held in the spring of 1990, the senior management group focused on the question of engineering capacity. The first step was to list the projects currently under development and try to attach some priority to each one. The discussion of priorities quickly focused on the question of product strategy. It was very difficult for the members of the group to determine the relative priority of alternative projects without a clear sense of direction with respect to the overall product line. For some time marketing and engineering had been discussing the increasing rate of product proliferation and the need to achieve coherence within the product line as well as in the manufacturing organization. While these ideas had occasionally been under discussion within the senior management group, the pressure to create a development strategy brought the issues of product line strategy to the fore. After extensive discussion, a consensus emerged around the strategy for next-generation new products. That strategy called for the creation of a platform product that would serve as the basis for several follow-on products in selected market niches.

Toward the end of the day's session, as managers began to discuss the implications of the platform strategy for engineering capacity, it became clear that pursuit of that particular product strategy would require some very tough choices. The problem was that many of the projects then under development did not fit with the emerging product strategy. Since a vast expansion of the engineering organization was out of the question, it was evident that pursuit of the platform product strategy would require Physio Control to eliminate several ongoing development projects.

Over the next few months, the heads of marketing, R&D, and manufacturing reviewed the existing projects, reevaluated the platform strategy, and developed better estimates of the resource requirements for various development efforts. This review of resource requirements was particularly crucial for support groups like the model shop, testing, and quality assurance.

In a series of discussions held in the summer of 1990, senior management not only reaffirmed its product strategy, but began to lay out a more detailed sequence of projects—including the platform project scoped a few months earlier—required to realize the strategy. One of the most difficult problems Physio Control confronted in developing the aggregate project plan portion of their development strategy was defining the relationship between its current and future generations of products. Significant engineering resources at Physio Control were devoted to the support of current products. Some of that support took the form of specific projects to improve or upgrade the current products, but much of it involved specific customer requests, fixing problems, responding to crises in the field and manufacturing plant, and, in general, undertaking engineering work in order to solve specific problems. Individual marketers and engineers could always justify spending time on the current product, since doing so generated cash and earnings immediately.

In order to resolve the conflict between current and future products, senior management at Physio Control did not start with a prioritized list of projects. Rather, they asked the question: "Given our strategy, the nature of our business, and our short- and long-term objectives, what is the appropriate mix of projects we ought to pursue?" The project options they examined included major projects (to create new platforms), smaller projects (to leverage off existing platforms and thus expand the product line or open up new market segments), and ongoing support of current products. After determining the fraction of resources they wished to see devoted to each type of project, the senior management group, working with data and analysis supplied by engineering, R&D, marketing, and manufacturing, identified a prioritized list of projects within each category. The priorities established for each type of project grew out of the overall product strategy, including the business plan and aggregate project plan for the next five years. These plans identified the sequence of projects required to realize the business and product strategies. They matched this prioritized list with an estimate of development resources required to complete the project, as well as an estimate of the available capacity (given the business plan). By matching estimated requirements for high-priority projects against capacity, senior management was able to determine the set of projects within each category that their resources could support and that would deliver the desired financial results.

The net effect of the series of discussions and analyses conducted within the senior management group was a development strategy that sharply reduced the number of projects in progress at Physio Control. But the process also resulted in a much higher degree of communication and greater shared understanding of the development process and development strategy among the senior management group and key functional executives in engineering, marketing, and manufacturing.

Changing the Development Process

In companies with complex development processes and a long history of development experience, a fruitful starting point for bringing about significant change is often the overall architecture of the development process. By introducing a restructured sequence of activities and redefining both the phases of development and the milestones that characterize completion of each phase, firms may create a new framework—a new context in which engineers, marketers, and manufacturers may see new opportunities for improvement. The Ford Motor Company's efforts—identified within the firm as "concept to customer" (or "C to C")—are illustrative of such an approach and its potential benefits.[3]

In the early 1980s, Ford faced a dismal future: quality was far below competitive standards and market share was falling. In addition, the company's financial position was precarious and layoffs were ongoing. By the end of the decade, however, Ford had introduced a string of successful new products. Indeed, the Ford Explorer, introduced in the spring of 1990, may prove to be Ford's most successful product introduction ever. Despite the fact that it debuted in a down market, the four-door, four-wheel-drive sport utility vehicle sold phenomenally well.

Behind the Explorer and other successful Ford products (such as the Lincoln Continental, Probe, and Taurus) lay a decade of changes in Ford's management culture, particularly their product development process. A pivotal event in this process of change was the development of the Taurus, a family sedan with the styling, handling, and ride of a sophisticated European car. As a product, the Taurus offered a distinctive yet integrated package in which advanced aerodynamic styling was matched with a new chassis, independent rear suspension, and a front wheel drive layout.

But the Taurus was also an important "vehicle" bringing about change in the development process at Ford. It was the initial project used to improve the development process. Traditionally, Ford's development efforts had been strongly functional in character and the architecture of the development process reflected this orientation: it was schedule driven, relatively sequential in the way it organized activities, and punctuated by a series of detailed reviews that were highly proceduralized and bureaucratic. In developing the Taurus, however, Ford sought to break down barriers between functions by creating "team Taurus," the core of which included principal participants from all the functions and activities involved in the creation of the new car. The team served to coordinate and integrate the development program at the senior management level, and was the first step on a long path of organizational, attitudinal, and procedural change. The team was initially headed by Lew Veraldi, at the time the director of large car programs at Ford. As the development of the Taurus proceeded, however, it became clear that integrated development, and, in particular, development that required much less time to complete, necessitated more than a high-level core team under the direction of a single manager.

In order to cut lead time, improve quality, and bring products to market that were distinctive and attractive to customers, Ford launched the C to C process in the mid 1980s. Led by a handpicked group of engineers and product planners, the C to C project took as its mission the creation of a new architecture for product development. Its specific focus was to create a sequence of development activities and associated milestones that would result in a forty-eight-month development time (a 20–25 percent cycle time reduction) on major new development programs while improving product quality and creating products with competitively attractive features and performance.

The C to C team was led by an experienced senior engineer, and its members were drawn from most of the important engineering groups as well as product planning and marketing. Through extensive interaction with senior functional managers, the group sought in the first instance to identify the overall structure of the current development process at Ford. They determined how the process actually worked, where the milestones were, and what materials were used to make decisions. The C to C team also became the focal point for significant benchmarking activities in which Ford compared itself to its major competitors and companies outside the auto industry whose success in product development was well documented. The benchmarking activities, as well as the intensive analysis of the internal process, revealed several opportunities for significant improvement. But the group also recognized the importance of establishing fundamental principles for the creation of a new development architecture. Through a series of presentations and extensive discussion within the development organization at Ford, the group articulated and sought to create consensus around critical milestones, decision points, and criteria for decision making, as well as around patterns of responsibility and functional involvement. The following statements illustrate the principles the C to C team developed:

- Senior management review of the program should be driven by the substantive milestones rather than the calendar schedule.
- Suppliers of the production parts should be responsible for the prototypes of those parts. They may subcontract production of prototype

parts, but the production suppliers remain responsible for quality, performance, cost, and delivery of prototype parts.
• Parts used to manufacturer pilot vehicles should be made with production tools.

Over the course of several months, the C to C team applied these and other similar principles to define the major development milestones as well as the critical sequence of activities and patterns of responsibility. This architecture was then implemented step by step in ongoing programs and in all new efforts. Thus, once the process was defined, it was implemented in every program (and adapted to where the particular program was in its development): if a program had passed the first prototype stage, the C to C process was implemented for subsequent development activities; brand new programs were launched with the full-scale C to C process as their underlying structure.

The implementation of the C to C process was one step in a long evolutionary path in Ford's development organization. The C to C process envisioned strong cross-functional interaction and involvement throughout the development process in order to eliminate significant engineering changes and rework occasioned by poor communication and lack of shared understanding. Thus the implementation of the C to C process motivated and necessitated continual organizational change as Ford sought to formalize the team structure that grew out of the Taurus experience.

Creating Building Block Skills and Tools

In most development projects, there are a handful of critical activities that have an important influence on lead time, product quality, process reliability, and other important dimensions of project performance. For example, in some products, complex parts are manufactured using dies or molds that require a long time to design and manufacture. In situations such as these, a focused effort to substantially improve an organization's capability in executing that critical activity can often result in significant development performance improvement. Improving such critical activities often requires creating new or improved capability in basic tools and skills.

In early 1987, Eastman Kodak launched a new development project that necessitated exactly that kind of improved capability.[4] The project's intent was to develop a single-use 35 mm camera (originally called the Fling but subsequently renamed the FunSaver). The Fling project was in part a response to Fuji Film's introduction of the QuickSnap, a 35 mm single-use camera expected to be available in volume in the United States within six months. The challenge facing the Fling project was considerable: the camera needed to produce high quality images, be rugged and reliable, sell for a relatively low price, and be completed in less than forty weeks (similar Kodak projects generally took sixty-five to eighty weeks).

The Fling team determined that the only way to complete the project was to use computer-aided design (CAD) for the entire development effort. While Kodak had used CAD for individual parts, they had never done a complete camera design from start to finish with all of the parts on CAD. The challenge went further. Not only did all parts need to be designed on CAD, but CAD needed to be used in such a way as to facilitate the design and development of the long lead time tooling for the parts. Thus, the challenge for the Fling team was not only to develop the Fling, but also to create tools and a design process that would allow full utilization of CAD for all parts and would integrate parts and tooling design.

Since the traditional methods of engineering involving drawings were generally regarded by engineers as less demanding and easier to complete than a full-scale CAD-based design, the team needed to attract design engineers fully committed to the use of CAD and experienced in its intricacies. The team decided to use a Unigraphics CAD/CAM system originally developed by McDonnell Douglas for aeronautical design work. This was the third generation of CAD at Kodak, and a crucial objective of the design team was to make the CAD system user-friendly. Parts were designed by creating a series of objects such as points, lines, surfaces, and dimensions that described the part. Objects could be grouped logically in a layer, and layers could be worked on individually or overlaid to generate a single part, a subassembly, or the entire camera. The use of layers allowed engineers to see how their work and the resulting parts fit with other parts being designed by the system. It also facilitated the organization of control and change responsibility, with each layer being assigned to a single engineer who had control of change authorization. Engineers at any time could access all of the design layers in order to generate a picture of the integrated parts and subassemblies. In addition, different colors could be assigned to the layers to help differentiate them and provide perspective on how the particular part being designed fit into the overall camera.

A second major thrust of the team was to make sure that all engineers involved in the project—including design, tooling, and manufacturing—had access to the designs of all the parts. Of course, only the designer assigned control over a particular part could make final changes or additions to that design. Every night, however, all the work done by the design engineers on the project was uploaded to a central data bank. Once a design for a part was uploaded, everyone had access to it and could examine on a daily basis updated versions of the complete design.

This common database and the facility to view and examine the implications of design changes for other parts and components was an important element in achieving significant manufacturing involvement early in the design. Along with the assignment of a tool designer and manufacturing engineer to the Fling team, the ability the system provided them to examine the evolving design easily and quickly on a daily basis meant that it was easy for them to understand the preliminary versions of the design, to catch manufacturing problems early, and to add value to the design activities.

The new design system was also used for designing the molds used to fabricate the parts. The tooling designers first designed the components of the mold on the CAD system using the part design done by the product designers as a starting point. On the Fling project this step was simplified substantially by the up-front work done by the tooling designers in conjunction with the parts engineers. In addition, the user-friendly design system facilitated the tool designer's work by aligning the layers developed by the parts designer with the corresponding surface of the mold design. That system also made standard adjustments and was particularly crucial in catching design mistakes or inconsistencies.

In order to facilitate communication and ensure consistency and discipline in design, the Fling team used the CAD system to capture all design changes. When a tool designer needed a change in a part in order to simplify the tool or support recommended changes in processing, that change had to be completed by the part engineer in the CAD system. This approach was consistent with the Fling project team's view that CAD was a communications tool. Moreover, CAD made ambiguities in the design evident and simplified the process of achieving a shared perspective and understanding of the design of the part and the tools. While CAD generally involved more up-front work on the part of the designers, the team believed that there were substantial long-term benefits during this project and on future projects. In particular, the CAD system reduced substantially the time to design the molds. Tool fabrication itself was also improved because of the greater involvement of tool designers early in development through the CAD system. The Fling estimated that tool fabrication could be reduced from five weeks to one week with this system.

By developing a user-friendly CAD system, requiring that all parts be designed with it, and creating tooling design in conjunction with parts design, the Fling team effected a substantial reduction in the development cycle. In addition, the introduction of this new set of tools created significant opportunities for change in other aspects of the development process. Such changes included the creation of a strong team structure with shared responsibilities and significant up-front involvement of all critical functions.

A possible future change the team now envisions is sharply reducing the distinction between a product and tooling design engineer. It was evident to the Fling team that the CAD system made it possible for a single engineer to accomplish part design and tooling design on relatively simple parts. While there might be a need for specialization on very complex items, the great bulk of parts developed for the Fling and their respective tooling could have been combined and developed by a single engineer, assuming the engineer had received some training in both parts and tooling design. The prospect at Kodak is for significant improvements in productivity and lead time as the organization conducts additional training, gains experience in working on cross-functional teams, and further refines the CAD system and its application.

The Demonstration Project

The need to effect improvements in product development often coincides in an organization with the need for specific new products to deal with competitive threats or exploit a technical opportunity. In such circumstances organizations often find it attractive to launch what might be called a "demonstration project." Such a project is designed to teach the organization a new mode of development by employing new concepts directed at a specific product or process.

In the mid 1980s Hewlett Packard's Vancouver Division was faced with such a challenge.[5] With responsibility for HP's low-cost printing products, the division felt boxed in between low-cost impact printers developed by Japanese firms like Epson on the low end, and very expensive, high-speed printers using laser technology on the high end. With its market share and financial fortunes declining and its future in question, the division embarked on a bold strategy to deliver to the market a personal computer-based printer that would sell for less than $1,000 but would offer laser quality printing. At the same time the division desired to make a substantial improvement in the development process to achieve both reduced lead times and lower-cost manufacturing. The project, called DeskJet, was to be based on the introduction of an innovative technology—inkjet printing—in a low-cost, high-quality form for the first time.

Recognizing the ambitiousness of the program, the HP Vancouver Division created a core team at the outset and gave them a twofold mission. First, they were to design and develop a breakthrough product for the division. Second, they were to create a new development process, with significant emphasis on speed, design for manufacturability, and teamwork.

The DeskJet team was a true heavyweight team. It was one of the two major development projects in the division, and was managed by the head of R&D. In addition to having a core team including key individuals from all the major functions, at the working level critical R&D designers, mechanical and electrical engineers, software developers, and manufacturing personnel, as well as individuals from purchasing and quality control, were dedicated to the project and co-located. The combination of strong leadership, a cross-functional team at the core, and the creation of a co-located working-level group provided the organizational context in which a new development process became a reality.

In the beginning, the team focused on developing a clear and consistent product definition. They were substantially aided by well-defined targets. The strategy was to bring to market a personal printer that would sell for less than $1,000 but would offer laser quality printing. Because HP's proprietary inkjet technology had only been used in very expensive, high-end products, the DeskJet product required substantial technical development to create a print head and printing process that could be offered to the market at low cost. The product also needed to offer substantial improvements in reliability over previous HP products as well as create a platform for subsequent product generations.

The need for speed as well as the product strategy of high-quality printing at low cost, with high-volume production, called for significant integration of product and process development. In contrast to normal practice at HP, the team chose to develop the product and process designs simultaneously. Design for manufacturability (DFM) was a critical theme linking product and process designers. Working with their process colleagues, design engineers simplified the mechanical design of the product and substantially reduced the number of parts in manufacturing. In one famous example, product designers combined more than thirty parts to create a new complex part that made up the base of the printer and provided significant mechanical functions.

In addition to DFM, the team also focused on the creation of early production tools. By integrating tooling design with part design in the CAD system, the team was able to cut substantial time off mold design and mold making, thereby reducing lead time substantially. The discipline imposed within the project by the drive to get to production tools early was complemented and supported by a significant change in the prototyping process. The team scheduled prototype builds once per month during the development phases of the project in order to focus attention on objectives, provide timely feedback, and facilitate the convergence of marketing, engineering, and manufacturing activities and thinking.

Through strong leadership, teamwork, and significant technical development, the DeskJet project met with considerable success. The project was completed in a twenty-two-month cycle, compared to a thirty-six to sixty-month cycle for similar projects in the past. Given the significant technical development and manufacturing development required for the DeskJet, the twenty-two month cycle was even more remarkable. The DeskJet won the HP corporate award for the best R&D design in 1987, as well as the Datek Industry Award as Printer of the Year in 1988. Furthermore, the project achieved its basic goal of providing the market with laser quality printing on plain paper at under $1,000 and met with considerable financial success. It achieved more than double the margins of earlier products, and created sales volume substantially in excess of forecast. Finally, the DeskJet project became a model for subsequent development efforts, having "demonstrated" what was possible and how it could be achieved at HP Vancouver.

Building Capability: A Comparison of Alternatives

The four approaches or starting points for building development capability—development strategy, development process, skills and tools, and demonstration project—each bring different opportunities and risks. Moreover, while the approaches ultimately are focused on substantially improving development capabilities by creating new ways of working, they differ in their focus and sequence, and thus one may be preferred over another in different contexts. Exhibit 12–1 outlines various circumstances in which a particular approach may be selected, and suggests the opportunities and risks that accompany each approach.

In the case of creating a development strategy, for example, such an approach may be most appropriate where the product line is complex and changing and where the organization has experienced substantial increase in development requirements in the face of resource constraints. Starting the process of building new capability and development with a development strategy serves to focus existing resources and establish priorities. However, in order to succeed, it almost always requires that the organization reduce the total number of active projects. Failure to do so creates the risk that initially the organization will have a plan with no substance and no leverage for real improvement. A complementary discussion of context, opportunities, and risks applies to all three remaining approaches.

The discussion in Exhibit 12–1 suggests that the preferred context for a given approach is driven by the character of the opportunity the organization faces as well as its legacy of organizational capability and historical experience. The approach selected should both fill gaps in the organization and exploit opportunities with large payoffs. Introducing a company-wide development process, for example, is likely to be important when products are complex or the organization is large and has a

Eᴄʜɪʙɪᴛ 12–1

Comparison of Alternative Approaches to Creating Development Capability*

Approach	Context Where Approach May be Preferred	Opportunities	Risks
1. Creating a Development Strategy	• Complex, changing product line; many project opportunities • Increase in development requirements in the face of resource constraints	• Focus resources • Establish priorities (reduce projects)	• Failure to reduce number of projects hinders change • "Staff" planning exercise with no real substantive impact
2. Introducing Substantial Change to the Company-Wide Development Process	• Large organization, complex product line • Functional organization with history of sequential development	• Communicate new pattern to entire organization • Focal point for organizational energy	• Difficult to phase into ongoing projects • Adds bureaucracy to "cure" existing bureaucratic process
3. Establishing Building Block Tools and Skills	• Smaller companies or projects with history of teamwork • Fabricated parts where molds or dies are crucial	• Leverage change across many paths • Create fundamental change in way tasks are done	• Local optimization – build local skill but don't tie it to larger system • Technical (or commercial) sandbox
4. Pursuing a Demonstration Project	• Well-defined technical or market opportunity • Demand for significant development improvement for project success	• Organization sees integrated process in action • Identify challenges and problems quickly	• Project idiosyncratic – rest of organization doesn't learn • "Once and for all" mentality

* While a wide variety of approaches can be pursued in improving development capability, these four are perhaps most common. Based on the experience of dozens of firms, the opportunities and risks of each and the settings where they might be most appropriate are outlined.

history of sequential development. In that context, a new development process has significant leverage.

The risks that each of these approaches poses to an organization share common elements. In each case the challenge is to build from the starting point defined by the approach and to spread insight and understanding—as well as skill and capability—to other parts of the organization. That challenge is particularly evident in the case of building block tools and skills. If the new tools become nothing more than a set of toys for the technical or commerical personnel, the tools will not have their desired impact. Moreover, if they are introduced effectively at the local level but without attention to the complementary actions that need to be taken to make them effective within the overall development system, they likewise will have only a limited impact, and one likely to diminish with time. But this issue of spreading the effect of an approach and extending its reach applies also to an avenue for change that starts at the top. For example, introducing a new, company-wide development process can easily get bogged down in the creation of new bureaucracy and procedures rather than becoming a framework within which other supporting and complementary changes to the new process can occur. Likewise, a demonstration project can be nothing more than a single project, and may fail to teach the organization lessons that spread and extend its influence.

Creating New Development Capability: General Observations

The four approaches discussed in Exhibit 12–1 represent starting points in an organization's effort to create new development capability. Although the starting points are different, we recognize that they are the beginning of a series of changes that will, if successful, build support and momentum and pervade the development system. Management must recognize that selecting an initial approach does not mean that it will be sufficient on its own. Indeed, depending on the circumstances in the organization, it is likely that more than one of the approaches may eventually come into play as the organization proceeds on its journey to truly outstanding development capability. Although the starting points have different implications for the timing of activities and entail different implementation problems, it is useful to see them as part of a larger process of organizational change. Viewed in these terms, the four different approaches to building capability represent different starting points along a similar journey. In this section, we examine the common themes that characterize this journey.

The Path of New Capability

Whichever point an organization chooses to launch its effort in creating new capability, it must recognize that that effort is not a single step, but one of many along a path. In spite of the fact that the initial effort may involve a focused set of charges in the organization, successfully building development capability is not a matter of a single demonstration project or the introduction of new tools such as a CAD system ("We are going to improve development by introducing the XYZ CAD system"). If it is to succeed, the first effort must be followed by other changes and projects as the organization seeks to change the entire pattern of development.

This notion that building capability is a long-term process representing a path for development's evolution represents a significant change from traditional assumptions that most companies have made about the way one improves development. We compare this new concept with the traditional approach in Exhibit 12–2. In the conventional paradigm, indicated by the dashed line in the figure, managers seem to assume that development performance (here represented by cycle time on the project) can be improved by a step function process in which major changes in either procedures or systems are implemented at periodic points in time, bringing about significant improvement almost immediately. The actual pattern of change under these assumptions, however, is quite different.

As indicated by the solid line on the graph, changes in development procedures or systems are often precipitated by deterioration in performance. As lead time on development projects rises because of the addition of procedures to "catch" past mistakes, the absence of appropriate skills, or a failure to integrate across functions, senior management focuses on the need for change and improvement. But instead of making fundamental changes along a development path, the organization typically revises procedures, modifies checkpoints, or redefines subsequences of activities without addressing the real underlying problems. The result may be a modest improvement in performance which occurs almost immediately as the organization tries very hard to improve itself. As time goes on, however, the normal processes within the development system reassert themselves and the underlying problems surface once again. A repetition of this creates a sawtooth pattern of gradual deterioration followed by modest improvement and subsequent deterioration.

In organizations that substantially improve their development systems, we see a different pattern. The starting point for improvement in development performance may be any one of the four avenues that we have identified above, and may include other activities discussed in

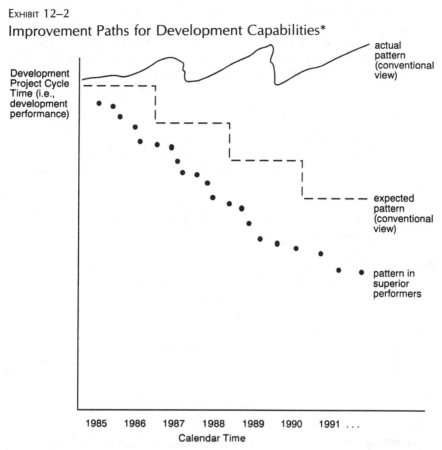

Exhibit 12–2

Improvement Paths for Development Capabilities*

Development Project Cycle Time (i.e., development performance)

actual pattern (conventional view)

expected pattern (conventional view)

pattern in superior performers

1985 1986 1987 1988 1989 1990 1991 . . .

Calendar Time

* Typically, firms envision an improvement path for product development that collects improvement ideas and periodically implements them. Unfortunately, the reality is that development processes often get encumbered over time until periodically they are simplified. Those firms that do achieve systematic improvement in development seem to do so on a continuous, incremental basis.

SOURCE: R. H. Hayes, S. C. Wheelwright, and K. B. Clark, *Dynamic Manufacturing* (New York: The Free Press, 1988), p. 337.

prior chapters. But what is striking about the high-performing organizations is the evolutionary, incremental, consistent, persistent improvement in performance in one project after another. In this approach, management focuses its attention on creating a context in which the initial starting point leads to learning and improvement, further understanding of the opportunities, and subsequent evolutionary changes in procedures that tighten, streamline, and make more effective the basic organization. Although at any one point in time the changes observed in the organization need not be radically different from previous practice, over a sustained period of time the organization not only takes on a very different character and builds a different set of capabilities, but also experiences dramatic performance improvements.

Competitive Benchmarking

Viewing the building of new development capability as a journey which is likely to extend over a significant period of time underscores the importance of fostering motivation and desire in the development organization. Managers can do several things to build this motivation and desire. Perhaps one of the most powerful levers managers can use is the process of *benchmarking* their organization against other similar organizations, thus building awareness of their competition.[6] Such efforts allow managers to channel a sense of rivalry and competition from the marketplace deep into the development organization. The effect is that individuals called on to make substantial changes in the way they work may see their efforts not in terms of some vague corporate goal, but rather in terms of very specific competitive realities. Subsequently, benchmarking against "best in class" may be especially helpful. This second type of benchmarking analysis identifies those who are best at some key aspect of development; not just from one's own industry, but from across all industries.

Benchmarking also has the effect of changing what people expect and what they see as possible. Particularly when an organization is confronted by the need to make major improvements in its process, the individuals who must bear the brunt of the change often go through a denial phase in which proposed targets for improvement (e.g., reducing development cycles or tooling lead times by 50 percent) are met with widespread skepticism and disbelief. To overcome this sense of "it can't be done," managers can use benchmarking to demonstrate that, indeed, it can be. Furthermore, benchmarking can often indicate exactly how one might go about making it happen. Establishing an external, dynamic base of reference through competitive benchmarking energizes the improvement process by giving it real-world "pull," not just the "push" of a few converted managers.

While recognizing that building capability is a path and will extend over a period of time, it is important that managers capitalize on their internal sources of insight and enthusiasm. This is likely to involve spotlighting important successes in the organization, conducting project audits in order to document improvements and learn from experience (see Chapter 11 for a discussion of project audits), and in general focusing management attention on the building process. An important element for achieving and maintaining such focus is measurement. Establishing measurements of development capability and performance that are credible may involve significant investment, but it will clarify what must be done and give an accurate idea of how the process has proceeded to date.

Building Capability Is a Development Process

Like the creation of a great product line or a significant series of outstanding manufacturing processes, building development capability occurs through a sequence of projects. Like new products and processes, building capability raises all of the questions about resource allocation, focus, capacity utilization, establishing an effective sequence of projects, priorities in development, concept leadership, and so forth. The implication is that the challenge of building capability requires a development strategy of its own. Such a development strategy for capability needs to include at least three kinds of efforts:

- *Building capability through product and process development projects.* Ongoing projects can often be a vehicle for introducing new skills or tools, and may be used as demonstration projects. Thus, as the organization creates its product or process development strategy, it needs to decide in which projects specific opportunities for improvement will be realized.
- *Independent efforts to build capability.* Outside of ongoing product and process development projects, the organization can undertake separate efforts to build new skills and tools, create new processes, and in general create new capability. For example, Ford's "concept to customer" process involved a significant effort on the part of a small team, working independently of ongoing development projects, to create a new development process. Development of CAD systems or rapid prototyping tools represents another type of separable project that builds capability. At some point, an organization must decide how to implement the capability developed in a specific product or process development project. But the creation of the capability itself may occur off-line in an independent effort.
- *Project audits.* As we emphasized in Chapter 11, project audits represent an opportunity for an organization to learn by experience. These ongoing efforts to identify opportunities for substantial change and improvement need to be coordinated with and linked to ongoing efforts in product or process development.

Taken together, a plan that lays out the organization's approach to these three kinds of efforts constitutes a kind of "development capability strategy." In addition to helping the organization focus its resources and establish priorities, the process of creating a capability strategy may help managers focus the organization's attention and communicate to the members of the organization the nature of the journey they have chosen to pursue. Thus, a capability strategy can also serve to improve identification, motivation, and desire within the organization.

Skills and Knowledge

Where it succeeds, a strategy for capability and a path for building capabilities does so because it increases the knowledge and skills of the individuals in the organization. Several kinds of knowledge and skills are crucial. In pre-project activities, for example, we have discussed in this book skills in creating strategic maps, building aggregate project plans, and creating a development strategy. To make these activities work, the people charged with their completion need to enhance their knowledge of the organization's market position, technologies, production processes, suppliers, and competitors. Moreover, they need to be educated in the fundamental principles that govern the creation of maps, development strategies, and aggregate project plans.

Within specific projects, we have identified many kinds of skills and knowledge that are essential to creating new development capability. Some are technical in nature, like those required to achieve effective product/process integration. Others are organizational, like those required to create a capability for managing heavyweight teams. Still others are commerical, like those required to develop effective product concepts and link customer requirements and unmet customer needs to the details of product planning and design.

The importance of personal knowledge and skills under any of the four approaches suggests that managers must pay close attention to the way in which individuals involved in building new capability are educated, trained, and endowed with requisite experience and perspective. First, the importance of skill and knowledge means that managers must carefully select the individuals who will lead those efforts and who will provide important guidance and input into the process. But since the building of capability is likely to occur over a period of time, it is essential that managers give attention to issues of career paths, education and training, and, in general, the development of human resources in the organization.

The issue of education and training is obvious when development improvement rests on the creation of new tools and techniques. If improvement and development involves introduction of a new CAD system, training people to use the system and educating them in the basic principles that govern its operation are straightforward. But other kinds of education are less obvious. For example, the introduction of joint product and process design requires the training of individuals in tech-

EXHIBIT 12–3
Skill and Knowledge Requirements for Improving
Development Performance

Development Participants	Skill or Knowledge Requirements		
	Technical	Organizational	Commercial
Senior Corporate Managers	Understand key technical changes	Recognize importance of creating a rapid learning organization; lead and provide vision	Identify strategic business opportunities
Business Unit General Managers	Understand depth and breadth of technology	Train and select leaders; champion cross-functional teams; adapt career pathing	Target key customer segments; architect product families and generations
Team Leaders	Provide breadth of capabilities; comprehend depth requirements	Select, train, and lead development team; recognize importance of attitudes and secure functional support	Champion concept definition; competitive positioning
Team Members	Use new tools and apply technologies	Integrate cross-functional problem solving; create improved development procedures	Operationalize customer-driven concept development; refine concept based on market feedback

niques of DFM and education in the principles underlying effective integrated problem solving. These principles have to do with attitudes as well as new skills and extend beyond the narrow technical tasks confronting the product and process designers. A theme that runs throughout this book is the need for project participants to add value to the work of others, as well as do their specific job.

In a similar way, management must endow its project leaders with the intuition, skill, and judgment required to play that role in development. Education is important in that process, but there is likely to be no substitute for experience in specific functions and activities. Thus, managers must look carefully at career paths for project leaders, providing both a range of functional assignments as well as a sequence of increasingly broad and challenging project assignments. Exhibit 12–3 summarizes many of the skills and much of the knowledge required for rapid, productive, high-quality developments.

Changing Behavior and Overcoming Obstacles

The path to superior development capability is often marked by potholes and other obstacles. Building capability requires change, not just in systems or procedures, but ultimately in individual behavior. A more integrated development process, new approaches to planning, new ways of conducting prototype cycles—all of the desired changes in an organization's development process—rest on changes in the way individuals do their work on a daily basis. Thus, the challenge is to build capability while creating processes that change behavior.

It is hard enough to define new modes of behavior in a completely new situation. In most companies, however, building new development capability occurs within an existing organization. That organization must support existing products and develop new ones while simultaneously reinventing itself; senior managers do not get to call "time out" and stop, regroup, and then start over. Change and the building of new capability must go on while the organization gets real work done.

Managers thus are confronted by an ongoing organization and its need for support and success, and by the need to motivate people to change their behavior to make a future desired organization happen. This combination of new and old poses significant challenges to building capability. Indeed, there are attitudes and practices that are effective "showstoppers." In Exhibit 12–4 we provide examples of showstoppers from different organizational levels and phases of development. The list is clearly incomplete. Indeed, if we were to try to list all of the showstoppers that one encounters in building development capability, we would need many pages. The intent here is to indicate the nature of obstacles likely to confront managers who embark on a path of improved capability.

Obstacles show up throughout the organization, but are probably most difficult and prevalent at the middle ranks. Take, for example, the problem of discipline in engineering. Often, improving development capability involves instilling a new sense of discipline within the engineering organization. In the case of a new emphasis on designing it right the first time, old practices of letting changes go until later in the development process are completely dysfunctional. As Quote 3 in Exhibit 12–4 makes clear, engineers often perceive that what their supervisors really care about are the old objectives like hitting release dates, even though the release will contain mistakes that the engineers know are there and could fix now, if they took the time to do it. Implicit in the problem is an underlying willingness on the part of supervisors and managers in the system to live with the consequences of failing to catch the changes early in the process. Those consequences include late engineering changes, delays in market introduction, and quality problems in the field. Years of experience in implementing quality programs in manufacturing have taught that unless the members of the organization are convinced that management really cares about the new approach— unless they see a match between the way management talks and the

EXHIBIT 12–4

Showstoppers: Examples of Obstacles to Building Development Capability*

	Symptoms	Function/Level of Organization	Issues/Obstacles
1.	I've asked Jerry [head of planning] to study this for us.	Senior management	Improvement as a staff responsibility
2.	You don't need to take me through the details, just give me the bottom line.	Senior management	Lack of knowledge at the top
3.	Look, forget the new procedure. What Jack cares about is hitting the release date. Let it go and we'll ECO it in pilot.	Engineering/ middle management	Lack of discipline/willingness to live with consequences
4.	Hey, don't tell the mechanical guys about this change. Just put it through. By the time we get to prototype, it'll be too late and they'll have to accept it.	Engineering/ middle management	Failure to accept responsibility/ adversarial relationships
5.	My people can't worry about training for new tools – we've got to get these drawings released by Wednesday.	Engineering/ middle management	Short term pressures/ time horizon
6.	Wait a minute – field service is completely overworked. There's no way I can free up someone to work on this project.	Field services/ middle management	Lack of resources
7.	That's design engineering's problem. It's not my job.	Process engineering/ working level	Poor understanding/ lack of incentives
8.	I have an idea that might work, but there's no way I'm saying anything. You know the old saying around here: the nail that sticks up gets hammered.	Manufacturing/ working level	Fear/lack of trust

* Numerous patterns of behavior, many of which are subtle and deeply ingrained, can be major impediments to improving development capabilities. Examples common to different organizational levels are shown here along with their representative symptom(s) and the challenges that must be addressed to overcome them.

actions they take—people will not change their behavior to make the tradeoffs called for by the new approach.

Like the problem of lack of discipline, obstacles at the working level may grow out of dysfunctional attitudes or perspectives. Take, for example, the last quote in Exhibit 12–4. The individual involved is dealing with one of the most important sources of leverage in building new development capability: individual initiative and creativity. But failure to take action here reflects a lack of trust in the actions of superiors and peers. It also suggests a fear that new ideas will be rejected. Such attitudes are especially critical in building development capability, because so much of what matters in creating outstanding performance involves the total pattern of activity—process, structure, skill, and decision making.

While senior management or even a team of individuals may lay down an effective architecture from the top, successful development of capability requires the concerted involvement, effort, and, in particular, initiative and creativity of people throughout the organization. Systematic efforts to learn and improve are, of course, important, but there must also be a broad, grassroots effort to refine, streamline, and make more effective. As we emphasized in Chapter 11, people in the organization must understand that learning is not just a nice thing to have, but an essential element of successful development. It is crucial, therefore, that managers embarking on a path of improvement and capability pay close attention to the critical interfaces where distrust may be present. They also need to take action to break down those barriers of distrust by transferring people across boundaries, establishing working teams so that people can build up relationships that will support trust, and taking extraordinary measures to encourage individual creativity.

These considerations suggest that attitudes may present important obstacles to building capability. But there are also systematic problems that have to do with incentives, information, and resource allocation. The sixth quote by the field service organization is typical. Support groups that are not directly involved in detailed engineering often find themselves with substantial new responsibilities, but no new resources to carry them out. Solving this problem often requires restructuring tasks in order to give the support organizations the time and energy to participate in the crucial up-front work that will make their work more effective later on. There also may be a need for investment in expanding the capacity of support organizations in order to achieve significant improvement in development. In a project we recently studied, a new product whose lifetime revenues for the company were expected to approach $500 million had been substantially delayed because of a shortage of critical resources (e.g., two mechanical engineers). Pressure to reduce costs through across-the-board head count reductions led to a management decision that was penny wise and pound foolish.

Systemic problems are also evident in Quotes 5 and 7. Effecting change requires an understanding of the incentives faced by the individuals whose behavior must change. Once again, managers must be sensitive to those aspects of their systems that get in the way of the kinds of changes the new capabilities require. The process engineer who says "that's not my job" when required to get involved early in the design phase of a product lacks information on the purpose of such involvement and incentives to undertake it. Indeed, what the engineer means is ". . . that it is not what I get paid for, that is not how I get rewarded, there is nothing in it for me." Unless individuals understand the value awaiting them in working within the new or improved approach, it will be a long uphill battle to bring about significant change. In fact, our experience has been that once product and manufacturing engineers get involved in working together in an integrated fashion, the benefits become apparent. If the atmosphere is right—if they have been trained and their understanding is accurate—getting involved creates opportunities for them to substantially improve their performance, the quality of their work, and the performance and quality of others' work. It also influences the quality of their lives at work.

Building Capability: Management Leadership

Sustained improvement in the ability to develop new products and processes provides significant advantage in the market place. Throughout this chapter, we have tried to develop a framework that will be useful in meeting the challenge of creating sustained improvement. Although there are many different starting points and means of launching a program of continuous improvement in development capability, successful efforts share common characteristics. Managers recognize in the first instance that building capability is a journey, not a destination. The critical problem is to chart a path and sequence of efforts over time that will address the organization's opportunities and needs effectively. Because superior performance requires attention to many different elements that cut across functions, disciplines, and organizations, sustained improvement requires fundamental change in the entire pattern of product and process development. That change involves systems, procedures, and organizational structure, and also includes the skills and behavior of key individuals involved in the process.

Since product and process development touch much of what a company does, and since sustained and fundamental change must be pervasive to be effective, management leadership is a critical determinant of success. The importance of management leadership has long been recognized in academic studies of organizational change and in the popular press, but leadership may take many forms. In our study of building product and process development capability, we have seen managers approach development improvement in several ways. We organize our observations below into three modes of management leadership that represent different objectives, styles, and perspectives on the role of development in competition.

- *Mode One: Seek relief.* In the first mode—what we call "seek relief"— senior managers look to product development to solve short-term problems in their markets. Change in this mode focuses on the product itself, not the development process. Leadership in Mode One often appears bold and decisive: senior managers may direct an overhaul of a product's image in the marketplace through redesign, or may develop an entirely new product line through acquisition (suitably trumpeted as a move filled with synergy and decisiveness); management may effect a repositioning of the product through the addition of new technology and features. In the short term such moves may have considerable impact, but because Mode One behavior does not focus on the underlying process of development, it does not deal with an organization's basic capability. Its focus is fundamentally short term and its impact on competitive position is unlikely to be lasting.

- *Mode Two: Close the gap.* In the second mode, managers define the problem they confront—and, therefore, the opportunity they face—in terms of a gap between their own and important competitors' performance. Comparisons with competitors, particularly those with outstanding capability, can provide managers with important information about how to focus attention and energy. Leadership in this mode often recognizes the importance of making fundamental change in development, but does so within the framework established by competitive comparisons. Any number of changes may be identified in such an analysis. Managers may focus on the introduction of a new CAD system, installing new approaches to managing teams and development, or launching an educational program to establish new directions for the organization. Compared to the "seek relief" mode, Mode Two has a number of advantages: It gets at important underlying issues and builds new capability. Leadership in this model is substantive. Managers focus on changing the organization's capacity to act in ways that will make it more effective relative to its competitors. It misses, however, some of the important long-term benefits that come when senior management understands that product and process development capability can be the basis for distinctive advantage.

- *Mode Three: Competitive advantage.* The hallmark of Mode Three is its focus on building lasting advantage in development. Managers operating in Mode Three, therefore, keep the entire horizon—both long and short term—within their purview. They recognize the importance of making immediate changes that will begin to change the organization's competitive position. They also recognize the importance of making those changes in a way that will be lasting and fundamental. They see product development as an integral part of business strategy, and recognize that building outstanding development capability can reinforce and capitalize on the things the firm does well. In doing so, development becomes a source of advantage in itself. Leadership in Mode Three is truly substantive. Managers focus not only on how work gets done, but also on helping the organization discover what new things it needs to do to be successful. While leaders operating in

Mode Two focus on adding a capability to close a gap with competitors, leaders in Mode Three rethink the organization's approach to development and create a gap that competitors may not have considered. Leaders in Mode Two may do established things better, but leaders in Mode Three concentrate on doing new things better.

While senior managers in Mode Three may do many of the things that their counterparts in Modes One and Two do (redesign products, make acquisitions, fill gaps in CAD systems, or modify organizational structure), they do so with a broad comprehensive focus. The leadership they exercise focuses on the expansive vision of what the organization ought to become in the future as well as on the substantive details of everyday work in development. In this context, effective leaders pay careful attention to both the whole and the part. The successful building of capability over a long period of time is a matter of consistency between detailed actions and the overall pattern and direction of the new development process. Creating and ensuring depth of consistency is not something even a powerful senior manager can do alone, however. Everyone involved in the development process—from the senior executive to the most recently hired bench-level engineer—must share an understanding of the overall pattern of development the organization seeks. Like a great orchestra conductor, senior managers charged with the challenge of building long-term development capability must offer the organization a powerful and compelling vision or "score" of the development future, and then direct the timing and nature of contributions of others, "bringing them in" at the appropriate time.

With a clear understanding of the development pattern that the organization seeks, senior managers can move to help the organization translate that pattern into projects designed to build specific kinds of capabilities. Moreover, their support of that effort must include actions to help solve particular problems. In this sense, effective managerial leadership is much more than encouragement. Senior managers must supply critical energy and focus for the organization's search for new capability. They not only coach and counsel with key individuals, but also help define principles and then move to educate the organization in their application.

Leadership that offers a compelling vision of the new development path—that provides energy and momentum to the organization; encourages, coaches, and supports; develops substantive principles and teaches them to the organization; and helps apply those principles in solving problems—is the kind of leadership essential to building development capability.

Study Questions

1. What are the major benefits of each of the four approaches—creating a development strategy, changing the development process, creating building block skills and tools, and the demonstration project—used as starting points for building development capability? How are the benefits likely to show up in the situations described at Physio Control, Ford Motor Company, Eastman Kodak, and HP Vancouver?

2. What are the major pitfalls in each of the four approaches to building development capability? How might they be minimized and overcome?

3. The demonstration project is a particularly common approach in focusing attention on improving development capability. Using the Motorola Bandit pager (Chapter 10) and HP Vancouver DeskJet (this chapter) as examples, why do you think the demonstration approach was chosen in each situation? What issues do you think management encountered when it sought to pass the lessons learned on these demonstration projects on to subsequent projects and to other parts of the organization?

4. For most organizations, competitive benchmarking is a hot, new concept and tool—not only in the area of development capability, but in other areas of functional excellence. What difficulties might a firm encounter in seeking to apply competitive benchmarking with regard to product and process development activities? Why? How might those difficulties be overcome?

5. If building development capability is itself viewed as a development process, how might the lessons of the first eleven chapters be applied to the process? For example, what kind of pre-project planning might be done? How might it be made a cross-functional effort? How might management organize and lead such an effort? What type of design-build-test cycles might be structured and applied?

6. Outline two approaches that a company might use to build technical, organizational, and commercial skills at each of the four human resource levels identified in Exhibit 12–3. Be specific as to who would be involved, what would be entailed, and the results expected.

Eli Lilly and Company: Manufacturing Process Technology Strategy (1991)

In October 1991, Joe Cook, vice president of Production Operations and Engineering at Eli Lilly and Company, leaned back in his chair to collect his thoughts before the upcoming Manufacturing Strategy Committee meeting. Cook believed that manufacturing could play a greater role in reinforcing Lilly's competitive position in the pharmaceutical industry. Among several appealing possibilities, he was most drawn to a program aimed at upgrading Lilly's manufacturing process technology.

The environment for making such a proposal at Lilly was encouraging: for three decades Lilly's revenue had consistently expanded, but 1990 had broken old records. Pharmaceutical sales jumped 26%, the highest rate in 34 years. Net income had climbed 20% and earnings per share were up 22%. To support this growth, capital expenditure, mostly for manufacturing, had been boosted by 82%, following a 49% increase in 1989.

Nevertheless, the committee could choose among many potentially lucrative investments, including more product R&D. Along with marketing, R&D was regarded as the linchpin of corporate strategy in most pharmaceutical companies; generally, senior management had either science or marketing backgrounds. In 1990, Lilly increased R&D expenditures by 16%, to 13.5% of sales, following an 18% increase in 1989. Manufacturing's traditional focus had been on providing sufficient capacity and developing better sourcing strategies. Cook's proposal regarding process technology, therefore, would have to be backed by persuasive evidence to win support over competing opportunities.

Background

Colonel Eli Lilly founded Eli Lilly and Company in 1876 with total capital of $1,400 and four employees, including his 14-year-old son, Josiah. Defying then-standard practice, Colonel Lilly sought to make medicine according to recognized scientific criteria: precise formulation, accurate compounding, standardization by assay, full disclosure of ingredients on the label, and honest claims.

The formula was successful. The company rapidly became a leader in the pharmaceutical industry, and 115 years later was the second-largest pharmaceutical concern in the United States and the eighth-largest worldwide. Its prosperity had long been based on a combination of strong research and careful management. A scientific division was formed in 1886, and a department of experimental medicine in 1912. Generations of the Lilly family promoted sound planning and fair treatment of personnel. Growth had sprung from internal development improvements and expansion, with modest diversification in technology areas related to the basic core strengths. All expansion was financed solely from within the company.

In 1991, Lilly, with headquarters in Indianapolis, Indiana, sold a broad line of human health care and agricultural products. It was committed to all essential aspects of the industry: discovery, development, manufacture, and marketing. Over one-third of its 1990 sales came from outside the United States: the company manufactured and distributed its products in 25 other countries and sold them in more than 110 countries. Pharmaceuticals accounted for 71% of total sales in 1990, while medical devices and diagnostics (19%) and animal products contributed the rest. Exhibits 1A and 1B outline recent financial results.

Ten Lilly pharmaceuticals sold more than $100 million each in 1990. Lilly's Ceclor™, the world's number-one selling antibiotic, saw a sales increase in 1990 alone of $100 million. Prozac™, the world's top-selling antidepressant, was introduced in 1988 and rapidly became one of the company's top-selling drugs. In its first year on the market, Prozac's sales topped $100 million, faster growth than any other product in Lilly's history. Humulin™, human insulin (and the world's first marketed human health care product based on recombinant DNA technology), was the company's third-largest seller.

The pharmaceutical industry was the most profitable sector of the U.S economy. Returns on equity had long been 50% higher than the median

Exhibit 1A

Balance Sheet ($ millions at December 31)

Assets	1990	1989
Current Assets		
Cash and equivalents	$ 350.2	$ 323.0
Short-term investments	$ 400.6	$ 329.0
Accounts Receivable	$ 770.7	$ 732.1
Other Receivables	$ 108.0	$ 113.7
Inventories	$ 673.0	$ 599.5
Prepaid expenses	$ 198.8	$ 177.1
Total current assets	$2,501.3	$2,274.4
Other Assets		
Investments	$ 480.7	$ 530.8
Goodwill & intangibles	$ 469.1	$ 453.6
Sundry	$ 755.0	$ 474.6
Property & Equipment (net of depreciation)	$2,936.7	$2,114.6
Total	$7,142.8	$5,848.0
Liabilities and Equity		
Current Liabilities		
Short-term borrowings[1]	$1,239.5	$ 134.0
Accounts payable	$ 259.9	$ 196.2
Employee compensation	$ 367.7	$ 290.9
Dividends payable	$ 143.8	$ 115.5
Other liabilities	$ 406.7	$ 323.1
Income taxes payable	$ 400.0	$ 269.1
Total current liabilities	$2,817.6	$1,328.8
Long-term debt	$ 277.0	$ 269.5
Deferred income taxes	$ 351.2	$ 300.4
Other liabilities	$ 229.5	$ 192.2
Shareholders' Equity		
Common stock	$ 177.6	$ 176.8
Retained earnings	$4,548.7	$4,065.4
Loan to ESOP	($ 109.9)	($ 122.9)
Currency adjustments	$ 28.6	($ 53.9)
Less common shares in treasury	($1,177.5)	($ 308.3)
Total	$7,142.8	$5,848.0

SOURCE: Eli Lilly and Company, 1990 Annual Report.

[1] The 1990 increase in short term borrowing was directly related to a special $1 billion share-and-warrant repurchase program announced and completed in 1990 as part of the terms associated with Lilly's earlier acquisition of Hybritech.

EXHIBIT 1B

Income Statement and Selected Ratios ($ millions at December 31)

Income Statement	1990	1989	1988
Net Sales	$5,1919.6	$4,175.6	$3,607.4
Cost of Sales	$ 1,523.3	$1,255.8	$1,125.3
Research and development	$ 702.7	$ 605.4	$ 511.6
Marketing and administrative3	$ 1,426.2	$1,149.6	$1,019.5
	$ 3,652.2	$3,010.8	$2,656.4
Operating income	$ 1,539.4	$1,164.8	$ 951.0
Other income (net)	$ 59.6	$ 165.1	$ 129.7
Income before taxes	$ 1,599.0	$1,329.9	$1,080.7
Income taxes	$ 471.7	$ 390.4	$ 319.7
Net Income	$ 1,127.3	$ 939.5	$ 761.0
Selected Financial Ratios and Other Data			
Net income (% of sales)	21.7	22.5	21.1
R&D (% of sales)	13.5	14.5	14.2
Return on shareholders equity (%)	31.2	26.9	24.3
Return on assets (%)	17.5	17.0	14.8
Long-term debt (% of equity)	8.0	7.2	12.0
Number of employees	29,900	28,200	26,700
Net sales per employee (thousands)	$ 173.6	$ 148.1	$ 135.1
Net income per employee (thousands)	$ 37.7	$ 33.3	$ 28.5
Capital Expenditures	$ 1,007.3	$ 554.5	$ 372.1
Earnings per share	$ 3.90	$ 3.20	$ 2.67

SOURCE: Eli Lilly and Company, 1990 Annual Report.

for the *Fortune* 500 and in the 1980s the gap had widened. Profits for most major drug companies surged in that decade, as world markets expanded and prices rose. In 1990, world pharmaceutical sales totaled $174 billion (U.S. sales were more than $50 billion), an increase of 14% over 1989, continuing a compound annual growth rate of more than 10% throughout the 1980s. Pharmaceutical sales in Europe had grown by 28% in 1990 alone. Between them, North America and Europe accounted for 61% of the total; Japan made up a further 25%.

Market expansion was expected to continue at 7.9% per year, adjusted for inflation, through the mid–1990s. People around the world were living longer and desired more and better health care. In 1990, 13% of the U.S. population was 65 or older, up by more than 10 million people since 1950, and other developed countries showed similar trends. Typically, people over 65 required three or four times more medical support than younger people. In addition, developments in medical technology, including recombinant DNA and monoclonal antibodies, were yielding entirely new approaches to diagnosis and treatment and were expected to produce a mounting flow of new products.

Lilly's major competitors in North America included Merck, Bristol Myers-Squibb, American Home Products, Johnson and Johnson, and Pfizer. Worldwide, the largest non-American firms were European, including Ciba-Geigy, Hoechst, Glaxo, Bayer, and SmithKline-Beecham. Most of these had enjoyed growth rates comparable to or better than Lilly's. United States-based firms accounted for 42% of world sales in 1990.

Companies in the pharmaceutical industry vied to be first to market, especially when another firm was working on a similar product. Competitors had a minimum two years' notice of imminent new drugs, because New Drug Applications (NDAs) filed with the Food and Drug Authority took at least that long to gain an approval status. In addition, the first years of a drug's life often determined its long-term success. If a company could establish its product firmly in the minds of doctors before another hit the market, the follow-on products would have a more difficult product launch. Moreover, maintaining a reputation as industry leader was vital to attracting people, as well as to winning the confidence of doctors and establishing credibility in academia and in government circles. The key was to be seen as consistently producing quality products and undertaking leading-edge research.

Companies also competed vigorously with sales calls to doctors. In the 1980s, the number of pharmaceutical sales representatives employed by U.S. companies increased by 50%. Some companies maintained three or four sales teams in each region, so that each product could be fully represented to physicians. Pharmaceutical sales representatives often were highly trained; many were licensed pharmacists. Drug companies, however, rarely competed on price, except occasionally when confronted with generic substitutes.

Firms specialized in different kinds of drugs, or in different therapeutic classes, which allowed for some segmentation of the industry and reduced the threat of price competition. Lilly, for example, concentrated on insulin and antibiotics. This enabled it to develop strong links with particular universities and other centers of research. Specialization also improved the chance that new drugs in that therapeutic group would be widely accepted.

Industry Trends in the 1980s

Along with higher sales and profits, the 1980s brought important changes in the competitive environment facing Lilly and other pharmaceutical companies. Many at Lilly felt that the company's response to these shifts could determine its fate in coming years.

Globalization

Increasingly affluent—and aging—populations in the developed countries meant new customers for health care providers. National differences in health care markets were disappearing as most major medical problems were found worldwide. In addition, government regulators were beginning to communicate and coordinate their evaluation procedures. The European Community, for example, was developing an application procedure that would accelerate approval in European national markets. While this trend could expand the number of buyers, falling trade barriers could reduce prices to the lowest levels in Europe.

Rising development costs also spurred many pharmaceutical companies to seek larger markets. Complicated government approval and testing procedures drove up the cost of drug development. At the end of the 1980s, companies needed 8 to 12 years between discovery of a compound and the launch date of a commercial product. The number of patient trials required prior to FDA release for a typical drug had risen from 1,500 in 1980 to 10,000 in 1990. Average development costs per product had risen to an estimated $250 million, which included the considerable research and overhead outlays for the thousands of compounds that did *not* make it to the market.

Slower Rates of Innovation

By the mid–1980s, only one-third as many new products were introduced each year as had been during the 1950s. Although stricter regulatory requirements were partly responsible, some people argued that the pace of innovation had slowed, as researchers found it increasingly difficult to identify promising new drugs. Industry experts estimated that only one of every 5,000 to 10,000 new chemical compounds discovered by researchers ever became a commercial product.

Government Involvement

In the 1990s, two forces seemed likely to push prices and profits lower. First, governments were becoming more interventionist. By 1991, the

United States was one of only a few developed countries that did not significantly intervene in the free market system. Escalating medical costs in many countries sparked new calls for cost containment. Price controls, restrictive reimbursement schemes, managed health care programs, and greater government involvement in medical and pharmaceutical reimbursement, especially for the elderly, poor, and uninsured, threatened to squeeze margins. In 1991, half of U.S. prescription users had part of their costs paid by a third party, up from only 25% five years earlier.

At the same time, the public in many countries was demanding higher standards of environmental and product safety. Governments insisted on ever-tighter systems to prevent environmental contamination and reduce the risk of dangerous or contaminated drugs reaching consumers. In the United States, Food and Drug Administration (FDA) officials had to approve any change to the manufacturing process that might affect the product.

Meeting these new standards often required major investments. In August 1989, the FDA inspected one of Lilly's tablet and capsule manufacturing facilities at Indianapolis and mandated a substantial overhaul of operating procedures and documentation systems. Lilly estimated that several hundred new employees and over $70 million of capital expenditures had been needed to ensure that the new requirements were met throughout the company.

Shorter Product Lifecycle

The second force threatening to hold down prices was intensifying competition from generic drugs introduced after patents expired. In 1984, the U.S. Congress passed the Drug Price Competition and Patent Restoration Act, which enabled generic manufacturers to gain accelerated approval for their products; generic copies of many drugs could now be made available almost literally on the day the patent expired, depending upon how long the approval process for particular drugs had taken. In 1990, patents expired on drugs with annual worldwide sales of about $363 million. In 1991, $541 million worth of sales would go off patent, and in 1992 and 1993, the figures were expected to rise to $1.9 billion and $2.6 billion, respectively. Major generic competitors included Abbott Laboratories, Warner-Lambert, and American Cyanamid, as well as numerous smaller firms.

Patents ran from the date of issue, which preceded much of the approval process, and came some years before market launch. Therefore, the profit secured from new drugs was, even more than in the past, a function of how long firms could fully harvest their patents. Speed to market and manufacturing ramp-up could be critical to extending that period. Moreover, most companies could charge higher prices during the initial years of their patents, when they often faced little real competition.

These trends, coupled with more sophisticated and complex manufacturing processes, had increased the minimum-efficient scale of a new bulk active ingredient plant (the initial bulk material production step in most pharmaceutical products). Company officials estimated that the average capital commitment needed for a new bulk chemical site had increased from $200 million to $400 million during the 1980s. Moreover, the time line for building such a plant was lengthened by two years. It was estimated that these trends would continue to escalate in the 1990s and beyond.

Creating Pharmaceutical Products and Processes

While the procedures for getting a new drug to market could vary significantly by product type, all went through three basic stages: development (including gaining regulatory approval), bulk manufacturing, and fill and finish operations. Exhibit 2 indicates a typical schedule for these tasks at Lilly. Each stage had distinct economics and offered different opportunities for performance improvement.

- *Development* took place mostly between the discovery of a promising compound and its market launch.

  Following pre-clinical work, in which chemicals were tested only on animals, clinical trails were done in three phases. Phase I of testing demonstrated that the drugs were safe for humans at recommended dosage levels. Phase II attempted to show that the drug actually worked in the specific application claimed for it. Phase III simultaneously tested the safety and efficacy of the drug, more thoroughly and in larger patient populations than the first two phases.

  When scientists initially explored and tested new drugs, they needed only very small amounts of that compound, which were generally produced using small-scale laboratory technologies. As potential compounds moved into clinical trials, larger volumes were needed, and process development was required to help produce these volumes. Development thus was also responsible for:

  1. Defining the process for manufacture of the bulk active ingredients and scaling it up for production volumes in time for product launch.
  2. Designing the final dosage form of a compound (capsule, tablet,

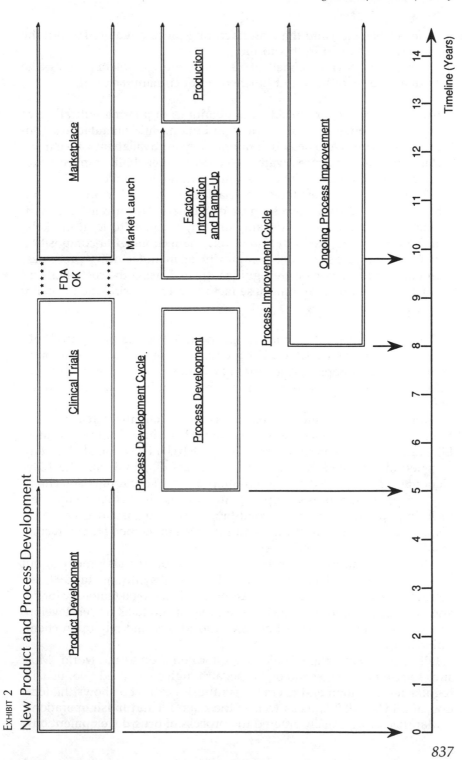

Exhibit 2
New Product and Process Development

Product Development

Clinical Trials

Marketplace

Production

FDA
OK

Market Launch

Process Development Cycle

Process Development

Factory
Introduction
and Ramp-Up

Process Improvement Cycle

Ongoing Process Improvement

Timeline (Years)

0   1   2   3   4   5   6   7   8   9   10   11   12   13   14

837

injectable, etc.) and the manufacturing process required to put the active ingredient in this form.
3. Ongoing activities aimed at reducing the cost of improving the quality of both bulk and finished product manufacturing.

- *Bulk manufacturing* produced large quantities of pharmaceutical active ingredients, often for worldwide distribution. Bulk manufacturing location decisions were heavily influenced by the availability of technical staff, the infrastructure (water, electricity, fuel, bulk transport) required for large-scale bulk operations, and tax incentives.
- *Fill and finish operations* took materials from the bulk plants and put them into the dosage form seen by consumers. Historically, the manufacturing facilities were usually smaller, oriented to local markets, and more flexible. Recently, however, the technological composition of newer products, greater complexity of manufacturing processes, and tighter regulations were significantly increasing the cost of fill and finish facilities. In addition, these factors were reducing the flexibility to make process changes.

The technology used to make drugs in the 1990s had progressed substantially from that available a decade before. Three separate (although occasionally overlapping) categories of technique were now available for bulk manufacturing: fermentation, chemical synthesis, and biotechnology.

Some compounds, such as insulin, could be manufactured by more than one of the processes and various firms had chosen different routes. Lilly (along with a biotech partner, Genentech) had developed Humulin, a genetically engineered form of human insulin, in 1978. The Lilly-Genentech process used genetically altered bacteria (through biotechnology) to produce a precise copy of human insulin. Other companies, including Novo Industri, the second-biggest seller of insulin, chose to develop and refine manufacturing and purification methods for extracting insulin from a yeast-based process.

Lilly utilized all three process technologies for various products, but was shifting toward biotechnology and chemical synthesis. In 1990, fermentation accounted for 25% of existing products, biotechnology for 7% and chemical synthesis for 68%. However, of products under development, 15% would use biotechnology, and 81% would rely upon chemical synthesis.

Lilly's manufacturing facilities were located around the world. Most sites focused on one technology type, although some used two, usually regular fermentation and chemical synthesis. Exhibit 3 shows the location of Lilly's bulk plants as well as the main fill and finish operations.

Manufacturing usually entered the process of drug development only

EXHIBIT 3

Manufacturing Plant Locations*

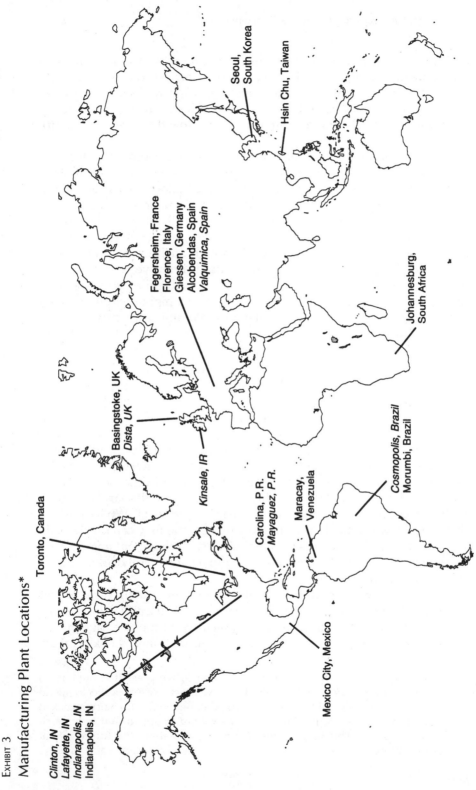

Clinton, IN
Lafayette, IN
Indianapolis, IN
Indianapolis, IN

Toronto, Canada

Basingstoke, UK
Dista, UK

Kinsale, IR

Fegersheim, France
Florence, Italy
Giessen, Germany
Alcobendas, Spain
Valquimica, Spain

Seoul,
South Korea

Hsin Chu, Taiwan

Johannesburg,
South Africa

Carolina, P.R.
Mayaguez, P.R.

Maracay,
Venezuela

Cosmopolis, Brazil
Morumbi, Brazil

Mexico City, Mexico

* Bulk chemical manufacturing facilities *underlined*. All others are fill and finish operations only.

after researchers had decided that the company should seek approval to market a new compound. This was partly because Lilly's decision to proceed with a potential product usually did not rely solely on manufacturing cost estimates, and partly a result of R&D's belief that any such involvement would constrain innovation and slow the development process.

While developing and scaling-up manufacturing processes for new drugs was the most exciting work done by Lilly's process technology group, improving existing manufacturing technologies was equally important. Typical improvements included combining or substituting steps in a production sequence, changing catalysts and solvents, developing additional process controls and control points, and refining parameter settings and operating procedures. Although such changes almost always required FDA approval, they could improve yields, reduce throughput times, eliminate costly inputs and solvent recycling requirements, increase quality, and achieve significantly higher output, thereby reducing or eliminating the need for additional capital-intensive production capacity.

Manufacturing at Lilly

During the 1980s, manufacturing priorities at Lilly had evolved through three phases. In the early and mid–1980s, the cost of idle plant was a continuing topic of senior management discussion and steps were taken to balance capacity. In the second half of the 1980s, however, rising sales for several products (Humulin, Prozac, Ceclor, and others) shifted the focus to growth. Capital expenditures were boosted sharply to cope with burgeoning demand for the company's products. While much of this capacity was added at existing plant sites, the new capacity usually involved different processes or more advanced equipment and thus required major new investment and substantial conversion of older equipment and facilities.

At the same time, strategic planning became increasingly important. An interesting question from Lilly's chairman, Richard D. Wood, at an August 1987 meeting of the company's executive committee triggered an intensive study of Lilly's past manufacturing planning. Cook recalled:

> Just after I took over my current responsibilities, we presented our capital budget for the year, carefully describing how much we proposed to spend and how the funds would be used. During the meeting, our chairman asked an interesting question: not how much we *wanted* to spend, but how much *should* we spend? This began a broader discussion about the future role of manufacturing at Lilly.

The company realized it had given manufacturing's contribution a relatively lower weight in corporate strategic thinking. To remedy that deficiency, management looked at where and how capital investments had been made in the past and concluded that key manufacturing decisions had mostly been reactive; immediate needs had predominated over long-term coordinated planning. One result was that critical manufacturing technologies were spread across numerous smaller-scale plants, rather than concentrated on key world-scale plants. Another was that manufacturing had not been able to coordinate fully its activities with other functions. This was thought to have resulted in significant lost opportunities—both in developing manufacturing processes for new drugs and improving existing processes.

Lilly's management also commissioned a consulting study to investigate the potential value manufacturing could add to the firm. The study concluded that more process development should take place earlier in the product life-cycle, preferably before Phase III trails, rather than after the decision had been made to introduce the product. Traditional thinking held that since 80% of pharmaceutical products failed to make it to market, spending more than the bare minimum needed to gain FDA approval would be a waste.

In late 1988 Lilly formed a Manufacturing Strategy Committee to help establish global manufacturing policies. The committee included top executives from manufacturing, engineering, R&D (development), marketing, finance, personnel, and international. The committee was to consider all aspects of manufacturing planning and their implications for the corporation as a whole, including human resource planning, process development, technology deployment, sourcing, capital investment, and vertical integration. (See Exhibit 4.)

By mid–1991, most committee members were confident that improvements in manufacturing could add substantially to the company's competitive position. However, even Lilly did not possess unlimited resources. A good strategy for manufacturing needed to sort out which options for improvement offered the greatest promise, long term as well as short term. It was decided that picking a central theme might provide the focus and leverage needed to energize Lilly's manufacturing strategy for at least the next five years.

Lilly's senior manufacturing managers were attracted to process development and improvement as a focal point for several reasons. *First,* if greater improvements in existing processes could be made, then the economic benefits of lower costs could be used to fund more new products and/or to maintain a strong market (and profit) position on mature products even after patent expiration.

Second, substantial process improvements achieved in the early years of a strong, new product would lead to two types of payoffs. One would

Exhibit 4

Manufacturing Strategy Committee (1988)

Manufacturing Vision

The Lilly manufacturing organization will provide a market advantage for the company by satisfying customer's requirements through recognized leadership and innovation in the worldwide development, production, and distribution of the highest quality products and services.

Manufacturing Strategy Committee Charter

- Serves as a focal point for all strategic manufacturing activities
- Coordinates, reviews, approves, and implements multiyear business planning
- Provides global direction for:
    - —Capital investments
    - —Human resources
    - —Sourcing
    - —Vertical integration
    - —Technology management

Membership—All Senior Executives

Manufacturing
Engineering
R&D (Development)
Marketing
Finance
Personnel
International

---

be higher margins as a result of lower costs and greater volumes. The other would be lower capital investment requirements. Better technology might allow more flexibility, reduced cycle time, and/or improved yields, with important implications for the amount of capability needed. Cook's staff had estimated that even a fraction of a percent increase in the overall yield of final bulk product in a typical manufacturing process could save $5 million of capital cost.

Even more important was the impact that process improvement could have on the total capital invested in a major new drug at its peak demand. Because market adoption for a new drug took time, even a very successful new product didn't reach its peak capacity volume until five or six years following introduction. Anything that could be done in those initial years to develop a less capital intensive process technology or to increase the effective output of the existing process technology (by improving yields or cycle times, for example) could significantly reduce the peak year's investment in capacity.

In the bulk chemical processing stage of most drug products, the basic unit of capacity planning was the standard chemical "rig"—or tankage that could produce 2,000 gallon batches. Although the cost of a new site varied widely, depending on the number of rigs to be included in that plant location, the type and complexity of the process technology to be employed, and so forth, Lilly estimated that an "average" rig of capacity cost about $40 million in 1991. In recent years, some of Lilly's very successful drugs had required 4 to 6 rigs in their peak year. Thus, improvements that reduced the peak requirement by 20% to 30%—something that Cook's staff considered quite possible—would have a big payoff.

Third, if Lilly's process development group could increase its ability to fully participate in the early stages of product development, there could be substantial payoff. Not only could product development be steered toward more effective and efficient process technologies, but the product required for clinical tests could be produced more quickly. Since production would be done with a process closer to that to be used for volume manufacturing, the entire FDA approval process might be shortened and the new product approved for introduction sooner. In the pharmaceutical industry, a few months head start in the market could be worth tens of millions of dollars of pretax profit.

In addition, more knowledge in process improvement would reduce the risk of failure in the critical early years of a patent. And, if Lilly could develop advanced proprietary technology it might be able not only to cut costs, but to reduce them in ways that would be more difficult for other companies to duplicate. In other words, Lilly might be able to achieve higher profit margins than other drugmakers, out of similar products. Developing proprietary technology also might permit more effective competition with generic manufacturers. Finally, if Lilly developed the capability to manufacture to very high environmental standards, it could meet new standards both more cheaply and more quickly than other firms.

Developing a Strategy for Process Technology

While the payoff from developing and improving process technology was significant, the benefits would be neither easy to obtain nor cheap. Senior management would not be likely to commit substantial corporate resources to manufacturing and process technology unless it could be convinced that the returns gained would be greater than those promised by other kinds of investment.

In order to provide the Manufacturing Strategy Committee with solid data and analyses, Cook wanted to put together specific illustrations of each of the three types of process technology efforts that had been identified. In addition, while he hoped that all three might eventually become central elements in Lilly's manufacturing strategy, he knew that senior management would probably initially agree to only one of them. By working through an illustration of each type, he thought the committee would be helped in deciding which to recommend.

As a starting point, he outlined what he considered the essence of each option:

- *Option 1: Improve the manufacturing process for a successful product that is already on the market.* This could be a product facing new price pressure from generics because of anticipated patent expiration, or a product for which lower prices could win greater market share. Typical of this option would be a product already on the market for five years and with four years remaining before patent expiration. (Such a product would have been patented long before market introduction.)
- *Option 2: Commit to process improvement for a product (or products) that is not yet on the market, but which appears overwhelming likely to succeed.* This could be a product in Phase III clinicals which, based on Phases I and II clinicals, was estimated to have a 90% chance of strong success and a 10% chance of medium success.[1] Such a product might have two more years of testing and approval before market introduction and then nine more years of patent protection after introduction.
- *Option 3: Commit substantial resources to a selected basket of products, very early in their development lifecycles.* This would entail investment in process development even before Phase I clinicals. It would be essential to invest in several products under this option, because only 20% of the product development projects put into Phase I ever got introduced to the market.

Because Lilly had never aggressively pursued these options, no historical data existed on which to evaluate and compare them directly. Traditionally, Lilly had invested in modest amounts of process improvement on promising new products, but only began such efforts during Phase II, when questions of scale-up received increased attention. Also, Lilly had invested substantial sums to improve the manufacturing processes of selected products after they were marketed. Recently, it had retained an outside consulting firm to take a major Lilly product and estimate what the impact would have been if an aggressive process improvement effort had begun five years before market introduction. The results of this study provided raw material for a systematic quantitative comparison of the three options.

---

[1] Medium success was generally considered to be about half the sales of strong success.

The consultants started by gathering the actual data on a major, successful new product introduced to the market in 1984 (see Exhibit 5A). Lily had patented the drug in 1974 and had started some process improvement efforts on that drug in 1979; for the next 12 years they committed approximately 5 full-time equivalents (FTEs) of process engineers per year to the endeavor. As shown in Exhibit 5A, the consultants also gathered data on the costs of that process improvement effort, as well as on the production volumes and product costs for the bulk active ingredients for that product for each of those years. These costs are plotted in Exhibit 6.

Next, the consultants conducted in-depth interviews and estimated the impact on costs of doubling that investment in process development during the first five years (1979–1984); in essence, they attempted to model Option 2. These estimates are shown in Exhibit 5B and included on the graph in Exhibit 6.

Cook also had asked his staff to work with the consultants in estimating the impact of increased, front-loaded process investment on the total capital investment needed to produce the same major product from 1979 out to the year 2000. The approach taken had been to estimate the productivity of a single rig assuming traditional process improvement levels and assuming more substantial, front-loaded process improvement efforts. These estimates and their resulting "rig requirements" for a major drug (see Exhibit 5) are shown in Exhibit 7A.

To show the impact that such a process improvement focus might have eventually on all of Lilly, the estimates for a single major drug were applied to Lilly's total requirements for bulk chemicals from 1979 through 2000 for all products introduced in 1990 or before. These results are shown in Exhibit 7B.

Finally, Cook's staff had brainstormed about what impact two other patterns of process improvement investment—those corresponding to Options 1 and 3—might have. For Option 1, which entailed increased investment in process development after market introduction, they concluded that adding five more process engineering full-time equivalents (FTEs) in years one through five following market introduction (for the major drug in Exhibit 5, this would be 1985–1989) would increase costs by approximately $580,000 per year and reduce the cost/kg by 3%–4% (as compared with the previous year) in each of those five years. In addition, the anticipated yield improvement would lead to an annual 2%–3% increase in the capacity of each rig.

For Option 3, their estimate assumed that, for the drug shown in Exhibit 5, process improvement would be staffed with 10 FTEs, at a cost of $1.6 million per year in 1977 and 1978. The pattern of increased, front-loaded investment would then be followed from 1979 onwards, assuming work on that drug was not terminated. The impact of this

EXHIBIT 5

Pharmaceutical Process Development and Manufacturing Costs

A. Actual Costs for a "Typical" Drug (Market Launch 1984)

Year	Unit Cost ($/kg)	Cumulative Volume (kg)*	Cumulative Process Development Expenses (1990 $m)	Cumulative Process Development Hours**
1979	$15,000	5,000	$0.58	9,600
1980	$14,000	6,000	$1.15	19,200
1981	$13,000	7,000	$1.73	28,800
1982	$12,000	8,000	$2.30	38,400
1983	$11,000	9,000	$2.88	48,000
1984 (launch)	$ 9,000	10,000	$3.46	57,600
1985	$ 7,000	20,000	$4.03	67,200
1986	$ 6,000	30,000	$4.61	76,800
1987	$ 5,000	40,000	$5.18	86,400
1988	$ 4,000	50,000	$5.76	96,000
1989	$ 3,000	75,000	$6.34	105,600
1990	$ 2,000	100,000	$6.91	115,200

B. Consultants' Estimates for Increased, Front-loaded Investment

Year	Unit cost ($/kg)	Cumulative Volume (kg)*	Cumulative Process Development Expenses (1990 $m)	Cumulative Process Development Hours***
1979	$12,000	5,000	$ 1.15	19,200
1980	$11,000	6,000	$ 2.30	38,400
1981	$10,000	7,000	$ 3.46	57,600
1982	$ 9,000	8,000	$ 4.61	76,800
1983	$ 7,000	9,000	$ 5.76	96,000
1984 (launch)	$ 5,000	10,000	$ 6.91	115,200
1985	$ 4,000	20,000	$ 7.49	124,800
1986	$ 3,000	30,000	$ 8.06	134,400
1987	$ 2,000	40,000	$ 8.64	144,000
1988	$ 1,000	50,000	$ 9.22	153,600
1989	$ 800	75,000	$ 9.79	163,200
1990	$ 600	100,000	$10.37	172,800

* Includes pre-launch clinical supplies.

** Assumes an average of 5 process engineers, 1979–1989, whose costs are included in "Cumulative Process Development Expenses."

*** Assumes 10 process engineers, 1979–1984, then 5 process engineers, 1985–1989, whose costs are included in "Cumulative Process Development Expenses."

EXHIBIT 6
Pharmaceutical Unit Costs (based on Exhibit 5)

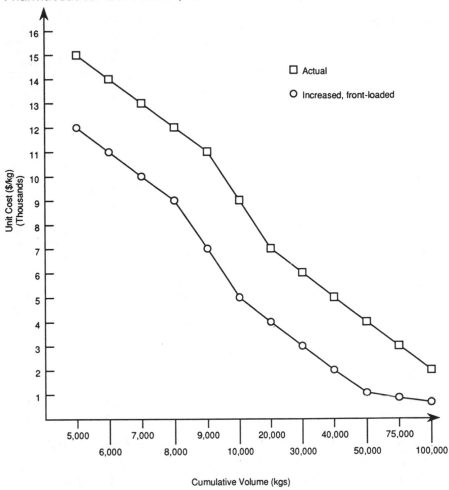

effort was estimated as 30%–40% improvement in cost/kg in 1979 (compared with the estimated costs achieved that year through the "front-loaded process investment" described earlier) and 10%–20% more output from each rig. These cost and yield improvements would result from a better "start point" for that process (by the percentages estimated), and then the cost and yield curves would simply follow those estimated for the front-loaded path shown in Exhibits 5, 6, and 7. If the drug were never introduced, there would be no significant benefit—other than

Exhibit 7

Capacity Planning and Investment in Bulk Chemical Facilities

A. Based on a Typical Major Drug

Year	Annual "Current" Yield ('000s kgs/rig)*	Annual "Front-Loaded" Yield ('000s kgs/rig)**	Volumes of Major Drug Required ('000s kg)	Projected Capacity Required "Current Yield" (# rigs)	Projected Capacity Required "Front-Loaded" Yield (# rigs)
1979	6	6	5	.83	.83
1980	6	6	1	.17	.17
1981	7	7	1	.14	.14
1982	6	8	1	.17	.13
1983	7	10	1	.14	.10
1984	8	13	1	.13	.08
1985	10	16	10	1.00	.63
1986	11	19	10	.91	.53
1987	12	22	10	.83	.45
1988	14	24	10	.71	.42
1889	16	24	25	1.56	1.04
1990	18	25	28	1.56	1.12
1991e	20	26	30	1.50	1.15
1992e	21	27	33	1.57	1.22
1993e	23	27	36	1.57	1.33
1994e	24	28	40	1.67	1.43
1995e	25	29	44	1.76	1.52
1996e	26	29	47	1.81	1.62
1997e	26	29	49	1.88	1.69
1998e	27	30	50	1.85	1.67
1999e	27	30	51	1.89	1.70
2000e	28	30	52	1.86	1.73

* Assumed volume needed to be processed, per year, based on market projections.

** Productivity: Volume capability, per standard rig.

Note: In 1991, the capital investment required for a new rig was $40 million.

---

experience—from having made that early process improvement investment.

With this information, the manufacturing management team was ready to evaluate each of the three illustrative options. The committee would then need to decide how to fold one or more of these options into Cook's recommendations for Lilly's manufacturing strategy.

EXHIBIT 7 (CONTINUED)
Capacity Planning and Investment in Bulk Chemical Facilities

B. All Lilly Pharmaceutical Manufacturing

Year	"Current" Yield ('000s kgs/rig)*	"Front-Loaded" Yield ('000s kgs/rig)**	New Tank Volume Required ('000s kg)	Projected Capacity Required "current" Yield" (# rigs)	Projected Capacity Required "Front-Loaded" Yield (# rigs)
1979	6	6			
1980	6	6			
1981	7	7	50	7	7
1982	6	8	70	12	9
1983	7	10	80	11	8
1984	8	13	100	13	8
1985	10	16	130	13	8
1986	11	19	170	15	9
1987	12	22	210	18	10
1988	14	24	240	17	10
1989	16	24	270	17	11
1990	18	25	300	17	12
1991e	20	26	310	16	12
1992e	21	27	290	14	11
1993e	23	27	250	11	9
1994e	24	28	240	10	9
1995e	25	29	220	9	8
1996e	26	29	200	8	7
1997e	26	29	180	7	6
1998e	27	30	150	6	5
1999e	27	30	110	4	4
2000e	28	30	90	3	3

* Assumed volume needed to be processed, per year, based on market projections.

** Productivity: Volume capability, per standard rig.

Note: In 1991, the capital investment required for a new rig was $40 million.

Intel Systems Group

On December 14, 1989, Jim Cole, vice president of manufacturing for Intel Corporation's Systems Group located in Portland, Oregon, hung up the telephone and took a bite from the stale sandwich that had been sitting on his desk for the past hour. The call had been from Pablo Rodriguez, manager of Intel's Puerto Rico plant. Rodriguez had sounded excited but tired. It was now past 10 P.M. in Puerto Rico, and Cole could imagine the tension at the plant: piles of circuit boards being reworked, exhausted employees on overtime, and engineers scrambling to track down yet another production problem. The X–2 production line in Puerto Rico had been down for over 10 hours after a problem was discovered by test engineers from UCC, a multinational computer and telecommunications equipment customer headquartered in London.

The X–2 was a personal computer Intel manufactured for UCC, which had stationed a small group of its engineers at the plant to test X–2 samples. Production had been plagued by a series of problems that suffocated valuable plant capacity and caused many hours of overtime to be spent on rework. Rodriguez called to inform Cole that the latest problem had finally been traced to a missing resistor in the design of the printed circuit board. The problem had apparently not been detected with the old UCC testing routines, and new routines had been in place for only a few days.

Pondering the information Rodriguez just provided, Cole returned to the presentation he was preparing for tomorrow's meeting, to be attended by members of Intel's top management team including CEO Andy Grove. The presentation would describe the prototyping runs of the X–4, the second product Intel was making for UCC, and recommend

This case was prepared by Professor Marco Iansiti; selected data have been disguised to protect the proprietary interests of the company.

---

whether it was ready to be transferred to the Puerto Rico plant for production.

It was no secret that both Intel top management and UCC were displeased by the many problems encountered during the X–2 introduction; UCC had even threatened to cancel its $200 million contract with Intel. Cole hoped that the X–4 would revive the relationship between the firms. He thus intended to present the "lessons learned" from the X–2 experience and to outline a 12-month improvement plan for addressing the challenges the UCC contract posed.

Intel Corporation

Intel was founded in 1968 by Robert Noyce and Gordon Moore, legendary figures in the early days of the transistor era. They had worked with William Shockley, who had coinvented the transistor while at Bell Labs, and had pioneered early semiconductor circuit design. Noyce and Moore were joined by Andy Grove, a Hungarian émigré with a Ph.D. in chemical engineering from Berkeley. At Intel, they established an environment of technical excellence that encouraged risk-taking and teamwork; many design innovations of integrated circuits (ICs) during the 1970s could be traced to the firm. Driven by its impressive rate of technical achievement, Intel grew quickly, approaching $3 billion in sales in 1988. (See Exhibits 1–3 for company data.) Over its history, Intel devel-

EXHIBIT 1

Intel Corporation: Consolidated Income Statements (millions of $)

	1988	1987	1986
Net Revenues	**$2,874**	**$1,907**	**$1,265**
Cost of sales	1,506	1,044	861
Research and Development	318	260	228
Marketing, general and administrative	456	357	311
Restructuring of Operations	—	—	60
Operating costs and expenses	2,280	1,661	1,460
Operating income (loss)	**594**	**246**	**(195)**
Interest and other	35	42	21
Income (loss) before taxes, extraordinary cumulative taxation correction	**629**	**288**	**(174)**
Provision for taxes	(176)	(40)	(9)
Extraordinary taxation correction	—	—	(20)
Net Income (loss)	**453**	**248**	**(203)**

Exhibit 2

Intel Corporation: Revenues and Operating Profits, by Product Line (millions of $)

Revenues

	1988	1987	1986	1985	1984	1983
Microprocessors	$1,554	$836	$478	$541	$701	$343
Memory ICs	334	266	259	312	392	335
Other ICs	276	254	198	206	209	123
Systems	710	550	329	319	327	321

Operating Profits (pretax)

	1988	1987	1986	1985	1984	1983
Microprocessors	$455	$189	$–5	$–1.4	$119	$63
Memory ICs	30	3	–170	–65	68	32
Other ICs	33	15	–10	4	43	26
Systems	76	38	–11	3	10	24

SOURCE: Analyst and case writer estimates. Yearly revenue and operating profit totals do not add to figures in Exhibit 1, due to internal transfers.

---

oped and manufactured a variety of integrated-circuit products, which by 1989 were the domain of Intel's Microcomputer Components Group and Controller and Memory Group. Intel also had integrated forward into producing complete computers, or "systems," under its Systems Group.

Intel Product Technology

In the 1970s and 1980s, the core of a computer comprised a complex network of electronic devices called transistors that were connected to each other to perform a variety of functions, such as information storage or the addition of numbers. In practice, thousands of transistors were fabricated simultaneously on a single piece of silicon, called a "chip" or integrated circuit.[1] To make up the core of a computer, a number of ICs were assembled on a printed circuit board (PCB); to complete the com-

[1] The integrated circuit was coinvented by Robert Noyce while at Fairchild.

Exhibit 3
Intel Corporate Organization Chart

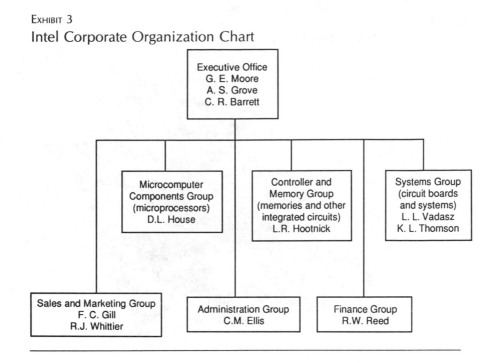

puter system, one or more printed circuit boards were mounted in a metal or plastic chassis. Other subsystems could also be integrated into the chassis, such as a disk drive or a power supply. In a personal computer (PC), most of the functions necessary to process the data were performed by a single IC, the *microprocessor*.

Intel Microprocessor Product Technology

Intel developed the first microprocessor in 1971, and remained a leader in the industry it created. Of the 17.4 million PCs shipped worldwide in 1988, 8 million were based on an Intel microprocessor. The development of the microprocessor had enabled the design of personal computers to be simple and compact: the microprocessor and all other ICs (a total of 20–50 chips) were often assembled on a single circuit board, along with other electronic components such as resistors and capacitors. (Typical PC circuit boards are shown in Exhibit 4.)

During the 1980s, the personal computer became a well-established business and engineering tool, and its performance advanced rapidly. Intel introduced increasingly powerful generations of microprocessors; the last three generations, the 80286, 80386, and 80486, introduced in

EXHIBIT 4

Typical Personal Computer Circuit Boards

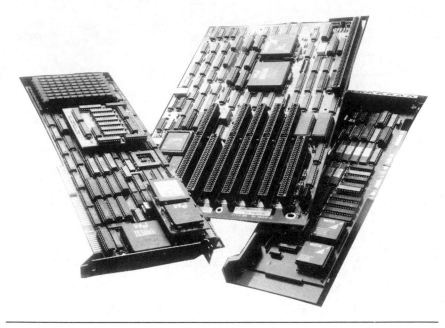

1982, 1985, and 1989, respectively, had each accomplished a performance improvement over the previous family of more than a factor of two in computing speed. Intel management strongly emphasized these developments: claimed CEO Grove, "if there isn't a new generation, there isn't an Intel."[2]

By 1989, the technology surrounding personal computers was changing, particularly in software. While in the 1980s software had been designed specifically for a family of personal computers, such as the IBM PC, new software applications were growing more similar in design and "look and feel" across personal computer families based on different microprocessors. Several applications, for example, were now available in IBM PC, Apple Macintosh, and Sun workstation versions, even though these computers were based on different microprocessors manufactured by different companies. Another interesting trend concerned printed circuit board design and assembly. Experts suggested that future personal computer performance would become increasingly depen-

[2] *Fortune,* 1989.

dent on the printed circuit board, whose technology was beginning to lag integrated circuit technology and limit the latter's performance; new circuit board technologies and manufacturing processes would thus be necessary to keep up with the personal computer performance race in the 1990s. Several Japanese firms, including Sharp, NEC, and Toshiba, had already mastered some of these technologies and introduced them in other products.

Intel Systems Product Technology

In the late 1980s, Intel's top management gave increased priority to their Systems business, which designed, manufactured, and marketed computers based on Intel's proprietary lines of microprocessors. This group had responsibility for developing and manufacturing printed circuit boards and completed computer systems. These responsibilities did *not* include designing or manufacturing the integrated circuits, which were provided by Intel's other groups or by outside vendors.

Grove's objective was that Intel Systems Group revenues become equal to those of the combined semiconductor component operations (all microprocessors and integrated circuits) by the early 1990s. Through this effort, Intel was hoping to pick up revenues that would offset the cyclical microprocessor business, as well as develop new capabilities and technical expertise deemed crucial to the 1990s.

The Systems Group had been founded in the early 1970s to develop a series of computer-based instruments for simulating and testing products based on Intel components. These "development systems" would enable emerging computer manufacturers to more easily design computers based on Intel's microprocessors. Intel managers had debated extensively whether the systems should be given away or sold to Intel microprocessor customers. Intel opted for the latter solution and, by the mid–1970s, the business had become significant and profitable.

In 1976, the Systems Group introduced a second family of computers: the *Multibus* line. Like development systems, these products were expensive (with prices usually above $10,000), designed for sophisticated users (mostly engineers), and built using Intel microprocessors and components. They were targeted at a somewhat broader set of mid-range computing applications, however, involving a number of industrial and technical tasks. For example, in the mid–1980s, an Intel Multibus System 310 monitored trading levels at the New York Stock Exchange. The products were usually relatively large, standalone units, not designed to fit on a desk top. The volumes produced of each model were small (at most a few hundred per month), but they satisfied the requirements of customers with many different customizable high-performance product designs.

Product design lives in the Multibus and development systems businesses were long, typically over five years. These two product lines were responsible for most of Intel Systems' sales and profits during the 1970s and 1980s, reaching a cumulative total of one million units shipped by 1988.

Intel Systems pursued other opportunities in the rapidly evolving computer business. Engineers developed a line of supercomputers, each using as many as 128 Intel microprocessors working simultaneously to perform certain calculations with extreme speed. By 1989, 150 supercomputers had been sold, but the business was not yet profitable. Intel also created a line of printed circuit boards that could be mounted in an existing personal computer to enhance its performance, by incorporating Intel high-performance ICs.

In the mid–1980s many Intel development and Multibus system functions could be performed by newly developed, less expensive products, such as high-end personal computers and workstations, manufactured by other companies. After peaking at around $200 million in sales in 1982, Intel's development system business had greatly diminished by 1986, and the Systems Group laid off about 1,000 employees, reducing its manufacturing force to about 800 people. Intel managers were concerned that Multibus sales had peaked and would begin to decline as well.

To supplement the lagging sales of its old product lines, Intel Systems introduced a new computer in 1987: the Intel 302. It was the System Group's first office desktop personal computer, and was based on an Intel 80386 microprocessor. The 302 was built without a screen or a keyboard and sold to a dozen different original equipment manufacturers (OEMs) for less than $3,000. Intel hoped to ship a million units by the mid–1990s.

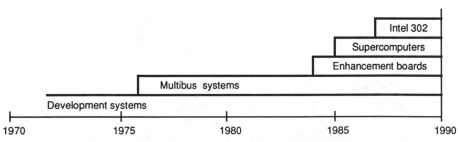

FIGURE 1　Evolution of Intel Systems Product Line

Also in 1987, Intel management began seeking large contracts for the design and manufacture of personal computers. Such contracts would help the Systems Group reach Grove's ambitious revenue goal, and might engender long-lasting relationships with large company customers that could offset the risks in the sometimes unpredictable computer business. Between 1987 and 1989, Intel contacted a number of major customers, including Prime, AT&T, Unisys, and UCC. The volume of each contract discussed was usually over $100 million. Intel was hoping to reach a yearly shipping rate of one million personal computers by 1992, thus acquiring a significant market share (total U.S. PC production in 1990 was projected to be about 12 million units).

Intel Systems Group Operations

In 1989, Intel Systems staff and the product and process development organizations for all major Systems product lines were located in Portland, Oregon (see Exhibit 5). The Oregon Microcomputer Division, organized in the late 1980s to emphasize the importance of the new high-volume personal computer business, was staffed mainly by Intel employees associated with the traditional Systems Group product lines, and was housed in the same complex as the rest of Intel's Oregon organization. Several Microcomputer Division managers also had responsibilities that extended beyond the Division. Jim Cole, for example, while formally within the Microcomputer Division, had line responsibility for all of the Systems Group plants, and was thus responsible for the production of all Systems Group products.

The Oregon complex was also the site of a pilot plant for refining new products before their transfer to Intel's manufacturing plants, one in Singapore, and one in Puerto Rico. The Singapore plant focused on the high volume production of printed circuit boards, and lacked the facilities to assemble and test completed systems in significant volumes. The Puerto Rico plant produced both circuit boards and completely assembled computer systems.

Intel Oregon: Product Development Process

Engineers staffing Intel's Oregon complex developed all of the existing Systems Group products; during the 1980s, they had designed over one hundred different new products each year. Designing these products demanded crucial in-depth knowledge of the characteristics and requirements of Intel microprocessors and ICs, expertise some Intel managers

Exhibit 5

Intel Systems Group Corporate Organization Chart (Simplified)

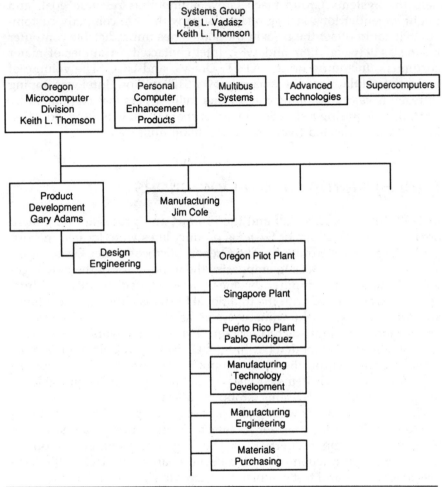

considered to be one of the Group's major assets. Most designers had backgrounds in electrical engineering, and had spent their careers designing printed circuit boards based on Intel components.

New products often were proposed by major customers or imaginative Intel engineers. Product development began with the definition of the most basic technical specifications of the new product, such as its functional and performance objectives. Once the definition was approved, a team from design engineering, led by an appointed project leader, developed the product design in detail. Engineers usually would have only part of their time allocated to the design of any single product. As the design evolved, early prototypes were built in engineering workshops to test the feasibility of the design. As the basic features in the product design stabilized, process engineers from the Manufacturing and Technology Development (MTD) group became involved on a part-time basis. MTD engineers were responsible for establishing the essential production techniques and specifying required equipment. The MTD group also followed emerging process technologies, and was responsible for incorporating them into the production process for the new products, whenever appropriate.

After the product design was officially completed, the product was *design released*. At this stage, manufacturing engineers began refining the processing guidelines established by the MTD organization, and developed a detailed set of procedures and instructions for product assembly. The Oregon pilot plant then assembled a few lots (batches) of the product in "pilot" runs designed to test the manufacturing process. The Oregon pilot facility was equipped to assemble products in low volumes, and used a relatively labor intensive process in both printed circuit board production and systems assembly.

Manufacturing engineers and Oregon pilot plant employees could suggest changes in the product design, though these were subject to the scrutiny of the design engineers and the approval of the project leader. Once the product and process designs were completed, the product would be *production-released* and transferred to the production plant. Both the design release and production release documents were the responsibility of the project leader. For a major new product introduction, the entire process (from definition of specifications to plant transfer), would take one to two years, depending on the urgency and complexity of the product. Figure 2 outlines the development process for multibus products.

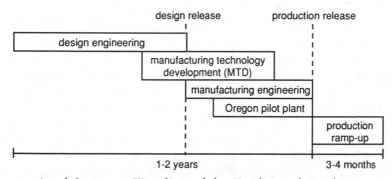

FIGURE 2   Intel Systems: Timeline of the Traditional Product Development Process

Product Transfer, Production Ramp-up, and Product Revisions

After the product was production released, a "transfer team" of Oregon manufacturing engineers usually traveled to the Puerto Rico plant to help ramp up production. The Puerto Rico plant would first perform a pilot run to test the Oregon engineers' manufacturing process, which was typically altered or further refined. Although plant engineers could request changes in assembly or testing procedures, these requests would have to be approved by Oregon manufacturing engineers before adoption. The typical response time of the Oregon organization to a change request by the Puerto Rico plant ranged from hours to over a month. Plant engineers complained it was difficult to obtain a response in less than a few days unless it was a serious emergency such as a line shut down. The usual schedule for production ramp-up involved a pilot run of about two dozen units, followed by the production of about a hundred units the next month; production would then be increased as the shipping schedule required. Further refinements to the product usually would continue after full production had begun. Quite often, major refinements might be made a year or more after the product had been transferred to manufacturing.

During the late 1980s, the Systems Group adopted new guidelines to ensure that products would be manufacturable in high volumes. In particular, the "Rites of Passage Document" (also called Product Transfer Checklist, see Exhibit 6) was written to ensure a clean transfer between the Oregon pilot plant and Puerto Rico. Intel engineers also had developed a manual of design for manufacturability guidelines for use by designers during the early stages of product development. A page from the manual is shown in Exhibit 7.

Intel Puerto Rico: Production Process

Intel's Puerto Rico plant had been in operation since 1979. While its traditional focus had been the production of Intel's Multibus line of products, Intel Puerto Rico had provided virtually all of the manufacturing capacity needed to support the recent contract business. Puerto Rico also was the production site for the recently introduced high volume OEM personal computer, the Intel 302. The plant did not employ any design engineers and was entirely dependent on the Oregon organization for new products and for product modifications: one Intel manager described the plant as "the baby bird waiting to be fed by the mama bird."

Intel Puerto Rico was accustomed to producing a very broad product line: in 1986, for example, about 400 different products were made, each at an average rate of about 3 units/month. Only rarely had production

Exhibit 6
Excerpt from Intel's Rites of Passage Document

INTEL	POLICIES AND PROCEDURES	No. 18478724	Rev. 3

TITLE: **RITES OF PASSAGE**

Product Code _____   Project Leader _____

Plant Site _____   Product Manufacturing Engineer _____

Date _____

No.	Product Transfer Checklist	resp.	done	not done

1.	Product Status:
	  a. Design Released
	  b. Production Released
		PL	☐
			☐
				☐
				☐

2.	No undispositioned engineering change requests	DE	☐	☐

3.	Documents available at systems document control center
	  a. engineering drawings
	  b. printed circuit board fabrication drawing
	  c. schematic
	  d. artwork
		DE	☐
			☐
			☐
			☐
				☐
				☐
				☐
				☐

4.	Full Compliance to Design and Process Rules
	  a. Printed circuit board guidelines IPP # 98797
	  b. Systems Design for Manufacturability IPP # 186870
		DE and ME	☐
			☐
				☐
				☐

5.	Product Performance Indicator Acceptable
	(must be within 10% of goal)
	           Goal Actual
	  a. First Pass Yield
	  b. Defects per Unit
	  c. % defective
	  d. assembly labor std. hrs.
	  e. test labor std. hrs.
		ME
		ME
		ME
		ME
		ME
			☐
			☐
			☐
			☐
			☐
				☐
				☐
				☐
				☐
				☐

6.	Compliance to maximum rework limit from engineering changes
	  a. printed circuit board: max (5) jumper wires and (5) cuts
	  b. systems: no open engineering change requests on plastic or metal items
		DE and ME	☐
			☐
				☐
				☐

DE = Design Engineering; ME = Manufacturing Engineering; PL = Project Leader.

---

exceeded 1000 units/month for a given product. In 1986, many of the products produced dated back to the 1970s; on the other hand, that same year 87 new products were introduced.

In 1989, the plant was divided into four separate facilities (see Exhibit 8(a) for a layout). The first facility produced printed circuit boards, while the second assembled circuit boards and other subcomponents into complete computer systems for the final testing of those systems. The third

EXHIBIT 7
Excerpt from Intel's Design for Manufacturability Guidelines (page 18)

INTEL	Project _____	IPP No. 186870	Rev. 3
System Design for Manufacturability Checklist	Date _____		

(Each violation requires completion of Rule Violation Form)

FASTENERS FOR IN HOUSE ASSEMBLY/MISC.

R = Rule G = Guideline	resp.	done	not done	n.a.
R8.1 When using screws, only use Philips drive screws	DE	☐	☐	☐
R8.2 For Systems over 20 pounds, do not locate fasteners such that they must be accessed from the bottom of the system	DE	☐	☐	☐
G8.1 Consider Snap Fasteners	DE	☐	☐	☐
G8.2 Use readily available standard screw lengths	DE	☐	☐	☐
G8.3 Minimize the variety of screw sizes and lengths used in an assembly	DE	☐	☐	☐
R8.3 Locate printed circuit board identification in visible location	DE	☐	☐	☐
R8.4 If a printed circuit board is reconfigured, it should be identified with an altered assembly number	DE	☐	☐	☐

G8.4 Design printed circuit board for assembly using this order of priority:
    1. Snap in
    2. 1/4 turn fastener
    3. Screws
	DE	☐	☐	☐

DE = Design Engineering.

---

facility was a warehouse used to store the inventory of components and subsystems needed for computer assembly. The final facility had been a semiconductor components plant, originally belonging to one of Intel's other groups. Closed for several years, the components plant was now empty.

The printed circuit board assembly facility included automated and manual production lines that placed and soldered various electronic components and integrated circuits onto printed circuit boards. (A simplified layout of the facility is shown on Exhibit 8(b).) Boards typically

Exhibit 8
Layout of Intel's Puerto Rico Plant

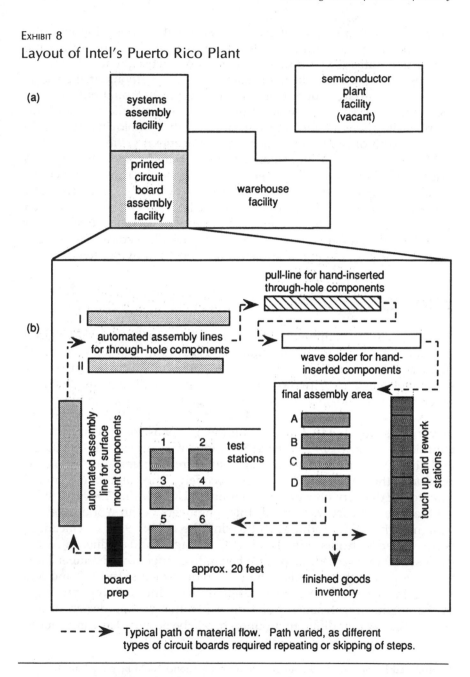

----▶ Typical path of material flow. Path varied, as different types of circuit boards required repeating or skipping of steps.

were processed in batches of about 75. Each batch traveled around the plant floor in a cart with a traveler sheet attached to it, indicating the completion dates for the different steps. The exact sequence of processing steps differed by product: for example, many Multibus circuit boards did not use surface mount components.[3] Typical throughput times in the circuit board facility ranged from three to seven days. The circuit board facility was of medium capital-intensity, employing about $43 million worth of capital equipment (at replacement value).

After boards were completed, they were transferred to the systems assembly facility, where they were mounted into the computer chassis, along with other subsystems, such as the power supply, disk drives, etc. The various steps in this process were quite labor-intensive and required modest amounts of capital equipment (about $10 million total). After assembly, the systems were tested and packed. Typical throughput times in the systems assembly facility ranged from five to ten days.

The UCC Contract

In early 1988, Intel approached UCC (whose 1988 sales were $23 billion) with an offer to design and manufacture a significant portion of the UCC personal computer product line. A contract was discussed in several high-level meetings between the two companies during the summer, when Intel was also in the process of designing two new products—the 300SX and the 303—to replace the Intel 302. These products appeared to be very close to what UCC needed for the first phase of the contract. The contract was signed in August 1988, and it was agreed that the 300SX and the 303 would evolve through *minor* refinements into the UCC products, the "X–2" and "X–4," respectively. The contract committed Intel to the delivery of over 100,000 units to UCC during 1989 and 1990.

Once the contract was signed, Intel engineers began working on the design of the UCC products, and during the fall of 1988, specifications were refined by teams of Intel and UCC managers and engineers. As the discussions progressed, the picture began to change. By December 1988, it was apparent that to satisfy the UCC requirements, the X–2 and X–4 were going to be very different in design from the Intel family of products. While engineering resources had been planned for the design of two products, now four different products had to be designed and introduced

[3] Introduced in the mid–1980s, surface mount components could be placed much closer together than traditional ("through-hole") components, allowing the design of more compact printed circuit boards. However, they were also more difficult to place and solder onto the printed circuit board, and required special equipment, usually characterized by a higher degree of automation.

by the end of 1989. (Ultimately, the 300SX and 303 production was delayed for a year while efforts were concentrated on the UCC products.)

Data on the projected cost and selling price (to UCC) of the X–2, X–4, and two other Intel products are shown in Exhibit 9. The projected production plan for the Puerto Rico plant in 1989 and 1990 is shown in Exhibit 10.

Development of the X–2

The X–2 incorporated the new Intel 80386SX microprocessor in a very compact design. This compactness posed challenges both for the chassis design, which had to fit snugly around the subcomponents, and for the circuit board design, which included a much higher percentage of surface mount components than traditional Intel Systems products.

The X–2 production was planned to fit in a market window bounded by the summer of 1989 and the summer of 1990. Expectations were high and UCC had already lined up some key high-volume customers who were expecting the product in the early fall of 1989. The X–2 was scheduled to be produced at a rate of about 8,000 per month in the fall of 1989.

A dedicated design team for the X–2 was established in December 1988. At that time a schedule for the development process was also defined: the X–2 was to be transferred to Puerto Rico in April 1989, and volume production would begin in mid-summer. Figure 3 provides a timeline for the development of the X–2.

Intel engineers worked day and night developing the new product. To help meet the early manufacturing deadline, a joint manufacturing engineering and MTD team was established in January 1989 to create a production process for the X–2. Early pilot runs for the product began in

EXHIBIT 9

Projected Cost Comparison of Four Different Intel Systems Products Manufactured (or planned) by the Puerto Rico Facility

Product	selling price ($)	standard cost ($)	material cost ($)
average for Multibus	11,754	5,640	3,384
302	2,865	1,701	1,544
X–2	1,784	1,691	1,538
X–4	3,005	2,102	1,855

Material cost included all purchased components and subsystems, as well as the integrated circuits purchased from Intel's semiconductor operations. These material costs were part of the total estimated standard cost of the product.

Exhibit 10

Intel Puerto Rico: Projected Production Plan

product	1989 production plan	1990 production plan
Multibus Line	14,000 units	13,000 units
302	30,000 units	20,000 units
X–2	30,000 units	48,000 units
X–4	0 units	48,000 units

Actual X–2 production for 1989 is shown in Exhibit 12.

February, at the Oregon facility. (The activity of the Oregon prototyping facility during 1989 is shown in Exhibit 11). These prototyping runs generated substantial feedback for the design team regarding key improvements in both circuit board and chassis design to make the product more manufacturable. From March until May, several task forces were assembled to address the low yields and manufacturability problems with the X–2, generating a flurry of design changes. These changes were subsequently tested in additional Oregon prototyping runs, shown in Exhibit 11, and further problems were detected. Meanwhile, UCC product specifications of the X–2 were still changing, as additional misunderstandings between Intel and UCC came to light.

Intel engineers were overwhelmed by the number of design changes and, as summer approached, some deadlines were missed. Design release of the X–2 was postponed from April to May, and finally to late June. An Intel manager described the situation:

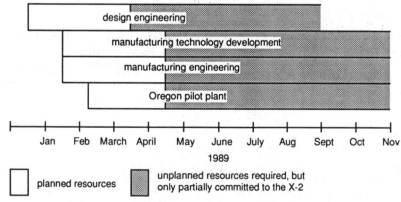

Figure 3   Intel Systems: Timeline of the Development Process for the X–2.

Exhibit 11

Number of X–2s Assembled at the Oregon Pilot Plant (each version denotes a different/refined product design)

Month in 1989

X–2 version #	Jan	Feb	Mar	Apr	May	Jun	Jul	Aug	Sep	Oct	Nov	Dec
1	0	0	17	2	0	0	0	0	0	0	0	0
2	0	0	6	32	28	6	0	0	0	0	0	0
3	0	0	0	12	0	0	0	0	0	0	0	0
4	0	0	0	0	0	43	7	80	17	4	0	0
5	0	0	0	0	0	11	21	4	0	0	0	0
6	0	0	0	0	0	65	23	50	55	2	0	0
7	0	0	0	0	0	0	79	18	0	1	0	0
8	0	0	0	0	0	0	0	80	18	2	0	0
9	0	0	0	0	0	0	0	0	52	0	0	0
10	0	0	0	0	0	0	0	0	144	6	0	0

. . . we simply got swamped; people were getting burned out. Schedules became "best case" schedules, and incomplete product revisions were transferred to the Oregon pilot plant. Engineering documentation was inaccurate. The development process became a contest between engineering and manufacturing and our relationship with the customer suffered.

By May, UCC's pressure on Intel had built to a disturbing level. Nine thousand units of the X–2 were due to ship by the end of September and UCC did not believe that sales lost due to late production could be recovered.

However, design of the X–2 started to stabilize in May, and first-pass pilot production yields (i.e., the percentage of units that passed Intel's tests without rework) increased to about 89%; Intel engineers had identified ways to correct problems that had caused low yields in the pilot assembly. The X–2 was partially design released[4] in late June, and a "Rites of Passage Document" was filed to allow the product to be transferred to Puerto Rico. Meanwhile, a UCC team was also set up

---

[4] While the design of the X–2 system, including the chassis configuration, was released, design release was still pending on the printed circuit board. At that time, the product had not yet been production released.

in Oregon to fully test and inspect X–2 prototypes. The transfer team from Oregon, however, did not include any of the original design engineers, who already were busy designing the next generation of products.

Production of the X–2

During July, the Puerto Rico plant performed its pilot run of 25 units, as both engineers and workers became accustomed to the X–2. First-pass production yields were below 60%, and additional manufacturability problems were identified. In particular, the computer chassis, provided by an outside supplier, did not fit well around the product (". . . in some cases we had to use a hammer to make the chassis fit . . .").

In August, the production rate was increased quickly to achieve high-volume production by September. A manager at Intel Puerto Rico described the ramp-up:

> When we were producing 50 X–2s a day, if there were some quality problems we could send the product to rework, and still comply with our schedule. Our structure was in a reactive mode, but by putting in a lot of extra hours we could meet the dates. As volume increased, however, we just couldn't keep reacting.

The clear urgency of the situation at Intel Puerto Rico served to marshall resources and concentrate efforts on achieving the production rates UCC expected. Engineers from Intel Puerto Rico, as well as additional teams flown in from Oregon, combined efforts on innumerable late nights and weekends to debug the process. After this tremendous effort from the Intel organization, X–2 production yields started rising, and production volume increased—1,805 units were produced in September. However, since 10% were found defective, even after rework, only 1,624 units were shipped.

The actual monthly production schedule of the X–2 during the last half of 1989 is shown in Exhibit 12 along with the percentage of units found defective each months. Only units not found defective were shipped. Unfortunately, the expected production quota of 8,000 X–2s for October was also not met. Carlos Novoa, who led the X–2 introduction in Puerto Rico, recalled:

> We were under tremendous pressure, and everything that could possibly go wrong did go wrong: there were problems with our chassis supplier, who was in Korea and was very hard to reach; we had a problem with electronic components cracking at high temperatures during our wave-soldering pro-

EXHIBIT 12

Actual 1989 X–2 Production and Yields

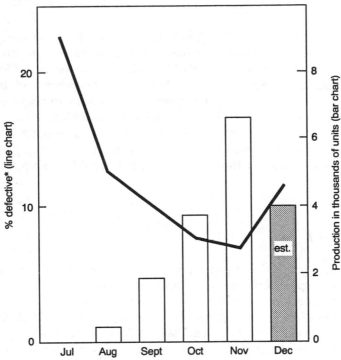

	July 1989	August	September	October	November	December
production (units)	25	470	1,805	3,741	6,505	4,000 (est.)
% defective*	24	12	10	8	7	12

* Note: Defective units had failed testing and inspection, even after rework.

cess; there were problems with training our workforce, and all of the people added to increase the capacity of the plant;[5] there were problems with our testing procedures, and problems that could have been detected at the board level were only found after the whole system had been assembled; finally, we had problems with changes in the board design—13 jumper wires were added

[5] Puerto Rico plant headcount increased from 500 to 830 during 1989.

after the basic board layout was completed.[6] The assembly of the system also was difficult: as many as 10 screws were necessary to attach the circuit board to the chassis. . . .

During October, 25% of the direct labor in the plant was assigned to rework, mostly on the X–2. In November, X–2 production improved and 6,050 units were shipped. By early December, however, about 5% of the units shipped in September, October, and November had been returned, after users registered a number of complaints. In response, UCC changed its final testing procedures at the plant, which caused another flurry of rework and design changes. The missing resistor found on December 14th was typical of the new wave of problems, and given their extent, it was expected that only 3,500 units would be shipped in December.

The X–4

The second personal computer product to be developed for UCC, the X–4, was a higher performance computer than the X–2 and used a faster Intel microprocessor. Expected production volumes for the X–4 were similar to those of the X–2. As it had done previously for the X–2, Intel had already set up large contracts with its suppliers for most of the volume of components and parts necessary for X–4 assembly. Of the parts included in the X–4, fewer than one-quarter were common to the X–2. The X–4 used a heavier duty power supply, a larger disk drive, a larger and heavier chassis, and a more aggressive circuit board design, requiring more high-performance components. Only two-thirds of the vendors used for the X–4 had been used on the X–2.

Developing the X–4 design had been similar to the X–2 struggle. In mid-December the product finally appeared close to design release, after eight months in development. There had been a few complaints from process engineers about the product's manufacturability, but most of the problems identified were corrected. A total of 510 X–4s (in eight different variations) had been built by the Oregon pilot plant, on a schedule similar to that for the X–2. The X–4 transfer team was scheduled to fly to Puerto Rico the week of December 18th, with the X–4 scheduled for volume production (4,000 units) in March 1990.

---

[6] "Jumper wires" were wires soldered to a circuit board to add new connections between the semiconductor components, usually in response to design changes. They were difficult to solder onto the board and sometimes unreliable.

December 14th, 1989

After finishing off the stale sandwich, Jim Cole went back to the presentation for the December 15th meeting. He wanted to propose both short- and long-term responses to address the challenges of the UCC contract. Although he could influence decisions concerning the product development organization, his primary responsibilities were in manufacturing and process engineering.

Cole knew that Intel management was very unhappy about his organization's performance on the UCC contract. During the fall of 1989, UCC and Intel managers had met on various occasions to discuss the reasons for the problems encountered with the X–2. UCC had accepted part of the blame, and promised that on the X–4 the specifications would be stable. A few Intel managers had also discussed with their UCC counterparts their concern that a few of the initial X–4s delivered might be defective, due to possible design and production problems. UCC managers had in return expressed that their number-one concern was having the products delivered on time. Intel thus promised on-time delivery of the X–4, according to the 1990 production plan for Intel Puerto Rico shown in Exhibit 10. Cole knew that Oregon engineers had learned a lot through their experience with the X–2. He also knew that the latest Oregon pilot run on the X–4 had achieved very high yields (95% first-pass production yield).

To help ensure that the problems encountered with the X–2 would not be repeated in the future, top management had decided to make a significant investment to upgrade Intel's Puerto Rico and Oregon facilities. The exact amounts were not yet defined, but Cole expected that given the crucial nature of the issues, as much as $50 million could be spend, if reasonable returns were projected.

Before leaving his office, Cole took one last look at the outline for his presentation. It was divided into three parts:

1. The X–4 transfer decision;
2. Lessons learned from the X–2;
3. Long-term improvements in Intel System's operations.

Notes

Chapter 1. Competing Through Development Strategy

1. For recent in-depth work on the world automobile industry, see Kim Clark and Takahiro Fujimoto, *Product Development Performance* (Boston: Harvard Business School Press, 1991); and James P. Womack, Daniel T. Jones, and Daniel Roos, *The Machine that Changed the World* (New York: Rawson Associates, 1990).
2. These data on technical diversity in automobiles come from William J. Abernathy, Kim B. Clark, and Alan M. Kantrow, *Industrial Renaissance* (New York: Basic Books, 1983).
3. For further information and analysis of developments in textiles and apparel, see Kurt Salmon Associates "Quick Response Implementation: Action Steps for Retailers, Manufacturers, and Suppliers," in Thomas Bailey, "Technology, Skills, and Education in the Apparel Industry" (Technical Paper No. 7, Conservation of Human Resources, Columbia University, November 1989).
4. Changes in the disk drive industry are examined in detail in Clayton M. Christensen, "The Development of the Magnetic Information Storage and Retrieval Industry, 1960–1987: An Analytical History," unpublished paper, Harvard Business School, December 1990.
5. The emphasis on speed is evident in the recent literature on product development. See especially George Stalk, Jr., and Thomas M. Hout, *Competing Against Time* (New York: The Free Press, 1990); and Preston G. Smith and Donald G. Reinertsen, *Developing Products in Half the Time* (New York: Van Nostrand Reinhold, 1991).

Chapter 2. The Concept of a Development Strategy

1. For more information about development experience at Plus Development, see "Plus Development Corporation (A)" (Boston: HBS Case Services, Harvard Business School), 9-687-001.

2. There is a large literature on technology strategy. Robert A. Burgelman and Modesto A. Maidique, *Strategic Management of Technology and Innovation* (Homewood, Illinois: Dow Jones-Irwin, 1988) provide a good overview, several cases, and references. For a European perspective see Ray Loveridge and Martyn Pitt (eds.), *The Strategic Management of Technological Innovation* (Chicester, England: John Wiley and Sons, 1990), who also provide an excellent bibliography.
3. For additional background on product/market strategy, see Glen L. Urban and John R. Hauser, *Design and Marketing of New Products* (Englewood Cliffs, New Jersey: Prentice-Hall, 1980).
4. Sony's product strategy is examined by Susan Sanderson and Vic Uzumeri, "Design-Based Incrementalism: The Walkman," Rensselaer Polytechnic Institute draft paper, 1990.
5. For an example of the implications of standards for product development in the electric motor industry, see "Reliance Electric Motor Division (A)" (Boston: HBS Case Services, Harvard Business School), 9-678-067.
6. For additional background on Honda's experience with the Today, see "Honda Today" (Boston: HBS Case Services, Harvard Business School), 9-692-044.

Chapter 3. Maps and Mapping: Functional Strategies in Pre-Project Planning

1. The cable story is based on real events, but names and circumstances have been disguised.
2. Maps have been discussed in several places. See, for example, Chapter 10 of Robert H. Hayes, Steven C. Wheelwright, and Kim B. Clark, *Dynamic Manufacturing* (New York: The Free Press, 1988); and Steven C. Wheelwright and W. Earl Sasser, Jr., "The New Product Development Map," *Harvard Business Review*, May–June 1989, p. 112.
3. The Coolidge example was first developed by Sasser and Wheelwright, "The New Product Development Map," although the focus in their article was on the product generation map. Here we examine the broad range of functional maps in the business.
4. For more information on the product-process matrix and its use in developing operations strategy, see Robert H. Hayes and Steven C. Wheelwright, *Restoring Our Competitive Edge: Competing Through Manufacturing* (New York: John Wiley and Sons, 1984).
5. This example was taken from Chapter 10 of Hayes, Wheelwright, and Clark, *Dynamic Manufacturing*.

Chapter 4. The Aggregate Project Plan

1. The concepts we develop in this chapter about aggregate planning for projects have analogies in other fields where aggregate planning and scheduling are important. For a review of the general problems in manufacturing, for example, see Thomas E. Vollman, William L. Berry, and D. Clay Whybark, *Manufacturing Planning and Control Systems, 2nd edition* (Homewood, Illinois: Dow Jones-Irwin, 1988). The canary cage analogy is one developed and described by John Bennion of Bain and Company.
2. Studies of time allocation among engineers have shown engineers in a typical setup where most people work on several projects and spend 25–30 percent of their time on value-adding activities (i.e., designing, testing, solving problems). The balance is taken up with travel, correcting mistakes, attending meetings, and so forth. For further analysis, see Jeffrey K. Liker and Walton M. Hancock, "Organization Systems Barriers to Engineering Effectiveness," *IEEE Transactions on Engineering Management*, EM-33(2) (1986), pp. 82–91.

3. For more background on the hospital bed market and Hill-Rom's strategy, see "BSA Industries—Belmont Division" (Boston: HBS Case Services, Harvard Business School), 9-689-049.
4. See Susan Sanderson and Vic Uzumeri, "Design-Based Incrementalism: The Walkman" (Rensselaer Polytechnic Institute draft paper, 1990), for more detail on Sony's strategy with the Walkman.
5. See Kim B. Clark and Takahiro Fujimoto, *Product Development Performance* (Boston: Harvard Business School Press, 1991), for details of this study.
6. For background on Kodak's FunSaver project, see "Kodak FunSaver" (Boston: HBS Case Services, Harvard Business School), N9-692-070.

CHAPTER 5. Structuring the Development Funnel

1. The concept of a development funnel is discussed in Robert H. Hayes, Steven C. Wheelwright, and Kim B. Clark, *Dynamic Manufacturing* (New York: The Free Press, 1988), Chapter 10.
2. There is a large literature on project selection in R&D, but our focus in this chapter is quite different. The project selection literature generally focuses on the problem of selecting among a set of projects that are relatively well defined. Here we examine the processes through which firms generate, review, and screen alternatives and determine the content of development projects as they move toward the market. For a review of this literature and a recent application see M. L. Liberatore and G. J. Titus, "The Practice of Management Science in R&D Project Management," *Management Science*, 29(8), August 1983, pp. 962–964; and Muhittin Oral, Ossama Kettani, and Pascal Lang, "A Methodology for Collective Evaluation and Selection of Industrial R&D Projects," *Management Science*, 37(7), July 1991, pp. 871–885.
3. For a much more detailed discussion of project selection and resource allocation, see Albert H. Rubinstein, *Managing Technology in the Decentralized Firm* (New York: John Wiley and Sons, 1989), Chapter 7. Variants of Model I have been discussed in the literature in terms of "technology push." See Edward B. Roberts, "Managing Invention and Innovation," *Research-Technology Management*, January–February 1988, for a review of the literature.
4. Of course, if the cost of development is sufficiently low, a strategy of market determined selection—offering many possible products to the market and letting customers decide which will succeed or fail—may be effective. This seems to be the case in the Japanese consumer electronics industry.
5. For further background on the problem of generating ideas and the influence of management in the process see Norman R. Baker, Stephen G. Green, and Alden S. Bean, "How Management Can Influence the Generation of Ideas," *Research Management*, 28(6), November–December 1985, pp. 35–42; and Rubinstein, *Managing Technology*, Chapter 6.

CHAPTER 6. A Framework for Development

1. Robert H. Hayes, Steven C. Wheelwright, and Kim B. Clark, *Dynamic Manufacturing* (New York: The Free Press, 1988), use the architecture metaphor in their discussion of the system of material and information flows within a factory. See especially Chapter 7.
2. The MEI case is a composite based on actual experience at several medical technology companies. Although the case captures the basic structure of the development process, the product and other aspects of the firms have been disguised.
3. For additional background on the development process at Kodak, see the chapter on

Kodak in H. Kent Bowen, Kim Clark, Charles Holloway, and Steven Wheelwright (eds.), *Vision and Capability: High Performance Product Development in the 1990's* (New York: Oxford University Press, forthcoming). Some of the details presented here also draw on a presentation by Al Van de Moere at the Boston University School of Management Manufacturing Roundtable Seminar, "The Kodak FunSaver Story," March 20, 1991.

4. See, for example, "General Electric Lighting Business Group" (Boston: HBS Case Services, Harvard Business School), 1-689-038; and "General Electric Company: Major Appliance Business Group (A)-(C)" (Boston: HBS Case Services, Harvard Business School), 9-585-053 to 9-585-055.

5. See, for example, "Motorola, Inc.: Bandit Pager Project" (Boston: HBS Case Services, Harvard Business School), 9-690-043; Tom Inglesby (ed.), "How They Brought Home the Prize—A Visit to Motorola's Bandit Plant," *Manufacturing Systems*, April 1989, pp. 26–32; Ronald Henkoff, "What Motorola Learns from Japan," *Fortune*, April 24, 1989, pp. 157–168; and "Motorola—Boynton Beach, Florida," *Industry Week*, October 15, 1990, pp. 62–64.

6. For a recent discussion of the skunkworks at Lockheed, see Ben R. Rich, "The Skunk Works Management Style—It's No Secret," *Product and Process Innovation*, 1(2), March–April 1991, pp. 28–35.

7. Kim B. Clark and Takahiro Fujimoto, *Product Development Performance* (Boston: Harvard Business School Press, 1991), discuss the application of these principles in automobile product development. See especially Chapter 10.

CHAPTER 7.   Cross-Functional Integration

1. There is a growing literature on cross-functional integration, including recent research and writing on topics such as concurrent engineering, simultaneous engineering, cross-functional teams, overlapping problem solving, and the engineering-manufacturing interface. The classic work on integration is Paul R. Lawrence and Jay W. Lorsch, *Organization and Environment* (Homewood, Illinois: Richard D. Irwin, 1967). For a more recent discussion, see Hirotaka Takeuchi and Ikujiro Nonaka, "The New Product Development Game," *Harvard Business Review*, January–February 1986, pp. 137–146; and Kim B. Clark and Takahiro Fujimoto, *Product Development Performance* (Boston: Harvard Business School Press, 1991).

2. For further discussion of the interface between manufacturing and engineering, see Martin E. Ginn and Albert H. Rubenstein, "The R&D/Production Interface: A Case Study of New Product Commercialization," *Journal of Product Management*, 3, 1986, pp. 158–170; and James B. Quinn and James A. Mueller, "Transferring Research Results to Operations," *Harvard Business Review*, January–February 1963, pp. 49–66.

3. For additional insight into engineering-marketing integration, see Ashok K. Gupta, S. P. Raj, and David Wilemon, "The R&D-Marketing Interface in High-Technology Firms," *Journal of Product Innovation Management*, 2, 1985, pp. 12–24.

4. This challenge has achieved recent recognition in the marketing literature. See, for example, Gerald Zaltman and Vincent Barabba, *Hearing the Voice of the Market* (Boston: Harvard Business School Press, 1991).

5. Clark and Fujimoto, *Product Development Performance*, develop this perspective in their study of the world auto industry.

6. See Clark and Fujimoto, *Product Development Performance*, for further discussion of the issues and framework presented in this section. Takahiro Fujimoto, "Organizations for Effective Product Development," D.B.A. dissertation, Harvard Business School, 1989, provides an in-depth review of the literature on communication in this context.

CHAPTER 8. Organizing and Leading Project Teams

1. For an example of recent literature related to leadership and organization, see Gloria Barczak and David Wilemon, "Leadership Differences in New Product Development Teams," *Journal of Product Innovation Management*, 6, 1989, pp. 259–267; Ikujiro Nonaka, "Creating Organizational Order Out of Chaos: Self-Renewal in Japanese Firms," *California Management Review*, 30(3), Spring 1988, pp. 57–73; Thomas J. Peters, *Thriving on Chaos* (New York: Alfred A. Knopf, 1988); and Robert H. Hayes, Steven C. Wheelwright, and Kim B. Clark, *Dynamic Manufacturing* (New York: The Free Press, 1987).
2. See Kim B. Clark and Takahiro Fujimoto, *Product Development Performance* (Boston: Harvard Business School Press, 1991).
3. These forms of organization were first developed in Fujimoto, "Organizations for Effective Product Development." Additional work includes Hayes, Wheelwright, and Clark, *Dynamic Manufacturing;* and Clark and Fujimoto, *Product Development Performance*. For further reading on the basis of organizing for development, see Paul R. Lawrence and Jay W. Lorsch, *Organization and Environment* (Homewood, Illinois: Richard D. Irwin, 1967); Jay R. Galbraith, *Designing Complex Organizations* (Reading, Massachusetts: Addison-Wesley, 1973); and Thomas J. Allen and Oscar Hauptman, "The Influence of Communication Technologies on Organizational Structure," *Communication Research*, 14(5), October 1987, pp. 575–578.
4. For a more extensive review of Motorola's experience with the Bandit line see "Motorola, Inc.: Bandit Pager Project" (Boston: HBS Case Services, Harvard Business School), 9-690-043.
5. For an extended discussion of this pattern of leadership and its impact in leading firms in the world auto industry, see Clark and Fujimoto, *Product Development Performance*.
6. Adapted from a description provided by Dr. Christopher Meyer, Strategic Alignment Group, Los Altos, CA.
7. For a more thorough discussion of Chaparral Steel's approach to development, see the chapter on Chaparral in H. Kent Bowen, Kim Clark, Charles Holloway, and Steven Wheelwright (eds.), *Vision and Capability: High Performance Product Development in the 1990's* (New York: Oxford University Press, forthcoming); and "Chaparral Steel: Rapid Product and Process Development" (Boston: HBS Case Services, Harvard Business School), N9-692-018.

CHAPTER 9. Tools and Methods

1. We are indebted to Geoff Gill and Michael Watkins for their help in formulating the gear design example.
2. The notion of fit between the parameters of design and the context of its use is an important theme in the literature on design. For one approach to this problem see Christopher Alexander, *Notes on the Synthesis of Form* (Cambridge: Harvard University Press, 1964).
3. The problem solving framework we use here has its roots in the work of Herbert Simon; see especially Herbert A. Simon, *The Science of the Artificial* (Cambridge: MIT Press, 1969). Design-build-test cycles and the logic of problem solving are discussed directly in Takahiro Fujimoto, "Organizations for Effective Product Development," D.B.A. dissertation, Harvard Business School, 1989; and Kim B. Clark and Takahiro Fujimoto, *Product Development Performance* (Boston: Harvard Business School Press, 1991).
4. This problem has been developed at length by Michael D. Watkins, "Managing Cross-Functional Problem-Solving in Product Development and Manufacturing: The Case of Liftgate Engineering at Ford of Europe," doctoral dissertation, Harvard Business School, 1991.

5. QFD is a methodology that originated in Mitsubishi's Kobe shipyards and was developed and extended by Toyota. There is a large literature on QFD, including works translated from Japanese. For an excellent introduction, see John R. Hauser and Don Clausing, "The House of Quality," *Harvard Business Review*, May–June 1988, pp. 63–73. In the paragraphs that follow we adapted the basic framework laid out by Hauser and Clausing and applied it to the gear design problem.

6. There is a large and growing literature on DFM. For a good introduction see Daniel E. Whitney, "Manufacturing by Design," *Harvard Business Review*, July–August 1988, pp. 83–91.

7. We have taken this example from Karl Ulrich, David Sartorius, Scott Pearson, and Mark Jakiela, "A Framework for Including the Value of Time in Design-for-Manufacturing Decision Making," M.I.T. Working Paper #3243-9-MSA, February 1991.

8. This method is described in Whitney, "Manufacturing by Design."

9. A similar concept is part of the framework developed in Hauser and Clausing, "The House of Quality."

Appendix to Chapter 9.

1. See, for example, Jeffrey K. Liker and Walton M. Hancock, "Organizational Systems Barriers to Engineering Effectiveness," *IEEE Transactions on Engineering Management*, vol. 33, No. 2 (May, 1986) pp. 82–91, who developed survey evidence that design engineers spend less than 10 pecent of their time designing new products "right the first time," and only 20 percent of their time doing actual engineering work. The rest was spent attending meetings, searching for people and information, and coordinating with other engineers.

2. This example uses the system developed by Steven Salzberg and Michael Watkins, "Managing Information for Concurrent Engineering: Challenges and Barriers," *Research in Engineering Design*, 2, 1990, pp. 35–52. We are grateful to Michael Watkins for his help with the work in this section. His work on computer-based systems provides a useful review of the literature and a detailed discussion of the computer system and its application. See Watkins, "Managing Cross-Functional Problem-Solving in Product Development and Manufacturing."

3. See Salzberg and Watkins, "Managing Information for Concurrent Engineering: Challenges and Barriers."

Chapter 10.   Prototype/Test Cycles

1. For additional information on prototyping in the workstation industry, see David Ellison and Steven C. Wheelwright, "The Prototyping of PCBs in Engineering Workstation Development Projects," Harvard Business School Working Paper, 1991.

2. This point of view—that prototyping is crucial to development—has been developed in work by Phil Barkan. See, for example, Phil Barkan, Marco Iansiti, and Kim B. Clark, "Prototyping as a Core Development Process," in H. Kent Bowen, Kim Clark, Charles Holloway, and Steven Wheelwright (eds.), *Vision and Capability: High Performance Product Development in the 1990's* (New York: Oxford University Press, forthcoming).

3. For additional background on prototyping in the automobile industry, see Kim B. Clark and Takahiro Fujimoto, *Product Development Performance* (Boston: Harvard Business School Press, 1991), pp. 176–182.

4. For the story of Coca Cola's introduction of a new version of Coke, see Thomas Oliver, *The Real Coke, The Real Story* (New York: Random House, 1986).

CHAPTER 11.   Learning from Development Projects

1. There is a large literature on learning in industrial settings. Much of it has to do with the "learning curve," or the observed tendency for costs (and other dimensions of peformance) to decline with increases in experience. Here we focus on directed, managed, systematic efforts to increase the firm's knowledge about development. For additional discussion of systematic learning, and learning in an organizational context, see Roger E. Bohn, "An Informal Note on Knowledge and How to Manage It" (Boston: HBS Case Services, Harvard Business School), 9-686-132; Roger E. Bohn, "Learning by Experimentation in Manufacturing," Harvard Business School Working Paper, 1987; C. M. Fiol and M. A. Lyles, "Organizational Learning," *Academy of Management Review*, 19(4), 1985, pp. 803–813; and Dorothy Leonard-Barton, "The Factory as a Learning Laboratory," Mimeograph, September 1991.
2. The themes we examine here are consistent with recent research on effective learning and organizational change. Michael Beer, Russell A. Eisenstat, and Bert Spector, *The Critical Path to Corporate Renewal* (Boston: HBS Press, 1990), for example, argue that effective learning and change needs to focus on the essential tasks and associated behavior in the organization, rather than on individual attitudes.
3. The notion that learning about new products involves a cycle of activities is a central theme in Modesto A. Maidique and B. J. Zirger, "The New Product Learning Cycle," *Research Policy*, 14, December 1985, pp. 299–313.
4. Robert H. Hayes, Steven C. Wheelwright, and Kim B. Clark, *Dynamic Manufacturing* (New York: The Free Press, 1988), discuss this issue and the general problem of creating a learning organization. See especially chapters 11 and 12 for examples that put learning about development in context.

CHAPTER 12.   Building Development Capability

1. For additional reading about organizational change along these lines, see Michael Beer, Russell A. Eisenstat, and Bert Spector, *The Critical Path to Corporate Renewal* (Boston: Harvard Business School Press, 1990).
2. Chapter 12 in Robert H. Hayes, Steven C. Wheelwright, and Kim B. Clark, *Dynamic Manufacturing* (New York: The Free Press, 1988), provides additional examples from manufacturing companies of strategies for bringing about fundamental improvement in operating performance. For additional insight from experience in service businesses, see James L. Heskett, W. Earl Sasser, and Christopher W. L. Hart, *Service Breakthroughs: Changing the Rules of the Game* (New York: Free Press, 1990), especially chapters 13 and 14.
3. Ford's recent experience is documented in the chapter on Ford's development process in H. Kent Bowen, Kim Clark, Charles Holloway, and Steven Wheelwright (eds.), *Vision and Capability: High Performance Product Development in the 1990's* (New York: Oxford University Press, forthcoming).
4. For additional background and detail on Kodak's FunSaver project, see "Kodak Fun-Saver" (Boston: HBS Case Services, Harvard Business School), N9-692-070.
5. For additional background on HP's development process, see the chapter on HP in Bowen et al. (eds.), *Vision and Capability*. Chapter 12 of Hayes, Wheelwright, and Clark, *Dynamic Manufacturing*, discusses the experience of the Vancouver plant in making broad improvements in manufacturing.
6. There is a growing literature on benchmarking. For a good example of the concept and its application, see Frances Tucker, Seymour Zivan, and Robert Camp, "How to Measure Yourself Against the Best," *Harvard Business Review*, January–February 1987, p. 8.

Index